MANY THOUSANDS GONE

The First Two Centuries
of Slavery in North America

MANY
THOUSANDS
GONE

*The First Two
Centuries of Slavery
in North America*

IRA BERLIN

THE BELKNAP PRESS OF
HARVARD UNIVERSITY PRESS
CAMBRIDGE, MASSACHUSETTS
LONDON, ENGLAND

Designed by Marianne Perlak

Library of Congress Cataloging-in-Publication Data

Berlin, Ira, 1941–
Many thousands gone : the first two centuries of slavery
in North America / Ira Berlin.
p. cm.
Includes bibliographical references (p.   ) and index
ISBN 0-674-00211-3
1. Slavery—United States—History—17th century.
2. Slavery—United States—18th century.
3. Afro-Americans—Social conditions—17th century.
4. Afro-Americans—Social conditions—18th century.
I. Title
E446.B49   1998
306.3′62′097309032—dc21
98-19336

CREDITS

For Martha

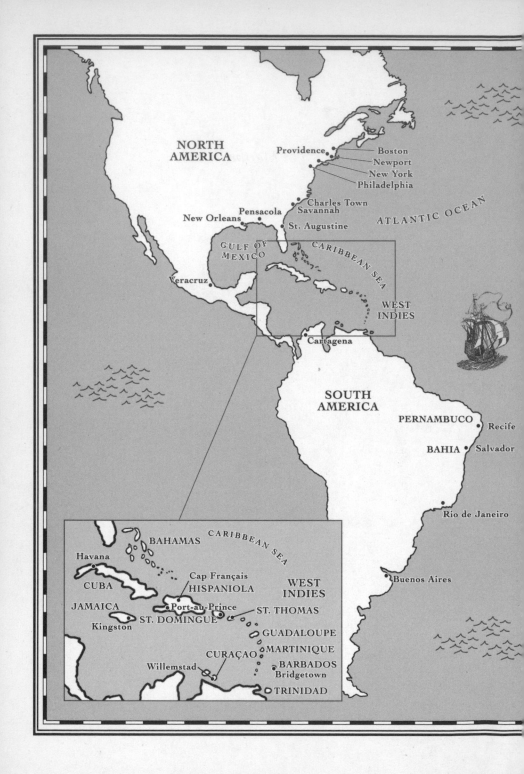

NORTH AMERICA

Providence • • Boston
• • Newport
• New York
• Philadelphia

ATLANTIC OCEAN

Charles Town
New Orleans • Pensacola • Savannah
• St. Augustine

GULF OF MEXICO
CARIBBEAN SEA
Veracruz •

WEST INDIES

Cartagena •

SOUTH AMERICA

PERNAMBUCO • Recife

BAHIA • Salvador

Rio de Janeiro •

Buenos Aires •

BAHAMAS
CARIBBEAN SEA

Havana •
CUBA
Cap Français
HISPANIOLA
WEST INDIES
JAMAICA
Port-au-Prince
ST. THOMAS
Kingston •
ST. DOMINGUE
GUADALOUPE
MARTINIQUE
CURAÇAO
Willemstad •
BARBADOS
Bridgetown
TRINIDAD

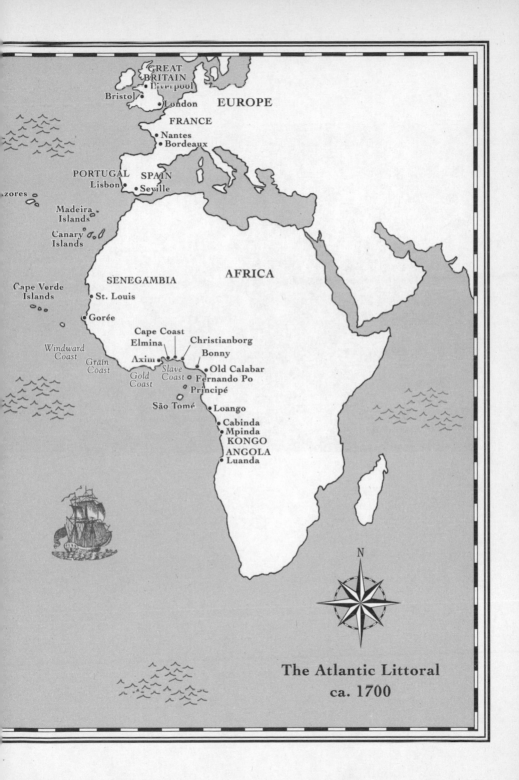

GREAT
BRITAIN
Bristol ● ● Liverpool
● London   EUROPE
FRANCE
● Nantes
● Bordeaux
PORTUGAL SPAIN
Lisbon ● ● Seville
Azores
Madeira
Islands
Canary
Islands
Cape Verde
Islands
SENEGAMBIA   AFRICA
● St. Louis
● Gorée
Windward
Coast
Grain
Coast
Cape Coast
Elmina   Christianborg
Axim ●   Bonny
Slave   ● Old Calabar
Gold   Coast ○ Fernando Po
Coast   ● Principé
São Tomé   ● Loango
● Cabinda
● Mpinda
KONGO
ANGOLA
● Luanda

N

The Atlantic Littoral
ca. 1700

Contents

✦

MAPS

MANY THOUSANDS GONE

*The First Two Centuries
of Slavery in North America*

No more auction block for me,
No more, no more,
No more auction block for me,
Many thousands gone.

No more peck o'corn for me,
No more, no more,
No more peck o'corn for me,
Many thousands gone.

No more driver's lash for me,
No more, no more,
No more driver's lash for me,
Many thousands gone.

No more mistress call for me,
No more, no more,
No more mistress call for me,
Many thousands gone.
Many thousands gone.

Making Slavery, Making Race

♠

Of late, it has become fashionable to declare that race is a social construction. In the academy, this precept has gained universal and even tiresome assent, as geneticists and physical anthropologists replace outmoded classifications of humanity with new ones drawn from recent explorations of the genome.[1] But while the belief that race is socially constructed has gained a privileged place in contemporary scholarly debates, it has won few practical battles. Few people believe it; fewer act on it. The new understanding of race has changed behavior little if at all.

Perhaps this is because the theory is not quite right. Race is not simply a social construction; it is a particular kind of social construction—a historical construction.[2] Indeed, like other historical constructions—the most famous of course being class—it cannot exist outside of time and place. To follow Edward Thompson's celebrated discussion of class, race is also "a fluency which evades analysis if we attempt to stop it dead at any given moment and atomize its structure." Race, no less than class, is the product of history, and it only exists on the contested social terrain in which men and women struggle to control their destinies.[3]

The reluctance to embrace the new understanding of race as socially constructed derives neither from a commitment to an older biological classification system, which in truth is no better understood than the newer genetics, nor from a refusal to acknowledge the reality of an ideological construct. Instead, it derives from the failure to demonstrate how race is continually redefined, who does the defining, and why. This book is in part an attempt to address that problem, first by recognizing the volatility of the experiences which collectively defined race, and then by suggesting how they shifted over the course of two centuries.

Many Thousands Gone is a history of African-American slavery in mainland North America during the first two centuries of European and African settlement. Like all history, it is a study of changing relationships. The emphasis on change is important. Philosophers, sociologists, anthropologists, and even some historians have provided extraordinary insight into how property-in-person specified once and forever the character of a slave's standing, personality, and relationship with others and gave slavery a meaning that transcended history. From such a perspective, slavery was both a model and a metaphor for the most extreme forms of exploitation, otherness, and even social death. Its unique character rested upon the slave's physical and cultural uprooting. But slaves were never "absolute aliens," "genealogical isolates," "deracinated outsiders," or even unreflective "sambos" in any slave society.[4] Knowing that a person was a slave does not tell everything about him or her. Put another way, slaveholders severely circumscribed the lives of enslaved people, but they never fully defined them. Slaves were neither extensions of their owners' will nor products of the market's demand. The slaves' history—like all human history—was made not only by what was done to them but also by what they did for themselves.

All of which is to say that slavery, though imposed and maintained by violence, was a negotiated relationship. To be sure, the struggle between master and slave never proceeded on the basis of equality and was always informed by the master's near monopoly of force. By definition, slaves had less choice than any other people, as slaveholders set the conditions upon which slaves worked and lived. Indeed, the relation between master and slave was so profoundly asymmetrical that many have concluded that the notion of negotiation—often freighted in our own society with the rhetoric of the level playing field—has no value to the study of slavery. Although the playing field was never level, the master–slave relationship was nevertheless subject to continual negotiation. The failure to recognize the ubiquity of those negotiations derives neither from an overestimation of the power of the master (which was awesome indeed), nor from an underestimation of the power of the slave (which rarely amounted to much), but from a misconstruing of the limitations humanity placed upon both master and slave.[5] For while slaveowners held most of the good cards in this meanest of all contests, slaves held cards of their own. And even when their cards were reduced to near worthlessness, slaves still held that last card, which, as their owners well understood, they might play at any time.

A number of corollaries follow from a recognition that even in slavery's cramped quarters there was room for negotiation. First, even as they confronted one another, master and slave had to concede, however grudgingly, a degree of legitimacy to the other. No matter how reluctantly it was given (or, more likely, extracted), such a concession was difficult for either party to acknowledge, for masters presumed their own absolute sovereignty and slaves never relinquished the right to control their own destiny. But no matter how adamant the denials, nearly every interaction of master and slave forced such recognition, for the web of interconnections between master and slave necessitated a coexistence that fostered cooperation as well as contestation.

Second, because the circumstances of such contestation and cooperation continually changed, slavery itself continually changed. The refusal of either party to concede the realities of master–slave relations meant that slavery was intrinsically unstable. No bargain could last for very long, for as power slipped from master to slave and back to master, the terms of slavery would again be renegotiated. Slavery was never made, but instead was continually remade, for power—no matter how great—was never absolute, but always contingent.

Thus, understanding that a person was a slave is not the end of the story but the beginning, for the slaves' history was derived from experiences that differed from place to place and time to time and not from some unchanging transhistorical verity. In some sense, this truism has become a staple of recent histories of all subordinate classes, not only slaves but also servants, serfs, and wage workers. Surely, it would come as no surprise to say that all wage workers at any particular moment had much in common, both in shared experiences and in opposition to their employers; but the lives of steel workers and cigar makers differed, as did their languages, institutions, and relationships with their employers, their fellow workers, and their families. If at times steel workers and cigar makers stood together against their employers on matters of compensation, working conditions, and political allegiance, few would expect their opposition to take precisely the same form. Yet, because slavery was such a powerful, all-encompassing relationship, scholars have often been transfixed by the commonalities that slavery produced, by the dynamics of the relationship between master and slave, and by the personality traits this most extreme form of domination appears to have generated.

Slavery's distinctiveness has been reinforced by its historic confrontation with free labor, a battle in which slavery—for good and ill—came to embody traditional society. The slave master's domination of the plantation order was seen as nothing less than monarchy writ small and patriar-

chy writ large. By extension, it represented hierarchy, discipline, and corporate control. Slaveholders understood their rule to be the incarnation
of the well-ordered society, which mirrored the well-ordered family. By
the same token, their slaves' interminable insubordination represented
not only a loss of labor and a threat of insurrection but also a direct assault on order itself.

Such an interpretation has propelled the relationship between master
and slave, generally in the guise of the question of paternalism (or sometimes patriarchalism or seigneuralism) to the center of the debate over
slavery, and has given the history of slavery a significance that reaches
beyond the bounds of the subject itself. The destruction of slavery and its
corporate ethos—as a means of organizing society as well as a means of
extracting labor—was a central event in the rise of capitalism and the
triumph of liberalism, certainly in the West and in other parts of the
world as well. Little wonder, then, that the discussions of the nature—
and sometimes the existence—of paternalism has preoccupied historians
during the last four decades.[6]

In contrasting the relations of slave labor to those of free labor, just as
in contrasting republicanism to monarchism or the patriarchal family
to the companionate one, historians have frozen their subject in time.
While they have captured an essential aspect of chattel bondage, they
have lost something of the dynamic that constantly made and remade the
lives of slaves, changing them from time to time and place to place. The
static model reified and reinforced the masters' vision of their hegemonic
power and the slaves' willing acceptance by removing from public view
the contingencies upon which power rested. The minuet between master
and slave, when played to the contrapuntal music of paternalism, was a
constant, as master and slave continually renegotiated the small space
allotted them. But the stylized movements—the staccato gyrations, the
seductive feints, the swift withdrawals, and the hateful embraces—represented just one of many dances of domination and subordination, resistance and accommodation. The essence of the slaves' history can be
found in the ever-changing music to which slaves were forced to dance
and in their ability to superimpose their own rhythms by ever so slight
changes of cadence, accent, and beat.

As always, close examination of the particulars of the human condition subverts general ideas, for it exposes contradictions and unearths
exceptions to the most powerful generalizations. The historicization of

the study of slavery inevitably calls into question many of the tropes that have guided the study of African-American slavery in mainland North America: African to creole, slave to free, sundown to sunup, and white over black, to name but a few. In reconsidering these general ideas, I have tried not merely to reverse them and argue instead for a progression from creole to African or from freedom to slavery, although such a course may at times be more accurate. Simply reversing the traditional formulations does little to advance knowledge of slave life and leaves the discussion of the African-American experience "encased," as Herbert Gutman once noted, "in snug and static historical opposites."[7]

As Gutman understood, binary opposites fit nicely the formulation of history as written, but they do little to capture the messy, inchoate reality of history as lived. Rather than proceed from African to creole or from slavery to freedom, people of African descent in mainland North America crossed the lines between African and creole and between slavery and freedom many times, and not always in the same direction. Similarly, although racial domination took many forms, at critical moments some white and black people met as equals and stood shoulder-to-shoulder against those they deemed a common enemy. And on some rare occasions, slaves enjoyed the upper hand. Although much of slave life took shape beyond the masters' eyes from sundown to sunup, slaves also created their own world under the owners' noses from sunup to sundown.

The latter point is of great importance. On mainland North America, as in the Americas generally, slaves worked. New World slavery did not have its origins in a conspiracy to dishonor, shame, brutalize, or reduce slaves on some perverse scale of humanity—although it did all of those at one time or another. The stench from slavery's moral rot cannot mask the design of American captivity: the extraction of labor that allowed a small group of men to dominate all. In short, if slavery made *race*, its larger purpose was to make *class*, and the fact that the two were made simultaneously by the same process has mystified both.[8]

Since labor defined the slaves' existence, when, where, and especially how slaves worked determined in large measure the course of their lives. But despite the centrality of their labor, the history of black people cannot be reduced to it. Slaves, like their owners, did not live by bread alone. Whether in moments stolen in the field, the dark of night, holidays granted by their owners, or harvest festivities, slaves, like other working peoples, expressed themselves in song, dance, prayer, and fables by which they understood their world and plotted to create another more to their liking. Such activities, often as separated from the world of work as day from night, were characterized by slaveowners—and not a few historians since—as escapist, mindless mimicry, or harmless distractions whose instinctive or impulsive basis reflected a resignation to a fate that could not be altered. Such depictions of the slaves' culture—with emphasis on the sensual, hedonistic, and exotic—had their point, particularly when viewed from the reserved, often prudish world of the Big House. But they badly underestimated the oppositional content of slave culture. The slaves' struggle to give meaning to their music, dance, and devotions were no less political than their struggle over work.

Matters of family, language, and spirituality were ensconced in the patches of tobacco and the fields of rice and indigo, just as questions of exploitation and compensation were articulated in the spiritual language of brush-arbor sermons and the vernacular of field chants. The weight of time alone—whether calculated as a portion of a day, a year, or a lifetime—does not automatically elevate work over any of the other manifestations of human existence, whether emanating from the quarter, household, and church rather than the field or workshop. Indeed, it is precisely in connecting the quarter, household, and church to the field and the workshop that the slaves' experience can be made comprehensible. The study of the workplace offers a practical point of entry to the slaves' social organization, domestic arrangements, religious beliefs, and medical practices, along with their music, cuisine, linguistic and sartorial style, and much else.

Observing slaves at work reveals differences in how slaves lived from place to place and time to time. For if no one would argue with the proposition that steel workers and cigar makers spoke different languages, created different institutions, and partook in different social relations, neither would anyone maintain that the language, institutions, or actions of each had always been the same. Nor would anyone contend that the struggles of steel workers in capitalist North America had been the same as those in communist Russia or even in capitalist Japan. What is true for steel workers and cigar makers is no less true for those enslaved people who chopped cotton, rotted hemp, winnowed rice, holed sugarcane, and cured tobacco. Slave life also differed from place to place and from time to time.

Viewing slavery through the perspective of what slaves did most of the time provides a means to draw some fundamental distinctions and find some essential commonalities among the varied experiences of North American slaves. In this study of the first two hundred years of slavery in mainland North America, I have distinguished four different slave societies: one in the North; another in the Chesapeake region; a third in the coastal lowcountry of South Carolina, Georgia, and Florida; yet another in the lower Mississippi Valley. In each region, slavery had its own geography, demography, economy, society, and—of course—history. Slave life evolved differently in the North, where slave labor supplemented that of family members and servants in an economy based on commerce and mixed agriculture; in the South Carolina lowcountry, where chattel bondage arrived with the first settlers and had little competition as the main source of labor on the great rice and indigo plantations; in the Chesapeake, where black-slave and white-servant labor developed in tandem within an economy organized around the production of tobacco; and in the lower Mississippi Valley, where an ill-defined labor system groped for a staple crop until the sudden emergence of sugar and cotton production transformed all. In such diverse circumstances, slavery's different development depended upon the nature of the terrain, the richness of the soil, the availability of markets, the demographic balance between white and black, free and slave, and men and women, and the diverse origins of both slaves and slaveholders.

Yet, whatever the geographic markers of slavery's development, time did not stand still for slaves any more than it did for free workers. The lives of slaves changed radically over the course of the two centuries between the time the first black people arrived in mainland North America and the beginning of the cotton revolution in the first decade of the nineteenth century. They would continue to change thereafter.

If the transformation of slave life was a continuous process, some moments were more important than others, as they altered the most basic relationships and set in motion conflicts that would take generations to resolve, if they could be resolved at all. Enslavement was one such moment, as was the final emancipation. Since the business of defining freedom remains unfinished nearly a century and a half after the ratification of the Thirteenth Amendment that abolished slavery at the end of the Civil War, it should come as no surprise that the meaning of slavery and the terms of the relationship between master and slave were still subject to contention on the eve of that war.

Two markers are critical for understanding the first two centuries of slavery in mainland North America. The first, drawn from the study of slavery in antiquity, distinguishes between *societies with slaves* and *slave societies*.[9] Societies with slaves are not societies in which, as one apologist for slavery in the North observed, "even the darkest aspect of slavery was softened by a smile."[10] Superficially, slavery in such societies might appear milder, as slaveowners—not driven by the great wealth that sugar, rice, or tobacco could produce—had less reason to press their slaves. Moreover, slaveholdings in societies with slaves were generally small, and the line between slave and free could be remarkably fluid, with manumission often possible and sometimes encouraged. But neither mildness nor openness defined societies with slaves. Slaveholders in such societies could act with extraordinary brutality precisely because their slaves were extraneous to their main business. They could limit their slaves' access to freedom expressly because they desired to set themselves apart from their slaves.

What distinguished societies with slaves was the fact that slaves were marginal to the central productive processes; slavery was just one form of labor among many. Slaveowners treated their slaves with extreme callousness and cruelty at times because this was the way they treated all subordinates, whether indentured servants, debtors, prisoners-of-war, pawns, peasants, or simply poor folks. In societies with slaves, no one presumed the master–slave relationship to be the social exemplar.

In slave societies, by contrast, slavery stood at the center of economic production, and the master–slave relationship provided the model for all social relations: husband and wife, parent and child, employer and employee, teacher and student. From the most intimate connections between men and women to the most public ones between ruler and ruled, all relationships mimicked those of slavery. As Frank Tannenbaum said, "Nothing escaped, nothing, and no one."[11] Whereas slaveholders were just one portion of a propertied elite in societies with slaves, they were the ruling class in slave societies; nearly everyone—free and slave—aspired to enter the slaveholding class, and upon occasion some former slaves rose into the slaveholders' ranks. Their acceptance was grudging, as they carried the stigma of bondage in their lineage and, in the case of American slavery, color in their pigment. But the right to enter the slaveholding class was rarely denied, because slaveownership was open to all, irrespective of family, nationality, color, or ancestry.

Historians have outlined the process by which societies with slaves in the Americas became slave societies.[12] The transformation generally turned upon the discovery of some commodity—gold being the ideal, sugar being a close second—that could command an international market. With that, slaveholders capitalized production and monopolized resources, muscled other classes to the periphery, and consolidated their political power. The number of slaves increased sharply, generally by direct importation from Africa, and enslaved people of African descent became the majority of the laboring class, sometimes the majority of the population. Other forms of labor—whether family labor, indentured servitude, or wage labor—declined, as slaveholders drove small farmers and wage workers to the margins. These men and women sometimes resisted violently—on the North American mainland most famously in Bacon's rebellion.[13] But mostly they voted with their feet and migrated from slave societies. Just as the "redlegs" had deserted Barbados in the wake of the sugar revolution of the mid-seventeenth century, the small planters and drovers fled lowcountry Carolina in the wake of the rice revolution of the early eighteenth century, and the yeomanry abandoned the blackbelt for the hill country of the South and the flatlands of the Midwest in the wake of the cotton revolution of the early nineteenth century.

In the absence of competitors, slaveholders solidified their rule. Through their control of the state, they enacted—or reinvigorated—comprehensive slave codes in which they invested themselves with near-complete sovereignty over their slaves, often extending to the absolute right over the slave's life. The new laws sharply reduced the latitude slaves previously enjoyed, and instead insisted that slaves defer to their owners at all times, without question. The prerogatives that slaves once openly maintained—among them the ability to travel, to meet among themselves, to hold property, and to trade at market—were also severely circumscribed or abolished, although they survived at the pleasure of individual slaveowners. That done, slaveholders narrowed the slaves' access to freedom, so that the previously permeable boundaries between slavery and freedom became impenetrable barriers. Finally, slaveholders elaborated the logic of subordination, generally finding the sources of their own domination in some rule of nature or law of God.

Since slavery became exclusively identified with people of African descent in the New World, the slaveholders' explanation of their own domination generally took the form of racial ideologies. But African descent and the racialist pigmocracy that accompanied it was only one manifestation of the slaves' subordination. Even in societies where slaveowner and slave admittedly shared the same origins, masters construed domination in "racial" terms. Russian serf masters mused that the bones of their serfs were black.[14]

Whereas elements of the process by which societies with slaves were transformed into slave societies were everywhere the same, the process itself was always different, except for its inherent brutality. Some societies with slaves passed rapidly into slave societies, so that the earlier experience hardly left a mark. Others moved slowly and imperfectly through the transformation, backtracking several times, so that the process was more circular than linear. Yet other societies with slaves never completed the transition, and some hardly began it. Moreover, slave societies did not always stay slave societies. The development of slavery did not necessarily run in one direction; slave societies also became societies with slaves as often as the opposite.

While acknowledging differences in the process by which societies with slaves became slave societies, historians have differed sharply as to the causes of the change.[15] A salable commodity alone did not in itself produce a slave society. The discovery or development of a staple crop predated the emergence of slave societies in some places; and once established, some slave societies outlasted their raison d'être. In the Chesapeake region, for example, tobacco was grown in a society with slaves before the 1670s and in a slave society thereafter. What distinguished the post-1670 Chesapeake was not the cultivation of tobacco or the employment of slave labor but the presence of a planter class able to command the region's resources, mobilize the power of the state, and vanquish competitors. A salable commodity was a necessary condition for the development of a slave society, but it was not sufficient. The slaveholders' seizure of power was the critical event in transforming societies with slaves into slave societies.[16]

The evolution of slavery in mainland North America took many forms, so that the moment (or moments) of transformation differed in the North, the Chesapeake, the lowcountry, and the lower Mississippi Valley. But the driving force behind the evolution of slavery remained the ever-changing nature of production. Alterations in the slaveholders' demands and the slaves' expectations opened the door to fundamental shifts in power. By definition, such moments were times of great stress, when the violence upon which slavery rested surfaced, sometimes with insurrectionary fury. The process of renegotiating the rules of the game put everything at risk.

Locating the seat of social change in the workplace, rooting those changes in the material circumstances of African-American life, and connecting such material changes to the development of African-American institutions and beliefs offer a structure for historicizing the study of slavery. The struggle over labor informed all other conflicts between master and slave, and understanding it opens the way to a full comprehension of slave society and the integration of the slave experience into the history of the American workingclass. It also provides the material basis for an appreciation of agency within the confines of slavery and how resistance that fell short of revolution could be effective.[17]

The conflict between master and slave took many forms, involving the organization of labor, the hours and pace of work, the sexual division of labor, and the composition of the labor force—all questions familiar to students of free workers. The weapons that workers employed in such conflicts—feigning ignorance, slowing the line, minimizing the stint, breaking tools, disappearing at critical moments, and, as a last resort, confronting their superiors directly and violently—suggest that in terms of workplace struggles, slave and wage workers had much in common. Although the social relations of slave and wage labor differed fundamentally, much can be learned about slave life by examining how the work process informed the conflict between wage workers and their employers. For like reasons, the processes of production were as much a source of workingclass culture for slave workers as for free workers.[18]

A second marker in the evolution of slavery had an effect that was as powerful as the transition from societies with slaves to slave societies. This was the great democratic revolutions of the late eighteenth century, which hit slavery hard. The Declaration of Independence, the Declaration of the Rights of Man, and the emergence of an independent Haitian Republic undermined the ideological foundation upon which slavery rested, and the wars that accompanied these ideological upheavals allowed slaves new leverage to contest their owners' power.[19] But the impact of the Age of Revolution was anything but uniform. In some places, the events that accompanied revolutionary change toppled slavery; in some places, they strengthened it; and in some places they pulled simultaneously in both directions. The new societies that emerged from the revolutionary era were as different from one another as those that emerged from the earlier transformation. In the North, most slaves were freed or eventually would be; in the Chesapeake, a large free black population increased in tandem with the region's slaves; in lowcountry South Carolina, Georgia, and Florida, slavery grew as never before, and few slaves gained their freedom; and in the lower Mississippi Valley, slavery expanded in the countryside while the number of free people of color grew in the cities. Again, the nature of each slave society and its interactions with the chronology of revolution made the difference.

The slaves' history thus took shape at the confluence of several diverse processes. Defining the markers of time and space by which slavery developed can only be contested terrain. While some would distinguish between New England and the Mid-Atlantic states, I have included them in a generalized North; while some would distinguish between tidewater and piedmont, I have joined the two together as part of a greater Chesapeake; and while some would divide lowcountry South Carolina from the upcountry (and even add a middlecountry), I have treated them as one, along with tidewater regions of Georgia and Florida. In a like fashion, the chronology of revolution can take a variety of different forms. While some might mark it with the outbreak of the French conflict, the ratification of the United States Constitution, or the triumph of Toussaint, I have begun with the War for American Independence.

The transformation of societies with slaves into slave societies and their metamorphosis during the Age of Revolution cannot be captured in the conventional formulations of "Africans to African Americans" or "slavery to freedom." Rather, the history of slavery on mainland North America was an uneven, convoluted process that can best be encompassed in three distinctive experiences: that of the *charter generations,* defined as the first arrivals, their children, and in some cases their grandchildren; the *plantation generations,* who were forced to grow the great staples; and the *revolutionary generations,* who grasped the promise of freedom and faced a resurgent slave regime. These successive experiences do not allow for a progressive history of black people on mainland North America, either in the linear or the optimistic sense of that word. But they do reveal how generations of people of African descent wrestled with the realities of slavery and freedom, trying to fashion a world of their own in circumstances not of their own making.

In presenting the diverse histories of the charter, plantation, and revolutionary generations, I have begun in each instance with an examination of the region that best exemplifies that generation's history. Thus, Part I, which covers the charter generations, starts with the Chesapeake region not simply because of its chronological primacy but because the character of the charter generations was most fully evident in seventeenth-century Virginia and Maryland. Succeeding chapters trace the history of the charter generations in the North, in lowcountry South Carolina and Florida, and in the lower Mississippi Valley, where it evolved along a different—and sometimes a diametrically opposite—path.

For like reasons, Part III, which chronicles the revolutionary generations, begins not in the Chesapeake but in the North or nascent free states. There, the full force of the Age of Revolution transformed slavery into juristical freedom, setting in motion both a reconstruction of African-American society and the growth of new forms of coercion. Variants of the same processes are then viewed in the Chesapeake (which by the mid-nineteenth century is called the Upper South), lowcountry (the Lower South), and lower Mississippi Valley, where some people of African descent secured freedom but most found themselves caught in slavery's tightening grip. By beginning where change was most evident and then exploring the permutations, this organization reveals how the very same processes—initial settlement, the advent of staple production, or social revolution—took different shapes.

Slave society in mainland North America did not cease to change in the first decades of the nineteenth century when this book concludes. Historians who have tried to hold time constant in order to explain the complex interactions of master and slave or the development of the slave personality have inevitably found their investigations stymied and their conclusions stereotyped by their very method. Even the most complex social relationships become caricatures when men and women—subalterns or superiors—are frozen in time. In the study of slavery, such static visions rob both slaves and slaveholders of their agency or, more strangely, allows agency but denies that their struggle changed the basic constellation of social relations. If the masters' hegemony is immutable, slaves and their owners are reduced to stock figures of the scholarly imagination. In mainland North America, slaves (like their owners) were simply not the same people in 1819 that they had been in 1719 or 1619, although the origins and color of the slave population often had not changed.

Indeed, the meaning of race itself changed as slavery was continually reconstructed over the course of those two centuries. Projecting the regimen of seventeenth-century tobacco production, the aesthetics of African pottery, or the eschatology of animistic religion into the nineteenth century is no more useful than reading the demands of blackbelt cotton production, the theology of African-American Christianity, and the ethos of antebellum paternalism back into the seventeenth century. It is important to remember that at the beginning of the nineteenth century, when this book concludes, the vast majority of black people, slave and free, did not reside in the blackbelt, grow cotton, or subscribe to Christianity. That the character of slave life in North America was reversed a half century later is a striking commentary on a period that historians have represented as stable maturity. This radical transformation affirms the notion that slavery's history can be best appreciated in terms of generations of captivity and the many thousands who suffered through the long night of American enslavement. Although it would take more than another half century before the last slave in the United States could intone the words, "No more auction block . . . No more hundred lash . . . No more Mistress call," the words of the great spiritual would remind all of the "many thousands" before the day of Jubilee.

I

SOCIETIES WITH SLAVES

The Charter Generations

Mainland
North America
ca. 1660

N

Connecticut R.
Hudson R.
Boston
Providence
Newport
Narragansett Bay
Delaware R.
New
Amsterdam
Philadelphia
Potomac R.
Rappahannock R.
Chesapeake Bay
James R.
Jamestown

Cooper R.
Ashley R.
Savannah R.
Charles Town
Mississippi R.
Tombigbee R.
Savannah
St. Johns R.
St. Augustine
Mobile
Pensacola
White Earth
New Orleans

ATLANTIC OCEAN

GULF OF MEXICO

Introduction

⚜

Black life on mainland North America originated not in Africa or in America but in the netherworld between the two continents. Along the periphery of the Atlantic—first in Africa, then Europe, and finally in the Americas—it was a product of the momentous meeting of Africans and Europeans and then their equally fateful rendezvous with the peoples of the New World. Although the countenances of these new people of the Atlantic—"Atlantic creoles"—might bear the features of Africa, Europe, or the Americas in whole or part, their beginnings, strictly speaking, were in none of those places.[1] Instead, by their experience and sometimes by their person, they had become part of the three worlds that came together in the Atlantic littoral. Familiar with the commerce of the Atlantic, fluent in its new languages, and intimate with its trade and cultures, they were cosmopolitan in the fullest sense.

Atlantic creoles traced their beginnings in the historic encounter of European and Africans on the west coast of Africa. Many served as intermediaries, employing their linguistic skills and their familiarity with the Atlantic's diverse commercial practices, cultural conventions, and diplomatic etiquette to mediate between African merchants and European sea captains. In so doing, some Atlantic creoles identified with their ancestral homeland (or a portion of it)—be it African or European—and served as its representatives in negotiations with others. Other Atlantic creoles had been won over by the power and largess of one party or another, so that Africans entered the employ of European trading companies, while Europeans traded with African potentates. Yet others played fast and loose with their mixed heritage, employing whichever identity paid best. Whatever strategy they adopted, Atlantic creoles began the process of integrating the icons and beliefs of the Atlantic world into a new way of life.[2]

The emergence of the Atlantic creoles was but a tiny outcropping in the massive social upheaval that joined the peoples of the eastern and western hemispheres. But it was representative of the small beginnings that initiated this monumental transformation, as the new people of the Atlantic soon made their presence felt. Some traveled broadly as blue-water sailors, supercargoes, interpreters, and shipboard servants. Others were carried to foreign places as exotic trophies to be displayed before curious publics eager for firsthand knowledge of the lands beyond the sea. Some were even sent to distant lands with commissions to master the ways of the newly discovered "other" and retrieve the secrets of their wealth and knowledge.[3]

Atlantic creoles first emerged around the trading factories or *feitorias* that European expansionists established along the coast of Africa in the fifteenth century. Finding trade more lucrative than pillage, the Portuguese Crown began sending agents to oversee its interests in Africa. These official representatives were succeeded in turn by private entrepreneurs or *lançados* who, with the aid of African potentates, established themselves sometimes in competition with the Crown's emissaries. The competition among the Portuguese was soon joined by other European nations, and the coastal factories became commercial rendezvous for all manner of transatlantic traders. What was true of the nominally Portuguese enclaves also held for those later established or seized by the Dutch (Fort Nassaw and Elmina), Danes (Fredriksborg and Christianborg), Swedes (Carlsborg), French (St. Louis), and English (Fort Kormantse).[4]

The transformation of the small fishing villages along the Gold Coast during the sixteenth and seventeenth centuries suggests something of the change that followed the arrival of European traders. Between 1550 and 1618, Mouri (where the Dutch constructed Fort Nassaw in 1612) grew from a village of 200 people to 1,500 and then to an estimated 5,000 to 6,000 at the end of the eighteenth century. In 1555 Cape Coast counted only twenty houses; by 1680 it had 500 or more. Axim, which had 500 inhabitants in 1631, expanded to between 2,000 and 3,000 by 1690.[5] Among the African fishermen, craftsmen, village-based peasants, and laborers attached to these villages were an increasing number of Europeans. Although the mortality and transiency rates in these enclaves were extraordinarily high even by the standards of early modern port cities, permanent European settlements developed from the corporate employees (from governors to surgeons to clerks), merchants and factors, stateless sailors and soldiers, skilled craftsmen, occasional missionaries, and sundry transcontinental drifters.[6]

Established in 1482 by the Portuguese and captured by the Dutch in 1637, Elmina was one of the first of these factories and a model for those that followed. A meeting place for African and European commercial ambitions, Elmina—consisting of the Castle São Jorge da Mina and the town that surrounded it—became headquarters of the Portuguese and later Dutch mercantile activities on the Gold Coast and, with a population of 15,000 to 20,000 in 1682, the largest of some three dozen European outposts in the region.[7]

The peoples of the enclaves—both long-term residents and wayfarers—soon joined together, geographically and genetically. European men took wives and mistresses (sometimes by arrangement) among the African women, and before long the children born of these unions helped populate the enclave. Elmina sprouted a substantial cadre of Euro-Africans (most of them Luso-Africans, that is, of Portuguese and African descent)—men and women of African birth but shared African and European parentage, whose swarthy skin, European dress and deportment, acquaintance with local norms, and multilingualism gave them an insider's knowledge of both African and European ways but denied them full acceptance in either culture. By the eighteenth century, they numbered several hundred in Elmina. Along the Angolan coast they may have been even more numerous.[8]

People of mixed ancestry and tawny complexion composed but a small fraction of the population of the coastal factories, but few observers failed to note their existence—which gave their presence a disproportionate significance. Africans and Europeans alike sneered at the creoles' mixed lineage and condemned them as haughty, proud, and overbearing. When they adopted African ways, wore African dress and amulets, or underwent circumcision and scarification, Europeans declared them outcasts (*tangosmãos* or *reneges* to the Portuguese). When they adopted European ways, wore European clothing and crucifixes, employed European names or titles, and comported themselves in the manner of "white men," Africans denied them the right to hold land, marry, and inherit property. Although the *tangosmãos* faced reproach and proscription, all parties conceded that the creoles were shrewd traders, with a mastery of the fine points of intercultural negotiations, and found advantage in dealing with them. Despite their defamers, some creoles rose to positions of wealth and power, compensating for their lack of proper lineage with knowledge, skill, and entrepreneurial derring-do.[9]

Not all *tangosmãos* were of mixed ancestry, and not all people of mixed ancestry were *tangosmãos*. Color was only one marker of this culture-in-the-making, and generally the least significant.[10] From common experience, conventions of personal behavior, and cultural sensibilities compounded by shared ostracism and mercantile aspirations, Atlantic creoles acquired interests of their own, apart from their European and African antecedents. Of necessity, they spoke a variety of African and European languages, weighted strongly toward Portuguese. But from this seeming babble emerged a pidgin form of speech that borrowed its vocabulary from all parties and created a grammar unique unto itself. Derisively called *fala de Guine* or *fala de negros*—literally "Guinea speech" or "Negro Speech"—by the Portuguese and "black Portuguese" by others, this creole language became the lingua franca of the Atlantic.[11]

Although jaded observers condemned the culture of the enclaves as nothing more than "whoring, drinking, gambling, swearing, fighting, and shouting," Atlantic creoles attended church (usually Roman Catholic), married according to the sacraments, raised children conversant with European norms, and drew a livelihood from their knowledge of the Atlantic commercial economy. In short, they created societies of their own, *of* but not always *in* the societies of the Africans who dominated the interior trade and the Europeans who controlled commerce in the Atlantic.

Operating under European protection but always at African sufferance, the enclaves developed a politics as diverse and complicated as the peoples who populated them and a credit system that drew on the commercial centers of both Europe and Africa. Although the trading castles remained under the control of European metropoles, the towns around them often developed independent political lives, separate from both African and European domination. Their presence enabled new men and women of commerce to gain social prominence; and intermarriage with established peoples allowed creoles to fabricate lineages that gained them full membership in local elites. The resultant political upheaval promoted state formation, along with new class relations and ideologies.[12]

New religious forms emerged and then disappeared in much the same manner, as Europeans and Africans brought to the enclaves not only their commercial and political aspirations but all the trappings of their cultures as well. Priests and ministers sent to tend European souls made African converts, some of whom saw Christianity as both a way to ingratiate themselves with their trading partners and gain a new truth. Missionaries sped the process of Christianization and occasionally scored striking successes. At the beginning of the sixteenth century, the royal house of Kongo converted to Christianity. Catholicism, in various syncretic forms, infiltrated the posts along the Angolan coast and spread northward. Islam filtered in from the north. Whatever the sources of the new religions, most converts saw little cause to surrender their own deities. They incorporated Christianity and Islam to serve their own needs and gave Jesus and Muhammad a place in their spiritual pantheon. New religious practices, polities, and theologies emerged from the mixing of Christianity, Islam, polytheism, and animism.

Agricultural practices, architectural forms, and sartorial styles of the enclaves, as well as their cuisine, music, art, and technology, were similarly syncretic.[13] Like the stone fortifications surrounding the castles, these cultural innovations announced the presence of something new to coastal arrivals, whether they came by caravan from the African interior or sailed by caravel from the Atlantic.[14]

As settlements such as Elmina expanded to provision the European-controlled castles and the sailing vessels that frequented the coast, they developed multifarious systems of social stratification and occupational differentiation. Residents included canoemen who ferried goods between ships and shore; longshoremen and warehousemen who unloaded and stored merchandise; porters, messengers, guides, interpreters, factors, and brokers or *makelaers* (to the Dutch) who facilitated trade; innkeepers who housed country traders; skilled workers of all sorts; and a host of peddlers, hawkers, and petty traders. Others chopped wood, drew water, prepared food, or supplied sex to the lonely men who visited these isolated places. African notables occasionally established residence, bringing with them the trappings of wealth and power: wives, clients, pawns, slaves, and other dependents. In some places, small manufactories grew up—like the salt pans, boatyards, and foundries on the outskirts of Elmina—to supply the town and service the Atlantic trade. In addition, many people lived outside the law; the rough nature and transient population of these crossroads of trade encouraged roguery and brigandage.[15]

Village populations swelled into the thousands. In 1669, at about the time the English were ousting the Dutch from the village of New Amsterdam, population 1,500, a visitor to Elmina noted that it contained 8,000 residents. The growth of the west African littoral continued to outpace that of the American colonies throughout the seventeenth and into the eighteenth century. During most of the eighteenth century, Elmina's population was between 12,000 and 16,000, larger than that of Charles Town, South Carolina, mainland North America's greatest slave port at the time of the American Revolution.[16]

The business of the creole communities was trade—brokering the movement of goods throughout the Atlantic world. Although island settlements such as Cape Verde, Principé, and São Tomé developed indigenous agricultural and sometimes plantation economies, the comings and goings of African and European merchants dominated life even in the largest of the creole communities, which served as both field headquarters for great European mercantile companies and collection points for trade between the African interior and the Atlantic rim. Depending on the location, the exchange involved European textiles, metalware, guns, liquor, and beads for African gold, ivory, hides, pepper, beeswax, and dyewoods. The coastal trade, or cabotage, added fish, produce, livestock, and other perishables to this list, especially as regional specialization developed. Everywhere, slaves were bought and sold, and over time the importance of commerce-in-persons grew.

As slaving societies (that is, societies that traded in slaves), the coastal enclaves were also societies *with* slaves. African slavery in its various forms—from pawnage to chattel bondage—was practiced in these towns. Both Europeans and Africans held slaves, employed them, used them as collateral, traded them, and sold them to outsiders. At Elmina, the Dutch West India Company owned some 300 slaves in the late seventeenth century, and individual Europeans and Africans held others. Along with slaves appeared the inevitable trappings of slavery—overseers to supervise slave labor, slave catchers to retrieve runaways, soldiers to keep order and guard against insurrections, and officials to adjudicate and punish transgressions beyond a master's reach. Freedmen and freedwomen, who had somehow escaped bondage, also enjoyed a considerable presence. Many former slaves mixed Africa and Europe culturally and sometimes physically.[17]

Knowledge and experience far more than color set the Atlantic creoles apart from the Africans who brought slaves from the interior and the Europeans who carried them across the Atlantic, on one hand, and the hapless men and women on whose commodification the slave trade rested, on the other. Maintaining a secure place in such a volatile social order was not easy. The creoles' genius for intercultural negotiation was not simply a set of skills, a tactic for survival, or an attribute that emerged as an "Africanism" in the New World. Rather, it was central to a way of life that transcended particular venues.

The names European traders called Atlantic creoles provide a glimpse of the creoles' cosmopolitan ability to transcend the confines of particular nations and cultures. Abee Coffu Jantie Seniees, a leading African merchant and politico of Cape Coast on the Gold Coast in the late seventeenth century, appears in various European accounts and account books as Jan Snees, Jacque Senece, Johan Sinesen, and Jantee Snees. In some measure, the renderings of his name—to view him only from the perspective of European traders—reflect phonic imperialism or, more simply, the variability of transnational spelling. Seniees probably did not know or care how his trading partners registered his name, which he may have employed for commercial reasons in any case. But the diverse renderings reveal something of Abee Coffu Jantie Seniees's ability to trade with the Danes at Fredriksborg, the Dutch at Elmina, and the English at Cape Coast, as well as with Africans deep in the forested interior.[18]

The special needs of European traders placed Atlantic creoles in a powerful bargaining position, which they learned to employ to their own advantage. The most successful became principals and traded independently. They played one merchant against another, one captain against another, and one mercantile bureaucrat against another, often abandoning them for yet a better deal with some interloper, all in the hope of securing a rich prosperity for themselves and their families. Success evoked a sense of confidence that observers described as impertinence, insolence, and arrogance, and it was not limited to the fabulously wealthy like Jantie Seniees or the near-sovereign John Claessen (who rejected a kingship in Fetu to remain at trade) or the merchant princes John Kabes (trader, entrepreneur, and dominant politico in Komenda) and John Konny (commanding ruler in Pokoso).[19] Canoemen, for example, became infamous among European governors and sea captains for their independence. They refused to work in heavy surf, demanded higher wages and additional rations, quit upon insult or abuse, and abandoned work altogether when enslavement threatened. Attempts to control them through regulations issued from Europe or from local corporate head-quarters failed utterly. "These canoemen, despicable thieves," sputtered one Englishman in 1711, "think that they are more than just labour."[20]

Like other people in the middle, Atlantic creoles profited from their strategic position. Competition between and among the Africans and European traders bolstered their stock, increased their political leverage, and enabled them to elevate their social standing, while fostering solidarity. Creoles' ability to find a place for themselves in the interstices of African and European trade grew rapidly during periods of intense competition among the Portuguese, Dutch, Danes, Swedes, French, and English and an equally diverse set of African nationals.

At the same time and by the same token, the Atlantic creoles' liminality, particularly their lack of identity with any one group, posed numerous dangers. While their middling position made them valuable to African and European traders, it also made them vulnerable: they could be ostracized, scapegoated, and on occasion enslaved. Maintaining their independence amid the shifting alliances between and among Europeans and Africans was always difficult. Inevitably, some failed.

Debt, crime, immorality, or official disfavor could mean enslavement —if not for great men like Jantie Seniees, Claessen, Kabes, or Konny, at least for those on the fringes of the creole community.[21] Placed in captivity, Atlantic creoles might be exiled anywhere around the Atlantic—to the interior of Africa, the islands along the coast, the capitals of Europe, or the plantations of the New World. In the seventeenth century and the early part of the eighteenth, most slaves exported from Africa went to the sugar plantations of the Americas. Enslaved Atlantic creoles, on the other hand, might be shipped to Pernambuco, Barbados, or Martinique, but transporting them to the expanding centers of New World sugar production posed dangers, which American plantation owners well understood. The characteristics that distinguished Atlantic creoles—their linguistic dexterity, cultural plasticity, and social agility—were precisely those qualities that the great planters of the New World disdained and feared in slaves. For their labor force, planters desired youth and strength, not experience and sagacity. Too much knowledge might be subversive to the good order of the plantation. Simply put, men and women who understood the operations of the Atlantic system were too dangerous to be trusted in the human tinderboxes created by the sugar revolution. Thus rejected by the most prosperous New World regimes, Atlantic creoles were frequently exiled to marginal slave societies where would-be slave-owners, unable to compete with the great plantation magnates, snapped up those whom the grandees had disparaged as "refuse" for reasons of age, illness, or criminality. In the seventeenth century, few New World slave societies were more marginal than those of mainland North America.[22] Liminal peoples were drawn or propelled to marginal societies, and creoles of African descent were among the first Africans transported to the mainland.

Atlantic creoles were not only the products of the meeting of Africans and Europeans off the coast of Africa. By the time Europeans began to colonize mainland North America, communities of creoles of African descent similar to those found around the West African *feitorias* had emerged all along the rim of the Atlantic. In Europe—particularly Portugal and Spain—the number of such creoles swelled as trade with Africa increased. By the mid-sixteenth century, 10,000 black people resided in Lisbon, where they composed 10 percent of the city's population. Seville had a slave population of 6,000 (although that number included a minority of Moriscos).[23] As the centers of the Iberian slave trade, these cities distributed African slaves throughout Europe.[24] But during the sixteenth and seventeenth centuries, the bulk of Europe's population of African descent resided on the Iberian peninsula, and the vast majority of them there lived the demeaning life of slaves.

Some, however, escaped bondage and took their familiar place among the Atlantic creoles as sailors, interpreters, peddlers, petty merchants, and artisans in the great Iberian ports. Drawing upon the traditional skills of middlemen and cultural brokers, they accumulated small estates and looked for ways to improve their possibilities. As Europeans expanded their reach across the Atlantic, creole peoples of African descent migrated with them, some willingly, some not. Men of color drawn from creole communities of Europe accompanied Columbus to the Americas and marched with Balboa, Cortés, De Soto, and Pizarro.[25] Some Atlantic creoles crisscrossed the ocean several times, as did Jerónimo, a Wolof slave who was sold from Lisbon to Cartagena and from Cartagena to Murica, where he was purchased by a churchman who sent him to Valencia.[26] Other Atlantic creoles traveled on their own, as sailors and interpreters in both the transatlantic and African trades. Some gained their freedom and mixed with Europeans and Native Americans. Wherever they went, Atlantic creoles extended the use of the distinctive language of the Atlantic, planted the special institutions of the creole community, and propagated their unique outlook.

With the settlement of the Americas, creole communities began to appear on the western side of the Atlantic. To be sure, the creole communities of Bridgetown, Cap Français, Cartagena, Havana, Mexico City, and San Salvador differed from those of Elmina or Seville in many respects, as almost all people of color were slaves. But they shared many of the characteristics of their counterparts in the Old World, exhibiting the same cosmopolitan qualities. They too were intimate with the languages and cultures of the Atlantic and understood something of its religions, trading conventions, and judicial systems. By the middle of the seventeenth century, they began to take their place as cultural brokers on the western side of the Atlantic.

Prior to the sugar revolution, Barbados, a small English settlement at the eastern end of the Antilles, was the home of many such men and women. The English, who seized the nearly uninhabited island in 1627, imported European servants and, when they had the opportunity, purchased African slaves. Until the 1650s, servants outnumbered slaves. Planters, who engrossed the best lands, put both servants and slaves to work growing tobacco and, when that failed, cotton and indigo. But internal divisions and international warfare frustrated the planters' commercial ambitions in Barbados, and until 1640 the island was more a settlement of farmers who produced for their own subsistence than of planters producing for an international market. Even during the 1640s, when the nascent planter class converted to the production of sugar and consolidated political power and staple production in their own hands, the Barbadian labor force continued to reflect its multiracial origins. Into the 1660s, plantations employed both black slaves and white servants.[27]

Although purchased for life, African slaves lived and worked alongside white indentured servants (many of them Irish), convicts, and occasionally political refugees. Their treatment differed little from the European underclass; and when given the opportunity, they stood with indentured servants against their owners. Planters appreciated the dangers of an alliance of servants and slaves, and they built their houses in the "manner of fortification in case there should be any uproar or commotion on the island, whether by the Christian servants or negroe slaves."[28]

But servant and slave rebels fared poorly in Barbados, as they did elsewhere in the Atlantic littoral. Although slaves ran away and plotted with the same spirit as indentured servants, and sometimes in concert with them, they also searched for other ways out of bondage. Since the line between freedom and slavery remained permeable prior to the sugar revolution, some traversed it. In 1654 Anthony Iland, a slave of sugar planter William Leachy, successfully sued for his freedom, claiming he was illegally held in bondage. Others, unable to win their freedom in court, hired their own time, and moved into the huckstering trade, particularly in the island's market towns. In time, they took control of the internal economy of Barbados. Visitors to the island found people of African descent becoming increasingly at home in the New World, as they mastered the terrain of the island, accepted Christianity, participated in the colony's internal economy, transformed it to meet their own needs, and, like Anthony Iland, learned enough about English law to win their freedom. Most importantly, they gained control of the word. An Anglican minister who toured the island in the 1670s noted that black people spoke English "no worse than the natural born subjects of that Kingdom."[29]

What was true for Barbados prior to the sugar revolution was equally true for other English colonies and for the possessions of France in the New World. The *Code Noir,* which France instituted in 1685 to regulate slavery, exhibited a greater concern with heretical Jews and Protestants than with race and slavery. In Martinique, Guadeloupe, and Saint Domingue, which would become the sites of some of the most oppressive plantation regimes in the western hemisphere, the lines between free and slave, black and white were porous prior to the arrival of sugar. Intermarriage between well-placed free people of color and ambitious French nationals was common. Indeed, census takers, notaries, and other officials regularly elevated free people of color to white, paving the way for their entry into the colonies' respectable society. Only after the establishment of the plantation order did the "social categories of Saint-Domingue," as one historian noted, "become increasingly based on genealogy rather than cultural identity."[30]

In short, the creole communities of the Caribbean followed the patterns established on the west coast of Africa and the port cities of Iberia. Like their counterparts in Elmina and Mpinda, Lisbon and Seville, the black people who arrived prior to the plantation revolution soon mastered the language of their enslaver and enough of their owner's customs to challenge them on familiar terrain. Upon occasion, they entered the marketplace, worked on their own, sued their owners in court, claimed Christian belief, and gained legal freedom. While they faced galling discrimination, they established a place in the societies of the New World.

Before long, Atlantic creoles created an intercontinental network of *cofradias* (*confradias* to the Spanish), or black religious brotherhoods, which by the seventeenth century stretched from Lisbon to São Tomé, Angola, and Brazil.[31] Although no known comparable institutional linkages existed in the Anglo- and Franco-American worlds, there were numerous informal connections between black people in New England and Virginia, South Carolina and Barbados, Louisiana and Saint Domingue. Like their African counterparts, Atlantic creoles of European, South American, and Caribbean origins also found their way to mainland North America, where they made up a large share of black America's charter generations. But their experience as first arrivals would take different forms in the colonies of the Chesapeake, the North, the lowcountry of South Carolina and Florida, and the lower Mississippi Valley.

Chapter One

Emergence of Atlantic Creoles in the Chesapeake

Atlantic creoles shaped black America's charter generations in the Chesapeake. They numbered large among the "twenty Negars" a Dutch man-o'-war sold to John Rolfe at Jamestown in 1619.[1] Like Rolfe's purchase, many of the first arrivals were transported to the mainland by Dutch carriers, dribbling into the Bay's inlets in small lots that rarely exceeded more than a score. Although some of the new arrivals hailed directly from Africa, most had already spent some time in the New World, understood the languages of the Atlantic, bore Hispanic and occasionally English names, and were familiar with Christianity and other aspects of European culture. Set to work alongside a mélange of English and Irish servants, little but skin color distinguished them from others who labored in the region's tobacco fields. Through the first fifty years of English and African settlement in the Chesapeake, black and white workers lived and worked together in ways that blurred racial lines. The small number of people of African descent (never more than 5 percent of the region's population during this period) combined with the peculiar demands of the tobacco economy to strengthen the bargaining position of black people, whose status as slaves remained undefined in law although not in practice.[2] Many escaped bondage and secured a modest prosperity. Reviled and disparaged, black America's charter generations nevertheless found a place in the society with slaves that emerged around the Chesapeake during the middle years of the seventeenth century.

The story of Anthony Johnson, sold to the English at Jamestown in 1621 as "Antonio a Negro," reveals something of the history of Atlantic creoles in the Chesapeake region. During the dozen years following his arrival, Antonio labored on the Bennett family's plantation, where he was among the few who survived the 1622 Indian raid that all but destroyed the colony, and where he later earned an official commendation for his "hard labor and known service." His loyalty and industry also won the favor of the Bennetts, who became Antonio's patrons as well as his owners, perhaps because worthies like Antonio were hard to find among the rough, hardbitten, if often sickly men who constituted the mass of servants and slaves in the region. Whatever the source of the Bennetts' favor, they allowed Antonio to farm independently while still a slave, marry, and baptize his children. Eventually, he and his family gained their freedom. Once free, Antonio anglicized his name, transforming Antonio a Negro into Anthony Johnson, a name so familiar to English speakers that no one could doubt his identification with the colony's rulers.[3]

Johnson, his wife Mary, and their children—who numbered four by 1640—followed their benefactor across Chesapeake Bay to the peninsula that composed the eastern shore of Virginia, where the Bennett clan had established itself as a leading family and where the Johnson family began to farm on its own. In 1651 Anthony Johnson earned a 250-acre headright for sponsoring the entry of servants into the colony; this allowed him to accumulate a substantial estate for any Virginian, let alone a former slave. Johnson's son John did even better than his father, receiving a patent for 550 acres, and another son, Richard, owned a 100-acre estate. When Anthony Johnson's plantation burned to the ground in 1653, he petitioned the county court for relief. Reminding authorities that he and his wife were longtime residents and that "their hard labors and knowne services for obtayneing their livelihood were well known," he requested and was granted a special abatement of his taxes.

Like other men of substance, Johnson and his sons farmed independently, held slaves, and left their heirs sizable estates. As established members of their community, they enjoyed rights in common with other free men, and they frequently employed the law to protect themselves and advance their interests. Still, when Anthony Johnson's own slave— a black man named John Casar (sometimes Casor, Cassaugh, or Cazara)—claimed his freedom and gained sanctuary with Robert and George Parker, two neighboring white planters, Johnson did not immediately attempt to retrieve his property. The Parkers had already exhibited considerable animus toward the Johnson family, accusing John Johnson of "fornication and other enormities." Antagonizing rancorous white men of the planter class was a hazardous business, even if Johnson could prove they had conspired to lure John Casar from his household. Eventually, however, Anthony Johnson decided to act. He took the Parkers to court and won Casar's return, along with damages against the Parkers.[4]

Johnson pursued Casar because, like the Parkers, he needed Casar's labor to grow tobacco, the fount of wealth and status in the Chesapeake.[5] The cultivation of tobacco offered considerable advantages to small planters like Johnson, as tobacco was a poor man's crop that could be grown as easily on small farms as on great plantations. Even when labor became available, planters gained few benefits from large units of production and other economies of scale, as good tobacco land occurred only in small, noncontiguous patches. Abandoning European agricultural practices, Chesapeake tobacco planters adopted a mixture of Native-American slash-and-burn and long-fallow hoe culture in part to reduce their labor needs. But such a regimen still required many ready hands.

The crop year began with the preparation of tobacco seedlings in late January and February. In late April, when the seedlings sported four leaves, they were carefully transplanted, the first of a series of movements before the young plants reached the field. Once they did, the plants had to be hilled and rehilled, checked for worms, primed, topped, and suckered to keep the number of leaves to about twelve. This labor occupied workers through the summer months. When the leaves ripened, the plants were cut and cured in specially designed barns or tobacco houses that maximized ventilation, minimized sunlight, and excluded rain. The cured leaves had to be stripped, stemmed, and packed in large bundles for shipping, a task which would occupy all hands into the winter months. In addition, since tobacco was hard on the soil, new land had to be cleared even as established fields were again being readied for cultivation.[6] As these diverse tasks required careful orchestration and reliable labor, losing Casar would be a blow to Anthony Johnson's economic aspirations, just as gaining his assistance—even his paid assistance—would elevate the Parkers.

But making tobacco was not Johnson's only concern. Integrated into the Chesapeake's annual tobacco cycle was the cultivation of corn, the region's subsistence crop. Tobacco and corn placed heavy demands on the men and women who wielded the hoe—particularly in the absence of animal power—but required only a primitive division of labor. There was little reason to employ overseers or stewards, distinguish among workers, or establish a hierarchical order in the fields. During the seventeenth and into the eighteenth century, master, servant, and slave worked shoulder-to-shoulder, with the mistress and her children frequently joining them in the field as well.[7] Although most planters appeared to presume people of African descent were slaves—since they were purchased from slave traders—no law yet enshrined African slavery in either Maryland or Virginia, and the laws that referred to black people were scattered and miscellaneous.

Since both white and black workers grew tobacco—subject to various degrees of coercion—black plantation hands labored according to customary English practices, themselves drawn from the Elizabethan Statute of Artificers. Indeed, as the Chesapeake settlement grew during the seventeenth century, servants expanded the customary rights of English laborers, so that by midcentury they rarely worked more than five and a half days a week during the summer. Winter marked a general reduction of labor, as there was seldom enough work to fill the shorter days. Throughout the year, tobacco hands had not only Sunday to themselves but also half of Saturday and all holidays, which were numerous. The workday itself was punctuated with a long mid-day break.

Custom also required masters and mistresses to provide their servants sufficient food, clothing, and shelter, and it limited the owners' right to discipline subordinates. When planters wished to discipline workers, whether black or white, they often used the courts; not until the next century did slaveowners presume that they were absolute sovereigns within the confines of their estate. Although no slave took his owner to court for ill-treatment, as servants did upon occasion, the law and "Customs of the Countrey" that safeguarded servants provided a modicum of protection for slaves as well.[8] In short, into the middle years of the seventeenth century and perhaps later, slaves enjoyed the benefits extended to white servants in the mixed labor force.

To be sure, the law was often ignored and customary practice forsaken; by all accounts, there was far more abuse of servants in the Chesapeake than in England, and slaves doubtless fared all the worse. Neither law nor custom could save some black people from the brutal exploitation that propertyless men and women faced as planters squeezed the last pound of profit from the tobacco economy. Thus, if the treatment of black laborers at the hands of planters differed little from that of white ones, it was in large measure because human beings could hardly be treated with greater disregard. While the advantages of this peculiar brand of equality may have been lost on its beneficiaries, it was precisely the shared labor regimen that allowed some black men like Anthony Johnson to obtain their freedom and join the scramble for land, servants, and status that characterized life in the seventeenth-century Chesapeake.[9]

While some slaveowners spurred productivity in this labor-short economy by laying on the lash, others offered more generous incentives to servants and slaves. Among the benefits planters extended was the opportunity to labor independently at least a portion of the time, with an understanding that servants and slaves would feed and clothe themselves or at least share the profits of their independent ventures. Such incentives did nothing to challenge the planters' domination or the system of servitude upon which it rested. Indeed, they strengthened the planters' hand by allowing them to transfer the burden of subsistence to their laborers, while they concentrated single-mindedly on tobacco.

If many slaveowners welcomed the exchange, gladly shrugging off their responsibilities as masters and mistresses while retaining their prerogatives, many slaves embraced the possibilities implicit in the bargain. Laboring to support themselves meant additional work, to be sure, but it provided a mechanism for them to control a portion of their lives, and it offered an opportunity—however slight—to buy their way out of bondage. The benefits that flowed to slaves from self-subsistence often extended beyond a richer diet and a larger wardrobe. In Virginia, the justices of one county court allowed a miscreant slave the choice of the lash or a fine, which he could pay "out of that hee calls his owne estate."[10]

The exchange of subsistence for time to labor independently marked the beginnings of the slaves' economy in the Chesapeake region, an elaborate system of exchange that complemented, overlapped, and sometimes competed with the owners' economy within the larger system of staple production.[11] Given time to attend to their own affairs in exchange for subsisting themselves, slaves gardened, tended barnyard animals, and hunted and fished on their own. Occasionally, they manufactured small items and sold them to their owners, neighbors, or other slaves.

Such arrangements had a long history in the evolution of plantation societies in the Atlantic world, reaching back to the emergence of the plantation in the Mediterranean and the islands off the coast of Africa in the fourteenth century. They were widely practiced in the Caribbean.[12] But in the colonial Chesapeake during the seventeenth century, the kaleidoscopic movement of tobacco prices, particularly their dramatic decline in the 1630s, encouraged planters to allow slaves to work independently in periods of economic depression, when demand for the slaves' labor fell while the cost of maintaining slaves remained constant. Indeed, the reduction of rations that slaveholders instituted during hard times may have made self-support more palatable, if not absolutely necessary, to hungry slaves.

Whatever might be gained for both master and slave from the growth of the slaves' economy, each party embraced these arrangements cautiously—as neither was certain of exactly to whom the benefits would accrue. Rather than concede an advantage, each would give only provisional approval to any agreement. No compact went uncontested for long, no matter how equitably the benefits were distributed. Slaves were quick to press for additional time for themselves, demanding Saturdays, early mornings, and evenings in addition to the traditionally free Sunday. Slaveholders not only resisted such exactions but also insisted that slaves accept greater and greater responsibilities for their own maintenance. In time, however, the slaves' economy took its place alongside the masters'. According to a seventeenth-century guide to the Chesapeake, the planter customarily permitted "his Servant a parcell of clear ground to plant some Tobacco in for himself, which he may husband at those idle moments he hath allowed him."[13]

As this guide suggested, some servants and slaves also gained access to provision grounds where they raised not only corn and vegetables to subsist themselves and their families but also tobacco, which they sold in conjunction with their owner's crop, and occasionally in competition with it. They also kept hogs and cattle, which they—like their owner—pastured in the region's open-range forests and swamps. Anthony Johnson was just one of many black men who acquired several head of cattle while still enslaved, and he later allowed his own slave, John Casar, to keep cattle as well—maintaining a part interest in Casar's stock.[14] Other slaves produced substantial crops of tobacco. In Virginia, an inventory for a plantation taken in 1658 revealed that two black slaves independently cultivated some 1,220 pounds of tobacco. The following year, their harvest almost doubled.[15]

The independent economic activities of Chesapeake slaves expanded during the middle years of the seventeenth century, taking a multiplicity of forms, as the Chesapeake's economy grew. Some slaves turned to handicrafts—shoemaking and carpentering seemed the favored trades—to complement agricultural production. Others bartered their free time for wages-in-kind or occasionally in tobacco (the region's proxy for cash), and still others became partners with their owners, ceding them a portion of the produce for the right to labor independently. Slaves thus entered fully into the growing network of exchange, buying and selling goods and services and lending and borrowing small sums from their owners, their neighbors, and one another. Such transactions required that they move freely about the countryside, thereby gaining a full knowledge of the physical and social geography of the Chesapeake. Slaves also traded directly with planter-merchants, assigned their debts to others, and rented land to add to their own fortunes. Transactions in which free people assigned property to slaves and slaves willed property to free people—nonsensical according to the logic of chattel bondage—could be found scattered through the records of seventeenth-century Maryland and Virginia.[16] Although the slaves' proportion of the region's wealth was small, perhaps infinitesimal, there was no part of the economic life of the Chesapeake in which they did not participate.

The social independence that flowed from the slaves' economic activities troubled some slaveowners. They disliked slaves traveling on their own and bargaining with strangers on the basis of equality. Slaveholders feared that too often their own crops became confused with those of their slaves, encouraging larcenous activities that linked slaves, servants, and former servants in unholy alliances detrimental to the slaveowning class. Yet, as customs associated with independent production became embedded in the economic life of the Chesapeake, slaveholders had difficulty extricating themselves from practices they found to be in their own interest. Officials—usually themselves substantial planters—railed against such practices and the evils they promoted. But while planters deemed other men's slaves unworthy of the prerogatives that might accrue from independent economic activities, they were reluctant to deny their own slaves the right to work independently, especially when such an exclusion would throw the burden of subsistence back upon them. Those who did often contradicted themselves in most embarrassing ways. A Virginia planter who publicly forbade his slaves the right to "truck or trade" violated his own edict in practice, and he was not the only one to do so.[17]

Still, the opposition to the slaves' economy was considerable, and over time it grew. Both Virginia and Maryland legislated against trading with servants, and local jurisdictions added their weight as well. When the regulations against illicit trading went unenforced, angry planters took their cases to court, where they generally received a sympathetic hearing. Yet, rather than halting the practice, official prohibitions became the occasion for documenting the extent of the slaves' economy. In 1652, after officials of one Virginia county reiterated the penalties against trading with slaves as a means of reemphasizing the county's long-established ban, two slaves, Emanuel Driggus and Bashaw Farnando, persuaded their owners to make a public avowal that "certaine cattle, hoggs, and poultrye nowe in their possession . . . [had been] lawfullie gotten" and "maye freely [be] dispose[d] of . . . either in their life tyme or att their death." Two weeks later, Driggus sold a cow to a Dutch merchant, certifying that it was his "owne breed and legally assured unto mee by order of the court."[18]

Such substantial holdings, beyond providing modest comforts or a chance to escape the lash, placed a few enterprising slaves within easy distance of purchasing their own liberty or that of their families, which Driggus and Farnando eventually did. More important, the numerous transactions that such accumulations represented provided slaves with critical experience in the larger world. Unrestrained by the confines of plantation life, slaves had the opportunity to connect with men and women of all social standing, and to construct networks of clients and customers who could vouch for their good character, front for them in forbidden transactions, and lend them money. More than cash-in-hand, such patrons provided the social capital that made it possible for some slaves to gain their freedom.

This is exemplified by Francis Payne, who began slave life in the Chesapeake in 1637 as "Francisco a Negroe" and ended it as Frank Paine, a free man. When Payne's owner, Jane Eltonhead, married a Maryland planter and left Virginia for her new husband's estate, Payne entered into an agreement that eventuated in freedom for himself and his family. Payne took control of his mistress's Virginia plantation, employing "the best meanes lawfully hee can for the further betteringe [of the] cropp" in exchange for "the power from tyme to tyme to make good use of the ground." From the first, there appeared to be a tacit understanding that Payne's profits would be applied to the purchase of his liberty, and a year later Payne's mistress and her husband formally agreed to sell him his freedom for "Three Suffict men Servants" age fifteen to twenty-four. The exchange of someone else's liberty for his own freedom was hardly an advance for the cause of freedom in general, but, at least in this case,

Payne cared only for freedom in particular. In 1656, after nearly twenty years in servitude, Francis Payne was a free man.[19] He later extended that arrangement to assure the freedom of his family.[20]

Payne had negotiated a near-impossible bargain, founded on a desperate desire for freedom and extraordinary entrepreneurial audacity. He faltered several times in fulfilling it, and only his mistress's willingness to grant two special extensions allowed him to complete the agreement. Even then, it took seven years for Payne to satisfy his mistress and secure his freedom, and another decade for him to secure the liberty of his wife and children. But when his obligations had been discharged, the Paynes took their place alongside the Johnsons in the ranks of the Chesapeake's free families.

John Graweere freed his child by brokering a similar arrangement with his owner, William Evans. Graweere's wife was the slave of Robert Sheppard, and their child followed its mother's status. "Permitted by his . . . master to keep hogs and make the best benefit thereof to himself provided the said Evans might have half the increase," Graweere had accumulated enough to purchase the child, but he needed Sheppard's assent. Perhaps to win it, he emphasized his desire for the child to "be made a christian" and, even more specifically, to be "taught and exercised in the church of England." Still, even after Graweere proclaimed his devotion to Jesus Christ and the Anglican Church, Sheppard or Evans or both hesitated in releasing the child. In the end, freedom was secured only after Graweere enlisted "the good liking and consent of Tho: Gooman's overseer," who agreed to stand as the child's godfather and "see it brought up in the christian religion."[21]

Aided by a knowledge of the Chesapeake's economy, an acceptance of the touchstones of Anglo-American culture, and hard cash, Payne and Graweere parlayed "the good liking and consent" of prominent planters or well-connected overseers into freedom. Unique in the details, their strategies exemplified the diverse schemes black men and women employed to secure their freedom during the middle years of the seventeenth century. Like other routes out of bondage—freedom suits, indenture enforcements, and manumissions of various sorts—these strategies required knowledge, determination, daring, a facility for shrewd trading, and, in the end, the ability to secure the patronage of some prominent man or woman.[22] These prerequisites to success were not easily obtained; yet, because they were precisely the attributes Atlantic creoles carried with them to the Chesapeake, the number of black free men and women expanded steadily.

By midcentury, the Johnsons, Paynes, and Graweeres were not alone among people of African descent who enjoyed freedom in the Chesapeake. Small communities of free blacks sprouted up all around the perimeter of the Chesapeake Bay, with the largest concentration on the eastern shore of Virginia and Maryland. The number remained tiny—in 1665 the free black population of Virginia's Northampton and Accomack counties amounted to less than twenty adults and perhaps an equal number of children—but as the black population of the entire region was itself small, totaling no more than 300 on the eastern shore and perhaps 1,700 in all of Maryland and Virginia, the proportion of black people enjoying freedom was substantial. And, perhaps more importantly, it was growing. In Northampton County, free people of African descent made up about one-fifth of the black population at midcentury, rising to nearly 30 percent in 1668.[23]

Although a minority, these free men and women defined the boundaries of black life and the character of race relations in the Chesapeake during the first fifty years of English and African settlement. The enslavement of most black people in the region—and, more importantly, the universal knowledge that people of African descent were enslaved throughout the Atlantic world—debased black people in the eyes of most whites, before Chesapeake lawmakers ruled that the children of enslaved black women were slaves for life and even prior to the enactment of other discriminatory legislation. But the free blacks' presence and growing numbers subverted the logic of racial slavery in the eyes of white and black alike. As long as the boundary between slavery and freedom remained permeable, and as long as white and black labored in the fields together, racial slavery remained only one labor system among many. If the stigma of color condemned some black people to lifetime servitude, so the stigma of poverty, criminality, immorality, uncertain lineage, and alien religion condemned others—men and women of European pedigree prominent among them—to terms of servitude in which they labored and lived no better than slaves. That black people could, and on rare occasions did, hold slaves and servants themselves suggested that race—like lineage and religion—was just one of many markers in the social order that Atlantic creoles understood well.

The names of these freed people of color attest to the broad influence of the larger Atlantic world: Domingo Mathews, John Francisco (later Sisco), Bashaw Ferdinando or Farnando, Emanuel Driggus or sometimes Drighouse (probably Rodriggus), and Anthony Longo (perhaps Loango).[24] These names traced the tumultuous experience that propelled creoles across the Atlantic and the Caribbean into the Chesapeake. They suggested that whatever tragedies befell these men and women before they reached the Chesapeake, they did not arrive as deracinated chattel, stripped of their past and without resources to meet the future. Unlike those who would follow them into slavery in the plantation era, these first arrivals were not denigrated by diminutives, labeled with names more appropriate to barnyard animals, or derided with the appellations of ancient notables. Instead, their names provided concrete evidence that they carried their dignity and a good deal more with them to the New World.

Like Antonio a Negro, they were creoles who had gained a familiarity with economic exchange, Christian religion, and slavery along the littoral of the Atlantic. For the most part, they entered the Chesapeake in small groups, as prizes of privateers and pirates, as unsalable portions of larger shipments to Barbados or other islands under English control, or as special orders to merchants in the coasting trade. Among the latter were transhipments from New Netherland, where slaves had landed in similar configurations via Curaçao and St. Eustatius. Few, however, derived directly from Africa. At the beginning of the eighteenth century, Maryland's governor, reviewing the history of his colony's slave trade, observed that "before the year 1698, this province has been supplyd by some small Quantitys of Negro's from Barbados and other of her Ma'tys Islands and Plantations, as Jamaica and New England Seaven." They arrived "eight, nine or ten in a Sloope, and sometymes larger Quantitys, and sometymes, tho very seldom, whole ship Loads of Slaves have been brought here directly from Affrica by Interlopers, or such as have had Lycenses, or otherwise traded there." Most of the latter had arrived in the last decade of the seventeenth century, a fact confirmed by "some ancient Inhabitants" who observed "that before the year 1680 what negros were brought to Virginia were imported generally from Barbados for it was very rare to have a Negro ship come to this Country directly from Africa."[25]

While most Atlantic creoles arrived in the Chesapeake as a part of the international trade in slaves, a few immigrated freely. One such man,

"John Phillip, A negro Christened in *England* 12 yeeres since," landed triumphantly in 1624, a member of the crew of a privateer with a Spanish merchantman in tow. Phillip did not stay long, but Sebastian Cain, another free black sailor, did. A former slave of Boston merchant Robert Keayne (hence his name), Cain had taken to the sea after gaining his freedom. Working the coasting trade, he alighted in Virginia several times in the 1650s and liked what he saw. In 1660 he liquidated his small estate in Massachusetts—taking time to purchase the freedom of a slave man named Angola from Keayne's widow—and settled permanently on Virginia's eastern shore as a neighbor and eventually kinsman of the Johnsons, Drigguses, and Paynes.[26]

Whether they came as free or slave, Atlantic creoles found the settlements around Chesapeake Bay little different from those they had left along the Atlantic rim, except perhaps for their isolation and small size. The mixture of farmers and merchants of largely English origins with a scattering of Dutch, Scottish, Irish, and Portuguese posed few problems for the new arrivals, as their working knowledge of the creole language, their understanding of commerce, and their experience in a multiplicity of social exchanges was as valuable in the Chesapeake as it was on the African coast or a Caribbean island. Whereas a later generation of transplanted Africans would be linguistically isolated and de-skilled by the process of enslavement, Atlantic creoles of the charter generations found themselves very much at home in the new environment.

The demography of the black migration—forced and free—contributed to this sense of well-being. Although Chesapeake planters, like slaveholders throughout the Americas, desired men rather than women and adults rather than children, their position as tobacco growers at a time when sugar magnates commanded the international market forced them to take what slaves they could get. Chesapeake planters could neither afford, nor could the tobacco economy absorb, the boatloads of direct African imports with their disproportionately male cargos that had begun to make their way to the sugar islands. As a result, the sexual balance of the Chesapeake's black population exhibited none of the wild disproportions that attended direct trade with Africa; and in fact, the sex ratio of the black population (meaning the number of men per one hundred women) may have been more evenly balanced than that of the white population during the seventeenth century. For like reasons, adults and children existed in normal proportions. This slow, irregular influx of

Atlantic creoles of both sexes allowed black men and women to marry and form families, or to keep established families intact.

Moreover, the creoles—perhaps because of their experience with the diseases of the Atlantic—seemed to be a remarkably healthy lot in a region known for its deadly fevers and towering mortality rates. Anthony Johnson, denominated "the old Negroe" in 1654, died in 1670. Some members of the charter generations survived better than European settlers. Mary, Anthony's wife of some fifty years, survived him by a decade. Anthony and Mary Johnson lived to see their grandchildren, an experience enjoyed by few European immigrants to the Chesapeake during the seventeenth century.[27]

Having established families and having begun to weave a larger web of kinship, Atlantic creoles ascended the social order of the Chesapeake in much the same way that they had won their freedom. Drawing upon knowledge gained in the larger Atlantic world and exhibiting a sure-handed understanding of patron-client relations, they searched the seams of a society whose commitment to chattel bondage had yet to be confirmed in law and whose dedication to white supremacy had yet to become an all-absorbing obsession. When they found the weak points, they burst the constraints of servitude, race, and impoverishment. The fluidity of colonial society, the ill-defined meaning of slavery, and the ambiguous notions of race allowed Atlantic creoles to carve a place for themselves in the Chesapeake and occasionally achieve a modest prosperity, despite the growing weight of discriminatory legislation.[28]

Free blacks cultivated their relationships with their former owners, landlords, commercial associates, creditors, sponsors, and patrons, not only to protect themselves in moments of peril but also to participate openly and freely in the routine transactions which, taken together, defined the economy and society of the Chesapeake region. Patrons rented or leased land to former slaves, lent them money, marketed their tobacco, purchased their livestock, and served as their advocates at law, often standing for their ambitious attempts to expand their liberty, much as did the Bennetts for Anthony Johnson or "Tho: Gooman's overseer" for John Graweere.[29]

Some patrons acted from respect or friendship for their clients, others from a sense of noblesse oblige, and yet others because the free people's gratitude could be profitable. Vulnerable black people paid premium prices for goods and services that white men and women bought cheaply.

Landlords who rented land to black planters often exacted higher rents from them than they did from white tenants, just as employers who hired free black craftsmen and laborers seemed to expect an extra measure of service.[30] Still, whatever the incremental cost of freedom, black people paid it willingly, and they openly deferred to the men and women who stood between them and the fearful possibilities of being defined outside of respectable society.

Atlantic creoles identified themselves with the colony's most important institutions—registering transactions in county courthouses and celebrating rites of passage in established churches. While they may have cared little for the precise nature of the Chesapeake's jurisprudence and religious observance, the existence of courts and churches carried great weight with the black men and women who struggled for a place in Chesapeake society. At every opportunity, free blacks had their property and debts recorded in the courthouse and their wills notarized. Such documentation afforded the occasion to certify Christian belief, in that acknowledging "the Lord Jesus Christ" was yet another marker of belonging. For like reasons, black people baptized their children and selected godparents from among the leaders of the colony. Occasionally, they adopted orphaned black children, giving them fictive parents in a manner that confirmed their adoptive parents' commitment to conventional family arrangements and once again provided the occasion for assuring their white neighbors that they raised their children "in knowledge of our Savior Christ Jesus."[31]

Identifying themselves with the community's most prominent icons and institutions, much as they connected themselves with the community's most prominent men and women, Atlantic creoles demonstrated a determination not to be excluded from Chesapeake society by intimations that they were libidinous heathens without language, lineage, or culture. Nowhere was this persistent drive for inclusion more evident than in their mastery of the law. Perhaps because of the fragile nature of their social position, creoles were extremely conscious of their rights at law.

Like their white neighbors, free people of color were a litigious people. Throughout the seventeenth century they sued and were sued with great frequency, testifying and petitioning as to their rights. Although many black men and women fell prey to the snares of Anglo-American jurisprudence—bastardy acts, tax forfeitures, and debt penalties—their

failure was rarely one of ignorance, as members of the charter generations proved adept at challenging the law on its own terms and rarely
abandoned a losing cause without appeal. On the eastern shore of Virginia, free blacks did particularly well before the bar of justice. According
to their historians, the free blacks' "record before the county court seems
neither better nor worse than that compiled by small white planters."[32]

In economy and society, Atlantic creoles—like ambitious white men
and women—strove to own their own land. Only a handful succeeded,
as most entered freedom financially, if not physically, exhausted from
the burdens of buying their way out of bondage. Francis Payne, who
gained his freedom after a near-heroic effort—like most former slaves—
was never able to purchase land on his own. Yet few whites rose from
servitude to landownership either. The most successful generally became
leaseholders, renters, and sharecroppers, which was the route that Payne
and most former slaves followed. And many landless free blacks had
property in cattle and tools. Cattle traders and artisans loomed large
among the most successful free blacks in the seventeenth-century Chesapeake.[33]

However achieved, independence allowed black men and women a
wide range of expressions that others termed arrogance—the traditional
charge against Atlantic creoles. Anthony Johnson exhibited an exalted
sense of self when a local notable challenged his industry. Dismissing
intimations of sloth and idleness, Johnson countered with a ringing assertion of his independence: "I know myne owne ground and I will worke
when I please and play when I please."[34] Such self-assurance was suffused
throughout free black society, for those men and women who had
crossed the Atlantic and scaled the barrier between slavery and freedom
were not easily intimidated. In 1655, when an officer of the Northampton
County Court served Tony Longo with a warrant, Longo, then busy in
the field, turned on him with a scathing "shitt of your warrant," a force-
ful reminder that he had better things to do than to be pestered by the
law. The stunned officer then reported that Longo's wife joined in "with
such noyse that I could hardly heare my owne words."[35] Such bravado,
blurted out in fits of exasperation, reflected both the creoles' confidence
in their ability to compete as equals and their frustration at the constraints that prevented them from doing so. Life in the margins was no
easier in the Chesapeake than it was elsewhere on the perimeter of the
Atlantic, even for the most successful people of color.

Yet, there were places where equality could not be denied. Marriage bans indicate that some whites and blacks ignored the strictures against what Chesapeake lawmakers later termed "shameful" and "unnatural" acts and instead joined together as man and wife without regard to color. On the eastern shore of Virginia, at least one man from every leading free black family—the Johnsons, Paynes, and Drigguses—married a white woman. There seems to have been little stigma attached to such unions: after Francis Payne's death, his white widow remarried, this time to a white man. In like fashion, free black women joined together with white men. William Greensted, a white attorney who represented Elizabeth Key, a woman of color, in her successful suit for freedom, later married her. In 1691 when the Virginia General Assembly ruled against such relationships, some propertied white Virginians found the legislation novel and obnoxious enough to muster a protest.[36]

Such relationships revealed the large social expanse where black men and women interacted with white people, if not with full equality, at least with open recognition that power had many sources, of which descent was but one. This was particularly true prior to 1640, when the absence of legal distinctions between white and black laborers allowed black slaves to take shelter in the laws and customs that protected white servants. But it remained true even after Chesapeake lawmakers began to codify racial distinctions.

In some measure, the tiny black population scattered across the landscape created a social demography that compelled interracial mixing. In many places, there were simply too few people of African descent to create a community with its own distinctive aspirations, ideals, and institutions. But the absence of such a community was more than just an artifact of the Chesapeake's population dynamics. Many blacks and whites appeared to enjoy one another's company, perhaps because they shared so much. Behind closed doors, far from the eyes of suspicious slaveholders, black and white joined together to drink, gamble, frolic, and fight. Indeed, it was the violence that followed long bouts of "drinkinge and carrousinge" that time and again revealed the extent of interracial conviviality.[37]

Inevitably, conviviality led to other intimacies. What was true for the most eligible free black men and women was no less valid at the bottom of black society. Bastardy lists suggest that the largest source of mixed-raced children in the seventeenth-century Chesapeake was not the imposition of white planter men on black slave women but the relations of black slaves and white servants. Fragmentary evidence from various parts of Maryland and Virginia affirms that approximately one-quarter to one-third of the illegitimate children born to white women had fathers of African descent. The prevalence of these interracial unions may have been the reason why one justice legally sanctified the marriage of Hester, an English servant woman, to James Tate, a black slave.[38]

The frequent and easy confederation of poor people of diverse color created a bank of trust which they drew upon in challenging their superiors. Throughout the seventeenth century, black and white ran away together, joined in petty conspiracies, and, upon occasion, stood shoulder-to-shoulder against the weighty champions of established authority. In 1676, when Nathaniel Bacon's "Choice and Standing Army" took to the field against forces commanded by Virginia's royal governor, it drew on both white and black bondmen in nearly equal proportions. Among the last holdouts were a group of eighty black slaves and twenty white indentured servants, who bitterly condemned as a betrayal the surrender of Bacon's officers.[39]

Thus, Atlantic creoles labored to incorporate themselves into the larger life of the Chesapeake in the hopes that participation would lead to recognition, and recognition would eliminate the threat of racial ostracism. Being defined outside of respectable society—not subordination—was what black people of the charter generations feared most. In 1688, when threats of enslavement—the "law made that all free Negroes should bee slaves againe" went the rumor—forced Sarah Driggus and some of her children to flee Virginia for Maryland, the Drigguses carried certificates of residence from a Virginia court and certificates of baptism from a Virginia church.[40] In her moment of greatest terror, Sarah Driggus reached for one of the oldest weapons in the creoles' arsenal. Such testimonials had allowed Anthony Johnson to farm independently while still a slave, secure his freedom, enter the landholding class, and even win a judgment against white men who would usurp his property. The patronage embodied in the testimonials Sarah Driggus carried from Virginia represented the remnants of a well-worn strategy that had secured a place for some black people in Chesapeake society and, in so doing, guarded all black people against the forces that would deny their humanity.

Unfortunately for Sarah Driggus, the design that had functioned effectively for more than five decades failed in the waning years of the seventeenth century. The testimonials that she hoped would shield her family offered no greater protection in Maryland than they had in Virginia. The Drigguses might run from the onrushing plantation regime, but they could not outrun it.[41]

Foreshadowing the transformation of Chesapeake society, during the last quarter of the seventeenth century the linkages among people of color—free and unfree—grew at the expense of connections with white patrons, on one hand, and white servants and free men, on the other. Ties among black people did not need to be invented, as black men and women had always lived and worked in close proximity, traded among themselves, given security for one another, socialized, shared memories, and exchanged gifts and other intimacies. Tight communities, bound together by blood and marriage and linked by connections of godparentage and guardianships, existed throughout the Chesapeake region.

But if black people knew one another well, they had not fabricated a culture, generated a social structure, or articulated an ideal that separated them from their European counterparts, unless a common desire for inclusion can be said to be the distinguishing mark of seventeenth-century black life. As that world collapsed, however, black people began to delineate the differences between themselves and those who would deny their birthright. In 1677 John Johnson, a third-generation Virginian whose grandfather had anglicized the family name, called his estate "Angola."[42] As the new markers of the black experience appeared, the foundation of a separate nation was established.

Chapter Two

Expansion of Creole Society in the North

⚹

Like their counterparts in Virginia and Maryland, the northern colonies began as societies with slaves, not slave societies, and remained such through the seventeenth and well into the eighteenth century. Slaves were few in number and marginal to commerce and agriculture in New England and the Middle Colonies. The multifarious character of the northern economy and the low ratio of blacks to whites allowed the charter generations to be incorporated into the larger life of the colonial North, even as they maintained their transatlantic linkages. Despite the burden of enslavement, Atlantic creoles—familiar with European ways and languages—established cultural roots in the port cities of the North and throughout the region.

The charter generations' creole origins, their small numbers, and the absence of plantation labor shaped black life in the northern colonies during the first century of settlement. Few slaves came directly from Africa, as the Dutch West India Company and later the Royal African Company enjoyed more profitable markets to the south. Instead, most slaves dribbled into the northern colonies from the Caribbean Islands or the mainland South, an incidental residue of the larger Atlantic trade. Since few northern traders specialized in selling slaves, slaves generally landed as special requisitions from merchants or farmers with connections to the sugar islands. Some of these were shipped northward as a last resort. "If you cannot sell all your slaves," a Rhode Island merchant informed his West Indies-bound supercargo, "bring some of them home; I believe they will sell well."[1]

Sometimes they did. But many of these slaves were the unsaleable "refuse"—as traders contemptuously demeaned them—of larger shipments. Broken, enfeebled, and generally unfit for plantation labor, they found their way to northern ports when no one else would purchase them.

47

In 1664 the governor of the colony of New Netherland—issuing a lament that would be echoed by northern slaveholders throughout the first century of settlement—described a cargo of slaves as "old and . . . rejected." Northern slaveholders generally disliked these scourings of the transatlantic trade who, one Massachusetts official opined, were "usually the worst servants." Authorities also feared that the West Indian re-exports had records of recalcitrance and criminality as well as physical defects. In 1708 Rhode Island acted against such imports, which the legislature declared "the worst sort of Negroes: some sent for murder, some for theft, some were runaways, and most were impudent, lame, and distempered."

In time, prospective slaveowners found virtue in necessity and declared their preference for seasoned slaves because of their knowledge of European languages, familiarity with work routines, or resistance to New World diseases. Dutch slaveholders in New Netherland eventually favored "Negroes who had been 12 or 13 years in the West Indies," deeming them "a better sort of Negroes" than slaves directly from Africa. Emigré planters, who carried their own slaves to the mainland, shared these biases. But whatever their preference, northern merchants and farmers, like Chesapeake planters, generally took what they got.[2]

Unable to compete directly with the wealthier staple-producing colonies for prime hands, northern merchants looked to other routes to secure the slaves they wanted. As a result, slaves also entered the North as the prizes captured by privateers and pirates operating out of northern ports. Some of these were Atlantic creoles taken on the high seas, and some of the captives may have been Africans on their way to the Americas. Others, however, were snatched while in transit between New World slave societies, as were a group of some thirty black and Indian slaves seized by a Dutch privateer off the coast of New Spain in 1704 and delivered to New York. Like so many products of the intra-American—rather than the transatlantic—trade, they were creoles, probably of American birth. Indeed, the so-called "Spanish Indians" promptly sued for their freedom in New York courts, exhibiting the Atlantic creoles' knowledge of the judicial system and litigious propensity.

Occasionally, northern traders reached across the Atlantic in their dealings with privateers and pirates. One group of New York merchants collaborated with pirates to bring slaves from Madagascar. But most pirated slaves were seized in American waters and had already spent considerable time in the New World.[3] The few slaves who entered the North directly from Africa generally arrived only when a temporary glut made sale impossible elsewhere in the Atlantic basin. Between 1659 and 1664 the Dutch West India Company—expelled from Brazil by the Portuguese—rerouted to New Amsterdam several shiploads of slaves that had been bound for Pernambuco. In 1684 some 150 Africans were delivered to Philadelphia. But these were singular events, and even in such special cases the Africans did not always remain in the North.[4] When conditions in the plantation colonies changed, merchants re-exported these slaves southward at a profit. Many of these transshipments ended up in the Chesapeake, affirming the parallel development of the charter generations in each of the two regions during the middle years of the seventeenth century.[5]

In the first decades of the eighteenth century, the nature of the northern slave trade shifted from the traditional pattern, but not enough to make a difference. A few northern merchants established direct ties with Africa. Even then, however, the richer markets to the south continued to drain off African arrivals. "Some times we have a vessell or two to go to the Coast of Guinea, & bring Negroes from thence," reported the governor of New York in 1708, "but they seldom come to this place, but rather go to Virginia or Maryland, where they find a much better market for their negroes than they can do here." In New York, with the largest slave population in the North, Caribbean imports continued to outnumber African arrivals well into the eighteenth century. Between 1715 and 1730 the count was more than three to one in favor of West Indian slaves; and during the first three decades of the eighteenth century, fully 70 percent of the slaves arriving in New York originated elsewhere in the Americas.[6]

Whatever their origins, slaves landed in the northern colonies singly, in twos and threes, or by the score, but rarely by the boatload. "As for blacks," remarked the governor of Connecticut in 1679, "there comes sometimes three or four in a year from Barbados."[7] Commission merchants, privateers, and pirates had neither the wherewithal nor the interest to fill their holds with slaves in the manner of transatlantic traders. Slaves thus arrived in the North chained and manacled but not under the horrific circumstances that accompanied the "tight packing" of the Middle Passage, the nightmarish journey between Africa and the New World.

Newly arrived slaves, most already experienced in the Atlantic world and familiar with their proscribed status, took advantage of the special circumstances of their captivity where they could. They quickly established families and increased their numbers by natural means during the first generation.[8] A perusal of the names scattered through archival remains of New Netherland reveals something of the dimensions of this transatlantic transfer: Paulo d'Angola and Anthony Portuguese, Pedro Negretto and Francisco Negro, Van St. Thomas and Francisco Cartagena, Claes de Neger and Assento Angola, Simon Congo, Christopher Santome, and Jan Guinea, and—perhaps most telling—Carla Criole, Jan Creoli, and Christoffel Crioell.[9]

As in the Chesapeake, the slaves' names tell much about their experience. To such men and women, New Amsterdam was not radically different from Elmina or Luanda, Bridgetown or Willemstad save for its inferior size. A fortified port controlled by the Dutch West India Company, New Amsterdam was a farrago of petty artisans, merchants, soldiers, and corporate officials scrambling for status in a frontier milieu that underscored the importance of intercultural exchange. On the tip of Manhattan, transplanted Atlantic creoles rubbed elbows with sailors of various nationalities and Native Americans with diverse tribal allegiances. Familiar with the milieu of New Amsterdam if not the place itself, Atlantic creoles almost immediately began the business of integrating themselves into society. Much like their counterparts in the Chesapeake, the black people arriving in New Amsterdam understood slavery as one of many forms of clientage. They connected themselves to the most powerful men and institutions in an effort to find the patrons who might assist their incorporation into mainland North American society. Members of the first generation were frequent visitors to the Dutch courts and were quick to sue for their freedom and, if possible, to expand their rights. Transplanted creoles, in short, seized every opportunity to improve the circumstances of their enslavement and where possible to gain their freedom.

In New Netherland, the diverse needs of the Dutch mercantile economy strengthened the slaves' hand relative to their owners. Far more than Maryland or Virginia in mid-seventeenth century, New Netherland rested upon slave labor. The prosperity of the Netherlands and the opportunities presented to ambitious men and women in the far-flung Dutch empire reduced the number of free Dutch immigrants available to New Netherland and limited its access to indentured servants. To populate the colony, the Dutch West India Company scraped the Atlantic basin for settlers, accepting German Lutherans, French Huguenots, and Sephardic Jews. Even those newcomers did little to sate the colony's need for farm workers, because, as an official of the West India Company reported in 1647, "agricultural laborers, who are conveyed thither at great expense . . . sooner or later apply themselves to trade, and neglect agriculture altogether." From this perspective, slave labor was absolutely necessary. Dutch officials imported all they could, so that in 1638 about 100 blacks lived in New Amsterdam, and they made up roughly 30 percent of the city's population. The proportion diminished over time, but at the end of the seventeenth century New Amsterdam (renamed New York by the English) still had a larger black population than any other mainland city. At the time of the English conquest in 1664, slaves comprised about 20 percent of the population of the city and about 5 percent of the population of the entire colony, a proportion not substantially different from that of the Chesapeake region at the time.[10]

At first, the Dutch West India Company housed its slaves in barracks and worked them under an overseer. But before long some of the company's slaves secured the right to live out and work on their own in return for a stipulated amount of labor and an annual tribute. Free to reside independently and frequently to work on their own, they mastered the Dutch language, took Dutch surnames, attached themselves to the Dutch Reformed Church, and, most importantly, established families. During the first generation, some twenty-six black couples took their vows in the Dutch Reformed Church in New Amsterdam, where they also baptized their children. Suggesting the strength of family ties, church records generally named the father, not the owner, of the newly baptized. Black families witnessed the baptisms of one another's children—rarely calling upon white people, owners or not, to serve in this capacity—and upon occasion legally adopted orphaned black children, knitting the community together with a web of kinship and, again, documenting their commitment to what the Dutch would deem conventional family relations. In 1644 the Dutch West India Company emancipated a group of slave men—probably the first male arrivals—their wives and children, so they could continue "to support their wives and children, as they have been accustomed to do."[11]

The aspirations of black people in New Amsterdam were not confined to family and church. In 1635, within less than ten years of the arrival of the first black people, a group of company slaves understood enough about the organization of the colony and the operation of the West India Company to petition the corporate headquarters in Amsterdam for payment of wages. Indeed, black people participated in nearly every aspect of life in New Netherland by the middle of the seventeenth century. They sued, and were sued, in Dutch courts, and they drilled in the Dutch militia. Slaves as well as free blacks traded independently, accumulating property and establishing the foundations of an independent economy.[12] Thus, the connections that Atlantic creoles established with English institutions in the Chesapeake were duplicated in New Netherland by other creoles who forged ties with similar Dutch institutions.

As in the Chesapeake region, escaping slavery was not easy in New Netherland, although there was as yet no legal proscription on manumission. Indeed, gaining freedom was nearly impossible for slaves owned by individuals and difficult even for those belonging to the West India Company. The company valued its slaves and was willing to liberate only the elderly, perhaps understanding that such aged survivors would soon—if they had not already—become a liability. Even when manumitting such slaves, the company demanded an annual tribute from adults and maintained legal ownership of their children, a practice that elicited protests from both blacks and whites in New Amsterdam. To black people, such "half-freedom," as the Dutch system came to be known, was no freedom at all.[13]

Half-freedom was calculated to benefit slaveowners, not slaves, by spurring youthful slaves to greater exertion and relieving owners of a responsibility to support the aged or infirmed. Still, slaves squeezed what benefits they could from the Dutch system. They accepted the company's terms and agreed to pay the corporate tribute, but they petitioned the West India Company to elevate the status of half-free slaves to full freedom. Hearing rumors that baptism assured freedom to their children, they sought church membership. A Dutch prelate complained that black people "wanted nothing else than to deliver their children from bodily slavery, without striving for piety and Christian virtues."[14] Although freedom never followed conversion in New Netherland, many half-free slaves reached their goal through other means. By the English conquest of 1664, about one black person in five had secured freedom in the colony, a proportion only slightly below that achieved by black people on the eastern shore of Virginia at about the same time.[15]

Some free people of African descent prospered. Building upon small gifts of land the West India Company provided as freedom dues, free blacks moved into the landholding class. A small community of former slaves established itself on the outskirts of the Dutch settlement on Manhattan, farmed independently, and sold produce in the public market. Other free people purchased farmsteads or obtained land as part of an effort to people the city's hinterland. In 1659 the town of Southampton granted "Peeter the Neigro" three acres. Somewhat later John Neiger, who had "set himself up a house in the street" of Easthampton, was given "for his own use a little quantity of land above his house for him to make a yard or garden." Upon occasion, the prosperity of free blacks enabled them to employ white men and women.[16]

The former slaves' position was precarious, and became more so as the Dutch commitment to slavery grew. The transformation of New Netherland from a string of trading posts to a settlement wedded to agricultural production placed a larger proportion of the slave population in the hands of individual planters, who had little interest in allowing them the benefits that once accrued to company slaves. Manumission became less frequent, and the place of those who had earlier obtained their freedom became increasingly marginal. The free people's place eroded more rapidly following the English takeover in 1664.[17] Nonetheless, some black people enjoyed the benefits of the earlier age. They maintained secure family lives, accumulated property, and participated as communicants in the Dutch Reformed Church, where they continued to baptize their children. When threatened, they took their complaints to court.

During the first century of settlement, no other northern colony developed as large a free black population as New York, although even there free people of African descent could not maintain their numbers into the eighteenth century. Traveling to the Bowery on the tip of Manhattan Island in 1679, a Dutch visitor observed that "upon both sides of this way were many habitations of negroes, mulattoes and whites. These negroes were formerly the proper slaves of the [West India] Company but, in consequence of the frequent changes and conquests of the country, they have obtained their freedom and settled themselves down where they have thought proper, and thus on this road, where they have ground enough to live on with their families."[18]

Slaves in New York also did remarkably well, informally enjoying the privileges of an earlier era well into the eighteenth century. Slaves had the right to hold property of their own—which greatly enhanced the ability to expand their independent economic activities as gardeners and provisioners in the city market. As a regular practice, slaveowners conceded the right of slaves to select their owners, so that slaves might live near kin or change an unsatisfactory situation. "The Custome of the Country," bristled a frustrated New York master to a West Indian friend in 1717, "will not allow us to use our Negroes as you doe in Barbados."[19]

Black people elsewhere in the North replicated the experience of those in New York. The same factors that mitigated the harshest features of bondage in New York strengthened the position of slaves in dealing with their owners. Small holdings, close living conditions, and the absence of gang labor allowed members of the charter generations to incorporate themselves into the mainstream of northern life and enjoy many of the rights of free people.[20]

During the first century of settlement in the North, black people composed a small fraction of the population of New England and the Middle Colonies. Only in Rhode Island did they approach the proportion of the population achieved in New York, and that did not occur until after midcentury. In most northern colonies, the proportion was considerably smaller. At its height, the black population totaled only 8 percent of the population of New Jersey and less than 4 percent in Massachusetts and Connecticut.[21] No visitor could confuse New England or the Middle Colonies with the plantation regimes of the sugar islands, where the slaves constituted upward of 80 percent of the population.

Still, slaves were neither an inconsequential element in northern economic development nor an insignificant portion of the northern population during the seventeenth and eighteenth centuries. Indeed, colony-wide enumerations diluted the significance of black people and underestimated the importance of slave labor. In some of the North's most productive agricultural regions and in the towns and cities, a large proportion of the free people held slaves, and slaves composed a large share of the population, sometimes as much as a third of the whole and half of the workforce.[22]

Slaves congregated in large numbers in northern cities and towns. New York City, Philadelphia, Newport, and Boston had substantial slave populations, as did lesser towns. During the first decade of the eighteenth century, slaves made up more than one-sixth of the population of Philadelphia, which seems to be representative of other northern cities at the time. During the middle years of the eighteenth century, New York lost its preeminence to Charles Town and then to New Orleans as the largest mainland slave city, but it remained a major site for urban slavery on the North American continent.[23]

Although most northern employers preferred bound European laborers to enslaved African ones, they had no principled objections to slaveownership. When prosperity discouraged potential European immigrants or war blocked their path, northern merchants, artisans, and farmers turned to African slaves, much as the Dutch had done early in the seventeenth century. In Pennsylvania, farmers and merchants shuttled between bound Europeans and enslaved Africans, exhibiting little concern for the origins, color, or status of their workers—save for availability and price. Moreover, some northern employers preferred slaves even when white indentured servants were available. Perhaps because of their early attachment, Dutch farmers in New York and New Jersey were particularly wedded to black bonded labor.[24] Although some white northerners never saw a black slave, others had daily, intimate contact with them. And, while some slaves found it difficult to join together with their fellows, others lived in close contact.

Although disproportionately urban, the vast majority of northern slaves—like white northerners—lived and worked in the countryside. A few labored in highly capitalized rural industries—tanneries, saltworks, lead and copper mines, and iron furnaces—where they worked alongside white indentured servants and hired laborers. Ironmasters, the largest employers of industrial slaves, also ranked among the region's largest slaveholders. Pennsylvania iron manufacturers manifested their dependence on slave labor when, in 1727, they petitioned for a reduction in the tariff on slaves so they might keep their furnaces in operation. Forges and foundries in other colonies similarly relied on slave labor.[25] But in an overwhelmingly agrarian society, only a small proportion of the slave population engaged in industrial labor.

Like most rural whites, most rural blacks toiled as agricultural workers. In southern New England, the Hudson Valley, Long Island, and northern New Jersey—areas which contained the North's densest black populations—slaves tended stock and raised crops for export to the sugar islands. Farmers engaged in provisioning the West Indies with draft animals and foodstuffs were familiar with slavery and had easy access to slaves. Some, like the Barbadian emigrés in northern New Jersey, had migrated from the Caribbean themselves. Others, particularly those around Narragansett Bay, styled themselves planters in the West Indian manner. They built great houses, bred racehorses, and accumulated slaves. Although they rarely held more than two or three slave families, slaveholdings could be found that numbered into the twenties or thirties and exhibited a complicated division of labor. The great estates of the Hudson Valley also depended on slave labor. The founder of the Philipse family in Westchester County—Frederick Philipse—died in 1702 holding twenty-one slaves; his son Adolophus had twenty-seven, and his grandson Frederick's estate eventually held forty-nine.[26]

But whatever the aspirations of this gentry, the provisioning trade could not support a plantation regime. Rural slaves generally lived on farms, not plantations; they never labored in large gangs; and frequently they worked alongside their owners at the various tasks of mixed cultivation. Following the seasonal demands of the northern agricultural regimen, they sowed in the spring and reaped in the fall. In slack times, slaves manured the land, chopped wood, broke flax, pressed cider, repaired fences, cleared fields, and prepared new land for cultivation. Slaves played an especially large role in the carrying trade, as boatmen and wagoners. Moving from job to job as labor demands changed, slaves found themselves in the field one day and in the shop the next, smithing horseshoes, tanning leather, making bricks, or repairing houses, barns, and furniture. On other days, they could be back in the field or driving a wagon, piloting a boat, or delivering a message. Upon occasion, men and women who worked in the fields and shops were assigned to domestic tasks as servants and gardeners. Although the sexual division of labor grew more pronounced with the rise of agricultural wealth, the division between house and field remained open and ill-defined.

The role of slaves in the agricultural North was reflected in the dwellings in which their owners housed them. No lines of slave cabins surrounded the slaveowner's Great House as an architectural embodiment of the relationship between master and slave. Instead, like other rural workers, slave farmhands were reduced to near invisibility by being stuffed into garrets, back rooms, closets, and outbuildings. An inventory for one Long Island estate described the main house as having a parlor, two bedrooms, and an adjoining "room of 14 by 16 foot for white servants, over it lodging rooms and a back stairs; behind it a kitchen with a room fit for negroes." Occasionally, large slaveholders designated a particular structure for their slaves, generally a small outbuilding distant from the main house. But most made no special provision, and, like Sojourner Truth's owner, packed their slaves away in a cellar where, Truth remembered, the "inmates, of both sexes and all ages" slept on "damp boards, like the horse, with a little straw and a blanket." Such dismal quarters afforded slaves neither comfort nor privacy.[27] In short, the life and labor of the North's charter generations were not radically different than that of other rural laborers. The knowledge that accrued to slaves as jacks-of-all-trades made their labor—like that of most other northerners—part of the larger system of exchange.

As in the Chesapeake region, northern slaves engaged in economic activities apart from those of their owners. According to one Anglican missionary, slaveholders regularly gave their slaves "one Day in a Week to clear Ground and plant it, to subsist themselves and Families to free themselves from the Trouble and Charge of Feeding and Cloathing their Slaves." Whatever the slaveowners' rationale, slaves seized the possibilities inherent in working for themselves. In addition to Sunday, some slaves gained "all Saturday, some half Saturday . . . to subsist themselves and Families." Before long, they had produced small surpluses and entered the market themselves.

Slaves throughout the northern colonies participated in the petty trade around town markets. Many—building upon the ongoing system of slave hiring—jobbed independently, sometimes compensating their owners for the right to control a portion of their own time and sometimes just pocketing their earnings. While their property accumulations remained small, they were recognized in practice and sometimes in law.[28]

The distinctive demands of northern agriculture shaped black life in the countryside. Where the provisioning trade predominated, black men generally labored as stock minders and herdsmen and wagoners and boatmen, while black women worked as dairy maids as well as domestics—cooking, cleaning, carding, spinning, and sewing. The large number of slaves demanded by the provisioning trade, and the ready access to horses and mules it afforded, placed black companionship within easy reach of most black men and women. This was especially true near towns or cities. Rural slaves commonly traveled to urban markets to sell produce from their own gardens and visit friends and relatives.

Slaveholders unwittingly abetted the dissolution of the rural–urban boundary by shuttling their slaves between the city and the countryside, particularly during periods of peak labor demand. The frequent sale of slaves due to an owner's changing labor requirements, economic ambitions, or death scattered slaves and spoke to the general insecurity of slave life in the colonial North. But it also suggests that even when slaves lived beyond easy reach of the towns or lacked access to horses and mules, they knew a good deal about the geography of the North.[29]

Nearly all rural slaves lived and worked in close proximity to white people. The jumble of workers, free and slave, black and white, militated against isolation. The provincial outlook that developed from plantation life was foreign to the experience of northern slaves, who moved easily through the countryside tending to their owners' business and to their own. Few rural slaves remained untouched by the larger currents of European-American life.

What was true for the countryside held even greater validity for black life in the cities. During the eighteenth century, one-fifth to one-quarter of all slaves in colonial New York lived in New York City. Portsmouth and Boston contained fully one-third of all slaves in New Hampshire and Massachusetts, respectively, and nearly half of Rhode Island's slave population resided in Newport. In these great seaports, which mediated between the northern interior and the Atlantic world, slaveownership was nearly universal among the urban elite and commonplace among the middling sort as well. During the late seventeenth and early eighteenth centuries, some three-quarters of Philadelphia's established families— wealthy merchants, professionals, and gentlemen and gentlewomen— owned slaves. Viewing urban life from the top of colonial society, one visitor to New England in 1687 noted that there was "not a house in Boston" that "has not one or two" slaves; with but slight exaggeration, this observation might be applied to every northern city at the turn of the century.[30]

Daily domestic responsibilities—cooking, cleaning, sewing, tending gardens and stables, running errands—kept slave women and a few slave men tethered to the owners' household or a nearby marketplace. But slave men could also be found laboring as teamsters and wagoners on the drays and stockmen in the warehouses that composed the core of the North's mercantile economy. The wharves were where most urban slave men spent their work lives. Slave men—in the tradition of Atlantic creoles—labored in the maritime trades not only as sailors on coasting vessels but also in the ropewalks, shipyards, and sail factories that supported the colonial maritime industry. Although much of this work required only brute strength, many urban slave men practiced skilled crafts.[31]

Like their rural counterparts, urban slaves lived in back rooms, lofts, closets, and occasionally makeshift alley shacks. To find potential black converts in New York City, a missionary was seen "creeping into Garrets, Cellars, and other nauseous places, to exhort and pray by the poor slaves." The cramped conditions of urban life encouraged slaveholders to allow their slaves to live out and hire their own time, thus expanding the slaves' independence. But even when they lived on their own, slaves rarely resided far from their owners. The small size of eighteenth-century cities and the demands of the owning class operated against residential segregation.[32]

The dense agglomeration of urban slaves made it possible for black people, many of whom had arrived with a knowledge of the Atlantic world, to join together with white northerners on many levels. The linguistic abilities of New York slaves provides one indicator of the cosmopolitan character of black life in the cities of the colonial North. Of forty New York runaways whose escape and whose language was noted between 1726 and 1814, nineteen spoke English with varying degrees of fluency and six spoke Dutch, French, or some African tongue. The remaining fifteen were bilingual, speaking combinations of Dutch and English, Welsh and English, French and English, and Spanish and English.[33] As with rural slaves, few black urbanites remained untouched by the larger currents of life in the New World.

Close proximity to European-Americans allowed the charter generations, urban and rural, to gain firsthand knowledge of their owners' world. Slaves learned trades as they worked, at the behest of their owners, alongside white journeymen, apprentices, and servants. Beyond their owners' eyes, slaves rubbed elbows with white men and women in taverns, at cockfights, and at "frolicks." Gossip, gaming, drink, crime, and lovemaking bonded the working people who gathered together in the ramshackle shanties that sprang up around the wharves and warehouses of northern ports. Sailors, to whom dockside taverns were but interchangeable parts of a larger Atlantic universe, were on particularly easy terms with black people. Conversing in the familiar creole patois, they renewed and refreshed knowledge of the Atlantic and the possibilities of life beyond the confinement of slavery.

The intermingling of these impoverished, often disaffected, men and women was made easier—particularly in the Middle Colonies—by the fact that many white men and women were also servants, the legal property of a master who could sell, trade, and discipline them at will. Bemoaning disorders caused by "servants, apprentice boys, and numbers of Negroes," authorities generally lumped white servants and black slaves together. The respectable class in the northern colonies widely shared the perception that the social cleavage ran between free and unfree—not white and black. Members of the lower orders found their fraternization profitable. Interracial gangs of thieves operated in every northern city, often out of clandestine dram shops, groceries, gambling dens, and brothels. Tavern keepers who encouraged slave thieves by purchasing their plunder were notorious throughout the urban North. These cultural brokers frequently orchestrated alliances between whites and blacks for their own benefit. New York officials surmised that such intrigue was behind the insurrections in 1712 and again in 1741, when authorities concluded that tavern owners not only confederated with black men and women but were also "the first movers and seducers of the slaves."

The periodic upheavals that peeled away the patina concealing interracial plebeian activities also revealed the complex underworld where black people, free and slave, gathered together for after-hours conviviality. White northerners might feign outrage at the extent of such activities, but they could hardly deny knowledge of their existence, since they had publicly condemned them from the first arrival of black people.[34]

But if urban slaves rubbed elbows with sailors and servants, they also interacted with their "betters" whenever an opportunity presented itself. Atlantic creoles' early identification with established churches arose perhaps more to secure a place in society than from a commitment to Christianity. Church fathers, suspicious of their motivation, rarely reciprocated. Although churchmen allowed slaves to register their marriages and baptize their children, they showed no systematic interest in slaves' conversion and sometimes went out of their way to denigrate people of African descent.[35]

The founding of the Society for the Propagation of the Gospel in Foreign Parts (SPG) in 1701 changed the relationship between black people and the Anglican Church, the most important Christian denomination in the Middle Colonies. Armed with a special brief to bring Christianity to the slaves, SPG missionaries commenced the work of conversion, often in direct opposition to owners, who feared that baptism would mean freedom. Although the missionaries had no truck with the leveling implications of conversion, their apologies did little to convince suspicious slaveowners. Nonetheless, black people saw allies among the missionaries. Early in the eighteenth century, black men and women crowded into Elias Neau's school in New York. Following Neau's death, his successor reported that "swarms of negroes come about my door . . . asking if I would be pleased to teach them and build on Mr. Neau's foundation." Although no one came forward to take Neau's place as catechist to the black people of New York, a steady stream of slaves— most of them connected to the city's wealthiest merchants—continued to be baptized, married, educated, and buried in Anglican churches in New York and other northern cities. However, Neau's estimate that one black person in ten had accepted Christ appears overly generous.[36]

While slaves mixed with whites at both the top and the bottom of the social order in the northern colonies, they preferred to spend their free time with those who most fully shared their own origins, status, and circumstances. During the 1690s, white New Yorkers complained repeatedly about the "tumultuous gatherings" of slaves on the Sabbath. According to one informant, "Philadelphia's blacks gathered on Sundays and holidays and were seen dancing after the manner of their several nations in Africa, and speaking and singing in their native dialects." To a considerable degree, such after-hours revelry was made possible by the anonymity of urban life. But rural slaves sometimes joined in the "great concourses," pushing the number of congregants into the hundreds.[37]

The frequency of such gatherings and their perceived threat to public order provoked nearly every northern jurisdiction to prohibit black men and women from congregating, especially on the Lord's Day. Some localities added restrictions on the sale of liquor to black people, and a few threatened special penalties for free blacks, extending to enslavement. As such penalties suggest, free blacks frequently took the lead in joining black people together. In 1671 New York authorities singled out Domingo and Manuel Angola, warning the public "that the free negroes were from time to time entertaining sundry of the servants and negroes belonging to the Burghers . . . to the great damage of the owners."

But the law did little to prevent black people from joining together, as twenty years later the Common Council complained about "the frequent randivozing of Negro Slaves att the houses of free negroes without the gates hath bin occasion of great disordr." As slaveholders feared, such meetings became a central element in black life in the northern colonies. Despite repeated efforts to prohibit such congregations, the circumstances of urban life foiled every attempt.[38]

The North's charter generations greatly expanded the culture of the

Atlantic littoral. By the early eighteenth century, most blacks in the North were brought into the world by a black midwife, married "by mutual Consent," and were buried in an African graveyard with what one Christian missionary called "some ridiculous Heathen Rites . . . performed at the Grave by some of their own People."[39] Indeed, because white northerners excluded black corpses from their burial grounds, the graveyard became the first truly African-American institution in the northern colonies, and perhaps in mainland North America. Confronted by the all too obvious mortality of their human property, slaveowners retreated in horror from the responsibility of interring slaves, a distasteful and often costly obligation. While slaveholders occasionally lamented the unceremonious dispatching of their slaves to eternity, and missionaries bemoaned the absence of Christian burial, slaves and free blacks acted. As early as 1699, less than twenty years after the first slaves arrived in Philadelphia, a separate section of the Strangers' Burial Ground had been allocated to black men and women, and slaves were protesting that they could not secure enough time off from work to bury their dead during daylight hours.[40]

As the protest suggests, black people were quick to put their own mark on these burial grounds. Combining remembered African customs with the special circumstances of northern life, black men and women formulated funerary practices that provided the dead with appropriate respect and gave the living a chance to join together. Dressed in their best finery, accompanied by music and song, black men and women generally marched en masse to the burial ground. Often they were led by a distinguished member of their community. Evoking practices of African memory, gifts were left for the dead, who were sometimes decorated with beads, amulets, and other talismans. Early in the eighteenth century, an elderly white resident of Philadelphia remembered seeing "Guinea slaves" "going to the graves of their friends early in the morning and there leaving them victuals and rum." The striking difference of such rituals and the memorials of white Philadelphians provoked scorn from those who observed that black men and women "are buried in the Common by those of their country and complexion without the office, on the contrary the Heathenish rites are performed at the grave by their countrymen."[41]

If the graveyard flourished, the wedding altar, birthing room, chapel, schoolhouse, and political clubhouse languished. Whereas slaveholders gladly conceded the right of burial to their slaves, they rarely extended such liberties to these other portions of the slaves' associational life, and free blacks were neither able nor willing to take up the tasks. To be sure, all of these institutions existed in some clandestine form. But from a public perspective, the institutional boundaries of African-American life coincided with the confines of the African burial ground. As in the Chesapeake, these developments would await critical changes in black life that accompanied the plantation revolution.

Chapter Three

Divergent Paths in the Lowcountry

ᛉ

The history of the charter generations in the lowcountry traced the paths initiated in the Chesapeake and the northern colonies but carried them to extremes. Atlantic creoles arrived in South Carolina and Florida in the seventeenth century much as they had landed in the mainland colonies to the north—entering slowly, and in small numbers from the Caribbean and elsewhere along the Atlantic rim. Most spoke English, Spanish, and some variant of creole along with their native language and had acquired knowledge of Christianity in either its Protestant or Catholic iterations. Often these first arrivals accompanied their owners, and, like them, they sometimes immigrated in family units, so that the slave population exhibited a healthy balance between men and women, with a sprinkling of children. As their language skills and family connections suggest, they understood how to navigate the convoluted shoals of European-American culture and, as elsewhere, immediately pressed for greater independence, within slavery if necessary, outside of it if possible.

Thereafter, however, the history of the first arrivals in the lowcountry diverged sharply, following two different paths. In South Carolina, the introduction of rice cultivation in the last decades of the seventeenth century and the rapid development of the plantation truncated the history of the charter generations. Atlantic creoles had no opportunity to register their marriages or baptize their children at established churches, bring suit in court, or establish relations with powerful patrons. Few gained their freedom. The history of South Carolina's charter generations was but a fleeting moment compared with that of the Chesapeake and northern colonies.

In Florida, however, the charter generations took a difference course; there, plantation culture made no inroads until late in the eighteenth century. Atlantic creoles, many of them fugitives from South Carolina, not only won their freedom in Spanish Florida but also gained a central place in the colony's principal institutions, the militia and the church.

Florida's charter generations survived into the late eighteenth century and dispersed only after the imposition of British rule.

Slaves arrived in Florida as part of Spain's effort to bolster its New World empire during the middle years of the seventeenth century.[1] In establishing the garrison Castillo de San Marcos at St. Augustine, Spanish officials exhibited a deep concern for the shipping lanes by which treasure from the mines of Mexico was transported to metropolitan Spain, but little interest in the men and women who would inhabit the post. During its first century, St. Augustine—the hub of Spanish settlement in Florida—remained preeminently a military outpost on the fringes of empire and only incidentally a center for farming and ranching. Its expansion in the late seventeenth and early eighteenth centuries was not a result of the discovery of an exportable staple but the threat to New Spain posed by the arrival of English settlers at the mouth of the Ashley and Cooper rivers farther north, at the site that would become Charles Town.[2]

Black slaves and a scattering of free blacks, most of them from New Spain, Hispaniola, and Cuba, constructed the fortification at St. Augustine and stayed to defend the garrison. In keeping with Spanish policy throughout the Americas, the governor of Florida commissioned a company of slave and free black militiamen. By 1683 it numbered forty-eight black men, some of whom gained their freedom in Spanish service. Three years later, black militiamen participated in the Spanish attack on English settlers at Edisto Island on the coast of South Carolina, and they remained active in the colony's armed forces thereafter. In quieter times, free black and slave men and women farmed and ranched, but military service continued to distinguish the small black population, which remained barely more than 1 percent of St. Augustine's population until the third decade of the eighteenth century.[3]

In South Carolina, as in Florida, Europeans and European-Americans —including English, Dutch, French Huguenots, Scottish, and Scotch-Irish—composed the majority of the English settlement, equaling almost two-thirds of the population at the end of the seventeenth century. During this period and into the first years of the eighteenth century, most white farmers—slaveholders and nonslaveholders alike—engaged in mixed agriculture and stock raising for export to the sugar islands, particularly Barbados, where many had originated. The majority of the un-free population were European servants, many of them refugees from Barbados, but Native Americans also numbered large in the ranks of the unfree. Slaves arrived in small groups, some at the hands of pirates eager to sell their human booty, some through the process of "salvaging" bankrupt and abandoned Barbadian plantations, some as Atlantic creoles from England—in short, the usual components of the charter generations.[4]

Slaveholders generally labored alongside a mixed workforce that was composed of Native-American and African-American slaves, Native-American and European-American servants, and occasionally European-American wage workers. Although slaveholders maintained an unshakeable commitment to racial servitude and yearned for the prerogatives of Barbadian grandees, the demands of the primitive, labor-scarce South Carolina economy frequently placed master and slave face-to-face on opposite sides of a sawbuck, where shared labor reduced—if it did not dissolve—the differences of status and color.[5] Such direct, egalitarian confrontations and the polyglot character of the laboring population mitigated the force of chattel slavery and provided Atlantic creoles with leverage to fend off the harshest features of racial domination during the initial period of settlement.

The dependence of white settlers on black slaves to defend their vulnerable lowland beachhead reinforced this "sawbuck equality." The threat of Spaniards to the south and Indians to the west hung ominously over South Carolina during its formative years, leading English officials to arm black men much as their Spanish counterparts had done in Florida. When the Spanish invaders and their black militiamen attacked Edisto Island, they likely faced black men defending the English colony. To bolster colonial defenses, officials not only drafted slaves in time of war but also regularly enlisted them in the colony's militia. In 1710 a knowledgeable Carolina Indian agent observed that "enrolled in our Militia [are] a considerable Number of active, able, Negro Slaves; and Law gives everyone of those his freedom, who in the Time of an Invasion kills an Enemey."

Between the settlement of the Carolinas and the conclusion of the Yamasee War almost fifty years later, black soldiers helped repulse every military threat to the colony. Although only a handful of slaves won their freedom through military service, and the English never formally incorporated black men into a regularly constituted militia as did the Spanish, the continued presence of armed, militarily experienced slaves weighed heavily on South Carolina slaveholders. During the Yamasee War, when the governor of Virginia demanded one black woman in return for each Virginia soldier sent to defend South Carolina, the beleaguered Carolinians rejected the offer, observing that it was "impracticable to Send Negro Women in their Roomes by reason of the Discontent such Usage would have given their husbands to have their wives taken from them which might have occasioned a Revolt."[6] The convoluted logic of the Carolinian's response revealed the power that accrued to slave militiamen.

The unsettled conditions that made the lowcountry vulnerable to external enemies strengthened the slaves' hand in other ways. Confronted by an overbearing owner or a particularly onerous assignment, slaves could take to the woods. Truancy was an easy alternative in the thinly settled, subtropical lowcountry. Forest dangers generally sent truant slaves back to their owners, but the possibility of another flight tempered the slaveholders' determination to discipline such fugitives and induced owners to accept the slaves' return with few questions asked.

Some slave men and women, however, took advantage of these circumstances to escape permanently. Maroon colonies existed throughout the lowland swamps and into the backcountry from the first years of settlement. Officials despised these fugitive communities, and they took great pleasure in putting the maroons to rout. But chasing maroons was difficult, dangerous, and expensive, even with the assistance of knowledgeable Indians. As long as the maroons distanced themselves from the plantations, officials turned a blind eye, allowing some illicit settlements to flourish. Maroons lived a hard life, perhaps more difficult than slaves, and few slaves chose to join these outlaw bands, made up almost entirely of young men. But the ease of escape and the existence of a maroon alternative made slaveowners chary about abusing their slaves.[7] The maroons' success gave slave resistance a strikingly different shape in lowcountry South Carolina than in the Chesapeake or in the northern colonies.

The structure of the fledgling lowland economy and the demands of stock raising, with deerskins the dominant "crop" during the initial years of settlement, allowed Atlantic creoles to stretch the military dependence of white settlers into generous grants of independence. On the farms and isolated cowpens (hardly plantations by even the most latitudinous definition), rude frontier conditions permitted only perfunctory supervision and the most elementary division of labor. Most units were simply too small to employ overseers, single out specialists, or benefit from the economies of gang labor. White, red, and black laborers of diverse legal status worked side by side at the dullest drudgery as well as the most sophisticated undertakings. Most slaves labored at a variety of tasks, and, as in the northern colonies, could best be characterized as jacks-of-all-trades rather than skilled artisans or prime field hands. Since cattle roamed freely through the woods until fattened for market, black cowboys—suggestively called "cattle chasers"—moved with equal freedom through the countryside, gaining full familiarity with the terrain.[8] The autonomy of the isolated cowpen and the freedom of movement stock raising entailed made a mockery of the total dominance that chattel bondage implied. Slaves set the pace of work, defined standards of workmanship, and divided labor among themselves, doubtless leaving a good measure of time for their own use.

Hard-pressed frontier slaveowners quickly laid claim to that time. Like their counterparts farther north, they demanded that their slaves provision themselves, as was the practice in the Atlantic islands off the west coast of Africa and the sugar islands of the Caribbean. Unintentionally, South Carolina planters thereby jump-started the slaves' economy in the new settlement. Objections were quick to follow, as many slaveholders disliked the independence such activities afforded slaves. In 1683, in perhaps the first legislation respecting slavery enacted in South Carolina, the General Assembly prohibited "Trading between Servants and Slaves." The law was repassed in 1687, with provisions against slaves expropriating and embezzling their owners' property. Later other strictures were added, including limitations on movement of slaves and penalties against white persons who traded with slaves. A recapitulation of these laws in the 1691 slave code forbade slaveowners from giving slaves Saturday afternoon free, "as hath been accustomed formerly."[9] In 1714 the South Carolina legislature denied slaves the right to hold "stock of hogs, cattle, or horses." But the numerous reiterations of the laws against independent trading by slaves only documented the extent of the slaves' economy, and, as elsewhere in the mainland, did little to curb these forbidden practices.[10]

By the first years of the eighteenth century, the slaves' economy had established deep roots in the Carolina lowcountry. Although centered in gardens and provision grounds—what one slaveholder called the slaves' "little Plantations"—it extended to hunting and fishing by slave men and to keeping barnyard fowl by slave women. Even if the new code had been enforced, which it was not, both it and laws protecting the slaves' right to enjoy Sunday for themselves legitimated the slaves' pioneer economy. Time allowed for gardening, hunting, and fishing both affirmed the slaves' independence and supplemented their diet. "There are many Planters who, to free themselves from the trouble of feeding and clothing their slaves," a knowledgeable cleric noted in 1712, "allow them one day in the week to clear ground and plant for themselves as much as will clothe and subsist them and their families."[11]

Perhaps if slaves only fed themselves and their families, the complaints would have been fewer. But as in the Chesapeake and northern colonies, slaves would not rest satisfied with mere subsistence. Their independent economic activities soon yielded a surplus, and they were quick to market it to whomever would pay their price. Slaves also sold their own labor: expanding upon the system whereby their owners hired them out, they hired themselves out. In 1712 lawmakers expressed their annoyance, moving against a practice that allowed "slaves to do what and go wither they will and work where they please, upon condition that the said slaves do bring their . . . masters as much money as . . . agreed upon."[12]

The restrictive legislation registered the planters' discomfort with the practice of slave hiring and the elaborate economies that slaves created. But if the planter class objected, individual planters did not. Slaveowners themselves were among the slaves' first customers, often violating the laws whose passage they had promoted. Indeed, some slaveowners employed their slaves as their agents, especially in dealing with Indians.[13] Generally, however, slaves marketed their own goods, setting up market stalls in Charles Town and other crossroads of commerce, thus giving their independence a firm material basis.

Slaveholders and other settlers complained bitterly and frequently about slaves traveling unsupervised through the countryside, congregating in the woods, and visiting Charles Town to carouse, conspire, or worse. But knowledge of the countryside and a willingness to hunt down cattle or stand up to Spaniards were precisely the qualities that slaveholders valued in their slaves. They complained, but they accepted. Indeed, to resolve internal disputes within their own community, European settlers sometimes promoted black participation in the affairs of the colony far beyond the bounds later permitted slaves or even black free men. "For at this last election," grumbled several petitioners in 1706, "Jews, Strangers, Sailors, Servants, Negroes, & almost every French Man in Craven & Berkly County came down to elect, & their votes were taken."[14] Such breaches of what would become an iron law of European-American racial policy reveal how the circumstances of the pioneer lowcountry life shrank the social as well as the cultural distance between Atlantic creoles and the mélange of European settlers. It suggests the independence that accrued to members of the charter generations, even when locked in slavery.

This was particularly true in Charles Town, an unimposing village at the confluence of the Cooper and Ashley rivers. Although it served as the seat of government, the colony's largest port, and the center of its social life, seventeenth-century Charles Town was a sorry, disheveled rendezvous for backcountry provisioners and transatlantic traders where the tavern was the largest public building and the wealthiest merchants were hardly better than shopkeepers. Town slaves, who worked the docks and served government officials, enjoyed a degree of independence that was the envy of even the most footloose cattle chaser. The attractions of this society were powerful, for it was easy to lose oneself in the labyrinth of warehouses and masts that crowded the city's wharves. In this maze were places enough for slaves to find a "drink in Charles towne for mony or what else they bring." In mixing with sailors, smugglers, Indian traders, and upward striving merchants—who one English official disparaged as "bankrupts, pirates, and decayed libertines"—slaves continually renewed and refreshed the culture of the larger Atlantic world.[15]

While something less than a metropolis, Charles Town was a magnet for runaways. Some only wanted a few days' respite, but others hoped to make a permanent escape on some visiting vessel. For Atlantic creoles it was the sea, not the backcountry, that provided the surest route to freedom. In Charles Town itself, few black people won their freedom, and Charles Town developed no free black population to compare with that of seventeenth-century New Amsterdam. Indeed, most town slaves had firsthand familiarity with farm work, as few slaveowners could afford the luxury of placing their slaves in livery. In short, Charles Town's significance for black life was not as an island of freedom in a sea of servitude but as a meeting ground in which slaves from throughout the lowcountry could gather on occasion—to the "prjudice of theire masters & mrses & apparent hazard of ye: peace & safety of ye: whole Contery."[16]

Thus, during the first years of lowcountry settlement, African-American and European-American culture and society evolved along parallel lines with a large degree of overlap. South Carolina's charter generations spoke far better English than slaves who succeeded them, indeed, perhaps better than any other black people to inhabit the lowcountry prior to the American Revolution.[17] Numbers combined with other circumstances to allow Carolina's charter generations a large role in shaping their society, creating striking similarities in the development of the lives of Atlantic creoles in the lowcountry and the colonies farther north.

During the last decade of the seventeenth century, however, economic and social changes undermined these commonalities and set the development of black life in lowcountry South Carolina on a distinctive course. The discovery of exportable staples, first naval stores and then rice and indigo, altered the lowcountry much as the tobacco revolution would later transform the Chesapeake. And, as in the Chesapeake, the transformation of the countryside that attended the inauguration of plantation production overwhelmed the development of a creole culture in South Carolina, bringing it to a sudden halt.

The very changes that truncated the charter generations in South Carolina and compressed its experience to a few decades at the end of the seventeenth century assured the survival—even the prosperity—of the charter generations in Florida. The rapid expansion of the English settlement in South Carolina only deepened the fears of Spanish officials. They searched for allies against the growing menace to the north, and could find only one reliable friend—their own slaves and those of the Carolinians. Atlantic creoles also were quick to recognize that the enemy of their enemy could be a friend. An alliance was sealed which spurred the growth of creole society in Florida.

Spanish raiders took the first steps toward that alliance in 1686 when, in assaulting Edisto Island, they carried off some dozen slaves. The governor of South Carolina demanded their return, along with those "who run dayly into your towns," but Spanish officials peremptorily refused—although they did offer to pay for the slaves. Instead, they put the fugitives to work for wages, instructed them in the tenets of Catholicism, and allowed them to marry—in short, providing runaways with all the accouterments of freedom but its legal title.[18]

That was quick in coming. In 1693 the Spanish Crown offered freedom to all fugitives—men as well as women—who converted to Catholicism. Thereafter, Spanish officials in Florida offered "Liberty and Protection" to all slaves who reached St. Augustine, and they consistently refused to return runaways who took refuge in their colony.[19]

The broad promise of liberty was not always kept. Indeed, some fugitives were sold in St. Augustine, and others were shipped to Havana. Nonetheless, the promise itself transformed Florida into a magnet for Carolina slaves. As the news spread, fugitives flocked to Florida from South Carolina, often requesting baptism into the "True Faith." Spanish officials delighted in the fugitives' choice of religion, smugly observing that they "want to be Christians and that their masters did not want to let them learn the doctrine nor be Catholics."[20] But, much as they might celebrate the runaways' desire for the true religion, Spanish officials did not allow their enthusiasm to blind them to the special skills these former slaves carried. The fugitives' knowledge of the countryside, linguistic facility, and ability to negotiate between the lowland's warring factions in a manner their forebears had made famous throughout the Atlantic littoral made the runaways into ideal allies against the English enemy.

Former Carolina slaves no sooner arrived in Florida than they were enlisted in the militia and sent to raid the plantations of their old owners, assisting black men and women—many of them friends and sometimes family—to escape bondage. When the raids boiled over into outright warfare, the new fugitives were incorporated into the black militia, fighting against the English in the Yamasee War and defending St. Augustine against an English assault that took the invaders almost to the walls of St. Augustine.[21]

The stream of fugitives grew with the expansion of slavery in South Carolina during the first decades of the eighteenth century.[22] Armed with the profits rice produced, South Carolina slaveholders entered the international market, purchasing slaves not by the handful but by the boatload. Charles Town became the largest mainland slave mart, and Africans disembarked on its wharves by the thousands. Generally deemed "Angolans," most were drawn from deep in the interior of central Africa, although some were Atlantic creoles with experience in the coastal towns of Cabinda, Loango, and Mpinda. Many spoke Portuguese, which, as one Carolinian noted, was "as near Spanish as Scotch is to English," and some were practicing Catholics at the time of their arrival.

At the end of the fifteenth century, the royal house of Kongo had converted to Christianity, and Catholicism, in various syncretic forms, had entered broadly into the life of the Kingdom of the Kongo, spread during the next two centuries by Portuguese missionaries and then by an indigenous Kongolese priesthood. Leaders of the Kongolese church corresponded with Rome and traveled to Europe, receiving the endorsement of Christ's vicar. Although Kongolese converts saw no reason to surrender their own deities, which were incorporated into the new system of belief, the Kongolese were knowledgeable believers who knew their catechism, the pantheon of saints, and the symbols and rituals of the Cross.[23]

The arrival of Christ's children in Charles Town had little effect on South Carolina slaveholders, who doubtless would have disapproved of their unique brand of Christianity if they noticed it at all. But if planters paid little attention to the beliefs of saltwater slaves as they put them to work in the rice fields, the presence of a Catholic sanctuary one hundred miles south of Charles Town gained the slaves' notice. No doubt the Church's presence in Florida made Spanish St. Augustine even more attractive to enslaved Catholics than it might have been if only freedom had been on offer. During the 1720s and 1730s, these Catholic slaves and other slaves—many newly arrived in South Carolina—defected in increasing numbers. In 1733 Spanish authorities reiterated their offer of freedom, prohibiting the sale of fugitives and commending black militiamen for their service in the struggle against the British. Five years later, the governor requested that the fugitives previously sold to Havana be returned to Florida and freed. Word of the new edicts may have stimulated others to flee the Carolinas.[24]

In 1739 a group of African slaves initiated a mass exodus. Pursued by South Carolina militiamen, the fugitives confronted their owners' soldiers in several pitched battles at Stono, only fifty miles from the Florida line.[25] Although most of the Stono rebels were captured or killed, others successfully escaped to Florida. Once they arrived, it became difficult for their owners to retrieve them, as Spanish officials would not surrender their co-religionists. The escapees were quickly integrated into the black community in St. Augustine—as they had already been baptized and knew their catechism—although they prayed, as one Miguel Domingo told a Spanish priest, in Kikongo.[26]

The former Carolina slaves did more than pray. As their numbers grew, black militiamen—augmented by the continued stream of Carolina fugitives—took an ever more active role in the border warfare against their former owners. The former slaves' presence and the Spaniards' promise of freedom, military commissions, and even a "A Coat Faced with Velvet," augmented the small but steady stream of runaways to Florida. Among those enlisted in the militia was one Francisco Menéndez, a former slave who may have adopted the name of one of St. Augustine's most powerful magistrates. Menéndez's heroics in repelling an English attack on St. Augustine in 1728 had won the attention of local officials and a special commendation from the Spanish Crown, along with the promise of freedom. When he was not freed, Menéndez and many of his fellow militiamen petitioned the governor of Florida and then the bishop of Cuba for their liberty, which they eventually received.[27]

To better protect St. Augustine, the governor of Florida established a black settlement to the north of the city. Gracia Real de Santa Teresa de Mose, a walled fort surrounding some ramshackle huts, was both a barrier against another English assault on St. Augustine and an agricultural settlement, for the former slaves soon planted substantial crops in nearby fields. The governor assigned a priest to instruct the newly arrived slaves and resident free blacks. Although the Spanish military supervised the town, the governor placed Menéndez in charge. Whatever their agricultural objectives and religious aspirations, the black men and women stationed at Mose understood that their future was tied to the strategic purposes of the settlement. They pledged to "shed their last drop of blood in defense of the Great Crown of Spain and the Holy Faith."[28]

Under Captain Menéndez, Mose became the center of black life in colonial Florida, as well as a base from which former slaves—sometimes joined by Indians—raided South Carolina. The settlement of some one hundred free black men and women was also the last line of defense against English assaults on St. Augustine, which came with a vengeance following the Stono Rebellion. The bloody struggle at Mose eventually forced the evacuation of the black population, and Spanish forces would not recapture the fort until reinforcements arrived from Cuba. However devastating to the fort itself, the militia's extraordinary bravery won Menéndez yet another commendation, this one from the governor of Florida, who declared that the black captain "had distinguished himself in the establishment, and cultivation of Mose."[29]

Menéndez was quick to capitalize on his fame. Writing in the language of patronage, he reminded the king that his "sole object was to defend the Holy Evangel and sovereignty of the Crown," and requested remuneration for the "loyalty, zeal and love I have always demonstrated in the royal service." In his petition to the king, Menéndez requested a stipend worthy of a militia captain.[30]

To secure his royal reward, Menéndez took to the sea as a privateer, with hopes of eventually reaching Spain and collecting his due. Instead, a British ship captured the famous "Signior Capitano Francisco." Although the captain had him stretched out on a cannon and threatened with emasculation for alleged atrocities during the siege of Mose, Menéndez had become too valuable to mutilate. His captors gave him two hundred lashes, soaked his wounds in brine, and commended him to a doctor "to take care of his Sore A-se." Menéndez was then carried before a British admiralty court on New Providence Island, where "this Francisco that Cursed Seed of Cain" was ordered sold into slavery. Still, even this misadventure could not undo the irrepressible Menéndez. By 1752, perhaps ransomed out of bondage, he was back in his familiar post in Mose.[31]

While Menéndez sought his fortune at sea, black men and women—joined by new arrivals, many of them Atlantic creoles from Spain, Cuba, and Africa—entered more fully into the life of St. Augustine. Free blacks continued to work for the Crown as sailors, soldiers, privateers, and trackers. Others labored independently as artisans, laborers, and domestics. They purchased property and, upon occasion, assisted others out of bondage, steadily increasing the proportion of black people who enjoyed freedom.[32]

Within St. Augustine, Florida's charter generations expanded in new directions. The disproportionately male former fugitives intermarried with Indians and newly arriving slaves—many of them Atlantic creoles from Spain, Cuba, and Mexico. As their connections grew, old hands and new arrivals created a tight community whose lives revolved around the militia and the church. In 1746 black people composed about one-quarter of St. Augustine's population of 1,500. Like the charter generations in the Chesapeake and New York, they sanctified their marriages and baptized their children in the established church, choosing godparents from among both the white and black congregants. From the perspective of the creole culture, that the church was Catholic rather than Anglican or Dutch Reformed was less important than that membership knit black people together in bonds of kinship and certified incorporation into the larger community. Militia membership—with its uniforms, flags, and martial rituals—served a similar purpose by amplifying the connections between black people and the colonial state. Much like Atlantic creoles elsewhere on the mainland, Florida's charter generations became skilled in pulling the lever of patronage, in this case royal authority. Declaring themselves "vassals of the King and deserving of royal protection," they continually put themselves in the forefront of service to the Crown with the expectations that the Crown would reciprocate.[33]

Hoped-for rewards were not always forthcoming. All "vassals of the King" were not equally favored. Beginning in 1749, a new governor of Florida forced black people to return to Mose, much against their will, as they had enjoyed the cosmopolitan life of St. Augustine, where their ability to converse in several European, Indian, and African languages gave them a place as cultural brokers in a multicultural society. Still, black men and women—many of them free—maintained a modicum of prosperity and respectability under the protection of the Spanish Crown, and Mose, with its own church, began to grow. Taken together, the black population of St. Augustine and Mose increased steadily so that in 1763 it totaled about 3,000, one-quarter of whom were free.[34]

While protests about the primitive conditions at Mose and pleas for permission to return to St. Augustine went unanswered, Spanish officials did not forget the colony's black defenders—at least as long as the English threat in South Carolina and, after 1732, Georgia loomed over Florida and the Spanish territory to the south. In 1763, when the English wrested control of Florida from Spain, black colonists retreated to Cuba with His Majesty's subjects, where the Crown granted them land, tools, a small subsidy, and a slave for each of the colony's leaders.[35] The evacuation, however, shattered creole culture in Spanish Florida. Far more than their counterparts in the Chesapeake or the northern colonies, Florida's charter generations had been incorporated as full—if yet unequal—participants in the life of mainland society. With the English occupation, South Carolina and later Georgia planters moved south en masse, bringing with them the social order of the plantation and obliterating the century-old history of the society that Atlantic creoles had created in Spanish Florida.

Chapter Four

Devolution in the Lower Mississippi Valley

🔥

From the perspective of white slaveowners on the Atlantic seaboard, the evolution of slavery in the lower Mississippi Valley during the eighteenth century ran backward, from slave society to society with slaves. In the process, black life in Louisiana changed from African to creole, rather than creole to African. From the days of the earliest military outposts in the Louisiana territory, French adventurers ached to establish a slave society along the lines of Saint Domingue. After several false starts, they succeeded in identifying a commodity, locating a market, and importing thousands of slaves, bypassing the Atlantic rim and drawing directly from the African interior. Although a few Atlantic creoles drifted into the region from metropolitan France, west Africa, and the Antilles, most of Louisiana's slaves derived from the African interior. Planters soon had them at work growing tobacco and indigo for the international market.

The sudden influx of so many African slaves within the course of a single decade—so different from the miscellaneous, piecemeal, and slow arrival of Atlantic creoles into the Chesapeake, northern, and lowcountry colonies during the initial period of settlement—made it seem for a moment that the plantation revolution had come to the lower Mississippi Valley. But the hastily constructed slave regime collapsed when African slaves joined with Native Americans to overthrow planter rule, leaving the nascent slave society to devolve into a society with slaves. The emergence of creole society, though belated, gave the charter generations of the Mississippi Valley a familiar form.

Far outside the Atlantic's main trading lanes at the extreme end of the French mercantile empire, French settlers in the lower Mississippi Valley had high ambitions and little else. Placed at the mouth of the Mississippi to outflank the English, they yearned to imitate the success of the sugar islands. But French metropolitan authorities had no plans for Louisiana

beyond the maintenance of a strategic military outpost, and they repeatedly rejected the pleas of Louisiana's settlers for the large-scale importation of African slaves, rebuffing a proposal to trade Indian captives to
Saint Domingue for African slaves at the rate of three for two. As a result,
few black slaves entered Louisiana during the first years of settlement. In
1715 Indians composed the bulk of a small slave population, and no more
than a handful of black slaves resided in the colony.[1]

Over the course of the first quarter of the eighteenth century, Native
American slaves were slowly joined by others who fit the mold of the
Atlantic creoles of the seaboard colonies. Some had European antecedents. Perrine, a black cook, arrived with other *engagés* from Lorient in
1720. Raphael Bernard, the manservant of a wealthy French emigré, followed his master from France for 200 francs and the promise of a new
suit. When his owner failed to respect the bargain and beat him to boot,
Bernard sued and recovered his back wages. A "mulâtress" accompanied
her French husband, a gunsmith who was deported from Gorée for
crimes unnamed. John Mingo escaped from South Carolina, but instead
of fleeing to Florida as did most fugitives from the lowcountry during the
eighteenth century, he traveled half a continent to Louisiana. There, a
patron assisted him in securing legal freedom, a small plot of land, and
the right to purchase a slave woman, whom he had taken for his wife.
When Mingo quarreled with his erstwhile benefactor over the terms of
the arrangement, he also sued; and although his larger claim was disallowed, Mingo won the right to purchase his wife. Louis Congo, a slave
whose name suggests his origins, gained his freedom by answering the
colony's need for an executioner. In return for assuming that gruesome
task, his employer freed Louis Congo and allowed him to live with his
wife (although she was not liberated, as he had demanded) on land of his
own choosing.[2]

Much like their counterparts on the eastern seaboard, these men and
women understood their rights, and—given their familiarity with the
language, religion, and legal codes of the Atlantic world—they did not
hesitate to exercise them. In this the French *Code Noir,* first promulgated
by the king in 1685 and introduced to Louisiana in 1724, provided a
small assist. The *Code* was weighted against manumission and discouraged self-purchase. It required manumitted slaves to defer to their former
owners, punished free black people more severely than white ones, and
barred interracial marriage. Still, free people of African descent enjoyed

many of the same legal rights as other free people, including the right to petition and testify in court. People of color—like Raphael Bernard and John Mingo—employed those rights to advance their interests, much as did their counterparts in Dutch New Netherland, English Virginia, and Spanish Florida. Occasionally they used the law to improve their collective status. During the 1720s, they successfully petitioned for the removal of a special head tax on free blacks and sued individual white colonists for alleged transgressions of various sorts.[3]

Free people of African descent could be found residing not only among the newly arrived Europeans but also among the tribes native to the lower Mississippi Valley. Some of these blacks may have been fugitives from the European settlement, but their presence early in the eighteenth century suggests they migrated from Spanish Mexico. Just as John Mingo traveled half a continent to the west to reach the Mississippi River, so some fugitives traveled half a continent to the east. French authorities disliked black people who resided among the Indians as much as they disliked those who resided within their own settlements. One black man who lived among the Natchez and instigated a series of raids against outlying French settlements made himself so odious that French authorities stipulated his elimination as part of a treaty with the Natchez Indians.[4]

The freed people's presence affirmed the frustrations of would-be planters eager to set Louisiana on the path blazed in Martinique and Saint Domingue. During the first two decades of settlement, attempts to transform Louisiana into a profitable staple-producing colony along the Caribbean model proved a dismal failure. Despite the best efforts to encourage agricultural production and domestic regularity, Louisiana remained an overwhelmingly male settlement dominated by corporate functionaries and military officers. While the ruling clique lined its pockets speculating and smuggling, colonists—most of them Canadian *coureurs de bois*—worked the forests and the swamps, oblivious to efforts to induce them to relinquish their nomadic ways.

Engagés, or indentured servants, paupers, and criminals—many of whom had entered the colony under duress—had a still weaker commitment to the arduous work necessary to transform the forests and swamps of the lower Mississippi Valley into productive farms. In the face of starvation, they rejected the notion that agriculture was the solution to domestic consumption, let alone the suggestion that production for the international marketplace would further their well-being. When forced to work, they resisted mightily, demanding their "natural rights to the fruits of their labor." Various experiments with sugar and silk or even tobacco provided little in the way of an exportable surplus. Instead, the colonists became more and more like the Native Americans with whom they resided and intermarried. The few French women transported to the colony went native, working barefooted and barebreasted in the fields. Missionaries who had hoped to convey superior Gallic ways to New World barbarians instead found French civilization unraveling before their very eyes. They worried about the creation of a "colony of half-breeds who are natural idlers, libertines, and more rascally than those of Peru." During the early years of European settlement, Louisiana, in the words of one historian, was "poor, unhealthy, dangerous, and uninviting."[5]

Although Indians might be denounced and disparaged, they could not be ignored. They were knowledgeable, numerous, and well armed. Unlike the French, Native Americans could feed themselves, and many French settlers relied on them for food, fuel, and medical care. The smaller tribes—the Apalachees, Mobilians, and Tunicas around Fort St. Louis on the Gulf coast and the Arkansas, Houmas, Natchez, and Yazoo in the lower valley—willingly supplied French settlers with corn, skins, and herbal remedies in return for liquor, guns, and protection. So did the powerful Choctaws. Awed and threatened by the mighty Chickasaw nation and its British allies, these smaller tribes even worked for the French and provided captives to do the labor no European would. A 1722 census counted more than 200 Indian slaves in French Louisiana.

But the natives also had their limits. As they slipped more deeply into alliance with the French and spent more time hunting pelts and making war on their neighbors, Native Americans became a less reliable source of provisions for European settlers, if not for themselves. By the end of the second decade of the eighteenth century, the shortfall of food was increasing, and the colony was becoming ever more dependent on France for its survival.[6] That dependence grew with the arrival of some 7,000 French and German settlers between 1717 and 1721—many of them former indentured servants with records of criminality, vagabondage, and military desertion. Few had an interest in cultivating the soil, and fewer still had training in agriculture.[7] Unable to forge the new arrivals into a cohesive workforce, would-be planters demanded African slaves and threatened to abandon the colony unless they got them. In 1719 French authorities finally bowed to the colonists' wish.

Between 1719 and 1731 the French-chartered Company of the West and Company of the Indies, which—like the Dutch West India Company—directed colonial affairs in both North America and west Africa, imported nearly 6,000 African slaves into Louisiana. Unlike the Atlantic creoles who populated the eastern seaboard during the seventeenth century, almost all of whom entered in small groups from the West Indies, the first black arrivals in Louisiana derived directly from Africa. They came by the boatload, with some ships carrying 400 slaves or more.[8] Although the first arrivals in Louisiana originated in the Gulf of Benin and Angola, they were soon overwhelmed by newcomers from Senegambia, where the Company of the Indies had an exclusive concession. In all, more than half of the slaves—almost 4,000 in total—derived from Senegambia and a good portion were Bambaras, a Malinke-speaking people from the upper reaches of the Senegal River, who had become deeply involved with French commerce in west Africa.[9]

The Bambaras had complex relations with the French. Although many Bambaras—usually captives of a nation whom the French also deemed Bambaras, although they often were not—became entrapped in the international slave trade and were sold to the New World, others worked for the French as domestics, boatmen, clerks, and interpreters in the coastal forts and slave factories. Their proud military tradition, honed in a long history of warfare against Mandingas and other Islamic peoples, made them ideal soldiers as well as slave catchers. Along the coast of Africa, "Bambara" became a generic word for slave soldier. Moreover, in Africa, French traders and soldiers sometimes married women of Bambaran and European descent, and at least one of these French nationals settled in Louisiana with his mixed-ancestry wife.

In a strange twist of logic, the same qualities that made Bambaras useful allies in the slave trade also made them desirable slaves. French traders sought them out, declaring Bambaras to be "strong, gentle, tractable, and faithful; not subject to sullenness, or to runaway as the Guinea Negroes frequently are." The high esteem accorded Bambara slaves, the direct ties between French commercial interests on the west coast of Africa and the lower Mississippi Valley, and the firm connections forged between shipmates on the long transatlantic crossing unified the slaves who entered Louisiana during the 1720s. Although a scattering of cosmo-

politan creoles were transported to Louisiana, most of the new arrivals
were peasant farmers and herdsmen with no experience in the Atlantic
world.[10]

With the entry of African slaves, French authorities relinquished their
wavering commitment to free labor in the lower Mississippi Valley.
Throughout Louisiana, Africans replaced European and Native-American laborers. In some places, African slaves supplanted European servants and wage workers in positions that required considerable skill.
White tradesmen often resisted the exchange, refusing to train black
journeymen because the white artisans believed it would work against
them in the long run. But most European workers gladly yielded their
places. Some fled the colony and retreated to Saint Domingue; others did
not stop until they reached France.

Yet others did not have a chance to escape, as European colonists died
at a frighteningly high rate in the lower Mississippi Valley. Those who
remained generally evacuated the countryside, settling in New Orleans,
which had become the Company's headquarters and the colony's capital
in 1722.[11] Once the slave trade was opened, the French never again tried
to populate Louisiana with European migrants. During the 1720s the
white population declined by 65 percent, so that in 1726 about 1,500—
settlers, soldiers, and *engagés*—remained in the colony. The French also
made but feeble effort to replace European workers with Indian slaves,
perhaps because the native population also declined catastrophically during the 1720s, owing to war, starvation, and disease. In 1728 the French
governor called for the termination of Indian slavery. As a result, black
slaves became an increasingly large share of the population and an even
larger share of the labor force of the lower Mississippi Valley.[12]

The black population did not grow easily. Of the first 2,000 slaves to
enter the colony, less than 700 were alive in October 1720. The terrible
toll taken by the long transatlantic crossing seemed to increase during the
1720s. Hundreds perished on the journey from the west coast of Africa to
the mouth of the Mississippi River. The sight of the great delta did not
assure survival, as it often took weeks, sometimes months, to navigate
the channel between the treacherous sandbars at the mouth of the river
and New Orleans. Those who survived that ordeal often died from starvation and exposure on the docks at New Orleans, as Company officials
in Louisiana failed to provide new arrivals with necessary provisions and
shelter.[13]

The nightmarish voyage of the *Venus* offers sobering evidence of the fate of many of the Africans whom French slave traders packed off to Louisiana. Of the 450 slaves loaded aboard the *Venus* in Africa in April 1729, only 363 reached the Mississippi River. Another forty-three succumbed before they disembarked in New Orleans. According to officials, the remaining slaves were so disease-ridden that "more than two-thirds of those who were sold at auction into the hands of the inhabitants . . . died" soon thereafter.[14]

The nature of the transatlantic slave trade left African slaves ill-prepared for life in the New World. Louisiana planters, like other would-be slaveowners in mainland North America, wanted adult men, and generally they got what they wanted. Some of the slavers that entered Louisiana carried three to four times as many adult men as women. A substantial sexual imbalance prevented slaves from establishing families. The Company of the Indies also instructed its agents "not to trade for any negro or negress who is more than thirty years of age, as far as possible, or less than eight," making for a youthful population.[15] But if slaves arrived young, the harsh realities of physical exhaustion, malnutrition, and rampant disease aged them quickly. Company officials in Louisiana had not the resources and perhaps not the desire to attend to the needs of newly arrived slaves. Probably little could be done to counter the physical rigors of the new environment. Although the sickle-cell trait provided some immunities against malaria, Africans had no more protection than Europeans from yellow fever, pleurisy, pneumonia, and a variety of subtropical diseases endemic to the lower Mississippi Valley. But if the Company of the Indies could not control the disease environment, its failure to provide food, clothing, and shelter for the newly arrived proved deadly to many of the forced immigrants.[16]

Nonetheless, Africans survived better than either Europeans or Native Americans in eighteenth-century Louisiana. Despite the sexual imbalance, some Africans formed families almost upon arrival, perhaps because they had been able to maintain Old World connections through the Middle Passage or because of the ease with which they combined with Native Americans. At first, slaves in Louisiana died faster than the slave trade could replace them and faster than they could reproduce themselves, but slowly the number of black slaves grew—augmented by importation and natural increase. In 1731 the black population stood at nearly 4,000, and black people outnumbered white ones, making up 60 percent of the colony's population.[17] In the decades that followed, the black population continued to increase more rapidly than the white, so that Louisiana acquired its distinguishing demographic characteristic: a black majority.

The Company of the Indies, like the Dutch West India Company in New Netherland, took the lead in employing African slaves. It acted from a narrow calculation of short-term profit, with little thought about how the Africans' arrival transformed the colony. The Company set some slaves to work on its own sprawling plantation across the river from New Orleans. It employed others on the Mississippi, delivering goods between the mouth of the river and the city, with some slave sailors traveling upriver as far north as the Illinois country. Canoemen who once navigated the Senegal may well have plied their trade on the Mississippi. But most of the Company's slaves worked around the Company's headquarters in New Orleans, shoring up levees, digging ditches and canals, and constructing docks. A large number were assigned to "cut down the trees at the two ends of the town as far as Bayou St. John in order to clear this ground and to give air to the city and to the mill." Another contingent toiled with French soldiers on the city's fortifications.

A few slaves transferred artisan skills to the New World, where they found employment in the mechanical trades. Animated by the belief that, once trained, slave craftsmen would "cost the company nothing," Company officials apprenticed slaves to blacksmiths, wheelwrights, saddlers, masons, and carpenters, creating a corps of skilled slaves. The governor even suggested that slaves be schooled in Paris for service in Louisiana. Although this proposal hardly received a hearing, the French Company of the Indies, like the Dutch West India Company, found slaves extraordinarily useful. It established a permanent force of some 200 and required all slaves in the colony to labor for the Company for thirty days each year.[18]

Thus, early on, New Orleans became a center of African life in colonial Louisiana as white settlers spread through the countryside while the Company kept tight control over slaves. New Orleans was small, even by eighteenth-century North American standards, but it stood at the crossroads of trade and commerce in the lower Mississippi Valley. On its streets and wharves and in its markets and taverns, company-owned African slaves—like their European slaveowners—rubbed shoulders with Indian trappers, Canadian woodsmen, French soldiers, and sailors of all nationalities. By their muscle and skill, African slaves played an ever-growing part in the city's economic life. The Company's practice of employing slaves as skilled workmen spread, and many European artisans employed them in the place of white journeymen and apprentices. Skilled slaves took control of artisan work in some trades. In 1743 the governor reported that the king's contractor "employs only very few French workmen."[19]

Drawn by the advantages of an urban venue and by employment in the Company's ranks, some Africans propelled themselves into positions of modest privilege and authority within the Franco-American world. They utilized connections with Company officials that reached back to Africa; and, not surprisingly, the most successful of these derived from the small Atlantic creole minority who had arrived amid the African majority. Samba, a Bambara who had labored for years as a boatman on the Senegal River in the employ of the Company of the Indies and had been enslaved and transported to the New World for leading a revolt against the French in Africa, used his knowledge of French and various African tongues as an interpreter before Louisiana's Superior Council, the colony's highest judicial and legislative body. Later, he became an overseer on the largest "concession" in the colony, the Company's plantation across the river from New Orleans.[20] Like urban slaves in New Amsterdam, Philadelphia, and Charles Town, the black men and women who resided in and around New Orleans quickly learned the white man's ways.

While most slaves lived within a boat ride of New Orleans, others caught only a fleeting glimpse of the city before they were shipped off to the concessions that lined the Mississippi—huge tracts the Company hoped would become the agricultural base of the colony. The entry of African slaves into the countryside during the 1720s breathed new life into the flagging attempts of the French to establish a staple-based economy in the lower Mississippi Valley. Unlike the men who directed the Dutch West India Company in New Netherland, Louisiana's ruling clique put aside its preoccupation with commercial speculation and shifted its energies to agricultural production. Urged on by subsidies that lowered the price of Louisiana tobacco below that of the superior Virginia leaf, they began to create a plantation regime. Before long, the tobacco estates spread upriver toward a fertile crescent between New Orleans and the Natchez village of White Earth, where Indians had worked the land for generations. South of New Orleans, planters tried their hand at indigo, although the capital investment in vats and kilns limited production to all but the wealthiest and best-connected planters.[21]

Because few settlers could afford to purchase slaves, the largest concessionaires and best-connected functionaries gained a lion's share of the newly arrived Africans. While three-quarters of the white inhabitants held no slaves in 1726, fifteen planters owned twenty or more.[22] By 1731 five tobacco and indigo plantations at Chapitoulas, above New Orleans, had a combined population of over 400 slaves, and the major landholders in the Natchez area, the primary tobacco-growing region, held 850 of the 955 slaves engaged in agriculture along that section of the Mississippi. The area across the river from Chapitoulas had the densest black population in the colony, with over 1,000 slaves operating some fifty plantations.[23]

Still, African slaves composed only a portion of the plantation labor force. Although the number of Africans grew steadily during the 1720s, the plantation labor force still included large numbers of white and red laborers—some servants for terms of years, some of them slaves, and some of them free. Moreover, French planters, eager to accelerate the process of plantation development, seized well-worked Indian lands and established their estates within the areas of densest Indian settlement, allowing African slaves to move easily between the Indian villages and their owners' plantations and thus to mix with Native Americans on their own terrain. Intermarriage between the largely male African population and Native-American women became common. The existence of such relationships worried planters and colonial officials, as they feared the Indians "may maintain relations with [African slaves] which might be disastrous to the colony when there were more blacks."[24]

Tobacco and indigo cultivation in a plantation setting made harsh demands on enslaved laborers, and the level of exploitation increased sharply with the advent of plantation production. As in the Chesapeake, tobacco required careful tending, as the plant moved from seedling to maturity. Indeed, the tobacco cultivation and processing was, if anything, more complicated in the moist subtropical environment of the lower Mississippi Valley than in the Chesapeake region.[25] Indigo did not take the season-long preoccupation of tobacco, but it too was a demanding crop whose cultivation required close attention for a portion of the year, and whose processing into dye required extraordinary attention.[26]

African slaves, most without experience in the cultivation of tobacco or indigo, lived a bleak existence on the frontier plantations. Slaveholders packed the newly acquired slaves into long barracks, with little regard for the traumatic transition between Africa and the New World. A 1730 plantation inventory listed twenty-seven men, twenty-one women, twenty-seven children—eighty-five slaves in all—living in two buildings no more than thirty-three feet in length. Planters, who had little money to pay wage workers or to feed *engagés,* appeared to have even less to expend on slaves. A visitor to the colony described the slaves as "walking skeletons."[27]

While seaboard planters stumbled in establishing a legal basis for chattel bondage, slaveholders in the lower Mississippi Valley knew no such problem. The *Code Noir* greatly enhanced the slaveholders' authority, giving them enormous power to discipline slave laborers, far more than they enjoyed over the fractious European *engagés* or native Indians. The *Code* provided some protection for slaves, requiring that slaves be instructed by the church and given the sacraments of baptism, marriage, and extreme unction and forbidding slaveholders from separating husbands from their wives and mothers from their young children. But there is scant evidence that slaveholders hewed to the law or that the slaves' erstwhile protectors—state and church—interceded on the slaves' behalf. If a handful of enlightened slaves in New Orleans employed the law to their own advantage, plantation slaves remained ignorant of its provisions. A close investigation of Louisiana's judicial records for the colonial period found not a single instance where abused slaves employed the *Code Noir* in an appeal to the Superior Council. Priests did no better against the planters' determination to squeeze what they could from newly arrived Africans. Slaves on the plantations distant from New Orleans, one Capuchin wrote his superior in 1725, "die without baptism and without any knowledge of the true God." Neither the state nor church exercised its legally constituted authority, leaving the field clear for planters to work their will.[28]

Nevertheless, slaves resisted the new plantation order. To escape the harsh regime, some fled, taking refuge in New Orleans or in the dense forests and swamps that stood behind the great riverfront estates. The region's impenetrable outback was particularly attractive to truants. Indeed, many fugitives were not content with a brief respite and instead found a permanent home in these forest retreats. Fed from the plantation larder by friends and relatives and assisted by friendly Indians, maroon settlements grew rapidly as slavery expanded during the 1720s, extending far beyond anything that existed in the Chesapeake piedmont or the South Carolina lowlands.

Louisiana's attorney general urged "prompt and sweeping action against runaway slaves, lest soon the community be raided by whole gangs thereof." By the time he spoke, however, the numerous maroon colonies had entrenched themselves as bases for interracial banditry, revealing close relations with plantations and Indian villages. In 1727 a recaptured fugitive betrayed Natanapallé, an armed settlement of Indians and Africans. Yet other Indians and plantation slaves supplied the maroons with necessary staples in return for game, pelts, and assurances of a home-away-from-home. Maroon villages not only served as a place to trade stolen goods but also as a marriage market for interracial liaisons, further cementing ties between Indians and Africans.[29]

Slaveholders combated such outposts of slave independence. The *Code Noir* provided stiff punishments for runaways, and planters did not hesitate to exceed them—cropping, hamstringing, and branding fugitives. Using their superior resources, slaveholders turned the maroons' allies against them, employing Indians and selected African slaves to hunt down runaways.[30] But try as they might, planters could not eradicate the maroon sanctuaries. As in the Carolina lowcountry, the possibility of maroonage greatly strengthened the slaves' hands by offering an alternative to the rigors of plantation life.

None of this slowed planters driven by visions of great wealth. During the 1720s, as planters usurped Indian lands, imported Africans, and established a new labor discipline, the specter of insurrection epitomized by the maroon colonies grew more omnipresent. In the fall of 1729, the fuming discontent broke its boundaries in deadly revolution. In November, Natchez Indians, pushed to the brink by the expanding plantation economy and fearful for their own enslavement, joined with newly arrived (mostly Bambara) slaves to massacre over 200 French settlers, more than 10 percent of the European population of Louisiana. Their initial success liberated hundreds of slaves, and many more joined the victorious Natchez.[31]

The Natchez, however, were not the only ones who saw African slaves as the balance of power in the region. From New Orleans, the governor sent a group of trusted black slaves on a preemptive strike against a small tribe south of the city to keep these Indians "in an attitude of respect." Encouraged by their success, he employed these same slaves, along with Choctaw Indians, against the Natchez, killing hundreds of rebellious Indians and their slave allies and recovering many of the slaves lost during the initial Natchez assault.

Even in victory, the critical role played by the African slaves impressed French officials. The governor conceded that the French success would have been more complete if not for the Indians' black allies; and in 1731, when the governor began negotiations for the Natchez's surrender, he demanded the return of all former slaves as a precondition for discussions. The Natchez tribe complied. Eager to inspire "a new horror of the Savages" among the slaves, French officials turned many of these returned black slaves over to the Choctaws, who promptly burned them at the stake with an appropriate "degree of cruelty."[32]

Seared flesh had a powerful impact, but not always the desired one. Although French authorities redoubled their vigilance at separating the slaves and the Indians, they hardly slowed the slaves' quest for freedom. Rumors of conspiracies by Africans and Indians ripped through the lower Mississippi Valley in the aftermath of the rebellion. Within months, new schemes to alter the balance of power among Europeans, Native Americans, and Africans boiled to the surface. At least one emanated from the Bambaras, who composed the majority of the slave population in Louisiana and whose reputation for military ferocity had been secured on both sides of the Atlantic. Led by Samba Bambara, the former Bambara rebel turned official interpreter, black slaves apparently hoped to reconstitute the recently defeated Indian–African alliance under their own leadership.[33]

Again, the French struck back with savage ferocity, and the usual bloodbath, culminating in Samba's dismemberment, squashed the conspiracy. But the French were careful to reward those slaves who had stood with them. Officials liberated the "fifteen Negroes, in whose hands we [the French] have put weapons" and who "performed prodigies of valor" and awarded them a permanent place in the colony's defense force. Like the employment of slave and free black soldiers in Spanish Florida, the establishment of a black militia in French Louisiana was more than compensation for services rendered; it was an attempt to assure the loyalty of all black people—free and slave—by stimulating among them "a great desire to deserve similar favors by material ser-

vice."[34] As in Spanish Florida, military service became the charter generations' entree to freedom in Louisiana. Black militiamen provided the nub
from which a free black population would grow.[35]

Although the Natchez rebellion and the Samba conspiracy failed to
oust the French or abolish slavery, they dramatically altered the course of
African-American life in the Mississippi Valley. In the years that followed, Louisiana maintained some of the trappings of a slave society,
most prominently the numerical dominance of slave over free, and black
over white. However, there was no confusing Louisiana with a plantation regime, as the Natchez revolt forced incipient planters to surrender
their vision of a slave society. Louisiana would devolve from a would-be
slave society to a society with slaves, where the culture of the Atlantic
would belatedly emerge. The Natchez rebellion, while it failed to over-
turn slavery, extended the experience of the charter generations well into
the eighteenth century.

But if during the middle years of the eighteenth century the slave society
of the lower Mississippi Valley continued to dissolve, the reverse process
gained momentum elsewhere in mainland North America. In the Chesapeake, lowcountry South Carolina and Florida, and northern colonies,
Atlantic creoles were on the defensive as a nascent plantation economy
emerged and with it a new class of men who were committed to the
plantation as both a model and metaphor for the organization of society.

Sensing there would be little room for them under the plantation
regime, Atlantic creoles began to decamp. Some fled as a group, as did
the creole community in St. Augustine that retreated with the Spanish
from Florida to Cuba following the British takeover in 1764. Others
merged with Native-American tribes and European-American settlers to
create unique biracial and triracial combinations and establish separate
identities. In the 1660s the Johnson clan abandoned Virginia for Maryland, Delaware, and New Jersey. John Johnson and John Johnson, Jr., the
son and grandson of Anthony Johnson, took refuge among the Nanticoke Indians and so-called Moors, among whom the Johnson name
has loomed large into the twentieth century. Near one Nanticoke settlement in Delaware stands the small village of Angola, the name of John
Johnson's Virginia plantation and perhaps Anthony Johnson's ancestral

home. Similar "Indian" tribes could be found scattered throughout the eastern half of the United States, categorized by twentieth-century ethnographers as "tri-racial isolates."[36]

Others moved west to a different kind of autonomy. Scattered throughout the frontier areas of the eighteenth-century were handfuls of black people eager to escape the racially divided society of plantation America. In upcountry South Carolina, backcountry Virginia, and piedmont Georgia, white frontiersmen with little sympathy for the nabobs of the tidewater sometimes sheltered such black men and women, employing them with no questions asked. People of African descent found refuge among the frontier banditti, whose interracial character—a "numerous Collection of outcast Mulattoes, Mustees, free Negroes, all Horse-Thieves," by one account—was the subject of constant denunciation by aspiring planters.[37]

While some members of the charter generations retreated before the expanding planter class, a few moved toward it. Given that at least one male member of every prominent seventeenth-century free black family on the eastern shore of Virginia married a white woman, the Atlantic creoles' descendants in that region would, perforce, be lighter in color. Whether or not this was a conscious strategy in Virginia and elsewhere, there remains considerable, if necessarily incomplete, evidence that these light-skinned people passed into white society.[38]

Retreat—geographic, social, and physical—slowly liquidated the charter generations. Their descendants who failed to escape were usually swallowed by the nascent slave regime. In 1667 a black man named Fernando, claiming "hee was a Christian and had been severall years in England," sued for his freedom in a Virginia court. The case, initiated just as tidewater planters were consolidating their place atop Virginia society, sent Virginia lawmakers into a paroxysm that culminated in the passage of a new law clarifying the status of black people: they would be slaves for life and their status would be hereditary. Some twenty-five years later, a similar case hardly made a ripple in the Virginia establishment. In 1691 one Don Francisco Condelarium, "a negro man sold by Mr Charles Ball unto Capt Tho: Brereton," appeared in a Virginia court to "complain he is unjustly made a slave." But "being not at present Capable to prove his assertion," he was returned to Brereton until the next court session when he might present "such evidence as he can produce in order towards cleering from or confirming him a slave." Needless to say, Condelarium did not appear at the next court session or any subsequent one and disappeared from the record thereafter.[39]

As the Atlantic creoles faded, but never quite disappeared, from mainland North America, so did an understanding of race in which black people were defined as cosmopolitan cultural brokers, familiar with the languages, religions, jurisprudence, and trading etiquette of the Atlantic. This view would soon be replaced by a new definition of race which would be less impressed with the achievements of peoples of African descent and more determined to limit the place of black people in mainland North America. Critical to that redefinition of race was the plantation revolution.

II

SLAVE SOCIETIES

The Plantation Generations

Mainland
North America
ca. 1763

N

MASSACHUSETTS

NEW YORK   NEW
            HAMPSHIRE

Boston
MASSACHUSETTS
Providence Newport
CONNECTICUT RHODE ISLAND

PENNSYLVANIA   New York
NEW
JERSEY
Philadelphia

Annapolis   DELAWARE
Alexandria
MARYLAND

VIRGINIA   Williamsburg
Norfolk
Great
Dismal
Swamp

NORTH CAROLINA

SOUTH
CAROLINA   Wilmington

GEORGIA   Georgetown
Charles Town

LOUISIANA
(SPAIN)   Savannah

Natchez   (CLAIMED BY
Pointe   SPAIN & GEORGIA)
Coupée   Mobile
WEST FLORIDA   Pensacola   St. Augustine
Baton Rouge   EAST FLORIDA
New Orleans

ATLANTIC OCEAN

GULF OF MEXICO

Introduction

✦

The first black people to arrive in mainland North America bore—or soon adopted—names like Anthony Johnson, Paulo d'Angola, Juan Rodrigues, Francisco Menéndez, and Samba Bambara. Although slaves, they established families, professed Christianity, and employed the law with great facility. They traveled widely and enjoyed access to the major Atlantic ports. Throughout the mainland, they spoke the language of their enslaver or the ubiquitous creole lingua franca. They participated in the exchange economies of the pioneer settlements and accumulated property, gaining reputations as knowledgeable traders and shrewd bargainers in the manner of creoles throughout the Atlantic littoral. A considerable portion of these first arrivals—fully one-fifth in New Amsterdam, St. Augustine, and Virginia's eastern shore—eventually gained their freedom. Some attained modest privilege and authority in mainland society.

Their successors were not nearly as fortunate. They worked harder and died earlier. Their family life was truncated, and few men and women claimed ties of blood or marriage. They knew—and wanted to know—little about Christianity and European jurisprudence. They had but small opportunities to participate independently in exchange economies, and they rarely accumulated property. Most lived on vast estates deep in the countryside, cut off from the larger Atlantic world. Few escaped slavery. Their very names reflected the contempt in which their owners held them. Most answered to some European diminutive—Jack and Sukey in the English colonies, Pedro and Francisca in places under Spanish rule, and Jean and Marie in the French dominions. As if to emphasize their inferiority, some were tagged with names such as Bossey, Jumper, and Postilion—more akin to barnyard animals than men and women. Others were designated with the name of some ancient deity or great personage like Hercules or Cato as a kind of cosmic jest: the more insignificant the person in the eyes of the planters, the greater the name.

Whatever they were called, they rarely bore surnames, which represented marks of lineage that their owners sought to obliterate and of adulthood that they would not permit.[1]

The degradation of black life in mainland North America had many sources, but the largest was the growth of the plantation, a radically different form of social organization and commercial production controlled by a new class of men whose appetite for labor was nearly insatiable. Drawing power from the metropolitan state, planters—who preferred the designation "masters"—transformed the societies with slaves of mainland North America into slave societies.[2] In the process, they redefined the meaning of race, investing pigment—both white and black—with a far greater weight in defining status than heretofore.

While new to North America, such planters had a long and notorious history. Beginning in the twelfth century in the Levant, planters discovered a commodity—sugar—for which the demand was nearly limitless. After centuries of experimenting, they devised a new way to grow, process, and market this great fount of sweetness, and though the plantation remained identified with sugar, its techniques and organization were eventually extended to other commodities, such as tobacco, coffee, rice, hemp, and cotton. Sugar planters moved steadily across the Mediterranean, perfecting their organization and technology as they transformed, by turns, Cyprus, Crete, Sicily, southern Spain, and northern Africa. By the fifteenth century, they had entered the Atlantic, first in the Azores, then Madeira, the Canary Islands, and Cape Verde Islands, traveling south until they reached São Tomé, Fernando Po, and Principé in the Gulf of Guinea. From there, it was just a short step across the Atlantic, where by the late sixteenth century the plantation economy had become entrenched on the coast of Brazil. Although hardly a seamless process and not always a progressive one, the possibilities inherent in drawing together European capital, African labor, and American lands became manifest. During the following century, planters turned northward, to the Antilles and mainland North America.[3]

Everywhere they alighted, planters transformed the landscape, creating new classes, remaking social relations, and establishing new centers of wealth and power. Armed with the power of the state and unprecedented agglomerations of capital, planters chased small holders from the countryside and monopolized the best land. To work their estates, they impressed or enslaved indigenous peoples or, in the absence of native populations, imported large numbers of servants or slaves, for sugar production was extraordinarily labor intensive.

Planters cared little about the origins, color, and nationality of those who worked the cane and processed its juices. When the locus of sugar production was on Cyprus and Crete, they employed—along with peoples native to those islands—white slaves transported across the Black Sea from southern and eastern Europe and black slaves transported across the Sahara from Africa. As the trade moved to São Tomé, Fernando Po, and Príncipe, planters used Africans imported from mainland Africa and Jews deported from Europe.[4] In the New World, Native Americans and imported Africans were the planters' laborers of choice. When native populations withered under the onslaught of European conquest and disease, plantation slavery became African slavery. "These two words, *Negro* and *Slave*," had "by custom grown Homogeneous and convertible," wrote an English prelate in 1680, affirming the way the growth of staple-producing plantations had redefined peoples of African descent in the eyes of Europeans.[5]

The plantation revolution transformed all before it. But what distinguished the slave plantation from other forms of production was neither the particularities of the crop that was cultivated nor the scale of its cultivation. Many crops identified with the plantation—tobacco and cotton, for example—had been grown and would continue to be grown on small units with the labor of freeholders and their families, occasionally supplemented by wage workers, indentured servants, and even one or two slaves. The farmers who directed such mixed labor forces enjoyed considerable success, producing bumper crops at costs competitive with the largest holders.

The plantation's distinguishing mark was its peculiar social order, which conceded nearly everything to the slaveowner and nothing to the slave. In theory, the planters' rule was complete. The Great House, nestled among manufactories, shops, barns, sheds, and various other outbuildings which were called, with a nice sense of the plantation's social hierarchy, "dependencies," dominated the landscape, the physical and architectural embodiment of the planters' hegemony.[6] But the masters' authority radiated from the great estates to the statehouses, courtrooms, countinghouses, churches, colleges, taverns, racetracks, private clubs, and the like. In each of these venues, planters practiced the art of domination, making laws, meting out justice, and silently asserting—by their fine clothes, swift carriages, and sweeping gestures—their natural right to rule. Although the grandees never achieved the total domination they desired, it was not for want of trying.[7]

Planters worked hard at play, for they needed to distinguish themselves from those who simply worked hard. From the planters' perspective, slaves were labor and nothing more. While the slavemasters took to their sitting rooms, book-lined libraries, and private clubs to affirm their gentility, they drove their slaves relentlessly, often to the limits of exertion. Those who faltered faced severe discipline. In the process, millions died.

Such a regime had to rest upon force. Violence was an inherent part of slave society, playing a role quite different from the one it had played in a society with slaves. To be sure, the use of force and even gratuitous brutality was endemic in societies with slaves, especially the rough pioneer societies of the New World, with their disproportionate numbers of armed young men. But violence was not only common in slave societies, it was also systematic and relentless; the planters' hegemony required that slaves stand in awe of their owners. Although they preferred obedience to be given rather than taken, planters understood that without a monopoly of firepower and a willingness to employ terror, plantation slavery would not long survive. The lash gained a place in slave societies that was not evident in societies with slaves.[8]

The planters' authority could not stand by force alone. Like every ruling class, the grandees legitimated their preeminence by the word—be it unspoken custom or written law. Indeed, the arrival of the planter class was generally followed by the creation or elaboration of some special judicial code.[9] Behind these laws, however, stood complex and sophisticated ideologies. Planters understood themselves not as economic buccaneers exploiting the most vulnerable, or as social parasites living on the labor of others, but as metaphorical fathers to the plantation community. Such ideologies came easily enough, as they were an extension of the time-honored traditions that undergirded the governance of the household, workshop, church, and state and bore a close resemblance to the system of patronage so much in evidence in societies with slaves. But small differences made for large distinctions, as slaves in plantation regimes were not just another subordinate group whose continuing loyalty could be assured by some gratuity. Slaves in plantation societies were an extension of their owners' estate in ways they never were in societies with slaves. As the "fathers" of their vast plantation families, paternalists granted themselves the right to enter into the slaves' most intimate affairs, demanded the complete obedience due a father, and consigned slaves to a permanent childhood. This domestication of domination became a central element in shaping slave life.[10]

There were other elements as well. Because slavery in mainland North America, as in the New World generally, was color-coded, novel notions of race accompanied the imposition of the plantation regime. To be sure, such new ideas were slow in developing in a world in which there were many other markers of difference. Nevertheless, slave societies—far more than societies with slaves—naturalized and rationalized the existing order through use of racial ideologies. *African* slavery was no longer just one of many forms of subordination—a common enough circumstance in a world ruled by hierarchies—but the foundation on which the social order rested. The structures of chattel bondage and white supremacy became entwined as they never had been in societies with slaves. Like plantation paternalism, the new racial ideologies distinguished slaves from all other subordinates. White supremacy demoted people of color not merely to the base of the life cycle as children, but to the base of civilization as savages.[11]

Slaves understood these ideologies and employed them on their own behalf. When playing the part of loving children redounded to their advantage, they adopted the role. In 1774, upon his return from a transatlantic sojourn, planter Henry Laurens was greeted by Old Daddy Stepney with a "*full* Buss of my Lips," along with "the kindest enquiries over & over again . . . concerning Master Jacky Master Harry Master Jemmy."[12] Doubtless Old Daddy Stepney was pleased to see his owner and to express his concern for Laurens's children. But the effusive show of devotion demonstrated that two could play the paternalist game. The negotiation between master and slave was no less evident in Daddy Stepney's embrace than it was in the wrathful fury of a slave insurrectionist or the fawning deference of a slave supplicant. Daddy Stepney expected his embrace would be rewarded, and it was.

Generally, the interplay between master and slave was neither the "kindest enquiries" nor a "*full* Buss" on the lips. The glad smile and tight clasp masked a bitter contest whose seething animosities periodically exploded with volcanic force. Planters threatened and cajoled, pressing their slaves to greater exertion through a combination of intimidation

and promises of better times. As long as slaveowners controlled the apparatus of coercion, slaves conceded what they could not resist. But such
concessions should not be confused with assent. Slaves continued to
struggle to take back piecemeal what their owners had appropriated at
once. The contest of master and slave was a never-ending war in which
the terrain changed frequently but the combatants remained the same.
The struggle in slave society was no different than in societies with slaves,
except that slaves labored at still greater disadvantage.

The slaves' disadvantage on the plantations of the New World was
compounded by changes in the Old, for the plantation revolution transformed Africa just as it transformed the Americas. The sharp increase in
demand for slaves during the eighteenth century—a demand to which
mainland North American planters contributed just a small part—revo-
lutionized west African society. Slaves, some of whom had previously
been carried northward from the savannah across the Sahara Desert in
caravans, moved south in ever greater numbers to the Guinea coast,
spurring the development of the great slave trading ports of Mina, Why-
dah, and, farther south, Loango (and later Bonny, Lagos, and Cabinda).
As they did, the economies of the African interior changed, and so did its
politics. Slaving came to serve a different function, as ambitious African
merchants and politicos constructed dynasties from the profits of slave
trading. In west Africa, new men rose to chiefdoms and paramountcies,
creating states like Asante, Dahomey, and Oyo which not only gained
control of the interior but also extended their reach north to the savannah and south to the aptly named "slave coast." Farther to the south,
Kongo and Mbundu merchants subverted the old kingdoms, allowing
the Portuguese to gain a foothold on the continent. New states arose as
these merchants and their mercenary allies pushed deeper into the interior of central Africa.[13]

As these predatory African slaving states grew in strength during the
eighteenth century, the character of the men and women forcibly transported across the Atlantic also changed. Whereas condemned criminals,
political prisoners, religious heretics, debtors, and others collectively denominated as "refuse" numbered large among the slaves drawn to mainland North America's societies with slaves, men and women innocent of
crime except for being in the wrong place at the wrong time were hunted
down for the purpose of sale to the great plantations. Especially commissioned armies and freelancing gangs, driven by the possibility of political

aggrandizement and great wealth, moved deep into the interior of Africa, kidnapping millions of men and women and killing millions of others. The kidnappers sometimes became the kidnapped, and the line between predator and prey became slim indeed. Large traders on the coast pressured the small traders in the interior towns, who in turn pressed the still more marginal traders in the hinterland, shaving their profit, forcing the most vulnerable merchants into more desperate measures. It was a world in which no one was safe. Families without large lineages, villages without powerful patrons, and weak polities were hard hit. Whatever degree of selectivity African slave raiders had once employed disappeared as the plantation revolution of the eighteenth century increased demand for slaves and pushed prices upward.[14]

But even at the height of the slave trade, African slave raiders were not indiscriminate kidnappers. If marauding slave traders swept up princes and paupers alike, one distinction was not lost: the slave trade was highly selective with respect to sex. Although a few men might be enlisted into the very armies that captured them and ravaged their homeland, slave traders generally considered men too dangerous to keep in close proximity. Women captives, on the other hand, could be incorporated into their captor's household, and, like children of both sexes, they could be employed as agricultural workers and domestic servants—the traditional tasks that fell to women and children. A few might gain full status within the household, since accumulating wives and other dependents added to a man's power and prestige. However, most were put to work in agriculture, which expanded greatly—with some units equaling the size of New World plantations. Captive men thus became the prime candidates for deportation, a welcome coincidence from the traders' perspective, as "men and stout men boys," "none to exceed the years of 25 or under 10," were the objects of greatest demand in the New World.[15]

Beyond the preference for adult men, almost all Africans were fair game. Nationality, religious beliefs, shared languages, and geographical propinquity counted for little, as slave captives were marched hundreds of miles from the interior to coastal factories. From these warehouses of humanity, the new moguls bartered away the captives' future and that of their posterity.

Although traders who operated the coastal factories also had little interest in distinguishing slaves by national, linguistic, or religious affiliations, the larger patterns of Atlantic commerce linked specific regions of

Africa to specific regions of the Americas. Some three-quarters of the slaves transported from west central Africa went to Brazil; two-thirds of slaves shipped from the Bight of Biafra landed in the British Caribbean; half of those leaving Senegambia alighted in the French Caribbean. Such linkages allowed European sea captains, who frequently came armed with requests for specific peoples, to satisfy planter preferences for particular "nations." But even with these connections, meeting the planters' requirements was difficult in the competitive world of international slaving. First, the ethnic composition of the slaves in any oceanside entrepôt had little necessary relationship to the ethnicity or nationality of its hinterland. In the long march from the interior, a trek that could take months, slave traders conscripted men and women of many peoples into their sad coffles, so that the ships leaving any particular port rarely carried the peoples of a single nation or language group. Once at sea, moreover, slavers often made additional stops, first along the African coast and then in the Americas, where slaves were bought and sold, increasing the heterogeneity of their cargoes. Finally, the internal and transatlantic trade changed over time. The result was a patchwork of African origins in the New World. Even on a plantation where most Africans derived from a single port, slaves could be found from places as distant as Senegambia and Madagascar. If the slave trade was not random, its outcome often was.[16]

But if neither planters in the Americas nor slave traders in Africa could fully control the commerce-in-person, the difference between newly arrived plantation slaves and those who had composed the charter generations was nonetheless striking. Atlantic creoles were cosmopolitans, for whom the Atlantic was a vast thoroughfare for commercial opportunity and a crucible for cultural interaction. The men and women drawn from the interior of Africa, by contrast, were provincials, for whom the Atlantic was a strange, inhospitable place, a one-way street to oblivion. Rather than broad connections with the Atlantic, it was deep roots in the village, clan, and household which shaped their world. Although their economies were complex, most enslaved Africans had been tied to the land as farmers or herdsmen.[17] They lacked the linguistic range and cultural plasticity of the charter generations. In their African villages, their family life, with its long lines of descent, took a different form from that of creoles along the Atlantic littoral, with their flexible households and fabricated genealogies. The sacred world of slaves taken from the interior was often an extension of their own households, and was inhabited by a variety of ancestors who might be called from the nether-life. Occasionally, these ancestors would act on their own, for they enjoyed an independent, if shadowy, existence. Their demands for obedience and sacrifice made long-departed forebears a formidable force in this world as well as the next, fusing the sacred and secular into a single irrefutable reality. Whereas creoles—with their knowledge of the religions of the Atlantic rim—had demonstrated a willingness to incorporate Christianity into their system of belief, the men and women of the interior were loathe to accept the religion of their enslaver.[18]

Captives taken from the interior also differed from the charter generations in another way, for if the Atlantic created unity, the interior spoke to divisions. Africa housed hundreds, perhaps thousands, of different "nations," whether defined by the languages they spoke, the religions they practiced, or the chieftains to whom they gave allegiance. Some were small states, hardly more than villages; others were great confederations extending over thousands of miles. The language, religion, domestic organization, aesthetics, political sensibilities, and military traditions that Africans carried from the interior to the plantations cannot be understood in their generality but only in their particulars, for the enslaved peoples were not Africans but Akan, Bambara, Fon, Igbo, or Mande.[19]

If Africa provided few common experiences, enslavement did. Above all, plantation slaves—especially in the early years of the plantation revolution—were immigrants. The immigrant experience, with all the difficulties of displacement and readjustment, shaped the lives of new arrivals. But the movement of slaves from Africa to the Americas was no ordinary migration. The slave trade fractured the Atlantic, creating profound discontinuities in the lives of those transported to the plantations of the New World. Attended by extraordinary levels of coercion, the forced transfer of "saltwater" slaves proved deadly to many and traumatic to all. The creoles' transit from the periphery of the Atlantic—whether from Africa, Europe, or the Caribbean—to mainland North America, no matter how frightening and disorienting, had none of the nightmarish qualities of the Middle Passage which the mass of plantation slaves experienced. Slavers bound for the plantations of the New World stuffed their human cargoes tight between the creaking boards of vessels specially designed to maximize the speed of transfer. Slaves were forced to wallow in their own excrement and were placed at the pleasure of the crew. Although conditions improved on slave ships over time, death stalked these vessels, and more than one in ten Africans who boarded them did not reach the Americas.[20] The survivors arrived in the New World physically depleted and psychologically disoriented. They were in a far poorer position to address the anarchic effects of long-distance migration than any other people who made the transatlantic journey.

With power and circumstance weighted against them, African slaves confronted planters who were certain that their prosperity depended upon the slaves' productivity. In time, saltwater slaves and their descendants shifted the balance of power, and in the process transformed themselves from Africans to African Americans. The growth of an indigenous slave population was a critical event in the history of the New World. But the long, complicated process of transformation was already under way by the time the captives were taken from the coastal factories. When the captives boarded ship in Africa, they did not think of themselves as Africans. Their allegiance was to a family, clan, community, or perhaps—although rarely—state, but never to the continent itself. By the time they reached American shores, that had begun to change; as they disembarked, the process by which many African nations became one had already gained velocity. The construction of an African identity proceeded on the western, not the eastern, side of the Atlantic, amid the maelstrom of the plantation revolution.

New identities took a variety of forms, shaped—but not determined—by slavery. If slavery loomed large among the new realities that confronted captive Africans, many other circumstances also weighed heavily upon them. The obvious differences with members of the owning class could not conceal differences among the new arrivals. Some of these had their roots in Old World animosities. Competition, as well as cooperation, within the quarter compounded the remnants of ancient enmities, giving nationality or ethnicity an ever-changing reality and with it new meanings to Akan, Bambara, and Fon identity. In this changing world, nationality or ethnicity did not rest upon some primordial communal solidarity, cultural attribute, or common experience, for these qualities could be adopted or discarded at will. In the Americas, men and women identified as Angolans, Igbos, or Males frequently gained such identities not from their actual birthplace or the place from which they disembarked but because they spoke, gestured, and behaved like—or associated with—Angolans, Igbos, or Males.

For most Africans, as for their white counterparts, identity was a garment which might be worn or discarded, rather than a skin which never changed its spots. While the color coding of New World slavery placed some identities off-limits, Africans still had many from which they might choose. Choice, as well as imposition or birthright, determined who the new arrivals would be. Indeed, rather than transporting a primordial nationality or ethnicity to the New World, the arrival of Africans often became the occasion for the creation of nationality that had little salience in Africa. Igbos or Angolans who searched out their countrymen in the Americas may have made more of those connections in the New World than they did in the Old precisely because of their violent separation from their homeland.

Whatever the new identity Africans accepted, adopted, or created, the process was hardly assimilation, if for no other reason than that the world around them was so diverse and was changing so rapidly that no single ideal to which to assimilate existed. Instead, there were many ideals from which Africans could select—among themselves, among the members of the owning class, and, for many, among the Native American population.[21] In short, identity formation for African slaves was neither automatic nor unreflective, neither uniform nor unilinear. Rather it was a slow process that proceeded unevenly and was often repeated as Africans were forcibly transferred from the Old World to the New.

The plantation revolution came to mainland North America in fits and starts. Beginning in the late seventeenth century in the Chesapeake, it moved unevenly across the continent over the next century and a half. In its wake, societies with slaves were transformed into slave societies. By the time the revolution had run its course, slave societies dedicated to cultivating tobacco in the Chesapeake, rice in lowcountry South Carolina, Georgia, and East Florida, sugar in the lower Mississippi Valley, and cotton across the breadth of the southern interior were the heart of mainland North America's economy and culture. Those areas not committed to plantation production, most prominently the North, became deeply enmeshed in the plantation economy as suppliers of capital, factorage, draft animals, food, technology, and—in the person of the plantation tutor—education, so much so that they took on the trappings of slave societies. Indeed, until urban-based manufacture eclipsed staple agriculture as a source of wealth during the nineteenth century, the plantation shaped society, economy, and politics throughout the mainland, as it did throughout the Atlantic.

As elsewhere, the emergence of slave societies in the North American mainland affected everyone, those who owned the vast estates, those who worked them, those who supplied them, and those who only wanted to avoid them. But it touched no one more deeply than African and African-American slaves. The degradation of black life that accompanied the plantation revolution on mainland North America put the charter generations—and other poor people—to flight. Those who did not escape the onrushing plantation regime shared the plight of the slaves imported to grow the great staples. But whether they fled the new regime or were incorporated into it, the creoles' history cast a long shadow over African-American life. Their economies and societies—the memory of their successes and the tragedy of their dispersion—would shape the evolution of slave societies.

As plantation production expanded and the planters' domination grew, slaves in mainland North America faced higher levels of discipline, harsher working conditions, and greater exploitation than ever before. Without question, members of the plantation generations worked longer, harder, and with less control over their own lives than did the members of the mixed labor force of slaves, servants, and wage workers who had preceded them. In a world where laboring men and women were commonly driven like beasts, the words "to work like a slave" took on a profound and chilling meaning for all working people.

If the plantation revolution escalated the level of exploitation and inaugurated a new, violent form of discipline, it also raised the level of resistance. The masters' gross violation of the ill-defined but nonetheless real boundaries of what might be imposed upon slaves elicited a vigorous response. The slaves' rejoinder took a variety of forms, from suicide to maroonage and from truancy to insurrection. Although the measurement of any of the various forms of resistance—by frequency, intensity, or even number—has proved illusive, the largest insurrections in mainland North America (at Stono, Manhattan, and the Parish of Saint John the Baptist) followed the emergence of slave society. None had the effect of the Natchez revolt in derailing slavery's transformation, but each shaped slavery's subsequent history.[22]

As in other slave societies in the Caribbean, mainland plantations devoted to staple production devoured labor. Unlike the largest agricultural units in societies with slaves, plantations required slaves not by ones and twos, the score, or even the dozens but by the hundreds, thousands, and eventually tens of thousands. But the Africanization of mainland slavery was neither a steady nor a uniform process. Of all the transatlantic slave routes between the eastern and western hemispheres, the one that transported Africans to the mainland North American colonies was the most indirect, producing heterogeneity that was perhaps unique in the Americas. In some places, Africanization took place within the course of a decade; in others, it was a century-long process.[23] And once accomplished, the Africanization of slavery was not necessarily completed, as in time creoles—in the form of native-born African Americans—reasserted themselves, only to be replaced by a new wave of African arrivals. Reafricanization frustrates any notion of a linear progression from African to creole. It also suggests that the Africanization of plantation society was not a matter of numbers, as small groups who arrived early often had greater influence than the mass of late arrivals. In short, the Africanization of mainland North American slavery was not a matter of who arrived or even who arrived where, but who arrived where and when.[24]

The peasants and pastoralists carried from the African interior to North American plantations confronted a host of new diseases and the harsh demands of staple production. Africans put to plantation production died by the thousands. Although slaves in mainland North America would be distinguished by their ability to reproduce themselves, few did so in the first generation.[25] With their numbers weighted heavily toward men, the first arrivals struggled to form families and reconstruct the institutions that had guided life in their former homeland. The new circumstances depreciated the strategies that had been employed by the charter generations; linguistic fluency, church membership, and juridical knowledge provided no advantage to those condemned to plantation labor. Rather than try to integrate themselves into the larger European-American world by adopting the languages, religions, and ethos of their enslavers, the plantation slaves turned inward, making the plantation itself—the slaveholders' home—the site for a reconstruction of African life. As elsewhere in the Americas, slaves made an African culture from their diverse memories of the Old World and the harsh realities of the New. As the plantation matured, *African* burial grounds, *African* churches, and eventually *African* academies appeared.

The name was of course significant, signaling an unprecedented joining together of African peoples. But that nascent culture was not of one piece, because the experiences of African people on the mainland was not of one piece. Rather, many different African "nations" emerged from the series of plantation revolutions that raked the continent between the late seventeenth and the early nineteenth centuries. Writing in the early eighteenth century, Alexander Garden, a keen observer of both the natural and human world, declared black people in lowcountry South Carolina "'twere a Nation within a Nation."[26] But what was true of Garden's nation in the South Carolina lowlands was equally true of black people elsewhere in mainland North America. The character of these diverse nations of African descent depended upon the requirements of particular plantation staples, the terrain on which they were grown, the numbers of slaves imported and their origins, the nationality of the slaveowning class and its ideology, the character of the white nonslaveholding population and its numbers, and the commitment of metropolitan authorities and their interest in settlement. As a result, the African nations of the mainland followed different paths in the Chesapeake, the lowcountry, the North, and the lower Mississippi Valley. In some parts of mainland North America, Africans replaced Atlantic creoles, and the charter generations sank swiftly into historical oblivion. In other parts of the mainland, Atlantic creoles maintained their place, and the charter generations' influence extended into the late eighteenth century. What Garden understood to be a single nation was in fact but one group of new nations aborning.

Chapter Five

The Tobacco Revolution in the Chesapeake

⚜

The plantation revolution came to the Chesapeake with the thunder of cannons and the rattle of sabres. Victory over the small holders, servants, and slaves who composed Nathaniel Bacon's motley army in 1676 enabled planters to consolidate their control over Chesapeake society. In quick order, they elaborated a slave code that singled out people of African descent as slaves and made their status hereditary. In the years that followed, as the number of European servants declined and white farmers migrated west, the great planters turned to Africa for their workforce. During the last decades of the seventeenth century, the new order began to take shape. The Chesapeake's economy stumbled into the eighteenth century, but the grandees prospered, as the profits of slave labor filled their pockets. A society with slaves gave way to a slave society around the great estuary.

Although black people grew tobacco as before, the lives of plantation slaves in no way resembled those of the charter generations. White indentured servants might graduate to tenantry or gain small holdings of their own, but black slaves could not. Planters restricted the slaves' access to freedom and stripped slaves of their prerogatives and free blacks of their rights. Rather than participate in a variety of enterprises, slaves labored single-mindedly under the direction of white overseers whose close supervision left little room for initiative or ambition. The slaves' economy withered and with it the robust network of exchanges that had rested upon the slaves' independent production. But even as the great planters installed the new harsh regime, African slaves and their descendants, sometimes in league with remnants of the charter generations, began to reshape black life. In the process, they created a new African-American society.

The triumph of the planter class began the transformation of black life in the Chesapeake.[1] Following the legalization of chattel bondage in the

1660s, slaves slowly but steadily replaced white indentured servants as the main source of plantation labor. Planters enslaved Indians where they could under new legislation that declared "all Indians taken in warr be held and accounted slaves dureing life."[2] But the Native-American population was dwindling fast at the end of the seventeenth century, so Africans became the object of the planters' desire. Between 1675 and 1695 some 3,000 black slaves entered the region. During the last five years of the century, Chesapeake tobacco planters—most of them located along the York River—purchased more slaves than they had in the previous twenty years. In 1668 white servants had outnumbered black slaves more than five to one in Virginia's Middlesex County and much of the Chesapeake region. By 1700 the balance of bound labor had been reversed, and the county of Middlesex—like many other jurisdictions in the Chesapeake—counted more black slaves than white servants. In all, slaves constituted one-third of the laborers growing tobacco in Maryland and Virginia, and, since the great planters could best afford to purchase slaves, slaves composed an even greater share of the workers on the largest estates. Still, black people remained a minority of the population. In 1720 no more than one-quarter of the region's population was black. Twenty years later, black people made up 40 percent of the population in parts of the Chesapeake. Although black people never challenged white numerical dominance, they achieved majorities in a few localities. For many whites it seemed like the Chesapeake would "some time or other be confirmed by the name of New Guinea."[3]

As demand for slaves surged upward, planters turned from the West Indies and other parts of the Atlantic littoral to the African interior as their primary source of slaves. During the 1680s some 2,000 Africans were carried into Virginia. This number more than doubled in the 1690s, and it doubled again in the first decade of the eighteenth century. Nearly 8,000 African slaves arrived in the colony between 1700 and 1710, and the Chesapeake briefly replaced Jamaica as the most profitable slave market in British America. The proportion of the Chesapeake's black population born in Africa grew steadily. By the turn of the century—eighty years after the first black people arrived at Jamestown and some forty years after the legalization of slavery—newly arrived Africans composed nearly 90 percent of the slave population, and their dramatic influx into the Chesapeake profoundly transformed black life.[4]

The transformation sped forward with increasing velocity in the

1730s. During that decade, the number of forced immigrants averaged over 2,000 per year and sometimes rose to twice that number, as slaves replaced indentured servants not only on large plantations but on smaller units as well.[5] Men and women with filed teeth, plaited hair, and ritual scarification (which slaveowners called "country markings" or "negro markings") were everywhere to be seen. Their music—particularly their drums—filled the air with sounds that frightened European and European-American settlers, and their pots, pipes, and other material effects left a distinctive mark on the landscape. An Anglican missionary stationed in Delaware found "difficulty of conversing with the Majority of Negroes themselves," because they have "a language peculiar to themselves, a wild confused medley of Negro and corrupt English, which makes them very unintelligible except to those who have conversed with them for many years." The language of black America turned from the creole lingua franca of the Atlantic world to the languages of the African interior—most probably various dialects of Igbo. Whereas Atlantic creoles had beaten on the door of the established churches to gain a modicum of recognition, the new arrivals showed neither interest in nor knowledge of Christianity. Their religious practices—probably polytheistic although sometimes Islamic—were dismissed as idolatry and devil worship by the established clergy, who placed them outside the pale of civilization as most white men and women understood it. Europeans and European-Americans found the manner in which the new arrivals spoke, prayed, married, and buried their dead to be foreign in ways the charter generations were not. Africa had come to the Chesapeake.[6]

The Africanization of slavery marked a sharp deterioration in the conditions of slave life. With an eye for a quick profit, Chesapeake planters imported males and females disproportionately, at a ratio of more than two to one, and by the end of the seventeenth century this sharply skewed sex ratio manifested itself in the plantation population. Such a sexual imbalance made it difficult for the newly arrived to establish families, let alone maintain the deep lineages that had framed so much of their African life. Since planters employed slave women much as they used slave men—dividing the labor force by age and physical ability but rarely by sex—the special needs of women during pregnancy went unaddressed, and this neglect undermined the ability of the slave population to reproduce itself. Moreover, just as direct importation drove birth rates down, it pushed mortality rates up, for the transatlantic journey left transplanted Africans vulnerable to New World diseases. As long as the main source of slaves was the African trade, fertility remained low and mortality high in the Chesapeake. Whereas Anthony and Mary Johnson, like other members of the charter generations, had lived to see their grandchildren, few of the newly arrived Africans would reproduce themselves. Indeed, within a year of their arrival, one-quarter of all "new Negroes," as they were called, would be dead.[7]

The trek across Africa and the Middle Passage left slaves not just physically weak but also mentally drained. Planters were determined to break the spirit of the new arrivals even further, by stripping Africans of ties to their homeland. Among the first objects of the planters' assault were the names Africans carried to the New World, and with them the lineage which structured much of African life. Writing to his overseer from his plantation on the Rappahannock River in 1727, Robert "King" Carter, perhaps the richest of the Chesapeake's new grandees, explained the process by which he initiated Africans into their American captivity. "I name'd them here & by their names we can always know what sizes they are of & I am sure we repeated them so often to them that every one knew their names & would readily answer to them." Carter then forwarded his slaves to a satellite plantation or "quarter," where his overseer repeated the process, taking "care that the negros both men & women I sent . . . always go by ye names we gave them." In the months that followed, the drill continued, with Carter again joining in the process of stripping the newly arrived Africans of the signature of their identity and inheritance.[8] For the most part, Carter designated his new slaves with a variety of common English diminutive and classical appellations, denying them access to the integrative path that "Antonio a Negro" had taken when he transformed himself into Anthony Johnson.[9] The names given African slaves embodied the distance between the experience of the plantation generations and that of the charter generations. There would be no Anthony Johnsons on Carter's plantation.

The loss of their names was only the first of the numerous indignities newly arrived Africans suffered at the hands of Chesapeake planters. Generally, planters placed little trust in Africans, with their strange tongues and alien customs. They condemned the new arrivals for the "gross bestiality and rudeness of their manners, the variety and strangeness of their languages, and the weakness and shallowness of their minds." Whenever possible, planters put the newly arrived African slaves to work at the most repetitive and backbreaking tasks in some upland quarter, denying them access to positions of skill that Atlantic creoles frequently enjoyed. Planters made but scant attempt to see that the new arrivals had adequate food, clothing, or shelter, because the open slave trade made "new Negroes" cheap, and the disease environment in which they were set to work inflated their mortality rate no matter how well they were tended. Residing in sex-segregated barracks, African slaves lived a lonely existence, without families or ties of kin, and often separated by language from supervisors and co-workers alike. Rude frontier conditions made these largely male compounds desolate, unhealthy places that narrowed the vision of their residents. The physical separation denied the new arrivals the opportunity to integrate themselves into the mainstream of Chesapeake society, and prevented them from finding a well-placed patron and enjoying the company of men and women of equal rank, as their predecessors had done. The planters' strategy of stripping away all ties upon which the enslaved persona rested—name, village, clan, household, and family—and leaving slaves totally dependent upon their owners was nearly successful.[10]

The ability of slaves to move unimpeded through the countryside had sustained the charter generations' broad view of the world, and had allowed them to interact openly with planters and servants, Europeans and Indians. Their wide social networks promoted a sense of self-confidence, even arrogance, which planters were determined to curb. In 1705 and 1723 new laws required slaves to carry a pass when they left the estate of their owner even for the most routine business and denied them the right to meet in groups of more than four, and then only for brief periods of time. Even more novel than the legislation itself was the determination of planter-controlled courts to enforce it, as county courts fined those planters who allowed their slaves "to goe abrod."[11]

But restrictions on movement were only one small indicator of the narrowing of slaves' lives. Whereas members of the charter generations had slept and eaten under the same roof and had worked in the same fields as their owners, the new arrivals lived in a world apart. Even the ties between black slaves and white servants atrophied, as blacks sank deeper into slavery while whites rose in aspiration if not in fact. The strivings of white servants necessitated their distinguishing themselves from African slaves, who were the recipients of harsh treatment that whites laborers would no longer accept. No matter how low the status of white servants, their pale skin distinguished them from society's designated mudsill, and this small difference became the foundation upon which the entire social order rested. Nothing could be further from the "drinkinge and carrousinge" that had brought black slaves and white servants together for long bouts of interracial conviviality than the physical and verbal isolation that confronted newly arrived Africans. Whiteness and blackness took on new meanings.[12]

Long before slaves were confined to remote upcountry quarters, the dynamics of the international slave trade had set them on this course of isolation. Between 1683 and 1721, roughly half of the slaves the Royal African Company sent to Virginia (and whose point of departure is known) sailed from Senegambia, at the mouth of the Gambia River. But it would be erroneous to presume that the port of exit had some necessary relation to the place of captivity, since points of departure were collection sites for slaves of many nations and provided only the roughest of guides to national origins. In addition, most slavers made other stops along the African coast and in the Caribbean, where they added some slaves and sold others. Independent traders, who worked outside the control of the African Company and whose points of origin are unknown, also brought slaves to Virginia, creating a somewhat different mix. During the second and third decades of the eighteenth century, changes in the source of most of the slaves entering the Chesapeake further reduced the possibility of reconstituting a single African nationality in the region. Between 1718 and 1728, so-called Calabars who derived from the Nigerian hinterland via captiveries on the Bight of Biafra made up 40 percent of new arrivals. In the following decades the trade moved southward, so that the largest group of African slaves—although still not the majority—originated not from the slave coast but from Angola. Through the entire period, the majority came from ports as distant from one another as Senegambia and Angola.

Perhaps because of the miscellaneous and changing nature of the trade into the Chesapeake, planters only occasionally considered national origins in deciding which slaves to purchase, as did Carter when he noted that Gambians were "preferable to any country by 40 shillings per head." Chesapeake planters maintained some crude stereotypes of various African nationalities—Coromantees revolted; Angolans ran away; Calabars destroyed themselves—but they rarely requested specific nationals, and once a sale had been completed, they rarely noted the nationality of their slaves, preferring to describe them simply as Africans or "new Negroes." "If they are likely young negroes, it's not a farthing matter where they come from," asserted one Virginia slaveowner upon the completion of a purchase in 1725.[13]

Slavers peddled their human cargo in small lots at the numerous tobacco landings that lined the Bay's extensive perimeter. Planters rarely bought more than a few slaves at a time, and larger purchasers like Carter frequently acted as jobbers, reselling their slaves to upstart planters. Once purchased, African slaves were further separated according to the various and changing circumstances of individual planters. Only occasionally did members of one nation congregate on a single plantation. Thus the slave trade in the Chesapeake operated to scatter men and women of various nations and diminish the importance of African nationality. And whatever fragile communities slaves had managed to create in their cramped, terrifying journey to the New World were also often disbanded as soon as the slave ships entered the Chesapeake Bay.[14]

Few Atlantic creoles could be found among these diverse arrivals. The touchstones of the charter generations—linguistic fluency, familiarity with the commercial practices of the Atlantic, knowledge of European conventions and institutions, and (occasionally) their partial European ancestry—vanished in the age of the plantation. The previous experience of most slaves as peasant farmers and pastoralists in the African interior provided little preparation for what was to follow in the New World. Unmediated by a common pidgin or creole language, newly arrived Africans often stood mute before their enslavers, estranged from the new land and from the white men who—like "King" Carter—asserted their domination in the form of the repetition of some unfathomable gibberish.

Such a social order required raw power to sustain it; and during the early years of the eighteenth century, planters mobilized the apparatus of coercion in the service of their new regime. In the previous century, maimings, brandings, and beatings had occurred commonly, but the level of violence increased dramatically as planters transformed the society with slaves into a slave society. Chesapeake slaves faced the pillory, whipping post, and gallows far more frequently and in far larger numbers than ever before. Even as planters employed the rod, the lash, the branding iron, and the fist with increased regularity, they invented new punishments that would humiliate and demoralize as well as correct. What else can one make of William Byrd's forcing a slave bedwetter to drink "a pint of piss" or Joseph Ball's placement of a metal bit in the mouth of persistent runaways.

But beyond the dehumanizing affronts, there were the grotesque mutilations. In 1707 "King" Carter requested court permission to chop off the toes of "two Incorrigible negroes . . . named Barbara Harry & Dinah." County officials readily granted him "full power to dismember," a penalty applied to white men only for the most heinous crimes. It was neither the last time Carter would so act nor the harshest penalty Chesapeake slaves would be assessed in the planters' campaign to terrorize their human property.[15]

The state ratified the planters' actions, affirming the masters' right to take a slave's life without fear of retribution. After 1669 the demise of a slave "who chance to die" while being corrected by his or her owner or upon orders of their owner no longer constituted a felony in Virginia. Such legislation soon became general throughout the region. In the years to follow, Chesapeake lawmakers expanded the power of the slaveholder and diminished the rights of the slaves in many other ways. The Virginia slave code, enacted in 1705, recapitulated, systematized, and expanded these sometimes contradictory statutes, affirming the slaveholders' ascent.[16]

Confined to the plantation, African slaves faced a new harsh work regimen as planters escalated the demands they placed on those who worked the tobacco fields. With the decline of white servitude, slaves could no longer take refuge in the standards established for English servants. During the eighteenth century, slaves worked more days and longer hours, under closer supervision and with greater regimentation, than servants ever had in the seventeenth. Although the processes of production changed but little during the first third of the eighteenth century, slaveholders reduced the number of holidays to three: Christmas, Easter, and Whitsuntide. Saturday became a full workday, and many slaves worked Sunday as well. Planters shortened or eliminated the slaves' mid-day break. In many places, planters extended the workday into the evening, requiring that slaves grind corn and chop wood for their masters on their own time. Winter, previously a slack season, became filled with an array of tasks, including grubbing stumps, cleaning pastures, and repairing buildings. Shorter winter days did not save slaves from the new regimen, as some planters required that they work at night, often by firelight.

Although they worked harder and longer than had English servants, African slaves rarely received equivalent food, shelter, and medical attention. The customary rights accorded English workers lost their meaning as the field force became increasingly African. Slaves might protest, but their appeals stopped at the plantation's borders. Whereas slaveholders in the seventeenth century had petitioned the courts to discipline unruly slaves, in the eighteenth century they assumed near sovereignty over their plantations. The masters' authority was rarely questioned, and, unlike white servants, African slaves had no court of last resort.[17]

The assumption of near absolute sovereignty reflected the rapid expansion of the planters' power during the first decades of the eighteenth century. Having enslaved black people and confined the remaining white servants to a subordinate place in Chesapeake society, the grandees knit themselves together through strategic marriages, carefully crafted business dealings, and elaborate rituals, creating a style of life which awed common folk and to which lesser planters dared not aspire. By midcentury, the great planters had forged an interlocking directorate, tied together by family loyalties, business partnerships, political allegiances, and grand displays at taverns, cotillions, and courthouses. Although Chesapeake planters were famous for their intramural disputes, their rule was complete. They would not be challenged—and then only briefly—until the evangelical awakenings of the late eighteenth century.

Meanwhile, the grandees steadily expanded their holdings and tightened their grip on colonial legislatures and county courts. Their plantations became the seats of small empires, as much factories as farms, which extended to mills, foundries, weaving houses, and numerous satellite plantations. Planters took on the airs of English gentlemen, making much of their sociability and cultivating a sense of stewardship. The seat of their domain—a large mansion house with accompanying "Kitchins, Dayry houses, Barns, Stables, Store hourses, and some . . . 2 or 3 Negro Quarters"—towered over the community with near perfect symmetry. It became the hub of the planter's universe. The home plantation, declared the tutor on one such estate, was "like a Town; but most of the Inhabitants are black." Writing after the Revolution, George Mason, himself a substantial planter, remembered that his father "had among his slaves carpenters, coopers, sawyers, blacksmiths, tanners, curriers, shoemakers, spinners, weavers and knitters, and even a distiller." The great plantation towns of the Chesapeake—Carter's Grove, Corotoman, Sabine Hall, Shirley, Stafford Hall, and eventually Doorhoregan, Monticello, and

Mount Vernon—dominated the countryside and symbolized the rule of the planter class.[18]

As planters consolidated their power, they no longer looked at themselves as mere patrons of their slaves and other subordinates, whose favors might be extended in return for loyalty and labor. From their new place atop Chesapeake society, planters began to spin out a vision of social relations that emphasized deference and authority. The creation of the plantation regime transformed patronage into paternalism, and a new sense of mastership emerged. The weight of tending numerous dependents reshaped the planters' self-image as the metaphorical fathers, whose benevolence could elevate those who accepted their rule and whose harsh retribution would humble those who challenged it. "I must take care to keep all my people to their Duty, to see all the Springs in motion and make everyone draw his equal Share to carry the Machine forward," wrote William Byrd in 1726. The vision of themselves as prime movers, fathers writ large, became the foundation of the planters' world.[19]

The growth of the paternalist ideology meant many things for slaves, but its first meaning was work. Regimented labor was all-encompassing. During the seventeenth century, few planters had owned more than one or two laborers, and most had worked in the field alongside their slaves and servants in a manner that necessarily promoted close interactions. African importation and the general increase in the size of holdings permitted planters—along with their wives and children—to withdraw from the fields. They hired overseers to supervise their slaves and sometimes employed stewards to supervise their overseers, dividing their workforce by age, sex, and ability. There were few economies of scale in tobacco culture, and planters—believing close supervision increased production—kept work units small by dividing their holdings into "quarters." But the small units rarely meant slaves worked alongside their owners. To squeeze more labor from their workers, planters also reorganized their workforce into squads or gangs, often placing agile young workers at the head of each gang. Rather than work at their own pace, slaves found their toil subject to minute inspection, as planters or their minions monitored the numerous tasks that tobacco cultivation necessitated. The demands placed on slaves to work longer and harder grew steadily throughout the eighteenth century as planters—particularly in the older, settled areas—encountered diminishing yields and rising production costs. Slaves suffered as planters prospered from the increased productivity, and the size of slave-grown crops far exceeded those previously brought to market.[20]

The time slaves spent working their owners' crop meant time lost tending their own gardens and provision grounds. The slaves' independent economy shriveled as the great planters expanded their domain. Whereas seventeenth-century planters had gladly allowed slaves to feed and clothe themselves, the new grandees—eager to cloak themselves in the patriarch's mantle and to maximize the time slaves spent in their fields—issued weekly rations and seasonal allotments of clothing, taking pride in the largess they bestowed on their slaves. Plantation slaves generally maintained gardens, raised barnyard fowl, and hunted and fished to supplement their allowance. But few cultivated provision grounds where they grew tobacco in competition with their owners, or kept hogs or cattle. If they did, they did so illegally, for in 1692 the Virginia legislature ordered owners to confiscate "all cattle, hoggs marked of any negro or other slave mark, or by any slave kept." When planters failed to act, the slaves' estate became the property of the parish church wardens and "forfeited to the use of the poore."[21]

Under such conditions, the slaves' economy only rarely reached beyond the boundaries of their owners' estates. Chesapeake slaves traded among themselves and occasionally offered some barnyard fowl to their owners, who—in a grand gesture—bestowed a few coins along with injunctions about frugality and the like. Those slaves who traded independently generally did so clandestinely, shrinking the distance between legitimate trade and theft—at least in their owners' eyes. As far as is known, none followed Emanuel Driggus's lead to request—and receive—judicial authorization to trade on their own. Instead, slaves became "the general Chicken merchants" of the Chesapeake. Their petty trade could rarely generate the income necessary to purchase freedom, as had Francis Payne and John Graweere in an earlier age.[22]

Violence, isolation, exhaustion, and alienation often led African slaves to profound depression and occasionally to self-destruction. But slaves contested the new regime at every turn—protesting the organization, pace, and intensity of labor and challenging the planters' definition of property rights. Over time, they perfected numerous techniques to foil their owners' demands and expand control over their own labor and lives.

If the imposition of plantation slavery required planters to escalate the level of violence, they often faced an equally violent opposition. During the first decades of the eighteenth century, the Chesapeake was rife with conspiracies and insurrectionary plots against slavery. In 1709 and 1710, 1722, and then for three successive years beginning in 1729, planters uncovered broad-reaching conspiracies to, in the words of Virginia's governor, "levy Warr against her majesty's Governmt," as black people struck back at the new oppressive regime.[23] But much as they might yearn for a violent confrontation with their owners, slaves soon learned that the planters' near monopoly of physical force—particularly their ability to call upon state authority—made victory a doubtful prospect.

Resistance required guile as well as muscle. If the imposition of the new regime began with the usurpation of the Africans' names, slaves soon took back this signature of their identity. While slaves answered to the names their owners imposed on them, many clandestinely maintained their African names. If secrecy provided one shield, seeming ignorance offered another. In the very stereotype of the dumb, brutish African that planters voiced so loudly, newly arrived slaves found protection, as they used their apparent ignorance of the language, landscape, and work routines of the Chesapeake to their own benefit. Observing the new Negroes on one Maryland estate, a visitor was "surprised at their Perseverance." "Let an hundred Men shew him how to hoe, or drive a Wheelbarrow, he'll still take the one by the bottom, and the Other by the Wheel." Triumphant planters had won the initial battle by gaining control over Chesapeake society and placing their imprint on the processes of production, but slaves answered that the war would be a long one.[24]

Rather than embrace Chesapeake society in the manner of the charter generations, transplanted Africans joined together to distance themselves from the source of their oppression—sometimes literally. Runaways fled toward the mountainous backcountry and lowland swamps. They generally traveled in large bands that included women and children, despite the hazards such groups entailed for a successful escape. As with African fugitives in lowland South Carolina and Louisiana, their purpose was to recreate the only society they knew free from white domination. During the 1720s, reports that fugitive slaves had established a settlement in the "Great Mountains" circulated widely in Virginia, and fear of maroonage grew among colonial officials. In 1729 a dozen slaves had left a new plantation near the falls of the James River, taking provisions, clothing, tools, and arms to a settlement of their own creation near Lexington. Two years later, Harry, a recently arrived African slave who had escaped from Prince George's County, Maryland, joined a small company of maroons beyond the line of European settlement. About the same time, a planter, surveying the Great Dismal Swamp on the south side of Virginia, stumbled upon a black family who "call'd themselvs free, tho' by the Shyness of the Master of the House, who took care to keep least in Sight, their Freedom seem'd a little Doubtful."[25]

Weather and topography conspired against the long-term viability of fugitive settlements in the Chesapeake. So too did planters. Whereas such settlements in a society with slaves were viewed as annoying growths, planters saw them as cancerous tumors that had to be excised. Few Chesapeake settlements lasted more than a year or two. With the discovery of the maroon colony near Lexington, officials moved quickly to dismantle the sanctuary. Virginia troopers smashed the main settlement, plowed up its crops, and retook the fugitives. According to the governor, their recapture "prevented for this time a design which might have proved as dangerous to this Country, as is that of the Negroes in the Mountains of Jamaica to the Inhabitants of that Island." Although the assault did not end attempts of black people to create independent settlements, such settlements survived only in a few isolated and impenetrable areas like the Great Dismal Swamp.[26]

Maroonage became less and less viable with the westward expansion of the plantation economy, but truancy continued to be a useful counter to the tyranny of plantation life. Withdrawing labor or threatening to withdraw labor, particularly at critical junctures in the productive process, enabled slaves to counter the ever-escalating demands that slaveholders made. Yet, like all of the slaves' weapons, withholding labor had to be used carefully. Chronic runaways faced brutal physical reprisals and, if they survived, were eventually sold to some distant place. Slaves thus calculated exactly how this weapon could be employed. Truants rarely fled in the winter. They almost always maintained ties with compatriots on their home estate, who supplied food, clothing, and information. They rarely remained at large so long as to be "outlawed," a circumstance that raised the ante in this most dangerous game and might bring reprisals that put the entire plantation community at risk.[27]

But the risk might well be worth the chance, especially for slaves caught up in the westward expansion of the plantation regime. Tobacco was hard on Chesapeake soils; and during the middle years of the eighteenth century, productivity had begun to slip, especially in the places of initial settlement. Unable to maintain the yields of earlier times, planters searched for ways to increase their return by finding fresh tobacco lands. Beginning in the 1720s, they pushed beyond the fall line, where the Atlantic coastal plain meets the piedmont, liquidating maroon villages and removing Indians to the west. The younger sons of great planters and ambitious small planters staked out new quarters and prepared to plant tobacco. Many took their slaves with them, and others purchased slaves from tidewater estates—dismembering nascent slave communities at their very point of formation. But upcountry planters also relied heavily on African imports. The hub of the slave trade moved from the York River to the upper James during the middle years of the eighteenth century. Between 1720 and the Revolution, slave traders and planters carried more than 15,000 Africans beyond the fall line, transferring the center of African life from the tidewater to the piedmont and making the upcountry the most thoroughly African portion of the Chesapeake region. Africans made up the majority of the black population in many places, and in some parts of the piedmont they composed the majority of the entire population.[28]

Africanization again marked the debasement of black life. As the piedmont's slave population grew, the familiar demographic characteristics of an open slave trade appeared: imbalanced sex ratios, low fertility, high mortality, and of course an African majority. In 1730, when the black population had begun to achieve a rough sexual parity in the tidewater, it stood at 120 males for every 100 female slaves in the piedmont. Reflecting the limited resources of upland planters and the desire of tidewater grandees to keep their most productive workers at home, the piedmont also had a disproportionately large number of children and young adults. Planters in general purchased "men boys" and "women girls," the words one slave trader used to characterize teenaged slaves.

The largely African, male, and youthful population distinguished black life in the piedmont during the early years of settlement. "You must understand there are great Quantities of those Negroes imported here yearly from Africa, who have Languags peculiar to themselves, who are here many years before they understand English," a frustrated Anglican missionary reported from upcountry Virginia in 1764. African arrivals kept their language, religion, music, and much else in the Chesapeake's backcountry. By the second half of the eighteenth century, much of the difference between African and creole slaves could be measured in the geography of the Chesapeake.[29]

Isolated from the mainstream of Chesapeake life, newly arrived Africans had no sense of the standards by which Chesapeake slaves had earlier worked. Old hands sometimes supplied guidance as to the established routine, but the forced migration to the upcountry was extremely disruptive, dividing established families and sundering communities. Even experienced hands faced new tasks, as the heavily forested piedmont had to be cleared, fresh land broken, cabins built, and crops planted—all in rapid succession.[30] In such circumstances, slaveholders found numerous ways to ratchet up the level of labor expected from slaves. While pressing slaves too hard might send them to the woods, slaveholders and their subordinates, eager to extend the tobacco kingdom, were quick to wield the lash.

The new regime left little room for free blacks, even those descendants of Atlantic creoles who had enjoyed freedom for generations. Chesapeake planters relied upon white nonslaveholders to serve as overseers and artisans and had no need for black militiamen. Unlike their counterparts in pioneer South Carolina, Florida, or Louisiana, tobacco planters collapsed all black people, free and slave, into one subaltern class, in which color—not nationality, skill, or religion—defined all. Chesapeake lawmakers systematically carved away at the privileges the free black members of the charter generations had enjoyed prior to the plantation revolution. To the extent that such liberties contradicted the logic of racial slavery, they would not be permitted. Only by fixing "a perpetual Brand upon Free-Negros & Mulattos by excluding them from that great Priviledge of a Freeman," declared the governor of Virginia in 1723, could white planters "make the free-Negros sensible that a distinction ought to be made between their offspring and the Descendants of an Englishman, with whom they never were to be Accounted Equal."[31]

During the half century following legal enslavement, lawmakers in the Chesapeake region filled their statute books with legislation distinguishing between the rights accorded black and white persons, barring free persons of African descent from the most elemental liberties, and denying slaves access to freedom. Free black people lost the right to employ white indentured servants, hold office, bear arms, muster in the militia, and vote. They were required to pay special taxes, were punished

more severely for certain crimes, and were subjected to fines or imprisonment for striking a white person, no matter what the cause.[32]

The opportunities for black people to escape slavery or enjoy liberty
all but disappeared. In the same motion that slaveowning legislators
degraded the free people's legal standing, they narrowed the avenues to
freedom. In 1691 the Virginia lawmakers transformed manumission into
a legislative prerogative and required slaveholders to transport former
slaves out of the colony, discouraging the freeing of slaves. Legislators
also tried to seal another route to freedom by confining the children of
white women and black men to thirty-one years of servitude and, as if to
make sure such men and women would never gain freedom, stipulating
that children born during this period—the grandchildren of the original
offenders—would also be enslaved for thirty-one years.[33]

Not content merely to prevent slaves from becoming free, some
whites evinced a desire to reduce free people of color to slaves. On Virginia's eastern shore, where the Johnson family once stood on a par with
other small landholders, white planters petitioned for the removal of all
free persons of African descent. The Johnsons, along with many other
families, did not wait for the legislative response before fleeing the colony. Others tried to pass into white society, a difficult task at which only
a few could hope to succeed. Yet others joined the remnants of declining
Indian tribes to create peoples who shared African, European, and Native-American ancestry.[34]

The exodus altered the size and character of the remaining free black
population. While the number of slaves in the Chesapeake grew ever
larger, the number of free people of African descent declined, if not in
absolute numbers, certainly as a proportion of the black population.
By midcentury, free people of African descent constituted a small and
shrinking share of the black population, probably not more than 5 percent. Nowhere did free people of color comprise more than 20 percent of
the black population, as they once had on Virginia's eastern shore.[35]

Along with their diminishing numbers, free people of African descent
acquired another distinguishing characteristic. In 1755 about 80 percent
of this group in Maryland were of mixed racial origins. Like white Marylanders, about half of the free colored population was under sixteen
years of age, and of these, almost nine out of ten were of mixed ancestry.
In other words, Chesapeake free blacks were becoming progressively light-
skinned. In the "bleaching" of the free black population, planters found
additional evidence of the identification of whiteness with freedom.[36]

While their tawny color indicated partial European ancestry, most free people of color had no kinship to the new planter class, men and women who, in an earlier age, might have served as patrons and benefactors. Instead, they generally descended from white servants, frequently women. Such impoverished people had little in the way of status, money, or connections to offer their children. Moreover, planter-inspired legislation further compromised the liberty of the offspring of white women and black men by requiring them to serve their mother's master for long terms. The racially mixed descendants of white women generally did not gain their freedom from servitude until they were nearly "past labour" and their owners could no longer wring a profit from them. The fine print of the law and the heavy hand of its enforcers assured that few black people arrived at freedom in full youthful vigor. Those who gained their freedom had difficulty maintaining it. Falling prey to numerous snares and legal chicanery—bastardy laws seemed to have been the favorite ploy—they frequently found themselves clapped back into servitude.[37]

A few men and women, mostly descendants of the charter generations, prospered. Azaricum Drighouse, the grandson of Emanuel Driggus, maintained a substantial plantation on the eastern shore; and when he died in 1738, the value of his estate placed him in the upper echelons of eastern-shore planters. But Drighouse was an exception. His counterparts—men like Humphrey Jones, John Rawlinson, and Edward Nicken —were rare indeed. Most of the descendants of the old charter generations, like most free blacks, spent their lives working and living alongside slaves, occasionally serving terms of servitude, and sometime plummeting into slavery.[38]

The close connection between free and slave blacks, their illegitimacy, and their inability to protect themselves at law made it easy for white planters to treat them as one. Unscrupulous planters and traders sold numerous free black apprentices and servants into slavery simply by removing them beyond the reach of evidence that they had a legal title to freedom, thereby demonstrating the disdain in which they held the liberty of people of African descent. A complaint brought by Moll, a black servant in the Virginia piedmont against her former owner, for "claiming her as a slave and Threatning to carry her out of the colony," captures the dangers free blacks regularly faced at midcentury.[39] Those black men and women who maintained their freedom could scarcely hope for the opportunities an earlier generation of free people of color had enjoyed. The transformation of the free black population in the century between 1660 and 1760 measured the changes that accompanied the plantation revolution in the Chesapeake. The growth of a slave society and the degradation of free people of African descent were part of the same process of making slavery and making race.

Enslavement, Africanization, the imposition of the new plantation regimen, and the destruction of the charter generations—the various elements of the plantation revolution—altered black life in the Chesapeake region, almost always for the worse. But during the fourth decade of the eighteenth century, black society was again transformed as a new generation of African Americans eclipsed the African majority, ending the era of African domination. Native-born black people were healthier and lived longer than the African newcomers. Like members of the charter generations, they too were familiar with the landscapes and economies of the region. Perhaps most importantly, the new creoles had control of the word, as English was their native tongue. They could converse easily with one another, as well as with their owners and other whites. Indeed, many native-born slaves had developed particular variants of English and spoke in a "Scotch-Irish Dialect" or "Virginia accent."

Language allowed them to adjust their inherited cosmology, sacred and secular, to the requirements of tobacco cultivation and the demands of their status. Traveling through the countryside as messengers, watermen, and jobbing tradesmen, native-born slaves exuded confidence as they mastered the terrain, perfected their English, and incorporated the icons and institutions of their owners' culture into their African inheritance. The culture that emerged enabled African Americans to challenge their owners from a position of knowledge.[40]

The passage from an African to an African-American majority began slowly. The transition had its demographic origins in the slaves' development of immunities to New World diseases and the steady growth in the size of slaveholding units. At midcentury, Chesapeake slaves not only lived longer but they also resided in units whose large size made it possible to find partners and form resident families. During the 1720s the slave population began to edge upward through natural increase. Planters, encouraged by the proven ability of Africans to survive and reproduce, strove to correct the sexual imbalance within the black population, importing a larger share of women and perhaps reducing the burdens on slave women during pregnancy. Although planters continued to purchase Africans at a brisk pace and the sex ratio remained imbalanced, by 1730 almost 40 percent of the black people in the Chesapeake colonies were native to the region. At midcentury, African Americans formed four-fifths of the slave population. On the eve of the American Revolution, the vast majority of Chesapeake slaves were native Americans, most several times over.[41]

Chesapeake planters delighted in the growth of an indigenous slave population, as it allowed them to transfer much of the cost of reproducing the workforce to the workers themselves. Thomas Jefferson declared that "a woman who brings a child every two years [is] more profitable than the best man on the farm [for] what she produces is an addition to the capital, while his labor disappears in mere consumption." Jefferson was not the only slaveholder who appreciated the value of a self-reproducing labor force. "Nothing is more to the advantage of my son," declared one ambitious planter in 1719 as he purchased two fifteen-year-old girls, "than young breeding negroes." Although mortality rates remained high, African importation declined steadily as the indigenous slave population increased. By the 1770s, only 500 of the 5,000 slaves added annually to the black population of Virginia derived directly from Africa.[42]

As the native population grew, the Chesapeake once again became a creole society, although its point of reference was not the Atlantic but the North American interior. The charter generations and their descendants had been all but obliterated by the plantation revolution, so that only small remnants survived. Its members' occasional presence—especially in the likes of Azaricum Drighouse—reminded both white and black that people of African descent had once played a different role in Chesapeake society. But the charter generations no longer shaped the course of black life.

Africans—or so-called saltwater slaves—also remained important, at least as long as an open slave trade continued to renew knowledge of the Old World. But even in those areas where Africans composed a majority—parts of the piedmont during the 1740s and 1750s, for example—their numerical dominance dwindled, as rapid settlement quickened the pace of creolization. The majority of black people in the piedmont had also become African American, living in families and working in a manner familiar to slaves of native birth. Rather than shaping the lives of the creole majority, Africans were incorporated into the ongoing evolution of black society.[43]

At midcentury, the African moment in Chesapeake history was passing, as the African population aged and the rising generation of African Americans came into its own. During the next two decades the linguistic and material evidence of an African presence, so visible in the early decades of the eighteenth century, would all but vanish. Slaves with teeth filed, hair plaited, or skin scarred in the ritual manner disappeared from the countryside. Some African words, gestures, and forms continued to shape speech, but no distinctive language emerged, and parents rarely gave African names to their children. The pottery they made, the pipes they smoked, and perhaps most importantly the way they celebrated rites of passage—particularly birth and death—incorporated ancestral Africa into everyday African-American life so thoroughly as to become almost invisible. African-American culture in the Chesapeake evolved parallel with Anglo-American culture and with a considerable measure of congruence.

The emergence of the new culture marked the transformation of the relationship between master and slave and with it the very definition of race. As Chesapeake slaves gained control of the word, the landscape, the productive processes, and much else, notions of blacks as a dull, brutish people fell away. In their place reappeared the stereotype of the artful, sensible charlatan, men and women who gain their way not through force but through guile and manipulation: forged passes, mimicked dialectics, and artfully constructed stories. The belief that such men and women could transform themselves—as erroneous as the older depiction of the brutish slave—was a product of the changing realities of slave life.

But cultural transformation was not assimilation to a European ideal. Black people kept their African ways as they understood them, worshipping in a manner that white observers condemned as idolatry and superstition. If a new generation of American-born peoples was tempted toward Christianity, an older generation would have nothing of it. Indeed, the distinctive nature of African-American culture led some white observers to conclude there could be no reconciliation of African and European ways. From his post in Delaware, an Anglican minister rendered the opinion that most slaves "seem to be of a species quite different from the whites, have no abstracted ideas, cannot comprehend the meaning of faith in Christ, the nature of the fall of man, the necessity of a redeemer, with other essentials of the Christian scheme."[44]

The slow, halting process of creolization also roiled black life. African Americans frequently flaunted their superior knowledge of the region and disparaged the African newcomers for their strange habits and ignorance of Chesapeake life. Occasionally, the disparagement went the other way. Writing in the nineteenth century, Charles Ball, a Maryland slave, remembered that his African grandfather "always expressed great contempt for his fellow slaves, they being . . . a mean and vulgar race, quite beneath his rank, and the dignity of his former station." Planters played on African–creole differences to divide slaves from one another. Stigmatizing Africans as "outlandish" and condemning them for their "various harsh jargons," slaveowners praised creoles for affecting "our language, habits, and customs."[45] Still, if such backhanded appreciations did not elevate creoles over Africans in any lasting way, it allowed the new creoles to confront planters on a more even ground than had their African predecessors. They understood something about the paternal aspirations of the planter class. Whether slaves took those aspirations at face value or dismissed them as cynical cant, slaves were not above employing the masters' beliefs against them.

Slaveholders grew more receptive to such supplications. During the last half of the eighteenth century, planters dwelled increasingly upon the responsibilities that accompanied mastership. Nowhere was this interplay between the aspirations of master and slave more evident than in the evolution of the slave family, as the desire for a stable domestic life joined all black people together. Planters too had a stake in the permanence of the slave family—at least insofar as domestic stability aided production and reproduction. But while planters applauded—and profited from—the slaves' natural increase, they had little direct interest in the organization of the slave family. Often they found it inconvenient for husbands and wives to reside together, and frequently they found it profitable to sell children away from their parents or divide families to satisfy their own dynastic aspirations. Likewise, planters disliked losing the labor of pregnant and postpartum women, even though the children added to their wealth. If some slaveowners were "kind and indulgent to pregnant women," others forced the "Bellyed" into the fields with the lash. Thus, however much planters profited from the domestic regularity in the slave quarter and the creation of an indigenous slave population, they remained the greatest enemy of the viability of the slave family.[46]

To create families to their liking, African-American slaves pressed their owners with demands for a modicum of domestic security. Husbands and wives petitioned for permission to reside together on the same quarter or to allow husbands to visit "broad wives" and other kin, often flattering masters and mistresses with their supplications. Such off-plantation relationships disrupted the smooth operation of plantation life, making slaveowners reluctant to acquiesce. However, if the appeals to planter benevolence failed, slaves—particularly slave men—raised the cost of disapproval by withdrawing their labor. When Sam, a thirty-three-year-old carpenter, fled his plantation in central Maryland, his owner knew he could be found "lurking in Charles County . . . where a Mulatto woman lives whom he has for some time called his wife." According to her owner, a young fourteen-year-old fugitive with an iron collar was "harbour'd in some Negro Quarter, as her Father and Mother Encourages her Elopements, under a Pretence that she is ill used at Home." The separation of family members was probably the single largest source of flight and the root cause of other dissension within the plantation.

In the end, few owners denied their slaves' requests to visit kinfolk on their own time. Where possible, slaveowners accommodated their slaves, allowing them to live together, and occasionally they purchased slaves to unite slave couples. By the middle of the eighteenth century, Chesapeake slaves had transformed their desire for domestic stability into a right, which, if not always honored by their owners, was recognized as a legitimate aspiration.[47]

Slaves established other conventions to provide them with a modicum of domestic stability. While slave women demanded time to feed their children at the breast, slave men saw to it that their families were fed beyond their masters' rations. Slaves also began to wrench control of the naming process from their owners, and parents increasingly named their children after a respected ancestor or other notable. A number of naming patterns appeared, but among the names that were missing from the quarter were those of the master and mistress. Few slaves named their children after the plantation's putative father and mother, a tacit recognition that the "family, black and white," were no kinsmen. Before long, a system of inheritance emerged within the slave community. By the middle years of the eighteenth century, it became common for slave artisans and domestics to pass their skills and special positions within the plantation hierarchy to their children.

Slaves also won a measure of privacy for their domestic lives. Unlike the barracks that housed newly arrived Africans, native-born slave families generally resided in individual cabins, often of their own construction. Most were small, rude buildings, little different from the outbuildings where slaveholders housed their animals and stored their tools, although they generally took a neater, more permanent form in the great plantation towns. But even when ramshackle and dilapidated, the separate slave quarter marked the acceptance of the slaves' demands for an independent family life and a grudging concession to the slaves' right to privacy—a notion that was antithetical to the very idea of chattel bondage.[48] With the maturation of the plantation generations, the family once again became the center of black life in the Chesapeake and the locus of opposition to the planter's rule.

The peripatetic nature of tobacco cultivation aided and abetted the expansion of family life. Tobacco needed fresh soils, and planters rarely worked the same ground more than three years running. Slaves no sooner established themselves on one piece of ground than they were off preparing another. As slaves moved from quarter to quarter, they crosshatched the countryside with ties of friendship and, before long, kinship. A growing network of roads that brought even small quarters within easy distance of one another facilitated the maintenance of these kin ties. Complaints by planters about the "continual concourse of Negroes on Sabboth and holy days meeting in great numbers" documented how black people maintained their families at a distance.[49]

Nevertheless, the slave family remained a fragile institution, as slaves had few resources to sustain ties and fewer still to protect—let alone advance—their interests. Slaveholders continually intervened in the slaves' family affairs, undercutting parents and other figures of authority, affirming their power as they rationed visitation rights and forced slaves to solicit their approval for the most routine engagements. Even under the best of circumstances, the long-distance relationships between husbands and wives were difficult to maintain and the authority of parents difficult to sustain, when they had no power to protect, few resources to reward, and little authority to punish. The frailty of family ties grew with the distance, as from afar kin relations did not even have the force of propinquity. Nonetheless, slaves recognized the centrality of their own domestic institution, and put it in the center of their own world.

With the reestablishment of the black family came responsibilities not only as husbands and wives, parents, and even grandparents but also as community leaders: men and women who set the standards and defined the norms of the slaves' society and then established strategies and created the tactics by which they might be achieved. Leadership placed some slave men and women squarely in opposition to the planters' belief that they were metaphorical fathers and mothers of the slave community. The development of black family life, and the restructuring of the black community which the new kinship patterns affirmed set in motion a new series of conflicts over the fruits of the slaves' labor, as slaves tried to roll back the stringent labor requirements that accompanied the growth of the plantation and to reinvigorate their own economy. The issues were many: customary workload and pace of labor, division of labor within slave families, the nature of supervision, character of discipline, all of which slaveowners claimed as their exclusive prerogative and all of which slaves determined to alter in their own favor.

The African-American family did not end at the household's edge. Sometimes extended families occupied a single plantation or quarter; sometimes slave families spilled across plantation boundaries. In Folly's Quarter of Charles Carroll's great Doorhoregan estate on the western shore of Maryland, Fanny lived surrounded by her children, grandchildren, and nephews and nieces, forty in number. Likewise, all but thirty of the 128 slaves residing on Riggs, Carroll's home quarter, belonged to two extended families. Sometimes the quarter took the name of the family matriarch or patriarch. But the small size of most Chesapeake estates forced slave men and women to look beyond plantation borders for a spouse. As slaves intermarried across plantation lines, the extended network of kin spread through the countryside, joined together by consanguinity and shared obligations. Scattered among the dozen quarters, mills, and forges that comprised Charles Carroll's vast holdings, some twenty slaves bore the names of their grandparents and others that of aunts and uncles and of course parents.[50]

The quarter, whether the home of a single extended family or a group of unrelated individuals who had been transmuted into kin, became the institutional embodiment of the slave community in the Chesapeake. On the home plantation, the quarter was generally neatly tended, often along a street that led to the planter's Great House. Outside the orbit of the great plantation towns, the quarter was little more than a ramshackle collection of huts and outbuildings. Surrounded by equally disorderly gardens, animal pens, and scrawny barnyard fowl, this farrago of small dwellings—each rarely more than a single spartan room with an earthen floor—was much like the west African villages or compounds from which slaves or their ancestors derived.[51] Within its bounds, slaves plotted their own ascent, socializing among themselves, educating their children to the harsh realities of enslavement, and honing the weapons which they would employ to reclaim what their owners usurped.

The slaves' weapons were many, and after a century in the tobacco fields they extended beyond revolt, maroonage, and truancy, for slaves understood the processes of tobacco cultivation as well as any owner. That many quarters took their names from the slave patriarchs or matriarchs who were their central figures and who often served as their foreman and occasionally as their forewoman suggests the degree to which black people had gained control over their work and their lives.[52] As knowledgeable agriculturalists, these men and women appreciated how their strategic interventions could destroy a season's crop and ruin their owners. In their understanding of the complex process in which tobacco was cultivated and cured, Chesapeake slaves found strength.

Initially, slaves secured some substantial gains. Slaves stabilized the workday, which planters had stretched substantially beyond what had been customary during the early years of the eighteenth century, and began the process of rolling back the number of hours they were expected to labor. The planters' effort to counter this trend by lengthening the number of hours spent in the fields or speeding the pace of labor elicited immediate protests—sometimes in the form of shoddy work, broken tools, or increased truancy. "The Negroes are very unwilling to give up the principles they were allowed in Wingfield's time," reported the manager of a Virginia estate upon the appointment of a new overseer. Slaves conspired to frustrate the new man, and finally determined to have him "turned off." When the manager dismissed their complaints, they sent a delegation directly to the master, so that eventually all conceded that the new man had to go.[53] Such small victories gave slaves a bit more control over their lives, and chastened those who desired to increase plantation productivity.

During the middle years of the eighteenth century, slaves recovered some of the prerogatives that members of the charter generations had taken for granted. The free Sunday had become an entitlement rather than a privilege, so almost all Chesapeake slaves had Sundays to themselves. According to a historian of eighteenth-century Chesapeake agriculture, "slaves had converted that practice into a right that could not be violated arbitrarily." Occasionally, slaves enjoyed part of Saturday as well. When owners impinged upon the slaves' free days, they generally compensated them in time or money.[54]

Still, planters resisted, refusing to surrender the very essence of slavery's value. To prevent slaves from elevating customary practices into entitlements and from manufacturing yet additional rights, slaveholders sought to confine the slaves' economy. They were especially adamant about the independent trading, as they understood how the slaves' entry into the marketplace enlarged their understanding of the value of their own labor and sharpened their appreciation of the planter's usurpation. Moreover, planters were not above countering with new demands of their own—for example, requiring slaves to process as well as grow tobacco and to manufacture candles and other necessities for the Great House. The maturation of tobacco culture did not end the contest between master and slave; it only moved the struggle to new ground.[55]

The new terrain was defined by three related changes in Chesapeake society during the middle years of the eighteenth century: the declining productivity of the older tobacco regions, the rise of small grain production, and the growth of towns. Each of these set in motion a series of other changes—the reorganization of the plantation, the growth of an artisan class, and the spread of slave hiring—that sometimes strengthened the slaves' hand at the expense of their owners and sometimes strengthened the owners' hand at the expense of the slaves. Whatever the balance of power, the struggle between masters and slaves—the continued renegotiation and contestation of the terms of life and labor—both sped the transition of African to creole and opened new avenues of resistance.

The same crisis that drove planters to the fresh tobacco lands of the piedmont also encouraged them to experiment with other crops. In many parts of the Chesapeake, tobacco—the universal staple in the seventeenth century—gave way to mixed cultivation that combined tobacco with a variety of small grains, corn, forest products, and livestock. The most dynamic element in the mix was wheat, which became increasingly attractive as a series of European crop failures swelled demand for American foodstuffs. During the 1720s planters—particularly those in the marginal tobacco areas—turned from tobacco to cereal production. In some parts of the Chesapeake region, most notably the eastern shore of Maryland and Virginia, planters eliminated tobacco from their repertoire altogether. As demand for rye, oats, and especially wheat spiraled upward throughout the Atlantic world, changes in the character of the Chesapeake's economy that had begun in a few marginal tobacco areas during the third and fourth decades of the eighteenth century became general. On the eve of the American Revolution, the value of cereal production exceeded that of tobacco in many parts of the region.[56]

The cultivation of wheat and other small grains transformed the nature of agricultural labor and, with it, slavery. Whereas tobacco farming required season-long labor, cereal agriculture employed workers steadily only during planting and harvesting. Laborers had little to do with the crop the remainder of the year. They were hardly idle, however, as grain cultivation also required a large, diverse, and skilled labor force to transport the grain, market it, store it, mill it, and reship it as bulk grain, flour, or bread. The wagons in which wheat were shipped and the draft animals that pulled the wagons all required maintenance. The presence of draft animals and other stock, in turn, produced new tasks, as their hides could be tanned and fashioned into harnesses, bridles, saddles, and shoes. Plantations dedicated to grain production not only fielded corps of wagoners but also blacksmiths, saddlers, harness makers, tanners, and shoemakers. Artisans also found employment in flour mills, iron foundries, weaving houses, and other nonagricultural ventures.[57]

At first, skilled labor was reserved for white nonslaveholders. Free and servant men took charge of artisanal work, while their wives and daughters did the weaving and dairying. But at midcentury, as the number of servants declined and as the planter's wife took on new social pretensions, slaves entered many of these trades, particularly in the great plantation towns, in which self-sufficiency was the goal if not quite the reality. Generally, slave workers followed the sexual division of labor of the white men and women who had preceded them. Slave men monopolized skilled plantation labor, along with almost all of the work as wagoners and boatmen. Slave women had a narrower range of occupations, but some also left the field, if only for domestic tasks, dairying, and weaving. Although slave artisans in the Chesapeake never dominated any craft, due in large measure to the active competition of white nonslave-holders, the number of slaves working outside of the field grew. Slaves like Jem, who was not only "a good workmen in a forge, either in finery or chafery," but could also "do any kind of smith's or carpenter's work . . . [and] any kind of farming business," became increasingly common in the region. Whereas during the first years of the eighteenth century, nearly all Chesapeake slaves worked in the field, by the Revolution only seven in ten men did field work. The proportion was higher for women, although it too fell from the earlier period.[58]

Changes in the structure of the labor force resonated outside of the plantation. Although many of the new enterprises that employed slave artisans were incorporated into plantation life, particularly on the great estates, others were located in towns. The Chesapeake, for the first time, developed a cadre of cities. Older administrative centers like Annapolis and Williamsburg became home—or, sometimes, a second home—to an increasingly affluent planter class. The newer cities depended upon commerce to sustain them. The first of these, Norfolk on the western shore of the Chesapeake and Chestertown on the eastern shore, were centers of the grain trade, as were upstart towns like Alexandria and Baltimore. With urbanization and the concomitant growth of manufacturing, the demand for artisans and laborers outstripped the number of available white men, many of whom saw opportunities in westward migration. The requirements of urban employers drew additional slaves into the urban sphere.[59]

The need for urban labor also created a market for hirelings, and the advent of mixed agriculture with its peculiar seasonal rhythms encouraged rural slaveholders to rent their slaves during slack time. Unlike those confined to the plantation, hired slaves generally worked independently, outside the direction of an owner or overseer. Control over their time also allowed hired slaves expanded opportunities to pursue their own interests. Some hired themselves to do odd jobs, earning cash or receiving payment for "overwork." The general acceptance of jobbing opened the door for slaves to travel freely, live on their own, and enjoy a measure of independence not possible in the rural plantation regimen.[60]

Self-hire and overwork payment marked the expansion of the slaves' economy in a new guise. The Chesapeake remained preeminently an "allowance society," with slaveholders doling out rations and clothing.

Slaves believed themselves entitled to their allowance and demanded what they understood to be their due. When customary levies of blankets, clothing, and food were not forthcoming, they protested, often vigorously.[61] However, slaves—with access to cash—were not satisfied with their owners' allotments. They pressed for what Jefferson called their "peculiam." Slaves enlarged their gardens and flocks of chickens, ducks, and geese, working "the Little Spots allow'd them" with great intensity. Occasionally, they kept a pig or two. In the region's foundries and forges, overwork payments became a regular practice, and skilled slaves established substantial accounts. Slaves expanded their market, selling their labor to nonslaveholders and others. John Harrower, a plantation-based tutor, hired a slave woman as a spinner. Harrower's slave employee worked for him at nights and on Sunday, allowing Harrower to set up a small enterprise of his own and giving his slave subcontractor a small income.[62]

Although the slaves' economy never equaled the level achieved in the seventeenth century when slaves traded in cattle and tobacco, it grew substantially after midcentury, with slaves dealing among themselves, with their owners, and with white nonslaveholders for cash and kind. Once again, planters complained about itinerant traders dealing with slaves and encouraging theft. The new laws that followed only reiterated the old and did little to address the planters' lament beyond documenting the reinvigoration of the slaves' economy.

The proceeds of their independent production permitted slaves to enrich their families' diet and expand their wardrobes. They purchased clothes beyond the standard issue of shoes, shirt and trousers or shift, and waistcoat. To prevent his slaves from "buying liquor with their fowls," one Virginia planter "obliged them to buy linnen" to make their clothes. It was an ingenious scheme, and yet another way to put the slaves' independent production in the planters' service, but, much to their chagrin, slaveholders were astounded to find their slaves dressing the gentleman, complete with watches in their pockets, powdered wigs on their heads, and silver buckles on their shoes. Although slaveholders appreciated and profited from the work of the skilled, many came to regret the creation of a new generation of slaves who, in the words of one slaveowner, had "an extra measure of pride" or, as another slaveholder expressed it, had "more Sense than Honesty." A visitor to North Carolina found that slave men used their earnings to "buy Hats, and other Necessaries for themselves, as *Linnen, Bracelets, Ribbons,* and several other Toys for their Wives and Mistresses."[63]

The slaves' economy made for a new sociability that transformed relations between master and slave and among slaves. Slaves presented chickens, eggs, melons, items of handicraft, and even small gifts to their friends, families, and occasionally owners. Such exchanges marked a leveling up of relations, as even the greatest paternalist understood that when their slaves presented them with a gift, the terms of the relationship shifted, however subtly. But if gifting strengthened the hand of some slaves in dealing with their owners, it left others at a loss. Indeed, participation in the exchange economy created new divisions within slave society, as access to the market distinguished the haves from the have-nots.[64]

As they took control of a larger portion of their labor, slaves also reformulated their religious life. Some discovered Christianity, another indicator of their movement into the mainstream of Chesapeake life. They were, to be sure, a tiny minority of the whole, as converts numbered in the tens or occasionally the hundreds and the slave population of the Chesapeake could be counted by the tens of thousands. Still, the new Christians seemed to be the very men and women most in touch with the changing currents of Chesapeake life: literate, skilled, well-traveled. A handful attended the schools established in Williamsburg and Fredericksburg by the Society for the Propagation of the Gospel. Anglican ministers converted—or baptized—many others, although even these did not amount to more than several hundred in total.[65] Many more, however, were attracted to the new evangelical Protestant sects that took root in tidewater Virginia and Maryland during the 1740s and then spread northward, first under the leadership of New Light Presbyterian, then Methodist, and finally Baptist preachers.

Whatever exactly African-American slaves thought of the evangelicals' religious aesthetic, they understood that the new religion recognized the spark of divinity in every man and woman, encouraged fellowship and mutuality, and respected the godly no matter what their status. In God's eyes, all were equal, for the greatest slaveholder was as corrupt as the lowliest slave. Slaves also appreciated that the evangelicals despised the opulence and pretension that was the hallmark of the planter class. Perhaps also a people who suffered much found attractive the notion that such abuse—like Christ's suffering—might have some larger purpose and that their suffering would be exchanged for everlasting glory, even if in some other world. No doubt the Old Testament story of the triumphant liberation of God's chosen resonated among those who themselves were slaves, and the prospect of the Great Jubilee that accompanied liberation was soon incorporated into African-American theology. Whatever the particular mix of theology and practice, some slaves embraced the new religion and grasped evangelical fellowship.

When the revival known as the Great Awakening began at midcentury, black people were at its center, celebrating spiritual equality in their search for the New Jerusalem. White preachers encouraged black converts and often welcomed their black brothers and sisters into the fold, as nothing so demonstrated the transformative power of Christ's message than the conversion of black heathens. Black people for their part saw new opportunities. They welcomed the chance to articulate openly their own religious vision and, occasionally, to participate as equals in matters of church discipline. Inevitably, the rush for spiritual equality became entwined with the profound desire for worldly equality—something that the rising class of slave artisans and hirelings had come to believe was their due. However carefully white evangelicals sought to separate the two messages—and many had no desire to do so—slaves inevitably combined the two. Samuel Davies, the Presbyterian evangelical from whose Virginia church much of the new religious radicalism emanated, found the slaves he had awakened eager to make the connection. "There are multitudes of them," asserted Davies, "who are willing, and even eagerly desirous to be instructed, and to embrace every opportunity for that end."[66]

The desire for instruction, however, went only so far. Before long, black people took control over their own religious education, interpreting the evangelical message in light of their unique experience and incorporating biblical stories into their own spirituality and remembered African theology. Such self-assertion was often discouraged by white evangelicals, especially as black men and women seized the spiritual initiative and created new forms of worship. Nonetheless, black preachers became an increasingly visible part of the evangelical awakening. When Jupiter, a six-foot insurrectionist, fled from his Southside Virginia plantation, his owner noted he was "a great Newlight preacher." He would be followed by others, like Primus, an active, artful young man of twenty who had "been a Preacher ever since he was sixteen Years of age, and has done much Mischief in his Neighborhood." By the American Revolution, black churches began to appear.[67]

The links between Christian piety and certainty in eventual salvation on one hand and artisanal skill and confidence in material advancement on the other grew steadily among the new converts. The heady mixture of spiritual validation and temporal revolution moved swiftly through the quarter as the mobile artisans, wagoners, and boatmen, whose numbers had swelled with the dramatic changes in the Chesapeake economy, accepted Christ. The combination awakened hopes of freedom in this world, as well as in the world beyond.

The self-assertion bred within the household, marketplace, artisan shop, and campmeeting incited increased dissatisfaction with slavery. The challenge to slavery implicit in the growth of the slaves' economy and the evangelical upsurge pushed slaves to confront their owners. The language of the free marketplace and open pulpit gave the slaves' disquietude a powerful voice. From the slaveholders' perspective, the insurgency took an insidious new form as independent traders, jobbing artisans, freewheeling wagoners and boatmen, and itinerant preachers did not avoid white society as had their African predecessors. Rather, like the charter generations, they strove to integrate themselves into the fabric of Chesapeake life—a society they believed to be their own.

Few men and women could save enough to buy their way out of slavery. Many more could flee, and flight became increasingly prevalent after midcentury. Confident of their ability to find shelter within the expanding web of kinship that blanketed the countryside or to disappear into the new towns where they could sell their services with few questions asked, African-American slaves searched for ways out of bondage. While the possibility of passing as free remained small in a society where free blacks were few in number, light-skinned, and well known, fugitives seemed increasingly willing to risk all, not simply for a few days' respite but for permanent freedom. The new pattern of flight signaled the reemergence of creole society, with its familiar linguistic fluency, cultural plasticity, social agility, and aggressive self-confidence.

The changes in African-American society in the Chesapeake during the middle years of the eighteenth century allowed black people to listen in on the debate between white Americans and their British overlords. The language of tyranny was one blacks well understood. When that debate broke out into open conflict, they would be quick to take advantage of it. In the summer of 1774 Bacchus, a Virginia slave, thought he saw a chance. A "cunning, artful, sensible Fellow," Bacchus was well acquainted with his native Virginia and the capital city of Williamsburg, where he had long worked for a leading physician "who trusted him much." Perhaps it was while waiting on his master's table that he overheard talk of the onrushing crisis, the complaints about enslavement, and the demands for freedom. Or perhaps the tocsin of liberty that had sounded in the debates in the House of Burgesses reverberated through the grogshops, back alleys, and forest retreats where black men and women congregated. In any event, the idea of freedom stuck in his mind and the possibilities of its realization summoned him to action.

When the weather turned warm, he responded. Assuming the name John Christian, he forged a pass, emptied his owner's purse, and collected his possessions. Apparently Bacchus never made it. Weighed down with "two white Russia Drill Coats . . . blue Plush Breeches, a fine Cloth Pompadour Waistcoat, two or three thin or Summer Jackets, sundry Pairs of white Thread Stockings, five or six white Shirts . . . A fine Hat cut and cocked in the Macaroni Figure," he was easily identifiable and probably soon taken up.[68] But his ability to forge a plausible pass and travel for a time through the countryside as John Christian indicates how black life had been remade in the years preceding the Revolution. With the coming of the Revolution, it was just such people as Bacchus who would again transform black life in the Chesapeake.

Chapter Six

The Rice Revolution in the Lowcountry

⚓

The plantation revolution in lowcountry South Carolina, Georgia, and East Florida marched only a short step behind that in the Chesapeake. Beginning in the last decade of the seventeenth century, the discovery of exportable staples, first naval stores and then rice and indigo, permanently altered the character of lowcountry South Carolina. Spurred by the riches that rice produced, planters consolidated their place atop lowcountry society, banished the white yeomanry to the upcountry, expanded farms into plantations, and carved even larger plantations out of the inland swamps and coastal marshes. Before long, African slaves began pouring into the region; and sometime during the first decade of the eighteenth century, white numerical superiority gave way to the lowcountry's distinguishing demographic characteristic: the black majority. No longer societies with slaves, lowcountry South Carolina, then Georgia, and finally East Florida became slave societies.

The transformation of slavery in the lowcountry followed the pattern established in the Chesapeake colonies—increased demand for slaves, direct African importation, and a general degradation of the quality of black life—but surpassed it in all respects. The demand for slaves was greater, the importation of Africans more massive, and degradation of black life swifter and deeper. Moreover, whereas in the Chesapeake the process of creolization—from African to African American—eventually unified eighteenth-century black society, changes in the lowcountry during that period left black people deeply divided. A minority lived and worked in close proximity to whites in the cities that lined the rice coast, fully conversant with the most cosmopolitan sector of lowland society. Heirs to the charter generations, this generally light-skinned urban elite pressed for incorporation into European-American society, perfecting their English, accepting Jesus, and mimicking the planters' sartorial style. From their clothes, separate residences, and mastery of numerous artisanal skills, they were confident they could compete as equals on the planters' own ground. The mass of black people, however, remained physically separated and psychologically estranged from the European-American world, and culturally closer to Africa than any other black people in continental North America.

Rice reshaped the destiny of black people in lowcountry South Carolina, Georgia, and Florida much as tobacco reformed the lives of Chesapeake slaves. Although the production of pitch and tar played a pivotal role in the early development of the staple-based economy in South Carolina, by the end of the seventeenth century rice was fast becoming the dominant plantation crop. In 1720 more than half of the value of all of South Carolina's exports derived from rice. Rice bankrolled the expansion of plantation society, brought thousands of Africans to American shores, and transformed the nature of slavery in the lowcountry.[1]

Rice cultivation evolved slowly during the late seventeenth and early eighteenth centuries as planters, aided by knowledgeable Africans, mastered the complex regimen necessary for commercial production. During the first half of the eighteenth century, rice culture was confined to the uplands, where successful cultivation depended upon ample and regular rainfall. It was a chancy business, and to reduce their risks planters learned how to drain marshy, low-lying inland swamps and then irrigate them through the use of slave-built reservoirs that drew water from the region's rivers. The migration of rice from the high ground to the coastal plain was largely complete by midcentury. Production increased immediately, and it shot upward again in the 1760s, when planters began to transfer production to the tidal swamps that lined the region's rivers, employing the ebb and flow of coastal rivers to water their fields. By the eve of the American Revolution, the rice coast stretched from Cape Fear in North Carolina to the St. John River in East Florida. Throughout the lowcountry, rice was king.[2]

As rice cultivation expanded, the polyglot labor force of the pioneer years disappeared. At midcentury, slaveholder and slave could rarely be found on opposite sides of a sawbuck. Instead, slaves became the mainstay of the lowcountry's working class, and Africans became the dominant element in the slave population. They also comprised an ever-larger share of the total population. By the 1720s slaves outnumbered whites by more than two to one in lowland South Carolina. In the heavily settled plantation parishes surrounding Charles Town, black slaves enjoyed a three-to-one majority, and that margin grew steadily during the 1730s. The rate of increase declined during the following decade, when fears of insurrection and a sharp decline in rice prices put a brake on slave importation, but the pause proved momentary. Imports expanded steadily from midcentury to the Revolution, and by 1760 black people made up 60 percent of the population in all but three lowcountry parishes. The South Carolina countryside, in the words of one visitor, "look[ed] more like a negro country than like a country settled by white people."

Georgia, where authorities in England had reined in planters' ambition, remained slaveless until midcentury. But once restrictions on slavery were removed, planters—"stark Mad after Negroes"—imported them in large numbers, giving lowland Georgia counties considerable black majorities. East Florida followed a similar path of development after the British assumed control in 1763, and South Carolina and Georgia planters expanded the plantation order southward. By 1770 more than one Florida estate boasted "no white face belonging to the plantation but an overseer."[3]

Slaves not only changed in number but also in kind. Although some creole slaves with origins in the Atlantic littoral continued to dribble into the lowcountry, their numbers dwindled to a small fraction of the whole. Indian slaves increased at first, as lowcountry planters—following a path pioneered in the Chesapeake—grabbed for the most available laborers. The many Indian wars in the region abetted this effort, and while large numbers of the Indians captured in the struggle with the Tuscaroras and the Yamasees were sold to the Caribbean, many fell to the mainland's plantation economy. By the second decade of the eighteenth century, South Carolina—in contrast with the Chesapeake—counted some 1,500 enslaved Indians.[4]

The enslavement of native peoples failed to satisfy the needs of the rapidly expanding rice economy, however. For that, lowcountry planters turned to Africa, and Charles Town took its place as the center of the lowland slave trade, quickly becoming the mainland's largest transatlantic slave market. Whereas slave imports had rarely exceeded 300 per year prior to 1710, by the 1720s they numbered more than 2,000 annually. Imports dropped in the 1740s, but the trade soon rebounded, and by the 1770s some 4,000 African slaves arrived annually in the lowcountry. Almost all of the slaves in South Carolina and later in Georgia and East

Florida—indeed, fully 10 percent of prerevolutionary black arrivals in mainland North America—entered through the port of Charles Town.[5]

The massive influx overwhelmed the Native-American population, and Indian slaves were swallowed in the tide, in much the same manner that new arrivals had earlier swamped the charter generations. Native-American slaves soon vanished from the census enumerations and plantation daybooks, as planters simply categorized their Indian slaves as Africans. This terminological hocus-pocus suggests how planters had redefined race so that slavery was equated with African ancestry, whether the slaves descended from Africa or not.

Whereas lowcountry planters cared little about the provenance of the native slaves, they became keenly attuned to the physical attributes and cultural origins of the new saltwater arrivals. Lowcountry planters developed preferences far beyond the usual demands for healthy adult and teenaged males. Both buyers and sellers dwelled upon the regional and national origins of their human merchandise, disparaging slaves from the Bight of Biafra or the so-called Calabars. Some planters based their choices on long experience and a considered understanding of the physical and social character of various African nations. Knowing that some west Africans cultivated rice, slaveowners naturally specified them. Others based their preferences on shallow ethnic stereotypes. Sometimes planters preferred just those slaves they did not get, perhaps because all Africans made unsatisfactory slaves and the unobtainable ones looked better at a distance. Mostly they desired Gambian people (sometimes referred to as Coromantees) above all others. "Gold Coast or Gambia's are best, next to them the Windward Coast are prefer'd to Angola's," observed a Charles Town merchant in describing the most saleable mixture. "There must not be a Calabar amongst them." Such notions were occasionally articulated by Chesapeake tobacco planters, but the grandees of the lowcountry not only dwelled upon their preferences, they also acted upon them, something their Chesapeake counterparts rarely did.

Still, even with their enormous resources, lowcountry slaveholders could not bend the international market to their will. Despite their preferences for Gambians, slaves deriving from central Africa—the much maligned Angolans—made up the largest proportion of the African arrivals early in the eighteenth century. Later in the century, slaves from Senegambia and the Windward Coast constituted the bulk of the forced migrants.[6]

Whatever their origins, the plantation was the destination of Africans entering the lowcountry. As the black majority grew, so did the size of plantation units. By 1720 three-quarters of the slaves in South Carolina resided on plantations of ten or more slaves. The size of plantations continued to swell, so that at midcentury more than one-third of all lowcountry slaves resided on units of fifty or more. In some places the units were larger still. By the time of the American Revolution, for example, better than half of the slaves in the Georgetown District lived on plantations of more than fifty, and more than one-fifth of the slaves lived in units of one hundred or more.[7]

As in the Chesapeake, the Africanization of slavery was accompanied by a transformation of the work regimen. With the rice revolution, lowcountry slaves were no longer jacks-of-all-trades or footloose cattle chasers. Instead, amassed on sprawling plantations, they labored in large, well-ordered gangs under close supervision, according to the seasonally determined routine that rice dictated. Sowing began in April and sometimes lasted into June, with barefoot slaves pressing the seeds into the waterlogged muck with their heels, a method familiar to their African forebears. Slaves then flooded the fields to encourage germination. Once the seeds sprouted, the fields had to be hoed to suppress the weeds. Thereafter, the fields were alternately flooded and drained to provide the crop with sufficient moisture, control the weeds, and keep the birds away. At least once during the growing cycle, weeds had to be hand-picked to prevent them from overtaking the rice. Thus, for a large portion of the year, slaves labored knee-deep in stagnant muck, surrounded by buzzing insects, under the scorching sun. In August, even after the fields were drained and the crops laid-by, there was little respite. If the fields were drained, the insects remained, and they were joined by a host of slithering reptiles that had been displaced by the movement of water and earth. Slaves returned to the fields to ward off the ravenous birds, often with a shotgun blast, until harvest began in September. Next, the rice had to be processed, and the lowcountry plantation—like that in the Chesapeake—was as much factory as farm. Almost as soon as the harvest was complete, the cycle began again. Slaves prepared the land for the next year's crop, cleared and extended the ditches and canals, rebuilt and augmented the embankments and dams, and repaired the trunks and floodgates.

The processing of rice began before the harvest ended and extended into the new year. Working late into the night during the winter months, slaves—generally women—beat the rice in large mortars to free the grain. Threshing was hard work, especially since planters forced their slaves to turn to it after they had finished a long day in the field. Planters, responding in part to the slaves' complaints about the ceaseless enterprise—which sent many of them fleeing to the woods and swamps for relief—experimented with a variety of mechanical means to separate the grain and the chaff. By the 1760s such machines were in place on the largest plantations, but even with mechanical aids the threshing process continued into the new year, and the overlap in cultivating the new and the old crops left slaves with little free time. In short, rice was a hard master.

As the profits from the sale of rice poured into the planters' coffers, they pressed slaves to increase production, expanding the rice fields and intensifying the slaves' labor. At midcentury, the discovery that the tides could be used to flood the fields and replenish the soils allowed planters to move the locus of production to the coast. But rice cultivation in the coastal marshes needed endless miles of canals to control the flow of water. The fragility of these massive earthworks required the slaves' constant attention and added to their burden. In 1775 a Scottish visitor first mistook a rice field for "that of our green oats." On closer inspection she discovered there was "no living near it with the putrid water that must lie on it, and the labour required for it is only fit for slaves, and I think the hardest work I have seen them engaged in."[8] However tedious and demanding tobacco cultivation, it never matched the exertion demanded by rice.

Rice production did not have an uninterrupted ascent. A sharp decline in prices that followed the loss of the French and Spanish markets in England's war with Spain, together with the insurrection at Stono in 1739, dulled the lowcountry's economy for almost a decade and induced planters to reconsider the dangers in surrounding themselves with an oppressed and profoundly alienated black majority. The South Carolina legislature slapped a nearly prohibitive duty on slave imports, and many planters believed themselves on "the Brink of Ruin." They turned inward toward greater self-sufficiency and tried to protect their fortunes from falling prices by putting slaves to the task of growing their own food, weaving their own cloth, and cobbling their own shoes. But planters also began experimenting with other crops, searching for a staple that would insulate them from a single-minded dependence on rice.[9]

The most promising of these new crops was indigo, a rapidly growing weed that could be transformed into a much-valued blue dye. By midcentury, slaveholders no longer viewed indigo as an experiment. Encouraged by an imperial subsidy, they incorporated it into their agricultural repertoire, generally growing indigo on the upland parts of their estates. By the time the United States had achieved independence, indigo accounted for one-quarter of South Carolina's exports.[10] The geography and seasonal rhythm of indigo production complemented that of rice, placing additional burdens on overworked field slaves.

Indigo was also a demanding crop; its short season and delicate nature required careful attention, although only at particular times during the growing cycle. After planting in the spring, indigo needed little tending in the field except for the periodic harvesting of the leaves in July, August, and occasionally September. But processing indigo was, if anything, even more arduous than processing rice. As fast as the leaves were harvested, slaves carried them to a series of great vats or tubs, where they fermented while slaves kept up a continuous pumping, stirring, and beating. The rotting indigo emitted a putrid odor and attracted clouds of flies that only slaves could be forced to tolerate. In time, the putrefied leaves were removed and the bluish liquid drained into a series of vats, where slaves "beat" the liquid with broad paddles. The process was repeated several times before the blue liquid was "set" with lime at just the right moment—a great skill by all accounts. After the sediment precipitated, the liquid was filtered and drawn off, leaving a dense blue mud, which was then strained, dried, cut into blocks, and dried again in preparation for shipping. The process was both demanding and delicate, requiring brute strength and a fine hand to create just the right density, texture, and brilliance of color. But slaves had little time to admire their handiwork, for like rice, indigo was a hard master.[11]

Indigo also required the support of multiple subsidiary trades to build the vats, maintain the pumps, and construct the numerous outbuildings necessary to sustain these complicated enterprises. Increasingly, planters turned these tasks over to slaves, creating a cadre of carpenters, brick masons, coopers, and machinists. Unlike the Africans who had grown rice prior to their capture, the slaves assigned to indigo production brought no knowledge of the task with them to the New World and often had to be directed by white artisans; still, their on-the-job training gave them a special expertise in the intricacies of making the blue dye. By the Revolution, if not before, slaves controlled indigo production, much as they superintended the growth and processing of rice.[12]

The demands of rice and indigo and the ready availability of Africans made for a deadly combination. Weakened by the rigors of the Middle Passage, the harsh labor regimen, and a new disease environment, slaves died by the thousands in the lowcountry's swamps. As long as the slave trade remained open and profits from rice allowed slaveholders to maintain—indeed, increase—their labor force as workers died, planters skimped on food, clothing, medical attention, and housing for their laborers, often packing newly arrived slaves into squalid dormitories where cramped conditions promoted the spread of infectious disease. The sickle-cell trait provided some immunities against malaria; but in combination with overexertion and dehydration, it could prove deadly. Africans had no more protection than Europeans from yellow fever, pleurisy, pneumonia, and a variety of subtropical diseases endemic to the lowcountry.

With men composing about two-thirds of the imports, slaves found it difficult to establish normal domestic relations and impossible to reproduce the complex extended household ties and deep lineages that characterized family life in Africa. Women, underfed, underweight, and overworked in the fields, conceived at low rates and miscarried at high ones. The slave population of the lowcountry experienced no natural increase in the 1720s, even as slaves in the Chesapeake began to reproduce themselves. The birth rates of lowcountry slaves continued to fall during the middle years of the eighteenth century, while mortality rates rose sharply. Between 1730 and 1760, deaths outnumbered births among lowland slaves, and only the steady importation of Africans allowed for population growth. Even with the reemergence of a creole population of African Americans after midcentury, the low fertility and high mortality of saltwater slaves ransomed the growth of the slave population to the continued importation of Africans. Not until the 1760s did the slave population begin again to reproduce itself naturally. "Plantation agriculture," as one historian has observed, "brought the demographic regime of the sugar islands to lowcountry South Carolina."[13]

As in the Chesapeake, among the first casualties of plantation slavery in the lowcountry were the slaves' own identities. Saltwater slaves found themselves tagged with placenames like Senegal, Pondicherry, and Quebec, or names with a classical ring like Othello and Claudius. One man became King Cole.[14] In addition to loss of identity, the plantation regime also meant a loss of independence for slaves. The casual and open exchanges between master and slave during the pioneer years disappeared, as did the possibility of enlisting slaves as soldiers. In the place of such open-handed interactions stood fear and contempt.

The slaveholders' jokes were no laughing matter. The process by which planters bent Africans to the demands of the new plantation were deadly serious. Much as in the Chesapeake, an escalation in the level of violence accompanied the emergence of a plantation economy. Christian missionaries decried the "profane & Inhumane practices," as planters turned to the lash, the faggot, and the noose to discipline slaves unfamiliar with the requirements of rice and indigo. Even punishment for "small faults" took on a monstrous quality, as with the planter who placed slave miscreants in a "coffin where they are almost crushed to death," keeping them "in that hellish machine for Twenty Four hours." Such atrocities disturbed a few clerics, but planters believed terror to be a critical element in sustaining their dominion over a people who, as one slaveholder professed, were "created only for slavery."[15]

The state—which was nothing more or less than the planters themselves—naturally affirmed this judgment. As early as 1690 South Carolina lawmakers had held slaveholders and their agents to be legally blameless for the death of a slave as a result of "correction." Even if a slave was killed as a result of "wilfulness, wantoness, or bloody mindedness," the murderer would face a maximum penalty of three months in jail and a fine of £50 to be paid to the owner. Since the murderer was often the owner, the financial penalty could hardly be considered onerous. The amount of the fine was later increased, but, as one student of slave law has noted, there was no capital punishment for the murder of slaves in South Carolina.[16]

The transplanted Africans who might be subjected to such abuse made no pretense of trying to adapt to the planters' ways. Slave unrest grew with the imposition of the new regime. Much as in the Chesapeake, the first decades of the eighteenth century were alive with rumors of insurrection and outbursts of violence, as slaves snapped back at their enslavers. Although the extent of the violence and the depth of the conspiracies are difficult to measure, there can be no doubt about what happened at Stono, where a group of Florida-bound fugitives turned on their pursuers with bloody results.[17]

Such direct confrontations, no more successful at Stono than any-where else in the Americas prior to Saint Domingue, were only one part of the slaves' counter-offensive. Even while they plotted rebellion, they bent their efforts to reformulate Africa in America. Domestic and reli-gious life were the most obvious manifestations of this determination to maintain the ways of the Old World even in the circumstances of the New. The polygamous practices of the largely male population scandal-ized Anglican missionaries, as did the saltwater slaves' unwavering an-tagonism to Christianity. Writing from Savannah in 1754, an Anglican missionary discovered that black people clung to "the old Superstition of a false Religion." Even when a handful of Africans demonstrated an interest in Christ's way, their reformulations of Christian eschatology appalled the mission men. The Reverend Francis Le Jau, perhaps the most resolute of the Anglican missionaries, found his star convert "put his own Construction upon some Words of the Holy Prophet's . . . [re-specting] the several judgmts. That Chastise Men because of their Sins." Indeed, his pupil's claim "that there wou'd be a dismal time and the Moon wou'd be turn'd into Blood, and there would be dearth of dark-ness" frightened Le Jau and many others who heard the pronouncement. Such specters reinforced the planters' adamant opposition to the Chris-tianization of their slaves. For all his effort, Le Jau touched but a handful of the thousands of slaves in his parish. Facing reluctant masters and equally reluctant slaves, no lowcountry missionary did any better.[18]

As the plantation system took shape, the lowcountry grandees re-treated to the region's cities, marking the growing social and cultural distance between them and their slaves. The streets of Charles Town—and, later, of Beaufort, Georgetown, Savannah, Darien, and Wilming-ton—sprouted great new mansions, as lowcountry planters, the wealthi-est people on the North American mainland, fled the malarial lowlands and its black majority. Although the cities of the lowcountry would even-tually have their own black majorities, they remained—even then—bas-tions of whiteness, compared with the overwhelming black countryside.

Moreover, by the 1740s, urban life in the lowcountry had become attractive enough that men who made their fortunes in rice and slaves gave little consideration to returning to England, as their West Indian counterparts had done. Instead, through marriage and business connec-tions, South Carolina's great planters, often joined by the most successful merchants, began to weave their disparate social relations into a close-knit ruling class, whose pride of place would become legendary. Charles Town, as the capital of this new elite, grew rapidly. Between 1720 and 1740 the city's population doubled, and nearly doubled again by the eve of American independence to stand at about 12,000. Charles Town's many fine houses, great churches, and shops packed with luxury goods bespoke the maturation of the lowland plantation system and the rise of a planter class.[19]

Planters, ensconced in their new urban mansions, their pockets lined with the riches rice produced, ruled their lowcountry domains through a long chain of command: stewards located in the smaller rice ports, overseers stationed near or on their plantations, and plantation-based black foremen or, in the idiom of the lowcountry, drivers. Insulated from the labor of the field by this considerable hierarchy, most planters could no more imagine working across a sawbuck from their slaves than they could envision enlisting them in the militia. The time when black and white fought side by side against the Spaniards and the Yamasees had passed.

But the planters' withdrawal from the countryside did not breed the callous indifference of West Indian absenteeism. For one thing, absenteeism in the lowcountry generally meant no more than a day's boat ride between townhouse and country estate. The very complexity of rice and indigo production required constant attention not only of overseers and stewards but planters as well. Indeed, even as they established their urban households, lowcountry planters built new, large plantation houses, often on the model of English country estates. They maintained a deep and continuing interest in their plantations, where they resided during the nonmalarial season.

This paternalism-at-a-distance operated differently than either the client–patron relationship that had framed the social order for the charter generations or the hands-on paternalist regime of resident planters in the Chesapeake. A handful of favorites might attract the attention of lowcountry planters, and troublemakers left their own mark, but the mass of slaves remained anonymous. Observing their small armies of laborers only intermittently and usually from afar, the grandees hardly knew their slaves. Their interaction with plantation hands was indirect at best, save for the regular notations of births and deaths in the plantation account book.[20]

Separation from their estates, both organizationally and geographically, forced lowland planters to cede some of their authority to underlings. Whereas stewards and overseers—almost always white—were the primary beneficiaries of this downward shift of authority, slaves gained some advantages. Planters allowed a few slave men to rise to the rank of driver or foreman. Although black drivers officially reported to resident white overseers, these young white men, who generally served for only a few years before striking off on their own, rarely gained the planters' confidence. Their motives and morals troubled planters, who saw much of themselves in the would-be slave masters. Planters often bypassed their overseers, allowing drivers to amass considerable power. For all practical purposes, drivers directed the day-to-day plantation operations on some estates, balancing the contradictory interests of the owner, overseer, and the mass of field hands.[21]

Only a select few slaves rose to the rank of driver, but many benefited from the task system, another consequence of the planters' long-distance relationship with the countryside. Under the task system, a slave's daily routine was sharply defined: so many rows of rice to be sowed, so much grain to be threshed, or so many lines of canal to be cleared. Such a precise definition of work suggests that city-bound planters found it difficult to keep their slaves in the field from sunup to sundown and conceded control over worktime in return for a generally accepted unit of output, especially when it could be measured from afar. With little direct white supervision, slaves and their black drivers conspired to preserve a portion of the day for their own use while meeting the planters' minimum work requirements.[22]

Shielding themselves from the brutal, often bloody, business of forced labor, lowcountry planters honed their sense of mastership. Increasingly during the eighteenth century, they saw their primary function as resolving grievances, rectifying injustices, and adjudicating disputes between overseer and driver, driver and slaves, while experimenting with new varieties of rice and testing the latest technological innovations. By midcentury the planter class—although less than a generation deep—had created its own ideal of the stern but fair patriarch whose long reach touched all aspects of plantation life, demanding deference and loyalty in return for benevolent oversight. As the conflict with Britain neared, some planters flirted with the new humanitarian ethos alive in the Atlantic world. It sharpened their concern for "their people" and reinforced a paternalist ethos that at once legitimated their rule and informed all social relations.[23]

Whatever advantages slaves could squeeze from their owner's evolving self-image, freedom was not among them. Seeing slaves as permanent children left little room for the possibility they might stand on their own, as independent men and women. The small, free black population of the pioneer years all but disappeared during the middle years of the eighteenth century. Ensnared in the web of racial proscriptions, some free blacks were swept into the rapidly expanding slave population. Others migrated to the backcountry, where they exchanged their African-American identity for that of a Native American—reversing the planters' terminological hocus-pocus. The region's largest free black population, the men and women of Gracia Real de Santa Teresa de Mose, retreated to Cuba with the Spanish in 1764, when the British takeover of Florida presaged the southward expansion of the plantation regime. Those who remained found their freedom sharply diminished.[24] The near invisibility of free black people, especially in the countryside, confirmed the planters' presumption that only black slaves could grow rice, a presumption no Chesapeake planter could make about tobacco.[25]

But if the distance between free and slave blacks narrowed in the eighteenth-century lowcountry as free men and women lost many of their former prerogatives, the division between urban and rural blacks expanded. The rice revolution that transformed the farms and pens of the lowcountry into plantations and the polyglot labor force into a black majority did not recast black life in a single mold. Rather than create a unified African-American culture, the plantation revolution in the lowcountry fractured black life.

Unlike in the Chesapeake region, no single black society emerged during the eighteenth century. One branch of black society took shape around the region's towns and cities. While planters lived removed from most of their slaves, they maintained close, intimate relations with some—the messengers who maintained the lines of communication between city and countryside, the boatmen who shuttled supplies to and from the lowland estates, the house servants who made life comfortable. Within the great rice ports, economy and society rested on slaves who transported and processed plantation staples, satisfied the planters' taste for luxury goods, and serviced the ships that bound the lowcountry to the rest of the world. Urban slaves, unlike their plantation counterparts, lived in close contact with their owners and other white people. The towns and cities of the lowcountry were almost equally divided between white and black throughout the eighteenth century. In 1720 Charles Town's 1,400 white people barely outnumbered black slaves. By the eve of the Revolution, the balance shifted the other way, as slaves—numbering nearly 6,000—had overtaken the whites. Savannah followed a similar pattern, although black people would not achieve a majority there until the beginning of the nineteenth century.[26]

Whereas slaveholdings towered into the hundreds on the lowland's great rice plantations, urban slaveholders rarely held more than a dozen slaves, and the great planters, with their dual residences, kept only a tiny fraction of their holdings in town. Like their counterparts in cities between Boston and New Orleans, slaves in the rice ports found themselves packed away in back rooms, garrets, and outbuildings, in close proximity to their masters, often in the same residence.[27] The small holdings, shared residence, and disproportionately large numbers of women—even when men dominated the plantation population—suggest that most urban slaves worked around the house, cooking, cleaning, and catering to the minute whims and physical needs of their owners. Under such circumstances, slaves learned well the ways of white people. In 1732 the executor of a Charles Town estate put two slave children up for sale. Both had been "bred up in Household Business." Like many other town slaves, they spoke "very good English," a marker of the reemergence of a creole society.[28]

Urban slavery extended beyond the owners' household, however. Slaves were central to the mercantile economy of the great rice ports. Nothing arrived or left Charles Town, Savannah, and the other lowcountry towns without some slave's handling it. Charles Town and Savannah housed a small army of slave porters, draymen, stevedores, and roustabouts. Slave men also worked as skilled craftsmen. The availability of trained slaves enabled some master artisans to retire from active participation in their trades. A visitor to Charles Town found "many of the mechaniks bear nothing more of their trade than the name." The proportion of the urban slave population engaged in skilled labor increased steadily during the colonial era, with the growth of the slave artisanry accelerating after midcentury. By the eve of the Revolution, complaints rang through the lowcountry about slaves who monopolized artisanal employment, fixed prices, and denied opportunities to white wage workers. Lawmakers answered the call with a variety of regulations aimed at limiting urban slaves to menial labor.[29]

By any account, these regulations failed, as the protests of white journeymen against slave competition were easily deflected by a shifting alliance of planters, master craftsmen, and urban consumers, all of whom benefited from the slaves' skill. Indeed, the large number of skilled slaves made it easy for fugitive craftsmen to hire their own time "in the Way of Business, without Controll." Some slave artisans forged passes, but most simply tended to their affairs, hardly bothering to present evidence—real or contrived—of their owners' permission. Rural craftsmen, confident of their abilities and having done a turn in some of the smaller rice ports, also took their chances in the bigger cities. Ishmael, "well known in Savannah as a jobbing carpenter," regularly worked the wharves at Yamacraw in 1774, "not withstanding he ha[d] no ticket" from his owner "or any other licence authorizing him to work out."[30]

As in the cities of the Chesapeake, urban slave artisans generally labored in the lower trades, with men working as carpenters, coopers, and shoemakers and women as seamstresses and weavers. But unlike in the Chesapeake, urban slaves in the lowcountry also entered the ranks of the most skilled as smiths, mechanics, and wood workers. Slave artisans were particularly important along the waterfront as shipwrights, ropemakers, and caulkers, so that when white journeymen attempted to oust slaves from the docks, master artisans countered that "his Majesty's Ships have been repaired and refitted only by the assistance of Our Slaves, And . . . without these Slaves the worst Consequences might Ensue."[31]

Slaves who were rented by their owners soon learned to arrange for their own employment, establishing a near-independent place in the urban economy. Some did overwork on their own account, pocketing a portion of their wages. Thousands more hired themselves on a full-time basis and paid their master a portion of their wages. Complaints first issued in the 1730s of the "common Practice" whereby slaveowners authorized their slaves "to work out by the Week" with the understanding that they would earn "a certain Hire" grew louder over the course of the eighteenth century. By 1771 a Savannah minister estimated that 10 percent of the adult slaves "live by themselves & allow their master a certain sum p. week." In Charles Town, where the proportion may have been even higher, authorities tried to regulate the rates by which slaves hired themselves, at one point barring slaveholders from hiring out more than two slaves—a concession that legitimated the larger principle.

Despite the best efforts of municipal officials—who added their own regulations to the colony's—slaves continued to set their own terms and fees, refusing to labor "unless it be such work as shall be agreeable to themselves and such pay as they may require." Planters, "defrauded" by slaves who pocketed their earnings, sometimes joined a chorus of white artisans in complaining about jobbing slaves, but they usually demanded an end to the practice for everyone's slaves but their own. By the 1760s Charles Town slaves had created "combinations amongst themselves" to raise wages, and housekeepers found that slaves "refuse doing their work, unless their exorbitant demands are complied with."[32] The slaves' economy thrived in the cities of the lowcountry.

Cash-in-hand endowed slaves with the means to distance themselves from their owners' control. Urban slaves often lived on their own. The ability to live independently allowed slaves to escape the crowded confines of their owners' home—a mixed blessing from the owners' perspective—and to establish their own households.[33] Slave men, free to work and live on their own, rented rooms on the edge of town—the Neck in Charles Town, under the Bluff in Savannah—and installed their wives and children, placing their domestic life on a sounder basis. Unbalanced sex ratios, distance, difficulties of visiting, and of course a lack of legal recognition of marriage played havoc with the slave family in the cities of the lowcountry, as they did elsewhere. But the independence afforded by wage work allowed urban slaves to reclaim a semblance of control over their domestic lives.

Urban slave women found employment outside of their owners' households as cooks, seamstresses, mantua makers, weavers, and dozens of other occupations. More importantly, they took control of the streets of the rice ports, monopolizing the markets by mediating between slave-grown produce from the countryside and urban consumption. Slave women not only purchased nearly everything that entered into their owners' kitchens, but they also sold all kinds of merchandise on their own. In every lowcountry town, slave women could be found hawking goods from street carts. Often these carts were family enterprises, with men butchering animals or catching fish and women preparing them for sale. Slave women dominated the public markets to such an extent that white patrons charged them with forestalling, engrossing, and extortion. The press rang with charges that slave women intercepted produce from the countryside and made consumers "pay an exorbitant Price for the same." Outraged white householders and white vendors protested that slaves interfered with "poor honest white people supporting themselves and families [by] being suffered to cook, bake, sell fruit, dry goods, and other ways traffic in the public market and streets," and lawmakers responded favorably to white hucksters who claimed they had been "ent[ir]ely ruined and rendered miserable." But the enforcement of the law came to nothing. In 1773 a visitor to Charles Town reported that black women controlled the markets in which they bought and sold "on *their own accounts,* whatever they please."[34]

White observers inevitably translated the license slave women enjoyed in the marketplace into the metaphor for sexual freedom. "Not only do both sexes walk around together on the streets," declared one scandalized prelate, "but whites and Negroes of both sexes act most shamefully and make much noise at night." The "great number of loose, idle, disorderly women" who owned the streets of Charles Town and Savannah after dark confirmed the fears of the priggish and the hopes of the licentious. As in all port cities, sex stood high on the list of commodities for sale. It was a desperate and tawdry business, mostly transacted in the back rooms of dramshops and taverns. But such activities were always more than opportunities for market women and laundresses to add to their income, for the demand for black sexuality promised new power and threatened great perils.[35]

The aggressive sexuality of young urban black women—"unmannerly, rude and insolent"—and their equally loud dress attracted sailors, country merchants, and other men alone in the great ports. Black women elevated the trade, often hosting dances that imitated—perhaps parodied—the planters' high style. Such balls were of course illegal, but the allegedly clandestine affairs appeared to be known to all. Patrons could be found among the men of the planter class, whose dual residences separated them from their white wives and sweethearts for a portion of the year. Not only did "many of the leading gentlemen . . . not marry," but they "commit their disgrace which is considered little or no shame."[36]

Freedom in the marketplace permitted slaves to enlarge their social life in other ways. Beyond their owners' eyes, slaves traveled freely and socialized as they wished. As in the North, funerals became an occasion for "meeting in large bodies in the night," and, at least in one instance, "rioting and in a most notorious manner and breaking the Lord's day." But urban slaves joined together in large numbers on many other occasions as well. In what one appalled white observer labeled "a County-Dance or Rout, a Cabel of [sixty] *Negroes*" met on the outskirts of

Charles Town, feasted on "Tongues, Hams, Beef, Geese, Turkies and Fowls, drank bottled liquors of all sorts . . . the men copying (or *taking off*), the manners of their masters and the women those of their mistresses."[37]

Slaves also established cookshops, groceries, and taverns to cater to their own people. Such places became notorious interracial meeting grounds, where white sailors and journeymen fraternized with city-bound slaves, and where the movement of liquor and sex transcended racial lines. Interracial gangs of thieves appeared to be as endemic in the cities of the lowcountry as they were in ports all around the Atlantic rim. Although urban officials continually redoubled their efforts, they failed to terminate these illicit ventures.[38]

Alongside these forbidden enterprises were a handful of respectable ones sponsored by the Society for the Propagation of the Gospel and other Anglican missionaries, occasionally with the aid of benevolent planters. In Charles Town and Savannah, Anglican ministers and various missionaries associated with the SPG found willing converts among the assimilationist-minded populace. So too did the first stirrings of evangelicalism, which was brought to the lowcountry by the Methodist George Whitefield and his most zealous converts, the planters Hugh and Jonathan Bryan. The promise of equality in the sight of God received an enthusiastic reception among the slaves of the rice ports. But for precisely the reason that urban slaves were attracted to the evangelical promise, lowcountry lawmakers came down hard on the few men who dared to present Christ's words to all comers. Slaveholders were even more suspicious of the missionaries than were their northern counterparts, and the interest urban slaves manifested in Christianity only reinforced slave-owner opposition.[39]

Mobile, skilled, and cosmopolitan, urban slaves improved their material condition and expanded their social life even while the circumstances of the mass of rural slaves deteriorated in the wake of the rice revolution. In the rice ports, the slaves' wealth far exceeded the modest prosperity of even the most successful slaves in the Chesapeake. Their conspicuous displays symbolized the independence that urban life allowed. The black men and women—some slaves, some slave hirelings, and some runaway slaves—who resided below the Bluff in Savannah and in Charles Town's Neck were free in everything but name. Some took the name as well, although the number of black people who gained legal freedom remained small.[40]

The incongruous prosperity of urban slaves jarred the planter class. By hiring their own time, living apart from their owners, controlling their own family life, riding horses, and brandishing pistols, these slaves forcibly and visibly claimed the privileges white men and women reserved for themselves. Perhaps no aspect of their behavior was as obvious, and hence as galling, to city-bound planters as the slaves' elaborate dress. While plantation slaves—men and women—worked stripped to the waist wearing no more than loin cloths (thereby confirming the white man's image of savagery), urban slaves appropriated their owners' taste for fine clothes and often the garments themselves. Tooling around Charles Town in their finery, displaying pocket watches, and sporting powdered wigs, they aroused the ire of countless self-proclaimed ladies and gentlemen who viewed the slaves' fine dress as a challenge to their exclusive claim to the symbols of civilization. Grand jury presentments offered a seemingly interminable list of laments about the "excessive and costly apparel" worn by slaves, particularly by slave women. Lowcountry legislators enacted various sumptuary regulations to restrain what they considered the slaves' penchant for dressing above their station. The South Carolina Assembly even considered prohibiting masters and mistresses from giving their old clothes to their slaves. But hand-me-downs were not the problem as long as the slaves' independent economic enterprises prospered. Frustrated by the realities of urban slavery, lawmakers passed and repassed the old regulations to no avail other than to document the difference between their expectations and the realities of urban slavery. On the eve of the American Revolution, a Charles Town grand jury again denounced the fact that the "Law for preventing the excessive and costly Apparel of Negroes and other Slaves in this Province (especially in *Charles-Town*) [was] not being put in Force." But how could the legislation be enforced when "the skilled negroes in Charlestown, who are used in the offices and shops or who are mistresses, are very well dressed"?[41]

Such outcroppings rattled the confidence of the planter class. In 1765, when white protestors against British taxes took to the streets of Charles Town with cries of "Liberty! Liberty and stamp'd paper," a group of slaves took up the chant. The slave trader and planter Henry Laurens dismissed the slaves who "mimick'd their betters," declaring they engaged in "thoughtless imitation." But the careful chronicle of the event belied his easy dismissal, and Laurens acknowledged that "all were Soldiers in Arms for more than a Week."[42]

Even as the shouts of "Liberty" subsided, urban slaves were redefining their place in lowcountry society. To be sure, their status was far from equal; indeed, it was rarely characterized by freedom. No matter how essential their function for city-based planters or how intimate their interaction with the urban artisanry or how far-reaching their independence based upon self-hire, relations between master and slave no longer smacked of the earlier sawbuck equality. Instead, urban slaves drew their status from their knowledge of urban society, which in the case of slave women often extended to the most intimate of connections. Like slaveholding men everywhere, lowland masters assumed that sexual access to slave women was simply another one of their prerogatives. Perhaps because of their origins in the West Indies, where such relationships were commonplace, or perhaps because their dual residence separated them from their white wives part of the year, white men frequently and openly established sexual liaisons with black women. These relations differed from the casual sex that might be purchased on the streets or the violent usurpations that might take place at any time. A few well-placed white men and black women formed stable, long-lasting unions, legitimate in everything but law. While such relationships existed in the Chesapeake, planters rarely acknowledged them; in the lowcountry, planters often recognized and provided for their mixed-race offspring. Although such provisions only occasionally extended to legal freedom, people of color enjoyed special standing in the lowcountry ports, and, as they did in the West Indies, officials sometimes looked the other way when such creoles crossed into white society.

For themselves, people of mixed racial origins were "terribly afraid of being thought Negroes." According to one observer, they "avoid as much as possible their Company or Commerce." Such pretensions never moved white people to acceptance, but even when they did not grant legal freedom, they usually assured the elevated standing of their mixed-race scions by training them for artisan trades or placing them in household positions. Barred from white society, the emerging "colored" elite wanted no part of black life on the plantations of the lowcountry.[43]

While one branch of black society stood so close to whites that its members sometimes disappeared into the white population, most plantation slaves remained alienated from the world of the masters, physically and culturally. A few—almost always recently arrived Africans—attempted to make that alienation complete through flight, taking "an East course as long as they could, thinking to return to their own country that way."[44] But the vast majority saw no alternative to the harsh realities of plantation slavery. Rather than reject the site of enslavement, plantation slaves slowly, if reluctantly, embraced it.

The expansion and elaboration of the plantation allowed slaves to create a world of their own. The slave quarter, standing at the center of these huge agricultural factories—the most highly capitalized enterprises in mainland North America during the eighteenth century—was the heart of African-American life in the countryside. Whereas urban slave-owners indiscriminately stuffed their slaves into back rooms and lofts or allowed them to live on their own, lowcountry planters carefully organized the slave quarter along well-tended streets or tidy squares to fit the overall design of their estates—keeping the slave quarter within sight of the Big House but separate nonetheless. But whereas planters designed their grounds, slaves constructed the buildings, employing materials and methods familiar to Africans. Built of a seashell muck of their own making or bricks fired in the plantation kiln, the slaves' houses and their distinctive configuration gave the slave quarter the appearance of a separate village or "Negro town," as more than one visitor observed. The seclusion of life in the quarter and its emulation of the texture, and often the form, of an African village imparted a sense of propriety, so much so that some lowcountry planters urged a return to the older barracks-style housing. What these planters feared as "too much liberty" was the emergence of a black community.

The residents not only labored together, but they lived "in separate houses," "converse[ing] almost wholly among themselves."[45] Having no experience of the close living arrangements that shaped slave life in the great rice ports or the interplay of master and slave that characterized plantation relations in the great plantation towns of the Chesapeake, lowcountry slaves re-created, as best they could, Africa in America.

The institutional presence of the plantation village bespoke the increasing permanence of black life in the rural lowcountry. By midcentury, as the fearful mortality of the early years began to subside, the ratio of slave men to women moved toward balance, and fertility rates edged upward. Planters, seeing advantages for themselves, acceded to the slaves' desire to establish stable families. As in the Chesapeake, some allowed family formation because of the profit to be made in a self-reproducing labor force. Others acted because they believed, along with the governor of South Carolina, that slaves who were "Native of Carolina, who have no Notion of Liberty, nor no longing after any other Country," and who had "been brought up among White People," made for a more pliable and obedient workforce. Clerics, entrusted with the task of Christianization, appreciated the planters' growing interest in slave families. "Among us Religious Instruction usually descends from Parents to Children," reported an Anglican missionary in 1740, "so among them it must first ascend from Children to Parents, or from young to old."[46]

Although the massive influx of African slaves continued, slave men and women took advantage of the changing demographic circumstance and of their owners' enthusiasm for a reproducing labor force to reestablish family life. The growing size of lowcountry plantations made a residential slave family a far greater possibility in the lowcountry than in the Chesapeake. The "broad wife" and long-distance visitation, so much a fixture of the slaves' domestic life in Maryland and Virginia, was much less in evidence in the lowcountry, where residential families became the foundation of thickly woven networks of kin.

Plantation slaves, determined to reclaim a semblance of domestic regularity, forced grudging concessions from their owners. By midcentury many planters agreed that slaves shared the same sentiments which underlay their own domesticity. Slaves "love their families dearly and none runs away from the other," admitted one South Carolina owner. Out of respect for their slaves' wishes to reside together, masters sometimes purchased slaves in family units. A South Carolina planter who had sold a disobedient slave man to Florida was so touched by the slave's distress at being forcibly parted from his wife that he reconsidered the sale, observing that "a separating of those unhappy people added still greater discomfort to their unfortunate condition." Indeed, planters even worried about slave men without wives.[47] As the plantation culture matured, slave masters recognized the legitimacy of the slave family, although they often honored it in the breach.

But from the planters' perspective, the slave family also had its drawbacks. The domestic relations that slaves pieced together, especially the claims black parents made to their own children, challenged their owners' dominion. If plantation patriarchs demanded the loyalty of their "children," so did slave parents. In the contest between the metaphoric parents of plantation and the parents of birth, the master and mistress fared poorly. The recognition of the slave family also provided a modicum of protection for slave women—at least married women—as planters came to understand that violation of the sanctity of the marriage bed wreaked havoc on plantation discipline. Most importantly, the emergence of the slave family created a powerful source of opposition within the plantation, as a cadre of respected elders bearing the titles of mother and father, aunt and uncle took their place at the top of the plantation order.

In creating their own world within the plantation, lowcountry slaves built upon the independence secured by the charter generations. During the pioneer period, hard-pressed slaveowners had required slaves to raise their own provisions. Planters regularly reaffirmed the slaves' right to free Sunday, and when they impinged on the slaves' time, they compensated them for the infringement.[48] With time to themselves, slaves regularly kept small gardens—"little Plantations," as one planter called them—and tended barnyard fowl. Moreover, since slaves could consume the lowcountry's great staple, owners also permitted them to grow rice on their own and to keep the broken grain that could be salvaged from their owners' fields. Slaves marketed their rice along with garden produce, greatly enlarging the slaves' economy.

Whereas the emergence of the plantation economy in the Chesapeake circumscribed the slaves' independent economic activities, the growth of the rice economy enlarged them. During the eighteenth century, lowcountry slaves expanded the established practice of keeping a portion of their time to work for themselves, transforming prerogatives won by the charter generations into a right that slaveholders violated at their peril. By midcentury, plantation slaves worked "as much land as they could handle," and generally they had Sundays to tend gardens of corn, potatoes, peanuts, and melons. The care slaves lavished on their own gardens and provision grounds stood in sharp contrast to their owners' fields, which appeared shabby and disheveled in comparison. Lowcountry slaves cultivated their "little piece of land . . . much better than their Master," noted a visitor from Scotland. "There," she added, "they rear hogs and poultry, sew calabashes, etc. and are better provided for in every thing than the poorer white people with us."[49]

As in the Chesapeake, lowcountry slaves expected their owners to issue regular allotments of food and clothing, maintain their housing, and meet their medical needs. At holidays such as Christmas, slaves looked forward to additional gifts. Lowcountry planters seldom shirked their provisioning duties. From their perspective, the regular issuances affirmed their authority and fulfilled the duties of mastership. But plantation slaves did not rest satisfied with their allowance. They insisted upon the right to produce for themselves, and saw it—not the planters' dole—as the key to their livelihood. Thus, if they expected the regular allotment of rations and played their part in the charade surrounding Christmas gifting, they guarded their rights as independent producers, pressing their owners for larger gardens and grounds and more time to work them. In short, the battle over the slaves' economy paralleled, complemented, and complicated the struggle over the masters' economy, with masters and slaves negotiating and renegotiating the rights to which each believed themselves fully entitled.

Although the lines of battle continually shifted, by midcentury planters had acknowledged the slaves' right to produce independently, understanding that the slaves' accumulation of property reinforced their attachment to their home estates and reduced the impulse to flight. Rather than hinder the slaves' attempts to accumulate, some planters encouraged—and protected—their slaves' property. Slaveowners occasionally purchased their slaves' breeding stock; and when slaves were sold, owners often either purchased the slaves' property or—upon the sale of a slave—provided for the slaves' property to be transferred with their person. The expansion of lowland rice cultivation from South Carolina to Florida could only take place with the movement of the slaves' "Little Estates."[50]

The growth of the slaves' economy did not go unnoticed. Nonslaveholders saw profit in the slaves' enterprise, and the plantation was soon beset with a host of peddlers bearing a seemingly endless supply of merchandise for barter or purchase, easy credit, and—from the planters' perspective—even easier morals. Fearful that such men carried insurrectionary ideas, lowcountry legislators repeatedly restricted such trade, but legislation had no more effect on the slaves' independent economic activities in the countryside than it did on the slaves' overwork and self-hire in the rice ports. Slave-produced goods reached markets beyond the plantations, sometimes allowing for a merger of the independent economies of rural and urban slaves. Some plantation slaves attended town-based markets, and others hawked their goods through the agency of slave watermen, who traversed the rivers between plantation and port. Thus, the growth of the lowcountry towns and the increasing specialization in staple production enlarged the market for slave-grown produce. Planters disliked the independence truck-gardening afforded plantation slaves, the tendency of slaves to confuse their owners' produce with their own, and the new friends slaves found among peddlers and other white non-slaveholders. Still, the ease of water transportation and the absence of white supervision made it difficult for even the most critical to restrain the slaves' independent activities.[51]

To keep their slaves on the plantation, planters traded with them directly, bartering manufactured goods for slave produce, paying them for Sunday work, and purchasing their handicrafts. Henry Laurens, who described himself as a "factor" for his slaves, exchanged some "very gay Waistcoats which some of the Negro Men may want" for grain at "10 Bushels per Waistcoat." Later, learning that a plantation under his supervision was short of provisions, he authorized its overseer "to purchase of your own Negroes all that you know Lawfully belongs to themselves at the lowest price they will sell it for." Planters thus found benefits in the slaves' participation in the lowcountry's independent economic production, but the small profits gained by bartering with their slaves also legitimated the slaves' customary right to gardens and provision grounds.[52] Although slave propertyholding generally remained small prior to American independence, it insulated plantation slaves from the harsh conditions of primitive rice production, improved their material circumstances, and provided social distance from the slaveholders' arbitrary authority.

The task system, initially a product of the planters' seasonal absence, supported the slaves' material ambitions and their desire for a richer life. Tasking permitted slaves, often with the aid of their black drivers, to preserve a portion of the day for their own use. Even at its most onerous, the customary task allowed slaves a measure of control over their work, both in terms of energy and time expended. Some slaves—mostly full hands—left the field in the early afternoon, a practice that protected them from the harsh afternoon sun and allowed them time to tend their own gardens and stock after the sun had reached its high point.[53]

But like gardens and grounds, tasking was a matter of continual contention. If, by midcentury, slaves and masters accepted the principle that underlay the task system, the precise definition of the task remained subject to endless dispute. Lowcountry slaves struggled to enlarge their own time at their owners' expense, and planters pressed for a like advantage. Although both slaveowners and slaves appeared to accept the standard quarter-acre task for planting and weeding rice by an able-bodied adult, other work might take more or less time and hence was subject to contest. Cleaning canals and threshing rice were particular sources of friction, with slaveowners or their representatives wielding the lash and slaves malingering, feigning illness, or taking to the swamps.

The lines of battle changed constantly, but some moments seemed more liable to dispute than others.[54] Attempts to introduce new crops, new implements, and new techniques nearly always initiated a new round of negotiations. So too did the arrival of a new overseer or steward, as slaves were quick to test the new man's mettle. Overseers were careful not to press slaves too hard. One Mr. Hewie did, and the slaves drowned him, a loss his employer and other planters did nothing but lament. While not many overseers lost their lives in struggling with slaves, numerous overseers lost their jobs—since slowdowns, truancy, and sabotage were viewed as reasons for dismissal.[55]

The control slaves gained over the productive process was enhanced by the growing elaboration of the division of labor that rice and indigo production required. The steep and carefully graded hierarchy of the lowcountry plantation grew steeper and fuller with the expansion of the plantation during the middle years of the eighteenth century. The enormous size of rice and indigo plantations compelled lowcountry planters to allocate their authority to selected members of the labor force. No matter how meticulously planters organized their estates, someone needed to enforce the regimen on workers who were uncooperative at best. Much of that work fell to the driver and to a growing number of slave artisans, technicians, and plantation specialists.

Despite the difficulties the position entailed, by midcentury the driver had become a fixture on the plantations of the lowcountry and had begun to consolidate power within the plantation, sometimes at the expense of white supervisors and fellow slaves. Evidence of the driver's growing prestige could be found in the small but significant differences in clothing and housing—along with small privileges that accrued to the driver's wife—that elevated the driver over the mass of plantation hands.[56]

Below the driver stood a corps of plantation-based technicians and craftsmen, as the absence of white nonslaveholders forced planters to turn to slaves for skilled labor. Sluice minders, really hydraulic engineers, built and controlled the canals that irrigated the rice fields. Slave coopers made barrels to house rice and vats to process the indigo; slave brickmakers and masons fashioned bricks and built the kilns to cure the indigo; slave blacksmiths cared for horses and mules, while slave carpenters kept the plantations in good repair. In addition, slave watermen connected the great estates with Charles Town and other lowland ports, bringing messages and supplies to the plantation and hauling staple produce away.[57]

The number of skilled and mobile plantation hands increased during the course of the eighteenth century, as the lowland plantation became larger, more complex, and technically sophisticated. By the 1730s slaves had taken control of so many trades that the entire political establishment of South Carolina—the governor, council, and assembly—saw fit to petition the king against the practice of training slaves to be "Handicraft Tradesmen." The effort was for naught. As the century progressed, planters introduced machines to increase production, including wind fans, mechanized mortars, and hydraulic pumps—all of which slaves serviced. When lowcountry planters expanded south into Florida, there was not the slightest pretense of employing white craftsmen. No one doubted that black people had "great capacities, and an amazing aptness for learning trades"—a shibboleth that was occasionally voiced in the colonies to the north. Planters regularly trained slaves "to be coopers, carpenters, bricklayers, smith, and other trades." The number of slave watermen also increased, as the growing rice trade required more and larger boats. By the last quarter of the eighteenth century, schooners with crews of twelve men or more—usually entirely black—coursed the rivers of the rice region.[58]

As in the Chesapeake, men monopolized almost all the skilled positions within the agricultural sector, leaving the field force disproportionately female, with young women assigned to the most arduous tasks. When equipping his Florida estate in 1769, a Carolina planter was pleased to see the arrival of "two very strong and able wenches, [who] will do as much work as any man." The sexual stereotypes—which barred women from most skilled labor—allowed slave women to have a small niche of their own, as planters assigned them a variety of tasks deemed woman's work. Some of this labor required considerable ability, learning, and deftness. Planters generally disparaged such work, defining it as "making Negro clothes, attending sick people, & a hundred things which new or Ship's Negroes cannot perform," but slaves appreciated the talents of plantation seamstresses, nurses, and midwives and honored them accordingly.[59]

Although drivers and artisans stood at the head of the slave hierarchy, they derived their authority from very different sources. Unlike drivers, the elevated status enjoyed by artisans, technicians, and watermen rested not on connections with the masters but on their own considerable achievements. The pride generated by their hard-earned knowledge infused them with an air of confidence that pushed plantation-based craftsmen into the first ranks of the runaways and rebels. It also propelled them into the marketplace to improve their lives and those of their families. Like their urban counterparts, rural artisans found that the demand for skilled labor offered opportunities to earn a little cash. The ability of rural slave artisans to hire their own time allowed them to translate their skill into substantial material benefits and a larger knowledge of the world. Jobbing slaves visited with one another and traveled together to fish, hunt, and oyster. An investigation of an alleged slave conspiracy in 1749 revealed dozens of encounters which took slaves far from their home plantation, where they "Eat and drank together . . . [and] only played and Laughed." The rice revolution propelled plantation slaves—by their numbers and their skills—into positions of authority few slaves could hope to achieve in the Chesapeake region. Lowcountry planters fully admitted that their slaves were "capable of the management of a plantation themselves."[60]

But however capable, slaves were rarely willing. Disaffection was the rule among enslaved workers. As in the Chesapeake, slaves found truancy a powerful weapon in the struggle to maintain control over their own lives. Perhaps it was more powerful in the lowcountry, because absconding for just a few days during a critical moment in the agricultural cycle was especially disruptive to the carefully choreographed production of rice and indigo. After several such experiences, Henry Laurens concluded that it was best to "indulge" potential runaways, as previous flights "cost me much Trouble & expence"; and to reassert plantation discipline, he had had to sell a valuable hand "to avoid a second Flight."[61] If slave truants walked a fine line to avoid being outlawed, slaveholders walked an equally fine line in preventing truancy from escalating into maroonage.

Nonetheless, maroonage remained a lively tradition among lowland slaves. Although the expansion of the rice economy shrank the swamps and forests, there remained many hiding places for fugitives. Such maroon colonies had all but vanished from the Chesapeake region by the middle of the eighteenth century, but they survived in the lowcountry, coexisting uncomfortably with the world of the plantation. The nexus could be observed in the discovery of a party of some forty runaways, including women and children, in a swamp north of the Savannah River in 1765. The group's organization was military, and the maroons began their day with the raising of the colors and the beating of a drum. Although they seemed to live peripatetically by hunting and fishing, their camp consisted of four substantial buildings. Their supplies were also substantial, and invading soldiers found "about 15 bushels of rough Rice, Blankets, Potts, Pails, Shoes, Axes & many others Tools." Such largess could not be accumulated without the assistance of plantation slaves, and its existence reveals the ways in which the two worlds—the plantation quarter and the maroon sanctuary—were linked together.[62]

Other fugitives from plantation society hoped to find independence in the upcountry, an untamed frontier where Native Americans mixed with European-American hunters, squatters, and pioneer farmers. Although aspiring planters made the upcountry the site of slavery's most dynamic growth after midcentury, most upcountry farmers owned no slaves and had little sympathy for the great lowcountry nabobs. Indeed, sheltered among the settlers were a handful of free black people—some descended from the charter generations—eager to strike a blow at their old tormenter. Frontiersmen, black and white, frequently welcomed fugitive slaves, employing them with no questions asked. Although demanding, the diverse nature of labor on a frontier plantation was no doubt a welcome relief from the discipline of the great lowland rice estates. Fugitive slaves also found a home among bandits, whose interracial character—a "numerous Collection of outcast Mulattoes, Mustees, free Negroes, all Horse thieves"—earned them the reproach of the region's aspiring planters.[63]

The alternatives offered by lowcountry maroon colonies and upcountry frontier farming or banditry, like the independence generated by the task system and truck gardening, provided the material basis for slave society in lowcountry South Carolina and Georgia. Within the confines of the overwhelmingly black countryside, the cultures of Africa survived well, as the open slave trade continually reawakened memories of the

Old World. Unlike the North, Chesapeake, and lower Mississippi Valley, Africanization in the lowcountry did not span a short generation in which newcomers dominated the black population. Instead immigration was a continuous process lasting a full century, during which wave after wave of new arrivals repeatedly remade lowland society. The continued influx of Africans, not merely their towering majority, gave black life its distinctive shape in the lowcountry.

The pattern of the lowland slave trade heightened the impact of Africans on the evolution of black culture. While African slaves arrived in the Chesapeake through a multiplicity of inlets and creeks, they poured into the lowcountry through a single port. The unicentered slave trade and large plantations on which most slaves resided assured the survival not only of the common denominators of West African life but also of many of its particular national forms. Planter preferences, shipboard ties, or perhaps the chance ascendancy of a single nation allowed specific African cultures to reconstitute themselves within the plantation setting. Indeed, some slaveowners controlled the trade on both sides of the Atlantic. Planter-merchant Richard Oswald, who owned a slave factory on the Sierra Leone River, shipped directly to his Florida estate, making much of his ability to keep his imports together. Common national identities also drew slaves together across plantation boundaries, and planters expected fugitives to be found with their former compatriots. March, who spoke "very broken English though he has been many years in the province," fled to a plantation "where he frequently used to visit a countryman of his." Ties of language, experience, and memory bound slaves together much as they did other immigrants, forced and free.[64]

Living in large units, often numbering in the hundreds, on plantations they had carved out of the malarial swamps, and working under the direction of black drivers with rarely a white man in residence, the black majority attained, needed, and perhaps wanted only fleeting knowledge of European-American society. Many slaves, particularly the newly arrived Africans, hardly knew their owners or any other white person, for that matter. Enjoying nothing of the multilingual fluency of the charter generations, they were walled off from whites—and sometimes from one another—by the barrier of language.

The language barrier protected plantation slaves from other impositions, most prominently Christianity. Even after midcentury, an Anglican minister long associated with the efforts to Christianize the African population observed that it "requires Length of Time, great Patience and much Industry before they can have a sensible Idea of our Language." "Our negros," reported another frustrated missionary in 1754, "are so Ignorant of the English Language . . . that it is a great while before you can get them to understand what the Meaning of Words is." In this circumstance, conversation, let alone conversion, was impossible beyond a few crude utterances.[65] Few plantation slaves accepted Jesus or even knew his name. In the countryside, they remained "as great strangers to Christianity, and as much under the influence of Pagan darkness, idolatry and superstition, as they were at their first arrival from Africa."[66] What plantation slaves knew about European-American life did not encourage them to learn more. African cultures survived well in the lowland countryside.

But it did not survive unchallenged. The planters' raw power and the missionaries' zeal to convert tested the slaves' efforts to maintain their African ways. As slaves pressed their case—boldly rejecting Christianity or quietly braiding their hair in the traditional manner—the conflict over work and over culture became one. The slaves' refusal to accept Christian baptism was but another manifestation of their struggle with their owners, no different than their rejection of the planters' task. Missionary complaints of "pagan rites"—which may have been polytheistic, animistic, or Islamic—in the slave quarter were as much indicators of the slaves' success in controlling their own lives as were planter laments of sloth and slipshod work. The conditions of lowcountry slavery—task labor, propertyholding, kin connections, maroon alternatives—that gave lowcountry slaves leverage in their workplace struggles also allowed them to honor the memory of their forebears.

In the long run, planters could no more ignore the slaves' religion than they could their work habits. As with the struggle over work, the struggle over religion was a constant, even if the lines of battle were forever changing. Anglican missionaries, who had scored successes in their efforts to win over black converts in the port cities, were much less successful in the countryside. When evangelical Christianity arrived in the person of Methodist George Whitefield in the 1740s, some slaves on the plantations of Hugh and Jonathan Bryan accepted Christ, perhaps because the message of salvation contained within it the possibility of deliverance from slavery. At least the Bryans' slaves thought so—and so did neighboring planters, who put a prompt end to the Bryans' activities. Still, they had sowed the seed of Christianity within the black community and—however inadvertently—forever linked salvation to liberation. But the seed would be long in germinating. After being dragged before the General Assembly and forced to recant their errors, the Bryans withdrew their public support for the conversion of slaves, although they continued to proselytize their own slaves. Still, taken as a whole, the evangelicals were no more successful than their Anglican predecessors. In 1775, when a New England minister took up residence in one lowcountry plantation parish, he found that not a single slave had been baptized, although the parish was overwhelmingly black.[67]

The failure of Christianity on the plantations of the lowcountry pointed to the slaves' success in insulating themselves against their owners' cultural domination. Lowcountry slaves incorporated more of African culture—as reflected in their language, religion, work patterns, plaited hair, filed teeth, and country markings—into their new lives than did black Americans in the Chesapeake region. Throughout the eighteenth century, they continued to work the land, name their children, and communicate through word, gesture, and song in a manner that openly combined African traditions with the circumstances of plantation life. The ubiquitous presence of Africa was nowhere more evident than in the names slaves called themselves. Although many lowcountry planters renamed slaves upon purchase, slaves clandestinely kept their "country names," revealing the degree of control slaves maintained over their own lives on the overwhelmingly black estates. When two slaves escaped from a Georgia plantation in the summer of 1767, their owner noted that one "calls himself GOLAGA," although "the name given him [was] ABEL," "while the other" calls "himself ABBROM, the name given him here BENNET." Seven years later, a similar announcement revealed that the practice had not ended, as the fugitive "SMART, commonly call[ed] himself by his country name LANDORA."[68]

Wrestling control of the naming process from their owners, plantation slaves fused their African inheritance with their experience in the New World. By midcentury, even after substantial growth of an American-born population on the plantations, more than one-fifth of the slaves on several large lowcountry estates had African names. Perhaps more significantly, the proportion of African names among these African-American slaves was even higher than among the African arrivals (at least as denoted in the planters' records), as African parents and grandparents tried to keep memories of the Old World alive among their children.

Even when European names gained ascendancy, black parents maintained traditional naming practices. Particularly prominent was the African practice of naming children after important days, events, and places. Thus on December 25, 1743, "Christmas" was born on one South Carolina plantation, taking the name of a holiday that derived from Europe but maintaining the traditional African form of naming.[69] By the late eighteenth century, lowcountry slaves had begun to name their children —especially their sons—after their fathers and grandfathers, employing an African tradition to fortify generational ties in the inhospitable world of plantation slavery.[70]

The transformation of the naming process was symptomatic of the larger change of black life in the eighteenth-century lowcountry. Absentee ownership and planter hostility to the Christianizing efforts of missionaries gave lowcountry slaves a large field to develop their own social and religious life and to reproduce their material culture in the form of metal work, pottery, and baskets.[71] While Chesapeake slaves could hardly avoid contact with their owners and the region's white majority, plantation slaves in the lowcountry enjoyed enough independence that by midcentury they had established their own cycle of festivals. "It has been customary among them," lamented one Anglican cleric, "to have their feasts, dances and merry meetings upon the Lord's Day."[72] From such gatherings, it was just a short step to the development of distinctive song, dance, and even language—Gullah, a variant of Atlantic creole. "Even had we spoken with the tongues of angels," a British soldier would observe in 1779, "none of us could manage to talk with these people because of their bad dialect"—a striking commentary on the distinctiveness of the rural slaves' language and much else in black life in the lowcountry.[73]

In sum, by the eve of the American Revolution, one branch of black culture in the lowcountry had evolved in close proximity to whites. Urbane, often skilled, well-traveled, and cosmopolitan, city-bound African Americans were heirs to the strategies of the charter generations. They knew European-American society, and they used their knowledge for personal improvement. Some—a well-connected minority—pressed for incorporation into the white world. They perfected their English, valued

stylish garments, and urged missionaries to tutor their children.[74] Plantation slaves, by contrast, shared few of those assimilationist aspirations.
By their dress, language, and work routine, they lived in a world apart.
Rather than demand incorporation into white society, they yearned only
to be left to themselves. Within the slave quarter, aided by their numerical
dominance, their plantation-based social hierarchy, and their continued
contact with newly arrived Africans, they developed their own distinctive
culture, different not only from that of their European-American owners
but also from the cosmopolitan world of their urban counterparts.

To be sure, there were connections between the black majority in the
countryside and the urban sophisticates, particularly as the participation
of slaves in the lowcountry's internal marketing system grew. Hucksters,
boatmen, and jobbing artisans moved easily between these two worlds,
and most slaves undoubtedly learned something of the world of the other
through chance encounters, occasional visits, and word-of-mouth.[75] A
common white enemy continually reduced the social distance between
people of African descent who sought to improve their lives through
incorporation into the European-American world and those who were
determined to keep their distance from it.

The revolutionary crisis brought to the surface many of the differences between town and country, Africans and creoles in South Carolina,
Georgia, and East Florida. Charles Town slaves quickly turned the new
political possibilities to their advantage. In late 1774 or early 1775, David,
a black Methodist preacher trained in England and sent to the lowcountry by the countess of Huntingdon, unleashed a powerful sermon, reminding an assemblage of slaves that "the Children of Israel were delivered out of the hands of Pharo and he and all his Host were drowned in
the Red Sea and God will deliver his own People from Slavery." David's
words were understood all too well in Charles Town, and, if they com-
forted his congregants, white evangelists hustled him out of the city to
save him from a lynch mob.[76]

David's themes, shorn of their Old Testament allusions, were echoed
in the overwhelmingly black countryside by a slave preacher, who translated the Anglo-American conflict into terms that spoke to the plantation experience. "The old King had reced a Book from our Lord by
which he was to Alter the World (meaning to set the Negroes free) but for
not doing so, was now gone to Hell & in Punishmt." With the king's
death, the preacher assured his flock, the world could be made anew.

"The Young King . . . came up with the Book, & was about to alter the World, & set the Negroes Free."[77] The preacher's words, like David's, also needed no translation, but, unlike David, this pastor had no well-placed friends to protect him. The message these black men preached did not die with their removal. It spread throughout lowcountry South Carolina, Georgia, and Florida. As in the Chesapeake colonies, the revolutionary crisis, melded with evangelical zeal for salvation and deliverance, would soon and once again transform black life in the lowcountry.

Chapter Seven

Growth and the Transformation of
Black Life in the North

⁂

No plantation revolution remade black life in the northern colonies. But beginning sometime in the second quarter of the eighteenth century, the character of northern slavery changed. The change was not nearly as dramatic and far-reaching as in the mainland colonies to the south, where the emergence of a planter class and the advent of staple commodity production remade the Chesapeake and the lowcountry from societies with slaves into full-fledged slave societies. Instead, the transformation proceeded slowly and unevenly across the northern landscape in the half century between 1725 and 1775 and was far less complete, affecting the Middle Colonies more than New England, the cities more than the countryside. Nonetheless, as the northern colonies were more fully incorporated into the Atlantic economy, the significance of slavery grew. In some places, the North itself took on the trappings of a slave society, with an economy that rested upon the labor of enslaved Africans and African Americans.

Although the course of slavery in the North stopped short of the transformation initiated by the tobacco and rice revolutions, it nonetheless reshaped the lives of black people, both deepening the nightmare of slavery and buffering its worst effects. Direct African importation brought with it higher mortality, lower fertility, stricter discipline, harder work, and other manifestations of the degradation of slave life that accompanied the open slave trade in the Chesapeake and the lowcountry. But the greatly expanded slave population allowed black people—slave and free—to unite as never before. The influx of Africans awakened black northerners to their African origins, and they freely drew on that inheritance as they remade their lives in the years preceding the Revolution. Distinctive African-American institutions emerged, so that on the eve of the American Revolution the African burial ground was no longer the only public place in which black people congregated.

*   *   *

Slavery edged toward the center of the northern economy during the middle years of the eighteenth century. The growing demand for labor, especially when war disrupted the supply of European indentured servants and military enlistment siphoned young white men from the labor force, increased the importance of enslaved workers. "All importation of white servants is ruined by enlisting them and we must make more general use of Slaves," asserted a Philadelphia merchant at the onset of the Seven Years' War in 1756. Such sentiment resonated elsewhere in the northern colonies, where merchants, farmers, and artisans found that the labor of family members, indentured servants, and wage workers no longer satisfied their requirements.[1]

Spurred by new demands, the number of slaves in the northern colonies increased steadily during the middle decades of the eighteenth century. In some places, the growth of the enslaved black population outstripped that of the free white population. Between 1720 and 1750 the number of slaves in Rhode Island swelled from around 500 to well over 3,000, and the black proportion of the population rose from 5 to 10 percent of the whole. In no other New England colony did slavery's growth equal that of Rhode Island, but everywhere the increase of the enslaved black population at least kept pace with that of the free white population. In the Middle Colonies, the demographic history of slavery took a different shape as the proportion of slaves in the population declined from the first years of settlement but then surged upward. In New York, for example, slaves never again equaled the 30 percent of the population they had achieved in the 1640s. But after an initial decline, the number of slaves rose steadily throughout the eighteenth century, fluctuating between 11 and 15 percent of the total population.[2]

The expansion of slavery followed the general development of the northern labor force with a precision that marked the emergence of an Atlantic labor market.[3] When opportunities for economic advancement contracted in Europe and the Atlantic sea lanes were clear, European labor—free and servant—poured into the North, and African slavery languished. But when the reverse was true—when opportunities for free workers expanded in Europe or when war blocked the passage of European servants to the North—slave imports through southern trade routes grew. Philadelphia was a case in point. During the first decade of the eighteenth century, slaves composed more than one-sixth of its population and an even larger share of the working population. The proportion declined thereafter, especially when economic depression drove demand down and a high impost pushed slave prices up. With the withdrawal of the tax and the revival of prosperity, however, the number of slaves began to increase steadily. By the 1740s, 15 percent of all workingmen in Philadelphia were slaves.

The slaves' share of the workforce continued to expand during the next two decades, especially after 1755, when the French and Indian War again drew young men to the army, closing off alternative sources of servile labor. By the early 1760s one worker in five was a slave. Dependence on slave labor declined thereafter in Philadelphia and other parts of Pennsylvania, but it remained strong in New York. More than one-third of the immigrants arriving in New York between 1732 and 1754 were slaves. At the time of the American Revolution, black people composed 12 to 14 percent of the population of New York.[4]

The general expansion of slavery revealed the trend but concealed its full impact, for slavery scored its greatest gains in the most economically productive portions of the North. While the overall expansion of slavery hardly affected New England, which remained wedded to family and wage labor, the Middle Colonies became increasingly committed to slavery. Indeed, slaves became the single most important source of labor in the North's most fertile agricultural areas and its busiest ports.

The commitment to slavery emerged first in the cities. Although 90 percent of Pennsylvania's population lived outside Philadelphia in 1750, the city contained more than 40 percent of the colony's slaves. Similar comparisons of Boston with Massachusetts, Newport with Rhode Island, and New York City with New York reveal the continuing affinity of slavery and urban life in the colonial North. As urban slavery expanded, slaveownership became nearly universal among the urban elite and commonplace among the middling sort as well, especially in the great port cities. The upper orders of society in New York, Newport, and Boston became fully invested in slavery.[5]

As their numbers increased, northern slaves moved from the periphery of urban productivity, as servants in gentry homes, to its center, as workers in artisan shops. Again, the change can be traced most fully in Philadelphia, where the wealthiest Philadelphians—merchants, professionals, and "gentlemen"—shed their slaves, and the middling craftsmen entered the slaveholding ranks in record numbers during the middle years of the century. By the 1760s tradesmen and artisans dominated the ranks of Philadelphia's slaveholding class, making up over one-third of all masters and controlling about 40 percent of the slave population and an even larger share of the slave men.[6] The importance of slave workers in New York City was, if anything, greater than in Philadelphia. New York artisans invested heavily in slave labor, and hardly any trade failed to utilize them. On the eve of the American Revolution, a visitor to New York complained that "it rather hurts an Europian eye to see so many negro slaves upon the streets." Even after the Revolution, with emancipation on the horizon, more than one-third of the membership of the city's General Society of Mechanics and Tradesmen held slaves.[7]

The movement of slave labor from the households of the gentry to the workshops of artisanry marked an important stage in the transformation of northern slavery. Some urban employers continued to view slaves as temporary substitutes for servant labor and reverted to servants or turned to free wage labor when they could, but others became wedded to slavery. Among the largest urban employers—particularly those connected to the maritime trades, like boat builders, sail makers, and rope spinners—the commitment to bonded labor deepened, perhaps because they had the most invested.

The presence of slaves in the workshops of the North, often practicing crafts that had previously been the province of white workers, free and unfree, drew increasingly noisy rebukes from those who felt the sting of slave competition. The complaints were loudest in New York City. In 1737 the city's free coopers petitioned against "the pernicious custom of breeding slaves to trades whereby the honest and industrious tradesmen [are] reduced to poverty for want of employ." Other like protests followed, and they were echoed throughout the northern colonies. But while some free craftsmen lamented slave competition, others relied heavily upon slave labor themselves, particularly when indentured labor was difficult to secure. In Philadelphia, artisans in every trade—both high and low—employed slaves in their shops. As in the slave societies to the south, slave men and women were an indispensable part of the economy.[8]

The expansion of slavery followed a similar trajectory in the countryside, eventually eclipsing that of the cities. Throughout the grain-producing areas of Pennsylvania, northern New Jersey, the Hudson Valley, and Long Island—the North's breadbasket—slavery spread swiftly during the eighteenth century, as farmers turned from white indentured servants to black slaves. By midcentury the transformation reached into parts of southern New England, especially the area around Narragansett Bay, where large slaveholders took on the airs of a planter class. In many of these places, slaves constituted as much as one-third of the labor force, and in some locations slaves composed more than half of the whole.

Chester County in southeast Pennsylvania provides an overview of the transformation. In the second decade of the eighteenth century less than 4 percent of Chester's decedents owned slaves, while more than 16 percent relied on servants. That balance shifted slowly in the years that followed, veiling the change. But between 1756 and 1763, when the Seven Years' War limited the availability of white indentured laborers, the switch from servants to slaves accelerated, becoming visible to even the most obtuse observer. Chester's slave population had swelled from under 300 to over 600. On the eve of the American Revolution, nearly one-fifth of decedents in Chester employed slave labor, while only one-tenth held servants.

Along the Maryland border as well, the slave population exploded; Lancaster County experienced an eight-fold increase between 1759 and 1780. With this rapid growth in the countryside, the proportion of the colony's slaves residing outside of Philadelphia increased from two-thirds in 1750 to three-quarters in 1760. There was no question which way the vectors of change were pointing. On the eve of the American Revolution, slavery in Pennsylvania would be fully identified with the countryside.[9] Slaves were no longer an adjunct to an agricultural economy based on family labor or white servitude but were the largest element in the rural labor force.

The growth of slavery in the mid-eighteenth century was even more profound in the Hudson River Valley, Long Island, and northern New Jersey, where farmers came to depend upon slave labor. By the middle of the eighteenth century, slave men outnumbered propertyless single white men 262 to 194 in Monmouth County, New Jersey. In the richer agricultural areas, the balance was even more skewed. Neighboring Middlesex County assessed 281 slave men and only 81 free wage workers, white and black; in Bergen County the count was 306 to 8. In a few smaller jurisdictions a black majority emerged, although countywide totals remained well below that mark.[10]

In replacing servants with slaves, northern farmers did not reorganize their productive system, as had occurred in the colonies to the south. Nor did the expansion of rural slavery transform the slaves' place within the working class, as it did in urban areas in the North. The new reliance on slavery did not create plantations nor inaugurate a system of gang labor. Slave workers in the agricultural North remained jacks-of-all-trades, engaging in all aspects of the northern agricultural regimen. They continued to labor in small groups in which indentured servants and wage workers, black and white, had a substantial presence. Their importance grew from the force of numbers, not from a change in kind—at least for slave men.[11]

While the labor of rural slave men conformed to the routine of free workers, the tasks assigned slave women did not. As the proportion of white servants declined, slave women migrated into domestic service. With the increased reliance on slave labor, slave women monopolized places in the kitchens and pantries of northern farmsteads. But even these women worked in the field part of the time, and Sojourner Truth's powerful iteration that she had "plowed and planted and gathered into barns, and no man could head me" rang true for eighteenth-century slave women throughout the North.[12]

With slaves everywhere in demand, importation increased. Slaves not only arrived in the North in greater numbers but they also comprised a larger share of the immigrant population. Between 1732 and 1754 black slaves made up fully one-third of the immigrants (forced and voluntary) reaching New York. In general, the slave trade expanded slowly during the early years of the eighteenth century, but given the minuscule size of the trade, even a small increase caused a stir. "We have *negroes* flocking in upon us since the duty on them is reduced," lamented one opponent of the slave trade in Philadelphia in 1720 following the Crown's revocation of the impost on slaves. But these modest increases were followed by more substantial ones, so that between 1757 and 1766 some 1,300 slaves disembarked in Philadelphia and on the wharves across the river in West Jersey. These totals hardly compared to the number of Africans arriving in Charles Town, where the annual influx exceeded Philadelphia's entire decade of extraordinary growth in new slaves. Nevertheless, the growth of the trade in Africans drove Philadelphia's slave population to its high point of nearly 1,400.[13]

As in the plantation colonies to the south, the character of the slave trade changed as its size increased. Northern merchants, who previously had accepted a handful of slaves on consignment, took shiploads, transforming the trade-in-persons from an incidental adjunct of the ongoing system of exchange to a systematic enterprise in and of itself. Moreover, slaves came directly from Africa, often in large numbers. Before 1741, 70 percent of the slaves arriving in New York originated in the Caribbean and other mainland colonies, and only 30 percent came directly from Africa. After that date, the proportions were reversed.[14]

Specializing in the slave trade, African slavers carried many times more slaves than did West Indian traders. Whereas slaves had earlier arrived in small parcels that rarely numbered more than a half dozen, direct shipments from Africa sometimes totaled over a hundred, and occasionally several times that. In the decade between 1755 and 1765, as Philadelphia merchants turned from the Caribbean to Africa for their slaves, African arrivals reached their highest level in history. In 1762 alone more than 500 slaves landed in Philadelphia in what one historian has called the city's "greatest infusion of African culture."[15]

Atlantic creoles, who made up the most visible portion of the first arrivals, could hardly be found among the newcomers. Even those slaves who arrived from the Caribbean or the mainland slave ports to the south had little experience in the New World. Transshipment of African slaves from the Caribbean was so swift as to make the West Indian layover little more than a short stop in the voyage between Africa and the northern colonies. Of the eighty slaves brought to Boston from Barbados in 1729, more than two-thirds had African names and only one-quarter Christian or English names of the sort that suggested New World origins.[16]

While the infusion of saltwater slaves into the Middle Colonies did not replace the polyglot labor force as it did in the Chesapeake and the lowcountry, the new Africans became an increasingly visible portion of the slave population. White men and women previously oblivious to the differences among black people became increasingly sensitive to the complex nature of African nationality. As in the lowcountry, slave traders not only distinguished between seasoned Caribbean slaves and Africans but among Africans themselves. A Pennsylvania master, speaking in a common parlance, observed his fugitive slave was "suppos'd to be as Whedaw Negroe," as she was "mark'd around the Neck with three Rows like Beads." When a boatload of "Gambia Slaves" arrived in Philadelphia in the spring of 1762, merchants hawked them as "much more robust and tractable than any other slaves from the Coast of Guinea, and more Capable of undergoing the Severity of Winters in the North-American Colonies."[17]

The African presence did more than enlarge the slave trader's stereotypes or provide an easy way for slaveholders to identify runaways. Africans, their faces often lined with tribal markings and their tongues laden with the languages of the continent, became the most visible element in the black population of the North. Of the fugitive slaves advertised in New York City's press between 1771 and 1805 and whose linguistic abilities were noted, more than one-quarter spoke English badly if at all. Africans replaced creoles not only in the centers of slavery's greatest growth but also in the peripheral areas like New England. As late as 1791, nearly 80 percent of the black vagabonds warned out of Boston were African born.[18]

Direct African importation transformed the black population in other ways as well. Viewing the influx of African slaves as substitutes for indentured European laborers, farmers and tradesmen naturally wanted them on the same terms. Indentured servants had generally arrived as young men without families, and slaves were imported in much the same manner. "For this market they must be young, the younger the better if not quite Children," declared a New York merchant in 1762. "Males are best." As a result, the sex ratio of the black population, which had earlier in the century achieved rough parity, swung heavily in favor of men. From virtual equality at the beginning of the eighteenth century, the sex ratio of New York's black population rose to 129 males for every 100 females in 1731 (for those over age 10) and 135 males for every 100 females in 1746 (for those over age 16). Elsewhere sex ratios of 130 or more became commonplace. In Boston, the ratio of males to females reached 169 in 1764.[19]

The impact of disease was also especially severe on newly imported African men and women, who had no exposure to the contagions of the New World—not even from a brief stop in the West Indies—or with the North's cold, damp winters. Ailments like measles and whooping cough, which Europeans sloughed off in childhood encounters, killed adult Africans by the hundreds. The deadly effect was compounded by poor diet, insufficient clothing, and inadequate shelter. Together, these disabilities pushed the death rate of slaves far above that of white men and women, especially in the cities where close living conditions promoted contagion. As African slaves proved unable to resist a whole new phalanx of microbes, their morbidity and mortality rocketed upward, creating a demographic disaster much like that which accompanied the plantation revolution in the colonies to the south. The crude death rate of black people in Boston and Philadelphia during the 1750s and 1760s was well over 60 per thousand, nearly one-third to one-half more than the death rate of white people. In 1763 more than one-quarter of the slaves who died in Boston were new arrivals. To insulate slaveholders from losses exacted by such an extraordinary death toll, Massachusetts lawmakers rebated the impost on slaves who perished within their first year in the colony.[20]

As the slaves' mortality rose, their fertility fell. The problem was not new. From the beginning of settlement, northern slaveholders, unlike their mainland counterparts to the south, showed little interest in creating an indigenous slave population and rejected even the reluctant concessions that planters in the Chesapeake and the lowcountry made to the slave family. The discomfort and expense of sharing their cramped quarters with slaves outweighed the profits offered by a labor force that reproduced itself. Northern slaveholders discouraged their slaves from marrying, by making it difficult for slave families to reside in the same abode. They routinely separated husbands from wives and parents from children, and only reluctantly extended visitation rights. Women with reputations for fecundity found few buyers, and some owners sold slave women at the first sign of pregnancy.

The unbalanced sex ratio and the higher mortality that accompanied the arrival of thousands of Africans threw additional obstacles in the path of slaves desirous of establishing families. An independent domestic life, which came so easily to the first black arrivals in New Amsterdam and was the hallmark of the charter generations throughout the North, became increasingly difficult for black northerners to sustain in the eighteenth century. Rural slaves worked in units so small that sharing a residence with their spouse and children was the exception rather than the rule in the countryside. Slaves resided in closer proximity in cities, but urban slaveholders rarely had space to lodge more than a few slaves, and large slaveholders either hired their slaves to others or allowed them to live on their own. Such practices may have increased the slaves' independence, but they constrained the development of residential family units. As in the countryside, slave husbands and wives, parents and children rarely lived in the same households in cities. Indeed, from the slaveholders' perspective there was no expectation that they should, and urban slaveholders—like their rural counterparts—routinely sold and traded family members with little consideration for the sanctity of the slaves' family life. A New Jersey owner, unusual for his solicitude, found it "most agreeable" to sell them as a unit, "they being man and wife." However, he added matter-of-factly, "a few miles separation will not prevent the sale." The absence of residential households diminished the chances of black men playing the role of the husband and father and black women the role of the wife and mother. Grandparenthood, given slave mortality, became unknown to most northerners of African descent. The attenuation of familial ties by distance and time, and the difficulties created by small work units, frequent sale, and meddlesome slaveowners made it difficult for slaves to maintain a normal family life by contemporary standards—whether colonial American, African, or European.[21]

Over the course of the eighteenth century, African-American domestic life fell into greater and greater disorder in the North. By the eve of the Revolution, slave women were having few children, and slaves' fertility fell to as low as one-half that of whites in some locations. Between 1767 and 1775 only 100 black children survived birth in Philadelphia, while the black community buried over 600 of its members.[22]

It was a vicious cycle. With deaths towering over births among young new arrivals and infants, slaves could not sustain their numbers; consequently, the weight of the black population fell toward the aged, who were too old, enfeebled, and disease-ridden to reproduce. Old people were susceptible to disease, and their susceptibility increased over time, for slaveowners exhibited no desire to provide medical support, food, clothing, and shelter for unproductive hands. Close observers like Benjamin Franklin understood that it would take "a continual Supply . . . from Africa" to maintain slavery. In its demographic outline, northern slavery at the middle of the eighteenth century bore a closer resemblance to the plantation colonies to the south half a century earlier than to the experience of the charter generations.[23]

The same forces that disrupted, distorted, and degraded slave family life also narrowed the slaves' avenues to freedom. With the heightened commitment to slavery, northern lawmakers obstructed the slaveholders' right to free their slaves. Although the first limitations on the right of manumission in the North dated from the seventeenth century, the thicket of restrictions grew over time. During the eighteenth century, New York, Pennsylvania, New Jersey, and then the New England colonies curbed manumission by requiring slaveholders to post heavy bonds for the good conduct of former slaves and to support those who fell to public charity.[24] Slaveholders, desperate for labor, needed few such obstacles to discourage them from donning the emancipator's garb. Few did. During the sixty-five years between 1698 and 1763, only ninety slaves were manumitted in Philadelphia; the number in New York was even smaller. Aged and sickly, many of these men and women were released by owners who had effectively emancipated themselves from the support of laborers they deemed nonproductive.[25]

Manumission restrictions had their effect. The old free black population, with its origins in the first generation of Atlantic creoles, withered, and few slaves exited bondage. The proportion of black people enjoying freedom in the North slipped. At the time New Amsterdam fell to the English in 1664, about one-fifth of the city's black population was free. No similar count was made in the century that followed, but fragmentary evidence indicates that free blacks in eighteenth-century New York did not regain that proportion until after the Revolution. New York City's experience was probably not in any way exceptional for urban slaves. In rural areas, the proportion of free black people shrank even further than in the cities. A generous estimate of the percentage of black people enjoying freedom in Monmouth County, New Jersey, is 3 percent. Moreover, the release of elderly, enfeebled slaves skewed the free black population toward the aged, so that the proportion of free blacks was not only smaller but also less able to compete in the vigorous northern economy than had been the previous generation of free blacks.[26]

As the free black population shrank, its prosperity waned, and white northerners slipped into the practice of equating bondage with blackness. Northern lawmakers reinforced that presumption by circumscribing the liberty of free blacks. In various northern colonies, free blacks were barred from voting, attending the militia, sitting on juries, testifying in court, and holding property. In various places, free blacks were required by law to carry special passes to travel, trade, and keep a gun or a dog. They were judged in special courts, along with slaves, and for certain offenses they could be punished like slaves. Often the punishment meted out to free blacks drove them back into bondage, as the Pennsylvania law enslaved those free blacks found to be without regular employment, and who "loiter[ed] and misspen[t]" their time.[27]

If not quite a slave society, the North—particularly the Middle Colonies—was no longer merely a society with slaves. During the middle years of the eighteenth century, one northern colony after another updated, refined, or consolidated the miscellaneous laws that had been passed during the seventeenth century and issued more comprehensive slave codes. While reorganizing and recapitulating the old legislation, colonial lawmakers took the opportunity to strengthen the hand of the slaveowner at the expense of the slave. Among the casualties of the new regulations was the slaves' economy, which came under ever tighter oversight. New York lawmakers, in an action that typified many northern colonies, again barred slaves from trading independently and punished free persons who "Trade or Traffic with any slave" with a fine of triple the value of the goods at issue plus a fine of £5. Lawmakers took special aim at slaves who oystered and peddled them from carts and stalls.[28]

Slaves frequently ignored the law, sometimes with the open connivance of their owners. But if some northern slaveholders were flexible and indulgent, the social order they supported was not. Nothing revealed this more dramatically than the names by which slaves were called. The Africans who entered the North in the eighteenth century were branded—as one abolitionist noted—by their owners "with such like Names they give their Dogs and Horses." Comic, classic appellations became as commonplace in the slave quarters of the North as in the plantation colonies to the south. Moreover, unlike the charter generations, the northern slave population of the eighteenth century rarely had two names, just as they rarely registered their marriages, baptized their children, or held property of any sort. Indeed, some places barred black people from the ownership of property altogether.[29] Rather than hold property, they *were* property, and little more.

As the North took on the trappings of a slave society, northern slaves turned inward. Manifestations of this transformation took two forms: first, an explosive thrust to cast off the weight of bondage—most prominently in New York in 1741; and, failing that, a determined effort to recast life in bondage.[30]

Resistance took a variety of forms. While creoles and other members of the charter generations moved quickly to Europeanize their names, adopting English or, in New Netherland, Dutch names, African arrivals struggled to maintain the touchstones of their homeland. When Quasho Quando's owner attempted to rename him Julius Caesar, Quando simply refused to accept the new identifier—despite his owner's threats, promises, and additional threats.[31] Similarly, whereas the charter generations had connived to gain admission to Christian churches to formalize their marriages and baptize their children, the new arrivals kept their distance from the Cross. Missionaries attracted few slaves, especially in the rural North. Taking office in Monmouth County in 1745 with a determination to bring black people into the fold, the Reverend Thomas Thompson, a former dean at Oxford, baptized only thirteen slaves before he left New Jersey on an African mission five years later. Other missionary-minded Anglicans also found "those born in Guinea strangely prepossessed in favor of superstition and Idolatry." Christian evangelicals, who made their first appearance in the North during the 1740s, fared little better, until the American Revolution. Even in New England, where a tradition of catechizing slaves developed, few slaves converted. In 1772 a Congregational minister who entertained "a very full and serious Meeting of Negroes . . . Perhaps 80 or 90" in his Newport, Rhode Island, residence reported that only "perhaps 26, and not above 30," blacks professed a belief in Christ, although the city had a black population of well over a thousand. Schools for slaves opened by Anglican missionaries and prayer meetings organized by pious women fared no better. Converts were few in number, and most of those derived from a select group of domestics whose owners were among the wealthiest, best-placed men and women. The privileged positions of these slaves gave them reason to see advantage in conversion, a view shared by few other black people.[32]

Outside this small circle of privileged bondsmen and women, slaves viewed Christianity with all of the suspicion and hostility due the religion of the owning class. The defiant opposition, if not contempt, of the mass of black people and their dedication to African practices frustrated and angered missionaries, who condemned African ways as superstition.

Perhaps even more lamentable from the cleric's perspective than their refusal to embrace Christianity, black northerners drew upon Africa in structuring their domestic relations. Polygamy persisted. An Anglican chaplain in New York maintained that black people shunned Christianity "because of their polygamy contracted before baptism where none or neither of the wives also will accept divorce." The commitment to multiple wives became a point of conflict between black New Yorkers and Elias Neau, who, by his own admission, repelled potential converts "because they know that I often insist on the 7th commandment, and that I thunder against polygamy."

The slaves' callous disregard for the possibilities of everlasting glory might have been accepted as merely additional evidence of African ignorance, had not their continued reliance on African religion been proved subversive. The investigation of the 1712 New York revolt revealed it had been instigated by "a free Negro who pretended to sorcery" and who gave the rebels "a powder to rub on their clothes to make them invulnerable." Less than one-tenth of the black population of New York City subscribed to Christianity after more than three decades of proselytization. The proportion was doubtless smaller in the rural North.[33]

The rejection of Christianity was just one manifestation of the reorientation of black culture stimulated by the importation of African slaves. Newly arrived Africans, although a minority of black society, had a powerful effect on the native black population, infusing it with knowledge of Africa and African ways. Sometimes it was just the presence of African men and women walking the streets of northern cities and the byways of the northern countryside, bearing ritual scars and speaking the language of a land most black northerners knew only from second- and third-hand accounts. At other times, newly arrived Africans reawakened black Americans to their African past by providing direct knowledge of west African society. In 1769 "Congamochu, alias Squingal" "talked much of his wives, and country" before he ran off.[34]

African Americans soon began to combine their African inheritance with their own evolving culture. In some measure, the easy confidence of white northerners in their own dominance speeded the synchronization of African and creole cultures by allowing black men and women to act far more openly than slaves in the plantation colonies. Black northerners incorporated African ways in the silent and unconscious way that generally characterizes the transit of culture. In Andover and Plymouth, Massachusetts, black people employed construction methods reminiscent of west Africa, designing their homes in the traditional African twelve-foot pattern, rather than the sixteen-foot lengths common to Anglo-American houses. Black northerners were often highly conscious of their African connections. They called themselves Sons of Africa, and adopted African forms to maximize their independence, to choose their leaders, and in general to give shape to their lives.[35]

To be sure, the Africanization of the northern colonies also created new fissures within black society. From their diverse experiences, Africans and African Americans frequently evinced different aspirations from one another, and their life-chances—as reflected in their resistance to disease and their likelihood of establishing families—also diverged sharply. Fragmentary evidence suggests that such differences had long existed in the North, and that the greater visibility of Africans merely sharpened them.[36] But Africans were too few in number to stand apart for long. Whatever conflicts these differences created, white northerners paid such distinctions little heed. The propensity of white northerners to lump black people together mitigated intraracial differences. Indeed, compared with the mélange of English, Scotch-Irish, Germans, Dutch, Swedes, French Huguenots, and Sephardic Jews who constituted the North's European populace, men and women of African descent had much in common. Rather than permanently dividing black people, the entry of Africans into northern society gave new direction to African-American culture.

This new African influence was manifested most fully in the emergence of a variety of festivals—Negro Election Day in New England and Pinkster Day in New York and New Jersey. These celebrations featured fetes of ritual role reversals of the sort that were common throughout Africa and Europe, and their emergence in the northern colonies during the middle years of the eighteenth century doubtless owed much to their dual heritage.[37]

Both Election Day and Pinkster Day took a variety of forms, but everywhere they were times of great merrymaking that drew black people from all over the countryside. "All the various languages of Africa, mixed with broken and ludicrous English, filled the air, accompanied with the music of the fiddle, tambourine, the banjo, [and] drum," recalled an observer of the festival in Newport. Drawing upon their own resources and those of their owners, black men and women dressed in all manner of finery "with cues, real or false, heads pomatumed and powdered, cocked hat," paraded in horse and carriage, marched in formation, danced with "the most lewd and indecent gesticulation," and sang with "sounds of frightful dissonance." Although such garish sensuality offended some white men and women, it attracted others.[38]

The festival culminated with the election and inauguration of black kings, governors, and judges. In some places, this was accompanied by great ceremony. The new governor rode through town "on one of his master's horses, adorned with plaited gear, his aides on each side *á la militaire* . . . moving with a slow majestic pace." Occasionally, incumbents were escorted by black militiamen, "sometimes a hundred in number, marching sometimes two and two" and "an indefatigable drummer and fifer of eminence." Athletic contests, cockfights, games of chance, music, and "the most fatiguing dances" followed inauguration ceremonies.[39]

Newly elected kings and governors assumed symbolic power over the whole community and a measure of real power over the black community. During their term of office, black governors held court and adjudicated minor disputes, displaying their authority in a seeming release from bondage. Such role reversal, like similar status inversions in Africa and elsewhere, confirmed rather than challenged the existing order, but it also gave black people an opportunity to express themselves more fully than the narrow boundaries of slavery allowed.[40]

Both Election and Pinkster days also provided a mechanism for black people to recognize and honor their own notables. Black kings and governors were men of moment in the black community. Most already enjoyed elevated standing. Sometimes this derived from their connections to powerful slaveholders, hence their ability to underwrite the merrymaking. More commonly, however, their status originated in reputations for wisdom, respectability, or physical prowess. Elections often honored special achievements, and in the postrevolutionary era, black veterans frequently gained office. Significantly, a disproportionately large number of elected officials were native Africans. Like King Pompey of Lynn (Massachusetts), Prince Robinson of Narragansett (Rhode Island), and Tobiah and Eben Tobias of Derby (Connecticut), all claimed royal lineage that reached across the Atlantic.[41]

These celebrations established a framework for an African-American politics. Black people carefully defined their electorate and their leaders, upon occasion requiring property ownership or other evidence of material success. Candidates mustered their constituents and assured their friends of patronage. The black militias that escorted black governors also gained recognition, and in a few places they were allowed to drill on Training Day, the time set aside for military exercises. Negro Election Day and Pinkster Day shaped the political life of the black community and merged with partisan divisions of American society.

In the 1760s and 1770s the politics of Election and Pinkster days became enmeshed with the nascent conflict between the American colonies and British imperial authorities. That struggle, laced with the language of enslavement and liberation, sharpened the political consciousness of African and African-American slaves. As the conflict intensified, slaves began to formulate their own case for liberty. In Massachusetts, where slaves retained the right of petition and many other civil rights, they took their case directly to the General Court, reminding colonial legislators that they expected "great things from men who have made such a noble stand against the designs of their *fellow-men* to enslave them." Pointing to their own unfortunate condition, black petitioners informed colonial lawmakers: "We have no Property! We have no Wives! No children! We have no City! No Country!" but "in common with all other men we have a natural right to our freedoms." When their petitions received no hearing, they regrouped and petitioned again. The following year "a Grate Number of Blackes" renewed their call, again reminding lawmakers they had been "stolen from the bosoms of our tender Parents and from a Populous Pleasant and plentiful country and Brought hither to be made slaves for Life in a Christian land." Playing off the hypocrisy of slaveholding by the great advocates of liberty, black memorialists enumerated the effects of slavery: the destruction of family ties, the denial of religious freedom, and the limitation on economic advancement. From that perspective, Massachusetts slaves demanded not only immediate emancipation but also "some part of the unimproved land, belonging to the province, for a settlement, that each us may there sit down quietly under his own fig tree."[42]

Not all northern slaves articulated their positions in formal petitions, but the meaning of their actions seemed all too obvious to anxious slaveholders. In rural New Jersey, slaveholders found themselves beset by growing unrest among slaves, who let it be known that "it was not necessary to please their masters, for they should not have their masters long."[43]

As northern slaveholders stiffened their opposition to discussion of abolition, slaves directed their appeals to the British. In 1774 black men in Massachusetts offered their services to Thomas Gage, the British commander for North America. Declaring their willingness to fight alongside the king's soldiers in return for their liberty, they changed their tone from the supplication of the earlier memorials to one of entitlement to freedom. Rejecting enslavement, they declared themselves "a freeborn Pepel" who had never forfeited their "naturel right to . . . freedoms." After listing the deprivations of slavery, they urged the enactment of legislation to assure their liberation.[44]

Formal petitions were just the outcroppings of a larger movement toward freedom that grew out of the transformation of black life during the fifty years before the Revolution. Changes that had tipped the delicate balance toward a slave society at midcentury moved in the other direction at century's end, toward a society with slaves, reopening the possibilities for freedom. In some parts of the North, slaves initiated legal suits for their liberty. In other places, they bargained with their owners or simply fled. The unrest that surfaced in rumors of insurrections and in veiled threats that slaves would side with the British in any contest for empire suggests how the simultaneous maturation and politicization of African-American culture cleared the way for the refashioning of black life and the transformation of the North from a society with slaves to a free society.

Chapter Eight

Stagnation and Transformation in the
Lower Mississippi Valley

↑

If the plantation revolution affected the northern colonies indirectly, it touched the lower Mississippi Valley—the colonies of Louisiana and West Florida—hardly at all. Following the Natchez revolt in 1729, the nascent plantation order unraveled, as the importation of Africans ceased and the great concessions fell into disarray. While the tobacco and rice revolutions were transforming the seaboard colonies in quick order, Louisiana continued its devolution from a slave society to a society with slaves. The slave trade abruptly ended, the headlong rush to create a plantation-based society faltered, and a polyglot labor force replaced the African majority in the lower Mississippi Valley. By midcentury a native-born black population had emerged, and, most importantly, some black people began to exit slavery.

As the slaveholders' economy faded, the slaves' economy flourished. Black people, slave and free, became full participants in the system of exchange that developed within the lower Mississippi Valley, trading the produce of their gardens and provision grounds, the fruits of their hunting and trapping expeditions, and a variety of handicrafts with European settlers and Indian tribesmen. The independence provided by the slaves' economy was reinforced by the expanding role of black men in Louisiana's militia. Playing off the European-Americans' vulnerability to foreign invasion and domestic insurrection, black militiamen gained special standing fighting the white man's battles—sometimes figuratively, often literally. As soldiers in behalf of the French and later the Spanish Crown, slave and free black warriors not only tamed European interlopers and hostile Indians but also disciplined plantation slaves and captured runaways. In the process, they became a political, cultural, and sometimes a physical extension of European-American society. However grossly discriminated against, their service in the white man's cause enabled them to inch up the colony's social ladder, and the free black population began to grow. In the failed attempt of the French to create a plantation society, the heritage of the charter generations gained a new life.

Although the Natchez rebellion and the Samba Bambara conspiracy neither ousted the French nor abolished slavery in Louisiana, they dramatically altered the course of African-American life in the lower Mississippi Valley. The French Crown stripped the Company of the Indies of its control of Louisiana, severing the ties between Africa and the lower Mississippi Valley. After 1731 only one African slaver arrived in Louisiana until the Spanish—who took formal control of Louisiana from their French ally in 1763, at the end of the Seven Years' War—reopened the slave trade in the 1770s. Although West Indian slaves continued to dribble into the colony through the ongoing trade with the sugar islands, their numbers were never substantial. Other slaves entered the region through Anglo-American settlements in West Florida, which also changed hands in 1763, from Spain to Britain. New arrivals from the Antilles—especially Saint Domingue and Jamaica—and from the mainland enlarged and diversified the slave population. But taken as a whole it remained small, insular, and indigenous to the lower Mississippi Valley. The close of the slave trade cut Louisiana planters off from new African laborers and Louisiana slaves off from direct knowledge of Africa, accelerating the process of creolization.[1]

The transfer of Louisiana from France to Spain under the first Treaty of Paris in 1763 promised to transform the slave trade in the lower Mississippi Valley. Determined to increase the slave population as a means of assuring the prosperity of their new colony, Spanish authorities broke with their protectionist past and allowed several boatloads of slaves to enter the colony from Jamaica and elsewhere in the Caribbean during the early 1770s. But the weight of Spanish mercantilism, fear of Yankee interlopers, and finally the outbreak of the American Revolution (as Spain entered the contest against Britain, along with France) stymied the Spanish policymakers and frustrated planters eager to enlarge their labor force. Not until the 1780s, when American merchants took de facto control of Louisiana's trade, did the number of slave imports increase substantially.[2]

The absence of a ready supply of slaves in the half century between the 1730s and the 1780s forced planters to reconsider their system of

labor recruitment and to reorganize production. While they did not surrender their commitment to chattel bondage or their desire to expand the
colony's tobacco and indigo fields, Louisiana planters could no longer
depend upon the slave trade to sustain and replenish their workforce.
If the colony's laboring population was to grow—or even maintain itself—planters understood they would have to create an indigenous slave
population by moderating the demands of plantation labor and allowing
slaves to establish families.

Such a policy was most fully articulated by Antoine-Simon Le Page
Du Pratz, a Swiss national appointed by the French Crown to direct the
plantations formerly under the control of the Company of the Indies. Du
Pratz proposed a traditional social order in which the mutuality of superiors and inferiors bound masters and slaves together in a community of
interest. He urged slaveholders to surrender the harsh regimen that had
characterized slavery in Louisiana prior to the Natchez revolt and instead
to provide their slaves with sufficient food, clothing, and shelter. When
slaves come home, he lectured Louisiana planters, "caress them . . . give
them something good to eat, with a glass of brandy . . . give them something to sleep on and a covering . . . Take care of them when they are sick
and give attention both to their remedies and their food . . . It is your
interest so to do," Du Pratz emphasized, "both for their preservation,
and to attach them more closely to you." Du Pratz had no doubts about
the eventual triumph of superior European civilization and Catholic religion, and therefore he was willing to allow slaves a large measure of
economic and cultural independence lest they be "undone" by the rigors
of servitude in the lower Mississippi Valley and the trauma of separation
from their native land. He encouraged planters to respect the slaves'
domestic arrangements, religious rituals, and other practices that Europeans usually condemned as uncivilized. To promote domestic responsibility among the slaves, he also urged planters to provide garden plots
where slave men and women could supplement their diet and, perhaps,
produce a little extra that might be traded to improve their material
condition.[3]

Although there is no evidence that planters heard Du Pratz's words,
they adopted his proscription, if only because the changes unleashed by
the Natchez rebellion left them no choice. To improve the circumstances
of their slaves, planters replaced barracks with small outbuildings, giving
the slave quarter a village-like appearance, much like slave compounds in

lowcountry South Carolina and Georgia.[4] To encourage family formation, planters provided a setting in which slave men and women could
join together, and they eased the slaves' workload—particularly that of
women, so that pregnancies might be carried to term. Slaveholders also
showed a new interest in the slaves' spiritual well-being. To remove the
stain of African barbarism and to save black souls, some planters allowed
Capuchin missionaries to solemnize slave marriage and baptize slave
children, not in the manner of the mass baptisms of the first arrivals but
in church ceremonies with owners in full participation. Although there is
no evidence that state authorities enforced the *Code Noir*'s long-ignored
strictures against the separation of husbands and wives or the sale of
children under fourteen from their parents, some highly placed officials,
including the governor, witnessed the marriages of their slaves, which
gave the slave family a new legitimacy. During the 1730s slave marriages
appeared with increasing regularity in parish registers. Ursuline nuns
schooled a handful of slave children, and planters began to stand in as
their godparents.[5]

Slaves took advantage of the new circumstances and joined together
as man and wife. With increased frequency, inventories listed men and
women as couples and women as "*sa femme.*" Before long, the black
population began to increase by natural means. By the 1740s the difference between the African-American creole majority in Louisiana and the
African-born population in the sugar islands had become a matter of
common knowledge among French authorities on both sides of the Atlantic. "This species survives almost entirely by procreation," one official
wrote from New Orleans in 1741. "In effect, among the approximately
4,000 blacks of all types and ages, two thirds are Creole. That is the
difference between this country and the French West Indies where there is
very little natural reproduction among slaves."[6] Fueled by natural increase, the black majority grew steadily—if slowly—in the years that
followed, while the white population stagnated. By 1746, estimates of the
white population of Louisiana stood at 3,200, while black people—almost all slaves—numbered 4,730. During the next two decades, as Louisiana's population expanded, its racial balance remained unchanged. At
the time of Louisiana's accession to Spain in 1763, there were under 6,000
black slaves in the lower Mississippi Valley—almost all of them native
born.[7]

Crucial to the slaves' success in reproducing themselves and establishing a distinctive African-American culture was the stagnation of the colony's economy during the middle years of the eighteenth century. After the Natchez rebellion, Louisiana slaveholders continued to grow tobacco for export, but without notable success. European markets preferred the Chesapeake leaf, and the loss of subsidies for tobacco that followed the demise of the Company of the Indies reduced the planters' profits to near invisibility.[8] By contrast, indigo production boomed during the late 1740s and 1750s, and the blue dye became the colony's most lucrative export. But only the largest planters had the capital to enter the indigo trade. The number of indigo plantations in Louisiana never exceeded sixty during the period of French rule. Even in its best years, Louisiana indigo faced competition from Guatemala and South Carolina. When the outbreak of the Seven Years' War in 1756 disrupted trade, the indigo boom collapsed, deflating the plantation economy. Production of tobacco and indigo revived at war's end with the encouragement of the colony's new rulers, who subsidized the crops and protected their markets within the Spanish empire. Still, Louisiana's export economy remained subject to fluctuations caused by international warfare and internal instability.[9]

The failure of the export economy stifled the development of the plantation. Rather than penetrating the backcountry and spreading evenly through the countryside, the population hovered around the port of New Orleans. In 1763 fully one-third of the white population and one-quarter of the black population of Louisiana resided in and around the capital city, and an even larger proportion of both lived within a day's boat ride of the city.[10] The tight confines of the plantation region and the close proximity of New Orleans gave most slaves access to and knowledge of the colonial port.

As the century progressed, slavery in the lower Mississippi Valley increasingly became an urban-centered institution, as in many other societies with slaves. Whereas slavery in the lowcountry, the Chesapeake, and even the northern colonies migrated from the cities to the countryside and became identified with agricultural production during the eighteenth century, the trend was just the opposite in the lower Mississippi Valley. Slaveownership became nearly universal among propertied European Americans in New Orleans, and some 60 percent of all households included slaves at the time of the Spanish accession. Although that figure declined as the city swelled with free immigrants at century's end, a 1788 census indicated a high concentration of slaveownership in the Mississippi's great port.[11]

New Orleans became the center for slave life in the lower Mississippi Valley. Although black people did not achieve numerical dominance until later in the century, by the 1740s they played a large role in the life of the city, not only performing all the heavy work to maintain its wharves and warehouses but also a good deal of the skilled labor. Black life in eighteenth-century New Orleans took on the familiar features of urban slavery elsewhere on the continent. The slaveholding units were small, with slaves crammed into dingy attics and dank cellars. Slave husbands and wives rarely had the opportunity to dwell within a single household, and everyone—men, women, and children—found it difficult to escape the watchful eye of master and mistress, at least within the household. But if life within the masters' house was close, the streets were open. Slaves mixed easily with Native-American traders, European merchants and planters, and sailors and dockside roustabouts whose racial origins defied categorization. They lived out and hired their own time. Urban slaves in the lower Mississippi Valley maintained their ties to the Atlantic, and they developed connections which reached into the interior—for the riverine plantations were but a short canoe ride away. The cosmopolitan universe of Atlantic creoles was easy to reproduce in the streets and back alleys of New Orleans.[12]

The growing urban focus also reflected developments in the countryside. As the market for Louisiana's tobacco and indigo waxed and waned, planters turned to the production of lumber, naval stores, and cattle. These commodities found a far readier reception in Saint Domingue, Martinique, and other Caribbean islands than either of the old standbys, although they never generated the level of return that planters hoped would accompany staple production. In the absence of bonanza profits, agriculture became less a way of making money—big money— and more a means of gaining a competency. Planters and farmers rested their livelihood on a broad mix of crops, stock raising, and logging. Absenteeism declined. Although the largest owners maintained residences in New Orleans, nearly all spent some time on their estates. At the time of the cession of Louisiana to Spain, the resident master had become ubiquitous. Almost universally, these owners directed their plantation operations through black overseers or *commandeurs*—only five white overseers were listed in the 1763 census.[13] The managerial hierarchy of owner, steward, overseer, driver or foreman—which was becoming synonymous with plantation life in the Chesapeake and lowcountry—had no counterpart in the lower Mississippi Valley at midcentury.

In the absence of a staple commodity of the kind that induced planters elsewhere in the Americas to drive slaves to the limit, the harsh regime of former years mellowed. Freed from devotion to a single crop and unconfined by the narrow alternatives of plantation life, slaves worked at a variety of trades. When one Louisiana planter described his slave as "a black-smith, mason, cooper, roofer, strong long sawyer, mixing with these a little of the rough carpentry with the rough joinery," no one thought this bondsman unusual.[14] Many slaves—particularly slave men—moved from the fields to the forest, where they felled the great cyprus, hewed shingles, collected pitch and tar, and tended cattle and various draft animals. Lumbering and cattle raising were exhausting and dangerous, to be sure, but they allowed slaves to work at their own pace far from their owners' eyes.

Other aspects of the new work regimen operated to the slaves' advantage. Slave lumbermen, many of them hired out for short periods of time, carried axes and, like slave drovers and herdsmen, were generally armed with knives and guns—necessities for men who worked in the wild and hunted animals for food and furs. Many men had access to horses, as did cowherds and drovers who tended cattle and swine. Periodic demands that slaveowners disarm their slaves and restrict their access to horses and mules confirmed what many believed to be dangerous practices but did nothing to halt them.[15] In short, slave lumbermen and drovers were not to be trifled with. Their work allowed considerable mobility and latitude in choosing their associates and bred a sense of independence from planter domination. Slaves found it a welcome relief from the old plantation order.

Slaves also found employment and a measure of independence in the cartage trades, particularly as boatmen and canoers. The Company of the Indies had employed them in this role from the first, hoping to "diminish the naval expenses every day by making only blacks, and a few white men, sailors." The number of black boatmen increased during the eighteenth century along with trade on the Mississippi. Like lumbermen and cowherds, the carrying trade gave slaves a good deal of freedom, familiarizing them with the countryside and placing them in close contact with Indians, who also plied the waterways.[16]

In the absence of a staple-based economy, planters turned to the production of foodstuffs for internal consumption and sometimes for export, first to Saint Domingue and Martinique and later to Mexico and Cuba. Cutting costs, they encouraged and sometimes required slaves to feed themselves and their families by gardening, hunting, and trapping on their own time. Indeed, some slaveholders demanded their slaves also clothe themselves and purchase other necessities. Such requirements stoked the slaves' economy, forcing slaveowners to cede their slaves a portion of their time to work independently on the Lord's Day. "It is because the slaves are not clothed that they are left free of all work on Sunday," argued one advocate in an affirmation of the slaves' right to maintain gardens, market produce, and work independently on Sunday. "On such days some of them go to the neighbors' plantations who hire them to cut moss and to gather provisions. This is done with the tacit consent of their masters who do not know the where-abouts of their slaves on the said day, nor do they question them, nor do they worry themselves about them and are always satisfied that the negroes will appear again on the following Monday for work."[17]

With the promise of such independence—the right to travel freely, earn money from overwork, hire themselves out, and sell the products of their own labor—slaves accepted the burden of subsisting themselves. Without relinquishing their claim to a regular allowance from their owner, plantation slaves established substantial gardens and raised barnyard fowl, crafted baskets and pottery, and hunted and fished. Eager to enrich the family diet and gain still greater control over their own lives, slaves pressed their owners to expand the time they could spend working for themselves. By midcentury, according to one account, slaves labored independently for as much as three of the thirteen hours of daylight in addition to Sundays. Some slaves gained Saturdays as well. Others worked long into the evening so they could extend their noontime break. "In this way," according to a Spanish officer, "they have time to attend for a short while to their crops and to their poultry, hogs, etc."[18]

Although planters permitted, even encouraged, the development of the slaves' economy, they, their church, and their state continued to view the independence it allowed slaves with trepidation. Clerics objected to slaves working on the Lord's Day. Again and again, they insisted that the seventh day be given over to prayer, not labor. To the Catholic hierarchy, it mattered not who benefited from the slaves' work.[19] Civil authorities supported these objections, reminding planters that the *Code Noir* obliged slaves to observe Sunday and other holy days and specified punishments for owners who forced—or even allowed—their slaves to labor on the Lord's Day. Indeed, the *Code* forbade slaveowners from substituting free days for rations and discouraged slaveholders from allowing slaves to work after hours.[20]

Official disfavor did not stop with the *Code Noir*. In 1751 the Superior Council, which had evolved from the chief judicial body into the colony's legislature, enacted a host of regulations barring slaves from marketing, and punishing them, their owners, and others involved in transactions with slaves. The new regulations cast a wide net, but they took careful aim at the practice of forestalling, whereby aggressive slave marketers intercepted goods before they were placed on sale, withheld them from the market, and then sold them at extortionate prices. Following accession to Spain, the Cabildo—the new municipal government in New Orleans—added its weight to old regulations by enacting legislation that incorporated many of the features of the French law. Under Spain, the regulation of the slaves' economic activities did not change substantially.[21]

But clerical and secular injunctions were poor guides to the realities of slavery in the lower Mississippi Valley. And, as elsewhere in mainland North America, laws governing the slaves' independent economic activities were rarely enforced and often openly flouted. Indeed, the repeated passage of similar statutes reveals their ineffectiveness and suggests the primacy of custom over the rule of law. In a close judicial inspection of the slaves' independent economic activities, both plaintiff and defendant conceded the slaves' customary right to work on their own behalf.[22]

Slaveholders respected, even promoted, the slaves' customary rights, but only to their own advantage. If buying and selling on an open market gave slaves a measure of independence, slaveholders considered it a convenient and sometimes profitable way to defray expenses. For the master, the slaves' free time was no right, and the slaves' property had no standing. Instead, slaveowners insisted that the slaves' petty enterprises were privileges, granted at the owners' pleasure and, as slaves occasionally discovered, revoked at the owners' pleasure. To affirm their own preeminence in these matters, slaveholders periodically reasserted their claims. In the late 1760s, perhaps stirred by rising indigo prices, a planter in Natchitoches "established new methods [of production], and took away

the slaves' Saturdays which formerly they had spent tending to their
own needs, such as food and chores." His slaves petitioned the planter's
mother-in-law, apparently a figure of some importance on the estate. The
appeal provided no relief, and when the planter "promised fifty lashes to
the first who complained . . . the complaints stopped"—at least for the
moment.[23]

Still, slaves took what they could get, and in the process gained just
what the master denied: a modicum of independence and a better life
for themselves and their families. As slaves expanded control over their
own time, they also enlarged their spatial domain. On many plantations, slaves not only secured the right to raise garden vegetables and
keep barnyard fowl but also to maintain provision grounds on marginal
lands along the edges of the owners' estates. "Most of the slaves clear the
grounds and cultivate them on their own account," noted one visitor to
eighteenth-century Louisiana, "raising cotton, tobacco, etc., which they
sell," sometimes in competition with their owners. On one plantation,
slaves maintained a barn of their own in which to store their produce.[24]

Slaves hiring themselves on their own time found a ready market
for their services in the labor-short Louisiana economy. Slaves took to
jobbing, laboring at nights and at odd hours in the forest, collecting
pitch and moss, and hewing logs for mill operators and slaveless farmers.
"Some [planters] give their negroes Saturday and Sunday to themselves,
and during that time the master does not give them any food," reported
yet another visitor to Louisiana, "they have them to work for other
Frenchmen who have no slaves, and who pay them."[25] In creating their
own economies, slaves built upon a system of petty exchange and occasional labor that had long been the province of the Native-American
population in the lower Mississippi Valley. As the tribal population
shrank and retreated in the face of the growth of the European-American
settlement, slaves and free blacks took over much of this trade, often in
association with Indians, some of whom in fact were slaves. They hunted
together, traded together, exchanged knowledge of the forests and fisher-
ies, and much else. Men and women of African descent intermarried with
native peoples, so that trading connections within the black community
reached into both European and Native-American societies.[26]

The routine nature of these transactions gave them a legitimacy that
transcended custom. When the issue came to court in Louisiana, the
argument that "in this colony it is known that a negro may, at his free

will, dispose of all day Sunday so as to make provisions for themselves by working for the neighbors and to gain the wherewith to clothe himself" swept away all challenges. Planters even denied clerical injunctions that slaves attend church, and instead contended "it would be idleness and dangerous to public welfare if a slave should be left on his plantation without any work." By the last quarter of the eighteenth century, the slaves' ability to work independently was so well entrenched that slaves on one plantation struck when they were not paid for their Sunday work. Simply put, "It was not practiced and not the custom for the negroes to ask the permission of their masters for what they should do on Sunday."[27]

Slaveholders also gave the slaves' property de facto recognition by paying slaves for commodities they had produced on their own time and de jure recognition by protecting their property in court against theft. The slaveowners' actions deepened the slaves' sense of proprietorship over the fruits of their own labor. In 1775, when the commander of the Spanish fort at Pointe Coupée expropriated the horses of two slave men whose nocturnal rambles had become notorious, the slaves fled to New Orleans to place their complaint before the highest officials in the colony. The commander assured his superiors that the proceeds from the sale of the horses would be used to repair the fort and urged that the slaves be punished in an exemplary manner. But before long the fugitives were back in Pointe Coupée boasting that they had prevailed, and the embarrassed commander was left to pen long letters of explanation. A year later, when a new officer took control at Pointe Coupée, he found the problem was not slave-owned horses but slaves with guns.[28]

As throughout mainland North America, the slaves' modest prosperity attracted a host of traders, shopkeepers, and peddlers—both Native-American and European—who were eager to exchange their wares for those that the slaves produced.[29] Small crossroads taverns and groceries sprang up to purchase those wares, but slaves preferred to sell their goods themselves, generally in the bustling market at the great entrepôt of the Mississippi Valley, New Orleans, and its satellites of Mobile and Pensacola.

Urban slaves developed an even more vigorous independent economy than did rural folk. Their labor—women as domestics and marketers, men as laborers, teamsters, boatmen, and artisans—allowed city-based slaves to expand their economic activities into all corners of urban life. In 1774 the court set aside a challenge to the slaves' independent economic activity, noting that it had long been "a custom, use and style for all the Negroes . . . in the cities to work for themselves . . . without being obligated to pay anything to their masters." As usual, white competitors from the nonslaveholder ranks, disenchanted slaveowners, and literal-minded officials continued to voice opposition. An occasional crackdown—when long-ignored laws were enforced suddenly and with a vengeance—revealed the fragility of the slaves' economy. But the importance of slave artisanry reduced such moments to little more than revelations of the contradictions of law and practice. The same Cabildo which had moved against slaves hiring themselves unanimously agreed to allow merchants to open their stores on Sunday so they could accommodate black customers. Likewise, the same court that ruled against slaves "rent[ing] themselves" qualified its approval "in the case of negroes such as blacksmiths, carpenters, et cetera, who are capable of carrying on their trades alone." Exceptions tended to prevail; once the moment had passed, authorities relaxed enforcement of restrictions new and old and slaves continued as before.[30]

Slaves found a great emporium for their labor and produce in New Orleans. The city's population had grown slowly in the middle years of the eighteenth century, reaching 3,000 on the eve of accession to Spain. Black people made up less than half of that number, but their ranks were growing and they would soon constitute a majority.[31] Although required by law to obtain passes to enter and leave New Orleans, slaves from throughout the colony traveled to the city to sell their produce and services on their own account. "Those who live in or near the capital," reported an acute observer of slave life in Louisiana, "generally turn their two hours at noon to account by making faggots to sell in the city; others sell ashes, or fruits that are in season." Officials continued to grouse about the role of slave marketers; but in 1784, when the Cabildo established a regular market in New Orleans, it was quick to assure all that slaves could peddle their wares as before.[32]

Slaves who worked the wharves and the streets of the port cities or who visited its markets carried away much besides a few sols or pesos earned from peddling their chickens and eggs. Market day broke the isolation of rural life and became a social occasion of the first rank. Free from the direct oversight of an owner or *commandeur*, plantation slaves mixed openly among themselves and with the black residents of the city, selling and trading goods and gossip. Once the haggling had ended, the merriment began. Dressed in their best attire, some pious men and women headed directly for the cathedral that dominated the city's main square. But others gravitated to drink, dance, and game. In the rear of the city, away from the river, a regular rendezvous developed on the site of the slaves' Sunday Market. *Place de Nègres,* later called "Congo Square," soon became a gathering spot where black people celebrated their African past.[33]

Urban slaves did not segregate themselves on market day. As in Charles Town and Savannah, Philadelphia and New York, "white and black, free and slave," according to one observer, "mingled indiscriminately" in New Orleans and the other Gulf ports. If white sailors, tradesmen, and market women who met together in taverns and cafés sometimes flaunted the prerogatives of a white skin, their own lowly position suggested that pigmentation itself commanded few privileges. Like black slaves, they had no great affection for the planter class.[34] While their confabs rarely went beyond the hard language of men and women whom life had used roughly, such chatter gave slaves a larger view of the world and perhaps a chance to contemplate a time when they would be slaves no more. The process of redefining their own interests, which began in their gardens and provision grounds, crystallized in market-day banter. Even when slaves left the market with no more in their pockets than when they arrived, they carried away ideas of incalculable worth.

The mixing of white and black sometimes went beyond conversation. As elsewhere on the mainland, slave women took control of the streets. For most, the trade in food was an outgrowth of their labor in the kitchens. But many found permanent employment in the market, earning the right to live independently by buying their time or sharing their profits with their owners.[35] Among the commodities slave women placed up for sale in the rough-and-tumble of the urban marketplace were their bodies. By midcentury, New Orleans and the other Gulf ports had developed reputations as sexually open cities, where relationships between white men and black women were not only tolerated but also accepted and occasionally celebrated. Officials opposed such interracial liaisons, and they were rarely legitimated in law under French or Spanish rule. But the peculiar demography of the Gulf ports—with their European population heavily weighted toward men and their African population heavily weighted toward women—encouraged white men and black women to join together in a variety of matches, licit and illicit. The presence of several hundred lonely, impoverished soldiers, along with dozens of sailors and boatmen and a continued stream of immigrant men, doubtless fueled the atmosphere of open sexuality. By the beginning of the nineteenth century, the city's stereotype of available and alluring women of color was in place.[36]

Others also recognized the commercial possibilities of selling sex. Before the end of the century, entrepreneurs began to promote mixed cotillions and masquerades, whose purposes were a matter of public scandal.[37] But interracial sex was not the exclusive preserve of the soldiers and sailors who, "failing in their duties [to enforce the ban], attend the dances dressed as civilians." Even men of high standing, complained one outraged cleric, lived "almost publicly with colored concubines." They "did not even 'blush'" when they carried their mixed-race descendants "to be recorded in the parochial registries as their *natural children*." But the prelate's exasperation was difficult to sustain when the director of the Capuchin's plantation kept a mixed-race housekeeper whose children called him "papa."[38]

In their willingness to recognize their black wives and mixed-race children, white men in the lower Mississippi Valley followed a pattern familiar in the Lower South. But the institutionalization of those relations went much further. By the end of the eighteenth century, the alliance of white men and black women—disallowed by law—was formalized under the name *plaçage*. Just short of marriage, the white suitor and the *plaçee's* mother (who by the end of the eighteenth century may herself have lived in a similar relationship) carefully negotiated the arrangement that assured free colored women a lifetime commitment, legitimate before all but church and state.[39] However achieved, interracial liaisons often propelled black women into places of significance, as their lovers and patrons supported their economic ventures in the market. By their numbers, their alliances with white men, and their economic successes, black women in the lower Mississippi Valley gained a strategic place in the region's cities.[40]

By midcentury, slaves in the lower Mississippi Valley—a largely creole group leavened by a sprinkling of African and Caribbean transplants—had begun to establish their own unique culture. That culture drew from Africa as well as Europe, the Caribbean, and Native America. It was most visible in the creole lingua franca that fused various African tongues with French and Native-American languages into a new language with an African grammatical structure and a French vocabulary. Describing the dialect employed to interrogate a group of slave conspirators, a French official called it "a mixture of the language of their nations and French pronounced with great diversity." Put to music, the new lingua franca could be heard in the sound that emanated from the *Place de Nègres*. And if the new culture could be heard, it also could be tasted in the rice-based cuisine, and seen in the distinctive style of dress. African beliefs manifested themselves in outcroppings of new religions, so much so that when the lawmakers of the Cabildo revised French slave law in 1777, they turned their attention from the suppression of heretical Protestants and Jews which had preoccupied the authors of the *Code Noir* to the expurgation of the "superstitious or foreign" rites brought to the lower Mississippi Valley by Africans.[41]

If slaveholders found advantages in the slaves' ability to subsist themselves, they despised and disparaged the new culture that the slaves' economic independence produced. They especially disliked the freedom with which slaves moved through the countryside and in and out of New Orleans. Certain that mobility promoted disorder and theft on a grand scale, planters denounced "the negroes of the town [who] come out at night . . . in order to assemble with those of the country, who come prowling through the town, to commit every kind of malfeasances." Periodically, they attempted to root out such enterprises, tightening regulations to control the slave population. Reassertion of the planters' authority, however, generally accompanied expansion in the staple economy. The sharp upturn in indigo prices during the 1740s and 1750s initiated one such effort. Planters who had invested in the vats and kilns that indigo required were unwilling to have their slaves wandering the countryside either to sell their produce in New Orleans or to visit with maroons in the swamps. They argued that black people, free and slave, should carry passes and be prohibited from riding horses and carrying guns, and that "country Negroes" should be forbidden "to assemble in the town of New Orleans . . . under any pretext whatsoever."[42] But such activities, and the racial and interracial camaraderie that accompanied them, proved impossible to eradicate as long as the urban merchants and city-bound planters needed the slaves' produce and services. The collapse of the indigo boom, combined with the beginning of the Seven Years' War, halted the new police efforts. With nothing to sell, with crops rotting in the fields, and with external enemies threatening the colony, planters and colonial officials realized they had little to gain from the strict enforcement of the new regulations.[43]

The failure to create a viable staple economy, a disciplined slave workforce, and a racial regime similar to that of Saint Domingue burdened the French in Louisiana. They transferred that burden to Spanish officials after 1763. Spanish authorities tried to reinvigorate the failing economy and win the support of suspicious francophone planters by systematically promoting immigration, subsidizing staple production, expanding trade, and enforcing slave discipline. Most importantly, Spain enlarged the bound workforce by reopening the slave trade. During the twenty years that followed Spain's arrival in the lower Mississippi Valley and England's takeover of West Florida, authorities progressively liberalized the regulations governing the slave trade, encouraging slave importation through tariff regulations and direct payment in specie.

The initial efforts bore some success. Immigrants from the Canary Islands and the Arcadian Coast accepted Spanish offers of cheap land, and Anglo-Americans embraced a similar deal from the British in West Florida. The new arrivals spurred staple production, particularly when aided by generous subsidies and protected markets. But free immigration slowed in the years prior to the American Revolution, and the beginning of war, in combination with imperial politics, stymied the hoped-for economic revival. The Spanish market proved no more receptive to Louisiana's exports than had the French market, and the number of slaves entering the colony increased only slightly during the 1760s and 1770s. In the end, the Spanish in Louisiana and the British in West Florida were no more successful than their predecessors at establishing an international staple economy. In 1777 a visitor affirmed the dominance of the local exchange economy over the international staple economy by observing that "the inhabitants neglect agriculture and generally employ themselves hunting and fishing."[44]

Rather than winning the loyalty of French planters, the efforts of Spanish authorities only increased the planters' estrangement. During the 1760s the colony's new rulers discovered that their greatest enemy was not the unruly slaves they hoped to discipline but the disenchanted planters they hoped to befriend. The open disaffection of the planter class drew the attention of Spanish authorities away from the slaves, leaving slaves pretty much on their own. The distinctive African-American culture that had emerged in post-Natchez Louisiana continued to grow under Spain, and with it the possibility that slaves might use the wealth garnered from their independent economic activities to free themselves.

Even in failure, the Natchez revolt had enlarged the free black population. Drawing on their experience in quelling the rebellion, the French had incorporated black men into Louisiana's defense force and had called upon them whenever the colony was threatened by powerful Indian confederations, European colonial rivals, or slave insurrectionists. On each such occasion—be it the Chickasaw war of the 1730s, the Choctaw war of the 1740s, or the threatened British invasion of the 1750s—French officials had mobilized black men, free and slave, with slaves sometimes offered freedom in exchange for military service. By 1739 at least 270 men of color were under arms in Louisiana, including some fifty free blacks.[45]

The black militia played an even larger role in Spanish Louisiana than it had under the French. Its importance became manifest in 1769, when, after six years of administrative temporizing, Spain asserted its claim over Louisiana and the French colonials revolted. The militia by that time included over 300 free men of color. Spanish authorities dispatched General Alejandro O'Reilly from Cuba to reestablish order. Accompanied by several companies of Havana-based free black militiamen, O'Reilly smashed the coup, executing some of the leaders and exiling others.[46] But the elimination of the conspirators failed to placate Spanish authorities, who continued to fret about the stirrings of indigenous French planters, Anglo-American settlers in the upper valley, and the British in West Florida, each of whom had their own Indian allies.[47]

With enemies everywhere, Spanish authorities needed friends. None seemed more eager to demonstrate their loyalty to the Spanish Crown than the free people of African descent. When O'Reilly demanded that Louisianans swear allegiance to the new government, free people of color were among the first to take the oath, simultaneously volunteering their military expertise. With the practiced hand of a colonizer experienced in the complexity of governing sharply segmented societies, Spanish officials embraced free people of African descent as allies against external and internal foes. O'Reilly, whose appreciation of the free colored militia had been nourished by long years of imperial service, recommissioned Louisiana's colored militia, adopting the division between *pardo* (or light-skinned) and *moreno* (or dark-skinned) units present elsewhere in Spanish America. He clad the militiamen in colorful uniforms and granted them *fuero militar* rights, thereby exempting militiamen from civil prosecution, certain taxes, and licensing fees—no mean privilege for black men in a slave society.[48]

The black militia thrived under Spanish rule, becoming an integral part of the colony's defense force and growing steadily in numbers. When not deploying them against foreign enemies, Spanish officials used free black militiamen to maintain the levees that protected New Orleans and the great riverfront plantations, extinguish fires in the city limits, and hunt fugitive slaves. While white settlers disdained military duty, black men delighted in their role as protectors of the king's domain. They wore their dress uniforms proudly and, long after the Spanish were ousted from the region, affixed their titles to their names with the added "que en Tiempo de la Dominación Española." As the value of the free black militia to Spain increased, so did the class from which the militia sprang.[49]

To provide a ready supply of colored militiamen and guarantee their loyalty, Spanish officials encouraged the growth of the free colored population. Unlike the French *Code Noir*, which discouraged manumission by requiring slaveowners to obtain permission of the colony's highest governing body—the Superior Council—before they could free their slaves, Spanish law allowed slaveowners to manumit with little more than a trip to the courthouse.[50] Given the opportunity, numerous slaveholders made the journey. Between 1769 and 1779, the first decade after Spain took effective control of Louisiana, slaveholders registered 320 deeds of manumission in New Orleans, many times the number issued during the entire period of French rule.[51]

Manumission began inside the slaveowners' household. Among the first to be freed were the products of *plaçage,* the lovers and children of the slaveowners. During the first decade of Spanish rule, numerous masters freed for reasons of "love and affection" their slave wives and the children they bore. More than half of the voluntary manumissions under Spanish rule were children, and three-quarters of these were of mixed racial origins. Most of the adults were women. In short, given the opportunity, slaveholders freed their families as a matter of course.[52]

But manumission was not confined to family members. Close living conditions, particularly in the cities, allowed some slaves—generally house servants, artisans, and tradesmen of various sorts—to gain the attention and respect of their owners. Slaveholders also awarded these privileged slaves freedom, although again manumitters favored women over men. Females, both women and children, composed 63 percent of the slaves freed.[53]

Spanish officials also loosened the strictures on self-emancipation, simplifying the purchase of freedom. Whereas the *Code Noir* made slave masters responsible for inaugurating slave freedom, the *Siete Partidas* and the *coartacion*—the latter an amalgam of customary practices that had gained the force of law in Spanish America in the eighteenth century—gave slaves the power to initiate their own emancipation through negotiations with their owners. Once the process of self-purchase began, it transcended the relationship between master and slave, and the slaves' right to freedom could not be denied, even in the face of an owner's opposition. If a slaveowner refused to negotiate freedom, the slave—or any interested party for that matter—could petition the governor's court and have a *carta de libertad* issued, thereby requiring the owner to manumit when the stipulated price was paid. The *carta,* moreover, remained in force no matter how many times a slave was sold or traded, and any contribution the slave had made toward freedom had to be recognized by future owners. Owners who refused to negotiate with their slaves could be carried before a judicial tribunal, which would fix a price for slaves to buy themselves.[54] Unlike most of the regulations that defined the slaves' rights, Spanish officials enforced the law respecting manumission, often in the face of the owners' steadfast opposition. With no special friend at law, slaveowners generally avoided official adjudication and settled with their slaves out of court.[55]

As Louisiana slaves grasped the implications of Spanish law and—most importantly—came to appreciate the willingness of Spanish officials to enforce it, more and more slaves took advantage of the new opportunities. Although voluntary, master-inspired manumissions outnumbered those initiated by slaves employing the law during the first decade of Spanish rule, the proportion of slave-initiated manumissions steadily increased during the decade. Drawing upon their own resources and joining together with free people of color—many of them just a step removed from slavery—slaves opened negotiations to buy their own liberty and that of their families and friends. If owners rejected the slaves' proposals to buy their way out of bondage, slaves did not hesitate to invoke their legal rights.[56]

Still, the right to purchase freedom, no matter how fully elaborated, would not have liberated a single slave without the expansion of an independent slave economy during the post-Natchez years. Drawing on the money they earned through jobbing, overwork, and the sale of produce and handicraft, Louisiana slaves—particularly those within easy reach of New Orleans—began to buy their way out of bondage in larger numbers than in any place in mainland North America. The free colored population, which had grown slowly under French rule, surged upward during the last third of the eighteenth century. In the first decade of Spanish rule, nearly 200 slaves initiated proceedings to purchase their freedom in New Orleans alone. As with master-sponsored manumission, a majority of the slaves who gained freedom through the courts were female, although they tended to be older and darker in color.[57] As a result, the proportion of black people who enjoyed freedom during the first decade probably doubled after Spain took control of the colony. In New Orleans, site of the greatest growth of the free community, this group grew from less than 100 in 1771 to more than 315 in 1777.[58]

The growth of the free black population created tension between those who escaped bondage and those who remained enslaved. Some of the tension had its roots in petty jealousies—real and imagined—as freed people flaunted their newly won status. But differences also had an undeniable reality in the legal distinctions that underlay the participation of black men in the colored militia and the employment of the militia against runaway slaves, particularly maroons. Yet many newly minted free people saw themselves as just a step removed from slavery, and they welcomed the opportunity to assist others in escaping bondage. The close confines of African-American life in Louisiana, where more than three-quarters of the black population lived within a day's boat ride of New Orleans and almost all enjoyed a native birth, mitigated the new divisions of status. Diversity did not yet divide black people in the lower Mississippi Valley. African-American unity allowed peoples of African descent to seize the moment, when the specter of revolution reached the lower Mississippi Valley.

While the plantation revolution bypassed the lower Mississippi Valley, it continued apace elsewhere on mainland North America. In the Chesapeake, in lowcountry South Carolina, Georgia, and East Florida, and even in the northern colonies, slave societies replaced societies with slaves, and a massive wave of new arrivals from the African interior swallowed the Atlantic creoles.

As the connections between mainland black society and the larger Atlantic world attenuated, the expansion of the great estates and the growth of the African population made the plantation the locus of African-American life. Within the plantation, slaves struggled fiercely against the growing power of the planter class and their determination to reduce black people to labor and little more. Countering the trauma of enslavement, towering rates of mortality, endless work, and omnipresent violence, slaves created new economies and societies that tried to protect them from the harshest aspects of the slave regime and provide a modicum of independence. As they listened in on the growing debates between European Americans and their European overlords, words like "freedom" and "liberty" attracted their attention, for they promised the reconstruction of black life on more favorable grounds. With the outbreak of revolutionary war, first in the English seaboard colonies, then in continental Europe, and finally in the Caribbean, those possibilities became a new reality.

III

SLAVE AND FREE

The Revolutionary Generations

Drittes Regiment Garde.
Chef. Se. Hochfürstliche Durchlaucht der Landgraf

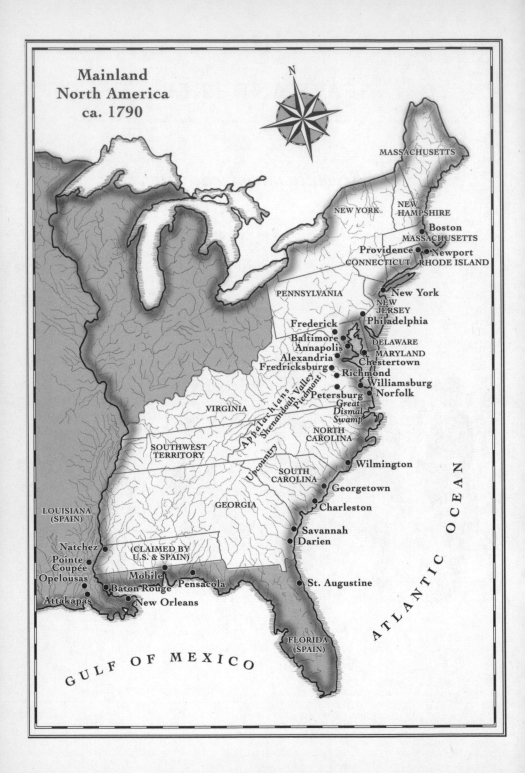

Mainland
North America
ca. 1790

N

MASSACHUSETTS

NEW YORK

NEW
HAMPSHIRE

Boston
MASSACHUSETTS

Providence
Newport
CONNECTICUT
RHODE ISLAND

PENNSYLVANIA

New York

NEW
JERSEY

Frederick
Philadelphia

Baltimore
Annapolis
DELAWARE
Alexandria
MARYLAND
Fredricksburg
Chestertown
Richmond
Williamsburg
Petersburg
Norfolk

VIRGINIA

Great
Dismal
Swamp

NORTH
CAROLINA

SOUTHWEST
TERRITORY

Upcountry

SOUTH
CAROLINA

Wilmington

Georgetown

GEORGIA

Charleston

Savannah
Darien

LOUISIANA
(SPAIN)

Natchez

Pointe
Coupée
(CLAIMED BY
U.S. & SPAIN)

Opelousas
Mobile
Pensacola
St. Augustine

Attakapas
Baton Rouge
New Orleans

ATLANTIC OCEAN

FLORIDA
(SPAIN)

GULF OF MEXICO

Introduction

✦

The age of the great democratic revolutions—the American, the French, and the Haitian—marked a third transformation in the lives of black people in mainland North America.[1] Seizing the egalitarian ideal that informed the revolutionary age, black people through mainland North America challenged the masters' ascendancy. Men and women who had been swallowed whole by the plantation struggled to remake themselves in often bloody contests with their owners. Slaves demanded freedom; free people demanded equality; and while not all succeeded, by the beginning of the nineteenth century, the structure of African-American society had been radically altered.

The War for American Independence in particular gave slaves new leverage in their struggle with their owners, offering the opportunity to challenge both the institution of chattel bondage and the allied structures of white supremacy. Slavery rested upon the unity of the planter class and its ability to mobilize the state and rally nonslaveholders to slavery's defense. But the American Revolution divided planters among Patriots and Loyalists and forced both to employ their slaves in ways that compromised the masters' ability to invoke state authority. In many instances, the state—whether understood as the planters' former British overlords or their own representatives—turned against the master class.

As the slaveholders faltered, so did the support once rendered them by nonslaveholders. Some nonslaveholders abandoned long-standing ties with planters to fashion new connections among themselves. A few forged alliances with slaves. The emergence of such combinations compelled some slaveholders to go so far as to arm their slaves, occasionally offering freedom in return for military service. The concessions, no matter how carefully hedged, eroded the planters' position atop slave society and opened the way for the transformation of African-American life.[2]

* * *

To a large degree, the nature of revolutionary warfare—the intensity of the fighting and the internal divisions it created—shaped the slaves' ability to challenge the old order. Where the fighting remained distant and invading armies little more than rumor, masters generally parried the slaves' threat. But where rival armies occupied large portions of the countryside, creating civil disorder and social strife, the advantage fell to the slaves. Often they found opportunities for freedom amid the chaos of war, camouflaging themselves among the tramping soldiers and occasionally becoming soldiers themselves.

The turmoil of war marked only the beginning of the slaveholders' problems. The invocation of universal equality—most prominently in the Declaration of Independence—further strengthened the slaves' hand. The Patriots' loud complaints of enslavement to a distant imperial tyrant and insistence on the universality of liberty overflowed the bounds of the struggle for political independence. How can Americans "complain so loudly of attempts to enslave them," mused Tom Paine in 1775, "while they hold so many hundreds of thousands in slavery?" Others, including many slaveholders, echoed Paine's unsettling query. Propelled by the logic of their own answers, some rebellious Americans moved against slavery, particularly in areas where slaves were numerically few and economically marginal.[3]

Revolutionary ideology was only one source of the new spirit of liberty and equality. An evangelical upsurge that presumed all were equal in God's eyes complemented and sometimes reinforced revolutionary idealism and placed new pressure on slaveholders. The evangelicals despised the planters' haughty manner and high ways, and they welcomed slaves into the fold as brothers and sisters in Jesus Christ. Black men and women who joined, and occasionally led, the evangelical churches considered worldly freedom an obvious extension of their spiritual liberation, and many white congregants enthusiastically agreed.[4]

The war and the libertarian ideology that accompanied it extended beyond the boundaries of the newly established United States, deeply affecting the rest of mainland North America. As the fighting spread to the lower Mississippi Valley and from there to the Gulf Coast, planters in those regions found themselves on the defensive, their position threatened by international rivalries among imperial powers and eroded by internal divisions. Events in Spain, France, the Caribbean, and South

America initiated new assaults on slavery and compounded such breaches.

Reacting to changes within their own empire and the new order that an independent United States portended, Spanish policymakers took up the cause of reform. Their plans to revitalize their American empire rested in good measure on the expansion of slavery. But the sudden growth of slavery posed dangers, both from an enlarged and independent-minded planter class and from the slaves, upon whose backs the revitalization rested. In 1789, to address these concerns and speak to the enlightened spirit of the age, the Spanish king issued a *cédula* concerning "the Education, Treatment and Occupations of Slaves." The *Código Negro,* which circumscribed the power of the master and protected slaves against abusive owners, met ferocious opposition from planters throughout the empire. It never went into effect and was eventually withdrawn. But news of the king's *cédula,* much of it disseminated by the planters' unbridled opposition, spread rapidly through the slave quarters, where it was interpreted as the beginnings of a general emancipation.[5]

The unrest stirred by the reformist Spaniards paled in comparison with that set loose by the revolutionary French. In 1789 the Bastille fell, and the Revolutionary Assembly promulgated its Declaration of the Rights of Man. Three years later, the Jacobin-controlled General Assembly declared against racial distinctions, and in 1794 it abolished slavery. Events in France resonated in French America. No colony was more affected than Saint Domingue, where *gens de couleur*—people of color—seized notions of liberty, equality, and fraternity and pressed their case for full citizenship. Planters denounced them as degenerates and incendiaries and imprisoned their leaders, executing many after torture and mutilation. Driven to the brink, in 1790 the free people took up arms and, when defeat loomed, armed their slaves, who needed no primer on revolution. The dispute between free people—white and brown—quickly escalated into a full-fledged slave insurrection, pitting white against black, free against slave. Interventions by the British and Spanish advanced the cause of the slave, as one belligerent after another bid for the slaves' support against their French overlords. By the time France tried to retake the colony and reimpose slavery, an independent Haiti had emerged under Toussaint L'Ouverture.[6]

Events in Saint Domingue echoed throughout the Atlantic world, deeply affecting the mainland, especially the former French colony of Louisiana and the nearby East and West Florida colonies, all three then under Spanish sovereignty. As in the United States, slaves in Louisiana and the Floridas quickly took advantage of the divisions created by Spanish reform and by the French Revolution—first between planters and the state and then within the slaveowners' ranks. Seizing the initiative, slaves plotted to enlarge their prerogatives, win their freedom, and—as free people—demand full equality. The possibilities of freedom that had been unleashed by the War for American Independence reverberated in the lower Mississippi Valley and the Gulf region.

Confronted by the realities of slavery's changing fortunes, some mainland slaveholders opted for abolition or manumission, sometimes for reasons of principle, sometimes for expediency. But even among the most principled opponents of slavery, those inclined toward emancipation represented a minority. Freedom rarely arrived without slaves' taking the initiative, actively pressing their owners for permission to buy freedom and threatening flight or rebellion if refused. Owners countered with threats of their own, often escalating the struggle, as neither slaveowners nor slaves recoiled from the use of force. Behind their violent encounters stood the reality of organized resistance and brutal repression, revealed most fully in Saint Domingue. With the slaves' success in creating the Haitian republic, neither master nor slave could doubt the possibility of a world turned upside down. The specter of Saint Domingue—whose long shadow reached the deepest recesses of mainland society—inflated petty violations of racial etiquette. Whispers of discontent became rumors of insurrection and sometimes bloody confrontations.

But it was not simply the disembodied idea of freedom or the embellished rumors of distant emancipation that moved mainland slaves. Events in Saint Domingue—starting with the claim of free people of color to full citizenship, the suppression of that claim, and the transformation of a conflict among free people into a slave rebellion, escalating to various foreign invasions and civil wars—had set loose a vast exodus. Great planters and small, slaves, free people of color, and *petits blancs* searched for shelter in the storm of revolution. The initial flight of close to 10,000 men and women from Cap Français in 1793 was followed by many more who abandoned the island during the next two decades. Although most settled on nearby islands, large numbers took refuge in mainland North America, finding shelter in ports from Boston to New Orleans. The emigrés carried a variety of messages, which, depending upon the recipient, hardened opposition to emancipation or encouraged demands for freedom. But whatever the refugees' message and however it was received, their presence and their firsthand accounts of a slave society gone awry informed all. No part of mainland North America was untouched.[7]

As the reality of Saint Domingue manifested itself, the ground for negotiation over slavery expanded, sometimes in legislative caucuses, sometimes in courtrooms, and sometimes directly between slaves and their owners. Slaves and masters positioned themselves to take best advantage of the new circumstances. With the winds of revolution at their backs, slaves pressed to fulfill the expectations of the new era, if not with freedom, then at least with a greater measure of control over life and labor. Bracing themselves against the gale of change, slaveowners labored to smother the slaves' rising expectations and, if possible, increase their control by extracting still greater draughts of labor. If the bloody events filled slaveholders with dread, they induced slaves to act with ever greater urgency and confidence.

Nothing strengthened the slaves' hand more than the growing number of black people who escaped bondage, some as manumittees, some as fugitives, some as emigrés from Saint Domingue. Although free black people quickly acquired interests of their own—and calculated them carefully before committing themselves to slave or slaveowner—their very existence demonstrated the possibilities of freedom far better than any revolutionary tract or evangelical sermon. Free blacks, moreover, were not content simply to lead by example. Most espoused the cause of universal freedom and the liberation of family, friends, and indeed anyone who had shared with them the bitter fruits of bondage. Those who labored against racism and discrimination believed that their success depended upon the liquidation of slavery.

Despite the myriad forces assaulting slavery, freedom progressed slowly and unevenly. The Age of Revolution witnessed the liberation of only a small fraction of the slaves in mainland North America. In many places, the advance toward freedom could hardly be noticed, and in others the process worked in reverse, as slavery grew more rapidly than freedom during the late eighteenth and early nineteenth centuries. Far more black people lived in slavery at the end of the revolutionary age than at the beginning. Much of this increase derived from the reopening of the African trade, as the number of Africans enslaved and carried to mainland North America rivaled the number of people of African descent freed by all the state-sponsored emancipations and individual acts of manumission. But much of this increase was the result of an ingenious construction of revolutionary ideology, carved from the very ideals of universal liberty, which presented slaveowners and their allies with a powerful defense against abolition. If indeed all men were created equal and some men were slaves—the argument ran—then, perhaps, those who remained in the degraded condition of slaves were not fully men after all. The implications of this twisted reading of the Declaration of Independence and the Declaration of the Rights of Man would have a powerful influence on Americans, black and white. The great declarations removed some men and women from the body politic even as they incorporated others, inciting repression along with liberation.[8]

The seeming opposition of freedom and slavery dissolved in the contradictions of the slaveholders' war for liberty. The very same slaveowners who liberated their slaves often purchased new ones, and the very same slaves who shed their shackles sometimes manacled others. Manumission, even emancipation, served masters as well as slaves, giving slaveholders new weapons to discipline their bondpeople, extract their labor, and maintain their subordination.[9] As in earlier eras, the transit between slavery and freedom was neither direct nor linear.

African-American life thus evolved along several different paths during the revolutionary era in mainland North America. The number of black people enjoying liberty increased manyfold as a result of military service, successful flight, self-purchase, manumission, and state-sponsored emancipation. Drawing on the century and a half of black experience in mainland North America, these newly liberated men and women created new worlds of freedom. But the same events that freed slaves also allowed slaveholders to consolidate their power and legitimate their claims to property-in-person. Although the free black population grew rapidly between 1775 and 1810, the boundaries of the slave regime in the new United States expanded far beyond those that existed under British, French, and Spanish rule, and the number of black people locked in bondage in North America grew ever larger.

The Age of Revolution inaugurated two profoundly different, overlapping, and sometime conflicting reconstructions. As slaves secured their freedom, they remade their lives, taking new names, new residences, and new occupations. In reconstructing families, they created new communities and with them new identities as free men and women. Former slaves gave meaning to freedom in a host of institutions: churches, schools, benevolent societies, newspapers, parades, and political caucuses. Older forms of solidarity and sociability like Election Day gave way to new ones, more attuned to the desire of black people for the full rights of citizens in the new republic. Ritual role reversal might be celebrated by those whose aspirations encompassed only the faint hope for some future liberation; it held little attraction for those who believed equality to be their birthright.[10]

But if the reconstruction of black life in freedom followed along the same path in different locations and under different conditions, it never took quite the same route. Some slaves shucked off the names of their masters; others adopted them. Some migrated to the city; others remained in the countryside. Some embraced their owner's Christianity; others created a religion of their own. Some added their voices to the call for abolition and universal equality; others labored hard to preserve their ties to the planter class, mimicking its manner, adopting its principles, and—upon occasion—entering into its ranks as slaveholders with hardly a backward glance. The nature of postemancipation reconstruction, like the character of emancipation itself, rested upon the various circumstances of black life.

Whatever form the reconstruction took, white Americans rarely welcomed the new order. On the one hand, they condemned newly freed slaves as dissolute wastrels whose unrestrained exuberance for freedom would reduce them to the penury they deserved. On the other hand, they mocked those who strove for respectability as feckless impostors whose ill-fitting periwigs and pretentious oratory would elicit the ridicule they deserved. The multifarious and nearly universal opposition of white people to the expansion of African-American freedom set in motion intense conflicts during which "African" nationality—the very meaning of race—was again redefined. As some black people claimed their place as citizens, others searched for new identities within their own community. A few looked to Africa for a fresh start. Like the plantation revolutions, the democratic revolutions transformed peoples of African descent. Black men and women who gained their freedom in the revolutionary era were as different from those of the plantation generations as the plantation generations had been from the charter generations.

If liberated people of color redefined freedom, the enslaved drew upon the ideals and events of the revolutionary age to redefine slavery. Slaves who lost the struggle for freedom did not surrender to the new order. Having failed to secure the great prize, they pressed for what advantages could be obtained. In the cities and on the farms and great plantations, slaves confronted their owners over matters of labor discipline, institutional autonomy, and cultural independence, employing traditional forms of resistance as well as revolutionary ones. Slaveowners opposed these incursions into their domain and labored to enhance the power they already enjoyed. Where possible, slaveholders restricted the prerogatives that slaves had secured during the war and ratcheted up the level of exploitation. As the conflict between owner and owned unfolded, the terms of bondage were rewritten.

A massive movement of the black population exacerbated the conflict between master and slave. The diaspora began with the war itself and the dislocation caused by invading armies. However, the flight of numerous slaves and the large-scale displacement of yet others did not end with the fighting. Peace saw planters reopen the transatlantic slave trade and gave the internal trade new velocity. By the beginning of the nineteenth century, the geography of African-American life—slave as well as free—had been radically altered, as the locus of black slavery shifted westward and the locus of black freedom shifted cityward.[11]

The new geography reflected a transformed economy. The reorganization of agricultural production, the introduction of new crops, the growth of manufacturing, and the expansion of commerce forced some black people into situations of extraordinary constraint, while it allowed others hitherto unknown independence. In either case, slaves and free blacks faced owners and employers on new terrain, once again contesting what was the slaves' and what was the masters', what was the employees' and what was the employers'. The reformulation of the American economy redrew the line between the slaves' independent production and the slaves' labor in the owners' behalf. It also demanded that free people of color master the role of wage worker, reopening questions of the division of labor, the definition of the stint, and the character of discipline.

The Age of Revolution also transformed relations among black people themselves, as the old criteria of status that structured black society in the wake of the plantation revolution dissolved. Differences between African-born and American-born black men and women mattered less as the number of Africans entering mainland North America dwindled, and differences among Africans—as between Igbos and Angolans—mattered hardly at all except in a few areas of the Lower South and the Lower Mississippi Valley. The American Revolution submerged such differences among black people in the common cause of freedom. As distinctions between Africans and African Americans disappeared, new differences—between free and slave—emerged, creating new fissures within the black community along with new points of alliance. And as the separate worlds of freedom and slavery solidified, legal standing mattered more and more. By the beginning of the nineteenth century, legal distinctions between slave and free had become the basis for social standing in black society. With such distinctions, a new politics emerged, for free and slave had different aspirations and strategies for achieving their goals. Their competing agendas complicated alliances and divisions within black society.

The new societies of free and slave did not emerge everywhere at once. Freedom triumphed only in the northern states and then only slowly and imperfectly. But nowhere did slavery enjoy an uninterrupted ascent. Even where it grew most vigorously, the presence of free people of color challenged the emergent notion that black people were naturally slaves. The chronology of freedom and slavery in the Age of Revolution was just as irregular as the chronology of the plantation revolution. The contradictory nature of a slaveholders' rebellion for liberty accounted for some of this diversity. But black society on mainland North America had already evolved in regionally distinctive ways by the eve of independence, causing the events of the revolutionary era to resonate differently in different places. Just as "African" and "African American" took on different cultural meanings in the colonies of the North, Chesapeake, lowcountry, and lower Mississippi Valley prior to 1776, so "free" and "slave" gained regionally distinctive definitions in the postrevolutionary era.

Chapter Nine

The Slow Death of Slavery in the North

▲

Nowhere on mainland North America did events and ideas of the Age of Revolution fall with greater force on black society than in the northern colonies. The American Revolution reversed the development of northern slavery—first, liquidating the remnants of slave society; then, revivifying the North as a society with slaves; finally, transforming the society with slaves into a free society. Between the beginning of the war and the first years of the nineteenth century, every northern state enacted some plan of emancipation. The North's free black population swelled from a small corps of several hundred in the 1770s to nearly 50,000 by 1810, while the number of slaves contracted. In time, the northern colonies became the free states.

But the demise of slavery was a slow, tortuous process. Often it was propelled more by atrophy of the slave population—owing to high mortality, low fertility, the close of the transatlantic slave trade, and the southward exportation of slaves for profit—than by the growth of liberty among blacks. In 1810 there were still 27,000 slaves in "free" states. For most northern slaves, more than a generation passed before they were able to exit chattel bondage, and more than two generations were required to extricate themselves from the various snares—legal, extralegal, and occasionally illegal—that allowed former owners and other white people to control their labor and their lives. In New York and New Jersey, the largest slaveholding states in the North, gradual emancipation left some black people locked in bondage or other forms of servitude until midcentury and beyond. Even then, former slaves faced a forest of proscriptive statutes and discriminatory practices, as white lawmakers limited the legal rights of former slaves and as white employers created new forms of subordination that kept black people dependent.

Still, whatever the limits northern lawmakers placed on their freedom, black people moved quickly to give meaning to their freshly won liberty and to give form to a rapidly maturing African-American culture.

They chose their own names, took their own residences, and found their own jobs. Having created individual identities as free men and women, they built institutions to protect and expand their liberty as a free people. Along with churches, schools, and fraternal societies, a leadership class emerged and labored to maintain the unity of African-American society. But even as these leaders struggled on their people's behalf, they began to develop interests of their own. Like every elite, they were both part of their society and—by their wealth, education, and social standing—apart from it. The social divisions within black society created fissures—between slaves and former slaves, between urban and rural cultures, and between blacks and people of mixed racial origins. With freedom, new sources of solidarity and division emerged within northern black society.

The denunciation of tyranny and the celebration of universal liberty ignited opposition to slavery in the North. Emboldened by their own claim as freedom's champion, some white Americans joined slaves and free blacks in a condemnation of slavery. Emancipation came quickly in northern New England, particularly in areas where slaves were numerically few and economically marginal. Vermont freed its slaves by constitutional amendment, while Massachusetts and New Hampshire freed theirs by legal processes so obscure that historians continue to puzzle over slavery's demise.[1] But in southern New England and the Middle Atlantic states—where black people were more numerous and slavery more deeply entrenched—slaveholders resisted efforts to eliminate chattel bondage. Instead, they sought ways to protect their property by enforcing long-neglected slave codes and implementing new harsh restrictions.[2] In such places, the war itself, more than its patriotic rhetoric, proved the greatest solvent to the master–slave relation. The massive movement of troops—particularly the British occupation and subsequent Patriot reoccupation of the great seaboard cities—and the resultant dispersal of civilian populations greatly disrupted slavery. Numerous slaveholders transferred their slaves to friends and neighbors for safekeeping. Others tried to remove or "refugee" (as the process became known) slaves to distant places where they might be safe from confiscation or sequestration from one or the other belligerent.[3]

Neither course had the desired effect. When the opportunity arose, Patriots and Loyalists confiscated one another's slaves, often selling them along with other property to punish enemies and finance military adventures. Rather than allow slaves to be so used, some slaveholders hastily sold their slaves before the enemy's advance. Others abandoned them to their own devices or, upon occasion, simply dismissed them. In 1777, when Patriots torched his house in New York, the Loyalist Oliver De Lancey gave his slaves "leave to work for their maintenance, and go where they pleased."[4]

Few slaves waited for their owners to act on their behalf. Seizing the moment, black men and women fled bondage by the thousands. Generally, they headed for free territory—northward to New England and southward to British lines—where in 1775 Lord Dunmore, Virginia's royal governor, had promised liberty to all who reached his camp. In July 1776, Cuff Dix, a black Pennsylvania iron worker, gathered his clothes, changed his name, and "march[ed] to join his Lordship's own black regiment," since Dix, like other slaves, believed "that Lord Dunmore [was] contending for their liberty." Farther to the north, slaves did not have to make the long trek to Dunmore's headquarters in Virginia. In the summer of 1776 Dunmore landed on Staten Island with the remainder of his African brigade, inciting numerous New York and New Jersey slaves to enter the British ranks.[5]

Once they reached the war zone, fugitive slaves found refuge with common soldiers of all persuasions who welcomed their assistance in doing the dirty work of the war. Former slaves scouted the countryside, dug trenches, built roads, loaded wagons, tended horses, cooked food, foraged for firewood, washed laundry, and sold sex in exchange for shelter, protection, and, they hoped, freedom. In time, both belligerents ratified the exchange, with the British generally acting first and Patriots rushing to match their enemy's largess.

Fugitive slaves, for their part, opportunistically chose the cause that best assured the success of *their* own cause: freedom. At times, they served the British; by war's end, several regiments of Black Guides and Pioneers had been enlisted in His Majesty's forces. At times, they served rebellious Americans; by war's end, several northern states enlisted black men, slave and free. Almost every state counted some black men under arms at one time or another, and Rhode Island enlisted 200 slaves into its First Regiment. Connecticut formed an all-black company. Many more fugitives—women as well as men—served irregularly. The former slave Titus, transformed by his alliance with British regulars and Loyalist irregulars into "Colonel Tye," bedeviled Patriots in central New Jersey, kidnapping their leaders, raiding their farms, and establishing himself and his Black Brigade as a "fearsome presence."[6]

Other slaves used the cover of tramping armies to break for freedom. When Loyalist soldiers occupied New York in 1778, Sarah was but one of many slaves who fled to the "1st. Maryland Regiment where she pretends to have a husband, with who[m] she has been the principal part of this campaign and passed herself as a free woman." In the spring of 1780, fearful of an influx of runaways into New York City, a British general warned the local ferry masters that "not only male but female Negroes with their children take advantage of your port in New Jersey to run away from masters and come into the city," and he ordered the ferry masters to "prevent their passing the North River." Patriot authorities issued an identical warning several months later.[7]

Successful flight struck slavery a mighty blow. During the war, the fugitive population doubled in Philadelphia and increased fourfold in New York City, even as the number of slaves declined. As soldiers, sailors, military laborers, and camp followers, thousands of slaves eluded their owners and passed into northern society as free men and women. Even those who avoided military service found the army's presence a useful subterfuge in securing their escape. Caesar, a fugitive from Chester, Pennsylvania, made his escape by claiming "he came last from the southern army, and that he is a freeman." When the British army left Philadelphia in 1778, residents complained that a "great part of the slaves hereabouts were enticed away." Between 1775 and 1780 Philadelphia's slave population fell by a quarter.[8]

Young men free of family responsibilities were the first to flee, eager for their freedom and the opportunity for martial experience. Women encumbered by children, for whom encampments of armed young men could be frightening and dangerous places, were slower to leave. But before long, they too fled slavery. Young women—probably single women —led the way, soon joined by older women and their children, suggesting that black people took the occasion of their liberation as an opportunity to reconstruct their families.[9]

The wartime erosion of slavery encouraged direct assaults against the institution itself. The heady notions of universal human equality that justified American independence gave black people a powerful weapon with which to attack chattel bondage, and they understood that this was no time to be quiet. "It is the momentous question of our lives," declared black Philadelphians in 1781. "If we are silent this day, we may be silent for ever."[10] Black people throughout the North made themselves heard. Echoing the themes sounded by black petitioners prior to the Revolution, slaves denounced the double standard that allowed white Americans to fight for freedom while denying that right to blacks. Indeed, slaves and free blacks not only employed the ideas of the Revolution but also its very language. Declaring that "they have in Common with all other men a Natural and Unalienable Right to that freedom which the Grat Parent of the Unavers hath Bestowed equalley on all menkind and which they have Never forfuted by any Compact or agreement whatever," black Bostonians amplified an idea respecting the "Naturel Right of all men" that was familiar to "every true patriot."

Success bred success. Black people who gained their freedom by legis-lative enactment, individual manumission, and successful flight pressed all the harder for universal emancipation, demanding first the release of their families and friends and then all black people still in bondage. In Pennsylvania, newly freed blacks—eager to secure an end to slavery—of-fered to pay a special tax to compensate slaveholders for their loss of property and thereby ensure that emancipation would not cost white taxpayers a cent. Formal petitions, augmented by informal but unmistak-able words and deeds, revealed that black people expected liberty would soon be theirs.[11]

Such actions could not be ignored easily by those who marched under the banner of Jefferson's declaration. Numerous northern slaveholders yielded to the logic of the Revolution and freed their slaves or allowed them to purchase their liberty. In 1780 the revolutionary government of Pennsylvania, spurred by reminders that slavery was "disgraceful to any people, and more especially to those who have been contending in the great cause of liberty themselves," legislated a gradual emancipation. Like all such half-measures, the act's ringing declaration of revolutionary principles was freighted with the dead weight of compromise that contra-dicted those very principles. The Pennsylvania law freed not a single slave born before emancipation day—March 1, 1780—and kept the children of slaves born thereafter locked in bondage until age twenty-eight, probably most of their productive lives. Under the new law, no slave would have to be freed until 1808; and in fact, many black people were retained in bondage long after that date. In 1811 a Chester County ironmaster registered the birth of a six-month-old black girl, in order to assure that she would serve him until 1839.[12] By controlling slave children, slaveholders maintained a hold on their parents, even those who were free, frequently forcing them to sign long-term contracts to work under disadvantageous terms in exchange for visitation rights with their children. Such arrangements slowed the progress of freedom in Pennsylvania and kept many free blacks under the domination of white men and women, often their former owners, after they had been legally freed. Try as they might, abolitionists failed to achieve full emancipation by legislative or judicial means in Pennsylvania until 1847.[13]

In 1780, at the time of the enactment of the gradualist program in Pennsylvania, the legal liquidation of slavery had not yet even begun in Connecticut, Rhode Island, New Jersey, or the largest northern slave state, New York. Slaves in these states—having glimpsed the possibility of freedom in the greatly enlarged free black population—pressed for abolition with ever greater vigor. Everywhere, slaveowners found their slaves working slower and answering quicker with a tone that chilled. By their formal petitions, frequent absences, willingness to turn fugitive, and acts of insolence and violence, slaves served notice that they took seriously the libertarian promise of American independence and would accept nothing less than the end of chattel bondage.

The number of runaways dropped briefly with the return of peace but then rose quickly to exceed wartime levels. Seeing their friends and relatives shed the shackles of slavery, many slaves simply abandoned their owners. According to one estimate, between half and three-quarters of the young slave men in Philadelphia absconded from their owners during the 1780s. With the aid of newly freed slaves and white opponents of slavery, they translated escape into permanent freedom with increased frequency. If retaken, they fled again and then again, until recalcitrant owners recognized the futility of retaining them in bondage. Social unrest among slaves manifested itself in other ways. During the 1790s, a wave of arson that spread up and down the seaboard—universally attributed to slaves—convinced many white northerners that chattel bondage could no longer be sustained.[14]

Still, slaveholders strenuously resisted emancipation. They mobilized their considerable political influence in legislative chambers, courts of justice, and the popular press. Slaveowners condemned emancipation as a subversive act that would saddle the state with a free people who would not work for their livelihood. Other defenders of slavery drew upon arguments ranging from biblical precedent and the "rules of economic necessity" to the sanctity of private property, repudiating the principles that underlay the Declaration of Independence in the process.[15] Debates over slavery gave opponents of emancipation the opportunity to con-struct—for the first time—a coherent defense of slavery and to organize themselves around that defense. Joined by those who doubted slavery's efficacy but who were determined to maintain the old order as long as possible, the opponents of abolition formed an important block in the legislatures of the Middle Atlantic states, especially New York and New Jersey.[16]

Progress toward emancipation in such circumstances could only be slow and piecemeal. In 1784 Connecticut and Rhode Island lawmakers legislated emancipation, adopting Pennsylvania's gradualist formula. A year later, New York legislators liberalized the state's manumission law; for the first time since the beginning of the eighteenth century, slave-holders could free their slaves without posting bonds to insure the state against freed people becoming a public charge. More than two decades would pass before lawmakers in New York and New Jersey, the remain-ing northern slave states, advanced beyond such token measures. The stalemate emboldened slaveholders, encouraging their representatives to derail the movement toward freedom and, where possible, throw the process of liberation into reverse, as when in 1794 the New Jersey Assem-bly restricted the right of slaves to sue for their freedom. The slavehold-ers' persistent opposition meant that when abolition finally came to New York and New Jersey, it arrived laden with delay, compromise, and often outright opposition to African-American freedom.

The New York abolition law of 1799 and the New Jersey act of 1804, like their Pennsylvania counterpart, mandated the eventual liquidation of slavery but actually freed no slaves. In New York, the children of slaves born after the law went into effect on July 4, 1799, would remain in the service of their mothers' owner until age twenty-eight for males and twenty-five for females. It would take nearly another twenty years for New York to free the slaves who had been born before 1799. A similar formula delayed even longer the arrival of freedom in New Jersey. Still, by 1804 every northern state had committed itself to emancipation in one form or another.[17]

The North's commitment—however grudging—armed slaves with

new weapons to fight for their liberty. Although the right to manumit formally expanded the rights of slaveowners, not slaves, slaves nonetheless took advantage of the new laws. They pressed their owners for the opportunity to purchase themselves and their families, promising fidelity and hard work for a term of years, or in some cases decades, in exchange for eventual freedom. If refused, slaves—drawing upon the customary right to select their own master—schemed for another, more compliant owner to purchase them. If those plans came to naught, slaves turned sullen, malingered, and in some cases simply walked away from slavery. Occasionally, they lashed out at their owners with violence and the threat of yet more violence. During the 1780s and 1790s the slaves' insistent demands broadened the avenues to freedom. The number of manumissions increased rapidly in New York and New Jersey, slavery's remaining northern bastions.[18]

Negotiating freedom was a complicated business. Slaveholders—with their knowledge of the law, material resources, and confidence bred of mastership—had an undeniable edge. But slaves were not without their own assets and experience, gained from hiring themselves, jobbing independently, and selling goods at market. Among their resources, none was more important than the support of family and community. Such mutuality belied the notion of *self*-purchase. Rather than being a solitary act, buying oneself was generally a collective effort of many individuals, beginning with immediate family members, extending to other kin, and sometimes reaching out to unrelated benevolent men and women, white as well as black.

Still, the resolution of the intense bargaining rarely fell fully in the slaves' favor. Few owners could resist squeezing their slaves one last time. Slaveowners added all manner of demeaning requirements that both forced slaves to recognize the old relationship even after it had legally expired and drained the nascent free black community of resources. For example, a New York slaveholder required his slave "to behave with fidelity and zeal for [her owner's] interest" for five years before agreeing to execute a promised deed of manumission. Others delayed freedom to ensure that their heirs would be properly supported. Often owners demanded hard cash as well as fealty, requiring their slaves to pay them directly for the grant of freedom. In Philadelphia, the painter Charles Willson Peale required his slave to beg door-to-door for money to pay for her freedom. A New York master promised to free his slave for $175 if he conducted himself "to the satisfaction of me and my family." Meeting the terms of such flinty benevolence took enormous discipline and years of hard work. It not only enabled slaveholders to exact additional value from their slaves but also allowed them to prolong slavery's existence well into the nineteenth century.[19]

However expensive and demeaning to the slave or lucrative and reassuring to the master, conditional emancipation eventuated in freedom. The greatly enlarged free black population camouflaged fugitives, allowing slaves to elude recapture. The greater the possibility of successful flight, the more carefully slaves plotted their escape. Many more fugitives aimed for permanent freedom rather than a brief respite in the woods or some back-alley retreat, taking food, clothing, and money—occasionally even a horse—before they fled. When Dan left his owner in Lancaster, Pennsylvania, in 1779, he not only carried "a good deal of money" but also several changes of clothing. His owner had "no doubt he will be particular in changing his dress," and, like so many postrevolutionary fugitives, would "endeavour to pass as a freeman." Others drew upon their wartime experience. Jack, who fled from Philadelphia in 1781, had been a "servant to Doctor Hutchinson when the army were at Valley Forge," and his owner thought he could be found in "some part of the country."[20] If unable to flee successfully, slaves took their owners to court, often with the assistance of abolitionist lawyers, who knew the law as well as their slaveholding counterparts and could turn it to the slaves' advantage. In at least one case, a slave openly demanded "that freedom, justice and protection, which I am entitled to by the laws of the state, although I am a Negro."[21]

A change in the nature of flight signaled slavery's demise. In 1781 a New Jersey slaveowner who had not bothered to advertise for his fugitive in the past, because the slave "had a trick of absenting himself for two or three weeks at a time and returning home," suddenly placed a notice in the press. In 1800 a New York mistress, driven by similar concerns about a runaway slave family, offered them the "privilege of working themselves free" if they returned.[22] Few fugitives did, and the number of attempted escapes, measured by the number of runaway advertisements, rose steadily in the 1790s. Often the increase was propelled by rumors that the emancipation had been promulgated by some legislative enactment, judicial fiat, or executive decree. The seeming inevitability of emancipation as one state after another opted for freedom and as news of the insurrection in Saint Domingue reached northern ports compelled slaves to act. In response, slaveholders instituted new controls, in one instance forming a "Slave Aprehending Society." Neither greater vigilance nor greater organization improved the slaveholders' cause, however. The promise of eventual emancipation had set slavery on the road to destruction.[23]

During the years of its lingering death in the North, slavery hardly behaved like a moribund institution. In 1788, while some pressed for abolition, the New York legislature enacted a comprehensive slave code, systematizing and strengthening the regulations underlying the system of chattel bondage. New Jersey lawmakers followed suit. As a result, progress toward legal freedom in the states that had enacted gradualist laws was painfully slow at best. While the number of free black people increased in New York in the postrevolutionary years, so too did the number of slaves. The slave population of New York grew by almost one-quarter and the number of slaveholders by one-third during the last decade of the eighteenth century. In 1790 "very few New Yorkers lived more than a few doors from a slaveholder." More than two-thirds of the black people in New York remained locked in bondage, and one in five New York households held at least one slave. Not until 1830 did free blacks outnumber slaves in parts of rural New York and New Jersey.[24]

Slavery survived especially well in the northern countryside. While urban slaveowners—particularly artisans—switched from slave to free wage labor, farmers in many of the North's richest agricultural areas increased their commitment to bonded labor. Between 1780 and 1810 the slave population of Pennsylvania dropped from nearly 7,000 to less than 800. In 1810 only two slaves resided in Philadelphia, which had once been the center of slavery in Pennsylvania. The remainder lived outside the city, most along the Maryland border. Slavery also flourished in rural New York. In 1800 more than half the white households in Kings County on Long Island held slaves, as did one-third of those in Richmond County and one-fifth of those in Queens. Those proportions declined slowly thereafter, so that ten years later more than one-third of the white households in Kings, one-quarter in Richmond, and one-eighth in Queens counties still owned slaves. In 1820, when 95 percent of the black people in New York City were free, only half of the slaves in Kings County had gained their liberty. In the county of Richmond, 600 black people—almost 90 percent of the black population—remained locked in bondage. In a similar fashion, emancipation in the Hudson Valley also lagged behind the arrival of freedom in the city of New York.

The concentration of slavery in rural areas provided opponents of emancipation with powerful political bases, stiffening resistance to the institution's eventual liquidation. At the beginning of the new century— the much-celebrated dawn of freedom and equality under law—the proportion of families that owned slaves was higher in the traditional slave-holding regions of New York, such as Long Island, than in most southern states.[25]

Black people who exited slavery often found themselves living in circumstances that looked suspiciously like the old bondage. Following the gradualist laws and conditional manumissions—which delayed freedom well into adulthood—many manumitters required their slaves to agree to long-term indentureships as part of the price of freedom, thereby reviving an older system of subordination and providing masters with a profitable exit from slaveownership. Even without prompting from their former owners, poverty forced many freed people to indenture themselves or their children to white householders. Often newly emancipated black people left bondage and entered servitude in the same motion. Whereas only five black people had been indentured in Philadelphia in 1780, five years later the number had risen to forty. During the 1790s, several hundred black people entered into long-term indentureships, with the number of indentures reaching its zenith in 1794, when over 300 black people, most of them children, entered into terms of servitude. Although servitude, unlike slavery, was not hereditary, servants lived under the control of a master or mistress, and the rights to their labor could be sold or traded like other property. The more closely that indentured servitude became identified with black labor, the smaller the difference between the treatment of slave and servant.[26]

Throughout the North, free blacks continued to reside in the households of their former owners, many of whom also held slaves. Indeed, as the emancipation process inched forward, the proportion of white slave-holders whose households included free blacks increased. By 1800 almost one-fifth of the slaveholders in New York City and one-third in Kings County housed free blacks. The overlap between householders who owned black slaves and those who held free black servants grew substantially in the following decade, suggesting that most free blacks merely replaced slaves in the social order and in the eyes of former owners. The line between servitude and slavery was fine indeed for black indentured servants, particularly since white servants rarely served more than seven years and rarely after age twenty-one. [27]

Unlike the Civil War emancipation, when Lincoln's Proclamation freed black people in the rebellious southern states in a single stroke, the process of emancipation during the Age of Revolution dragged on for years in most northern states, for decades in many, and for generations in some. Slavery's slow demise had powerful consequences for African-American life in the North, handicapping the efforts of black people to secure households of their own, to find independent employment, and to establish their own institutions. It encouraged the notion that black free people were no more than slaves without masters, thus hardening racial stereotypes, giving former slaveowners the time to construct new forms of subordination, and preventing the integration of black people into free society as equals. Moreover, while the old slave codes disappeared with the liquidation of slavery, many of the constraints remained. In many places, free blacks continued to be governed by the same regulations as slaves, subjected to curfews, restricted in their travels, and denied the right to vote, sit on juries, testify in court, and stand in the militia. The shift of slavery from the city to the countryside and from the workshop to the household severed blacks' ties with the most productive segments of the northern economy and denied many former slaves the opportunity to practice their trades. Finally, slavery's protracted demise created divisions within black society, between those who had early exited bondage and those who remained locked in slavery's grip until its final liquidation. For northern black people, the arrival of freedom in the postrevolutionary years was tempered by the continued reality of slavery and the emergence of newer forms of domination.

Legal freedom, however imperfect and slowly realized, was freedom nonetheless. Recognizing their new circumstances as a signal event in African-American history, black men and women determined to make the best of it. Former slaves commonly celebrated emancipation by taking new names. A new name was both a symbol of personal liberation and an ac of political defiance; it reversed the enslavement process and confirm d the free black person's newly won liberty, just as the loss of an Afric n name had earlier symbolized enslavement.

With a single stroke, former slaves claimed their freedom and obliterated lingering reminders of their past, in slavery *and* in Africa. The processes of emancipation and Americanization were one for northern black people, as biblical and common Anglo-American names replaced both African names and the derisive names slaveowners had forced upon them. In place of Caesar and Pompey, Charity and Fortune, Cuffee and Phibbee stood Jim and Betty, Joe and Sally, Bill and Susie. And as if to emphasize the new self-esteem that accompanied freedom, freed people usually elevated their names from the informal to the full form—to James, Elizabeth, Joseph, Sarah, William, and Susan.

The dual process of social and cultural change could also be seen in the choice of surnames. In bondage, most black people had but a single name; freedom allowed them the opportunity to select another. The Freemans, Newmans, Somersets, and Armsteads scattered throughout the North suggests how a new name provided an occasion to celebrate freedom. The names of the black soldiers in the Fourth Connecticut Regiment made the point directly: Pomp Liberty, Cuff Freedom, and Primis Freeman. Other black people, following an ancient tradition, borrowed surnames from their trades and skills, and a few took names that identified them with their color—most prominently Brown. But black people usually took common Anglo-American surnames—Jackson, Johnson, Moore, and Morgan—to accompany forenames of like derivation. These names, like the singular absence of the names of the great slaveholding families, again suggest how black people identified with free society as they shucked off their old status.[28]

The process of naming followed the chronology of emancipation, racing ahead where slavery fell and lagging where slavery remained in place. In Boston and Philadelphia, where emancipation was well advanced in the postrevolutionary years, most black families had surnames at the time of the first federal census in 1790. But few had taken surnames—or, if they had, census takers refused to recognize them—in New York City, where emancipation had yet to begin. Just ten years later, with freedom a reality for many more black people in New York City, surnames had become nearly universal. And, as in so many other ways, the transformation of black life in the countryside lagged behind the city. In rural New York, another decade would pass before most black people would be recognized by their surnames.[29]

For many former slaves, establishing a new address was also a part of the process of securing freedom. Freed people tried to escape the stigma of slavery by deserting their owner's abode for a new residence. For them, fleeing the memory of slavery and the subtle subordination that the continued presence of a former master entailed was reason enough to abandon old haunts. For others, however, freedom required a return to the site of their enslavement. During the war, many slaves had been refugeed to distant places by owners to prevent their escape, while others had fled precisely to make good their escape. Separated from family and friends and the familiar landmarks of their past, some of these displaced persons returned to their old homes, hopeful of resuming their old lives. Diverse motives mobilized thousands of black people in the years following the Revolution and gave the movement of the black population a helter-skelter appearance. Although former owners liked to employ the image of a people in disarray, most former slaves knew where they were going. The great thrust of postrevolutionary black migration in the North was from country to city.

The sources of urbanization could be found in the harsh conditions of rural life. Although some rural black men and women joined together to form small, close-knit villages, with their own churches and schoolhouses, most fell into new forms of dependency. They took their place among the North's landless farmhands who annually contracted with farmers in exchange for the right to a cottage, a garden, a woodlot, and occasionally a token sum of money. Over time, some black cottagers accumulated household furnishings, agricultural implements, and barnyard fowl and stock, but few purchased or even leased land of their own. During the fifty years after the Revolution, fewer than 10 percent of the black household heads owned land in Pennsylvania's Chester and Delaware counties, and most of this land was worthless scraps that no one else seemed to want.

The impoverishment of rural black men and women worked to the advantage of white farmers. Northern farmers encouraged the settlement of black cottagers by providing them land enough for a garden to give "employment and comfort to the wife and children; but not an inch of ground . . . for *cultivation* of any sort, which might tend to draw the cottager from the farmer's business, to attend to an enlarged employment of his own." While this arrangement aided those dependent on black laborers, who had a ready supply of hands at planting and harvest time, it left little room for black people to escape poverty. "You do not see one out of a hundred . . . that can make a comfortable living, own a cow, [or] a horse," observed a visitor to the New Jersey countryside in 1794.[30]

Poverty, isolation, and the accompanying insecurity limited the liberty of rural black people. Although they had the right to move freely and contract with whom they wished, the annual shuffling between employers or landlords rarely improved their prospects. And whatever they accumulated or achieved slipped away in times of economic hardship. Then, harsh realities forced rural black families to surrender their hard-won household independence. Black parents apprenticed their children to white farmers; black women moved into white households as domestics; black men took to the road or to the sea. The least fortunate found refuge in the county almshouse.[31] The poverty and isolation of rural life provided but a weak foundation for an independent black community. For that, black men and women turned to the city.

With the countryside increasingly identified with both the lingering remnants of slavery and new forms of dependency and coercion, rural black men and women gravitated toward the cities upon receipt of their freedom. In the years following the Revolution, the black population of the rural North declined and that of the cities shot upward. Boston's black population grew fastest in the 1770s, Philadelphia's in the 1780s, and New York's in the first decade of the nineteenth century. "Whole hosts of Africans now deluge our city," declared a white New Yorker in 1803, echoing complaints of white Bostonians and Philadelphians of previous decades.[32]

Refugees from the slave societies to the south added to the influx. Many of these former slaves had followed the British army as it traversed the continent. At war's end, the British evacuated thousands of black men and women—many of whom had served the Loyalist cause—from St. Augustine, Savannah, Charleston, and Yorktown to New York City. Fearful of reenslavement, most of these, including some 250 black New Yorkers, accompanied white Loyalists to Canada.[33] But some black Loyalists remained in the North. Other black southerners came northward on their own, following the North Star and making it—for the first time—into a symbol of freedom. This northward migration increased during the 1790s, when one southern state after another barred the entry of free blacks and made manumission contingent upon removal from the state. Would-be southern manumitters, prohibited from freeing slaves within their own jurisdictions, sent their former slaves to the North.[34]

To these mainland migrants were added several hundred, perhaps as many as a thousand, black refugees who had been caught in the insurgency that transformed Saint Domingue into the world's first black republic. The great exodus from Hispaniola, which began in 1791, continued for more than a decade, spurred by a cruel civil war that engulfed the island. In 1793 the first mass evacuation—a flotilla of nearly 200 ships bearing approximately 4,000 white refugees, nearly 2,000 slaves, and several hundred free people of color—stopped at the nearby Caribbean and mainland ports of Havana, Kingston, Charleston, Norfolk, and New Orleans. But hundreds also landed in Philadelphia, New York, and Boston. The entrance of refugees into the mainland grew as the exiles were chased away from one refuge after another by slaveholders fearful of the contagion of revolution. During the 1790s and into the first decade of the nineteenth century, many free people of color settled in the North.[35]

Unhappy with the new arrivals, northern officials did their best to bar the entry of black refugees—particularly those touched by the revolutionary events in Saint Domingue. Boston authorities "warned out" black migrants, expelling over 200 in 1800. Pennsylvania lawmakers, supported by the mayor of Philadelphia, debated prohibition on the entry of black people and the creation of a registration system that would require free black people to carry freedom papers.[36] But with no place else to go, desperate refugees continued to flood the mainland.

Their numbers swollen by the influx, northern blacks, who had always been disproportionately urban, became even more so. The black population of Philadelphia, New York, and Boston grew faster than the black population of their respective states of Pennsylvania, New York, and Massachusetts. By 1810 almost one-quarter of the black population of Massachusetts lived in Boston, nearly one-third of New York's in New York City, and two-fifths of Pennsylvania's in Philadelphia. The number of black people residing in secondary cities like Salem, Albany, Camden, and Pittsburgh also increased, as did a host of small, isolated black communities.

The cityward migration of black people from the North and South and the arrival of emigrés from Saint Domingue gave black life in the North an overwhelming urban bias. By the third decade of the nineteenth century, black northerners had almost entirely abandoned the countryside. In 1826 a Hudson Valley newspaper observed that while a "few of this ill-fated race, more wise and faithful than the rest, still remain in their old chimney corners to spend their days in comfort; [black people] are all gone to that paradise of negroes, *the City of New York!*"[37]

In some cities, such as Philadelphia, the black population grew faster than the city's white population. In 1780 fewer than one in twenty-five of Philadelphia's residents was black; by 1820 that proportion had grown to almost one in nine. Located on the crossroads between freedom and slavery, Philadelphia attracted numerous fugitives, immigrants, and refugees, but similar changes took place in other cities. Of the major seaports, only in New York did the black population fail to keep pace with the white. After growing more rapidly than the white populace in the 1780s, the proportion of the population that was black leveled off in the 1790s before sliding backward after 1800. But even in New York, black people remained a dynamic element in the city's population.[38] Throughout the North, emancipation permanently altered the geography of African-American life, fusing the transformation from slavery to freedom with the cityward movement that characterized nineteenth-century American society generally.

The sexual balance of black society also shifted with the movement of people set loose by emancipation. During the prerevolutionary period, black men generally outnumbered black women in the North, in large measure because of the disproportionate importation of African men. By the beginning of the nineteenth century, however, the sexual balance had shifted in the urban North. In 1806 black women outnumbered black men four to three in New York City. (Among slaves the imbalance was even more pronounced than among free blacks.) The disequilibrium grew thereafter. By 1820 there were many more black women than men in northern cities, an imbalance that remained well into the twentieth century. Notably absent were young men in their late teens and twenties, many of whom had been sold south as slaves and some of whom had found economic opportunity at sea, as the maritime industry became the largest single employer of free black men. In New York City, for example, women between the ages of fourteen and twenty-six outnumbered men two to one. In the countryside, the black population remained heavily male.[39]

Sexual imbalances within northern cities could be traced back to the legacy of slavery, the distortions created by gradual emancipation, and the economic opportunities available to freed people. As slaves, black workingmen had played a central role in the labor force of prerevolution-

ary northern cities. But unlike in colonial Charles Town and New Orleans, slave artisans in colonial Boston, New York, and Philadelphia
never monopolized any skilled trade. Except perhaps in New York City,
most slaves were confined to menial and irregular labor. Emancipation
did little to elevate the status of former slaves and in many ways weakened the place of black men in the northern economy.

As slavery waned in the North, slaves moved from the artisan shop to
the merchant household, severing the ties between black men and the
most lucrative urban work.[40] Newly freed slaves, particularly emigrants
from the countryside, had to establish ties that urban slaves of a previous
generation had enjoyed as a matter of course. Moreover, while revolutionary ideology promised freedom, it made no provision for former
slaves to be trained in a craft, and it offered them no guarantees of steady
work or a living wage. Slaveholders, who freed their slaves because they
believed that slavery was inconsistent with the Declaration of Independence or that all men were equal in the sight of God, saw in that belief no
further requirement that they provide their former slaves with a trade or
patronize their shops or stores. Once having freed their slaves, slaveowners expressed little or no concern for their fate. But the newly freed slaves
did not merely fall in occupational standing. Many slave craftsmen had
difficulty finding work at their old trades once they were free, as white
employers refused to hire free blacks for any but the most menial jobs.

In freedom, most black northerners remained confined to the unskilled and service sectors of the economy, laboring as cooks, washer-
women, seamstresses, coachmen, gardeners, and valets. The opportunities of the marketplace, so plentiful in the states to the south, were
severely limited in the North, where white farm women controlled the
trade in butter, eggs, and garden produce. While black women might
occasionally peddle oysters and cakes, in no northern city did they mo-
nopolize the market as they did in Charles Town and New Orleans. The
wide expanse of the marketplace, which black women occupied in the
ports to the south and which served as an important source of wealth and
social opportunity for black women, was largely closed to them in northern cities.

White northerners, who had a long acquaintance with black people
in the role of servants, simply exchanged enslaved servants for free ones.
Thus, as free blacks replaced slaves in the population, they also replaced
them in the domestic labor force, assuring employers of a steady supply

of household workers and maintaining racial perceptions of servitude that had been formed in slavery. The demand grew for domestics during the postrevolutionary years, as the merchants and professionals separated home and residence and as a new mercantile elite escalated the requirements of a comfortable domestic setting. In New York City, the number of white households with resident free blacks—most of them headed by merchants and professionals—increased threefold between 1790 and 1800. The laundress who labored within those homes became a ubiquitous black figure in every northern city, the very symbol of black womanhood. "The women," reported the Pennsylvania Abolition Society flatly in 1795, "both married and single, wash clothes for a living."[41]

The range of economic opportunities was only slightly greater for black men who, in addition to laboring as coachmen and valets, found work as day laborers. In 1800 at least 40 percent of the free black heads of households in New York and Philadelphia were "laborers," a broad category that included almost every black man without an identifiable skill.[42] At best, such work was hard, dirty, irregular, and unremunerative. Often it could be demeaning and shameful, as with the black laborers who cleaned streets, swept chimneys, and disposed of night soil. The arrival of new competitors—particularly Irish immigrants—placed black men on the defensive in the search for steady employment. If all workers had difficulty finding work in the years after the Revolution, black workers had more trouble than most. Some fell out of the ranks of the employed and into dependency or charity.[43]

Unable to find work on land, black men took to the sea in increasing numbers. Work on merchant ships, coasting vessels, whalers, and even some men-o'-war provided a broad avenue of economic opportunity for newly freed men without capital or place in society. In the years following the Revolution, one-fifth of Philadelphia's maritime workforce was black, and one-quarter of Philadelphia's adult black men (and still a larger proportion of the able-bodied) were sailors. Opportunities for sailors grew in the 1790s as the Napoleonic wars increased European demand for American goods and with it employment for merchantmen of all sorts.[44] The large number of men who took to the sea further shifted the sexual balance of the urban black population toward women, whose limited economic opportunities and poor pay—even when compared with black men—assured impoverishment.

Nonetheless, some black men and women found a niche in the middle ranks of American society, entering the professions and mechanical trades and securing small proprietorships. A handful became merchants and manufacturers of the first rank. Of the hundred black people listed in the 1795 Philadelphia directory, four were ministers and teachers, ten artisans, and seventeen tradespeople. In New York, where black people had deep roots in the mechanical trades, the proportion of black men practicing skilled trades may have been about twice as great as in Philadelphia, with approximately one-third of the adult black men working as skilled craftsmen in 1800.

The number of black artisans and tradespeople increased slowly but steadily during the postrevolutionary decades, as skilled slaves worked their way out of bondage and unskilled free blacks improved their standing. In Philadelphia, professionals advanced in number from three in 1795 to twelve in 1811; artisans increased from twelve in 1795 to over one hundred by 1816. Most of the advances were in the trades connected with the preparation of food and clothing. Butchers, brewers, cigar makers, confectioners, tailors, hatters, and shoemakers numbered high among the black artisan class. Along the docks and wharves, black men labored as ship joiners, caulkers, and ropemakers. Philadelphia's most successful black artisan, James Forten, employed about thirty workmen—white and black—in his sail-making operation.[45]

To white northerners, catering food, cutting hair, cleaning chimneys, and driving coaches seemed fitting roles for newly freed black men and women, since it kept black people at the service of white people in many of the very jobs where they had labored as slaves. Although some free blacks found such work embarrassing reminders of the past, others saw opportunities as well as an occupational refuge. Many of the most successful black businessmen took up and then expanded these trades. In New York City, black men dominated the oystering trade, working first as street vendors and then opening shops of their own. Black men and women played a similar role in the catering business. Robert Bogle, a former slave, began in Philadelphia as a waiter, contracting food for weddings, funerals, and parties; eventually he became a successful undertaker as well as caterer.

No trade better revealed the ability of black entrepreneurs to occupy the service sector of the economy than did hairdressing. Black barbers, in addition to cutting hair, operated bathhouses, pulled teeth, and lanced boils, all at a healthy profit. Likewise, the purchase of a horse—by which means a day laborer transformed himself into a carter or a drayman and, with hard work and luck, a stable keeper—provided yet another avenue of advancement. Although regulations in some cities (most notably New York) barred the entry of black men into the carting trades, in most places drayage allowed ambitious black men to escape the harsh reality of the pick, the shovel, and the broom.

Many of these service trades were closed to women, black or white. But some black women operated boardinghouses and brothels, serving the hundreds of black sailors who passed through the great port cities. Others, playing upon their reputations as cooks or seamstresses, commanded substantial prices for their product. Such work was necessary, for black households generally needed two incomes.[46]

Economic independence provided the basis of family security, and no goal stood higher among the newly freed than establishing a household under their own control. Given the opportunity, newly freed slaves legitimated relations which previously had no standing in law, joining together to celebrate weddings and to register their marriages in official records often of their own making.[47] The legitimatization of long-standing relationships gave black people a freer hand in performing familiar duties, as husbands and wives, parents, and sons and daughters. In Philadelphia, the Pennsylvania Abolition Society reported that some freed people "were found supporting their aged parents and grandparents" and "others providing for orphans and destitute children."[48]

But giving family life a basis in fact as well as in law was generally the last step in the process of family reconstruction. Before a family could be united under one roof, spouses, parents, and children had to be located. Slavery had separated them, and the Revolution added to the divisions, as young men and women marched off to war or took flight and as children and the elderly were refugeed or carried by their owners to distant places. The disruption of the fragile domestic arrangements that sustained slave family life can be measured by the fact that only twenty-three black children were born in Philadelphia between 1775 and 1780.[49] Wartime disorder assured that the postrevolutionary process of family reconstruction would be slow, tedious, and—for many—incomplete.

Much as they desired to achieve household independence, northern blacks generally began their life in freedom by residing with white employers—often their former owners—who might agree to hire both parents and provide space for their children. In Boston, nearly two decades after slavery had been abolished, more than one-third of all black people resided in households headed by white men or women. The process of securing household independence was even slower in Philadelphia, where in 1800, two decades after the Pennsylvania legislature enacted its gradualist plan, more than half of the black population resided in white households. But some freed people were unable to find an employer willing to lodge all family members. Urban employers—much like urban slaveholders—generally wanted only healthy adults in their households, and viewed children and old people as unwarranted encumbrances. Newly freed slaves often had to apprentice their children and allow elderly parents to shift for themselves; thus, black families were divided in freedom as they had been divided in slavery. In 1790 at least one-quarter of the black households in Philadelphia bound their children into long-term apprenticeships with white families.[50]

Slowly, as they gained competencies, black people escaped white households, but many of these black families were not yet able to survive on their own. Low wages and irregular employment required black families to double up, with two or more families living in a single household. Numerous black families took in boarders to make ends meet. Although black families were generally smaller than white ones—reflecting a later age of marriage, a lower birth rate, and the necessity of apprenticing children—black households contained many more "extra people" under the same roof than did white households.[51] Black families continued to bear the burden of slavery as they confronted the reality of poverty.

Still, the reconstructed African-American family was far healthier than the black family in slavery. When black people came together under one roof, they ate better and lived longer. Infant mortality fell as parents devoted more time to their children. During the 1790s, there were over 400 more births than deaths among black people in Philadelphia, and the city's African-American population grew through natural increase.[52]

Household formation in the postrevolutionary North followed the staggered pace of emancipation, taking more than a generation to complete. Since the chronology of emancipation differed from place to place, the process of family reconstitution continued well into the nineteenth century, as black families accumulated the capital to provide for household independence. In Boston, where slavery had been eliminated during the Revolution, one in three black persons still dwelled in a household headed by a white person in 1790; thirty years later, 85 percent of the black population lived independently. In Philadelphia, where most black people had escaped slavery during the 1780s, over 50 percent of the free blacks had achieved independent household status in 1790 and nearly 75 percent reached that goal by 1820. The process was still slower in New York City. Between 1800 and 1820 the proportion of free black families residing in white households remained steady at about one-third. Newcomers to the city followed the same pattern: finding a residence in a white household, apprenticing their children while they gained competence, establishing a household with another black family, and finally achieving the long-desired household independence.[53]

The cost of household independence was high. However galling and degrading, living under another's roof guaranteed subsistence. On their own, former slaves had trouble supporting themselves, particularly in times of economic distress, which came frequently to men and women proscribed from all but the most menial labor. The movement out of white households was accompanied by a sharp rise in the number of black residents in poorhouses and asylums. Almost simultaneous with the achievement of household independence in 1815, the proportion of black residents of the Philadelphia almshouse outstripped the black share of that city's population for the first time. It increased steadily thereafter, as did the proportion of black inmates in the state penitentiary.[54]

As black men and women escaped white households and set up housekeeping on their own, the residential distribution of black people shifted. In the great seaports, black people left their owners' neighborhoods for the same reasons they had abandoned the countryside—to escape the daily reminders of their former status. In New York, as in other northern cities, the heaviest slaveholding wards had the fewest free blacks. But the new pattern of residence was hardly a ghetto. No single area of residential concentration emerged in any northern city. Instead, clusters of three or four black families appeared, generally set in older commercial areas that were residentially undesirable to whites or in newer suburbs that had not yet become fashionable or accessible. In these neighborhoods, black people found rents affordable and, for some, homeownership possible.

Before long, however, neighborhoods with high concentrations of black families developed. By 1810, two-thirds of black Philadelphians—men and women who had previously been scattered throughout the commercial district—resided in the Cedar Street Corridor. Within ten years, the proportion of Philadelphia's black people who resided around Cedar Street had risen to three-quarters. A similar area of residential concentration emerged in New York City (between Mulberry and Orange Streets) and in Boston (behind Beacon Hill). Although the majority of residents of such neighborhoods were white, the high proportion of black people made them centers of the nascent African-American community.[55]

Such urban concentrations soon sported a host of institutions—themselves a lure to new black residents—which addressed the problems of the newly freed slaves. Many of these new institutions rested upon the informal, clandestine associations black people had created in slavery. Others drew on the experiences slaves gained interacting with white abolitionists who had assisted their passage from slavery. Yet others were a product of the novel circumstances of freedom.

The new institutions were a consequence of both the waning of the old and the emergence of the new. By the beginning of the nineteenth century, few Africans could be found in the North, and these aged men and women could no longer be relied upon to lead their people. Their memories of the old country, which had served as a bulwark against the adoption of Anglo-American forms, no longer carried the weight they once did. Opposition to conversion, which had kept most black people out of Christian churches despite the best efforts of Anglican mission men and a host of evangelicals, wore thin as newly freed black people searched for ways to organize their communities, create a sense of belonging, and give voice to their moral and social commitments.

But freedom also created new problems which required new solutions. Still ranking high among these was the need to bury the dead and provide for the departed's kin. As slaves, black people had labored to gain full control of the burial rites, but even their successes rested upon the sufferance of their owners and was subject to the oversight of municipal authorities. With freedom, the responsibility was fully theirs. During the postrevolutionary years, every black community established some association to meet this essential human need. The Free African Society of Newport, Rhode Island, a quasi-religious benevolent association founded in 1780, was a prototype of such organizations, as was the Free African Society of Philadelphia established seven years later. In 1790 the leaders of the Philadelphia group attempted to lease the Strangers' Burial

Ground, where Philadelphia black people had been buried since the early eighteenth century. When that failed, they purchased ground of their own.[56]

But like many similar associations, Philadelphia's Free African Society soon turned to the problems of the living. The Society instituted regular procedures respecting marriage and established a register to record them. As its role in burying the dead and marrying the living suggests, the Free African Society was fast transforming itself into a church. In 1790 its members organized a "Union" congregation, with the aim of incorporating the entire black community within a single body. The process—sped by the growing antagonism to free blacks within the established churches and the desire of black people to worship by themselves—foundered upon social as well as denominational differences within the black community. By 1794 Philadelphia's Union Church had metamorphosed into St. Thomas's African Episcopal Church under the leadership of Absalom Jones, while Richard Allen had established an independent Methodist congregation that would eventually become "Mother Bethel" of the African Methodist Episcopal Church.[57]

African churches quickly emerged as the central organization in what Absalom Jones called the struggle to "throw off that servile fear, that habit of oppression and bondage train us up in."[58] For almost a century, white missionaries had tried without notable success to introduce northern black people to Christianity, and there were proportionately fewer black people attached to Christian churches in 1750 than there had been in 1650. But black leadership changed the dynamic of conversion. Drawn by the promise of salvation and the prospect of controlling their own destiny, black people rushed to join the new churches. Members of white-controlled organizations abandoned them, and unchurched black people enrolled for the first time. By century's end, both Jones's African Episcopal Church and Allen's African Methodist Church had nearly doubled their memberships from their beginnings less than a decade earlier. The process of Christianization took on new speed as leadership passed from white to black churchmen.[59]

In other cities the institutional development within the African-American community took a different course, measured to some degree by the timing of emancipation. In some places, benevolent societies or fraternal orders, rather than churches, became the central community organizations. In Boston, Prince Hall's Masonic Lodge preceded the appearance of the African church. But whatever the organizational form, these institutions served as platforms from which to address the problems black people faced in freedom. Within their walls, black people educated themselves and their children, insured themselves against disaster, protected themselves against kidnappers, planned for their future, and, perhaps most important, set the standards for their deportment as a free people. Newport Society ordered its members to "dress themselves and appear decent on all occasions so that they may be useful to all and every such burying . . . That all the spectators may not have it in their power to cast such game contempt, as in times past." Everywhere such associations turned political, issuing condemnations of slavery and racial discrimination and demanding the vote and other elements of citizenship. In confronting the problems of the black community, a few men and women came to the fore, articulating their identity as a free people.[60]

The new organizations marked the emergence of a new leadership class in the black community. Fired in the furnace of Revolution, these men and women came of age with freedom. Many owed their liberty to the changes unleashed during the Age of Revolution, and they shared the optimism that accompanied independence. Generally wealthier, more literate, and better connected with white people than most former slaves, these upward-striving and self-consciously respectable men took the leadership of the enlarged free black population and stood in the vanguard of those advocating the liberation of black people. Pointing to the Declaration of Independence, they petitioned for a ban on the slave trade, demanded that the rights to manumission be enlarged, and pressed for a general emancipation. Where gradual emancipation laws had been enacted, they labored to speed slavery's final demise. When Pennsylvania slaveholders attempted to amend the Act of 1780 and reenslave many of those who had recently been emancipated, black petitioners successfully petitioned the state legislature not to return former slaves to "all the horrors of hateful slavery" after restoring "the common blessings they were by nature entitled to." And once freedom was achieved, black people demanded complete equality, attacking limitations on their right to sit on juries, testify in court, and vote.[61]

Proud of their achievements and certain their experience provided a guide that would elevate the race, the new leaders did not hesitate to lecture "their people" on the importance of hard work, temperance, frugality, and piety. Turning their back on the saturnalia of Election Day, they established new forms of social action, celebrating not the coronation of a surrogate king but their own emancipation. Their disciplined caucuses with their careful adherence to parliamentary rules and precisely worded memorials with their classical references demonstrated that they were not a heathen, uncivilized people but respectable working people worthy of citizenship in the republic.[62]

Much of their intended audience hardly heard the message. Outside of a small circle of abolitionists, white northerners ignored their meetings, dismissed their petitions, and ridiculed their parades. More important, many of their black compatriots also paid them no mind. Eager to enjoy the immediate rewards of freedom, they spent their wages on new frocks and waistcoats. While the respectables met in the quiet decorum of their sitting rooms to debate the issues of the day, the newcomers joined together in smoke-filled gaming houses and noisy midnight frolics. Their boisterous lifestyle, colorful dress, plaited hair, eelskin queues, and swaggering gait scandalized the respectables. While the respectables saw such behavior as a calumny upon the race and a special threat to their own efforts to secure full recognition, the newcomers disdained the pretensions of black men and women who acted "white."[63]

The division within black society manifested itself in many ways. While the respectables protested with decorous petitions, passed through the friendly hands of well-connected members of the abolitionist and manumission societies, the newcomers were more likely to act directly, suggesting a connection with the streets rather than the church and indicating the different routes black people took to protect their newly won freedom.[64]

The most successful black leaders, such as Richard Allen or Prince Hall, managed to unite these diverse elements of African-American society. In some ways, the African-American churches became a point of mediation between the lives of the upward-striving middle class and the poor. But church membership remained low in the black community, and a large proportion of the male black population was off at sea.

The almost universal adoption of the term "African" in the designation of African-American institutions marked the final creation of an African nationality in the New World. In much the same way as the Dutch Reformed Church affirmed Dutch nationality or the Anglican Episcopal Church affirmed English nationality on the western side of the Atlantic, the designation "African" affirmed the distinctiveness and confirmed the unity of black people. If black men and women in the North no longer called themselves or named their children in the traditional African manner, they celebrated their origins on the placards that adorned the largest buildings and the biggest organizations in the black community. The Free African Society of Philadelphia began its articles of incorporation with the words: "We, the free *Africans* and their descendants." Some spoke earnestly about returning to Africa, although few actually made the journey.[65] The acceptance of "African" as the institutional designation also denoted the passing of distinctive national identities—the descendants of Africa were no longer Igbos, Coromantees, or Gambians. Henceforth, all people of African descent would be one people.[66]

Chapter Ten

The Union of African-American Society in the Upper South

✞

The revolutionary crisis transformed African-American life in the Chesapeake, or, as it was called when Marylanders, North Carolinians, and Virginians moved west into Kentucky and Tennessee, the Upper South. As in the northern colonies, the struggle for political independence—both the war itself and the changes that accompanied the establishment of an independent republic—challenged slavery, as slaves and their allies hammered at chattel bondage with the mallets of revolutionary republicanism and evangelical egalitarianism. But unlike in the North, slavery in the Upper South did not crack. The slave society that had emerged in the wake of the plantation revolution of the late seventeenth century hardly faltered, even as the region's periphery—mostly prominently the area surrounding Baltimore—devolved into a society with slaves. Thousands of slaves gained their freedom in the Upper South, and the greatly enlarged free black population began to reconstruct black life in freedom. But the expansion of slavery and with it a host of new forms of racial dependencies more than counterbalanced the growth of freedom.

The simultaneous expansion of freedom and of slavery defined black life in the Upper South and united free and slave as in no other region of the United States. The nascent class lines—informed more by notions of propriety and respectability than by material standing—that divided black people in the free states did not materialize in the Upper South; freedom and slavery evolved in a parallel course that entwined free and slave blacks in the same families, workplaces, churches, and communities. A two-caste system with rigid divisions between black and white came to exemplify the Upper South following the Age of Revolution.

Even before the war began, black people in the Chesapeake understood the importance of the revolutionary conflict to their own independence, and they seized the divisions within the slaveowning class to improve their lot, perhaps even to secure their liberty.[1] In April 1775 a delegation of slaves visited Lord Dunmore, the royal governor of Virginia, and offered to exchange their services for freedom. Dunmore sent them packing, but their bold stroke confirmed the governor's belief that slaves could be counted among the king's friends. That November, when the long-smoldering dispute between colony and metropolis burst into open warfare, Dunmore freed all slaves willing to bear arms in His Majesty's service, and black men and women flocked to his headquarters in Norfolk harbor. Their numbers grew steadily until early December, when Patriot troops routed Loyalist forces, including a large number of black men wearing sashes emblazoned with the words "Liberty to Negroes." The loss broke the back of Dunmore's attempt to discipline the rebellious Virginians and depreciated his emancipationist pledge.[2]

Despite military failure and Patriot propaganda that the British would sell their black followers to the sugar islands, Dunmore's promise stirred slaves throughout the continent. It echoed loudly in the North, and had an even more powerful resonance in the Chesapeake region. At George Washington's Mount Vernon estate, Washington's steward frankly confessed that the general's slaves found liberty to be "sweet" and "there is not a man of them, but woud leave us, if they believ'd they coud make their escape." Indeed, whenever Dunmore's flotilla neared the coast, slaves—as one dejected master put it—began "flying to Dunmore." Slaveholders became so distraught about the loss that they addressed an article in the *Virginia Gazette* directly to their slaves in which, by turns, they denied complicity in the slave trade, threatened death to runaways, and enjoined their slaves to "be content with their situation, and expect a better condition in the next world." Robert Carter of Nomini Hall, the grandson of "King" Carter and himself one of the largest slaveholders in Virginia, assembled his slaves and lectured them on Dunmore's treachery. Upon receiving assurances of their loyalty, Carter instructed them in their duties in the event of a British invasion. His lecture appeared to have the desired effect, but when the opportunity arrived, Carter's slaves fled.[3]

Dunmore used his black recruits to raid the Virginia coast, and his black soldiers aided hundreds of slaves to escape, sometimes assisting the evacuation of entire plantations. In August 1776, when Dunmore retreated to Bermuda, 300 black fugitives sailed north with him, hoping for future military service and freedom. All told, about 800 slaves escaped to join Dunmore, and more importantly, hundreds more heard of his promise of freedom and were infected with the dream of liberty.[4]

But until its final months, the war touched the Chesapeake region lightly, compared with the extended military occupation suffered by New York and Philadelphia to the north and Charleston and Savannah to the south. Still, military operations in the Chesapeake greatly disrupted the plantation regime and created an opportunity for some slaves to flee their owners. The royal navy was omnipresent—controlling the Chesapeake Bay throughout the war, implementing a blockade beginning in 1777, and allowing British troops to make periodic landed incursions. At the war's end, vast armies ravaged the countryside.[5]

Primed by Dunmore's earlier promise, slaves saw the Union Jack as a standard of freedom. When it appeared on the horizon, they fled their owners' homes. In February 1777—soon after the royal navy established its blockade—British warships gave refuge to over 300 fugitives off the coast of Virginia, and the number who sought British protection hardly diminished in the months that followed. In August, with the sight of General William Howe's armada sailing up the Chesapeake to assault Philadelphia, the number of runaways escalated. Slaveholders confiscated even the smallest dinghies, posted militiamen "to stop the Negroes flocking down from the interior parts of the country," and, in desperation, summarily executed captured fugitives. But there was no way to guard all of the Chesapeake's numerous creeks and inlets, and not even the closest surveillance or rumors of abuse at the hands of their owners' enemy could stem the flood of runaways. Slaves, bemoaned one prominent planter in 1781, "continue to go to [the British], not withstanding many who have escaped and inform others of their ill treatment."[6]

Losses that had been confined to the tidewater during the first years of the war spread to the interior as the war widened, allowing slaves earlier refugeed from the coast to fulfill the hope that Dunmore had aroused. When Prince escaped from his piedmont plantation, his owner "expected he tried to get to Howe's army, as he once attempted to join Dunmore." After a British raid up the James River, a prominent clergyman reported that "the families within the sphere of this action have suffered greatly. Some have lost 40, others 30, every one a considerable part of their slaves." Few of the great Chesapeake planters—the Carters, Harrisons, Jeffersons, Nelsons, and Washingtons—survived the war without losing at least part of their slaves. Indeed, British raiders took special delight in liberating the slaves of the great Patriots. Most of George Washington's slaves never had a chance to taste the "sweet liberty" that Dunmore offered, but when the British raided Mount Vernon in 1781, seventeen slaves fled, including some of Washington's most trusted artisans and house servants.[7]

Some slaveholding Patriots recognized the hypocrisy of their war for liberty. James Madison freed his slave Billy, who had been captured while fleeing to the British, observing that the young man desired only "that liberty for which we have paid the price of so much blood, and have proclaimed so often to be [the] right, and worthy pursuit of every human being." But even Madison's magnanimity came grudgingly with the opinion that flight had "thoroughly tainted" Billy, and that he was no longer "a fit companion for fellow slaves in Virga." Most of Madison's compatriots would not concede even that. Frustrated and bitter over their losses, slaveowners tried to discourage runaways with predictions of a "more heartless captivity" in the West Indies than any known in the Chesapeake. Some took perverse satisfaction when slaves—probably thousands—died of epidemic disease in British encampments. Though such dangers gave slaves pause, they never dammed the stream of fugitives, and before long some runaways were returning to their old estates, not to beg forgiveness but to lead family members and friends to British lines.[8]

Not all losses could be attributed to the slaves' initiative. Tories, privateers, and banditti, often allied with fugitive slaves, went out of their way to seize the Patriots' slaves. One such expedition featured several barges, manned by "tories and Negroes," which sailed up the Nanticoke River on Maryland's eastern shore and "plundered the inhabitants . . . of their slaves and valuable effects." British raids during the summer of 1779 on the Virginia coast—particularly on the peninsula between the James and the Rappahannock rivers—cost Patriot slaveowners an estimated one thousand slaves and convinced one master that "if a stop is not put to those cruisers . . . our most valuable Negroes will run away." And so it seemed to Virginia planters when another expedition, this one commanded by the turncoat Benedict Arnold, began a series of incursions along the James, reaching Richmond in January 1781 and taking hundreds of slaves along the way.[9]

But those assaults were only the beginning. With the arrival of Lord

Cornwallis and his army in Virginia, still more slaves took leave of their owners, emptying the quarters of many plantations. "Your neighbors Col. Taliaferro and Col. Travis lost every slave they had in the world, and Mr. Paradise has lost all but one," observed Richard Henry Lee in tracing Cornwallis's progress through Virginia. "This," he added, "has been the general case of all those who were near the enemy." By the time Cornwallis's doomed army reached Yorktown, 4,000 to 5,000 slaves were in his train.[10]

Once under royal protection, slaves ingratiated themselves to their hosts by making the king's cause their own. In some respects, it was an easy task, as the manpower shortage that had induced Dunmore to employ black troops worsened as the war dragged on. British officers put hundreds of slaves to work. Benedict Arnold employed 300 black men to fortify Portsmouth and protect it from counterattack by Patriot forces. Large numbers of black men and women tendered their services as personal servants. "Every officer," noted one Hessian soldier, "had . . . three or four Negroes, as well as one or two Negresses on horseback for his servants. Each squad had one or two horses and Negroes, and every noncommissioned officer has two horses and one Negro." The enlisted soldiers also had "his Negro, who carried his provisions and bundles." Black men, many of them recent fugitives, manned the barges and skiffs that raided the Chesapeake coastline, and black women cleaned, laundered, and did other necessary work around army camps.[11]

As in the North, Patriot commanders were slower than their British counterparts to recruit slaves as soldiers and laborers. Rather than enlist black men in the revolutionary cause, they offered those who returned from British service a full pardon and threatened those who did not with jail, exile, mutilation, and death. But as the war lengthened and manpower grew critically short, the rebel colonies in the Upper South—following the North's lead—yielded to grim necessity. Maryland lawmakers authorized slave enlistment and subjected free blacks to the draft. Virginia legislators, while shunning James Madison's proposal to create a black regiment, allowed free black men to enlist in its army and navy. Delaware, Maryland, and Virginia permitted slave men to serve as substitutes for their masters. The black men who enlisted as soldiers in the Patriot cause never totaled more than several hundred, but thousands left their plantations to work on Patriot fortifications.

Such actions, of course, no more challenged the Patriots' commitment to the institution of slavery than did the earlier presence of black militiamen in the service of the French and Spanish Crown. Instead, Patriot commanders believed they were using black labor as they always had: to support a way of life based on chattel bondage. Nonetheless, the presence of black men and women in Patriot service revealed how war had forced slaveholders to act in previously inconceivable ways. The shocking turn of events was not lost on those slaves who remained with their owners.[12]

Slaves who marched off to war, whether in British or American service, faced a hard regimen with scant assurances of eventual liberation. Both sides employed black men and women opportunistically, lavishing fugitives with promises when they were needed and cruelly dismissing them when they were not. Rather than secure their freedom, fugitive slaves found themselves used as bounties to recruit white soldiers and compensate loyal slaveholders for their losses. Military officers, with no personal stake in the well-being of their charges, worked black laborers hard. Like Dunmore's black recruits, the black men who followed them into military service were "kept constantly employed in digging entrenchments in wet ground, till at length the severity of their labour forced many of them to fly." Such hardships—compounded by scanty rations, shabby clothing, wretched housing, and epidemic disease—convinced many to avoid both belligerents and wait out the war on their old plantations.[13]

Fearful that the war would bypass them but unwilling to chance the dangers of military life, some runaways lived off the land, a dangerous practice for black men and women at any time and more so in wartime. The maroon population of the Great Dismal Swamp and other backwaters increased once again, as slaveholders had neither time nor the resources to pursue fugitives. Others joined bands of guerrillas or Tories. The number of interracial bandits plundering the countryside rose during the last years of the war and became a growing problem for slaveowners, who found that such gangs enjoyed "great success in procuring our slaves." A few slaves plotted rebellions of their own, often with the aid of disaffected white men whose allegiance to the planter class atrophied as the war dragged on. "The insolence of the Negroes in this county is come to such a height," wrote one Patriot from the eastern shore of Maryland, "that we are under a necessity of disarming them." The local Committee of Safety collected eight guns, along with swords and bayonets.[14]

As the possibility grew that they would lose their slaves, planters refugeed them to distant places in hopes of removing slaves beyond the chance of successful flight. In addition to those impressed to meet some emergency, potential fugitives—slaves "merely suspected of a design to . . . escape"—were exiled to the west to work in the lead mines of Virginia. Others were sent for safe-keeping to remote upcountry quarters. Such actions sped the shift of population from the tidewater to the interior and helped to unify the region. But removal, no matter what the cause, separated slaves from their loved ones, sundering families and friends. Indeed, the disruptions often became another inducement to flight.[15]

Under such circumstances, few planters could continue business as usual. Although the British rarely chased slaveholders from their estates, their blockade severed planters from their most lucrative markets, causing severe economic dislocations at the very moment when wartime property losses and high taxes stressed their resources and threatened their prosperity. While some of the great planters who were isolated from the main field of battle did well, many of the smaller ones suffered, as the disruption in trade eroded their assets and sometimes left them clad in threadbare clothes with nothing but garden vegetables for their tables.[16]

To compensate for wartime disruptions, planters reshuffled their crops and revamped their agricultural practices in ways that accelerated the ongoing transformation of the region's economy from a tobacco monoculture to a mixed-farming regime. They generally reduced tobacco production and increased production of foodstuffs, cloth, and various other necessities, manufacturing many items they had once imported from Britain. As home industries increased, slaves found themselves practicing new trades, such as weaving cloth, churning butter, molding candles, cobbling shoes, boiling salt, and carding wool. A visitor to Virginia noted that spinning was "the chief employment of the female negroes."[17]

Such alterations might assure planters a full larder in hard times, but home production still left them strapped for cash. To provide some extras, they lit upon other work for their slaves, driving them hard. Often the new duties in the weaving houses and shoemaking shops did not come as substitutes for customary tasks but as additions to them. Weary slaves found themselves laboring far into the night to complete their assignments. Even then slaves discovered that their basic allotment of food, clothing, medicine, and salt was sharply reduced. With slaveowners themselves wearing homespun clothes and running short of provisions, they no longer would—or could—dole out the standard issue of rations. To ward off hunger, slaves hunted and fished, expanded their gardens, peddled handicrafts, and raided their owners' larder more than once.[18] The modest expansion of the slaves' economy was costly to master and slave.

As slaveholders piled new tasks upon the old, increasing the slaves' duties and lengthening their workday, wartime changes evoked new struggles between master and slave over the terms of labor and the circumstances of slave life. The renegotiation proceeded unevenly as the balance of power between slave and slaveowner shifted with the winds of war. Where planters remained insulated from wartime events, they might adjust the burden of subsistence to the slaves and institute additional labor requirements. But even then they moved with great care, and often proposed changes with an entreaty, not a command. Where slavery was threatened by British incursions or the possibility of flight, the initiative shifted to the slaves, who made their demands known by working more in their own gardens than in their owners' fields. Attempts to reestablish the old order or to rebalance it in the planters' favor soon elicited complaints of demoralization and charges of insolence from the master class. Proximity to British lines hardened the slaves' resolve to work less than before. In the summer of 1779 the slaves on a Maryland plantation struck back when overseer William Elson pressed them too hard. Turning on him, they "cut his throat from Ear to Ear with an Axe." With every slave a potential runaway or violent rebel, few overseers were as foolish as Elson.[19]

War's end confirmed the wisdom of the planters' caution. When the British evacuated Yorktown, they took hundreds of slaves with them. Many of these stalwarts of the British cause were betrayed and given to soldiers as bounties or to Loyalist planters in compensation for property confiscated by the Patriots.[20] But the British also allowed slaves to make their way to freedom in the North and the West Indies. In 1783, when the British evacuated New York, they carried over 1,000 black Virginians and Marylanders to freedom in Canada and elsewhere. In all, more than 5,000 Upper South slaves escaped slavery during the war and perhaps as many remained in the South as free men and women.[21]

This paltry loss—a tiny fraction of the region's slave population—

hardly affected the long-term development of the Upper South. By re-fugeeing some slaves, disciplining others, and renegotiating the basic la-bor arrangements with still others, Chesapeake slaveholders kept their major holdings intact. In time, they recovered some fugitives from places as distant as Charleston, St. Augustine, and New York, dragging them from freedom's doorstep back into slavery.

More significantly, over the course of the war the number of slaves in the Upper South increased by natural means. In Maryland the slave population inched up from 80,000 at the beginning of the war to 83,000 in 1783, as did Virginia's—from about 210,000 at the commencement of the war to 236,000 at its end. Despite all of the wartime turbulence that increased mortality and allowed some slaves to escape, the Chesapeake's slave population continued to increase at an annual rate of about 2 per-cent. In the last quarter of the century, the slave population of the Chesa-peake had nearly doubled. As more children were born to slaves on plantations and as some states, following the North, banned importa-tion, the Chesapeake became a net exporter of slaves.[22]

The steady expansion of the slave population in the Upper South during the wartime years allowed many nonslaveholders to enter the slaveholders' ranks. Between 1782 and 1790 the proportion of property-holders owning slaves increased from 47 to 60 percent in Charles County, Maryland, and it followed a similar path in other rural jurisdictions, so that two-thirds of white householders held slaves. But the greatest growth in slaveholding came not among new entries to the owning class but among the grandees, whose expanding holdings swelled the popula-tion of the great plantation towns. On many estates, the number of slaves soon exceeded the number of workers needed. George Washington spoke for his class when he observed that it was "demonstratively clear that . . . I have more working Negros by a full moiety, than can be employed to any advantage in the farming system."[23]

Enjoying a surfeit of bound labor, Chesapeake planters became the great opponents of the African trade, smugly condemning both Lower South planters who were eager to repopulate their plantations after the disruptions of the war and the northern merchants who were equally eager to supply them. In condemning the international slave trade while embracing the interstate trade, Upper South planters could lament slav-ery as an evil that had been foisted upon them by their former British overlords while reaffirming their commitment to chattel bondage.[24]

Indeed, the internal slave trade proved to be a source of enormous profit, what one Maryland newspaper called "an almost universal resource to raise money." Planters not only collected quick cash from the sale of "excess" slaves, much of which was promptly invested in the region's expanding industrial economy, but it also provided them an opportunity to reconfigure their labor force in ways that improved productivity. Edward Lloyd, the largest slaveowner on Maryland's eastern shore, regularly sold a portion of his holdings—generally teenaged children—to keep his plantation workforce at what he believed to be the appropriate level. The practice was adopted by many others, as even the most conscientious masters found it necessary to reduce the size of their holdings periodically. Smaller planters followed suit, although some of them migrated with their slaves to seek new opportunities in the West. Yet others migrated cityward.

The migration to the Virginia piedmont, begun before the war, continued in its aftermath. But the Blue Ridge could not contain the ambitions of Chesapeake planters and farmers, who spilled into the Great Valley of the Shenandoah and up to the edge of the Alleghenies. Before long they had vaulted into Kentucky and Tennessee, and some were headed down the Mississippi with slaves in tow. By century's end, slaves whose ancestors had worked the tobacco fields of the Chesapeake for a hundred years or more were growing hemp in Kentucky and Tennessee, cotton in the Lower South, and sugar in the lower Mississippi Valley. In 1790 Kentucky counted 13,000 slaves, almost all of them from the Chesapeake region. Ten years later the total was nearly 40,000. Other slaves could be found in Tennessee, Missouri, and Louisiana. The exodus accelerated in the first decade of the nineteenth century. In all, an estimated 115,000 slaves left the tidewater region between 1780 and 1810.[25] The long-distance migrations from the tidewater to the piedmont and from the seaboard states to Kentucky and Tennessee created havoc as thousands of slave families were dismembered and communities set adrift.

Still, even with this massive exodus, the slave population of the tidewater region continued to grow. Not all tidewater slaveholders had the inclination to migrate or to sell their slaves into exile. Some appreciated the devastating effects such migrations had on their slaves, and others feared that even a hint of the despised deportation would encourage flight. Instead, they sold excess slaves to nearby estates, which allowed slaves to maintain their families at a distance. Other slaveowners apprenticed young slave men and women to trades or rented them out, adding to their income while satisfying their consciences. The largest planters transferred their slaves between quarters to optimize their employment.[26]

The new mobility within the Upper South—like the great migrations to the West and Southwest—added yet another trauma to the lives of thousands of slaves. Families, sometimes whole communities, were destroyed by the planters' desire to place their economy on a firmer footing. Even those slaves untouched by the inauguration of the interstate slave trade—and few slave families in the Upper South would not be directly affected by the southward sale of some loved one—felt the chill of uncertainty that the trade engendered. Those who left the region found themselves cut off from their African roots. This rupture both sped the process of creolization and spread the Chesapeake's peculiar variant of African-American culture to the rest of the continent. For those who remained, it dissolved communities, disrupting long-established networks of families and friends.

Hardly noting the massive upheaval they had set in motion, Upper South slaveholders labored to reestablish the prewar status quo on their own plantations and farms. Many of the slave men who had left the field for the shops and slave women who moved to the weaving houses abruptly found themselves returned to the tobacco fields after the war, as planters believed tobacco provided the quickest route to riches. Tobacco production reached prewar levels by the end of the first postwar decade.[27]

Yet wartime changes continued to resonate on the region's plantations and farms. The Upper South's economy never returned to the prerevolutionary preoccupation with tobacco production; and with the advent of European war in the 1790s and the subsequent collapse of tobacco prices due to the loss of the French market, mixed farming—corn, wheat, dairying, and in some cases vegetables and other produce—permanently unseated tobacco monoculture. During the final decade of the eighteenth century, tobacco—for the first time—made up less than half of Maryland's exports. A similar pattern could be found in nearby portions of Virginia. Even in the region's richest tobacco areas, farmers raised corn, small grains, livestock, and vegetables. In some parts of the Upper South, little tobacco was grown. Although the transition was nowhere easy, agricultural changes a half century in the making relentlessly transformed the nature of the slaves' work, life, and life chances in the Upper South.[28]

As before the war, the dynamic element in the new agricultural regime was wheat, the demand for which increased alongside the deepening European crisis. Wheat required steady work only during the planting and harvesting seasons. For the remainder of the year, laborers had little to do with the crop, and planters scrambled to keep their slaves profitably occupied. This down-time contributed greatly to the sense of excess labor and the need to reduce the number of slaves.[29]

Wheat cultivation accelerated a switch from hoe to plow cultivation. The use of draft animals to pull the plows required pens and barns, pasturage in the summer, and forage in the winter, which satisfied another requirement of cereal farming in the region, the need for manure to fertilize the region's easily depleted soils. A variety of new plantation-based specialists—stockminders, dairy maids, herdsmen, and of course plowmen—were suddenly needed, as was a larger, more mobile, and skilled labor force to transport the grain to market and store it, mill it, and reship it as bulk grain, flour, or bread. The wagons in which wheat was shipped and the animals which pulled wagons all required maintenance.[30]

Slaves performed most of these new tasks, moving with relative ease from the single-minded cultivation of tobacco to the complex multifaceted division of labor of the new mixed economy. On the plantations and farms, they sowed, mowed, plowed, broke flax, pressed cider, sheared sheep, and did dozens of other chores. Off the estates, they drove wagons, sailed boats, serviced inns and taverns, and labored in a variety of nonagricultural enterprises, increasing the proportion of slaves employed in manufacturing. Planters established flour mills and invested profits derived from cereal cultivation into ironworks and other enterprises. As millers, blacksmiths, machinists, and coopers, some slaves became highly skilled craftsmen. Yet, if there were many specialties in the new economy, there were few specialists among the slaves. Most slaves moved from job to job over the course of the year to meet the demands of an increasingly diverse and complex economy.

Movement became the defining feature of black life in the postwar Chesapeake. Those who were not sold to the South shifted from job to job and place to place with greater frequency. Often their owners hired them out, sometimes by the year, sometimes by the month, week, or day, and sometimes by the job. Such movement often came as a welcomed relief from the narrow confines of plantation life, suggesting it was not simply the ability of slaves to accept the new changes but also their willingness to seize advantages in the new order.[31]

The new economy broke the isolation of the Chesapeake plantation in other ways as well. White workers also cultivated wheat and other small grains. Seasonal demands, especially at harvest time, were such that planters put every available hand in the field. Slaves who had worked only among their own suddenly found themselves laboring alongside white laborers, hired by the day or the job.[32] The re-creation of a mixed labor force returned the Chesapeake to its seventeenth-century agricultural beginnings when white and black worked side by side. While the world of the Atlantic creoles could not be reproduced quite as easily as this new propinquity suggests, the interaction of white and black field hands hinted at new possibilities to a generation of slaves who had previously labored for white men but seldom beside them.

As they adjusted their labor force, slaveholders also tried to reclaim prerogatives that had been lost during the tumult of war. Styling themselves "improving farmers," planters introduced new managerial techniques to rationalize production and increase the profitability of their estates—all in the name of the genius of the new enlightened age.[33] From the slaves' perspective, such enlightened agriculture doubtless looked like much of the same, and "improvement" was the masters' euphemism for their slaves' working harder and longer. According to a historian of the Chesapeake's agriculture, planters "scaled up to the old prewar standard." At Mount Vernon, Washington set a pace that left slaves little time but to work, ordering his overseers to have his slaves "at their work as soon as it is light—work 'till it is dark—and be diligent while they are at it . . . The presumption," he emphasized, "being, that, every Labourer (male or female) does as much in the 24 hours as their strength, without endangering their health, or constitution, will allow of." While Washington disdained the lash and offered a variety of incentives to encourage his slaves to meet his imposing standard of industry, he also implemented a system of close supervision. "If the Negroes will not do their duty by fair means, they must be compelled to do it," declared the leader of the new republic.[34]

Slaves resisted this intensification of labor under the new order as they had resisted it under the old, frustrating and infuriating those who had been charged with implementing the new regimen. If masters like Washington contrived to speed the pace of work, slaves conspired to maintain what they had come to understand as the traditional stint. More than one overseer felt like James Eagle, who supervised slaves on a Maryland plantation, when he complained that the slaves under his direction "Get much more Dissatisfied Every year & troublesome for they say that they ought all to be at there liberty & they think that I am the Cause that they are not." Eventually, Eagle quit, muttering about being unable to "Conduct my business as I ought to do."[35]

Eagle's frustration reveals the advantages slaves found in the new regime. The growing size and density of the black population made it easier for slaves to maintain an active community life. The isolation of the early eighteenth century was a thing of the past. The very mobility which added uncertainty into slave life also gave slaves a fuller knowledge of the world beyond the plantation's boundaries. Indeed, some slaves seemed to enjoy the new possibilities that movement allowed, and became, in the words of one disturbed slaveowner, "great Ramblers."[36] In addition, the new economy permitted a growing number of slaves to escape backbreaking field labor entirely and move into artisanal positions previously reserved for white men and women. Plantations and farms fielded not only wagoners but also blacksmiths, saddlers, harness makers, and tanners. Many tanners doubled as shoemakers. Throughout the Upper South, plantations and farms housed many more skilled workers and many fewer field hands.[37]

Slaves were as quick as their owners to see profit—and a measure of control over their lives—in filling the demands created by the new markets. Ned, who had previously labored in the field on the eastern shore of Maryland, was only one of many slaves to attach his star to the new order. He informed his overseer that he had "a great desire to be hired out to go by the water & says that he will not stay hear," more than implying that he would run away rather than work in the field. Rather than risk the loss, Ned's owner obliged his slave. While the bay's open waters held an attraction of their own, many slaves opted for the boating trades because—like artisanal labor and the carting trades—they allowed slaves to earn cash, jobbing either with their owners' permission or on their own.

The slaves' economy grew especially rapidly in the iron manufactories, an industry that expanded greatly during the Revolution and then kept growing thereafter. Forges and furnaces required large numbers of skilled laborers who worked independently and usually beyond the direct supervision of an owner or overseer. The nature of their work rendered the lash ineffectual as an inducement to labor, so ironmasters developed a variety of incentives to encourage productivity among their slave workmen. Prominent among them was payment for overwork, which itself was incorporated into the regular routine. Skilled slaves could expect to earn at a rate that most free workers would have envied. Moreover, once established, the system of overwork payment could not be confined to the most skilled. Unskilled slaves demanded an opportunity to earn a bit of cash or at least some chit that might be traded at the ironmaster's store. While the earning of these hands never equaled the remuneration gained by forge men and puddlers, it revealed how, once slaveowners conceded the smallest point, slaves pressed for some greater advantage.[38]

Overwork was but a small outcropping of the growth of the slaves' economy. Entering the marketplace, slaves sold items of handicraft and produce from their gardens, along with their labor, and thereby accumulated property of their own. Although the economy of Chesapeake slaves rarely advanced beyond the "ground . . . allowed them for gardening, and privilege given them to raise dung-hill fowls," farming and handicraft provided new outlets for the slaves' entrepreneurial energies. Slaveholders raised few objections to these practices or challenged the slaves' right to market goods produced on his or her own time. In fact, petitioners from the Virginia piedmont complained that many slaveholders permitted their slaves to "own, possess and raise stock of horses and hogs" and allowed them to exercise "all the rights of ownership in such stock."[39] Writing at the turn of the century, one observer declared that the right to produce and market such crops was "*permitted* (and greatly *confirmed* by custom)." Indeed, some slaveholders regularly purchased produce from their slaves. The reinvigoration of the slaves' economy entangled masters in endless negotiations with their slaves, who tenaciously protected what they believed was rightfully theirs.[40]

Changes in the slaves' economy rippled through the quarter, affecting men and women differently. In field and manufactory, almost all of the new positions went to men, who plowed, tended the draft stock, drove the wagons, and occupied most of the skilled trades. The removal of men from the fields left the field gangs even more disproportionately female than before the Revolution, and women found themselves performing the onerous and distasteful work of collecting manure, grubbing stumps, and breaking ground that a plow could not penetrate. Slave women also labored in various household tasks, washing, cooking, spinning, making candles, and the like, but these jobs were almost always in addition to their regular field work. Only rarely—for the very young and the very old—did household labor occupy slave women on a full-time basis. Except on the largest estates, few adult women took the position of cook or maid, and they too were in the field at harvest time. The world of the mistress was closed to most slave women. Meanwhile, the benefits of the new regime—travel off the plantation and the practice of skilled crafts—fell disproportionately to men.[41]

Such changes reverberated within the slave family, which faced a host of new threats in the wake of the forcible removal of members through apprenticeship, rental, and especially sale to the Lower South. The slaves' ability to resist these changes revealed both the depth of their commitment to kin and the limitations on their power. Confronted by the possibility of domestic dismemberment, slaves petitioned owners to preserve the plantation-based family and withheld their labor by running away if their pleas were ignored. While such measures might work in an emergency, they did not address the precariousness of a domestic life that rested upon the master's whim. So slaves searched for yet other ways to gain a measure of domestic security.

Some slave parents tried to endow their children with a necessary trade. During the postrevolutionary years, artisanal crafts and privileged domestic positions in the great plantation towns—and perhaps elsewhere as well—became lodged in selected families, with fathers passing them on to sons, and occasionally mothers to daughters.[42] Although such tactics did little to prevent the large-scale dislocations that accompanied the planters' reordering of slave life, they delayed sales and divisions and perhaps prevented permanent separations. They also secured regular visiting rights to slaves, so that in the 1790s an English observer noted that "it is an usual practice for the negroes to go to see their wives on the Saturday night."[43]

As a result of such concessions, slaves won considerable control over their domestic lives. By the beginning of the nineteenth century if not before, slave parents, along with—and sometimes rather than—slaveowners, approved marriages among young men and women, oversaw wedding ceremonies, and blessed the new couple. Explaining the regime he hoped to establish at his forge, ironmaster David Ross projected a world in which "young people might connect themselves in marriage to their own liking, with consent of their parents who were the best judges." Increasingly, slave grannies, rather than white midwives, brought slave children into the world, and slave parents cared for their children through infancy.[44]

But the growth of parental authority could hardly stabilize a foundation that rested on long-distant visitation. That foundation shook when the slave family became a much more sexually differentiated unit, as the new division of labor in the workplace separated husbands and wives, parents and children. It collapsed entirely with sale to the West.[45]

Changes in the structure of slave domestic life were paralleled by changes in religious life. The evangelical awakenings that had begun prior to the Revolution reignited in the 1780s. Beginning with a series of revivals along the James River in 1785, the movement spread quickly, stoked by the growth of the Baptist Church in Virginia and the Methodist Church in Maryland and Delaware. Even more than in the prerevolutionary period, the movement's rough egalitarianism became harnessed to a growing antislavery sentiment and a willingness to allow slave and free black members to participate in some aspects of church governance and discipline. Indeed, within the white populace, evangelical preachers were the most determined opponents to slavery. But whether it was the hope of eternal grace or temporal equality that drew slaves, black men and especially black women came to Christianity in unprecedented numbers.[46]

The evangelicals' antislavery moment soon passed. Antislavery preachers faltered in the face of planter opposition and their own quest for respectability. White evangelicals bridled at the equation of slave and slaveholder as brother and sister in Christ. The fear that spiritual resurrection would lead to social insurrection necessitated a withdrawal of the hand of Christian fellowship. But the slaves who had adopted Christ as the savior maintained their commitment to the evangelicals' spiritual and social promise. Although still but a tiny portion of the slave population— not more than 10 percent at the turn of the century, according to a generous estimate—black converts filled churches and camp meetings. In the portion of the Upper South west of Maryland, black people composed 40 percent of all Methodists in 1794 and 1795. They were even more prominent in some Baptist congregations. Black believers took to the pulpit themselves, and a small cadre of black ministers could be found scattered throughout the region, preaching openly to black, and occasionally mixed, congregations. Their clandestine services were even more active. Not a few—like the fugitive Nat, who "pretends to be very religious, and is a Baptist teacher," or Peter, "who was fond of conversing on religion, and professes to be the Baptist church," or George, who could "deliver many text of Scrpture, which he is fond of doing"—became leaders of the nascent black church.[47]

The process by which New World Christianity gave form to an African religious sensibility had just begun in the Upper South as it had in the North. The evangelical retreat from abolition and its acceptance of slavery doubtless slowed, if it did not reverse, the rate of conversion. The hollow responses of evangelicals to black men and women who asked "What have you got for me?" did nothing to aid the cause. Nonetheless, a small cadre of black Christians began the process of joining Christ's mission to the advancement of their people and themselves.[48]

Like many ambitious black men and women, black preachers gravitated toward the growing towns and cities of the region. Prior to the Revolution, the emergence of Norfolk and Chestertown alongside the administrative centers of Annapolis and Williamsburg provided the Chesapeake with the beginnings of an urban network. The postwar expansion of cereal cultivation and mixed farming stimulated the development of a host of greatly enlarged and sometimes new urban places: Alexandria, Frederick, Fredericksburg, Lynchburg, Petersburg, Richmond, and, most importantly, Baltimore. Almost nonexistent before the war, Richmond was named the capital of Virginia in 1779 and became a town of several thousand by the turn of the century. By 1810 Richmond hosted a population of nearly 10,000. Baltimore, which was fast becoming the great metropolis of the Chesapeake, exhibited an even more pronounced growth. In 1810 its 35,000 residents made it the fourth largest city in the nation. Whereas only a small fraction of the region's population resided in these places, the towns became the hub of the Upper South's politics and economy, housing the institutions of government and the region's fastest-growing industry, flour milling.[49]

Artisans stood at the heart of the economic changes in the cities, just as they did in the countryside. The urban workshops that had sprung up in the absence of British imports expanded rapidly in the postwar years, and they expanded again during the tumult of the European wars. Processing wheat and other small grains required the support of a host of ancillary industries to supply the wagons and carriages, saddles and harness, barrels and boxes to the farmers who grew the grain, the millers who processed it, the wagoners and boatmen who carried it, warehousemen who stored it, and the host of stablemen, innkeepers, and others who served these town-based industries. At the crossroads of commerce, the mill towns also became centers of transport, with shipyards, sail lofts, ropewalks, blockmakers, riggers, and caulkers to serve the maritime industry as well as wagon-makers, saddleries, foundries, and machine shops to support the land-based trade. Unprecedented urban growth attracted members of the building trades—carpenters, masons, brickmakers, roofers, plasterers, and painters. Before long, these agglomerations themselves became important markets for truck from the countryside and manufactured goods from city-based shops.[50]

Urban slavery expanded with the new towns, as slaves—particularly the slave hirelings—offered ambitious businessmen a quick entry into the rapidly expanding economy. On the eve of the Revolution, Norfolk residents employed about 750 adult slaves; by century's end that number had at least doubled. In Richmond, the black population grew apace the white. During the 1780s, slaves composed almost half of the population in the new towns, and by the 1790s they outnumbered whites in places like Petersburg. Similar patterns of growth could be found in all the towns of the Upper South, especially the newly incorporated cities. The slave population of Baltimore exploded upward, quadrupling between 1790 and 1810 to stand at nearly 4,000.[51]

The largest town-based enterprises—grain mills, shipyards, and tobacco factories—relied upon slave labor, as did many tradesmen and shopkeepers. Slave men were particularly prominent in the new towns, where the building boom required large numbers of carpenters, sawyers, and roofers. Unlike in most northern cities, urban slave men equaled or outnumbered women in some of the new towns of the Upper South, as the mills needed factory hands almost as much as householders needed domestics.[52] Little wonder the region's leaders viewed the towns as subversive to the good order of plantation society. Jefferson's famous exaltation of the virtues of rural life takes on a different meaning in the context of the growing black population of the cities of the Upper South.

The changing demand for labor pushed and pulled slaves from the countryside to the city. As planters reconfigured their labor force, urban employers bought or hired many of the excess rural slaves, transforming agriculturalists into urbanites. The market for short-term rentals was particularly lively. Planters and farmers—whose seasonal labor requirements left their slaves idle portions of the year (and who did not sell them out of the region)—found they could profitably rent slaves in towns. Urban slaves who were hired out by their owners discovered they could sell their own time, returning only a portion of their wages to their owners. The growth of hire and self-hire soon spawned a new class of men whose business it was to rent slaves, seasonally, annually, and occasionally for shorter periods. The appearance of such brokers, as well as the willingness of others to purchase slaves for the sole purpose of hiring them out, affirmed the acceptance of a practice which had once been frowned upon and which remained illegal. But slaveholders and slave hirers scoffed at the law. "Many Persons have suffr'd their Slaves to go about to hire themselves," lamented the citizens of Richmond in 1782, "and pay their Masters for their hire and others under pretence of putting them free."[53]

Such complaints reveal that rural slaves were not simply pulled into the region's new cities to meet the needs of urban entrepreneurs. Aware of the new possibilities offered by city life—artisanal labor, self-hire and living out, the right to choose one's own master, and, most prominently, the possibility of freedom—slaves positioned themselves to gain urban employment. In 1794 Barnet ran off with intent to "impose himself upon the public as a free man . . . in Richmond or the neighborhood thereof." Although he was "by no means a master craftmen," Barnet "sometimes undert[ook] to make shoes."[54]

Like Barnet, others transferred rural skills to the new towns. But once in the city, they also practiced a variety of trades unknown to the countryside, from printing to mill work, taking advantage of the wider range of occupational opportunities that urban life presented. Slaves were also deeply involved in the service trades, finding employment as bakers, butchers, and especially barbers, stable keepers, and caterers. White artisans held more than three-quarters of Richmond's slave men, who—if they followed the occupations of their owners—composed about one-quarter of the city's skilled workers in 1784. A similar pattern could be found in Baltimore. Thus, in a period when the process of emancipation was stripping newly liberated black craftsmen of their skills in the North,

slave artisans were becoming more attached to the shops and manufactories in the Upper South.[55] While newly freed slaves were being forced
from northern workshops, black men and women were becoming the
backbone of the Chesapeake region's growing urban industrial workforce. The tobacco factories of Richmond and Petersburg, the brickyards
of Alexandria and Baltimore, and the shipworks in every port city and
river town depended upon slave laborers who were sometimes owned
directly by the new industrialists or, more generally, hired from the countryside on an annual basis.[56]

The growth of town-based marketing expanded the female domain,
allowing black women—free and slave—economic opportunities long
enjoyed by their counterparts in the Lower South and the lower Mississippi Valley. Sunday markets grew with the expansion of urban life.
While the demand for domestics drew slave women from the countryside, once in the city they proved as entrepreneurial as slave men. Women
fulfilled their role as cooks, seamstresses, and washers but also took their
places in the city markets. They became such familiar features that runaways found it easy to camouflage themselves in the bustle of stalls and
wagons. Phebe's owner was but one of many masters to report that his
fugitive had "been seen frequently . . . about the market, selling cakes,
oysters, etc." The ability to move freely through the streets of the new
towns was a liberating experience for all slaves, and women seemed to
take special advantage of the change. With freedom of movement came
familiar charges that black women "ruined the morals as well as the
Health of the younger part of the community."[57]

But black women—slave and free—in the Upper South found employment of a sort that rarely existed anywhere in mainland North
America. Tobacco factories hired black women in large numbers, allowing slave women to participate in the system of overwork that had generally been the provenance of men. Industrial development in the Upper
South transformed women's work in the region.[58]

The expansion of the slave's economy—be it overwork, marketing, or
handicraft—disturbed both slaveholders, who feared it would disrupt the
social order of the towns, and nonslaveholders, who bridled at the competition. In Richmond, white journeymen shoemakers refused to work
for master craftsmen who employed slaves. Baltimore draymen and Norfolk carpenters, fretful of the competition, wanted blacks excluded from
their trade, much as had been done in New York. But such fears paled

beside concerns for another aspect of the slaves' economy—theft. Towns-people, particularly small traders and peddlers, had little compunction about dealing with stolen goods, and slaves were only too glad to engage in the exchange. From his vantage point at Mount Vernon, George Washington believed he had identified a deep conspiracy. "To be plain, Alexandria is such a receptacle for everything that can be filched from the rightful owners, by either blacks or whites," complained Washington. "I am perfectly sure not a single thing that can be disposed of at any price, at that place, that will not, and is not, stolen, where it is possible; and carried thither to some of the underling shop keepers, who support themselves by this kind of traffick." Washington's fellow citizens agreed. Municipalities throughout the Upper South moved to regulate the sale of goods by slaves, as did the newly impaneled state legislatures.[59]

Washington's near obsession focused not so much on the petty losses as on the growing ties between shopkeepers and their slaves. If competition between white journeymen and skilled slaves kept them apart, the alliance of shopkeepers and slaves flourished. The interracial camaraderie of the back-alley taverns, gaming houses, and brothels created an atmosphere that subverted plantation discipline. For slaves, towns became great emporiums in which everything was for sale. Among the commodities that might be purchased was freedom. For most, it was a short respite from the master's harsh glare. Others, however, cherished a more expansive notion of liberty.

The economic transformation that accompanied the growth of wheat culture and the concomitant urban development reignited the growth of the free black population in the Upper South. The proportion of black people enjoying freedom had declined steadily during the eighteenth century with the near termination of manumission and the charter generations' failure to reproduce itself. The free black population dwindled to a handful, whose numbers and circumstances bespoke the equation between enslavement and African descent that planters had come to believe natural if not providential. By the last quarter of the eighteenth century, "the number of free negroes was so small that they were seldom to be met with."[60]

The changes that accompanied the Revolution—the war, the transformation of the countryside, and the growth of towns—allowed large numbers of slaves to take their liberty, reversing the downward slide of African-American freedom. Some of the slaves who escaped during the war remained at large, changing their names and creating a new life for themselves as free people, generally in the new mill towns. Although such freedom was precarious at best and difficult to maintain, numerous men and women made the exchange. "There is reason to believe," complained angry Virginians in 1781, "that a great number of slaves which were taken by the British army are now passing in this Country as free men."[61]

Others secured freedom—and legal documentation of it—by fighting in the war, often as substitutes for their owners. In recognition of their wartime service, a few grateful slaveowners freed their slaves, and occasionally state legislatures liberated black veterans by special enactment. The Virginia General Assembly, drawing back in horror at reports that some owners had reenslaved their black substitutes, proceeded to order the emancipation of all such veterans. In other states, slave men who had served in their owners' place had only a verbal promise of freedom. As in the North, some owners kept their word; others did not. But most slave substitutes did not wait around long enough to find out. At war's end, they quietly passed into a growing population of free blacks.[62]

More important, the changes unleashed by the war—especially the creation of a new class of mobile slave artisans, wagoners, and boatmen—allowed some slaves to seize upon the egalitarian ideology of the Revolution and press for their freedom. As in the North, slaves and their allies never ceased to advertise the stark contradiction between fighting for one's own freedom while denying it to others. Although the opponents of slavery in the Upper South nowhere overthrew slavery, the region's slaveowners publicly agonized over the dilemma of living with an evil that was also a necessity. If their handwringing often served as a cover for inaction, it nevertheless helped to put the door ajar. In 1782 Virginia lawmakers repealed the state's fifty-nine-year-old prohibition on private acts of manumission. Slaveowners were free to manumit any adult slave under forty-five by will or deed. Five years later, Delaware passed a similar act, and in 1790 Maryland, which already permitted manumission by deed, expanded the law to include manumission by will. Liberalized provisions for manumission were extended to the new states west of the Great Valley.[63]

The half measures suggest that the antiabolitionist sentiment that slowed emancipation in the states to the north deeply affected the Upper South. The transformation of slavery in the Upper South—the acceptance of a mobile slave labor force, the growth of slave hire, the expansion of slave skill—assured slavery's viability, strengthening the hand of abolition's opponents. The doctrine of natural rights, which gave impetus to emancipation sentiment, also sanctified property rights, so that slaveholders, like abolitionists, found comfort in the words of the Declaration of Independence. As the century drew to a close, slaveholders in the Upper South—like those in the North—began haltingly to systematize all the crude and perfunctory arguments that had been used to justify African slavery. In 1810, when Daniel Coker, a founder of Baltimore's African Methodist Church, penned a dialogue between a black minister and a Virginia planter, the minister's imaginary opponent articulated the full range of slavery's defense.[64]

The emancipationist impulse and the defense of slavery played themselves out in complex, contrapuntal ways, for in the Upper South as in the North, manumission was both a means to end slavery and a means to extend its life. There was no contradiction between the growth of manumission and the expansion of slavery. For thousands of Upper South slaveowners, the promise of freedom contingent on good behavior was a useful weapon in managing slaves during a period of slavery's decline, particularly in the northern edges of the Chesapeake region, where slaves could gain their freedom by simply crossing the border to Pennsylvania.

If freedom came to black people in the northern states in the compromised half-measures of gradual emancipation, it arrived in the Upper South through equivocations of contingent manumission. In almost half of the over 1,000 manumissions registered in Baltimore County between 1789 and 1814, freedom was deferred until some later date, giving rise to a new form of servitude called "term slavery." Emancipation in the North delayed the arrival of freedom for a generation or more; manumission in the Upper South promised to extend slavery's demise for a century or more.[65]

But if slaveholders believed they had found a powerful new weapon in the promise of future freedom, so too did slaves. Almost immediately, slaves took advantage of the liberalized laws, imploring their owners to free them. Some slaveholders responded favorably, troubled by the contradictions between slaveholding and the Declaration of Independence, the sanctity of the family, the inalienable rights of man, and the lessons of the gospel. A Maryland slaveholder emancipated her slaves in 1802 because, she insisted, slavery contradicted the "inalienable Rights of Mankind." A Virginia master manumitted his slaves because to keep them was "contrary to the command of Christ to keep fellow creatures in bondage." Often revolutionary ideology and Christian ideals were so entwined that a slaveholder blurted them out in the same breath.

To be sure, some emancipators merely mouthed antislavery rhetoric while ridding themselves of unwanted slaves. Indeed, economic changes seemed to reduce the cost of subscribing to abolitionist principles, as the seeming surplus of slaves allowed for selective manumission without affecting the economy of the region. The growth of a class of free blacks—who would support themselves most of the year but be available for hire at planting and harvest time—seemed to fit better with the new agricultural regime than with the old monoculture.

But the opponents of slavery—slaves most prominently among them—cared little about the slaveowners' motives. Indeed, they appreciated the intersection of self-interest and high principle, observing that the commitment to emancipation seemed greatest wherever wheat had replaced tobacco or, in the idiom of the day, where the plow had replaced the hoe. The more the economy shifted toward mechanization, the more likely were doubtful slaveowners to embrace freedom. "The history of emancipation in Maryland," one overly optimistic abolitionist observed, "has proved that manumission begets manumission, that they increase even in geometrical proportions."[66] Still, the hoped-for increase, which never quite reached geometrical proportions, was accompanied by a pattern of manumission which extended slavery's existence. Conditional manumission robbed black men and women of their most productive years by delaying freedom, and often by requiring them to compensate owners for the monetary loss of their labor.

When slaveowners refused to act, some slaves took matters into their own hands with threats of flight, malingering, and sabotage. Like their owners, they too combined the carrot with the stick, mixing their threats with promises of good behavior and even the prospect of monetary payment. As freedom, like slavery, became a matter of intense negotiation, slaves drew on their experience hiring their own time or marketing their garden produce, hopeful that the combination of warnings and assurances would seal the bargain. Even then, negotiations often had to be carried on at a distance, through the agency of a third party. So-called honest brokers hammered out the complex agreements wherein free people—many of them recently liberated—literally mortgaged themselves to ensure the freedom of their families and friends. It was a chancy business, and when it failed, free people slid back into bondage.[67]

The numerous collaborators necessary for a slave to purchase freedom challenged the notion of *self*-purchase in the Upper South as it had in the northern states. Mostly, the acquisition of freedom was a family matter, with husbands purchasing the freedom of their wives and parents paying to liberate their children. Through long years of work and underconsumption and by pooling their savings and borrowing against future earnings, numerous black men and women freed themselves and their loved ones. Of the slaves freed in Norfolk between 1791 and 1820, more than one-third—a conservative calculation—purchased themselves or were purchased by others, mostly by their families. Even then the rising price of slaves put the purchase of freedom out of the reach of most industrious black families.[68]

A few slaves sought liberation through the courts. Although freedom suits provided only piecemeal emancipation, the creation of a single precedent often led to the liberation of many slaves. "Whole families," recalled one opponent of slavery, "were often liberated by a single verdict, the fate of one relative deciding the fate of many." Awakened to the possibility of freedom, slaves rummaged through their family trees searching for a connection to freedom in the charter generations. Many found it in Indian ancestry, and others in descent from a white woman, often an indentured servant who had taken a black man as a husband or lover. Knowledge of the charter generation which had been submerged for years came rushing to the fore as slaves searched for roots in freedom. Armed with that information and aided by abolitionists with knowledge of the law, slaves petitioned the courts. Confronted with a growing number of freedom suits, state courts responded sympathetically by liberalizing the rules of descent and expanding the range of evidence acceptable in freedom suits. Moreover, as such suits suggest, the increased legal actions required white sympathizers who were willing to take the slaves' side in lengthy and expensive legal battles.[69] The archetypal suit was brought by the descendants of the slave Charles and Irish Nell, a white servant woman, who claimed their freedom by reason of descent from a white woman. The Butlers and some 300 other slaves traced their origins back to the union of Charles and Nell, and when they won their freedom, numerous other slaves who claimed to descend from Irish Nell went free as well.[70]

The rapid increase in the number of black people freed in the years following the Revolution—along with rumors of abolition to the North—swelled the expectations of those remaining in bondage. For the first time since the seventeenth century, freedom was the property of a large class of black men and women in the Chesapeake region. Many slaves who saw their friends and relatives shed the shackles of slavery began thinking of what had previously seemed unattainable. Slaves given conditional freedom demanded it all; masters who delayed manumission to some future date frequently found their slaves absconding to liberty. Some fled to freedom, but for others flight was just another counter in the continuing negotiation between master and slave—to improve conditions, assure the sanctity of family life, and perhaps gain liberty.[71]

Whatever a fugitive's strategy and goal, the greatly enlarged free black population enhanced his or her chances of success by blurring the lines between freedom and slavery. With so many newly and illegally freed blacks traveling the countryside, white people could no longer identify every black man or woman in their neighborhood or assume every unknown black person was a slave. Although many whites stopped strange black men and women as a matter of course, the rising number of unknown, but legally free, black people taxed even the most vigilant. This novel situation forced slaveholders to append a special caution to their runaway advertisements: "It is probable this fellow may endeavour to pass for a free man, as there are many free blacks passing about this country."[72] Runaways challenged the presumption that all blacks were slaves by hiding themselves among the growing free black population.

The enlarged free black population not only camouflaged fugitive slaves but also actively encouraged and aided their flight. Just as *self*-purchase was the effort of more than a single individual, so too was successful flight. When Manuel, Landon Carter's best plowman, ran off to join Dunmore's Brigade, he took his son Billy with him and—Carter was certain—connived to bring the rest of his family to freedom. Indeed, so often did runaways take refuge with free friends and relatives that masters usually looked first to them when searching for their missing property. Thomas Jones thought his slave Sam would go to Baltimore, where he had "several relations (manumitted blacks), who will conceal him and assist him in making an escape," and "Bet went off with a free fellow named Tom Turner, who follows the water for a living and calls her his wife." As Bet's escape suggests, kinship ties motivated many of the free Negroes who aided slaves. Black men and women often took extraordinary chances to free their families. "Hankey (alias Hagar Sexton)" found shelter with "a family of free Mulattoes" in piedmont Virginia who "protected and harboured" her. Yet, even more important than the protection, shelter, food, and passes that free blacks provided was their example: they were living proof that a black people could be free. "Henny," noted a Maryland slaveholder in 1793, "will try to pass for a free woman, as several have been set free in this neighborhood."[73]

Once they had made their escape, fugitives often headed north to test the rumors of freedom. But perhaps even more remained in the Upper South, if only to be near friends and relatives. Everywhere slaveholders found hundreds of unfamiliar black men and women living "under the name and character of Free Negroes." With the aid of free people of color or a white friend, fugitive slaves turned the new system of surveillance against its makers. In forging passes and registration papers, fugitives became officially free. "I will venture to assert," complained the neighbor to one prominent manumittor, "that a vastly greater number of slave people have passed & are passing now as your free men than you ever owned." Everywhere, slaveholders found hundreds of new black faces living "under the name and character of Free Negroes."[74]

Free black emigrés from Saint Domingue added to the growing number of freed slaves. The first arrivals, several hundred strong, entered Baltimore and Norfolk with the exodus flotilla in the summer of 1793. But others added to the group during the next decade, so that free people of color with roots in Saint Domingue could be found in nearly every town in the Upper South. To the numbers of newly arrived free people could be added slaves refugeed from Saint Domingue, many of whom took leave of their owners almost upon arrival.[75]

The spectacular increase in manumission, self-purchase, freedom suits, flight, and immigration altered the size and character of the free black population in the Upper South. Maryland, which was fast being transformed from a slave society into a society with slaves, best exemplified the change. Between 1755 and 1790, the state's free black population grew 300 percent to about 8,000, and in the following ten years it more than doubled. By 1810 nearly 34,000 black Marylanders were free, giving the state the largest free black population in the nation. The gains registered by free blacks elsewhere in the Upper South never equaled that of Maryland, but they were substantial. In 1782, the year Virginia legalized private manumission, St. George Tucker estimated the presence of about 2,000 free blacks in the state. By 1790, when the first federal census was taken, the free black population had grown to 12,000. Ten years later, it numbered 20,000, and in another ten years it stood at over 30,000. During the twenty years between 1790 and 1810, the free black population of Virginia had more than doubled. In all, the number of free black people in the states of the Upper South grew almost 90 percent between 1790 and 1800 and another 65 percent the following decade, so that they made up more than 10 percent of the region's black population. By the end of the first decade of the nineteenth century, there were over 108,000 free black people in the Upper South, and better than 10 percent of the black population enjoyed freedom.[76]

The sexual ratio of the free black population, which had long weighed heavily toward women, moved steadily toward balance, as men and women gained their freedom in roughly equal numbers.[77] Large-scale indiscriminate manumission and the successful flight of many black slaves allowed dark-skinned men and women to enter the ranks of the previously light-skinned population. The balance between free people of mixed racial origins and free black people may have tilted toward the latter.[78] Since most runaways were young men and women, the increased number of successful fugitives infused the newly freed population with a large group of restless youths. By the beginning of the nineteenth century, free people of African descent were no longer the tiny group of mixed-race and crippled people they had been in the years immediately before the Revolution. It included more people of darker skin, the vigorous young as well as elderly former slaves.

As in the North, freedom arrived burdened with the heavy weight of slavery's continuing presence. New forms of dependency emerged even more quickly than the old ones could be liquidated. In the countryside, many free blacks continued to reside with their former masters, suffering the oversight of an owner even after they no longer were owned. Planters appreciated the advantages of power without responsibility. They held tight to the spouses and children of former slaves, seeing them as a lever to access the labor of free blacks. Some planters sold or rented small plots of land to former slaves to secure the benefit of their labor during planting and harvest. In the cities, term slavery provided a means for owners to exact the labor of energetic young men and women and make them responsible for themselves in old age. Much like gradual emancipation and apprenticeship in the northern states, contingent manumission and term slavery delayed the arrival of freedom and strengthened the masters' hand.[79]

But if the continued presence of slavery burdened black people, so did freedom. As slaves, black men and women were fully integrated into the economy and society of the Upper South. As free people, they faced ostracism and discrimination. To the new forms of subordination that equated free blacks with slaves, lawmakers added the new proscriptions that distinguished free blacks from white people. Free black men were barred from voting, sitting on juries, testifying in court, and attending the militia, and all free blacks, women as well as men, were barred from owning dogs and guns and trading without a permit. A pass system prevented free blacks from traveling freely and required them to register themselves annually with county authorities. Many of these restrictions had long existed, but the new legislation reinforced them, reminding all that freedom would not mean equality.[80]

But even the weight of delayed freedom and the straightjacket of new forms of subordination could not prevent former slaves from celebrating emancipation. Free blacks, following their northern counterparts, took new names, deserted the site of their enslavement, reunited their families, found work, and created the institutions worthy of a free people. Reconstruction in the Upper South after the Revolutionary War thus reflected both the new possibilities that accompanied freedom as well as the consequences of economic and social changes, giving a unique regional shape to the postemancipation transformation of black life.

With freedom, a new pattern of naming emerged. Day names and placenames became less prominent, and common Anglo-American names became the norm. The classical names of slave times made their final exit among free people, as did various diminutives. The aspiration for full manhood and womanhood represented by the elevation of diminutives into their proper form was also manifest in the selection of surnames. Rarely present in slave times, surnames became nearly universal among free blacks during the first decade of the nineteenth century. Although Upper South free blacks took the names of former masters with greater regularity than did their northern counterparts, such names were never the rule. Indeed, census enumerators identified a disproportionately large number of black people who celebrated their liberation by declaring themselves Freeman, Freeland, and Liberty.[81]

A new address often accompanied a new name. Former slaves migrated cityward, causing urban officials in the Upper South to join their northern counterparts in bemoaning the "large numbers of free blacks flock[ing] from the country to the towns." Without exception, the free black population of every Upper South city grew faster than its rural counterpart and generally faster than the urban white and slave populace. Norfolk's free black population increased from 8 in 1782 to 61 in 1790 to over 352 in 1800; Richmond's population grew from 265 in 1790 to more than 600 in 1800, and Baltimore—with the nation's largest free black population—totaled some 5,600 in 1810, a gigantic increase from the 323 free blacks who resided in that city twenty years earlier. As the balance of free black life swung to the cities, the proportion of the urban black population that enjoyed freedom likewise increased. In 1782 less than 7 percent of black people in Richmond enjoyed freedom. By 1790 the proportion had more than doubled, and in 1810 almost one-quarter of black Richmonders were free. In Petersburg the free black population tripled between 1790 and 1810 and made up one-third of the city's black population.[82]

As the change of black population in Petersburg suggests, the great growth in the numbers of free black people did not emancipate the cities of the Upper South. Unlike in the North, there was no rural evacuation in the Upper South, as newly liberated slaves were unwilling to abandon friends and relatives still in slavery. The rural majority distinguished free black life in the Upper South from that in the North. In most cities, the number of slaves continued to tower over the number of free people of color. Even in Baltimore, where free people would eventually outnumber slaves, the enslaved black population grew more rapidly than the free one during the late eighteenth and early nineteenth centuries. It was not until after 1800 that the number of free blacks surpassed that of slaves.

As black people understood, migration within the Upper South provided no escape from slavery. Slavery's continued presence shaped the efforts of former slaves to reconstruct their families. Household independence in the Upper South lagged behind the North, as newly freed men and women continued to reside with slaveowners, many of whom were former masters. In 1810 almost one-third of the Baltimore free blacks lived with slaveowners. The proportion was still higher in the country-side. But where they could, free people gathered their families under their own roof, taking in boarders where necessary to create financially viable households. The proportion of free blacks living independently in 1810 was far greater than in 1790. Homeownership followed the same pattern. While it remained infinitesimal, it increased sharply in the first years of the nineteenth century, from eight in 1798 to fifty-eight in 1815.[83]

The slow rate of household formation pointed to the difficulty free blacks had in earning a living. In the countryside, free blacks, like their northern counterparts, generally worked as farmhands. A few entered into sharecropping agreements and a handful even negotiated tenantries, hoping to ascend the agricultural ladder to landownership. However hard they labored, few black croppers and tenants joined the landowning class. In Baltimore County, as favorable an environment as free blacks might find in the region, black propertyowners composed only 4 percent of the landowners in 1790.[84]

Economic opportunities were far greater in the city, although urban free blacks also remained poor and propertyless. Whereas blacks became increasingly marginal to the northern economy in the years following emancipation, free blacks—and slaves—grew more important in the Up-per South. The continued presence of slavery, which stymied the aspira-tions of black people for an independent domestic life, strengthened their place in the urban economy. Behind the shadow of slave labor, particu-larly the growing use of hired slaves, free blacks maintained their toehold in the artisanal crafts and urban services. Most Upper South free blacks pushed a broom and shouldered a shovel, but they enjoyed greater access to skilled employment than did their northern counterparts. Although the niches free blacks occupied in the Upper South—barbering, shoemak-ing, drayage—were much the same as in the North, they were consider-ably larger.[85]

Within the towns and cities, free blacks began to create a society worthy of their new status. A new leadership class soon emerged from within the ranks of the black artisans and shopkeepers, much as it did in the North. Men like Daniel Coker in Baltimore and Christopher McPher-son in Richmond were as much a product of the transformation of black life in the Upper South as were Richard Allen in Philadelphia and Prince Hall in Boston. Like Allen and Hall, the new men of the Upper South eagerly pressed for full citizenship. Indeed, Upper South blacks stepped beyond any inroads made in the northern states, entering into the partisan electoral arena. In 1792 Thomas Brown, a veteran of the Revolution, offered himself to Baltimore's electorate, declaring that his candidacy for the Maryland House of Delegates would "represent so many hundreds of poor Blacks as inhabit this town, as well as several thousands in different parts of the state."[86]

Before long, the institutional scaffolding of African-American life from schools to cemeteries appeared, all bearing the name "African." As in the North, the African church played the central role. The forced segregation of blacks in congregations which had once allowed open seating and equal access to the church burial ground precipitated the creation of independent organizations in the Upper South, as it had in the North. The first of the independent black churches appeared during the 1780s in Williamsburg, the product of the division of a mixed Baptist congregation. Another followed in Petersburg, when in 1797 the black congregants withdrew from the Gillfield Church to create their own Afro-Baptist congregation.

Perhaps the greatest growth of an independent black church took place in Baltimore, under the aegis of black Methodists. Black congregants, who once worshipped alongside white Methodists, found themselves denied access to their own church. Before long, the insurgency had begun, and black Methodists demanded, according to one bishop, "a church, which, in temporals, shall be altogether under their direction." Although the Methodist hierarchy bridled at first, it eventually conceded, and a separate African Methodist Episcopal Church flourished in Baltimore under Daniel Coker much as it did in Philadelphia under Richard Allen.[87]

But if institutional change followed the same vector in the Upper South as it did in the North, the structure of black society was strikingly different. The sharp divisions between the respectables and the poor, so evident in the postemancipation North, never emerged with the same force in the Upper South. To be sure, there was a powerful tavern culture along the docks and in the back alleys of the new towns that challenged the aspirations of the upward-striving, church-going respectables. Poor free blacks and slaves marched to a different drummer than did the likes of Daniel Coker and Christopher McPherson. But the continued existence of slavery muted the differences within black society. Many free people of color—men and women—married slaves and lived, worked, and prayed together. Independent African churches were usually joint ventures of free and slave. If the ability of free people to hold property propelled them into positions of leadership in these organizations, slaves participated fully and often took leadership roles as deacons and ministers. Everyday experience reinforced the ties between free and slave peoples. Measured by church membership, family formation, wealth distribution, and aspirations and ideas, black society was much more of one piece in the Upper South—despite the formal divisions of freed and slave—than in the North. The shadow of slavery assured continued African-American unity. As perhaps nowhere else in mainland North America, the fate of free and slave blacks was entwined. Slavery defined freedom, and freedom defined slavery, in the Upper South during the Age of Revolution.

Fragmentation in the Lower South

▲

The revolutionary changes that transformed the North from a slave to a free society and stimulated the expansion of the free black population in the Upper South resonated differently in lowcountry South Carolina, Georgia, and East Florida, or—as settlement spread west—the Lower South. Although the War for Independence greatly disrupted slavery, the Patriot victory affirmed the power of the planter class and armed slave-owners with new weapons to protect and expand slavery. Unlike in the North, the region's leading men did not associate in abolition societies and press for the liquidation of slavery. Indeed, they did not even muse about the possibility of slavery's eventual demise, as did slaveholders in the Upper South. Nowhere in the Lower South did lawmakers scheme to invent new forms of racial subordination, be they apprenticeship, contingent manumission, or term slavery. Nowhere—not even in the periphery of the region—did the features of a society with slaves reemerge.

Instead, planters pressed to reopen direct trade with Africa, thereby reiterating their commitment to the expansion of slave society. Lowcountry grandees extended their domain to the upcountry and consolidated their place as the region's ruling class. By the beginning of the nineteenth century, planters had repaired the damage the war had wrought and had primed slavery for a half century of explosive growth.

The reconstitution of slavery and its expansion reshaped African-American life in the Lower South. On the plantations, the black majority—augmented by newly arrived Africans—extended and deepened the connections between Africa and America, simultaneously enlarging the cultural distance between themselves and their owners. But while fresh infusions of saltwater slaves reinvigorated African life in the quarter, some people of African descent—most of them born in America and residing in rice ports, many of them of mixed racial origins—escaped bondage and labored to integrate themselves into European-American society. These free people of color joined with urban slaves to expand their liberty. Unlike free African Americans in the North, those in the Lower South dared not adopt the language of the Declaration of Independence, for Lower South planters interpreted the merest whisper of racial egalitarianism as a tocsin for servile revolt. Instead, free people of color appealed for a place in Lower South society, and in the process abandoned plantation slaves to fend for themselves. Colored people found a niche in which predominantly brown free people stood apart from black slaves on one hand and from white free people on the other. The unity of black people—free and slave—so manifest in the Upper South had no place in the region. Instead, the Lower South was transformed into a three-caste society of white, black, and brown.

As nowhere else on the North American continent, the War for American Independence in the Lower South became a bitter civil war, filled with a savage, fratricidal violence that tore the fabric of society. For more than seven years, Loyalist partisans backed by the might of the world's greatest military power and the Patriot forces supported by the revolutionary army bloodied each other. Tossing aside military conventions, the two combatants fought one another with ambush and midnight raids; assassination, arson, butchery, pillage, and plunder became the common mode of warfare. Between the Loyalists and Patriots stood thousands of men and women who desired nothing more than to stay out of harm's way. When they could not, many turned Tory and initiated their own war of all-against-all, forming bands of guerrillas and banditti who had no permanent allegiance but to their own narrow interests. Such fierce warfare exposed slaves to unspeakable atrocities, but it also revealed the divisions within the planter class.[1]

With their owners pitched against one another, slaves moved quickly to secure their liberty. Bolstered by rumors that they would "be all sett free on the arrival of the New Governor," some slaves confronted their owners directly. Before he ran off in the fall of 1775, Limus boldly announced his determination to be his own man. "Though he is my Property," reported Limus's stunned owner, "he has the audacity to tell me, he will be free, that he will serve no Man, and that he will be conquered or governed by no Man."[2] With that, Limus was gone.

Such insurrectionary outcroppings convinced planters that they were besieged by slave rebels. "To keep those mistaken creatures in awe" and "to guard against any hostile attempts that may be made by our domes-ticks," lawmakers expanded the watch, raised militias, organized pa-trols, and mobilized Indian allies. In 1775 three companies of militiamen patrolled the streets of Charles Town (soon to be renamed Charleston). At the northern boundary of the rice belt, the Wilmington Committee for Safety authorized patrols "to search for & take from Negroes all kinds of Arms whatsoever." Individual owners also acted with dispatch. Henry Laurens, a leader of the Patriot faction in South Carolina, gathered his brother's slaves together in June 1775 and "set before them the great risque of exposing themselves to the treachery of pretended freinds & false witnesses," admonishing "them to behave with great circumspec-tion in this dangerous times."[3]

Laurens was pleased to find that the "Poor Creatures . . . were sensi-bly affected, & with many thanks promised to follow [his] advise & to accept the offer of Protection." However, not all slaveowners were as confident of their slaves' continued loyalty. Rather than rely on the devo-tion of their slaves, slaveholders intensified surveillance and increased discipline. Throughout the Lower South, black people—free and slave—found that regulations which had gone unenforced for years were given new life. Violators were scourged, whipped, cropped, and hanged for offenses that previously received but scant notice. Scapegoats were nu-merous. Thomas Jeremiah, a successful free black pilot in Charleston—called by South Carolina's royal governor "one of the most valuable, and useful men . . . in the Province"—was arrested for conspiring to lead slaves into an alliance with the British. When the governor protested the gross miscarriage of justice, Charleston's Committee for Safety brazenly threatened to hang Jeremiah on the doorpost of the executive mansion. The governor thereafter held his tongue, but his silence did nothing to save Jeremiah, who was hanged and then burned.[4]

Plantation slaves faced the same harsh reality, as slaveowners took their own measures to reduce the possibility of insurrection or flight. Lowcountry slaveowners—even more than those in the North or Upper South—carried their slaves away from the war zone, refugeeing them to areas from which flight would be impossible. Some lowcountry planters transported their slaves as far north as Virginia, while others exiled their slaves to the lower Mississippi Valley. Yet other masters instituted new restraints to check mass escapes. One Georgia planter separated men from the women and children to prevent flight in family groups, although, like many similar measures, it did little to prevent such escapes.[5] The exodus of slaves fed the sense of a regime unraveling.

Such fears generally owed more to the feverish imagination of besieged slaveholders than to the reality of slavery's imminent collapse, but the wild trashing of hysterical slaveholders convinced many black men and women that freedom's jubilee was at hand. What else could they make of the house-to-house searches for guns and ammunition, the night-long patrols, and the refugeeing of thousands of their number to distant places, all punctuated by the trial of alleged conspirators whose sentence—like Thomas Jeremiah's—was inevitably death, often by mutilation.

Although few slaves willingly risked all for the possibility of freedom, the rumors of revolt persisted, and in the aftermath planters condemned suspected participants to bloody retribution. From Beaufort, North Carolina, came reports of "a deep laid Horrid Tragick Plan for destroying the inhabitants of this province without respect of persons, age or sex." Forty black men and women were jailed; many were whipped, some cropped. In Pitt County, North Carolina, near the South Carolina border, the local Committee of Safety authorized patrollers to "shoot one or any number of Negroes who are armed and doth not willingly surrender their arms" and gave the patrol discretionary power to "shoot any Number of Negroes above four, who are off their Masters Plantations, and will not submit."

The hysteria had hardly died when rumors spread that an army of some 250 black men had reached Wilmington—although "none [were] taken nor seen tho' they were several times fired at." Fears exacerbated by such reports were heightened by the slaves' enthusiastic response to Dunmore's proclamation. In December 1775 several hundred runaways who had been collecting under British protection on Sullivan's Island in Charleston's harbor began to raid plantations along the coast. The assaults continued into the new year, when Patriot regulars finally chased them off the island with a murderous show of force.[6]

Slaves deserted their owners in droves. The first fugitives were men, much as they had been in the northern colonies. But as the social order frayed with the intensification of internecine warfare, and as the possibilities of successful flight grew, slaves fled en masse—with extended families or the populations of entire plantations abandoning their old estates. Unlike in the North or the Upper South, where slaves ran away singly, fugitives in the Lower South frequently moved in large groups, revealing how ties of kinship and friendship on the great plantations had knit slaves together. David George, who eventually found a refuge on the island of Jamaica, "recalled that when his owner fled at the approach of the British army, he, his family, and fifty or more of my master's people" marched to the encampment of "the king's forces."[7] When Thomas Pinckney, South Carolina's representative to the Continental Congress, returned home in the spring of 1779, he discovered his plantation empty of slaves except for a handful of pregnant women and old people. Pinckney's experience was no exception. Carrying guns, farm implements, and substantial supplies of food and clothing, slaves headed for the swamps to join established maroon bands or migrated west with hopes of confederating with friendly Indians.[8]

Thousands more set off in search of royal army and navy units, drawn by rumors—many of them unwittingly spread by indignant Patriot slaveowners—that the British would sponsor a general emancipation. Some fugitives found their way to British lines, entering army encampments or canoeing to patrolling warships and announcing—as did one group—that "they were come for the King." Large numbers of slaves also migrated to the great rice ports, especially after the British occupied Savannah in 1779 and Charleston a year later. Slaveowners in search of their property knew where to look. "Not a day has elapsed," reported a British official from Savannah, "without some persons comeing in from South Carolina, to enquire after Negroes." The success of fugitive slaves induced slaveowners to append a novel notice to the standard runaway advertisement: "If they will return to their duty they will be forgiven." Such pathetic pleas revealed how wartime events had compromised the masters' authority and reduced the great planters to suppliants.[9]

Flight was a familiar strategy for many revolutionary fugitives. Some runaways were up to "past tricks," as one owner put it. Like York and Portious, they were already so "well known in town, [as to] render any description unnecessary."[10] Other fugitives were new to the business of flight, but whether old hands or new, runaways found it easy to elude capture amid the hundreds of new black faces that crowded into the refugee-infested rice ports. Even with a "clog on his leg," Abraham escaped to Charleston early in 1778, where he passed as free, finding employment "in the brick business for . . . three months" before his owner discovered his whereabouts and advertised for his return. He was still at large six months later.

Once safely within city lines, fugitive slaves changed their names, clothing, and status, passing "for one that has been out on hire." Earning a bit of cash, they frequently took passage on one of the numerous ships that weighed anchor in Charleston, Savannah, and the lesser ports, renewing contact with the Atlantic in hopes of securing freedom in some distant place. But most remained, often assisting other fugitives in gaining their liberty. When some fifteen slaves fled to Charleston from a nearby plantation in 1781, their owner reported they were "haboured in the Quartermaster-General's different Departments by six fellows of mine, who are employed there for his Majesty's service."[11]

Urban life had its dangers, as kidnappers lurked everywhere and disease was rampant in the crowded shanties where black refugees congregated. Smallpox and malaria swept through Charleston several times during 1779 and 1780, and fugitive slaves appeared to be the primary victims. Still, opportunities abounded in these war-torn urban enclaves, and fugitives were prepared to take the risks necessary to secure them. Black men and women found numerous white tradesmen and housekeepers who were willing to hire them with few questions asked. Employment by army officers, soldiers, and camp followers was particularly easy to arrange. In Savannah, former slaves squatted in abandoned buildings, openly "selling and otherwise dealing or trading without any limitation or check." Deepening their control over Charleston's market, fugitive slaves became a major supplier to the British commissary. The soldiers and their officers not only welcomed the slaves' labor but also their companionship. In 1782 a group of fugitive women in Charleston elevated their wartime liaisons to a new level when they invited resident officers to what one outraged slaveholder called "an Ethiopean Ball." The Cinderella-like atmosphere saw black women "dressed up in Taste, with the richest silks, and false rolls on their heads, powder'd up with the most pompous manner" and conveyed to the cotillion by these "Gentlemen." The old axiom that "city air made free men" took on new meaning in revolutionary Charleston, particularly for slave women.[12]

The actions of British officers suggested that freedom-minded slaves had indeed found friends. In June 1779, on the eve of the British invasion of South Carolina, General-in-Chief Henry Clinton promised slaves who abandoned their rebel owners "full security to follow within these Lines, any Occupation which [they] shall think proper."[13] Whatever Clinton meant, slaves interpreted the British commander's proclamation as the long-rumored general emancipation. So did some of the general's subordinates. Common soldiers especially welcomed fugitive slaves, who willingly relieved them of the burdensome duties of military life in return for food, protection, and the possibility of eventual freedom. According to one observer, not only did every British soldier seem to have his own servant "who carried his provisions and bundles," but "every soldiers woman . . . also had a Negro and Negress on horseback for her servants." Personal servants composed but a small portion of the slaves who found refuge within British lines, however. In desperate need of laborers to build fortifications, drive wagons, chop wood, tend draft animals, clean clothes, and cook food, British officers approved the actions of their men and joined in impressing slaves into military service, rarely distinguishing between the slaves of Patriots and Loyalists.[14]

Although slaves were assigned the dirtiest and most difficult work, circumstances occasionally transformed drudges into warriors. In 1776 Florida's royal governor commissioned four black militia companies who fought in units that mixed white, black, and Indian soldiers. Three years later, when a joint Franco-American force laid siege to Savannah, British commanders armed black servants and laborers to repulse the invaders. Later, Georgia's Loyalist governor singled out black soldiers for their valor in defense of the city, and the Loyalist legislature authorized the arming of slaves in defense of the colony, although only at "time of Alarms actually fixed."[15]

Once armed, black men refused to relinquish their weapons. When the "Rebel Partizan [Thomas] Sumpter made his long projected attack on the post of Congarees . . . he was disgracefully beat off, and once by a party of sequestered negroes." The British employed armed black men in defense of their fortifications near Augusta, Georgia, and black cavalry units fought alongside the British regulars outside of Charleston in April 1782. By the end of that year, over 700 black soldiers were under arms in the Lower South, and black dragoons roamed the countryside pillaging estates to keep Charleston supplied. Lord Dunmore, now in Charleston, plotted to arm yet more slaves for an assault on Spanish West Florida and Louisiana.[16] The successful employment of black troops convinced British commanders of the utility of a permanent force of former slaves, and they organized one in the West Indies following the war.[17]

But the British proved to be unreliable liberators. The influx of fugitives frightened them, as they feared identification as the slaves' friend would drive slaveholding Loyalists into the Patriot camp. Caught between the need to mobilize slave laborers and the fear of alienating slaveholders, British commanders wavered, developing no consistent policy. Although some officers and soldiers continued to harbor fugitives, others did not, and while fugitives sometimes found themselves welcomed into British lines, others were jailed, whipped, and returned to their Loyalist owners in exchange for promises of loyalty, supplies, and information respecting the movement of Patriot forces.[18]

To facilitate the restoration of slave property, the British command published monthly lists of fugitive slaves who had taken refuge in Charleston. In Savannah, British authorities jailed arriving fugitives in "a strong and convenient house or prison" and returned them to their Loyalist owners at the first opportunity.[19] Slaves of "unfriendly persons" were frequently forced to work on sequestered estates or awarded to Loyalists in compensation for slaves they had lost. British commanders also employed slaves as bounties to recruit white men to His Majesty's service, or they simply sold runaways for profit. Loyalist partisans—aided and abetted by British authorities—raided rebel plantations, taking as many as 8,000 slaves to East Florida, where they invigorated the plantations of the British-controlled province. Yet others were carried or sold to the sugar islands, West Florida, and Louisiana, sometimes by Loyalists and sometimes by privateers with no loyalty except to themselves.[20]

To satisfy their planter allies, demonstrate they were the friends of good order, and reap the benefit of plantation labor, the British also created police boards that sequestered plantations abandoned by Patriot slaveowners and operated them under the auspices of resident Loyalists, military officers, and specially appointed overseers. In South Carolina alone, approximately 5,000 slaves worked on the sequestered estates.[21] Business-as-usual was the watchword of these operations. The Charleston-based board of overseers, established in May 1780, issued regulations that confined slaves to the plantations. Slaves who wandered from their estates were apprehended as fugitives and returned to their owners. On at least one occasion, British regulars quelled a rebellion on a Patriot-owned plantation, rescuing the white overseer from angry slaves.[22]

The reconstitution of the plantation order under the royal army thus offered slaves few benefits. Police commissioners worked slaves hard to turn a profit and demonstrate the utility of their operations. Overworked and underfed, slaves on the sequestered estates were susceptible to the epidemic diseases that stalked the Lower South, and when they fell ill there was little medical care to be had. Indeed, the police commissioners had few resources. Since they enjoyed neither authority nor power to protect the plantations under their supervision, the slaves—along with other property under their protection—were frequently carried off by Patriot, Tory, and occasionally even British raiders. When the commissioners complained to their superiors, military officers ridiculed them, dismissed their memorials, and asserted their own claim to supervise sequestered property. Sometimes, field officers forcibly appropriated slaves from the sequestered estates to fill the army's insatiable need for labor.[23]

Black men and women employed by the British as laborers enjoyed a measure of protection, but little else. Military camps were scarcely one step removed from the charnel houses, as Patriot slaveholders—like their counterparts in the Upper South—took every opportunity to reiterate. Crowded together in rude shelters, poorly nourished and clothed, given scant medical attention, and supervised by men who had even less interest in their well-being than their former owners, black refugees died by the thousands.[24] Those who survived were liable to be stolen back and forth between Loyalist partisans and Patriot rangers, their families divided, and their friends and loved ones scattered in different directions— some to the West Indies, some to the Floridas, and some to the lower Mississippi Valley.

By sometimes welcoming black men and women and sometimes clapping them into bondage, British officials made it impossible for fugitives to predict whether they would be greeted as freed people or slaves, treated as allies or spoils of war. The uncertainty created by the maze of contradictory policies and practices slowed the fugitives' movement toward British lines, kept many slaves on their home plantations, and sent others deep into the swamps. Yet despite the contradictory policies and inconsistent practices, slaves clung to the belief, however uncertain or misguided, that the enemy of their enemy was their friend.

If the British were unreliable friends, slaves knew what to expect from the Patriots. Although John Laurens, an aide-de-camp to George Washington and the son of South Carolina's greatest slave trader, proposed arming slaves in defense of American independence, Lower South planters rejected the sable arm, even in their own cause. Whatever concessions the war would force slaveholders to make, freedom would not be among them.[25] Seeking to avoid the loss of their human property, slaveowners instead hurried them off to distant places. Loyalist planters carried their slaves to East Florida and various West Indian islands, where they had numerous connections, but Patriots had fewer options, especially after the fall of Savannah and Charleston. With Loyalists firmly in control of much of the Lower South, some planters marched their slaves north to Virginia and Maryland and threatened to take them as far away as New England to prevent their escape.[26]

Refugeeing was a far more difficult process in the Lower South than in the North, where it entailed little more than boarding a slave or two with a distant relative or friend. The transfer of plantation units that numbered into the hundreds required massive mobilizations which, even under the best of circumstances, sundered slave families and separated friends. Black people despised such divisions, and they understood that removal reduced their chances of escaping to freedom. Thus, the merest hint of removal set some slaves in motion. Others refused to budge. A South Carolina Loyalist who had retreated with his slaves to Florida and planned to move them to New Providence Island found they "were unwilling to go thither." When he threatened to transport them by force, "they determined to go to the Woods and to see their way [back] to South Carolina by land." Rather than risk the loss, he eventually sold out. His course appeared to be the better part of wisdom, for slaveholders who were determined to refugee their slaves discovered that they simply ran off, hid in the woods and swamps until their owner had left, then returned to occupy the abandoned plantation, working as before except under their own direction and for their own benefit.[27]

Remaining on the old estate, however, posed problems. Slaves who did so were fair game for impressment officers and kidnappers, and often it was difficult to distinguish between the two. Like the British, Patriot officers early recognized the need for slave labor. They seized slaves by the thousands from their enemies. Patriots confiscated over 500, on eleven plantations, from James Wright, the royal governor of Georgia. Patriot quartermasters and commissary officers—who needed laborers as desperately as their British counterparts—understood that even these thousands would not be enough, and they impressed the slaves of owners sympathetic to their own cause.[28]

Patriot officers employed slaves in every sort of labor: building fortifications, driving wagons, chopping trees, nursing wounded, and cooking food. Those slaves who could not be employed were sold for a profit. Captured slaves were also used as bounties to attract white recruits and to compensate Patriot slaveholders for lost property.[29] When the Patriots reestablished civilian government, they sold captured slaves to raise revenue and sometimes gave them away to compensate soldiers.[30]

Black people caught in this bloody free-for-all suffered badly whether in the hands of Patriots or Loyalists. Whenever possible, slaves dodged both belligerents, taking refuge with free blacks, Indians, or white non-slaveholders. Such practices grew more common as the war undid the social order, causing aggrieved planters to append yet another special notice to runaway advertisements, this one respecting the crime of harboring fugitives: "It is hoped so scandalous a practice will be discountenanced by all well wishers to the community, by discouraging the persons concerned in such practices, that they may be brought to condign punishment."[31]

Many young slave men rejected the safe harbors provided by the "scandalous practice" and instead joined the gangs of bandits that ranged across the countryside, raiding plantations and selling their booty —including slaves—to the highest bidder. Occasionally, these bandits combined forces with maroons or Indians (sometimes the two being the same), lodging their families in established maroon villages while they foraged in the countryside. By 1782, fifty to one hundred "Black Dragoons" were "plundering & robbing" in the neighborhood of Goose Creek, South Carolina. In the backcountry, slaves and free blacks combined forces with Loyalist raiders, where a tradition of interracial banditry had its roots in the westward migration of displaced members of the charter generations. The specter of armed black men outside the control of constituted authority frightened Patriots and Loyalists alike and filled lowland planters with panic—which was no imaginary hysteria. After a gang of black bandits robbed her home, assaulted her with "the most abusive language imaginable," and threatened "to hew us to pieces with their swords," a woman planter did not sleep for weeks. A British general complained that "the Banditis of Negroes who flock to the conquerors . . . [have done] ten thousand times more Mischief than the whole Army put together."[32]

But the bandit's life was not for everyone. Women, the very young, and the old had but small place among the rough men who roamed the countryside. Separation from family and the dangers that accompanied warfare discouraged even the stout-hearted. In trying to avoid the risks military labor entailed, many slaves—perhaps the majority—remained under the protection of their owners. Some adamantly refused to leave their old estates, resisting both military impressment and the lure of fugitive bands.

Slaveholders celebrated this attachment to home, particularly when it implied loyalty to the old regime and to them personally. "Not one of them left me during the war," boasted William Moultrie, the famed Patriot guerrilla, in his postwar reminiscences. "Nay, some were carried down to work on British lines, yet they always contrived to make their escapes and return home."[33] But most planters were not as comfortable as Moultrie with the reconstitution of plantation life that took place in their absence. Patriot owners who ventured back to their estates during a lull in the fighting or who tried to sustain plantation operations at a distance discovered that their slaves had become, according to one grandee, "ungovernable." And in some cases they literally were. In 1781, while the slaves on one lowcountry plantation attempted to cut their overseer's throat, others "beat out his brains with his own musket."[34]

Such incidents—and rumors of many more such incidents—had a powerful effect. Often plantation slaves ignored their owners and their representatives—be they overseers, elder sons, or wives—and worked under a driver or an older hand, who by age, accomplishment, or reputation had earned their trust. Eliza Lucas Pinckney, who managed her family's estate during her husband's absence, found her slaves "insolent and quite their own masters." Some simply quit work and, as Thomas Pinckney complained, were "now perfectly free & live upon the best produce of the Plantation."[35] With men off at war, women—even those as experienced in plantation affairs as Eliza Pinckney—may have had special difficulty controlling their slaves, but the problem was not confined to the slaveowners' wives and daughters. Men confronted many of the same difficulties, as slaves admitted "no subjection to Overseers."[36] The impressment of draft animals and the sequestering of tools gave slaves numerous excuses to avoid work—especially the much-despised marling of the fields and tending of the canals. No matter what the sex or age of their supervisor, slaves spent their time doing "now what they please every where." When planters tried to muster a field force in the regular manner, their slaves disappeared. In 1780 Eliza Pinckney estimated that her crop would be "very Small by the desertion of Negroes in planting and hoeing time." Many planters surrendered all hope of making a crop in the chaotic years of 1780 and 1781.[37]

While the war disrupted plantation life in the Upper South and forced master and slave to renegotiate the terms under which slaves labored, it altered plantation life and labor in the Lower South in far more fundamental ways. With slave discipline in disrepair, slaveholders bowed to the slaves' demands, allowing them to enlarge their own economies. Slaves expanded their gardens and provision grounds, growing the crops that fed them and their families rather than those that made their owners rich. From the planters' perspective, such concessions came easily enough, as wartime disruption and the British blockade made it all but impossible to market the region's great staples. In South Carolina, rice production slipped from a prewar 155,000 barrels annually to fewer than 25,000 barrels in 1782. Indigo all but disappeared when the Continental Congress prohibited its export to England, and producers in Louisiana and Central América filled the vacuum.[38] Indeed, with few markets for their staples and with foodstuff in short supply, slaveholders saw wisdom in their slaves' action. The slaves' gardens and provision grounds grew at the expense of the owners' fields, and spinning and weaving houses sprouted up on the great estates. If planters saw advantages in harnessing the slaves' economy for their own purposes, slaves welcomed the chance to increase the time they spent working to feed and clothe themselves. Although neither master nor slave embraced the new order, both found benefits in the changes the war had brought.[39]

Among the crops that benefited from the new collaboration was cotton. Small amounts had always been cultivated in South Carolina and Georgia and had long been a favorite in the slaves' gardens and provision grounds, enabling them to clothe themselves beyond the meager allotment provided by their owners. Planters had also experimented with cotton, although their probes never amounted to much. But with cloth in short supply and homespun in patriotic favor, the production of cotton increased, almost entirely for internal consumption. Planters purchased tools for cleaning, carding, spinning, and weaving the fiber, and occasionally put women and children to work in special weaving houses. The coalescence of interest established important precedents that, much to the slaves' distress, planters would draw upon in the postwar years. But for the short term, slaves welcomed the fact that their owners' fields had become more like their own gardens.[40]

For slaves who remained in the countryside—whether working for themselves or their owners—reformulating plantation life in the midst of civil war was no easy task. Departing owners stripped plantations of livestock, draft animals, agricultural implements, and supplies, and foraging soldiers and other marauders took much of the remainder, picking the bones of an already gaunt carcass. Soldiers and partisan gangs periodically forced slaves to take to the woods from fear they would be assaulted, kidnapped, or worse. When they returned, slaves discovered their gardens plundered, their henhouses empty, and their furnishings destroyed. Without regular issuances from the plantation larder, the slaves' clothes became threadbare and their diets meager. Cold and hungry, low-country slaves suffered through a succession of winters on scraps of what the soldiers left and on the bounty of the streams and woods, hopeful that the next year's crop would sustain them. Yet, the following year, the cycle whereby slaves sowed and soldiers reaped only repeated itself. During the last years of the war, slaves starved on some of the richest agricultural land on the continent.[41]

Lulls in the fighting brought no respite, only the return of armed white men—sometimes Loyalist, sometimes Patriot, sometimes Tory—who tried to enrich themselves by expropriating the fruits of the slaves' labor and sometimes the slaves themselves. Soldiers of both armies and bandits without partisan allegiance raided plantations and carried slaves off for quick sale.[42] Indeed, the ruthlessness of foraging soldiers and banditti may have made the arrival of former owners like Moultrie a welcome sight.

Nonetheless, few slaves celebrated the return of their owners at war's end. Rather than await their reappearance, large numbers of slaves fled the Lower South with the royal army and navy. The retreating British carried thousands—perhaps as many as 20,000—slaves from the Lower South as they evacuated, some 5,000 to 6,000 slaves from Savannah and another 10,000 to 12,000 from Charleston. They funneled many of these slaves through St. Augustine—which was in the process of being returned to Spanish rule—from which the British removed another 6,000 slaves, and then to New York. At each of these ports, British and American authorities debated the fate of black people who claimed freedom under Clinton's proclamation. With slaveholders petitioning for the return of their slaves, the ports of evacuation became scenes of mass hysteria, as desperate slaves searched for some way to assure their safe passage. When the evacuation fleet finally departed, slaves were seen clinging to the sides of the vessels, grasping at their last opportunity.

Once on board British ships, freedom was not assured. Turning their backs on their black allies, British commanders allowed Loyalist and Patriot slaveholders to reclaim their property, and military officers sold numerous black people as the spoils of war to the West Indies and the developing plantations of West Florida and Louisiana. Yet others were taken to various sugar islands. But many black people—perhaps the majority of the fugitives—escaped the reimposition of slavery, often with the aid or connivance of British soldiers and sailors who refused to play the slave catcher. A few of these black men and women followed white Loyalists to Canada, from whence they migrated to England and later to Sierra Leone, a colony established for former slaves on the west coast of Africa by English abolitionists.[43] Others remained in Florida, which was returned to Spain in 1784 as part of the peace settlement. Acting under the Crown's old offer of sanctuary, at least 250 were manumitted by Florida's governor and reentered the society that Francisco Menéndez and the old charter generations had been forced to abandon, joining the militia and converting to Catholicism. Others remained at large, often taking up residence among the Seminole Indians.[44] Still others remained as a free people in the northern and the southern states. But for every slave freed, several died as a result of wartime butchery, brutality, or disease.

Wartime death, flight, and evacuation sharply reduced the slave population of the Lower South. Between 1775 and 1783, the number of slaves in Georgia fell from 15,000 to 5,000, a loss of two-thirds.[45] In South Carolina, the loss was 25,000, according to some estimates, or approximately one-quarter of the prewar slave population. In areas where the revolutionary struggle was particularly intense, the decline was even more precipitous. Planters in South Carolina's St. John Berkeley Parish lost almost half of the 1,400 slaves they had held in 1775. Since men were most able to escape and most liable for military impressment, the decline in the number of slave men may have been proportionally greater.[46]

While George Washington and his fellow slaveowners bemoaned the excess of slaves in the Upper South, Lower South planters issued complaints of a different sort. Delegates to the Constitutional Convention in 1787 from the lowcountry denounced attempts to prohibit the international slave trade by representatives from the Upper South, stating firmly that "South Carolina and Georgia cannot do without slaves."[47]

At war's end, returning slaveholders found their estates tattered and their labor force depleted—a consequence of "the absence of many of our most valuable inhabitants and [their] slaves," according to a leading

Savannah merchant. They also confronted the new economic realities of American independence, which barred their products from numerous markets and deprived them of bounties the British imperial system had supplied.[48] But even before they began rebuilding their shattered economy, reconstructing the labor force, and establishing new markets, planters had to restore order on their estates. Slaveowners who expected that they could operate as they had before the war faced new struggles, as slaves—who had greatly expanded their independence in their owners' absence—did not willingly surrender wartime gains. Some fled on their owners' approach, making it clear that the terms of their labor would have to be renegotiated before they would again submit to their owners' rule. Andrew, the driver on the Georgia estate of one Mrs. Graeme, had protected his people throughout the war, avoiding British, Patriot, and Tory marauders. When Graeme returned in 1783, Andrew again led the slaves off the estate, and "Mrs. Graeme could not get them back, until she made terms with Andrew."[49]

Not all black leaders came to terms peacefully. Some, armed and organized, maintained their military presence. Maroon colonies had increased in size during the war, and in parts of the Lower South black irregulars continued to operate openly. Twenty miles north of the mouth of the Savannah River, one hundred maroons established a fortified encampment from which they raided neighboring plantations. Calling themselves "the King of England's soldiers," black veterans of the siege of Savannah attacked the Georgia militia directly. As planters well understood, the presence of armed black men informed slaves of alternatives to plantation labor and increased general insubordination on the great estates. "If something cannot be shortly done, I dread the consequences," a white militia captain warned the governors of South Carolina and Georgia.[50]

Even more than in the states of the Upper South, the level of plantation violence in the Lower South appeared to rise sharply in the immediate postwar years, as slaves struggled to enlarge wartime gains in the face of the planters' attempt to reassert the old order. The violence did not diminish in the 1790s, as news of the great slave revolt in Saint Domingue passed from the Atlantic ports to the countryside. The subsequent arrival of refugees—white and black—and the interjection of revolutionary politics into the partisan divisions within the Lower South provided planters with firsthand accounts of the world turned upside down. Encouraged by Toussaint's victory, slaves were well in advance of their owners in these matters.[51]

Faced by the slaves' challenge, planters closed ranks and mobilized the newly established state authority. They sent the militia—often led by veterans of the revolutionary army—against the black irregulars and the maroons, defeating them in pitched battles, beheading their leaders, driving the maroons more deeply into the swamps, and flushing the bandits from the backcountry.[52] On the plantations, slaveholders confronted insubordination with the same overwhelming force, wielding the lash with special ferocity as they reestablished sovereignty over their estates.[53] Slaves resisted the imposition of the new order with ingenuity and determination, but planters soon revived staple production, consolidated their control over the lowcountry, and expanded the plantation system to the backcountry. In 1786, when Johann Schopf toured South Carolina, the reconstruction had proceeded far enough that he could favorably compare lowland planters to the Russian nobility whose estates contained "the most necessary handicraftsmen, cobblers, tailors, carpenters, smiths, and the like, whose work they command." During the 1790s, rice production caught and then surpassed the greatest prewar years, as slaveholders completed the transition from inland to tidal fields, a process that had begun at midcentury.[54] Although the lowcountry's golden age had passed and lowcountry planters would never again command the proportion of America's wealth they had prior to the Revolution, prosperity had returned. Rice was back.

The success of planters in South Carolina and Georgia reveals the powerful role of the slave state. In Florida, Spanish officials had no such commitment to the plantation regime. Florida's plantation economy languished, and many of the South Carolina and Georgia planters who had migrated to Florida under prewar British control returned home during the 1780s. Others left in the 1790s, perhaps disgusted when Spanish authorities provided a refuge for Georges (soon to be Jorge) Biassou, a leader of slave forces in Saint Domingue who broke with Toussaint and associated himself with the Spanish Crown in Santo Domingo. Biassou immediately took command of the black militia in Florida and forged an alliance with the communities of fugitives through the marriage of his brother-in-law with the daughter of Prince Witten, a carpenter formerly of South Carolina.

The revival of the black militia with Jorge Biassou occupying a place once held by Francisco Menéndez could hardly cheer the planters who had emigrated from South Carolina and Georgia. Ill at ease in a society in which the black militia played such an important role, they began to decamp. When Florida's governor burned all the plantations north of the Saint John's River rather than surrender them to an invading force of American adventurers, many of the remaining planters departed. The revival of plantation society in Florida would await that colony's incorporation into the United States.[55]

But even in South Carolina and Georgia, the Revolution transformed society. While rice revived quickly, indigo did not. The loss of British subsidies, competition from Louisiana and Central America, and a series of natural disasters destroyed the indigo industry in the lowcountry.[56] Searching for a profitable substitute, planters lit upon cotton. Slaves, who had gladly expanded their own cotton patches during the war, found their owners transforming cotton from a garden crop to a staple crop. In what one scholar called a "terrible irony," cotton took its place alongside rice and tobacco as the mainstays of the slaveholders' regime. Along the coast, planters succeeded in cultivating the long-staple variety, whose flat, smooth seed was easily separated from the luxuriant, silky fibers. Sea-island cotton became the main crop of the estuarine region. Long-staple cotton could not be grown in the interior, however, leaving tobacco and small grains as the most important upcountry exports. But with the perfection of a gin that could separate the sticky green seeds from the shorter fiber, backcountry planters surrendered their attachment to tobacco and grain and gave themselves over to cotton. So too did many lowcountry planters. Cotton gins and presses took their place next to rice fans in the inventories of lowcountry estates. The new attachment to cotton pushed production upward. Between 1790 and 1800, South Carolina's annual cotton exports rose from less than 10,000 pounds to some 6,000,000, the backcountry being the greatest source.[57]

The resumption of staple production fired the demand for slaves, as planters replaced the laborers lost during the war and added new ones. "The Negro business is a great object with us, [and] the Planters will as far in his power sacrifice every thing to attain Negroes," observed one lowcountry merchant with an eye on the main chance.[58] Planters imported thousands of slaves into the region. Some 10,000 entered South Carolina (until the foreign slave trade to South Carolina was closed in 1787), and others were carried into the lower Mississippi Valley.[59] Lower

South planters imported slaves from all quarters. Slaveholders retrieved many from exile in Virginia, North Carolina, and East Florida, where they had been refugeed during the war. Others were brought back from the Bahamas, Barbados, and more distant portions of the Antilles. Low-country planters even retook a few slaves in New York, just as they were about to disembark with their erstwhile British protectors.

They gathered yet others by securing wartime fugitives who had remained at large. In May 1783 a South Carolina planter advertised for five slaves who had absconded with the British army four years earlier. He understood that they had taken refuge in Savannah and then retreated "with the Indians two or three days before the attack on that place." Although they were reportedly still lodged in Indian country, he believed there was a chance they might be retaken. A year later, a Georgia slave-owner tried to recover a slave who had been captured by marauding Loyalists in 1778 and transported to St. Augustine, and then had managed to migrate silently back to Savannah, where he worked "as a jobbing carpenter" and "endeavoured to pass for a free person."[60]

Retrieving slaves scattered by the war failed to satisfy the planters' needs, and they looked outside the Lower South for the means to reconstitute their labor force. Planters purchased many slaves from the northern states, where the on-rushing emancipation encouraged southward sale at bargain prices. So many northern slaves entered the Lower South in the postwar years that in 1792 South Carolina slaveholders complained that the nascent "free states" were dumping "infamous and incorrigible" slaves on them. Chesapeake planters, who were switching from tobacco to wheat, expelled thousands of slaves whom they deemed redundant. Most were carried into the Lower South by a new class of professional slave traders, which was destined to become an ever larger part of the plantation landscape.[61]

Even with the advent of the interstate slave trade, the demand for slaves pressed hard against domestic supplies, and African slave traders found a welcome reception in Charleston and Savannah. South Carolina barred the African trade in 1787, and Georgia followed ten years later. But in 1803 the dam burst. South Carolina reopened the transatlantic slave trade, and Africans poured into the lowcountry. Between 1803 and 1808, when the constitutional prohibition went into effect, over 35,000 slaves entered South Carolina, more than twice as many as in any similar period in its history as a colony or state. As a result of this influx, the lowcountry more than recouped its wartime loses. In all, between 1782 and 1810, South Carolina alone imported nearly 90,000 slaves.[62]

The resumption of staple production and the reconstitution of the slave labor force allowed lowcountry planters to reassert their commitment to slavery. Whatever wartime events had forced them to yield to their slaves, their retreat was tactical at best. Abolitionists might defeat northern masters and Upper South slaveowners might negotiate the liberation of individual black men and women, but the lowland planters had no intention of surrendering their slaves. For them, slavery was no peculiar institution. When questioned about its alleged evils, they rarely apologized, and many began to defend chattel bondage as a positive good.[63]

With the restoration of their shattered labor force, Lower South grandees enlarged their landholdings by purchasing the estates of departed Loyalists and by ousting small holders. Lowcountry plantations—already the largest, most capital-intensive, and technologically advanced agricultural institutions on the continent—grew still larger and more complex as planters learned to monitor the estuarial flows necessary for tidal rice production. As they did, their plantation populations swelled to still greater proportions. In All Saints Parish, one of the most productive rice-producing districts in lowcountry South Carolina, over half of the slaves lived on units of more than 100 in 1790; by 1820 the proportion had increased to eight in ten. The large units squeezed out small holders—perhaps the only year-round white residents—and barred the entry of new ones. The slave majority far increased beyond the bounds established in prerevolutionary years. By 1810 four of five residents in the South Carolina lowcountry were slaves, and in the three most productive rice-producing parishes the black population towered to over 90 percent.[64]

As planters consolidated their rule in the lowcountry, the merger of lowcountry and upcountry proceeded apace. Putting aside the wartime interruption, the plantation regime resumed its westward march. During the 1760s only a small fraction of the region's slaves had resided in the backcountry. That changed dramatically in the decade following the war, and by the first decade of the nineteenth century the upcountry had been fully incorporated into the plantation zone. Although the majority of the upcountry's population remained white, by 1800 slaves composed one-third of the population of the lower-backcountry or so-called middlecountry, and slaveholders constituted a like share of the white population. Some portions of the upland region, like the area around Camden, South Carolina, resembled the lowcountry in their demographic features, with slaves making up two-fifths of the population. As the slave population swelled, white squatters, small farmers, and even substantial yeomen fled, increasing the slaves' proportion of the total population. Between 1790 and 1810 the number of slaves in the backcountry increased from 29,000 to more than 85,000. Whereas less than one-tenth of South Carolina's slaves resided outside the lowcountry in 1760, by 1810 almost one-half did.[65]

The expansion and unification of the plantation regime strengthened the planters' place in the state and the nation. But try as they might, Lower South planters could no more re-create the prerevolutionary social order than could their counterparts in the Upper South. Men like the driver Andrew, emboldened by their revolutionary experience and exploiting their owner's eagerness to reestablish production, protected wartime gains. In the process, drivers elevated their own standing on the plantation. Throughout the lowcountry, the driver's authority over plantation routine grew during the postwar years. Often drivers directed day-to-day operations without the presence of a white supervisor. Even in the presence of white overseers, drivers often enjoyed a place of superiority. "A *Driver* is more *Absolute* than the *Deay of Algiers*," declared one lowcountry overseer who came up short in a tangle with the plantation driver.[66]

As before the war, tasking enhanced the control slaves enjoyed over their daily work routine. The task system survived as the primary mode of labor organization and became more deeply embedded in the system of rice production. Even more than inland rice production, the tidal organization with its gridlike fields lent itself to a precise division of labor by the task. Tasking was also extended to long-staple cotton production.[67] The entrenchment of the task system assured slaves that they would continue to control a portion of their own time. As one observer reported from Georgia in 1806, once a slave had completed his task "his master feels no right to call on him," leaving the slave to spend "the remainder of the day at work in his own corn field."[68]

The introduction of cotton to the upcountry, and its rapid expansion in the last decade of the eighteenth and first years of the nineteenth century, however, changed the terrain upon which slaves and slaveholders confronted one another. For one thing, most upcountry slaveholders resided on their estates. In some measure, these upstarts could hardly afford not to, but they appeared to have no taste for the absenteeism of the lowlands. The planter's presence changed the dynamic of the master–slave relationship. The distance from which lowland grandees adjudicated plantation disputes disappeared and with it any pretense of objectivity.

Upland cotton also called forth a new design for production. Gang labor, which was subordinate to tasking in the lowlands, became the dominant mode for organizing production. Indeed, the advantages of the gang in driving slaves led some lowcountry rice planters to experiment with it, too. Slaves, however, intensely disliked the regimentation gang labor required and the close supervision that accompanied the new order. Much of the postwar struggle between master and slave revolved around the conversion from the task to the gang system as lowcountry slaves moved to the uplands.[69]

In the lowcountry, where the task system survived well, the switch to tidal production also allowed slaves to escape some of the backbreaking drudgery that accompanied prewar rice cultivation. Tidal production, which depended upon irrigation to suppress the weeds, freed lowcountry slaves from endless hoeing that characterized work on the inland rice plantations. At the same time, it created a need for workers who could tend the network of dikes and locks that regulated the tidal flows. Large plantation units also allowed for greater specialization; the division of labor in the Lower South was, to a considerable degree, a function of plantation size.

As a result of the changes in lowcountry work organization, technology, and plantation size, the proportion of slaves who labored in the field declined from over 80 percent to less than 75 percent during the postrevolutionary years. By the turn of the century, about one in four slaves worked at some skilled trade. The decline was particularly sharp with respect to men, who took up work as blacksmiths, boatmen, carpenters, carters, coopers, and machinists. Some slave men became famous for their engineering expertise in building and regulating the complex hydraulic system. The introduction of new, large mills to clean and process rice also created jobs for slave artisans—again mostly for men—as the mills were complicated enterprises that required constant servicing. Slave women did not share in the benefits of these changes, and, with men monopolizing the various crafts, the field population became increasingly female.[70]

The occupational structure of the slave workforce took a different shape where cotton predominated. Cotton, unlike rice, required few skills, and the intensive labor needed to carve new plantations out of the upland wilderness decreased the number of slaves who were removed from the field. As a result, while the slave artisanry expanded in the lowcountry, it declined in the uplands. The absence of skills and requirements of gang labor set the history of black life in the upcountry onto a different track. African-American life in the cotton South evolved in ways that broke sharply with life on the rice plantations of the lowcountry.[71]

New skills and the maintenance of the task system allowed lowcountry slaves to sustain their independent productive activities, even against the novel demands slaveholders placed upon them. Preserving the greatly expanded gardens and provision grounds they had staked out during their owners' wartime absence often required long hours in the field. Not every slave could maintain the pace. Young men and women frequently had to return to the fields to assist their elders in completing required tasks. Often, gardening and provisioning only added to the slaves' burden, with little improvement in their standard of living. Still, slaves refused to surrender their own economies. The priority which slaves assigned their independent productive activities surprised and angered many slaveholders. In midseason, a South Carolina planter was astounded to discover his slaves had left the fields "to finish planting their crop."[72]

With surpluses derived from their independent economic activities, Lower South slaves entered the marketplace more openly and aggressively than before the Revolution—selling and trading with one another, their owners, and with white and black in the great rice ports. In the postwar years, the slaves' trading networks extended even farther from their plantation base, perhaps because the physical mobility allowed during the war gave them a greater familiarity with the countryside. Slaves enjoyed a near monopoly control over the market in the rice ports. In Charleston, postwar grand jury presentments denounced the practices of slave marketers who engrossed goods entering the city from the countryside, increasing prices for city-bound planters and other urban consumers to what some claimed was extortion. Complaints of "negroe patroons . . . in the constant habit both by night and by day of trading with your petitioners negroes and of carrying of[f] sundry Valuable articles of Cattle, hogs, & other articles of Considerable value" were equally common in the countryside.[73]

Planters addressed the slaves' growing participation in the market in two ways. First, they attempted to subvert the slaves' entrepreneurial activities by establishing plantation-based stores. Such stores harnessed the slaves' material aspirations to the masters' pecuniary advantage, pouring the profits of the slaves' economy into the pockets of the owning class. They also kept slaves at home. However reasonable, plantation stores still conceded far too much for some planters. Rather than regulate the slaves' independent productive activities, they wanted to quash them entirely.

Opposition to the slaves' independent productive activities was especially intense in the upcountry, where cotton planters feared their slaves would develop their own cotton economy. In 1796 South Carolina lawmakers restated and elaborated the prohibition against shopkeepers and peddlers trading with slaves. But even with their substantial penalties, the new ordinances hardly stopped traders, who saw a chance to deal directly with slaves. In 1806 planters along the Combahee River exclaimed against "pedling boats which frequent the river . . . for the purpose of trading with The Negroe Slaves, to the very great loss of the Owners, and Corruption of such Slaves." As before, protests were issued, laws passed, but to little effect. In time, upcountry planters, like their lowcountry counterparts, not only accepted the slaves' economy but also found ways to profit from the slaves' independent production.[74]

As much as lowcountry planters benefited from the slaves' economy, they continued to condemn it as criminal. They particularly disliked the back-alley cookshops and groceries that doubled as taverns and gaming houses in which slaves, free blacks, and white laborers and sailors mixed easily. These ramshackle meeting places spawned everything from prostitution to insurrection, subverting the planters' "good order." Urban and rural slaves moved freely through these portions of town, especially since slaveholders and their agents preferred not to linger in such areas. When stopped and asked to present a badge or pass, slaves had dozens of explanations: an itinerant artisan required assistance; their master needed a message delivered; they had to visit a sick child. The outpouring made it impossible to maintain the discipline of the plantation.[75]

Just as slaveholders could not roll back the slaves' wartime gains, so slaves could not keep everything they had secured. Slaves found that the changing repertoire of plantation staples and alterations in the processes of production wiped away some of the wartime gains and returned the advantage to the owning class. The new requirements of cotton production, so strikingly different from those of rice or indigo, threatened to undermine the shards of independence slaves had secured. While the task system was extended to the sea-island or long-staple variety in the lowcountry, upcountry planters preferred gang labor. The gang organization—with its lockstep discipline—not only jeopardized the slaves' control over their work routine, but also restricted their access to the marketplace.

The arrival of thousands of black newcomers complicated the slaves' struggle against the planters' reorganization of production. Most came with no knowledge of the precedents established through long years of on-the-ground negotiations between slaves and owners. Creole slaves drawn from all over the North American continent had generally worked under different circumstances. Africans, who by 1810 composed more than one-fifth of the slaves in South Carolina, had even less of an understanding of what was at issue. Both master and slave contended for the allegiance of the new arrivals. Slaveholders used the occasion of the entry of new slaves to ratchet up labor demands, apply new standards of discipline, and create an order more to their liking; old hands countered these new demands, tutoring the newcomers in the contest between master and slave.

While the new arrivals entered into the ongoing conflicts within the quarter, they also brought something of their own to the struggle. The reafricanization of the Lower South informed all aspects of black life. This was especially true in the upcountry, where planters located most of the new arrivals. But no part of the Lower South was untouched by the reopening of the African trade, and many Africans entered the lowcountry, where their presence slowed and finally reversed the steady creolization of the black population. In South Carolina the proportion of Africans in the slave population, which had declined to nearly 10 percent in 1790, increased sharply in the first decade of the nineteenth century, so that in 1810 one lowcountry slave in five had been born in Africa.[76] Once again, black society in the lowcountry society was transformed from creole to African.

The peculiar pattern of the slave trade in the Lower South reinforced the effects of reafricanization. Although Savannah and Georgetown developed an active direct trade with Africa, most slaves continued to enter the region through Charleston. As in earlier years, funneling the trade through a single port allowed for the maintenance of national groups and shipboard ties, increasing the impact of the recent African arrivals. But changes in the trade in the early nineteenth century altered the origins of the African population, with increasing numbers arriving first from the Gold Coast (1783 to 1787) and then from Angola (1804 to 1807).[77] The ethnic coherence of the postrevolutionary trade reemphasized the solidarities of the Old World. Once again, countrymarks and plaited hair became common on the estates of the Lower South, and some creoles may have adopted the style.

Newly arrived Africans were quickly integrated into established African-American society. Unlike the initiation of African importation a century earlier, the postrevolutionary reafricanization of the Lower South's slave population was not accompanied by radical changes in the demography of the slave community. Whereas the influx of Africans had earlier been followed by a sharp drop in the slave birth rates and an equally steep increase in slave mortality, rates of natural increase among slaves grew steadily in the Lower South during the 1790s and into the nineteenth century. Drawing on their past experience, planters no longer relied upon Africa to enlarge their labor force. Indeed, even as they revived the transatlantic trade, slaveowners encouraged their slaves to bear children. Thus, although the newly arrived Africans were disproportionately young men, the slave population continued to move steadily toward sexual equality.[78]

From a cultural perspective, the integration of Africans into the established African-American life in the Lower South suggests how deeply African ways had already been incorporated into life in the quarter. From an institutional perspective, the steady increase of the native population suggests how quickly established African-American communities absorbed the newcomers. From a social perspective, the maintenance of African-American dominance suggests how fully creole society guided the development of plantation life.

As the black majority in the lowcountry and the black plurality in the uplands grew, as the power of the black drivers increased, as tasking and independent economic production became more entrenched, plantation

slaves increased their control over life in the quarter. In the years following the Revolution, slave cemeteries appeared much more frequently on
plantation plats, signaling planters' recognition of the permanency of the
slaves' sacred grounds—an event that could be likened to the official
recognition of an African graveyard in a northern city. Likewise, the
paths and byways slaves employed to visit neighboring estates also
gained greater prominence on plantation maps, as slaveholders acknowledged the limitations of sovereignty over their estates and accepted the
interplantation connections among their slaves.[79] Not all planters found
the changes to their liking. Complaints mounted about the new powers
enjoyed by the drivers, the absence of white men from the great estates,
and the assertiveness of slave marketwomen. But the rapidity with which
slaveholders reinitiated plantation production assuaged many hurts.

As if to acknowledge the slaves' dominion over their plantation envi-
rons, planters retreated more fully to the rice ports. The reafricanization
of the countryside and slaves' domination of the quarter made Charleston and the other rice ports even more attractive to planters. The retreat to the cities and the pattern of seasonal absenteeism was more evident after the war than before. Eventually, urban residence became
common not only for the lowcountry grandees but also for their upcountry cousins, many of whom became cousins in fact as the regional elites
knit themselves together in ties of matrimony, education, and commerce.
The planters' withdrawal assured that slaves would continue to have a
good deal to say about daily life on the plantation. The distinctive plantation-based culture of African-American slaves that had developed in the
first century of settlement became more pronounced after the Revolution.

Slaves also married across plantation lines, so that the ties of kinship
that joined plantations together did the same for the countryside more
generally. Just as the family had been the building block of the black
community within the plantation, so the growing network of domestic
relations linked plantations and expanded the black community beyond
the bounds of individual estates. The steady expansion in the region's
internal economies suggests that the pattern of inheritance and larger kin
relations grew as lineages expanded.[80]

As planters retreated to cities, the physical and social estrangement of
urban creoles and plantation slaves—long a feature of lowcountry life—

intensified. Although Charleston and Savannah surrendered the transatlantic slave trade to their northern counterparts, they nonetheless grew rapidly in size and complexity during the postrevolutionary years, with the expanding markets for cotton and rice. The number of laborers required to service this growing commercial activity increased the demand for urban slaves. Charleston's slave population doubled between the Revolution and the beginning of the nineteenth century, and in Savannah, as in other rice ports, black people achieved a numerical majority.

Although some of the most ambitious and talented black men and women had fled with the British at war's end, those who remained parlayed wartime liberties and postwar economic opportunities into a considerable measure of independence. The small army of black teamsters, stevedores, and roustabouts—free and slave—who worked the docks, wharves, and warehouses of Charleston, Savannah, and their satellite cities grew in number. Slave artisans continued to play a large role, particularly in the urban service trades as bakers, butchers, tailors, and shoemakers. They also maintained a substantial presence in the maritime and building trades. Most strikingly, however, they strengthened their position in the crafts critical to the lowland's staple economy.

Slaveholders found a large market for hiring their slaves, and, according to one visitor, "many persons obtain[ed] a handsome living by letting out their slaves, for 6 to 10 dollars per month." Slaves also hired their own time, reinforcing a sense that "the poor craftsmen cannot succeed"—at least not the white ones.[81] In Charleston, white workingmen petitioned against "Jobbing Negro Tradesmen" who worked on "their own Account . . . free from the Direction or Superintendence of any white Person." Such appeals met with no more success than they had prior to the war, but still the attacks continued. Black coopers seemed to be the favored target, although their prominence may have had more to do with the active opposition of white competitors than their unique place within the expanding black artisanry.[82] Self-hire seemed to increase in the postwar years, and few of the semiannual presentments to Charleston's grand jury failed to decry the practice. Similar complaints could be heard in Savannah, where municipal officials campaigned to rid the city of black-run market stalls, gaming houses, and taverns whose operation was an open secret. When the campaign failed, officials fell back on more selective regulations, but with no more success.[83]

Able to live and work independently, urban slaves became their own masters and mistresses to a considerable degree. They collected wages, established residences, and governed their families apart from their owners. The wartime expansion of black artisanship allowed black craftsmen, often in cahoots with slave domestics, to take control over a number of trades, laying the basis for monopolies that lasted well into the nineteenth century. "Many of the most opulent Inhabitants of Charleston, when they have any work to be done, do not send it themselves, but leave it to their Domestics to employ what workmen they please," observed one group of displaced white artisans during the 1820s. "It universally happens that those Domestics prefer men of their own color and condition, and, as to a greatness of business thus continually passing through their hands, the Black Mechanics enjoy as complete a monopoly, as if it were secured to them by law."[84] Such prosperity made the fact of slavery all the more galling, since it provided the material basis for increasing independence.

Charleston's Neck, Savannah's Bluff, and countless back-alley retreats in both cities and in other rice ports had long been the site of black communities. After the war, however, these places seemed to expand geometrically, and with them complaints about "a dangerous tendency, the number of Negroes who are suffered to erect and inhabit houses in and about the town . . . and who harbour, and even protect with fire arms, Negroes who run away from their owners." Amid the tangle of rough shacks and jerrybuilt tenements, black men and women established a life apart from white people, masters and mistresses included.[85]

As in the states to the north, black people in the Lower South also began to create an infrastructure to give meaning to their independent communities. The religious awakenings of the eighteenth century had been slow to come to the lowcountry; but following the Revolution, evangelical Christianity garnered a new legitimacy. Slaves were among the first converts. Although plantation slaves were incorporated within the churches of their owners, urban life afforded the opportunity for black-controlled institutions.

The handful of black men and women who had converted prior to the Revolution took up the leadership of African-American Christianity and succeeded where a generation of white missionaries had failed. Their ability to rally large numbers of slaves to the Cross won the respect of the white evangelicals and the grudging acceptance of planters. While some—like the black preachers David George and George Liele—followed the retreating British to Jamaica, others transformed their wartime gains into more permanent institutional forms on the mainland. The most successful was Andrew Bryan, who not only founded the largest black Baptist church in North America but also nurtured a cadre of leaders who would follow him to his Savannah pulpit.[86]

Christian religion, tight community ties, and independent economies allowed some black men and women—generally American-born, often artisans, and almost always urban-based—to translate de facto independence into de jure freedom. Although the possibility of emancipation, which had expanded greatly in the states to the north, remained barely possible in the Lower South, the changes that accompanied the Revolution widened the avenues to freedom. Manumission increased in the last quarter of the eighteenth century. Only forty-two slaves had been freed in South Carolina during the 1760s; that number more than doubled in the 1770s, and it nearly doubled again the following decade. Self-purchase followed the same upward trajectory, and over one-third of the slaves freed in the postrevolutionary decades bought their own liberty or that of a loved one, trading the accumulations of decades for liberty.[87]

The influx of refugees from Saint Domingue during the 1790s added to the number of free people of African descent in the region, a population whose mixed origins gave them the name "free people of color." Propinquity made the ports of Charleston and Savannah, far more than New York and Baltimore, natural havens for refugees from the great slave rebellion. Although these free people of color—many of mixed racial origins and light skin—met a hail of restrictions and then outright prohibitions to their entry, the bans proved to be only partially successful. A census of Savannah taken in 1798 counted over 200 adult "French Negroes" in the city, and Charleston officials "had reason to suspect" a large refugee populace. The presence of French Negroes became a constant concern of urban authorities in the 1790s.[88]

The increase of manumission, self-purchase, and immigration encouraged and abetted fugitives, who eluded their owners and thereby expanded the free black population. Runaways who had made their escape during the Revolution were still being sighted in Charleston and Savannah during the 1790s, doubtless evading capture with the aid of newly freed black people. New fugitives augmented their numbers, as there always seemed to be slaves and free blacks willing to hide escapees in the maze of back alleys, warehouses, and lofts that crowded around the wharves of the rice ports. According to aggrieved planters, runaways also gained the aid of other "despicable characters in the city who harbour and encourage the desertion of negroes from their owners . . . by furnishing them with tickets in their master's names, [and who] render their recovery extremely difficult." White men and women who broke ranks with the slaveholding class helped to expand the number of black free people, sometimes by harboring fugitives.[89]

Nearly invisible prior to the Revolution, free people of color seemed ubiquitous thereafter—at least in the eyes of urban-based planters. In fact, free people of African descent remained a tiny fraction of lowland society, composing barely 2 percent of the total black population of the Lower South in 1790. Nonetheless, the increase was striking. At the first federal census enumeration in 1790, census takers counted nearly 400 free blacks in Georgia and 1,800 in South Carolina. During the next decade Georgia's free black population more than doubled and that of South Carolina increased 75 percent. Thereafter the rate of increase declined sharply, but by 1810 over 6,000 free people of African descent resided in the Lower South. The growth of freedom was particularly great in the port cities. The Charleston free black population went from 25 in 1770 to nearly 600 in 1790 and increased by another 400 to 1,000 in 1800. At the turn of the century, there were more free black men and women in Charleston than in Boston.[90]

But unlike in the North, where ideologically sponsored emancipation freed all slaves, manumission in the Lower South was selective, with slaveholders freeing those slaves whom they knew best. House servants numbered large among the freed, suggesting the intimate ties between such slaves and their owners. Women composed the majority of manumitted adults, and the children who were manumitted tended to be of mixed racial origins, often half European.[91] Generally, the women were house servants and artisans with whom slaveholders had daily domestic intercourse and perhaps sexual intercourse.[92] When they did not free these favorites outright, slaveholders often placed them in positions from which these privileged slaves could buy their way out of bondage, giving those who purchased themselves the same social origins and somatic attributes as the manumittees.[93]

The influx of colored refugees from Saint Domingue reinforced the ongoing development of free black life in the Lower South. Like most freed people in the Lower South, the refugees were tied to the slaveholding class. Many fought alongside the slaveholders in Saint Domingue, and a few had been slaveholders themselves. These men and women, generally light-skinned, urban, and born in the New World, separated the free colored population even further from the world created by plantation slaves. Whatever aspects of language and culture free people of color shared with urban slaves—many of whom were just a step away from legal freedom—they had little in common with the newly arrived darker-skinned Africans who populated the plantations in ever-increasing numbers.[94]

Once free, former slaves reconstructed themselves and their communities. Expectations pushed free people toward a new life, leading them to take new names, seek new residences, find new work, establish new institutions, and perhaps even forge new identities. But the selective, paternal manumission of slaves in the Lower South—unlike the universal, ideologically sponsored emancipation of the North or the massive contingent manumission in the Upper South—shaped the way black people defined their lives in freedom. Free people of color in the Lower South did not jettison the names of their former owners or shed their identification with the slaveholding class. Instead, they labored to preserve the evidence of those connections, knowing full well that ties with powerful planters could serve as a protection and perhaps even a source of patronage. April Ellison, a South Carolina slave who had been freed by one William Ellison, petitioned the court to change his given name. "April" smacked of slavery, the former slave told the court. A change would "save him and his children from degradation and contempt which the minds of some do and will attach to the name of April." Ellison, however, had no wish to surrender his surname. Keeping his master's (perhaps his father's) name would not only be a "mark of gratitude and respect" but would also "greatly advance his interest as a tradesman." Although rarely revealing their motives as fully as the former April Ellison, many lowcountry free blacks followed his practice. While few black Van Cortlands, Livingstons, and DeLanceys could be found in New York, many black Draytons, Hugers, Kinlochs, Manigaults, and Middletons could be located in Charleston.[95]

For much the same reason, former slaves continued to reside in close proximity to their former owners. Free people of color were no more urban in 1810 than they had been two decades earlier, although in both periods they were more urban than either black slaves or white free people. For example, while fewer than 7 percent of slaves and whites resided in the state's largest city, one-third of South Carolina's free black population resided in Charleston in 1790; a similar pattern existed in Georgia. But the nearly complete evacuation of the countryside that accompanied the growth of freedom in the North did not follow manumission in the Lower South. Many former slaves in the Lower South did not stray far from the site of their enslavement, where a patron would be most effective.

The freed people's strategy worked. Far more than in the North or even the Upper South, manumitters maintained an active interest in the welfare of their former slaves. Some smoothed their former slaves' transition from slavery to freedom with small grants of cash, household furnishings, clothing, and occasionally even long-term annuities. More importantly, the interest of former owners assured freed people a market for their services, as their old masters and mistresses continued to patronize their shops and encouraged friends to do the same. Many free people of color labored in the trades they had long practiced as slaves, and some even continued to work in the same trades as the craftsmen who manumitted them, accumulating substantial propertied estates.[96]

Identification with the slaveholding class bought free people of color a measure of physical security, economic prosperity, and social status. A close association with a white patron provided the only barrier between slavery and freedom. As the fate of Thomas Jeremiah revealed, free people of color, no matter how wealthy or well-placed, were vulnerable, for whites presumed them to be more black than free. Without a patron—or, in Thomas Jeremiah's case, with the wrong patron—a free black was in mortal danger. The paternalist shield not only afforded protection but also assured others—the patron's allies and other clients—of the reliability of the former slave. In a practical way, such patronage kept vigilantes from the freed people's doors and encouraged customers to enter their shops. Perhaps for that reason, the radical de-skilling that accompanied manumission in the North had no analogue in the Lower South, and former slaves maintained their high occupational standing, continuing to work as artisans and tradesmen.[97]

Fragile economic advances based upon ties with the slaveholding elite did not bring equality. Indeed, the free peoples' middling position precluded openly expressing even an aspiration for equality. The political affairs of free people of color tended to be conducted in private, behind the curtain of clientage. When they did venture into the public arena, they did so with great circumspection. The free people's memorials were marked by neither angry invocations of the great principles of the Declaration of Independence nor ringing demands for equal justice of the sort that characterized the protestations of black northerners. Rather, their appeals for the opportunity to prove their accounts at law, testify in court, or travel freely had more the tone of supplications than demands.[98] In a society where planters and their white nonslaveholding allies interpreted any challenge to their rule as an incipient insurrection, free people of color dared not let their petitions take any other form. If newly freed blacks in Philadelphia quickly rushed to the rescue of their enslaved brethren when the Pennsylvania legislature hinted that emancipation might be reconsidered, Charleston's free people of color watched silently as slavery expanded and occasionally joined in the process by purchasing slaves of their own. The hoped-for jubilee, which northern blacks solemnized in annual parades, remained a well-hidden wish in the Lower South.

Rather than contemplate the fate of those still in slavery, free people turned to their own struggle to climb the racial ladder by emulating their benefactors' speech, dress, and deportment as best they could. In their pursuit of acceptance, slaveownership was not simply an economic convenience but indispensable evidence of their determination to break with their slave past and of their silent acceptance—if not approval—of slavery. From the slaveholders' perspective, nothing more fully demonstrated the free people's reliability than their entry into the slaveholding class. During the early years of the nineteenth century, Charleston's free blacks invested heavily in slaves; almost one-third of the free black families entered the slaveholding class. Of these, most purchased family members, as a means of ensuring their freedom. But for some, slaveholding was business, as it surely was for the handful of free black planters on the outskirts of Charleston. Most of these black agriculturalists were small holders, hardly more than prosperous farmers, but their eagerness to emulate their white benefactors bespoke their highest aspiration.[99] A few of the lightest skinned managed to sneak quietly under the largest barrier of all—that of color—to become in all manner white.[100]

Most free people of African descent failed to cross the color line. Excluded from the parlors of the planters and repulsed by the culture of the quarter, they had no choice but to form their own society at the interstices of the Lower South's two great social formations. Perhaps no institution spoke more to the reality of free people's aspirations than the Brown Fellowship Society, an exclusive caste-conscious mutual association founded in Charleston in 1790. Limited to fifty "bona fide free brown men of good character," the Society became the institutional embodiment of the free colored elite in South Carolina. Like similar associations in the North, its origins were in the exclusion of free people of color from white institutions. Unable to inter their dead in the graveyard of St. Philip's Episcopal Church, which many attended, leading free people of color created their own burial association under the maxim of "Charity and Benevolence."

The Brown Fellowship Society provided its members and their families a final resting place and granted small annuities to support widows and children. And, like the friendly associations established by newly freed slaves in the North, it soon became much more. The Society's hall became a meeting place for the most successful free people, and its members undertook to assist other free people. Its burial ground became a resting place "not only for themselves, but for the benefit and advantage of others." In 1803 its members joined together to form the Minor's Moralist Society to support and educate indigent and orphaned children of color.[101]

Still, rather than draw the community together, as did African-American friendly associations in the North, the Brown Fellowship Society fragmented black society by excluding slaves and dark-skinned free people. Before long, dark-skinned people established a similar association, the Humane Brotherhood. Thus did the color divisions that supported slavery became suffused throughout the black community: what whites did to browns, browns would do to blacks. The racial pecking order assured that all lighter-skinned people of African descent would stand not with but above those with darker skin. The racial unity, so much a part of black society in the Upper South, proved elusive in the Lower South. Instead, status divisions bisected African-American life.

As their numbers grew and their place in the Lower South solidified, the free peoples' world took shape. It was defined not only by the conflicting pulls of master and slave but also by the free people's experience. By the beginning of the nineteenth century, free people had begun to draw upon that experience in articulating their own distinctive ideology. Although planters accused the free people of being the slaves' agents and slaves denounced them as the planters' surrogates, the interest they defended was their own. A three-caste society had emerged in the Lower South.

Chapter Twelve

Slavery and Freedom
in the Lower Mississippi Valley

The sharp division between plantation-based slaves who rooted their culture in Africa and urban creoles who looked to the European-American world also developed in Louisiana and the neighboring colony of West Florida during the revolutionary era. As in the Lower South, such a division emerged slowly in the lower Mississippi Valley during the eighteenth century. But events unleashed by worldwide revolution accelerated the process and gave the new order a more permanent form, perhaps even more commanding than in the Lower South.

War and revolution redounded to the benefit of free people of color, whose military significance increased with the threat of foreign invasion and internal insurrection. Under Spanish and then United States rule, the free black population expanded greatly, as New Orleans and the nearby cities of Mobile and Pensacola became refuges for free people from throughout the Caribbean. Urban colored communities grew in wealth and pressed for full equality.

The expansion of the free colored population and its egalitarian aspirations did not, however, slow the expansion of slavery in the lower Mississippi Valley any more than it did in the Lower South. Quite the opposite. The century-long effort by the French, Spanish, and then Americans to find a marketable staple finally succeeded in the last decade of the eighteenth century, as planters lit upon commodities that could compete with any in the Atlantic marketplace. The swift ascent of sugar and cotton moved the lower Mississippi Valley from the periphery of the plantation world to its center. Driven by the possibilities of great wealth, Spanish authorities (and then their American successors) reopened the slave trade, and African and African-American slaves once again entered the region in large numbers. In the 1790s, the lower Mississippi Valley was transformed to a slave society, liquidating the oldest society with slaves in mainland North America.

The plantation revolution debased slave life in the lower Mississippi Valley much as it had elsewhere in mainland North America. Slaves worked harder, died earlier, had less opportunity to form families, and fewer chances to establish institutions of their own, as planters imposed the regimen of sugar and cotton. Even as the number of men and women of African descent exiting bondage increased, the noose of slavery tightened.

The expansion and reafricanization of the slave labor force widened the distance between plantation slaves and urban free blacks, both Africans and creoles. While plantation slaves renewed and refreshed their ties with Africa, urban creoles gained their freedom and integrated themselves into the evolving European-American world—becoming fluent in the fashions and manners of the metropolis, familiar with its religion and literature, conversant in its culture, and at one with the material aspirations of other mainland colonists. A few ventured into the countryside and became planters themselves. As in the Lower South, the cities of the lower Mississippi Valley became three-caste societies, where free people of mixed racial origins stood socially and culturally between white free people and black, often African, slaves. And as in the Lower South, free peoples developed their own unique perspective, even as they balanced the world of the slave and the world of the slaveowner.

The distance between the African plantation slaves and the assimilationist-minded urban people of color reflected the explosive convergence of the plantation revolution with the Age of Revolution in the lower Mississippi Valley. Nowhere else on mainland North America did these two great climacterics coincide. Their intersection gave black life in the lower Mississippi Valley its unique form, simultaneously increasing the possibilities for racial alliance and expanding the social distance that separated slave and free.

The wars of the Age of Revolution that resonated throughout the lower Mississippi Valley in the last quarter of the eighteenth century and the first decade of the nineteenth threatened to wrest slaves from their masters. Echoes of the colonial rebellion in the newly proclaimed republic of the United States deeply affected Spanish Louisiana and British West Florida. Loyalist planters from South Carolina and Georgia, eager to protect their property from the lowcountry's bloody civil war, refugeed thousands of slaves into West Florida, marching some of them as far west as the Anglo-American enclave of Natchez on the Mississippi River. Nearly 400 slaves from the South Carolina lowcountry arrived there in October 1778. They were soon joined by others ejected from the nascent free states, where progress toward emancipation had placed slave property at risk, and from the West Indies, where a growing subsistence crisis required a reduction in the slave population. Although planters settled most of these slaves in the British colonies east of the Mississippi, they transferred some to the Spanish-controlled west bank. The influx of slaves reinvigorated the plantation economy on both sides of the divide.[1]

Neither slaveholders nor slaves found peace in the lower Mississippi Valley. The war that slaveholders sought to escape was soon upon them. The new United States struck first, sending raiders down the Mississippi, assaulting the British at Natchez and Manchac on the great river and threatening Mobile and Pensacola on the Gulf coast. Bolstered by reinforcements, British regulars eventually reclaimed Natchez and sent the Patriots packing, but not before the interlopers created enormous havoc. The Americans confiscated over a hundred slaves—including fifty on board a recently arrived Jamaican slaver—whom they sold along with other booty in New Orleans with the blessing of Spanish authorities. Many slaves fled on their own, taking refuge in Pointe Coupée and other Spanish enclaves. In response, some Loyalist planters again refugeed their slaves, this time into Spanish Louisiana. A few built stockades around their estates and armed their slaves to defend their plantation fortresses. Slaves often fought bravely in the masters' cause, but when the fighting subsided they no longer accepted the old order with the same alacrity. Some plotted their own liberation—a notion that was much in the air as the whiffs of revolution blew from the east.[2]

The struggle between the colonial Americans and their British overlords had hardly begun when the governor of Louisiana, eager to strike at Spain's enemies and consolidate Spanish control of the Gulf coast, attacked the British colony of West Florida. In 1779—at the head of an army of Spanish regulars and colonial volunteers, including large numbers of free colored militiamen—he captured Mobile. Three years later, Pensacola fell to Spain. By 1783 all of West Florida—including the settlements around Natchez, Mobile, and Pensacola—was incorporated into the Spanish empire.[3]

Once again, tramping armies gave slaves the opportunity to seize their freedom. Before the Spanish conquest, fugitive slaves from Spanish Louisiana crossed the Mississippi to take refuge in British territory, while slaves from British West Florida traversed the river in the opposite direction, each taking advantage of the national boundary that divided the region's slaveholders. Even after the dispossession of the British dissolved the jurisdictional lines that sheltered runaways, slaves continued to flee. Planters on both sides of the Mississippi complained bitterly about their losses and demanded new protection for their property. But the number of runaways grew, as newly arrived slaves found refuge in the region's numerous maroon colonies.[4]

Maroon settlements, which had been present from the introduction of slavery early in the eighteenth century, flourished amid the revolutionary warfare. By the 1770s they were no longer just small enclaves of African and Indian raiders; they had become permanent fixtures of the interior of Louisiana and West Florida. Their residents were well armed and well connected with other sectors of slave society. Moving freely through trackless swamps and dense forests, maroons in the lower Mississippi Valley created their own world, importing their families from the plantations and establishing independent settlements that equaled plantations in complexity. While some maroons lived on the bounty of the forest and streams, others cultivated corn and rice and traded on the open market, surreptitiously selling cyprus logs and finished lumber to mill operators and working for slaveless farmers and woodsmen.[5]

Rather than distancing themselves from the plantations as did fugitives in the Chesapeake and the lowcountry, maroon colonies in the lower Mississippi Valley cemented relations with plantation slaves by mutually advantageous exchanges. Deep in the bayous and forests, plantation slaves and fugitives joined forces, hunting and fishing together beyond the masters' eyes. Plantation hands provided maroons with supplies that could not be secured otherwise—food in times of need and information that assured the maroons' safety. They occasionally acted as agents for the maroons, peddling their baskets and other handicrafts in the public square at New Orleans. Maroons, in return, offered a market for stolen goods and a resort in hard times. They even assisted slaves in completing their tasks. Maroon colonies thus became both an alternative to and an extension of the slave quarter, and maroon settlements or *pasaje* were literally passages that connected the lives of maroons and plantation slaves. Friendships and kinship linked the two worlds.[6]

Maroons welcomed the wartime influx of fugitives, and the maroon settlements expanded greatly. The largest of these sanctuaries was Gaillardeland, located in the Bas de Fleuve, a sprawling, overwhelmingly black region between New Orleans and the mouth of the Mississippi. Led by one Juan Maló, a fugitive from the German Coast north of New Orleans, Gaillardeland included several settlements, some of which—like the Ville Gaillarde and Chef Menteur—achieved enough permanency to merit placenames. Maló, who christened himself Saint Maló, secured a reputation as a fierce warrior and a shrewd commander who could both travel undetected through the countryside and enter New Orleans in broad daylight to purchase arms within the shadow of the governor's mansion.[7]

Aided by both free and slave blacks, Saint Maló's followers grew during the revolutionary warfare, and by the early 1780s they numbered into the scores, perhaps the hundreds. Gaining confidence from their numbers, the maroons raided plantations and rustled cattle, daring Spanish soldiers, colored militiamen, and Indian trackers to catch them. Maló's reputation grew to mythic proportions among the slaves of the lower Mississippi Valley. Fearful of the maroon's success, Louisiana's governor worried that the Bas might be transformed into "a *palenque* such as the one in Jamaica . . . that could be easily defended by 500 men against any number."[8]

Saint Maló's success strengthened the hand of plantation slaves. Plantation discipline deteriorated as maroonage became a viable option for disenchanted slaves. Louisiana officials observed that several estates had been abandoned because of the slaves' new-found independence, and planters admitted that they had been forced to temper their rule lest their slaves take the maroon alternative.[9] The growth of maroonage revealed how war and revolution had compromised the planter's authority and imperiled metropolitan plans to revive the economy of the lower Mississippi Valley.

The reverberations of revolutionary warfare not only allowed some slaves in the lower Mississippi Valley to gain independence in the swamps and woods but also expanded the possibilities of legal freedom in the region's cities and towns. Threatened by internal and external enemies, Spanish officials again turned to their ally of last resort, the free people of color. The free colored militia participated in every military action undertaken by the Spanish during the 1770s and 1780s, distinguishing itself in the campaign against the British at Baton Rouge and Natchez in 1779. Black militiamen also served in the expeditions against Mobile in 1780 and Pensacola the following year. When not fighting foreign enemies, Spanish officials employed these men to hunt maroons, maintain the levees that protected New Orleans, and extinguish fires—since arson had become as great a problem in New Orleans as it was in New York and Charleston. If anyone doubted the militia's utility, authorities were quickly rushed to its defense. "The colored people have served during the late war with great valor and usefulness," asserted the governor of Louisiana, "and in time of peace they are the ones used to pursue the runaway negro slaves and destroy their camps, an activity virtually impossible for regular troops to accomplish because of the well-hidden sites." As the militia's value increased, so did its size. By 1781 the small force Spain had inherited from France had more than doubled, to stand at almost 300. In the outlying posts of Opelousas and Natchitoches, authorities incorporated the handful of black recruits into regular units along with white soldiers. But in the cities, with their larger free colored population, they followed established Spanish policy and created separate colored units, which were divided into *pardo* and *moreno* companies.[10]

By the beginning of the nineteenth century, several generations of free black men had served, establishing a tradition of military service that was passed from father to son. Although armed service often took these men far from their homes on dangerous and unrewarding missions, membership in the militia elevated their social position and that of the free black community generally. Led by officers of their own color and backed by the authority of imperial Spain, colored militiamen enjoyed a privileged place in Louisiana society. The coveted *fuero militar* insulated them from the aspersions of white Louisianans regarding their origins and color. Regular wages and pensions, along with relief from some taxes and licensing fees, provided black militiamen a steady—if modest—income and may well have assured them the patronage of white commanders. Experience in battle, along with the splendid dress uniforms—white jackets inlaid in gold, matching trousers set off by gold buttons, and a crimson cockade—elevated them in their own estimation, that of their fellow free people of color, and that of the larger community.[11]

Official reliance on the colored militia required that the door to freedom—unlocked by the French following the Natchez revolt and opened wider by the Spanish in the 1770s—be kept ajar in the Age of Revolution. But the sharp increase of manumission that had begun in the first decade of Spanish rule slackened as slaveholders lost their enthusiasm for the slaves' freedom. Perhaps the pool of white slaveowners with colored mistresses and offspring whom they were inclined to free diminished. Perhaps the rising price of slaves induced slaveholders to reconsider their generosity. Perhaps there was not much generosity or enthusiasm in the first place. In any case, whereas manumission increased with the growth of revolutionary egalitarianism in the new American republic, it sputtered in the lower Mississippi Valley. Unmoved by the principles that spurred the liquidation of slavery in northern portions of the new United States and manumission in the Upper South, Louisiana slaveholders freed their slaves at an ever slower rate during the last two decades of the eighteenth century. By the first decade of the nineteenth century, manumission was no longer the wellspring of the free black population.[12]

The emancipator's mantle passed from slaveholder to slave. As slaveholders ceased to free their slaves, slaves took responsibility for freeing themselves. Self-emancipation, which had accounted for one-fifth of the total acts of liberation in the 1770s, made up over three-fifths by the first decade of the nineteenth century and had become the dominant route by which slaves exited bondage in the lower Mississippi Valley. The proportion of slaves freed through the activities of slaves, their friends and relatives, and their allies within the white community spiraled upward as knowledge of Spanish law increased.[13]

But if self-purchase grew in importance as the eighteenth century ended, it did not grow easier—especially as the price of slaves shot upward. As elsewhere in mainland North America, it took extraordinary industry and iron discipline to accumulate the funds necessary to buy freedom. Slave men and women worked long hours beyond their normal duties and postponed their most pressing needs. Even industrious and determined slaves needed the assistance of family and friends who contributed cash, employment, and sustenance, along with advice and encouragement. Such cooperation made it clear that self-purchase was no more a solitary act in New Orleans than it was in New York or Baltimore.[14]

As in the new United States—and indeed throughout the Americas— the terms of manumission were set by slaveholders, for the benefit of slaveholders. In the northern states they delayed universal emancipation, tied black people to their owners after the general liberation began, and assured that freedom would not dramatically alter the racial status quo. In like fashion, manumission protected the slaveholder's commitment to chattel bondage in the Lower South, allowing only a handful of urban creoles to gain their freedom. So too in the lower Mississippi Valley, where fewer than one in twenty slaves was able to take advantage of the liberal regulations. Still, black people grasped the possibilities offered by Spanish policies. Nothing speaks more strongly of the black community's commitment to freedom than the fact that the complex regulations set forth by the *coartación* were never officially publicized in Louisiana but were nevertheless universally understood by slaves and free blacks and employed with great sophistication against an adversary whose superior resources and familiarity with the law provided obvious advantages.[15]

Changes in Louisiana society during the first decade of Spanish rule provided the basis for this collective effort. The initial growth of the free black population during the first years of Spanish rule created a core of knowledgeable men and women, familiar with the operation of the *Siete Partidas* and the *coartacíon*, well connected with sympathetic whites, and, most importantly, able to provide substantial material assistance. The wars of the Age of Revolution enriched many free blacks and slaves. Upon returning from the front, colored militiamen used their bounties and back pay to buy their families and friends. Those who remained on the homefront also prospered, as the movement of men and material through New Orleans—and, with their incorporation into the Spanish empire, Mobile and Pensacola—expanded the slaves' economy.

After the war, urban slaves and free blacks continued to benefit from the quickening of commerce. The reconstruction of New Orleans follow-ing a series of destructive fires increased the demand for labor, especially in the slave-dominated building trades, and promoted overwork and self-hire. Increased earnings allowed slaves and free blacks to accumulate considerable sums, much of which they invested in securing freedom. Historians estimate that black people spent over one-half million Spanish dollars to that end, most of it in the last two decades of the eighteenth century. Nowhere else on mainland North America did slaves have the resources to buy their way out of bondage in such large numbers, and nowhere else was there such a massive transfer of resources from black to whites. Through self-purchase, the free colored population of the lower

Mississippi Valley—which had spurted upward during the first decade of Spanish rule—continued to increase at a rapid pace. Some 1,500 black people purchased their liberty or that of family and friends in New Orleans between 1769 and 1803.[16]

The growth of the free black population took place in and around New Orleans and, to a lesser extent, the other Gulf ports. Those cities grew rapidly during the last quarter of the eighteenth century and the first years of the nineteenth. Between 1771 and 1805 the population of New Orleans more than doubled to reach 8,500, its black majority (mostly slaves) growing ever larger. Mobile and Pensacola expanded at a similar rate. The booming, labor-short ports presented numerous opportunities for slaves to work on their own and earn the cash necessary to buy their liberty. The free black population of New Orleans—which had tripled during the first decade of Spanish rule—more than doubled between 1777 and 1791 to stand at over 850. It continued to grow, so that by the time the United States took control of Louisiana in 1805, over 1,800 people of color enjoyed freedom in the territorial capital. Whereas free blacks composed only 7 percent of the black population and a minuscule 3 percent of the total population of New Orleans in 1771, by 1805 over 37 percent of the black population was free, and free black people composed more than one-fifth of the city's population.[17]

The purchase of Louisiana by the United States ended the great wave of manumissions and self-purchases that had spurred the increase in the number of free people of color. The planter-controlled territorial legislature abruptly terminated the rights slaves enjoyed under the *coartación*.[18] But even as manumission and self-purchase slowed, the free colored population continued to grow, as refugees from Saint Domingue flowed into the Gulf ports. The same flight from the western end of Hispaniola fueled the growth of the free black populations in seaboard cities between Boston and St. Augustine, but Louisiana's historic relationship with Saint Domingue made the lower Mississippi Valley an especially attractive haven for free people of color. Despite the opposition of Spanish and later United States officials, the number of immigrants grew steadily throughout the first decade of the nineteenth century. Indeed, many of the free blacks who migrated first to New York and Philadelphia eventually found their way to New Orleans.

In 1809 Spanish officials in Cuba, angered by Napoleon's deposition of Ferdinand from the Spanish throne, ousted the large community of

Saint Domiguean refugees from Havana. Once again the losers of the Haitian Revolution were set adrift. Many took refuge in New Orleans, and their numbers almost doubled the city's free black population. The new arrivals, over 3,000 strong, dwarfed the existing free population and by the end of the decade may have composed as much as 60 percent of Louisiana's free black community.[19] In 1810 free people of color made up nearly 30 percent of the city; they composed a similar proportion of Mobile and Pensacola.[20]

Despite the massive increase in manumission, self-purchase, and migration, the growth of the free black population was a highly selective process. As in the Lower South, masters who freed their slaves for paternal rather than ideological reasons generally picked and chose whom they liberated. And, as during the first years of Spanish rule, slaveholders selected their wives and mistresses, along with their racially mixed children, to be freed first. Self-purchase had a similar bias toward women and female children of mixed racial origins, as market women accumulated considerable sums that allowed them to purchase themselves and their families. But perhaps more importantly, when family members clubbed together, they generally purchased women—or women first—in order to assure the liberty of future generations since, by law, slave children followed the status of the mother. During the period of Spanish rule, nearly two-thirds of the slaves—manumitted and purchased—in New Orleans were women, and more than half of voluntary manumissions after 1769 were children and three-quarters of these were of mixed racial origins.[21]

The free colored population of the lower Mississippi Valley was disproportionately urban and female, and it was also lighter-skinned than the slave population. Over the course of the eighteenth century, the free colored population moved in the opposite direction from that of the North and Upper South, where universal emancipation and wide-scale manumission darkened the free colored population. Whereas census enumerations described little more than one-fifth of Louisiana's free people of African descent as "mulattoes" in 1769, more than two-thirds were so identified in 1791. Migration from Saint Domingue reinforced this somatic marker, as the free people of color of Saint Domingue also tended toward the light-skinned.[22]

Still, the free people were not of one piece. While the urban population grew larger, lighter-skinned, and more female through the selective processes of manumission, self-purchase, and migration, a different dynamic promoted the development of free colored society in the countryside, particularly in the frontier districts of Attakapas and Opelousas. There, pioneer planters and military officers took slave women for their wives. When the soldiers received new assignments, they often left behind free black wives and mixed-race offspring, investing them with substantial holdings. Black plantation matriarchs thus guided the development of free colored life outside the Gulf ports, at least during the first generation. They generally willed their property to their sons, who married within a tight circle of propertied free colored people. By the beginning of the nineteenth century, a small class of colored planters had established itself and begun to forge connections—often through the instrumentality of militia service—with the free colored population of New Orleans.[23] However, the transit from countryside to city only added to the differences within free black society. For while many free people prided themselves in their white ancestry, others were equally proud to claim unblemished African descent. During the 1790s, nearly one-fifth of the spouses listed in the marriage registers maintained for free people of color in New Orleans were African-born.[24] What distinguished free people of color from slaves and even whites was not so much color, sex, former status, or origins but their unique experience.

United by the collective enterprise of buying freedom, former slaves stood together with those yet to be freed, especially in the Gulf ports. Urban slaves, seemingly just a short step behind the free colored people in exiting bondage, had risen through the slave hierarchy, often propelled by the same forces that had earlier allowed the free people to escape slavery. Indeed, as the process of emancipation gathered momentum, numerous black families included both free and slave members. Connected by kinship and shared experience, enslaved market women and craftsmen not only shared the same urban residence but also the same aspirations and ideals of those who had already gained freedom. Hiring their own time, urban slaves worked on their own, lived on their own, and sanctified their marriages and baptized their children in the Catholic faith. Slave and free people witnessed each other's weddings and stood as godparents for each others' children. A visitor to New Orleans at the beginning of the nineteenth century captured something of their camaraderie when he noted that people of color—free and slave—"never approach each other without displaying signs of affection and interest, without asking each other news of their relations, their friends, or their acquaintances." "To the best of their ability," he added, "they try to do to each other as much good as they can."[25]

The men and women who greeted each other so effusively on the streets of New Orleans set about creating a community to address the aspirations and needs that accompanied freedom. In so doing, they traced the steps taken by other newly liberated black people. They adopted new names, created new neighborhoods, found new employment, and established organizations which spoke to their newly won status. Still, taken as a whole, the postemancipation reconstruction of African-American life in the lower Mississippi Valley followed a unique course.

As in the northern states, free black life became increasingly urban. Not only was manumission in the lower Mississippi Valley a disproportionately urban phenomena, but the slaves in the countryside who won their freedom also migrated to the port cities. The balance of the free black population, largely rural under French domination, shifted to the cities under Spain, and the trend continued under United States rule, especially since colored migrants from Saint Domingue rarely ventured into the countryside. By the beginning of the nineteenth century, free people of color in the lower Mississippi Valley—like those in the northern states—were fully identified with urban life.[26]

But like those in the Lower South, these free people maintained their ties with the powerful white men and women who had sponsored or assisted their passage to freedom. To that end, former slaves kept their old surnames, linking them with the region's great slaveholding families. For like reasons, they maintained their membership in the militia, keeping their *fuero* rights. They married and baptized their children in the Catholic Church, affirming their identification with the touchstone of European civilization. Many former slaves continued to reside with their former masters, patrons, or white employers because, as in other parts of the mainland, newly freed slaves could not afford to establish separate households. But even when they left their former owners, freed people continued to reside near them, often calling upon their former masters and mistresses to stand as godparents at their children's baptism, to notarize their legal documents, and to give bond for their business loans.[27] As in the Lower South, free people of color in the lower Mississippi Valley looked to white society for their patrons and protectors.

The strategy succeeded to a considerable extent, for with the arrival of freedom, black men and women maintained their economic standing in the lower Mississippi Valley. In many instances, they improved upon it. Free people of color in the Gulf ports controlled an even greater share of the artisanal and retail trades than did their counterparts in Charleston and Savannah. The visibility of free colored craftsmen and shopkeepers convinced one visitor to New Orleans that black men had a "great aptitude" for the "mechanical arts, . . . or in some little retail trade." Of the sixty-one free black men listed with occupations in the 1795 census, more than one-third were carpenters, another six shoemakers, and the rest divided among a variety of crafts—mostly in the lower trades. Between 1804 and 1819, fully 80 percent of the black bridegrooms whose occupations were registered in New Orleans found employment in the mercantile or manufacturing sector of the city's economy. Few free women of color had occupations listed in the 1795 census, and those who did were divided between domestic services and retail trades, but the presence of these women on the streets and in the markets was acknowledged by nearly every visitor. Relying on the skills and connections accumulated in slavery and the continued patronage of former masters and mistresses, free people of color aspired to, and often attained, the middle ranks of urban society in the Gulf ports.[28]

The free people's interstitial occupations—like their tawny color and their middling legal status—represented their position in the social order of the lower Mississippi Valley. As in the Lower South, they were uncomfortably sandwiched between white free people and black slaves, a third caste in a social order designed for but two. The divisions so evident in the Lower South between slaves and free people and among free people of African descent—by color, residence, and aspiration—grew wider as free people secured their place in the lower Mississippi Valley and developed an interest of their own apart from either slaves or slaveowners.

The free people's social position was unstable, subject to pulls and pushes from above and below. While some free people worked to liberate family and friends, others saw their elevation as being dependent upon slavery. They staked their claim to equality not, in the manner of northern free blacks, in abolitionist ideals but in the partisan regime of the slaveholders. To such men and women, nothing more fully demonstrated their rights as subjects or as citizens than their ability to own slaves. Slaveownership refuted the planters' oft-stated belief that free blacks were nothing more than slaves without masters by demonstrating their allegiance to the slaveholder's ideal. Like ambitious whites, free blacks bought and sold slaves, used slaves as bequests, donations, and gifts in marriage contracts, and employed slaves as collateral in mortgages and other transactions. If in the process, families were divided and men and women shipped to distant parts, black slaveowners—like white ones—accepted those consequences as an unfortunate necessity.[29] Presenting slaveownership as evidence of their political reliability, these free people of color rested their case for enfranchisement and equality.

Not everyone took this route. To others, the union of free blacks and slaves was no calumny. Rather than own slaves, they lived and worked with them, extending the camaraderie which joined free people of African descent together to the mass of plantation slaves. Indeed, such men and women condemned the assimilationist aspirations of black slaveholders, their willingness to hunt down maroons as members of the militia, and their desire for their daughters to be placed with some white gentlemen. Instead, they pressed for a general emancipation in which all would be free and equal. In so doing, they established a radical egalitarian tradition that would inform black life for the next century and a half. The possibility for free people to realize this most profound aspiration waxed and waned with the transformation of the lower Mississippi Valley.[30]

The divergent tugs on free people's allegiance intensified with the settlement between Britain and the new United States in 1783. In quick-fire order, the Age of Revolution merged with the plantation revolution, transforming the economics, politics, and society of the lower Mississippi Valley in the process. The relationship of slave and slaveholder was realigned, the place of free people of African descent reconfigured, and the meaning of race redefined.

With the end of the American Revolution, Europeans and Americans—drawn by Spain's promise of economic opportunity and assurances of cultural freedom—flowed into the lower Mississippi Valley. American planters and farmers migrated across the continent into the settlements around Natchez, Mobile, and Pensacola. When Spain ceded the area east of the Mississippi and north of the thirty-first parallel to the United States, the population increased still faster. By 1803 some 8,000 white settlers—mostly Americans—resided in the Natchez District. A similar development took place on the west side of the Mississippi River, where Spanish authorities welcomed several thousand Acadians, along with others from mainland North America, the Caribbean, and the Canary Islands.[31] By the end of the century, the white population of the lower Mississippi Valley totaled over 25,000.[32]

Newly arrived immigrants required food and clothing for the short term, and tools, draft animals, wagons, lumber, and slaves for the long. Authorities further encouraged economic growth by liberalizing Louisiana's previously restrictive trade policies, allowing British and American merchants to take control of the New Orleans market and, with it, the commerce of the Mississippi Valley. Spanish authorities offered similar incentives to agriculture, providing technical support for new staples like flax and hemp and subsidies for traditional exports. The Crown granted Louisiana tobacco planters a monopoly of the Mexican market and special license to supply their leaf to snuff manufacturers in Seville. Louisiana lumbermen won a similar right to sell sugar boxes in the Spanish Caribbean.[33]

To assure planters a disciplined labor force, officials—both local and metropolitan—resolved to terminate the lax regime that characterized slavery in the half century following the Natchez rebellion. To that end, Spanish authorities assured the largely French planter class that there would be no retreat from the *Code Noir.* Indeed, in 1777 the governing body of New Orleans, the Cabildo, had issued its own regulations, *Code Noir ou Municipale,* which combined the *Code Noir* and the Law of 1751, along with additional proscriptions. The 1777 regulations restated the restrictions on the slaves' mobility and denied their right to hold or inherit property, contract independently, and testify in court. It added explicit prohibitions against slave assemblage, gun ownership, and travel by horse, along with new restrictions on manumission and self-purchase. It concluded by admonishing free people of color against confederating with slaves for any purpose whatsoever.[34]

To demonstrate their commitment to a more disciplined slave regime, officials next turned on the maroon settlements that had proliferated amid the warfare of the Age of Revolution. Between 1782 and 1784 the governor sent expedition after expedition against Saint Maló and his followers, with some units numbering over 100 soldiers—white, red, and black. At first, these incursions into the Bas de Fleuve only substantiated the maroon leader's seeming invincibility. The maroons remained united and plantation slaves loyal to Saint Maló, whom they kept informed of the movement of soldiers and slave catchers. But successive military offensives attenuated the bonds between the maroon settlements and the slave quarters. Traitors among the maroons and slaves—often tempted by the promise of freedom—turned against Saint Maló. In the summer of 1784, after several pitched battles, Saint Maló was defeated and, with scores of followers, captured. In a triumphant procession, soldiers marched him back to New Orleans, where he was publicly hanged. Officials then turned on other maroon bands, raiding their encampments and carrying fugitives to New Orleans. In June 1784 over forty men and twenty women awaited trial in New Orleans. Some of them followed Saint Maló to the gallows, but most were too valuable to be executed and instead were lashed, mutilated, and banished from the colony.[35]

The capture of Saint Maló and the destruction of the Gaillardeland maroons opened the way for the expansion of the slave regime. Both the Spanish in Louisiana and the British in West Florida were already committed to such a course. Beginning in 1771, metropolitan authorities in Spain and local functionaries in Louisiana, operating through a series of royal edicts and provincial decrees, had progressively widened the routes by which slaves could be brought into the lower Mississippi Valley, so that by 1786 slaves could freely enter Louisiana and West Florida from anywhere in the world. After 1786 both Spanish authorities and planters—fearful of revolution-tainted slaves from the Caribbean—began restricting the trade; by 1796, in the wake of the great revolt in Saint Domingue, the entry of all slaves was forbidden.[36]

Even the strictest legal prohibitions were no match for planters, slavers, and smugglers eager to profit from the trade in persons. Indeed, slavers found little reason for subterfuge, as Spanish officials repeatedly granted special exceptions to legitimate traders and turned a blind eye to smugglers. In 1795, when the United States gained control of the east bank of the Mississippi above the thirty-first parallel and the right to navigate the Mississippi to its mouth, slave traders secured easy access to the Louisiana market through the American-controlled Natchez District. With Americans pressing to sell their wares, Spanish officials reconsidered their restrictions and, during the last years of the eighteenth century, again reopened their ports to slave traders of various nationalities.

Americans reversed the trend in 1804, prohibiting the entry of foreign slaves into Louisiana. But American authorities proved as compliant as their Spanish counterparts had been. When refugee planters from Saint Domingue petitioned for permission to bring their slaves into the United States, Congress agreed and permitted the entry of some 3,000 slaves. More important, the ban on international trade did not hinder the movement of slavery to the lower Mississippi Valley. Territorial law allowed United States citizens to carry slaves (either those native-born or those imported prior to 1798) into the Orleans territory, stoking the great migration from the seaboard to the interior.[37]

The slave trade grew steadily, even as rules regulating it gyrated wildly from open encouragement to strict prohibition and back. Within the valley, Louisiana planters imported large numbers of slaves first through West Florida and then the American Natchez District. The American settlements at Manchac and Natchez became transit points for slaves from both the seaboard and the West Indian colonies. Accompanying their owners, some of these slaves had traveled overland from Virginia or down the Mississippi from as far north as New York. The influx which began with the arrival of refugeed slaves from South Carolina and Georgia during the American Revolution gained momentum after the end of the war, as slaveholders small and large pulled up stakes and migrated west. Benjamin Farrar, a South Carolina planter, was but one of many who transported his entire lowcountry operation to West Florida. In 1783 he worked 150 slaves on his Natchez plantation. Other slaves arrived in long coffles led by interstate slave traders operating out of the North, where emancipation threatened to render slave property valueless, and out of the Chesapeake, where agricultural change diminished the need for labor. For numerous slaves, New Orleans and Natchez were the last links in a chain that extended from Louisiana back through the Caribbean and South Carolina or Georgia to Africa. At least sixty-six slavers carried approximately 2,700 slaves to New Orleans between 1787 and 1803. Doubtless many more came overland and still others entered illegally. British merchants viewed West Florida as "a very considerable extension of the African trade" and a base from which to sell "Negroes for the cultivation of the land . . . to the Spaniards throughout the whole bay of Mexico."[38]

For the first time since the 1720s, the slave population, which had edged upward through natural increase for more than a half century, began to multiply rapidly. The number of slaves in the Natchez District increased from about 500 in 1784 to over 2,000 in 1796. On the west bank, the slave population expanded from less than 10,000 to more than 20,000 between 1777 and 1788. In the next decade the number of slaves climbed another 25 percent, to stand at nearly 25,000 in 1806. Under American rule, the slave population in Louisiana reached 35,000 at the time of the 1810 census, and the Mississippi Territory contained a substantial slave population, most of which was concentrated in the Natchez District. Large-scale importation allowed the black population to keep pace with a rapidly growing white population, and the region, as a whole, maintained its black majority into the nineteenth century.[39]

Planters put the slaves to work growing tobacco and indigo, which breathed new life into a plantation economy that had stagnated for more than half a century. Sustained by subsidies and spurred by the Carolinas' and Georgia's withdrawal from the indigo trade, slaveholders in the lower Mississippi Valley prospered during the 1780s. Exports of tobacco and indigo, along with lumber and naval stores, reached new heights. But, as in previous years, the boom could not be sustained. Within a decade, overproduction of tobacco, the loss of its privileged position in the Mexican market, and the failure to meet the specifications of Spanish snuff manufacturers destroyed Louisiana's tobacco industry. Concurrently, bad weather, insects, and poor management sent indigo production into a decline from which it never recovered. By the 1790s Louisiana planters found themselves in a familiar if distressing position—searching for a marketable staple.[40]

But this time they did not have far to look. In 1791 rebellion removed Saint Domingue from the international sugar market and allowed marginal producers from Pernambuco to Veracruz to enter the business of growing and processing cane.[41] Louisiana planters, who had already been experimenting with sugar cultivation, received an infusion of new capital from the former grandees of Saint Domingue, many of whom had taken refuge in the lower Mississippi Valley. Aided by technical assistance from some of the world's most experienced sugar growers, mainland planters began converting indigo and tobacco estates into cane fields.

Caribbean expertise in league with mainland ambition launched the sugar revolution in the lower Mississippi Valley. The revolution-scorched refugees were particularly eager to exchange their know-how or rent their slaves for a portion of the crop or perhaps a share of the plantation. Local planters added their own innovations, improving the processing of sugar with such inventions as the vacuum pan. Between 1796 and 1800 at least sixty plantations converted from tobacco and indigo to sugar production. Although cane could be grown in only a small part of southern Louisiana—and then with a much shorter growing season, hence with greater uncertainty than in Saint Domingue and other Caribbean islands —sugar flourished. By 1803 Louisiana produced more than 4,500,000 pounds of sugar worth three-quarters of a million dollars. Sugar became king in lower Louisiana.[42]

North of the sugar country, another commodity aspired to royalty. Cotton had long been grown on a small scale in the lower Mississippi Valley, but planters there, like seaboard producers, had been stymied by the seemingly intractable difficulty of separating the fiber from the seed. Tinkerers—many of whom took up residence in the Natchez District— solved the problem in the early 1790s, and by mid-decade Natchez mechanics were competing to produce the most efficient cotton gin. One planter employed a black mechanic to build a gin from a drawing furnished by a passing traveler. In 1796 the first public cotton gin was established in Natchez. Cotton production began to climb, and a year later a horse-powered gin cleaned 500 pounds of cotton per day. Production in the Natchez District increased from fewer than 3,000 bales (at roughly 250 pounds per bale) in 1796 to 10,000 bales (now weighing 300 pounds each) in 1801. Cotton also prospered on the west side of the Mississippi, so that between October 1801 and May 1802 the combined production of cotton for export from New Orleans was over 18,000 bales. At the turn of the century Andrew Ellicott, a surveyor drawing the southern boundary of the United States, described cotton as "the staple commodity of the settlement of Natchez."[43]

Just as tobacco had earlier remade the Chesapeake and rice the low-country, the sugar and cotton revolutions forever altered the livelihood and lives of blacks and whites in the lower Mississippi Valley. Ousting small farmers from the rich flatlands and sending them into the hill country, planters tamed the wild bayous and open prairies, metamorphosing them into grand estates with names like the Briars, Elgin, Linden, Montebello, and Stanton Hall. In time this newly minted ruling class would marry among themselves and fill their houses with fine furnishings and their barns with blooded stock. Some would affect the manner of the aristocrat, and issue edicts on proper treatment of slaves and adjudicate disputes between aggrieved slaves and harried overseers.

But in the early years, with the prices of sugar and cotton skyrocketing and with land to be cleared for new fields, few would-be grandees yet had the time for such niceties. The lower Mississippi Valley remained a hard-scrabble frontier for another generation. As one planter noted at the beginning of the nineteenth century, sugar "require[d] large plantations, long and hard work, expensive equipment, and such a quantity of men that anyone undertaking its cultivation by day-laborers would be ruined within a year." The day of the patriarch had not yet arrived in the lower Mississippi Valley.[44]

Success in the plantation business rested upon success in constructing a labor force, and success in constructing a labor force rested upon the ability to amass slaves. But even with the reopening of the slave trade, securing the labor necessary to grow sugar and cotton tested the ingenuity and drained the purses of the most resourceful planters. Few could rely on a single source. As a result, the slave population of the Mississippi Valley became an amalgam of various creole and African nationalities. If slaveholders had preferences for particular slaves, the circumstances of the plantation revolution in the lower Mississippi Valley gave but scant opportunity to exercise them, as slaves arrived from all directions—from the northern states, the Chesapeake, the lowcountry, and the Caribbean. A good many of the Caribbean slaves were transshipments, who, after a brief stay in the layover in the sugar islands or a few hours docked in Charleston's harbor, embarked for New Orleans, Natchez, Mobile, or Pensacola. Indeed, with fear of revolution running high, Louisiana planters—certainly Spanish and later American policymakers—preferred African imports to Caribbean creoles, and they were particularly loath to take those from Saint Domingue.[45]

The proportion of Africans in the slave population increased steadily during the last decade of the eighteenth century and the first years of the nineteenth century, reafricanizing the lower Mississippi Valley. Of the 26,000 slaves who entered between 1790 and 1810, more than two-thirds, or 18,000, derived from Africa, according to one estimate. Nearly three-quarters of the 157 slaves registered for sale in Natchez between 1786 and 1788 were Africans. Even planters who carried slaves with them into the region added Africans to their holdings. Benjamin Farrar's slave force grew at a rate far faster than that of natural increase during the late 1780s and the 1790s. When Farrar died in 1800, many of his 225 slaves were listed in his inventory as *bozals*. An inventory of a West Florida planter revealed that six of his eleven slaves originated in Senegal, Calabar, Temene, Papa, or Cornanco. Such different places on the coast of Africa pointed to an even greater diversity of origins in the interior. The reafricanization left no one African nationality dominant, numerically or socially.[46]

Reafricanization followed a geographical pattern earlier established in the Chesapeake and the lowcountry. Newly arrived Africans rarely settled in established plantation areas but were quickly marched to the frontier. Just as piedmont Virginia and upcountry Carolina had become the sites of the greatest African settlement in those regions, so most of the Africans entering the lower Mississippi Valley in the late eighteenth and early nineteenth centuries made their way upriver from New Orleans. At Pointe Coupée, a rough frontier some 100 miles north of New Orleans, Africans composed one-third of the slave population in 1777; by 1782 that fraction had grown to three-quarters. Of the roughly 260 slaves sold at the Natchez courthouse between 1788 and 1790, 56 percent were African-born.[47]

Almost all the men and women sold at Natchez during the last quarter of the eighteenth century were purchased as individuals, and only rarely as families or couples. Those few slaves who arrived as families, or fractured families of mothers and children, were often separated, even when the children had barely reached their teens. Planters wanted a labor force heavily weighted toward men, and the influx of slave men, many of them African, upset the sexual balance of the long-established creole population, undermining the integrity of existing slave families and denying many the opportunity to form new unions. Men and women, particularly among the newly arrived, had difficulty finding spouses. The new disease environment faced by newcomers left them susceptible to a variety of ailments, and as mortality rates increased for adults as well as children, fertility fell.[48]

Their weakened condition did not reduce the demands placed on the new arrivals. If anything, the boom in sugar and cotton increased the slaves' burden, especially where new plantations had to be carved out of previously uncultivated land. Felling trees, grubbing stumps, draining swamps, and breaking the prairie were brutal work that could crush the strongest men and women. The introduction of new crops also provided planters with an occasion to ratchet up labor demands. Planters stretched the workday and added new tasks, as they imposed the order of a slave society on the mainland's longest-lived society with slaves.

Even among the uninitiated—men and women who were unaware of how a day's labor had been defined through years of tense negotiation—extracting such large draughts of labor required extraordinarily coercive measures. The level of violence increased, and a visitor to Louisiana at the turn of the century found the whip much in evidence.[49]

The lash was not enough, however. As in the Chesapeake and the lowcountry, planters turned to the state to bolster the plantation regime. Brushing aside the Spanish Crown's attempt to impose new strictures on abusive masters, planters instead lobbied for a free hand in dealing with slaves, complaining that extant slave codes did not "endow masters with the legitimate authority they should have over their slaves." Spanish authorities complied, first establishing a fund to compensate slaveowners for the execution of slave felons. The French, when they regained control of Louisiana in 1800, proved even more compliant, reimposing the *Code Noir* during their brief ascendancy. The hasty resurrection of the old code pleased slaveholders; and although it lost its effect with the American accession in 1803, planters—in control of the territorial legislature—incorporated many of its provisions into the territorial slave code.[50]

Transplanted African and Caribbean slaves did not face the new realities of plantation life alone. American-born slaves—mostly natives of the lower Mississippi Valley, but many drawn from the Chesapeake, lowcountry, and even the northern states—also found themselves on alien territory under the plantation regime. The introduction of gang labor on both sugar and cotton plantations, along with the dawn-to-dusk workday, not only imposed a new, foreign mode of discipline on slaves but also trespassed on a host of customary prerogatives that slaves held dear. For example, from the planters' perspective, the large units on which sugar and cotton were grown made movement from plantation to plantation—a prominent feature of slave life in eighteenth-century Louisiana—unnecessary and undesirable. The same was true of the slaves' free Sundays and half-Saturdays, gardens and provision grounds, and right to sell their labor and market its product independently. Planters who once saw advantages in allowing slaves to subsist themselves pressed to convert the lower Mississippi Valley into an allowance society in which rations replaced subsistence farming. Slave codes promulgated by the Spanish in the 1790s, although reiterating proscriptions that dated back to the *Code Noir*, took special aim at the slaves' independent economic life. So did the regulations introduced by Americans after 1803. The expansion of the masters' economy put the slaves' economy at risk.

Still, slaves held their ground and occasionally won some victories. Writing in 1803, a French emigré noted that the cotton planters around Pointe Coupée had "abandon[ed] the land to their slaves." Plantation slaves maintained substantial garden plots, which they "cultivate . . . at their own account, and get their food from it. They also raise and fatten hogs and fowls which they sell on their own account." Indeed, by the end of the second decade of the nineteenth century, the internal economies initiated by the charter generations and maintained through the eighteenth century remained intact. Visiting Louisiana in 1819, Benjamin Latrobe noted that "slaves are by no means obliged to work, any where in this state on Sunday . . . excepting in the Sugar boiling season, and when the river rises on the Levee to prevent danger from inundation." When they did such work, they were "guaranteed" wages. Moreover, the slaves' role in provisioning New Orleans was so large that Latrobe believed "the city would starve" without it—a claim usually reserved for West Indian, rather than mainland, cities.[51]

Some slaves even found advantages in the new plantation regime. As Latrobe observed, sugar production generated numerous opportunities for skilled workers. Encouraging plantation self-sufficiency, many of the new grandees employed slaves as shoemakers and seamstresses, boatmen and draymen. The ranks of domestic servants also began to grow, as the planters' growing wealth enabled them to take a few slaves out of the field and employ them exclusively in the Big House.[52]

The achievement came at considerable cost. Under the new regime, plantation slaves frequently worked from dawn to noon and then, after a two-hour break, until "the approach of night." As the planters' demands expanded, the time left for slaves to work their gardens and provision grounds grew shorter. To sustain them took an extraordinary commitment. The frantic pace at which slaves worked in their own plots was captured by an emigré from Saint Domingue in 1799, who observed that a slave returning from the field "does not lose his time. He goes to work at a bit of the land which he has planted with provisions for his own use, while his companion, if he has one, busies herself in preparing some for him, herself, and their children." "Many of the owners take off a part of that ration," noted another visitor. Slaves "must obtain the rest of their food, as well as their clothing, from the results of their Sunday labors." Planters who supplied their slaves with clothes forced them to work on Sunday "until they have been reimbursed for their advances," so that the cash that previously went into the slaves' pockets went to the masters'.[53]

Cotton's seasonal demands created opportunities for overwork, as planters established quotas to increase the productivity during planting and harvest. Work done "over and above that amount," noted one observer, "their good master pays them for their accoutrement." However, when slaves ventured into the cotton business for themselves, growing the staple on their own provision grounds, they met fierce opposition. A hail of legislation passed in the first years of the nineteenth century barred slaves from "raising and Vending cotton."

The new cotton region abutted Indian territory, and Native Americans, longtime partners with African and African-American slaves in the exchange economies of the lower Mississippi Valley, soon found themselves targeted by the new restrictive legislation. It not only prohibited trade between "slaves and Indians" but also barred the two from meeting except in the presence of "some reputable white person."[54] As planters asserted their sovereignty and sealed off their estates from outside influence, they sought to shrink the slaves' world and isolate them from all but the masters' dominion.

Among those from whom slaves had to be sequestered were free people of color, whose very being, planters believed, was subversive in a slave society. If Spanish authorities found value in a free colored militia, "armed and organized," planters saw nothing but danger, especially in the wake of events in Saint Domingue. Much to the slaveholders' delight, the degradation of slave life increased the social distance between plantation slaves and urban free people of color. Nothing seemed to be further from the cosmopolitan world of New Orleans, Mobile, Pensacola, or even Natchez than the narrow alternatives of the plantation, with its isolation, machinelike regimentation, and harsh physical discipline. As free people of African descent strived to establish themselves in the complex world of the urban marketplace and master the etiquette of a multilingual society, they drew back from the horrors of plantation life and the men and women forced to live the nightmare.

The repulsion may have been mutual. Plantation slaves, many of them newly arrived Africans, had little appreciation for the intricacy of urban life and little desire or ability to meet its rarified standards. If free people of color faced a world of continued innovation, changing markets, and new fashions, slaves—residing close to the soil—were governed by the demands of particular crops and the rhythms of the season. The white men and women they knew were generally owners and overseers with no purpose but to extract labor and assure adherence to the harsh plantation code. The accoutrements of mastership—the great houses and fine clothes—were not so much objects of desire as symbols of the power of planters to lord over their slaves. Rather than embrace these European-American values, plantation slaves sought to escape them. Their cultural practices—embodied in their filed teeth and tribal markings—pointed toward Africa.

Similarly, if free people of color embraced Christianity and identified with the Catholic Church, there was little evidence of Jesus's presence in the quarter. The new planter class, most of whom subscribed to some Protestant denomination, demonstrated but slight interest in proselytizing slaves. The awakenings that were drawing some seaboard slaves to Christianity had yet to reach the Mississippi Valley.[55]

Planters, ever eager to divide the black majority, labored to enlarge these differences between the city-bound free people of color and the plantation slaves. Rewarding with freedom those men and women who displayed the physical and cultural attributes of European-America spoke exactly to their purpose, as did the employment of free colored militiamen against maroons and other slave rebels. It was no accident that free people of color expanded their privileges when the danger of slave rebellion was greatest. Nor was it an accident that the free colored population grew lighter-skinned as the slave population—much of it newly arrived from Africa—grew darker. But somatic coding was just one means of dividing slave and free blacks. Every time that black militiamen took to the field against the maroons, and every time that free women of color joined together with white gentlemen at a colored ball, the distance between slaves and free black people widened.

The two great black migrations of the late-eighteenth and early-nineteenth centuries reinforced the division. While the importation of thousands of African slaves was renewing the ties of plantation slaves with Africa and isolating them from the Gulf ports, the arrival of thousands of free people of color from Saint Domingue was alienating urban colored peoples from the plantation and its hard-pressed residents. The colored refugees from Saint Domingue had even less in common with plantation slaves than did native free people of color. The shared history reaching back to the Natchez revolt had but slight meaning to the newcomers. Men and women chased from their homes and dispossessed of their property—often including slaves—by Toussaint's armies could hardly identify with saltwater Africans and the plight of the plantation slave. Indeed, colored refugees from Saint Domingue may well have tutored their mainland counterparts—the freed creole slaves—on the dangers that an alliance with plantation slaves posed to free people of African descent.

Yet, if the growth of the plantation attenuated relations between free people of color and slaves, it never severed them. Slaves still traversed the great river to sell their produce and their labor in the port cities. Some free blacks knew the countryside well, as peddlers, hunters, trappers, and soldiers. If free people of color lost badly to Toussaint's success in Saint Domingue, they also remembered the planters' unyielding opposition to their liberty and their crude denunciations of free people as a bastard race whose sinister scheming had sparked the great revolt and ruined all. Many free people of color—both natives and emigrés—were attracted to the newly arrived Africans, who represented their own origins; and, like the African arrivals, they too could be moved by the syncopated beat of drums and tambours in Congo Square.

The connections among black people, slave and free, received a boost from the upsurge of revolutionary egalitarianism that obliterated differences of status and color in the name of human equality. The successful establishment of a revolutionary republic under a proclamation that declared that "all men are created equal," and the bloody enactment of those principles, provided an ideological umbrella under which slaves, free blacks, Indians, and even disaffected white men and women could band together. The confluence of the plantation revolutions of sugar and cotton with the democratic striving of the Age of Revolution made for new, explosive possibilities in the lower Mississippi Valley.[56]

Revolutionary republicanism spread rapidly throughout North America during the last decade of the eighteenth century. American and French nationals, who celebrated the triumphs of their own revolutions and compared their new governments favorably to that of the decadent Spanish royalists, were the primary emissaries. But there were numerous others. French planters, who squirmed under Spanish imperial domination, found republicanism an attractive basis for opposition to the aliens who had ruled the lower Mississippi Valley since the arrival of Alejandro O'Reilly. So too did free blacks and slaves, especially after the French revolutionary assembly and the northern states abolished slavery.

French planters dreamed of independence from Spain, free blacks anticipated full citizenship and racial equality, and slaves hoped for liberty, but revolutionary republicanism could not serve all masters. The politics that joined rulers and ruled, natives and newcomers, free and slave fractured under the weight of the sharp divisions of Louisiana society. "The Rights of Man," which French planters employed against the Spanish governors of the colony, took on a different meaning in the slave quarter than it had in the parlors of the plantocracy. In a like fashion, while free people of color might doff a revolutionary cockade, wave the tricolors, sing the Marseillaise, and ask rhetorically, "Are we not all equals?" they could not soon forget that the Spanish Crown had been their most reliable patron, that they owed their freedom to Spanish law, and that the only thing standing between them and the slave-hungry French planter class was the good will of Spanish imperial bureaucrats.[57]

As French planters, free blacks, and slaves weighed the implications of revolutionary republicanism, its full meaning hove into view with the arrivals of the first refugees—white and black, free and slave—from the island of Hispaniola. The emigré's tales of a world turned upside down both excited and chastened the peoples of the lower Mississippi Valley and forced all parties to consider again the ramifications of revolutionary politics. As the events in Saint Domingue were relived by planter-legislators in the Cabildo, by militiamen in their barracks, and by slaves everywhere, the contagion of revolution was upon Louisiana. Copies of "The Rights of Man" were found in the streets of New Orleans, a series of fires of suspicious origin swept through the city, and the governor increased patrols, transferred troops from Veracruz and Havana, barred the importation of slaves, deported free people with roots in Saint Domingue, and closed cafés and cabarets. Planters, free blacks, and slaves had reason enough to welcome revolutionary change; but in the end, all except the slaves found that such changes threatened more than they promised.[58]

While planters, free people, and slaves postured, the Spanish rulers grabbed the initiative. Frightened by the ominous presence of American settlers to the north, British gunboats in the Gulf, and a host of internal subversives—French planters, Anglo-American settlers, remnants of once-powerful Indian tribes, and overworked plantation slaves—Spanish authorities confirmed their alliance with the free people of color. Don Francisco Luis Hector, baron de Carondelet, who assumed the governorship of Louisiana in 1791, enlarged the free colored militia and promoted several well-placed free men of color to the officer corps.[59] More than any previous Spanish governor, Carondelet took the role of the slaves' protector, listening to their complaints, often in the presence of their owners. Harboring a deep distrust of the French planters and strong belief that the roots of the great conflagration in Saint Domingue could be found in their abusive practices, he attempted to rein in Louisiana slaveholders, first by exiling the most openly disloyal planters and then by offering slaves and free blacks the protection of the Spanish Crown.[60]

Black people—slave and free—welcomed Carondelet's initiative. Slaves carried complaints of abuse directly to the governor, whose willingness to entertain their grievances sparked rumors of a general emancipation, perhaps already promulgated by the king in Seville or the Revolutionary Assembly in Paris but suppressed by colonial slaveowners.[61]

As in Saint Domingue, however, the initial challenge to the existing order came not from slaves but from free people of color, who had often claimed Indian ancestry to escape the stain of an African past. Seizing upon this precedent and upon Carondelet's promise to enforce an old edict against Indian slavery, free blacks saw an opportunity to increase their own numbers and secure equality. As in the Chesapeake, knowledge of the mixed ancestry of the charter generations that had been long suppressed came rushing to the fore. Between 1790 and 1794, slaves claiming mixed racial origins—aided by free people of color—introduced more than a dozen freedom suits in Louisiana courts. The first actions involved slaves in the upper valley distant from the new cane fields and cotton plantations. But the precedent worried planters. They appreciated that the success of one "Indian" slave gave hope to many others, as almost all the Indians were of mixed African and Native-American origins. While free people of color saw the benefits primarily for their enslaved kin and friends, planters understood how the success of a few could subvert the entire fabric of chattel bondage at the very moment the plantation revolution required the implementation of a new discipline.[62]

The planters' concerns multiplied as the freedom suits moved to a region just north of New Orleans and as the number of slaves involved grew substantially. A suit in 1793 by a recently freed Indian woman threatened to liberate twelve slaves owned by four different planters. The success of the enslaved "mulattoes," as the planters called the slaves of Indian descent, put hundreds of slaves who might legitimately claim Indian ancestry within easy reach of New Orleans, where free blacks and urban slaves had already demonstrated their skill in using the law to widen the avenues to freedom. The suits thus threatened the planters' rule at a time when all authority—and especially slaveholding authority—was under attack. The "continuous unjust lawsuits, fomented by malignant seducers," declared a group of leading planters in 1793, encouraged "many slaves [to claim] exemption from servitude under the specious pretext of supposing themselves to be descendants of free Indians."[63]

The planters' fears grew as slaves carried angry complaints to the capital, mixed with free people of color in the streets of New Orleans, and became familiar with the events and subversive ideas of the revolutionary age. The remarkable success of the early suits prompted planters to denounce Spanish law respecting Indian slavery and to demand an end to the liberation of all so-called Indians. Governor Carondelet bowed to their demand, suspended litigation on the subject, and proposed a compromise that would have freed some slaves of Indian descent and allowed others to purchase their freedom. The compromise, although never acted upon, pleased no one and merely stoked the smoldering discontent among all parties: slaveholders, free people of color, and slaves. Indeed, the growing resentments forced Carondelet to withdraw from his alliance with free people of color, abandon his efforts to protect the slaves, and retreat toward a more traditional union with the planter class.[64]

While some slaves struggled to exit slavery through freedom suits, others—drawing on the memory of Saint Maló and the reality of Toussaint—tried to smash the door down. Runaways grew in number and maroon colonies began to reappear in the outback. Maroons mixed openly with plantation slaves at taverns and grogshops, where they bartered stolen goods for guns and ammunition. As slaveholders attempted to seal off their plantations from outside influences and institute a strict regime, their rule was unraveling. Unrest increased and rumors of rebellion bubbled to the surface. During the 1790s and into the new century, the lower Mississippi Valley was alive with news of revolt, as one intrigue after another came to light. In 1791, 1795, and again in 1804 and 1805, planters uncovered major conspiracies.[65]

Revolutionary activities had many venues. The primitive frontier plantations, where newly arrived Africans reformulated their common African heritage, were the sites of many intrigues. Others took shape in the streets and back alleys of the port cities, where disenchanted black and white workers drank and gamed together. Yet others were hatched in the barracks, where white and black militiamen—mobilized against the very threat of revolution—had been joined together. Almost all the plotters talked the language of the revolutionary age. But while some linked their cause directly to the revolutions in the United States, France, and Saint Domingue, others drew on their memory of Africa.[66]

The largest of the conspiracies, a plot devised at Pointe Coupée in 1795, touched on all of these themes. Led by newly arrived African slaves who had reformulated African nationality on the plantation frontier, it joined together Europeans of various nationalities, European-Americans, free people of color, and even some Tunica Indians. The Pointe Coupée conspirators were familiar with the revolutionary events in Boston, Paris, and Cap Français, having worked alongside slaves imported from the North American seaboard and Saint Domingue. They had listened to a local schoolteacher recite "The Declaration of the Rights of Man," and they understood the division among French planters and Spanish governors. At least one of the plotters had sued for freedom on the basis of Indian ancestry, and many others had access to guns or the possibility of purchasing guns. Asked how slaves could obtain the weapons necessary to secure their freedom, one conspirator laughed off the question, declaring, "Don't be like stupid cows. We have pigs and chickens, and we can sell them and buy guns, powder, and balls." Drawing material support from their own economies, the conspirators brought together the many threads of black life in the lower Mississippi Valley. The governor's investigation culminated in the execution of several dozen slaves, the banishment of at least three free people of color, and the imprisonment of several white men.[67]

Yet, despite the planters' deepest fears, free people of color generally kept their distance from slaves and anything that smacked of servile insurrection. If individual free men were involved in the Pointe Coupée conspiracy, the leaders of the free colored community in New Orleans and its military arm played no role. When militiamen became involved in revolutionary activity, they acted from a deep sense of anger at their own subordination and their attraction to the "maxims of the new French constitution." But whatever the appeal of revolutionary ideals, free people exhibited little concern for the plight of the slave.

A close investigation of one free colored conspirator, militia lieutenant Pedro Bailly, exposed only discontent with white domination and a profound desire for equality, although his inquisitors were eager to find evidence of an alliance with slaves. Bailly was proud that his people—the free people of color—had confronted their white tormentors in Saint Domingue, but there was no evidence he desired to see a repetition of Toussaint's triumph in Louisiana. He himself was a slaveholder, as was his father and many of his comrades in the militia. Convicted of treason, Bailly was imprisoned in Havana in 1794. Two years later, upon his return to Louisiana, he continued to agitate for free colored equality—and he continued to hold slaves.[68]

If free people of color exhibited little sympathy for slaves, the new French constitution and the events in Saint Domingue stoked their own desire for enfranchisement and full incorporation into Louisiana society. The arrival of the Americans in 1803 only increased their egalitarian aspirations. Understanding that the treaty which transferred Louisiana to the United States promised that the free inhabitants would enjoy "all the rights, advantages and immunities of citizens," free blacks believed they beheld a new and unfettered opportunity. "We are duly sensible that our personal and political freedom is thereby assured to us for ever," declared New Orleans free people in one of their numerous memorials to the new American ruler, "and we are also impressed with the fullest confidence in the Justice and Liberality of the Government towards every Class of Citizens which they have here taken under their Protection." To demonstrate their loyalty and to underline their willingness to defend their rights, free black militiamen "universally mounted the Eagle in their hats" and marched in force at the ceremony transferring Louisiana to the United States, an action that the American governor read more as a threat than a declaration of loyalty.[69]

If Spanish authorities, who had sustained the free colored militia, doubted its loyalty in the Age of Revolution, Americans were certain the colored militiamen could not be trusted. "In a country like this, where the negro population is so considerable, they should be carefully watched," warned one American administrator. Although in time the American governor, William C. C. Claiborne—like his Spanish predecessors—came to appreciate the free people of color as a counterweight to the French planter class, he feared for the safety of Louisiana. The arrival of free people of color from Saint Domingue—many of whom had served in that colony's militia, been politicized by the events of the 1790s, and participated in the great revolt—deeply frightened Claiborne. The growth of pirate communities along Louisiana's coast, many of which welcomed the colored refugees from Saint Domingue, compounded Claiborne's uneasiness. Like Carondelet, Claiborne feared a replay of Saint Domingue, with French planters pushing free people of color into the arms of insurrectionary slaves.[70]

Planters were more than willing to play their role in the drama. Enfranchised by the creation of a popularly elected territorial legislature, they achieved far more power than they ever had under Spanish or even French rule, and they were quick to turn it on free people of African descent. In 1806, within three years of the American accession, the planter-dominated legislature contained the growth of the free black population, severely circumscribing the rights of slaves to initiate manumission. Thereafter slaves could be freed only by special legislative enactment. That done, the legislature struck at the privileges free people had enjoyed under Spanish rule, issuing prohibitions against their carrying guns, punishing free black criminals more severely than white ones, and authorizing slaves to testify in court against free blacks but not whites. In an act that represented the very essence of the planters' contempt for people of African descent, the territorial legislature declared that "free people of color ought never to insult or strike white people, nor presume to conceive themselves equal to whites, but on the contrary . . . they ought to yield to them on every occasion and never speak or answer them but with respect."[71]

With planters in control, the free people's position in the society of the lower Mississippi Valley slipped sharply. Claiborne slowly reduced the size of the black militia, first placing it under the control of white officers and then deactivating it entirely, when the territorial legislature refused to recommission the militia. The free black population continued to expand, but—with limitations on manumission and self-purchase—most of the growth derived from natural increase and immigration. The dynamism of the final decades of the eighteenth century, when the free black population grew faster than either the white or slave population, dissipated; prosperity also declined, and the great thrust toward equality was blunted as the new American ruler turned his back on free people of color.

In the years that followed, white immigrants flowed into the Mississippi Valley, and the Gulf ports grew whiter. American administrators found it easier to ignore the free people or, worse yet, let the planters have their way. Occasionally, new crises arose, suddenly elevating free blacks to their old importance. In 1811, when slaves revolted in Pointe Coupée, and in 1815, when the British invaded Louisiana, free colored militiamen took up their traditional role as the handmaiden of the ruling class in hopes that their loyalty would be rewarded.[72] But long-term gains were few. Free people of African descent were forced to settle for the meager benefit of their middling status, below whites and above slaves.

The collapse of the free people's struggle for equality cleared the way for the expansion of slavery. The Age of Revolution had threatened the growth of slavery in the lower Mississippi Valley, as it had elsewhere on the mainland. Planters parried the challenge. As in the Upper and Lower South, African-American slavery expanded far more rapidly than freedom in the lower Mississippi Valley during the postrevolutionary years. The seaboard planters' westward migration soon connected with the northward expansion of plantation culture in the lower Mississippi Valley to create what would soon become the heartland of the plantation South. As the Age of Revolution receded, the plantation revolution roared into the nineteenth century.

Making Race, Making Slavery

⚔

Slavery survived the Age of Revolution, but its course in mainland North America had been permanently altered. The twin legacies of the democratic revolutions—the demise of slavery in the North and its expansion in the South—transformed African-American society yet again. With that, race once more took on new meanings, as blackness and whiteness were redefined. If in the sixteenth and seventeenth centuries transplanted Europeans denounced Atlantic creoles as audacious rogues and if in the eighteenth century the nascent planter class condemned the newly arrived Africans for their "gross bestiality and rudeness of their manners," nineteenth-century white Americans redefined blackness by endowing it with a new hard edge and confining people of African descent to a place of permanent inferiority. Just as slavery had continually redefined notions of race, so notions of race would inform a new servitude.

Slavery and race were reconfigured in the decades prior to the Civil War. The division of the American republic that followed the demise of slavery in the northern states created a base from which abolitionists, black and white, could attack slavery. But slavery died slowly in the so-called free states, as the various mechanisms of coercion that accompanied its death throes persisted. Well into the third decade of the nineteenth century, the North remained a society with slaves, undergoing an extended transition to freedom. Not until the remnants of the old regime had been liquidated and values associated with free labor—legal equality, social mobility, and political democracy—gained ascendancy did the assault on slavery begin in earnest. Beginning in the 1830s, however, antislavery activists found new friends among the proponents of free labor, who conveniently suppressed the North's long commitment to chattel bondage. Whether they marched under the banner of radical abolition, Free Soil, or Republicanism, the opponents of slavery turned on the slave South as representative of everything they despised: ascribed status, unearned privilege, and rigid hierarchy.[1]

While the demise of slavery was transforming the North, its expansion was having an equally potent effect on the so-called slave states—another new entity. Emboldened by the power that national independence conferred, slaveholding planters transported their domain across the continent, glorifying the benefits of African slavery with each step. By the time northern abolitionists launched their assault, planters had encased the institution of slavery in an ideology that neither apologized for property-in-person nor conceded its eventual demise. At the same time, planters denounced free labor as a shabby excuse for the derogation of social responsibility. They celebrated the plantation as the model community in which masters fulfilled their historic obligations to their dependents—be they women, children, or slaves.[2] The "Old South" and its plantation ideal were as much the creation of the nineteenth century as were the "free states."

The emergence of the North–South dichotomy reshaped the lives of black people. On the eve of the Civil War, most black northerners lived in cities, the wellsprings of northern prosperity. But they gained little from their urban residence. Barred from the workshops and factories that enriched white northerners, black people seldom benefited from capitalism's expansive cornucopia. The mixing of white and black in the workshops and farms of the eighteenth century and the large role black people played in the colonial economy dissipated as they exited slavery. Competition from newly arrived immigrants further undermined the position of former slaves. Free black men and women sank to the base of northern society, marginalized, impoverished, and despised.[3]

On the eve of slavery's final destruction black southerners were anything but marginal to southern productivity and politics. By 1860 the locus of African-American society had been forcibly transported from the Chesapeake and the lowcountry to a band of rich prairie that stretched from Georgia to the Mississippi Valley and then through the Great Valley from Arkansas in the north to Louisiana in the south. The second great migration of blacks in America had dwarfed the first. More than a million men and women—almost double the number of Africans carried to mainland North America—had been carried from the seaboard states to the dark, loamy soil of the blackbelt.[4] There, slaves mastered the cultivation of short-staple cotton, a crop their seventeenth- and eighteenth-cen-

tury forebears hardly knew. The cotton revolution—like the earlier tobacco and rice revolutions—eroded the traditional constraints on the
masters' power. Limitations on the slaveholders' authority achieved
through years of arduous negotiations disappeared in an instant, as
planters used the new demands of cotton cultivation to revoke long-established prerogatives, strip slaves of skills, and ratchet up the level of
exploitation.[5]

In time, slaves reclaimed—and sometimes even enlarged—the rights
they deemed customary. They reconstructed their families and communities, salvaging what they could from the wreckage of the cotton revolution. In the process, they created a host of new institutions. The most
important of these, the African-American church, grew quickly as the
small cadre of eighteenth-century converts found power in the promise
of everlasting glory and the assurance that their children—if not themselves—would celebrate the Great Jubilee. Blackbelt residence, cotton
cultivation, and African-American Christianity set antebellum slavery
apart from the bondage suffered by the charter, plantation, and revolutionary generations. The novelty of the antebellum experience speaks to
the re-creation of African-American slavery during its last half century.

The passage from the revolution of 1776 to the revolution of 1861 did
not come easily. Only with consistent purpose and the application of
great force could planters and their allies crush the hopes aroused in the
Age of Revolution. Taking their place atop the republic's new state and
federal governments, planters systematically sealed the exits from slavery. Throughout the southern states, legislators tightened restrictions on
manumission that had been relaxed during the revolutionary era. In the
North, where the progress toward emancipation slowed, slaveholders
concocted new subterfuges to stay the final triumph of liberty. Throughout the nation, the courts turned away from judicial emancipation, often
rewriting the rules of evidence to assure the failure of suits for freedom.
In 1793 a new national fugitive slave law, mandated by the Constitution,
required local authorities to return fugitives to their owners. The possibilities of escaping bondage declined, and in most places would not revive again until the crisis of union sent federal soldiers into the South.[6]

Men and women who secured their freedom by revolutionary wartime service, law, or judicial degree discovered the revolution's promised
liberty to be circumscribed and stunted. State lawmakers welcomed
black people to freedom with a hail of restrictive legislation that denied

black men the elemental rights of citizenship afforded to white men, including the right to vote, sit on juries, testify in court, and serve in the militia. Various states further shrank the bounds of freedom by prohibiting free people of color from traveling freely, requiring them to carry identification papers, and limiting their ability to hold property. The federal government added its weight to the degradation, prohibiting black men from entering the national militia or even delivering the mail. The constraints on legal freedom spilled into the most mundane aspects of everyday life. Law and practice excluded free people of color from many public places and segregated them in others.[7]

As the revolutionary hopes dissipated, the black people's friends disappeared. Prominent among those who had once opposed slavery and pumped for equality but who now disavowed their earlier stance were evangelical Christians. White Methodists and Baptists surrendered their waning abolitionist commitment and deprived black congregants of their place in previously biracial churches. "The degraded state of the minds of slaves render[s] them totally incompetent to the task of judging correctly the business of the church," declared one Virginia Baptist association in 1802, as it disfranchised its enslaved membership. The institutional bulwarks which separated spiritual and secular equality were put in place, so that God's common purpose for master and slave would not impede the function of slave society.[8]

Slaves and free blacks did not relinquish the promise of the Age of Revolution. Their hopes sparked bitter resistance to the new regime. Black people petitioned, paraded, and protested for their rights. In the process, they extended the egalitarian legacy of the Declaration of Independence and became its great champion.[9] Where they were denied redress, however, their frustration frequently boiled over into violent resistance. Much as the plantation revolution had sparked a wave of insurrection, the liquidation of the revolutionary ideals ignited new insurgencies.

Fires that smoldered in Charleston, New Orleans, and New York in the 1790s again burst into flames, as the conspiratorial and insurrectionary activity continued into the new century. In 1800 Virginia officials uncovered a wide-ranging conspiracy in their own capital. The execution of its prime movers, the blacksmith Gabriel and some dozen of his co-conspirators, hardly ended the plotting. Within months, authorities discovered similar intrigues south of Richmond, and during the next decade

their successors unearthed more conspiracies in the slave states and terri-
tories. Cool heads dismissed many of these as the feverish reaction of
alarmists, but an uprising by several hundred armed slaves upriver from
New Orleans in the parishes of St. Charles and St. John the Baptist shook
even the most confident. Led by one Charles Deslondes—a slave whose
roots may have reached into Saint Domingue—the insurgents marched
on New Orleans. When confronted by United States regulars, they did
not break and run but "formed themselves in a line" and returned the
fire.[10]

Eventually, American soldiers subdued the rebels and hanged and
beheaded Deslondes and his confederates. Their mutilated remains hung
in public as an object lesson to those who dared to challenge the slave
regime. But the tremors Gabriel and Deslondes set in motion were not
confined to the slave states. In 1801, when a New York slaveholder, herself a refugee from Saint Domingue, tried to evade the recently enacted
emancipation law by removing her slaves south, black people took to the
streets. Led by Marcelle Sam, Isaac Pierre, and Ceneall, they refused to
countenance the reenslavement of refugees of Toussaint's revolution.[11]

Slave discontent continued into the second decade of the nineteenth
century, especially as a second war with Britain increased the slaveholders' vulnerability. When the British invaded the Chesapeake and the
lower Mississippi Valley in the War of 1812, they found slaves eager to
ally with the enemy of their enemy. Scarlet-coated former slaves, hastily
enlisted in the Colonial Marines, took part in the torching of Washington
and assisted other fugitives in making their escape from bondage. When
the British retreated, many of these men and women followed them to
freedom in the Caribbean, Canada, and Sierra Leone.[12] In 1814 the Treaty
of Ghent settled the Anglo-American conflict and reduced the risks of
internal subversion, but echoes from the Age of Revolution continued
into the third decade of the nineteenth century. In 1822 Denmark Vesey—
a Charleston free black who could quote liberally from the Declaration
of Independence, knew well the history of Saint Domingue, and planned
his rebellion for July 14—joined urban free people of color and plantation slaves, creating the planters' greatest nightmare. Vesey met the same
grim end as the other slave rebels.[13] Thereafter, conspirators and insurrectionists who drew their inspiration from the Age of Revolution went
underground, only to surface again with the arrival of the Union army in
1861.[14]

In the period between the Age of Revolution and the American Civil War, blackness and whiteness gained new meaning, as masters and slaves renegotiated the terms of life and livelihood. Familiar struggles over the division of labor, the organization of work, the definition of the stint, and the nature of discipline, along with rights to gardens and provision grounds, to travel off the plantation, and to family security and cultural autonomy, were played out yet again. Whether those negotiations resulted in a more confining enslavement or eventual liberation, new representations of black people emerged.

Such representations rarely depicted black people in a favorable light. In the eyes of most white Americans, the standing of black people had fallen dramatically by the middle years of the nineteenth century. Many, perhaps most, believed that the inferiority of black people originated not in their circumstance—be it enslavement in the South or poverty in the North—but in their nature. In this view, people of African descent were not simply less privileged but were congenitally different from people of untainted European ancestry. Proponents of such beliefs bolstered their case with a hodge-podge of conflicting biblical and scientific interpretations of human origins. The tangled illogic of their arguments did little to shake the belief that peoples of color were in all meaningful ways inferior to whites, a notion that flowed as much from authoritative reasoning to popular opinion as the reverse. White supremacy manifested itself in every aspect of antebellum society, from the ballot box to the bedroom.[15]

Slaveholders discovered much of value in supremacist ideology. The inferiority of black people confirmed the necessity, if not the benevolence, of mastership. Planters elaborated such notions, sometimes endowing black men and women with a vicious savagery and sometimes with a docile imbecility. From either perspective, the vision of the natural inferiority of peoples of African descent became a mainstay of the defense of slavery and proof certain that the proper—and most humane—place for black people was under the watchful supervision of a white master.[16]

But white supremacy was not simply a production of slave societies. The limitations on black life grew along with the celebration of democracy in the free states as well. The rambunctious democratic order that elevated the "common man" to new heights also fostered the growth of racism. When the property-based suffrage fell before the forces of democratization, racial restrictions rose. Either through exclusion or segregation, black people played a far smaller role in northern society in 1850 than they had in 1750.[17]

A new cult of whiteness affected even the opponents of black slavery. Although many, true to the Declaration of Independence, rejected demeaning representations of black peoples, others subscribed to the new racial ethos. Their objections to slavery rested not on the subordination of black people, which they accepted as inevitable, but on the unfortunate effects that this peculiar form of subordination had on the white citizenry. Slavery, in short, was wrong for what it did to white people, not for the injury inflicted on black men and women. Racism thus became embedded in the opposition to slavery as well as in its defense, giving it a life separate and apart from chattel bondage. Such racialist beliefs easily survived the destruction of slavery and gained new life in postemancipation society.[18]

Nineteenth-century racial thought was both ubiquitous and novel. Only rarely had such sentiment been articulated in the years prior to the cotton revolution. Although whites disparaged the charter, plantation, and revolutionary generations, they readily accepted a common humanity. Lowly status and miserable conditions were enough to account for the alleged indolence, stupidity, and libidinous heathenism of black people as seen through the eyes of whites. Behind the most vicious assaults on the character of people of African descent during the first two hundred years of American slavery stood a firm belief that, given an opportunity, black people would behave precisely like whites—which was what made African and African-American slaves at once so valuable and so dangerous.[19] The new racism rejected this logic.

Whether viewed from the perspective of the past or the future, the transformation of black society in the years that followed the Age of Revolution underscored the dynamic nature of slavery and its reciprocal relations to notions of race. Looking forward from the beginning of the nineteenth century to the era of the Civil War, slavery's changing character reveals how much of the antebellum experience was presaged in the first two centuries. The renegotiation of slavery would continue as black people marched across the blackbelt, learned the mysteries of cotton, and remade Christianity from remembered African cosmologies. However, looking backward from this same perspective, slavery's changing character suggests that the first two centuries of African-American captivity were no prolegomenon to an antebellum quintessence. Instead, the first two hundred years of African-American life embraced a distinctive experience which gave master and slave, black and white, unique definitions. Slavery's changing reality continually transformed race through the half-century prior to emancipation. The fresh representations of black and white that emerged in the blackbelt reflected the new circumstances, but they were also inescapably anchored in a past that reached back across the Atlantic. The history of the "many thousands gone" would guide slavery's last generation and would inform African-American life to the present day.

Table 1. Slave Population of Mainland North America, 1680–1810
(% of total population)

Region and colony/state	1680[a]	1700[a]	1720[a]	1750[a]	1770[a]	1790[n]	1810[p]
NORTH	1,895 (2)	5,206 (4)	14,081 (5)	30,172 (5)	47,735 (4)	40,420 (2)	27,081 (<1)
New Hampshire	75 (4)	130 (3)	170 (2)	550 (2)	654 (1)	158 (<1)	0
Vermont	—	—	—	—	25 (<1)	16 (<1)	0
Massachusetts	170 (<1)	800 (1)	2,150 (2)	4,075 (2)	4,754 (2)	0	0
Connecticut	50 (<1)	450 (2)	1,093 (2)	3,010 (3)	5,698 (3)	2,764 (1)	310 (<1)
Rhode Island	175 (6)	300 (5)	543 (5)	3,347 (10)	3,761 (6)	948 (1)	108 (<1)
New York	1,200 (12)	2,256 (12)	5,740 (16)	11,014 (14)	19,062[f] (12)	21,324 (6)	15,017 (2)
New Jersey	200 (6)	840 (6)	2,385 (6)	5,354 (7)	8,220 (7)	11,423 (6)	10,851 (4)
Pennsylvania	25 (4)	430 (2)	2,000 (8)	2,822[f] (2)	5,561[f] (2)	3,787 (1)	795 (<1)
CHESAPEAKE/ UPPER SOUTH	4,876 (7)	20,752 (20)	42,749 (24)	171,846 (36)	322,854 (37)	520,969 (33)	810,423 (34)
Delaware	55 (5)	135 (5)	700 (12)	1,496 (5)	1,836 (5)	8,887 (15)	4,177 (6)
Maryland	1,611 (9)	3,227 (11)	12,499 (19)	43,450 (31)	63,818 (32)	103,036 (32)	111,502 (30)
Virginia	3,000 (7)	16,390[b] (28)	26,550[b] (30)	107,100[g] (46)	187,600[b] (42)	292,627 (39)	392,518 (40)
North Carolina	210 (4)	1,000[c] (4)	3,000[c] (14)	19,800 (27)	69,600 (35)	100,572 (26)	168,824 (30)
Kentucky	—	—	—	—	—	12,430 (16)	80,561 (20)
Missouri	—	—	—	—	—	—	3,011 (14)
Tennessee	—	—	—	—	—	3,417 (10)	44,528 (18)
District of Columbia	—	—	—	—	—	—	5,395 (23)

(continued)

Table 1. (continued)

Region and colony/state	1680[a]	1700[a]	1720[a]	1750[a]	1770[a]	1790[n]	1810[p]
LOWCOUNTRY/ LOWER SOUTH	200 (17)	3,000 (36)	11,828 (60)	39,900 (57)	92,178 (58)	136,932 (41)	303,234 (46)
South Carolina	200 (17)	3,000[d] (44)	11,828[d] (64)	39,000 (61)	75,178 (61)	107,094 (43)	196,365 (47)
Georgia	—	—	—	600[h] (20)	15,000[h] (45)	29,264 (35)	105,218 (42)
East Florida	—	—	—	300[i] (13)	2,000[k] (67)	574[o] (26)	1,651[o] (54)
LOWER MISSISSIPPI VALLEY	—	—	1,385 (36)	4,730 (60)	7,100	18,700 (52)	51,748 (47)
Louisiana	—	—	1,385[e] (36)	4,730[j] (60)	5,600[l]	18,700[l] (52)	34,660 (50)
West Florida	—	—	?	?	1,500[m] (27)	?	?
Mississippi	—	—	—	—	—	?	17,088 (42)
MAINLAND	6,971	28,958	70,043	246,648	469,867	717,021	1,190,835

a. Unless otherwise indicated, populations are drawn from U.S. Bureau of the Census, *Historical Statistics of the United States, Colonial Times to 1970,* 2 vols. (Washington, D.C., 1975), 2: 1168.
b. Douglas B. Chambers, "'He Is an African but Speaks Plain': Historical Creolization in Eighteenth-Century Virginia," in Alusine Jalloh and Stephen E. Maizlish, eds., *Africa and the African Diaspora* (College Station, Tex., 1996), 110.
c. Marvin L. Michael Kay and Lorin Lee Cary, *Slavery in North Carolina: 1748–1775* (Chapel Hill, N.C., 1995), 307 n13 (1700) and 19 (1720).
d. Peter H. Wood, *Black Majority: Negroes in Colonial South Carolina from 1670 through the Stono Rebellion* (New York, 1974), 152.
e. 1726: Daniel H. Usner, Jr., *Indians, Settlers, & Slaves in a Frontier Exchange Economy: The Lower Mississippi Valley before 1783* (Chapel Hill, N.C., 1992), 49.
f. Gary B. Nash and Jean R. Soderlund, *Freedom by Degrees: Emancipation in Pennsylvania and Its Aftermath* (New York, 1991), 7.
g. Allan Kulikoff, "A 'Prolifick' People: Black Population Growth in the Chesapeake Colonies, 1770–1790," *Southern Studies,* 16 (1977), 45.
h. Betty Wood, *Slavery in Colonial Georgia, 1730–1775* (Athens, Ga., 1984), 89.
i. Peter H. Wood, Gregory A. Weselkov, and M. Thomas Hatley, eds., *Powhatan's Mantle: Indians in the Colonial Southeast* (Lincoln, Neb., 1989), 38.

Table 1. (continued)

j. Gwendolyn Midlo Hall, *Africans in Colonial Louisiana: The Development of Afro-Creole Culture in the Eighteenth Century* (Baton Rouge, La., 1992), 177.
k. 1775: J. Leitch Wright, Jr., "Blacks in British East Florida," *Florida Historical Quarterly*, 54 (1976), 427.
l. 1776, 1788: Paul F. Lachance, "The Politics of Fear: French Louisiana and the Slave Trade, 1786–1809," *Plantation Society*, 2 (1979), 196.
m. 1774: Usner, *Indians, Settlers, & Slaves*, 112.
n. Unless otherwise indicated, 1790 populations are drawn from *Return of the Whole Number of Persons within the Several Districts of the United States* (Philadelphia, 1791).
o. Jane L. Landers, "Traditions of African American Freedom and Community in Spanish Colonial Florida," in David R. Colburn and Jane L. Landers, eds., *The African American Heritage of Florida* (Gainesville, Fla., 1995), 37 n11.
p. Unless otherwise indicated, 1810 populations are drawn from *Aggregate Amount of Persons within the United States in the Year 1810* (Washington, D.C., 1811).

Table 2. Free Black Population of Mainland North America, 1790–1810

Region and state	1790[a]			1810[b]		
	Free black population	Total black population	Free blacks as % of black population	Free black population	Total black population	Free blacks as % of black population
NORTH	27,054	67,474	40	75,156	102,237	74
New Hampshire	630	788	80	970	970	100
Vermont	255	271	94	750	750	100
Massachusetts	6,001	6,001	100	7,706	7,706	100
Connecticut	2,808	5,572	50	6,453	6,763	95
Rhode Island	3,407	4,355	78	3,609	3,717	97
New York	4,654	25,978	18	25,333	40,350	63
New Jersey	2,762	14,185	20	7,843	18,694	42
Pennsylvania	6,537	10,324	63	22,492	23,287	97
CHESAPEAKE/ UPPER SOUTH	30,258	551,227	6	94,085	904,508	10
Delaware	3,899	12,786	30	13,136	17,313	76
Maryland	8,043	111,079	7	33,927	145,429	23
Virginia	12,866	305,493	4	30,570	423,088	7
North Carolina	4,975	105,547	5	10,266	179,090	6
Kentucky	114	12,544	1	1,713	82,274	2
Missouri	—	—	—	607	3,618	17
Tennessee	361	3,778	10	1,317	45,845	3
District of Columbia	—	—	—	2,549	7,944	32
LOWCOUNTRY/ LOWER SOUTH	2,199	139,131	2	6,355	309,589	2
South Carolina	1,801	108,895	2	4,554	200,919	2
Georgia	398	29,662	1	1,801	107,019	2
East Florida	?	574	?	?	1,651	?

Table 2. (continued)

Region and state	1790[a]			1810[b]		
	Free black population	Total black population	Free blacks as % of black population	Free black population	Total black population	Free blacks as % of black population
LOWER MISSISSIPPI VALLEY	?	18,700	?	7,825	59,573	13
Louisiana	?	18,700	?	7,585	42,245	18
West Florida	?	?	?	?	?	?
Mississippi	?	?	?	240	17,328	1
MAINLAND	59,511	780,310	8	183,421	1,374,256	13

a. 1790 populations are drawn from *Return of the Whole Number of Persons within the Several Districts of the United States* (Philadelphia, 1791).
b. 1810 populations are drawn from *Aggregate Amount of Persons within the United States in the Year 1810* (Washington, D.C., 1811).

Table 3. Black Population of Major American Cities, 1770–1810

City	1770–1784		
	Black population (% of total)	Free blacks as % of black population	Free blacks as % of total population
Boston	682 (2)[a]	—	—
Providence	536 (12)[b]	—	—
Newport	947 (9)[b]	—	—
New York	3,137 (14)[c]	—	—
Philadelphia	842 (3)[d]	14	<1
Baltimore	—	—	—
Charleston	6,300 (55)[e]	<1	<1
Savannah	—	—	—
St. Augustine	574 (29)[f]	—	—
Pensacola	212 (36)[g]	13	5
New Orleans	1,466 (46)[h]	21	10

a. 1776: Lorenzo Johnston Greene, The Negro in Colonial New England (New York, 1942), 337.

b. 1783: William D. Piersen, Black Yankees: The Development of an Afro-American Subculture in the Eighteenth-Century (Amherst, Mass., 1988), 165.

c. 1771: Edgar J. McManus, Black Bondage in the North (Syracuse, N.Y., 1973), 210.

d. 1775, including Southwark and North Liberties: Jean R. Soderlund, "Black Importation and Migration into Southeastern Pennsylvania, 1682–1810," Proceedings of the American Philosophical Society, 133 (1989), 148.

e. 1770: Peter A. Coclanis, Shadow of a Dream: Economic Life and Death in the South Carolina Low Country, 1670–1920 (New York, 1989), 115.

f. Jane L. Landers, "Traditions of African American Freedom and Community in Spanish Colonial Florida," in David R. Colburn and Jane L. Landers, eds., The African American Heritage of Florida (Gainesville, Fla., 1995), 37 n11.

Table 3. (continued)

	1790			1810		
	Black population (% of total)[i]	Free blacks as % of black population	Free blacks as % of total population	Black population (% of total)[k]	Free blacks as % of black population	Free blacks as % of total population
	761 (4)	100	4	1,464 (4)	100	4
	475 (7)	90	7	871 (9)	99	9
	640 (10)	65	6	630 (8)	100	8
	3,262 (10)[j]	33	3	9,823 (10)	83	8
	1,721 (6)	83	5	6,354 (12)	100	12
	1,578 (12)	21	2	7,686 (22)	48	10
	8,271 (51)[e]	7	4	13,143 (53)	11	6
	—	—	—	2,725 (52)	19	10
	574 (29)[f]	—	—	1,773 (58)[f]	7	4
	70 (26)[g]	19	5	646 (46)[g]	31	14
	2,651 (53)[h]	33	17	10,991 (63)	45	29

g. 1784, 1788, 1805: William Coker and Douglas Inglis, *The Spanish Censuses of Pensacola, 1784–1820: A Genealogical Guide to Spanish Pensacola* (Pensacola, 1980), 45, 48, 90.

h. 1777, 1791: Kimberly S. Hanger, *Bounded Lives, Bounded Places: Free Black Society in Colonial New Orleans, 1769–1803* (Durham, N.C., 1997), 22.

i. Unless otherwise indicated, 1790 populations are drawn from *Return of the Whole Number of Persons within the Several Districts of the United States* (Philadelphia, 1791).

j. U.S. Bureau of the Census, *A Century of Population Growth* (Washington, D.C., 1909).

k. Unless otherwise indicated, 1810 populations are drawn from *Aggregate Amount of Persons within the United States in the Year 1810* (Washington, D.C., 1811).

Abbreviations

AA	*American Anthropologist*
AH	*Agricultural History*
AHQ	*Alabama Historical Quarterly*
AHR	*American Historical Review*
AJLH	*American Journal of Legal History*
AR	*Alabama Review*
Catterall, *Judicial Cases*	Helen Catterall, ed., *Judicial Cases Concerning American Slavery and the Negro*, 5 vols. (New York, 1926–1937)
CS	*Caribbean Studies*
Donnan, *Slave Trade*	Elizabeth Donnan., ed., *Documents Illustrative of the Slave Trade to America*, 4 vols. (Washington, D.C., 1930–1935)
EHR	*Economic History Review*
FHQ	*Florida Historical Quarterly*
GHQ	*Georgia Historical Quarterly*
GHSC	*Georgia Historical Society Collections*
GR	*Geographical Review*
Gray, *So. Ag.*	Lewis Cecil Gray, *History of Agriculture in the Southern United States*, 2 vols. (Washington, D.C., 1933)
HA	*History in Africa*
HAHR	*Hispanic American Historical Review*
HArch	*Historical Archeology*
Historical Statistics	U.S. Bureau of Commerce, *Historical Statistics of the United States, Colonial Times to 1970*, 2 vols. (Washington, D.C., 1975)
HJ	*Historical Journal*
HMPEC	*Historical Magazine of the Protestant Episcopal Church*
HSSH	*Histoire Sociale—Social History*
IRSH	*International Review of Social History*

JAAHGS	*Journal of the Afro-American Historical and Genealogical Society*
JAF	*Journal of American Folklore*
JAH	*Journal of African History*
JAmH	*Journal of American History*
JAS	*Journal of American Studies*
JEH	*Journal of Economic History*
JIH	*Journal of Interdisciplinary History*
JLS	*Journal of Legal Studies*
JMH	*Journal of Mississippi History*
JNE	*Journal of Negro Education*
JNH	*Journal of Negro History*
JRT	*Journal of Religious Thought*
JSH	*Journal of Social History*
JSoH	*Journal of Southern History*
JUH	*Journal of Urban History*
LH	*Louisiana History*
LHist	*Labor History*
LHQ	*Louisiana Historical Quarterly*
LHR	*Law and History Review*
LL	*Labour/Le Travailleur*
LS	*Louisiana Studies*
MHM	*Maryland Historical Magazine*
Miss. Arch.	Dunbar Rowland and A. G. Sanders, eds. and trans., *Mississippi Provincial Archives: French Dominion,* 5 vols. (Jackson, Miss., 1919–1984)
MP	*Marxist Perspectives*
MVHR	*Mississippi Valley Historical Review*
NCHR	*North Carolina Historical Review*
NGSQ	*National Genealogical Society Quarterly*
NLR	*New Left Review*
NYGBR	*New York Genealogical and Biographical Register*
NYH	*New York History*
NYHQ	*New-York Historical Society Quarterly*
NY Documents	E. B. O'Callaghan, ed., *Documents Relative to the Colonial History of the State of New-York,* 15 vols. (Albany, 1853–1887)
NY Manuscripts	E. B. O'Callaghan, *Calendar of Historical Manuscripts in the Office of the Secretary of State, Albany, N.Y.* (Albany, 1865)

NY Manuscripts, Dutch	E. B. O'Callaghan, ed., *Calendar of Historical Manuscripts in the Office of the Secretary of State, Dutch Manuscripts,* 2 vols. (Albany, N.Y., 1865–1866)
PAH	*Perspectives in American History*
PAPS	*Proceedings of the American Philosophical Society*
PAS	*Pennsylvania Abolition Society Papers,* Historical Society of Pennsylvania, Philadelphia
PH	*Pennsylvania History*
PMHB	*Pennsylvania Magazine of History and Biography*
PS	*Plantation Society*
PSQ	*Political Science Quarterly*
RFHOM	*Revue Française d'Histoire d'Outre-Mer*
RIH	*Rhode Island History*
RKHS	*Register of the Kentucky Historical Society*
RL	*Revue de Louisiane*
Runaway Advertisements	Lathan A. Windley, comp., *Runaway Slaves Advertisements: A Documentary History from the 1730s to 1790,* 4 vols. (Westport, Conn., 1983)
S&A	*Slavery and Abolition*
SCDA&H	South Carolina Department of Archives and History, Columbia, S.C.
SCHM	*South Carolina Historical and Genealogical Magazine*
SES	*Social and Economic Studies*
SH	*Social History*
SS	*Southern Studies*
SSH	*Social Science History*
T&C	*Technology and Culture*
THQ	*Tennessee Historical Quarterly*
VMHB	*Virginia Magazine of History and Biography*
VQR	*Virginia Quarterly Review*
WMQ	*William and Mary Quarterly,* 3rd series

Notes

∧

Prologue: Making Slavery, Making Race

1. For a powerful statement, see Barbara Jeanne Fields, "Race and Ideology in American History," in J. Morgan Kousser and James M. McPherson, eds., *Region, Race, and Reconstruction: Essays in Honor of C. Vann Woodward* (New York, 1982), 143–77. Also see Henry Louis Gates, Jr., ed., *"Race," Writing, and Difference* (Chicago, 1986), 1–20; Stuart Hall, "Cultural Identity and Diaspora," in Jonathan Rutherford, ed., *Identity* (London, 1990), 222–37; and Evelyn Brooks Higginbotham, "African-American Women's History and the Metalanguage of Race," *Signs,* 17 (1992), 251–74. A handy discussion of the new biology can be found in Jonathan M. Marks, *Human Biodiversity: Genes, Race, and History* (New York, 1995); also see Steven Jay Gould, "Why We Should Not Name Races—A Biological View," in Gould, *Ever Since Darwin: Reflections on Natural History* (New York, 1977).

2. Although Barbara Fields's original formulation and later elaborations on the meaning of "race" ("Slavery, Race and Ideology in the United States of America," *NLR,* 181 [1990], 85–118) were aggressively historical, not all scholars have taken that tack. See, for example, Michael Omi and Howard Winant, *Racial Formation in the United States: From the 1960s to the 1980s* (London, 1986), which situates race in a specific historical setting but ignores the processes that are continually transforming it.

3. E. P. Thompson, *The Making of the English Working Class* (New York, 1964), 9.

4. Claude Meillassoux, *Anthropologie de l'esclavage: le ventre de fer et argent* (Paris, 1986), translated as *The Anthropology of Slavery: The Womb of Iron and Gold,* trans. Alide Dasnois (Chicago, 1991), 99–100; Orlando Patterson, *Slavery and Social Death: A Comparative Study* (Cambridge, Mass., 1982), 5–6; M. I. Finley, *Ancient Slavery and Modern Ideology* (New York, 1980), 74–75; Stanley M. Elkins, *Slavery: A Problem in American Institutional and Intellectual Life* (Chicago, 1959).

5. Any discussion of slavery which emphasizes the doubleness of slavery—as property and person—must begin with Georg Wilhelm Hegel, *Phenomenology of the Spirit,* trans. A. V. Miller (New York, 1977), and continue though the work of David Brion Davis, *The Problem of Slavery in Western Culture* (Ithaca, N.Y., 1966).

6. The literature on paternalism is vast, even when confined to the master–slave relationship, but the contemporary debate starts with Eugene D. Genovese, *Roll, Jordan, Roll: The World the Slaves Made* (New York, 1974). For the struggle against

slavery and the development of capitalism, see David Brion Davis, *The Problem of Slavery in the Age of Revolution, 1770–1823* (Ithaca, N.Y., 1975).

7. Herbert G. Gutman, *The Black Family in Slavery and Freedom, 1750–1925* (New York, 1976), 335.

8. The same point has been made about the relationship between race and gender; see Kathleen M. Brown, *Good Wives, Nasty Wenches, and Anxious Patriarchs: Gender, Race, and Power in Colonial Virginia* (Chapel Hill, N.C., 1996).

9. Keith Hopkins, *Conquerors and Slaves: Sociological Studies in Roman History* (Cambridge, UK, 1978), 99; Moses I. Finley, "Slavery," *International Encyclopedia of the Social Sciences* (New York, 1968), and Finley, *Ancient Slavery and Modern Ideology* (New York, 1980), 79–80.

10. Anne Grant, *Memoirs of an American Lady* (New York, 1809), 26–29.

11. Frank Tannenbaum, *Slave and Citizen: The Negro in the Americas* (New York, 1946), 117.

12. Although they differ in their emphases, two particularly clear statements are Richard S. Dunn, *Sugar and Slaves: The Rise of the Planter Class in the English West Indies, 1624–1713* (Chapel Hill, N.C., 1972), and Richard B. Sheridan, *Sugar and Slavery: An Economic History of the British West Indies, 1623–1775* (Baltimore, 1973).

13. Edmund S. Morgan, *American Slavery, American Freedom: The Ordeal of Colonial Virginia* (New York, 1975), ch. 13.

14. Peter Kolchin, *Unfree Labor: American Slavery and Russian Serfdom* (Cambridge, Mass., 1987), 170.

15. The debate over the origins of the plantation revolution is reviewed by Barbara Solow, "The Transition to Plantation Slavery: The Case of the British West Indies," in Serge Daget, ed., *De la traite a l'esclavage: Actes du Colloque International sur la traite des Noirs, Nantes, 1985,* 2 vols. (Nantes, 1988), 1: 89–110.

16. In the nineteenth-century North American South, small holders grew cotton, but large planters dominated its cultivation. The critical importance of the planter to the maintenance of plantation production has led some scholars to argue for a plantation mode of production which encompassed slavery but superseded it as well outlasting chattel bondage. See, in particular, the work of Jay R. Mandle, "The Plantation Economy: An Essay in Definition," in Eugene D. Genovese, ed., *The Slave Economies,* 2 vols. (New York, 1973), 1: 214–28.

17. Much of what follows draws from the papers and discussions at the "Cultivation and Culture" conference held at the University of Maryland in the spring of 1989. Many of those papers have subsequently been published in Ira Berlin and Philip D. Morgan, eds., *The Slaves' Economy: Independent Production by Slaves in the Americas* (London, 1991), and *Cultivation and Culture: Labor and the Shaping of Slave Life in the Americas* (Charlottesville, Va., 1993). My ideas have been especially influenced by Philip D. Morgan and are elaborated in a somewhat different form in the jointly written introductions of those two volumes. The centrality of labor in the formation of slave life was made forcefully in Stuart B. Schwartz, *Sugar Plantations in the Formation of Brazilian Society* (Cambridge, UK, 1986).

18. While there has been little study of the ways in which slaves worked and the relationship between work process and slave culture, those connections have been much at issue in the study of wage workers. On the debate over the role of work process and workingclass activism, see David Montgomery, *Workers' Control in America: Studies in the History of Work, Technology, and Labor Struggles* (Cambridge, UK, 1987), and *The Fall of the House of Labor: The Workplace, the State, and American Labor Activism, 1865–1925* (Cambridge, UK, 1987); Patrick Joyce, *Work, Society and Politics: The Culture of the Factory in Later Victorian England* (New Brunswick, N.J., 1980); Bryan Palmer, *Skilled Workers and Industrial Capitalism in Hamilton, Ontario, 1860–1914* (Toronto, 1979); and Richard Price, "The Labour Process and Labour History," *SH,* 8 (1983), 57–75, and the subsequent exchange between Price and Patrick Joyce.

19. Davis, *The Problem of Slavery in the Age of Revolution;* Robin Blackburn, *The Overthrow of Colonial Slavery* (London, 1988); David Barry Gaspar and David Patrick Geggus, eds., *A Turbulent Time: The French Revolution and the Greater Caribbean* (Bloomington, Ind., 1997).

Part I. Societies with Slaves: The Charter Generations

1. In studies of the acculturation of peoples in the New World, "creole" has been used to distinguish those of native American birth from those of foreign, generally European, birth. But the use of the term has taken on various other meanings and been applied, for example, to people of mixed racial descent, non-English descent (as in the creoles of Louisiana), and even African people who had some experience in the New World—the so-called recaptives or liberated "Africans"—in Sierra Leone. It has also been extended to animals, things, and processes: "sugar cane, rats, styles of cooking, among other things," Philip Curtin notes. Philip Curtin, *Economic Change in Precolonial Africa: Senegambia in the Era of the Slave Trade* (Madison, Wisc., 1975), 138-39 n5. The term is thus mined with difficulties, since there is no universally accepted usage.

In the United States, "Afro-American" and more recently "African American" have come into common usage as synonyms for "black" and "Negro" in referring to people of African descent. "Creole" derives from the Portuguese word "crioulo," meaning a slave of African descent born in the New World. It has been extended to native-born free people of many national origins, including both Europeans and Africans, and diverse social standing. It has also been applied to people of partly European, but mixed racial and national origins in various European colonies and to Africans who entered Europe. In the United States, "creole" has also been specifically applied to people of mixed but usually non-African origins in Louisiana.

Staying within the bounds of the broadest definition of "creole" and the literal definition of "African American," I have used both terms to refer to black people of Native American birth, and I have adopted the term "Atlantic creole" to refer to those of African descent but connected to the larger Atlantic world. John A. Holm, *Pidgins and Creoles: Theory and Structure,* 2 vols. (Cambridge, UK, 1988–89), 1: 9.

On the complex and often contradictory usages in a single place, see Gwendolyn Midlo Hall, *Africans in Colonial Louisiana: The Development of Afro-Creole Culture in the Eighteenth Century* (Baton Rouge, 1992), 157–59; Joseph G. Tregle, Jr., "On that Word 'Creole' Again: A Note," *LH,* 23 (1982), 193–98.

Part I is based upon "From Creoles to African: Atlantic Creoles and the Origins of African-American Society in Mainland North America." These notes provide only essential references; for full citations see *WMQ,* 53 (1996), 251–88.

2. For a ground-breaking work which argues for the unity of the Atlantic world, see Peter Linebaugh, "All the Atlantic Mountains Shook," *LL* 10 (1982), 82–121, and Marcus Rediker and Peter Linebaugh, "The Many Headed Hydra," *Journal of Historical Sociology,* 3 (1990), 225–53. From the perspective of the making of African-American culture, see John Thornton, *Africa and Africans in the Making of the Atlantic World* (Cambridge, UK, 1992). A larger Atlantic perspective for the formation of black culture is posed in Paul Gilroy, *The Black Atlantic: Modernity and Double Consciousness* (Cambridge, Mass., 1993).

3. A. C. de C. M. Saunders, *A Social History of Black Slaves and Freedmen in Portugal, 1441–1555* (Cambridge, UK, 1982), 11–12, 145, 197 n52, 215 n73; G. R. Crone, ed., *The Voyages of Cadamosto and Other Documents on West Africa in the Second Half of the Fifteenth Century* (1937, rpt. New York, 1967), 55, 61; P. E. H. Hair, "The Use of African Languages in Afro-European Contacts in Guinea, 1440–1560," *Sierra Leone Language Review,* 5 (1966), 7–17; George E. Brooks, *Landlords and Strangers: Ecology, Society, and Trade in West Africa, 1000–1630* (Boulder, Col., 1993), ch. 7; Kwame Yeboa Daaku, *Trade and Politics on the Gold Coast, 1600–1720: A Study of the African Reaction to European Trade* (Oxford, 1970), ch. 5, esp. 96–97. For the near-seamless, reciprocal relationship between the Portuguese and the Kongolese courts in the sixteenth century see, John K. Thornton, "Early Kongo-Portuguese Relations, 1483–1575: A New Interpretation," *HA,* 8 (1981), 183–204.

4. For an overview see Thornton, *Africa and Africans,* ch. 2, esp. 59–62. See also Daaku, *Gold Coast,* ch. 2; Brooks, *Landlords and Strangers,* chs. 7–8; Philip D. Curtin, *Economic Change in Precolonial Africa: Senegambia in the Era of the Slave Trade* (Madison, Wisc., 1975), ch. 3; Ray A. Kea, *Settlements, Trade, and Polities in the Seventeenth-Century Gold Coast* (Baltimore, 1982); John Vogt, *Portuguese Rule on the Gold Coast, 1469–1682* (Athens, Ga., 1979). *Lançados* from a contraction of *lançados em terra* (to put on shore); Curtin, *Economic Change in Precolonial Africa,* 95. As the influence of the Atlantic economy spread to the interior, Atlantic creoles appeared in the hinterland, generally in the centers of trade along the rivers that reached into the African interior.

5. Kea, *Settlement, Trade, and Polities,* ch. 1, esp. 38.

6. *Ibid.;* Vogt, *Portuguese Rule on the Gold Coast;* Harvey M. Feinberg, *Africans and Europeans in West Africa: Elminans and Dutchmen on the Gold Coast during the Eighteenth Century,* American Philosophical Society, *Transactions,* 79, No. 7 (Philadelphia, 1989). For mortality see Curtin, "Epidemiology and the Slave Trade," *PSQ,* 83 (1968), 190–216.

7. Kea, *Settlements, Trade, and Polities,* ch. 1, esp. 38–50, 133–34; Vogt, *Portuguese Rule on the Gold Coast;* Feinberg, *Africans and Europeans in West Africa.*

8. Brooks, *Landlords and Strangers,* chs. 7–9, and Brooks, "Luso-African Commerce and Settlement in the Gambia and Guinea-Bissau Region," *Boston University African Studies Center Working Papers* (1980); Daaku, *Gold Coast,* chs. 5–6; Curtin, *Economic Change,* 95–100, 113–21. For the development of a similar population in Angola see Joseph C. Miller, *Way of Death: Merchant Capitalism and the Angolan Slave Trade, 1730–1830* (Madison, Wisc., 1988), esp. chs. 8–9.

9. Daaku, *Gold Coast,* chs. 4–5; Brooks, *Landlords and Strangers,* chs. 7–9, esp. 188–96; Curtin, *Economic Change,* 95–100. See also Miller's compelling description of Angola's Luso-Africans in the eighteenth and nineteenth centuries that suggests something of their earlier history, in *Way of Death,* 246–50. Brooks notes the term *tangomãos* passed from use at the end of the seventeenth century, in "Luso-African Commerce and Settlement in the Gambia and Guinea-Bissau," 3.

10. Speaking of the Afro-French in Senegambia in the eighteenth century, Curtin emphasizes the cultural transformation in making this new people, noting that "the important characteristic of this community was cultural mixture, not racial mixture, and the most effective of the traders from France were those who could cross the cultural line between Europe and Africa in their commercial relations," in *Economic Change,* 117. Peter Mark in his study of seventeenth-century Luso-African architecture describes the Luso-Africans "physically indistinguishable from other local African populations." Peter Mark, "Constructing Identity: Sixteenth- and Seventeenth-Century Architecture in the Gambia-Geba Region and the Articulation of Luso-African Ethnicity," *HA,* 22 (1995), 317.

11. Holm, *Pidgins and Creoles;* Thornton, *Africa and Africans,* 213–18; Saunders, *Black Slaves and Freedmen in Portugal,* 98–102 (see the special word—*ladinhos*—for blacks who could speak "good" Portuguese, 101); Brooks, *Landlords and Strangers,* 136–37. The architecture of the Atlantic creole villages was also called "à la portugaise." Mark, "Constructing Identity," 307–27.

12. Daaku, *Gold Coast,* chs. 3–4; Feinberg, *Africans and Europeans,* ch. 6; Kea, *Settlements, Trade, and Polities,* esp. pt. 2; Curtin, *Economic Change,* 92–93.

13. Vogt, *Portuguese Rule on the Gold Coast,* 54–58; Daaku, *Gold Coast,* 99–101; Thornton, "The Development of an African Catholic Church in the Kingdom of Kongo, 1491–1750," *JAH,* 25 (1984), 147–67; Hilton, *Kingdom of Kongo,* 32–49, 154–61, 179, 198; MacGaffey, *Religion and Society in Central Africa: The BaKongo of Lower Zaire* (Chicago, 1986), 191–216; quotation in Feinberg, *Africans and Europeans,* 86.

14. Mark, "Constructing Identity," 307–27.

15. The history of one element of this population, the canoemen, is discussed in Peter C. W. Gutkind, "The Boatmen of Ghana: The Possibilities of a Pre-Colonial African Labor History," in Michael Hanagan and Charles Stephenson, eds., *Confrontation, Class Consciousness, and the Labor Process: Studies in Proletarian Class Formation* (Westport, Conn., 1986), 123–66, and Gutkind, "Trade and Labor in Early

Precolonial African History: The Canoemen of Southern Ghana," in Catherine Co-query-Vidrovitch and Paul E. Lovejoy, eds., *The Workers of African Trade* (Beverly Hills, Calif., 1985). For bandits see Kea, "'I Am Here to Plunder on the General Road': Bandits and Banditry in the Pre-Nineteenth Century Gold Coast," in Donald Crummey, ed., *Banditry, Rebellion, and Social Protest in Africa* (London, 1986), 109–32.

16. Feinberg, *Africans and Europeans,* 84–85 (for Elmina); Joyce D. Goodfriend, *Before the Melting Pot: Society and Culture in New York City, 1664–1730* (Princeton, N.J., 1992), 13 (for New Amsterdam); Peter A. Coclanis, *The Shadow of a Dream: Economic Life and Death in the South Carolina Low Country, 1670–1920* (New York, 1989), 115 (for Charles Town).

17. Feinberg, *Africans and Europeans,* 65, 82–83; Kea, *Settlements, Trade, and Polities,* 197–202, 289–90.

18. Kea, *Settlements, Trade, and Polities,* 233–35, 315–16, 319–20. Daaku notes that "difficulties arise in establishing the exact nationalities" of Gold Coast traders, as European "writers tended to 'Europeanize' the names of some of the Africans with whom they traded and those in their service, while some of the Africans fancifully assumed European names," in *Gold Coast,* 96.

19. Daaku, *Gold Coast,* chs. 5–6; David Henige, "John Kabes of Komenda: An Early African Entrepreneur and State Builder," *JAH,* 18 (1977), 1–19.

20. Gutkind, "Boatmen of Ghana," 131–39, quotation on 137, and Gutkind, "Trade and Labor in Early Precolonial African History," 40–41.

21. Gutkind, "Trade and Labor in Early Precolonial African History," 27–28, 36; Kea, *Settlements, Trade, and Polities,* 243; Curtin, *Economic Change,* 302–8.

22. The northern North American colonies often received "refuse" slaves. For complaints and appreciations, see Goodfriend, "Burghers and Blacks: The Evolution of a Slave Society at New Amsterdam," *NYH,* 59 (1978), 139; Lorenzo J. Greene, *The Negro in Colonial New England, 1620–1776* (New York, 1942), 35; William D. Pierson, *Black Yankees: The Development of an Afro-American Subculture in Eighteenth-Century New England* (Amherst, Mass., 1988), 4–5; Edgar J. McManus, *Black Bondage in the North* (Syracuse, N.Y., 1973), 18–25; James G. Lydon, "New York and the Slave Trade, 1700 to 1774," *WMQ,* 35 (1978), 275–79, 381–90; Darold D. Wax, "Negro Imports into Pennsylvania, 1720–1766," *PH,* 32 (1965), 254–87, and Wax, "Preferences for Slaves in Colonial America," *JNH,* 58 (1973), 374–76, 379–87.

23. Charles Verlinden, *The Beginnings of Modern Colonization: Eleven Essays with an Introduction* (Ithaca, N.Y., 1970), 39–40; Saunders, *Black Slaves and Freedmen in Portugal,* ch. 1; Ruth Pike, "Sevillian Society in the Sixteenth Century: Slaves and Freedmen," *HAHR,* 47 (1967), 344–59, and Pike, *Aristocrats and Traders: Sevillian Society in the Sixteenth Century* (Ithaca, N.Y., 1972), 29, 170–92; P. E. H. Hair, "Black African Slaves at Valencia, 1482–1516," *HA,* 7 (1980), 119–31; Thornton, *Africa and Africans,* 96–97; James H. Sweet, "The Iberian Roots of American Racist Thought," *WMQ,* 54 (1997), 162–64; A. J. R. Russell-Wood, "Iberian Expansion and the Issue of Black Slavery: Changing Portuguese Attitudes, 1440–1770," *AHR,* 83 (1978), 20. During the first two decades of the sixteenth century, about 2,000 African

slaves annually entered Lisbon and were sold there. By the 1530s, most slaves brought to Lisbon were sent to the New World via Seville.

24. In the mid-sixteenth century, black people entered the periphery of Europe; Verlinden, *Beginnings of Modern Colonization,* ch 2. England developed a small black population that grew with English involvement in the African trade; see James B. Walvin, *Black and White: The Negro and English Society, 1555–1945* (London, 1973), ch. 1; F. O. Shyllon, *Black Slaves in Britain* (London, 1774); and Shyllon, *Black People in Britain 1555–1833* (London, 1977). For France see William B. Cohen, *The French Encounter with Africans: White Response to Blacks, 1530–1880* (Bloomington, 1980), and Sue Peabody, *"There Are No Slaves in France": The Political Culture of Race and Slavery in the Ancien Regime* (New York, 1996).

25. J. Fred Rippy, "The Negro and the Spanish Pioneer in the New World," *JNH,* 6 (1921), 183–89; Leo Wiener, *Africa and the Discovery of America,* 3 vols. (Philadelphia, 1920–1922).

26. Saunders, *Black Slaves and Freedmen in Portugal,* 29; for sailors see 11, 71–72, 145, and Hall, *Africans in Colonial Louisiana,* 128. A sale of six slaves in Mexico in 1554 included one born in the Azores, another born in Portugal, another born in Africa, and the latter's daughter born in Mexico; Colin A. Palmer, *Slaves of the White God: Blacks in Mexico, 1570–1650* (Cambridge, Mass., 1976), 31–32; "Abstracts of French and Spanish Documents Concerning the Early History of Louisiana," *LHQ,* 1 (1917), 111.

27. Hilary McD. Beckles, *A History of Barbados: From Amerindian Settlement to Nation-State* (Cambridge, UK, 1990), ch. 2; Richard S. Dunn, *Sugar and Slaves: The Rise of the Planter Class in the English West Indies, 1624–1713* (Chapel Hill, N.C., 1972), chs. 1–2; Robin Blackburn, *The Making of New World Slavery: From the Baroque to the Modern, 1492–1800* (London, 1997), ch. 6, esp. 240–43.

28. Dunn, *Sugar and Slaves,* 50, 57, 67–76; Hilary McD. Beckles, *White Servitude and Black Slavery in Barbados, 1627–1715* (Knoxville, Tenn., 1989), quotation on 110. For the dismal conditions of servitude, see Alexander Gukel and Jerome S. Handler, eds., "A German Indentured Servant in Barbados in 1652: The Account of Heinrich von Uchteritz," *Journal of the Barbados Museum and Historical Society,* 33 (1969), 91–99.

29. Morgan Godwyn, *The Negro's and Indians Advocate* (London, 1680), 101, quoted in Breen and Innes, *"Myne Owne Ground,"* 70, 130 n8.

30. Léo Elisabeth, "The French Antilles," in David W. Cohen and Jack P. Greene, eds., *Neither Slave nor Free: The Freedmen of African Descent in the Slave Societies of the New World* (Baltimore, 1972), 134–71; Gwendolyn Midlo Hall, *Social Control in Slave Plantation Societies: A Comparison of St. Domingue and Cuba* (Baltimore, 1971); Thomas N. Ingersoll, "Slave Codes and Judicial Practice in New Orleans, 1718–1807," *LHR,* 13 (1995), 48; quoted in John D. Garrigus, "'Sons of the Same Father': Gender, Race, and Citizenship in French Saint-Domingue, 1760–1792," in Christine Adams, Jack R. Censer, and Lisa Jane Graham, eds., *Visions and Revisions of Eighteenth-Century France* (University Park, Pa., 1997), 137–52.

31. Saunders, *Black Slaves and Freedmen in Portugal,* 152–55; Russell-Wood,

"Black and Mulatto Brotherhoods in Colonial Brazil," *HAHR*, 54 (1974), 567–602, and Russell-Wood, *The Black Man in Slavery and Freedom in Colonial Brazil* (New York, 1982), ch. 8, esp. 134, 153–54, 159–60. See also Pike, *Aristocrats and Traders*, 177–79. In the sixteenth century, some 7 percent (2,580) of Portugal's black population was free; Saunders, *Black Slaves and Freedmen in Portugal*, 59.

1. Emergence of Atlantic Creoles in the Chesapeake

1. Rolfe quoted in Alden T. Vaughan, "Blacks in Virginia: A Note on the First Decade," *WMQ*, 29 (1972), 470. Also Wesley Frank Craven, "Twenty Negroes to Jamestown in 1619?" *VQR*, 47 (1971), 416–20; Craven, *White, Red, and Black: The Seventeenth-Century Virginian* (Charlottesville, Va., 1971), 77–80; Craven, *Dissolution of the Virginia Company: The Failure of a Colonial Experiment* (New York, 1932), 124–35; and Engel Sluiter, "New Light on the '20 and Odd Negroes' Arriving in Virginia, August 1619," *WMQ*, 54 (1997), 395–98.

2. The literature on the status of the first black people to arrive in the Chesapeake is extensive, formidable, and inconclusive, in large measure because the incomplete evidence and the ambiguous language of "slavery" and "servitude" has become entangled in an all-encompassing discussion of the origins of racism in British North America. The wide-ranging debate and some of its implications are reviewed and extended in Alden T. Vaughan, "The Origins Debate: Slavery and Racism in Seventeenth Century Virginia," *VMHB*, 97 (1989), 311–54. Admitting that little is known about the first arrivals and that only imperfectly, I have presumed them to be slaves in that they were sold by international slave traders and purchased by men familiar with the existence of African slavery in the Atlantic. That they were treated like servants in a society in which servants composed the vast majority of bound laborers and that some gained their freedom or acted as free men and women (as did servants) does not alter this presumption, since slavery took many different forms in early Virginia, as it did throughout the Atlantic world. Such a presumption, of course, does not resolve the debate over the origins of racism, the chronology of slavery's codification, or the changing nature of bondage—whether slavery or servitude—in early America. It does, however, speak directly to the condition of these men and women.

3. Anthony Johnson's primacy and "unmatched achievement" have made him and his family the most studied members of the charter generation in the Chesapeake. The best account of the Johnsons is in J. Douglas Deal, *Race and Class in Colonial Virginia: Indians, Englishmen, and Africans on the Eastern Shore of Virginia during the Seventeenth Century* (New York, 1993), 217–50. Also useful are T. H. Breen and Stephen Innes, *"Myne Owne Ground": Race and Freedom on Virginia's Eastern Shore, 1640–1676* (New York, 1980), ch. 1; Ross M. Kimmel, "Free Blacks in Seventeenth-Century Maryland," *MHM*, 71 (1976), 22–25; Vaughan, "Blacks in Virginia," 475–76; James H. Brewer, "Negro Property Owners in Seventeenth-Century Virginia," *WMQ*, 12 (1955), 576–78; Susie M. Ames, *Studies of the Virginia Eastern Shore in the Seventeenth Century* (Richmond, 1940), 102–5; John H. Russell, *The Free Negro in Virginia, 1619–1865* (Baltimore, 1913), and Russell, "Colored Freemen as Slave Owners in Virginia," *JNH*, 1 (1916), 234–37. Evidence of the bap-

tism of the Johnsons' children comes indirectly from the 1660s, when John Johnson replied to a challenge of his right to testify by producing evidence of baptism. He may, however, have been baptized as an adult. Breen and Innes, *"Myne Owne Ground,"* 17.

4. Deal, *Race and Class*, 218–22. Breen and Innes, *"Myne Owne Ground,"* 8–11, makes a convincing case for Johnson's connections with the Bennetts, although the evidence is circumstantial. Also see *ibid.*, 12–15. On Mary Johnson, see Kathleen M. Brown, *Good Wives, Nasty Wenches, and Anxious Patriarchs: Gender, Race, and Power in Colonial Virginia* (Chapel Hill, N.C., 1996), 107–9, 112–13.

5. "Tobacco is our meat, drinke, cloathing and monies," wrote an observer of Maryland life in 1669. Quoted in Lorena S. Walsh, "Slave Life, Slave Society, and Tobacco Production in the Tidewater Chesapeake, 1620–1820," in Ira Berlin and Philip D. Morgan, eds., *Cultivation and Culture: Labor and the Shaping of Slave Life in the Americas* (Charlottesville, Va., 1993), 170.

6. Gray, *So. Ag.*, 1: 215–33; Lois Green Carr, Russell R. Menard, and Lorena S. Walsh, *Robert Cole's World: Agriculture and Society in Early Maryland* (Chapel Hill, N.C., 1991), chs. 2–3; Lois Green Carr and Lorena S. Walsh, "Economic Diversification and Labor Organization in the Chesapeake, 1650–1820," in Stephen Innes, ed., *Work and Labor in Early America* (Chapel Hill, N.C., 1988), 150–53; Lois Green Carr, "Diversification in the Colonial Chesapeake: Somerset County, Maryland, in Comparative Perspective," in Carr, Philip D. Morgan, and Jean B. Russo, eds., *Colonial Chesapeake Society* (Chapel Hill, N.C., 1981), 344–50; Walsh, "Slave Life, Slave Society, and Tobacco Production," 170–99. Also see David O. Percy, *The Production of Tobacco along the Colonial Potomac* (Accokeek, Md., 1979).

7. For the integration of tobacco and corn, see Carr and Walsh, "Economic Diversification and Labor Organization," 150.

8. *Ibid.*, 145–75, esp. 154–57 (for workday and treatment of servants); Lorena S. Walsh, *From Calabar to Carter's Grove: A History of a Virginia Slave Community* (Charlottesville, Va., 1997), 31–32; Mechel Sobel, *The World They Made Together: Black and White Values in Eighteenth-Century Virginia* (Princeton, N.J., 1987), 33 and ch. 4. For a telling description of the treatment of indentured servants, see Darrett B. and Anita H. Rutman, *A Place in Time: Middlesex County, Virginia, 1650–1750* (New York, 1984), 130–38. Note, however, whereas English servants complained repeatedly to the local courts about their treatment at the hands of their masters, "not one such complaint was lodged by a black during the same period." Deal, *Race and Class*, 167, 288. On the rights of servants, see Russell R. Menard, "From Servant to Freeholder: Status Mobility and Property Accumulation in Seventeenth-Century Maryland," *WMQ*, 30 (1973), 48–49.

9. Edmund S. Morgan, *American Slavery, American Freedom: The Ordeal of Colonial Virginia* (New York, 1975), 108–79, 215–49; Craven, *White, Red, and Black*, 75–99.

10. Quotation in Deal, *Race and Class*, 292.

11. The literature on the slaves' economy in the Americas—sometimes called the "internal economy," "informal economy," or "peasant breach"—begins with the pioneering work of Sidney Mintz and Douglas Hall. See Mintz and Hall, *The Origins*

of the Jamaican Internal Marketing System, Yale University Publications in Anthropology, no. 57 (New Haven, 1960), 3–26, and Mintz, "The Jamaican Internal Marketing Pattern: Some Notes and Hypotheses," *SES,* 4 (1955), 95–103; Mintz, "Internal Marketing Systems as a Mechanism of Social Articulation," *Proceedings of the American Ethnological Society* (1959), 20–30. For a general overview of the development of slave economies, see the introduction to Berlin and Morgan, eds., *Cultivation and Culture,* 1–45, and for the seventeenth-century Chesapeake slave economy, see Breen and Innes, *"Myne Owne Ground,"* 73–74, and Deal, *Race and Class,* 187. In emphasizing the difference in the scale between the internal economies of the British Caribbean and the British mainland settlements, Michael Mullin argues that the slaves' independent productive and marketing activities played a disproportionately important role in shaping slave society in the sugar islands. While the comparison is instructive, it masks how the mainland slave economies, although generally less extensive, also shaped slave life and how their evolution was central to the transformation of slavery on the mainland. Michael Mullin, *Africa in America: Slave Acculturation and Resistance in the American South and the British Caribbean, 1737–1831* (Urbana, Ill., 1992), ch. 6.

12. In addition to the works cited in the preceding note, see Ciro Flamarion S. Cardoso, "The Peasant Breach in the Slave System: New Developments in Brazil," *Luso-Brazilian Review,* 25 (1988), 49–57; Gabriel Debien, *Les esclaves aux Antilles Francaises (XVIIe-XVIIIe siecles)* (Basse-Terre, Fort-de-France, 1974), 178–79; Marian Malowist, "Les débuts du systemme de plantations dans la période des grandes découvertes," *Africana Bulletin,* 10 (1969), 9–30.

13. For the continued negotiation of the slaves' economy, see "Introduction: Labor and the Shaping of Slave Life in the Americas," in Berlin and Morgan, eds., *Cultivation and Culture,* 1–45; John M. Jennings, ed., "The Poor Unhappy Transported Felon's Account Sorrowful of his Fourteen Years Transportation at Virginia in America," *VMHB,* 56 (1948), 182. Quotation in John Hammond, *Leah and Rachel, or, the Two Fruitful Sisters Virginia, and Mary-land* (London, 1656), cited in Breen and Innes, *"Myne Owne Ground,"* 73.

14. Deal, *Race and Class,* 219–22.

15. Quotation in Breen and Innes, *"Myne Owne Ground,"* 73; Deal, *Race and Class,* 222. For evidence that the property accumulated by slaves went with them when they were sold to another owner, see Breen and Innes, *"Myne Owne Ground,"* 81–82.

16. Deal, *Race and Class,* 284, 292–93, 346. For complaints about the free movement of slaves around the countryside, see "Management of Slaves, 1672," *VMHB,* 7 (1900), 314.

17. Deal, *Race and Class,* 337; "Management of Slaves, 1672," 314.

18. William Waller Hening, comp., *Statutes at Large, Being a Collection of all the Laws of Virginia,* 13 vols. (Richmond, Va., 1800–23), 1: 274–75. Quotation in Deal, *Race and Class,* 282, also see 219, 252–54, 272, and Breen and Innes, *"Myne Owne Ground,"* 81-2. Eventually, Driggus's presumption that his prerogative was a right exasperated his owner, who again went to court, this time to declare that no one

could buy, sell, or trade with Driggus without first securing his approval. Deal, *Race and Class,* 282.

19. Deal, *Race and Class,* 265–78, and Breen and Innes, *"Myne Owne Ground,"* 73–75. Payne was acting as a free man prior to 1656.

20. The liberation of Payne's family is a matter of some dispute. Breen and Innes note that Payne's agreement with his mistress was to buy "himselfe, his wife and children." But upon liberation, Payne married a white woman, and they do not appear to have had children. Breen and Innes, *"Myne Owne Ground,"* 72–75; Deal, *Race and Class,* 268–69, 276 n20.

21. Catterall, *Judicial Cases,* 1: 78; Robert McColley, "Slavery in Virginia, 1619–1660: A Reexamination," in Robert H. Abzug and Stephen E. Maizlish, eds., *New Perspectives on Race and Slavery in America: Essays in Honor of Kenneth M. Stampp* (Lexington, Ky., 1986), 21–22; A. Leon Higginbotham, Jr., *In The Matter of Color: Race and the Legal Process: The Colonial Period* (New York, 1978), 24–26.

22. Breen and Innes, *"Myne Owne Ground,"* 72–79; Brown, *Good Wives,* ch. 7.

23. Deal, *Race and Class,* 187–88; Breen and Innes, *"Myne Owne Ground,"* 68–69; Edmund S. Morgan, "Slavery and Freedom: The American Paradox," *JAmH,* 59 (1972), 18 n39; Allan Kulikoff, "A 'Prolifick' People: Black Population Growth in the Chesapeake Colonies, 1700–1790," *SS,* 16 (1977), 392–93.

24. Breen and Innes, *"Myne Owne Ground,"* esp. ch. 4 (names 69); Deal, *Race and Class,* 163–405; Douglas Deal, "A Constricted World: Free Blacks on Virginia's Eastern Shore, 1680–1750," in Carr, Morgan, and Russo, eds., *Colonial Chesapeake Society,* 275–305; Michael L. Nicholls, "Passing Through This Troublesome World: Free Blacks in the Early Southside," *VMHB,* 92 (1984), 50–70.

25. Quotation in Donnan, *Slave Trade,* 4: 21–23, 88–90, also 3: 414–15; 4: 49–50; quotation in Russell R. Menard, "From Servants to Slaves: The Transformation of the Chesapeake Labor System," *SS,* 16 (1977), 363–67; Deal, *Race and Class,* 164–65; Breen and Innes, *"Myne Owne Ground,"* 70–71. The largest group of slaves imported prior to 1680 may have been the forty-one slaves who arrived in 1656.

26. On Phillip, see McColley, "Slavery in Virginia, 1619–1660: A Reexamination," 15–16, and Vaughan, "Blacks in Virginia," 470; on Cain, see Deal, *Race and Class,* 254–55, 317–19, and Robert C. Twombly and Robert H. Moore, "Black Puritan: The Negro in Seventeenth-Century Massachusetts," *WMQ,* 24 (1967), 236.

27. Deal, *Race and Class,* 171–74, 222–23, 228, quotation on 222; Breen and Innes, *"Myne Owne Ground,"* 83. For mortality of Chesapeake settlers, see Russell R. Menard, "Immigrants and Their Increase: The Process of Population Growth in Early Colonial Maryland," in Aubrey Land et al., eds., *Law, Society, and Politics in Early Maryland* (Baltimore, 1977), 88–110; Lorena S. Walsh and Russell R. Menard, "Death in the Chesapeake: Two Life Tables for Men in Early Colonial Maryland," *MHM,* 69 (1974), 220–23; Craven, *Red, White, and Black,* 100–2; Kulikoff, "'Prolifick People,'" 403–6; Brown, *Good Wives,* 412 n52.

28. The most important of the discriminatory laws, according to Kathleen Brown, was a tax on free black women, which distinguished them from white women, at once shaping notions of gender and race. *Good Wives,* ch. 3.

29. For discussion of patron-client relations on the eastern shore of Virginia, see Breen and Innes, *"Myne Owne Ground,"* 97–101.

30. For example, Breen and Innes, *"Myne Owne Ground,"* 77; Deal, *Race and Class,* 285–86.

31. Quotations in Breen and Innes, *"Myne Owne Ground,"* 87, 75.

32. Breen and Innes, *"Myne Owne Ground,"* 26, 79–82, 86–97, quotation on 89. Free people of color not only employed the law against whites, but also against one another. See, for example, Deal, *Race and Class,* 268. For the long-term effects of bastardy acts, tax forfeitures, and debt penalties, see Deal, "A Constricted World," 275–305. Even in defeat, black men and women seized the opportunity to reiterate their place in society, for their appeals to higher authority were but another claim of the right to participate.

33. On landholding, Deal, *Race and Class,* 163–405 and esp. 337. Breen and Innes, *"Myne Owne Ground,"* 79–80, and the cattle economy 81–83. For a comparison with the success of white servants, Menard, "From Servant to Freeholder," 37–64.

34. Quotation in Breen and Innes, *"Myne Owne Ground,"* 6. The statement is generally attributed to Johnson, but may have been uttered by Francis Payne. See Deal, *Race and Class,* 266–67.

35. Morgan, *American Slavery, American Freedom,* 155; Morgan, "Slavery and Freedom: The American Paradox," 17–18.

36. Deal, *Race and Class,* provides numerous examples. Also see Morgan, *American Slavery, American Freedom,* 329–37; Warren M. Billings, "The Cases of Fernando and Elizabeth Key: A Note on the Status of Blacks in the Seventeenth Century," *WMQ,* 30 (1973), 467–74. On the dynamics of interracial sexual relations, see Winthrop D. Jordan, *White over Black: American Attitudes toward the Negro, 1550–1812* (Chapel Hill, N.C., 1968), chs. 3–4, esp. 78–82, and Morgan, *American Slavery, American Freedom,* chs. 15–16. Free black men may have married white women because they—unlike black women—were not subject to the tax on able-bodied laborers. Brown, *Good Wives,* 125–28.

37. Deal, *Race and Class,* 331–32, also see 179, 182.

38. Deal, *Race and Class,* provides numerous examples; Morgan, *American Slavery, American Freedom,* 329–37; Morgan, "Slavery and Freedom: The American Paradox," 17–18; Kimmel, "Free Blacks in Maryland," 20–21.

39. T. H. Breen, "A Changing Labor Force and Race Relations in Virginia, 1660–1710," *JSH,* 7 (1973), 3–25; Stephen Saunders Webb, *1676: The End of American Independence* (New York, 1984), 6–7, 66, 121–23; Sobel, *The World They Made Together,* 44–45.

40. Deal, *Race and Class,* 295–98; Deal, "A Constricted World," 281–91. Kimmel, "Free Blacks in Maryland," 21–25, on baptism see 248.

41. Deal presents the story of Sarah Driggus's flight to Maryland and return to Virginia in *Race and Class,* 295–304.

42. On John Johnson's Angola see Kimmel, "Free Blacks in Maryland," 23.

2. Expansion of Creole Society in the North

1. William D. Piersen, *Black Yankees: The Development of an Afro-American Subculture in Eighteenth-Century New England* (Amherst, Mass., 1988), 3–4; Jackson Turner Main, *Society and Economy in Colonial Connecticut* (Princeton, N.J., 1985), 305; David E. Van Deventer, *The Emergence of Provincial New Hampshire, 1623–1741* (Baltimore, 1976), 113, 256n; Joyce D. Goodfriend, "Burghers and Blacks: The Evolution of a Slave Society at New Amsterdam," *NYH,* 59 (1978), 126–29, and Goodfriend, *Before the Melting Pot: Society and Culture in Colonial New York City, 1664–1730* (Princeton, N.J., 1992), 112–14; Vivienne L. Kruger, "Born to Run: The Slave Family in Early New York, 1626 to 1827," unpublished doctoral diss., Columbia University, 1985, chs. 1–3; Graham Russell Hodges, *Slavery and Freedom in the Rural North: African Americans in Monmouth County, New Jersey, 1665–1865* (Madison, Wisc., 1997), 7; Gary B. Nash, *Forging Freedom: The Formation of Philadelphia's Black Community, 1720–1840* (Cambridge, Mass., 1988), 9; Jean R. Soderlund, "Black Importation and Migration into Southeastern Pennsylvania, 1682–1810," *PAPS,* 133 (1989), 144–45; Gary B. Nash and Jean R. Soderlund, *Freedom by Degrees: Emancipation in Pennsylvania and Its Aftermath* (New York, 1991), 10–11, 22; Jean R. Soderlund et al., eds., *William Penn and the Founding of Pennsylvania, 1680–1684: A Documentary History* (Philadelphia, 1983), 179–81; quotation in Piersen, *Black Yankees,* 4. For privateering, see Johannes Menne Postma, *The Dutch in the Atlantic Slave Trade, 1600–1815* (Cambridge, UK, 1990), 17–18.

2. Piersen, *Black Yankees,* 4–5, 178 n6; Lorenzo Johnston Greene, *The Negro in Colonial New England* (New York, 1942), 34–38; Edgar J. McManus, *Black Bondage in the North* (Syracuse, N.Y., 1973), 18–25, and McManus, *A History of Negro Slavery in New York* (Syracuse, N.Y., 1966), 35–39; James G. Lydon, "New York and the Slave Trade, 1700 to 1774," *WMQ,* 35 (1978), 381–94; and Darold D. Wax, "Negro Imports into Pennsylvania, 1720–1766," *PH,* 32 (1965), 254–87; Wax, "Africans on the Delaware: The Pennsylvania Slave Trade, 1759–1765," *PH,* 50 (1983), 38–49; Wax, "Preferences for Slaves in Colonial America," *JNH,* 58 (1973), 374–76, 379–87; Sharon V. Salinger, *"To Serve Well and Faithfully": Labor and Indentured Servants in Pennsylvania, 1682–1800* (Cambridge, UK, 1987), 75–78; quotations in Goodfriend, "Burghers and Blacks," 139; in Cecil Headlam, ed., *Calendar of State Papers, Colonial Series,* 40 vols. (Vaduz, 1964), 1: 110, also in Greene, *Negro in New England,* 35; in A. J. F. Van Laer, ed., *Correspondence of Jeremias Van Rensselaer Correspondence, 1651–1674* (Albany, N.Y., 1932), 167–68, and 175. See a 1714 New York law favoring the importation of African over West Indian slaves because of the large number of "refuse" and criminal slaves, *Journal of the Legislative Council of the Colony of New-York, 1619–1743,* 2 vols. (Albany, N.Y., 1861), 1: 433–34.

3. Donnan, *Slave Trade,* 3: 405–6, 410–11, 416–17, 421, 439–443; Goodfriend, "Burghers and Blacks," 128–29, 132; Goodfriend, *Before the Melting Pot,* 112–14; *NY Documents,* 1: 576–78, 580–81; 2: 1–4, 23–48; Ernst Van Den Boogaart, "The Servant Migration to New Netherland, 1624–1664," in P. C. Emmer, ed., *Colonialism*

and Migration: Indentured Labour Before and After Slavery (Dordrecht, 1986), 58–59. On trade and piracy around Madagascar see also Robert C. Ritchie, *Captain Kidd and the War against the Pirates* (Cambridge, Mass., 1986), 83–85, 112–114; Kruger, "Born to Run," 78–79; James A. Rawley, *The Transatlantic Slave Trade: A History* (New York, 1981), 280–81.

4. Donnan, *Slave Trade,* 3: 428, 417–34; Oliver A. Rink, *Holland on the Hudson: An Economic and Social History of Dutch New York* (Ithaca, N.Y., 1986), 163–64, 169; Nash and Soderland, *Freedom by Degrees,* 10. On the changing pattern of slave importation to New Netherland with the expulsion of the Dutch from Brazil and the Dutch West India Company's plans to make New Amsterdam an entrepôt for slaves going to other mainland colonies, including English ones, see Rink, *Holland on the Hudson,* 169, and Goodfriend, "Burghers and Blacks," 136–38. New Amsterdam merchants apparently desired to trade directly with Africa, but they never received permission to do so. *Ibid.,* 143.

5. Until New Netherland developed an agricultural base, slavery did not take hold; and in 1649 settlers admitted that slaves imported at great cost "just dripped through the fingers" and "were sold for pork and peas." *NY Documents,* 1: 302. On the change that took place during the 1650s with the beginning of direct African importation in 1659, see *NY Manuscripts,* 268, 289, 293, 307, 331.

6. Piersen, *Black Yankees,* 4–5; McManus, *Black Bondage in the North,* 18–25, and McManus, *New York Slavery,* 24, 28; Lydon, "New York and the Slave Trade," 375–79, 381–90; Greene, *Negro in New England,* 35–45; Soderlund, "Black Importation," 144–45; Wax, "Negro Imports into Pennsylvania, 1720–1766," 254–87, and Wax, "Preferences for Slaves in Colonial America," 374–76, 379–87; Salinger, *"To Serve Well and Faithfully,"* 75–78. Quotation in Goodfriend, *Before the Melting Pot,* 113. For an exception to the pattern of importing slaves from elsewhere in the Americas, see the importation of several hundred Madagascar slaves into New York at the end of the seventeenth and beginning of the eighteenth centuries, in Virginia Bever Platt, "The East India Company and the Madagascar Slave Trade," *WMQ,* 26 (1969), 548–77, and Jacob Judd, "Frederick Philipse and the Madagascar Trade," *NYHQ,* 55 (1971), 354–74.

7. Quotation in Piersen, *Black Yankees,* 1.

8. Although the slave family—at all times and in all places in mainland North America—remained a fragile enterprise that was hostage to the slaveholders' economic fortunes and moral standards, northern slaves managed to create a modicum of domestic stability during the first generation. By 1708 the governor of Rhode Island observed that the colony's planters were "supplied by the offspring of those [slaves] they have already, which increase daily." Quoted in William Davis Miller, "The Narragansett Planters," *American Antiquarian Society Proceedings* 43 (1933), 68 n2; and Greene, *Negro in Colonial New England,* 191–95, 201, 208–99. A similar situation appeared to exist in New Amsterdam in the forty years before the English conquest. Joyce D. Goodfriend, "Black Families in New Netherland," *JAAHGS,* 5 (1984), 94–107; Henry B. Hoff, "Frans Abramse Van Salee and His Descendants: A

Colonial Black Family in New York and New Jersey," *NYGBR,* 121 (1990), 65–71, 157–61; Kruger, "Born to Run," 46–50, 270–77.

9. An abstract of the black population between 1630 and 1664 by name can be found in Robert J. Swan, "The Black Population of New Netherland: As Extracted from the Records of Baptisms and Marriages of the Dutch Reformed Church (New York City), 1630–1664," *JAAHGS,* 14 (1995), 82–98. A few names suggest the subtle transformation of identity as the creoles crossed the Atlantic. For example, Anthony Jansen of Salee or Van Vaes, a dark-skinned man who claimed Moroccan birth, became "Anthony the Turk," perhaps because Turks were considered fierce—as Anthony's litigious history indicates he surely was—but importantly, alien and brown in pigment. Leo Herskowitz, "The Troublesome Turk: An Illustration of Judicial Process in New Amsterdam," *NYH,* 46 (1965), 299–310.

10. Goodfriend, *Before the Melting Pot,* 10 and ch. 6, esp. 124–132; Van Den Boogaart, "Servant Migration," 58; quotation in *NY Documents,* 1: 246. "Negroes would accomplish more work for their masters, and at less expense, than farm servants who must be bribed to go thither by a great deal of money and promises," declared the Board of Accounts on New Netherland in 1644. *Ibid.,* 1: 154.

11. Goodfriend, *Before the Melting Pot,* ch. 6; Goodfriend, "Burghers and Blacks," 125–44; Goodfriend, "Black Families in New Netherlands," 94–107; McManus, *New York Slavery,* 2–22; Michael Kammen, *Colonial New York: A History* (New York, 1995), 58–60; Van Den Boogaart, "Servant Migration," 56–59, 65–71; Rink, *Holland on the Hudson,* 161n. (Between 1639 and 1652, marriages of slaves and free blacks [including one interracial marriage] in New Amsterdam churches represented 28 percent of the marriages in that period); I. N. P. Stokes, *Iconography of Manhattan Island, 1498–1909,* 6 vols. (New York, 1914–25), 4: 82. For baptisms, see "Reformed Dutch Church, New York, Baptisms, 1639–1800," *Collections of the New York Genealogical and Biographical Society,* 2 vols. (New York, 1901), 1: 10–27, 2: 10–38; Kruger, "Born to Run," 44–50; 270–77, quotation on 48 (note that baptismal records [1639–1684] identify the father [68 percent], mother [4 percent], and both parents [27 percent]). In marriages (1641–44), all fifty-two spouses had surnames, although only one couple was clearly free. In freeing some of its slaves in 1644, the Dutch West India Company emancipated by name the male heads of household and made them responsible for their wives and children (who were not named) and the annual tribute to the company. Edmund B. O'Callaghan, comp., *Laws and Ordinances of New Netherland, 1638–1674* (Albany, 1868), 36–37.

12. Goodfriend, *Before the Melting Pot,* ch. 6; Goodfriend, "Burghers and Blacks," 125–44, and Goodfriend, "Black Families in New Netherlands," 94–107; Van Den Boogaart, "Servant Migration," 56–59, 65–71; McManus, *New York Slavery,* ch. 1; and Gerald Francis DeJong, "The Dutch Reformed Church and Negro Slavery in Colonial America," *Church History,* 40 (1971), 430; Kruger, "Born to Run," ch. 2, esp. 40–48, and also 270–78; Hoff, "Van Salee," 65–71, 157–61; Kammen, *Colonial New York,* 58–60. For black people using Dutch courts see Rink, *Holland on the Hudson,* 160–61. (In 1638, Anthony the Portuguese sued one Anthony Jansen

for damages done his hog; soon after, one Pedro Negretto claimed back wages.) *NY Manuscripts,* 1: 87, 105, 269 (for manumission, dubbed "half slaves"), 222 (adoption), 269 (granted land); Berthold Fernow, ed., *Minutes of the Orphanmasters Court of New Amsterdam, 1655–1663,* 2 vols. (New York, 1907), 3: 42; 5, 172, 337–40; 7, 11 (for actions in court). For adoption of a black child by a free black family, see Scott and Stryker-Rodda, eds., *The Register of Salmon Lachaire, Notary Public of New Amsterdam,* 22–23; *NY Manuscripts,* 222, 256; Kruger, "Born to Run," 44–51; A. Leon Higginbotham, *In the Matter of Color: Race and the American Legal Process* (New York, 1978), 104–5. For the 1635 petition see Stokes, *Iconography of Manhattan,* 4: 82, and No. 14, Notulen W1635, 1626 (19–11–1635), inv. 1.05.01. 01. (Oude), Algemeen Rijksarchief, The Hague. The petition by "five blacks from New Netherland who had come here [Amsterdam]" was referred back to officials in New Netherland. Marcel van der Linden of the International Institute of Social History in Amsterdam kindly located and translated this notation in the records of the Dutch West India Company.

13. See petition for freedom in *NY Manuscripts,* 1: 269. In 1649 white residents of New Amsterdam protested the enslavement of the children of half-free slaves, in that no one born of a free person should be a slave. The Dutch West India Company rejected the claim, noting that only three such children fit the complaint's description and the demands on them were not great. *New York History,* 1: 302, 343; O'Callaghan, comp., *Laws and Ordinances of New Netherland,* 36–37 (for the Dutch West India Company "setting them free and at liberty, on the same footing as other free people here in *New Netherland,*" although children remained property of the company); Van Den Boogaart, "Servant Migration," 69–70. For adoptions, see *NY Manuscripts, Dutch,* 1: 222, 256.

14. For black men paying tribute to purchase family see *NY Manuscripts, Dutch,* 1: 45, 87, 105; *NY Documents,* 1: 343; Goodfriend, "Black Families in New Netherland," 94–107; McManus, *New York Slavery,* 13–15; quotation in DeJong, "Dutch Reformed Church and Negro Slavery," 430; Kruger, "Born to Run," 49–50, 52–55; Hoff, "Van Salee," 65–71, 157–61.

15. Goodfriend estimates that seventy-five of New Amsterdam's 375 blacks were free in 1664, in *Before the Melting Pot,* 61.

16. Kruger, "Born to Run," 52–55, 591–600, tells the story of the creation of a small class of black landowners via gifts from the Dutch West India Company and direct purchase by the blacks themselves. Quotation on 592. Also Goodfriend, *Before the Melting Pot,* 115–17; Peter R. Chrisoph, "The Freedmen of New Amsterdam," *JAAHGS,* 5 (1984), 116–17; Stokes, *Iconography of Manhattan,* 2: 302; 4: 70–78; 100, 104–6, 120–48, 265–66; Gehring, ed., *New York Historical Manuscripts;* Van Den Boogaart, "Servant Migration," 69–71. For the employment of a white housekeeper by a free black artisan, see *ibid.,* 69; Fernow, ed., *Minutes of the Orphanmasters Court,* 2: 46; Roi Ottley and William J. Weatherby, eds., *The Negro in New York: An Informal Social History, 1626–1940* (New York, 1967), 12.

17. Between 1664 and 1712, when a restrictive manumission law was enacted, not more than two dozen slaves were freed in the southern six counties of New York.

Kruger, "Born to Run," 592–94; Goodfriend, *Before the Melting Pot,* 116. However, Goodfriend cautions against seeing the English conquest as the only cause of the change in the nature of slavery in the mid-seventeenth century. With their ouster from Brazil, the Dutch focused their attention on New Amsterdam as a market for slaves and, with that change, the nature of slavery began to change as well. Goodfriend, "Burghers and Blacks," 126–28, 134–39.

18. Quotation in Bartlett Burleigh James and J. Franklin Jameson, eds., *Journal of Jasper Danckaerts, 1679–1680* (New York, 1913), 65. Also see Goodfriend, *Before the Melting Pot,* 115–16.

19. Shane White, *Somewhat More Independent: The End of Slavery in New York City* (Athens, Ga., 1991), 106–11, 128–30; quotation in Arthur Zilversmit, *The First Emancipation: The Abolition of Slavery in the North* (Chicago, 1967), 22. On the right to choose a master, see Billy G. Smith and Richard Wojtowicz, comps., *Blacks Who Stole Themselves: Advertisements for Runaways in the Pennsylvania Gazette, 1728–1790* (Philadelphia, 1989), 7, 68.

20. Robert C. Twombly and Robert H. Moore, "Black Puritan: The Negro in Seventeenth-Century Massachusetts," *WMQ,* 24 (1967), 224–42; Greene, *Negro in Colonial New England.*

21. For a collection of the relevant censuses, see U.S. Bureau of the Census, *A Century of Population Growth* (Washington, D.C., 1909), 149–84. Also see Robert V. Wells, *The Population of the British Colonies in America before 1776* (Princeton, N.J., 1975), 69–143, and Wells's correction of the 1731 enumeration, "The New York Census of 1731," *NYHQ,* 57 (1973), 255–59. For estimates of the northern black population predating these censuses, see *Historical Statistics,* 756.

22. Soderlund, "Black Importation," 147–50; Nash, *Forging Freedom,* 8; White, *Somewhat More Independent,* 18–23; Piersen, *Black Yankees,* 14–18; Greene, *Negro in New England,* ch. 3.

23. Jean R. Soderlund, *Quakers & Slavery: A Divided Spirit* (Princeton, N.J., 1985), 64; Soderlund, "Black Importation," 147; Nash, *Forging Freedom,* 9; Elaine Forman Crane, *A Dependent People: Newport, Rhode Island in the Revolutionary Era* (New York, 1985), 76; White, *Somewhat More Independent,* xxv–xxix, 3–4, 25–27. Even in Connecticut—an overwhelming rural colony—slavery tended to be disproportionately a phenomenon of the towns rather than the countryside. Main, *Colonial Connecticut,* 82.

24. Nash, *Forging Freedom,* ch. 1; Salinger, *"To Serve Well and Faithfully,"* chs. 2–4; White, *Somewhat More Independent,* 19–21.

25. McManus, *Black Bondage in the North,* 42–43; Zilversmit, *The First Emancipation,* 36–38; Charles S. Boyer, *Early Forges and Furnaces in New Jersey* (Philadelphia, 1963), 30–31, 149, 166, 194–99, 239; Hodges, *Rural North,* 8–9; Frances D. Pingeon, "Slavery in New Jersey on the Eve of Revolution," in William C. Wright, ed., *New Jersey in the American Revolution: Political and Social Conflict* (rev. ed., Trenton, N.J., 1974), 51–52, 57; Wax, "The Demand for Slave Labor in Colonial Pennsylvania," 334–35; and Arthur Cecil Bining, *Pennsylvania Iron Manufacture in the Eighteenth Century* (New York, 1970), 122–25.

26. Greene, *Negro in Colonial New England,* 103–8; McManus, *Black Bondage in the North,* 40–41; Zilversmit, *The First Emancipation,* 33–36; Pingeon, "Slavery in New Jersey on the Eve of Revolution," 51; John E. Pomfret, *Colonial New Jersey, A History* (New York, 1973), 29; Miller, "The Narragansett Planters," 67–71; Christian McBurney, "The South Kingston Planters: Country Gentry in Colonial Rhode Island," *RIH,* 45 (1987), 86, 89–90; Masur, "Slavery in Eighteenth-Century Rhode Island," 144–45; Alan Tully, "Patterns of Slaveholding in Colonial Pennsylvania: Chester and Lancaster Counties, 1729–1758," *JSH,* 6 (1973), 284–303; Wax, "The Demand for Slave Labor in Colonial Pennsylvania," 332–40. On the Philipse family see, Kruger, "Born to Run," 150–55; for the Livingstons, see Roberta Singer, "The Livingstons as Slaveowners: The 'Peculiar Institution' on Livingston Manor and Clermont," in Richard T. Wiles, ed., *The Livingston Legacy: Three Centuries of American History* (n.p., 1986), 75–76.

27. Kruger, "Born to Run," 164–67, quotation on 165; Olive Gilbert, *Narrative of Sojourner Truth* (Battle Creek, Mich., 1878), quotation on 14; Hodges, *Rural North,* ch. 2, esp. 51–52; Peter O. Wacker and Paul G. E. Clemens, *Land Use in Early New Jersey: A Historical Geography* (Newark, N.J., 1995); Susan E. Klepp, "Seasoning and Society: Racial Differences in Mortality in Eighteenth-Century Philadelphia," *WMQ,* 51 (1994), 485–86; Main, *Colonial Connecticut,* 180. Also Edwin Olson, "Social Aspects of the Slave in New York," *JNH,* 26 (1941), 68. On housing see Robert K. Fitts, "The Landscapes of Northern Bondage," *HArch,* 30 (1996), 54–73; Rosalie Fellows Bailey, *Pre-Revolutionary Dutch Houses and Families in Northern New Jersey and Southern New York* (New York, 1936), esp. 272–75, 288, 306, 314, 326–27, 370, 377.

28. For slave marketing, see Olson, "Social Aspects of the Slave in New York," 67–68; Hodges, *Rural North,* 20–21; quotation in David Humphreys, *An Historical Account of the Incorporated Society for the Propagation of the Gospel in Foreign Parts* (London, 1730), 234. "How can the Negroe attend Instruction, who on half Saturday and Sunday is to provide Food and Rayment for himself and Family for the Week following?" *Ibid.,* 234–35. For attempts to regulate or prohibit the slaves' independent economic activities see, Herbert L. Osgood, ed., *Minutes of the Common Council of the City of New York, 1675–1776,* 8 vols. (New York, 1905), 1: 85–86, 93, and Charles Z. Lincoln, William H. Johnson, and A. Judd Northrop, comps., *The Colonial Laws of New York from the Year 1664 to the Revolution,* 5 vols. (Albany, N.Y., 1896), 1: 157–58, 519–20, 845. For the state's recognition of slave property, see McManus, *Black Bondage in the North,* 62–63.

29. Nash, *Forging Freedom,* 15–16. Hints about the extent of the slaves' mobility and their knowledge of the countryside can be gleaned from runaway advertisements. See for example a fugitive slave woman who was "well acquainted in Philadelphia, Jerseys, and Willmington." Smith and Wojtowicz, comps., *Blacks Who Stole Themselves,* 79–80, also 39.

30. Goodfriend, *Before the Melting Pot,* ch. 6; Van Den Boogaart, "Servant Migration," 59, 65–71; U.S. Bureau of the Census, *A Century of Population Growth,*

149–84; Greene, *Negro in Colonial New England,* 78, 81–82, 84–88, 92–93; Gary B. Nash, *The Urban Crucible: Social Change, Political Consciousness, and the Origins of the American Revolution* (Cambridge, Mass., 1979), 13–16, 106–111, 320–21; Nash, "Slaves and Slaveowners in Colonial Philadelphia," *WMQ,* 30 (1973), 226–52; Nash and Soderlund, *Freedom by Degrees,* 14–16; Soderlund, *Quakers and Slavery,* 58, 64; Thomas Archdeacon, *New York City, 1664–1710: Conquest and Change* (Ithaca, N.Y., 1976), 46–47; Van Deventer, *Provincial New Hampshire,* 113–14; Lynne Withey, *Urban Growth in Colonial Rhode Island: Newport and Providence in the Eighteenth Century* (Albany, N.Y., 1984), 71; Crane, *A Dependent People,* ch. 3; Main, *Colonial Connecticut,* 82, 181, 269, 283–84, 294–95, 305, and 366. Quotation in Carl Bridenbaugh, *Cities in the Wilderness: The First Century of Urban Life in America, 1625–1742* (New York, 1938), 49.

31. Goodfriend, *Before the Melting Pot,* 118–20; Richard G. Morris, *Government and Labor in Early America* (New York, 1965), 182–84. For complaints about skilled workers, see *A Report of the Records of Commissioners of the City of Boston,* 13 vols. (Boston, 1881–1909), 7: 5; Osgood, ed., *Minutes of the Common Council,* 1: 179.

32. Quotation in Goodfriend, *Before the Melting Pot,* 128; Richard B. Morris, ed., *Select Cases of the Mayor's Court of New York City, 1674–1784* (Washington, D.C., 1935), 237; Salinger, *"To Serve Well and Faithfully,"* 101–3; Nash, *Forging Freedom,* 13–16.

33. For analysis of the linguistic abilities of New York and Philadelphia slaves, see Kruger, "Born to Run," 85–87; Nash, *Forging Freedom,* 16.

34. Osgood, ed., *Minutes of the Common Council,* 1: 222–4, 276–77; John F. Watson, *Annals of Philadelphia,* 2 vols. (Philadelphia, 1830), 1: 62, 2: 265; Morris, *Select Cases,* 408–9; Goodfriend, *Before the Melting Pot,* 120–22; Nash, *Forging Freedom,* 18–20; Nash, *Urban Crucible,* 135; Frank Klingberg, *Anglican Humanitarianism in Colonial New York* (Philadelphia, 1940), 120–86, for slave participation in religious revivals. The connections between disaffected whites and black slaves in New York is explored in Thomas J. Davis, *A Rumor of Revolt: The "Great Negro Plot" in Colonial New York* (New York, 1985), quotation on 53. Further connections can be glimpsed in Daniel Horsmanden, *The New-York Conspiracy,* ed., Thomas J. Davis (Boston, 1971).

35. Hugh Hastings, comp., *Ecclesiastical Records, State of New York,* 7 vols. (Albany, N.Y., 1901–1906), 1: 548–55.

36. Sheldon S. Cohen, "Elias Neau, Instructor to New York's Slaves," *NYHQ,* 55 (1971), 7–27, quotation on 27; Goodfriend, *Before the Melting Pot,* 126–31; Frank Klingberg, *Anglican Humanitarianism in Colonial New York* (Philadelphia, 1940), 120–86, Neau's estimate on 131, quotation on 149; John C. Van Horne, ed., *Religious Philanthropy and Colonial Slavery: The American Correspondence of the Associates of Dr. Bray, 1717–1777* (Urbana, Ill., 1985); Nash, *Forging Freedom,* 16–24; Richard I. Snelling, "William Sturgen, Catechist to the Negroes of Philadelphia," *HMPEC,* 8 (1939), 388–401. Between 1705 and 1780, SPG officials baptized some 1,400 in the southern six counties of New York—a substantial number to be sure but an average

of less than twenty per year. For schools established by Anglican missionaries and other sympathetic whites, see Nash, *Forging Freedom*, 16–24. The complex relation between the Dutch Reformed Church and black people—free and slave—is traced in DeJong, "The Dutch Reformed Church and Negro Slavery in Colonial America," 423–36. Calculation of baptisms in Kruger, "Born to Run," 77, and Neau's estimate in Goodfriend, *Before the Melting Pot*, 129.

37. Watson, *Annals of Philadelphia*, 1: 62, 2: 265; Goodfriend, *Before the Melting Pot*, 120–21; Nash, *Forging Freedom*, 12–14, quotation on 13; Klingberg, *Anglican Humanitarianism*, 155.

38. After warning Domingo and Manuel Angola not to repeat their behavior, the court ordered them to communicate its admonition to "the other remaining free negroes." Fernow, ed., *Records of New Amsterdam*, 6: 146, 286; Osgood, ed., *Minutes of the City Council*, 1: 133–134, 276–77; Lincoln, Johnson, and Judd, comps., *Colonial Laws of New York*, 1: 356–57; Goodfriend, *Before the Melting Pot*, 120–21; Nash, *Forging Freedom*, 12–14; Klingberg, *Anglican Humanitarianism*, 155.

39. Humphreys, *An Historical Account*, 238. Humphreys added that slaveowners demonstrated no desire to attend to sick and dying slaves and instead, "rather than attend sick slaves," they were ignored and "frequent Discourses were made in Conversation that they had no souls and perished as the Beasts." In so noting, Humphreys echoed the comments of the Reverend John Sharpe, another SPG missionary, of twenty years earlier, see "Rev. John Sharpe's Proposals, March 1713," *Collections of the New York Historical Society*, 1880 (New York, 1881), 355. Although both Humphreys and Sharpe addressed conditions in New York, there is no reason to believe they did not apply elsewhere in the North. For an informed, pioneering overview of African-American funerary practice, see David R. Roediger, "And Die in Dixie: Funerals, Death, & Heaven in the Slave Community, 1700–1865," *Massachusetts Review*, 22 (1981), 163–83.

40. Goodfriend, *Beyond the Melting Pot*, 91, notes that in 1697 black people could be baptized in the Church but not buried in Trinity Church graveyard. Also see *ibid.*, 122; Stokes, *Icongraphy of Manhattan*, 2: 207, 197; 4: 88, 130, 193. A like process of exclusion from white burial grounds promoted the establishment of cemeteries for black people in other northern cities. Nash, *Forging Freedom*, 13; Klepp, "Seasoning and Society," 486 n46. In 1721 Boston limited the number of bells tolled for black funerals in order to restrict attendance, in Piersen, *Black Yankees*, 78. Laws were passed regulating burial in New York in 1721 and again in 1731 to restrict them to daylight hours and limit the number of people attending. See Osgood, ed., *Minutes of the Common Council*, 3: 296; 4: 88–89. In Philadelphia, black people were denied burial in white cemeteries until after the gradual emancipation act of 1780. Susan E. Klepp, *Philadelphia in Transition: A Demographic History of the City and Its Occupational Groups, 1720–1830* (New York, 1989), 32–33; Fitts, "Landscapes of Northern Bondage," 62–63.

41. Nash, *Forging Freedom*, 13; Cheryl J. Laroche, "Beads from the African Burial Ground, New York City: A Preliminary Assessment," *Beads*, 6 (1994), 3–20; "Rev. John Sharpe's Proposals," 355.

3. Divergent Paths in the Lowcountry

1. Probably the first African to arrive in Florida was one Esteban, a member of an expedition that landed near Tampa Bay in 1528. Richard R. Wright, "Negro Companions of the Spanish Explorers," *AA,* 4 (1902), 217–28.

2. Eugene Lyons, *The Enterprise of Spanish Florida: Pedro Mendendez de Aviles and the Spanish Conquest of 1565–1568* (Gainesville, Fla., 1974); John J. TePaske, *The Governorship of Spanish Florida, 1760–1763* (Durham, N.C., 1964), 135–54; Verne E. Chatelain, *The Defenses of Spanish Florida, 1565–1763* (Washington, D.C., 1941), ch. 13, esp. 59–75; Jane L. Landers, "Traditions of African American Freedom and Community in Spanish Colonial Florida," in David R. Colburn and Jane L. Landers, eds., *The African American Heritage of Florida* (Gainesville, Fla., 1995), 18–19; Charles W. Arnade, "Cattle Raising in Spanish Florida, 1513–1763," *AH,* 35 (1961), 116–24, and Arnade, *The Siege of St. Augustine in 1702* (Gainesville, Fla., 1959).

3. Theodore G. Corbett, "Migration to a Spanish Imperial Frontier in the Seventeenth and Eighteenth Centuries: St. Augustine," *HAHR,* 54 (1974), 414–18, 420–21; Jane G. Landers, "Acquisition and Loss on a Spanish Frontier: The Free Black Homesteaders of Florida, 1784–1821," *S&A,* 17 (1996), 85–87; Landers, "Traditions of African American Freedom," 19–20. On the employment of black militia men in the New World, see Herbert S. Klein, "The Colored Militia of Cuba: 1568–1868," *CS,* 6 (1966), 17–27; Allan J. Kuethe, "The Status of the Free Pardo in the Disciplined Militia of New Grenada," *JNH,* 56 (1971), 105–17; Lyle N. McAlister, *The 'Fuero Militar' in New Spain, 1764–1800* (Gainesville, Fla., 1957). For the creation of a black militia at St. Augustine, Jane Landers, "Gracia Real de Santa Teresa de Mose: A Free Black Town in Spanish Colonial Florida," *AHR,* 95 (1990), 13.

4. Peter H. Wood, *Black Majority: Negroes in Colonial South Carolina from 1670 through the Stono Rebellion* (New York, 1974), 13–24, 43–47, and Wood, "The Changing Population of the Colonial South," in Peter H. Wood, Gregory A. Waselkov, and M. Thomas Hatley, eds., *Powhatan's Mantle: Indians in the Colonial Southeast* (Lincoln, Neb., 1989), 38–39, 46–51; Russell R. Menard, "Slave Demography in the Lowcountry, 1670–1740: From Frontier Society to Plantation," *SCHM,* 96 (1995), 282–91.

5. Wood, *Black Majority,* 13–24, 94–97; Richard Waterhouse, "England, the Caribbean, and the Settlement of Carolina," *JAS,* 9 (1975), 259–81. The polyglot character of the workforce is emphasized by Russell R. Menard, "The Africanization of the Lowcountry Labor Force, 1670–1730," in Winthrop D. Jordan and Sheila L. Skemp, eds., *Race and Family in the Colonial South* (Jackson, Miss., 1987), esp. 84–93, 98–101. The image of sawbuck equality is derived from an account of a French refugee living near the Santee River who reported in 1697 that "he worked many days with a Negro man at the Whip saw." Alexander S. Salley, ed., "Journal of General Peter Horry," *SCHM,* 38 (1937), 51–52, as quoted in Wood, *Black Majority,* 97. In 1709, after South Carolina had become a slave society, Indians accounted for 1,400 of the 5,500 slaves in the lowcountry. In 1710 Native Americans accounted for one quarter of the bound laborers. Although the proportion dropped thereafter, in 1720 they still

represented 17 percent of the unfree population in South Carolina. Menard, "Africanization of the Lowcountry Labor Force," 86, 98–101.

6. Quotation in Clarence L. Ver Steeg, *Origins of a Southern Mosaic: Studies of Early Carolina and Georgia* (Athens, Ga., 1975), 105–7, 146 n7; Maurice Mathews, ed., "A Contemporary View of Carolina in 1680," *SCHM,* 55 (1954), 158; Wood, *Black Majority,* 124–301.

7. John D. Duncan, "Servitude and Slavery in Colonial South Carolina, 1670–1776," unpublished doctoral diss., Emory University, 1971, 587–601; Herbert Aptheker, "Maroons within the Present Limits of the United States," *JNH,* 24 (1939), 167–84.

8. John J. McCusker and Russell R. Menard, *The Economy of British America, 1607–1789* (Chapel Hill, N.C., 1985), 170–75; Converse D. Clowse, *Economic Beginnings in Colonial South Carolina, 1670–1730* (Columbia, S.C., 1971), 61; Gary S. Dunbar, "Colonial Carolina Cowpens," *AH,* 35 (1961), 125–30; John Soloman Otto, "Livestock-Raising in Early South Carolina, 1670–1700: Prelude to the Rice Plantation Economy," *AH,* 61 (1987), 13–24.

9. Thomas J. Cooper and David J. McCord, comps., *The Statutes at Large of South Carolina,* 10 vols. (Columbia, S.C., 1837–41), 2: 22–23; 3: 395–99, 456–61; 7: 343, 345–47, 356–68, 385–97; Thomas J. Little, "The South Carolina Slave Laws Reconsidered, 1670–1700," *SCHM,* 94 (1993), 98.

10. Cooper and McCord., eds., *Statutes at Large of South Carolina,* 7: 368, 382.

11. Frank J. Klingberg, *An Appraisal of the Negro in Colonial South Carolina* (Washington, D.C., 1941), 6–7; Klaus G. Leowald, Beverly Starika, and Paul S. Taylor, trans. and eds., "Johann Martin Bolzius Answers a Questionnaire on Carolina and Georgia," *WMQ,* 14 (1957), 235–36, 256; Margaret Washington Creel, *"A Peculiar People": Slave Religion and Community-Culture among the Gullahs* (New York, 1988), 68; Cooper and McCord, comps., *Statutes at Large of South Carolina,* 7: 404; Wood, *Black Majority,* 62. *Laurens Papers,* 12: 368; Mark Caterby, *The Natural History of South Carolina, Florida and the Bahama Islands,* 2 vols. (London, 1731–43), xviii; Evangeline Walker Andrews, ed., *Journal of a Lady of Quality* (New Haven, Conn., 1921), 176–77.

12. Marcus W. Jernesgan, *Labor and Dependent Classes in Colonial America, 1607–1783* (Chicago, 1931), 20–21. Quotation in Leila Sellers, *Charleston Business on the Eve of the American Revolution* (Chapel Hill, N.C., 1934), 99–100.

13. Cooper and McCord, comps., *Statutes at Large of South Carolina,* 2: 693; Duncan, "Servitude and Slavery in Colonial South Carolina," 33–35.

14. Quotation in Ver Steeg, *Origins of a Southern Mosaic,* 38, n13, 137–38 (italics removed); Wood, *Black Majority,* 54, 96, 102–3.

15. See Carl Bridenbaugh, *Cities in the Wilderness: The First Century of Urban Life in America, 1625–1742* (New York, 1938), 4–5, 201–1; quotations in Frank J. Klingberg, ed., *Carolina Chronicle: The Papers of Commissary Gideon Johnston, 1707–1716* (Berkeley, Cal., 1946), 99; Wood, *Black Majority,* 96 n5.

16. Wood, *Black Majority,* 99–103, 157, 159, quotation on 96 n5.

17. *Ibid.,* 95–96, 175.

18. J. G. Dunlap, "William Dunlop's Mission to St. Augustine in 1688," *SCHM,* 34 (1933), 24; Jane Landers, "Spanish Sanctuary: Fugitives in Florida, 1687–1790," *FHQ,* 62 (1984), 296–302; John J. TePaske, "The Fugitive Slave: Intercolonial Rivalry and Spanish Slave Policy, 1687–1764," in Samuel Proctor, ed., *Eighteenth-Century Florida and Its Borderlands* (Gainesville, Fla., 1975), 2–12. Quotation in Landers, "Mose," 13–14.

19. Landers, "Spanish Sanctuary," 296–302; Landers, "Mose," 14; Landers, "Traditions of African-American Freedom," 22–23; TePaske, "The Fugitive Slave," 2–12; Corbett, "Migration to a Spanish Imperial Frontier," 428–30.

20. Landers, "Spanish Sanctuary," 296–302, and Landers, "Mose," 13–15; TePaske, "The Fugitive Slave," 2–12; I. A. Wright, comp., "Dispatches of Spanish Officials Bearing on the Free Negro Settlement of Gracia Real de Santa Teresa de Mose, Florida" *JNH,* 9 (1924), 144–93, quotation on 150; Zora Neale Hurston, "Letters of Zora Neale Hurston on the Mose Settlement and the Negro Colony in Florida," *JNH,* 12 (1927), 664–67; Duncan, "Servitude and Slavery in Colonial South Carolina," ch. 17, quotation on 664; Dunlop, "William Dunlop's Mission to St. Augustine in 1688," 1–30. Several of the slaves who rejected freedom and Catholicism in St. Augustine and returned to South Carolina were rewarded with freedom, creating a competition between English and Spanish colonies that redounded to the fugitives' advantage. See Duncan, "Servitude and Slavery in Colonial South Carolina," 381–83. For the African conversion of South Carolina slaves, see John K. Thornton, "On the Trail of Voodoo: African Christianity in Africa and the Americas," *Americas,* 44 (1988), 268.

21. Landers, "Mose," 13–15; Wood, *Black Majority,* 304–5.

22. Wood, *Black Majority,* 239–98, 304–7, 310.

23. For the pre-transfer conversion of slaves from central Africa to Christianity, see John Thornton, "The Development of an African Catholic Church in the Kingdom of Kongo, 1491–1750," *JAH,* 25 (1984), 147–67; Anne Hilton, *The Kingdom of Kongo* (London, 1985), ch. 2, 154–61, 179–98; Wyatt MacGaffey, *Religion and Society in Central Africa: The BaKongo of Lower Zaire* (Chicago, 1986), 191–216. John K. Thornton, "African Dimensions of the Stono Rebellion," *AHR,* 96 (1991), 1101–11, quotation on 1102. Thornton makes a powerful case for the Kongolese origins of the Stono rebels, in their military organization and in the nature of their resistance. In 1710 an Anglican missionary in Goose Creek Parish, South Carolina, observed that the black slaves had been "born and baptized among the Portuguese." Klingberg, ed., *The Carolina Chronicle,* 69.

24. Wright, "Dispatches of Spanish Officials," 173–74; Landers, "Gracia Real de Santa Teresa de Mose," 17; "The Mose Site," *Escribino,* 10 (1973), 52. In 1749 slave conspirators plotting rebellion in St. Thomas Parish, South Carolina, planned to escape to Florida after setting fire to Charles Town. Philip D. Morgan and George D. Terry, "Slavery in Microcosm: A Conspiracy Scare in Colonial South Carolina," *SS,* 21 (1982), 122.

25. Wood, *Black Majority,* chs. 11–12; Edward A. Pearson, "'A Countryside Full of Flames': A Reconsideration of the Stono Rebellion and Slave Rebelliousness in the

Early Eighteenth-Century South Carolina Lowcountry," *S&A*, 17 (1996), 22–50; Larry W. Kruger and Robert Hall, "Fort Mose: A Black Fort in Spanish Florida," *Griot*, 6 (1987), 42.

26. Thornton, "African Dimensions of the Stono Rebellion," 1107; Landers, "Mose," 27.

27. Landers, "Mose," 15–17.

28. Landers, "Mose," 17–18; "Mose Site," 53; quotation in Wright, "Dispatches of Spanish Officials Bearing on Mose," 146–49. Menéndez commanded Mose until 1740, when another English assault, in response to the Stono rebellion, forced a Spanish retreat and the evacuation of Mose's black population to St. Augustine.

29. Landers, "Mose," 15–21, quotation on 20.

30. *Ibid.*

31. *Ibid.*, 21–22, quotation on 22.

32. *Ibid.*, 23–24.

33. John R. Dunkle, "Population Changes as an Element in the Historical Geography of St. Augustine," *FHQ*, 37 (1958), 5; Landers, "Traditions of African American Freedom," 22–23; Landers, "Mose," 24–28, quotation on 21; Kruger and Hall, "Fort Mose," 41–42.

34. Theodore J. Corbett, "Population of Structure in Hispanic St. Augustine, 1619–1763," *FHQ*, 54 (1976), 268; Corbett, "Migration to a Spanish Imperial Frontier," 430; "Mose Site," 52–55.

35. Corbett, "Migration to a Spanish Imperial Frontier in the Seventeenth and Eighteenth Centuries," 420; Wilbur H. Siebert, "The Departure of the Spaniards and Other Groups from East Florida, 1763–1764," *FHQ*, 19 (1940), 146; Robert L. Gold, "The Settlement of the East Florida Spaniards in Cuba, 1763–1766," *FHQ*, 42 (1964), 216–17; Landers, "Gracia Real de Santa Teresa de Mose," quotation on 21, 23–30; Landers, "Acquisition and Loss on a Spanish Frontier," 88.

4. Devolution in the Lower Mississippi Valley

1. Mathé Allain, *"Not Worth a Straw": French Colonial Policy and the Early Years of Louisiana* (Lafayette, La., 1988), chs. 5–6; Gwendolyn Midlo Hall, *Africans in Colonial Louisiana: The Development of Afro-Creole Culture in the Eighteenth Century* (Baton Rouge, La. 1992), 2–10, 57–59; Daniel Usner, Jr., "From African Captivity to American Slavery: The Introduction of Black Laborers to Colonial Louisiana," *LH*, 20 (1979), 25–27, and Usner, "Indian-Black Relations in Colonial and Antebellum Louisiana," in Stephan Palmié, ed., *Slave Cultures and the Cultures of Slavery* (Knoxville, Tenn., 1995), 146–47; James T. McGowan, "Planters without Slaves: Origins of a New World Labor System," *SS*, 16 (1977), 5–20. No black people—free or slaves—appeared in the 1708 census of Louisiana. Charles R. Maduell, Jr., comp. and trans., *The Census Tables for the French Colony of Louisiana from 1699 through 1721* (Baltimore, 1972), 16–17.

2. Glenn R. Conrad, comp. and trans., *The First Families of Louisiana*, 2 vols. (Baton Rouge, La., 1970), 1: 117; Daniel H. Usner, Jr., *Indians, Settlers, & Slaves in a*

Frontier Exchange Economy: The Lower Mississippi Valley Before 1783 (Chapel Hill, N.C., 1992), 47, and Usner, "From African Captivity," 36–38; Thomas N. Ingersoll, "Free Blacks in a Slave Society: New Orleans, 1718–1812," *WMQ*, 48 (1991), 175–76; Henry P. Dart, ed., "Records of the Superior Council of Louisiana," *LHQ*, 4 (1921), 236; Hall, *Africans in Colonial Louisiana*, 128–32.

3. Under the *Code Noir*, manumitted slaves had "the same rights, privileges, and immunities which [were] enjoyed by free-born persons," but they could lose their freedom for harboring a fugitive slave and a variety of other crimes. Thomas N. Ingersoll, "Slave Codes and Judicial Practice in New Orleans, 1718–1807," *LHR*, 13 (1995), 28–36, 38–39; Carl A. Brasseaux, "The Administration of the Slave Regulations in French Louisiana, 1724–1766," *LH*, 21 (1980), 141–42, 151–53; Donald E. Everett, "Free Persons of Color in Colonial Louisiana," *LH*, 7 (1966), 23–27. An abstract of the *Code Noir* is published in Charles Gayarré, *History of Louisiana*, 4 vols. (New York, 1854), 1: 531–40.

4. Hall, *Africans in Colonial Louisiana*, 100.

5. Allain, *"Not Worth a Straw,"* chs. 5–6; Dunbar Rowland and A. G. Sanders, eds. and trans., *Mississippi Provincial Archives: French Dominion*, 5 vols. (Jackson, Miss., 1919–84), 2: 82, 101–2, 111, 168; Hall, *Africans in Colonial Louisiana*, ch. 1, quotation on 11; McGowan, "Planters without Slaves," 5–26, quotation on 16, and McGowan, "Creation of a Slave Society: Louisiana Plantations in the Eighteenth Century," Unpublished doctoral diss., University of Rochester, 1976, ch. 1, quotations on 47, 58 n6; Antoine-Simon Le Page Du Pratz, *The History of Louisiana*, ed. by Joseph G. Tregle, Jr. (Baton Rouge, La., 1975), 3–34, 183–203.

6. Usner, *Indians, Settlers, & Slaves*, chs. 1–2; Patricia Dillon Woods, *French-Indian Relations on the Southern Frontier, 1699–1762* (Ann Arbor, Mich., 1980), 1, 9–12, 30–31, 34–40, 45–48, 69–73; Hall, *Africans in Colonial Louisiana*, 14–20.

7. Conrad, comp. and trans., *The First Families of Louisiana*, 1: 1–140; Carl Brasseaux, "The Image of Louisiana and the Failure of Voluntary French Emigration, 1683–1715," and Glenn R. Conrad, "Emigration Forcée: A French Attempt to Populate Louisiana, 1716–1720," both in Alf A. Heggy and James J. Cooke., eds., *Proceedings of the Fourth Meeting of the French Colonial Historical Society* (Washington, D.C., 1979), 57–66; McGowan, "Planters without Slaves," 7–11; Hall, *Africans in Colonial Louisiana*, 5–9, 18.

8. Jean Mettas, *Repértoire des Expéditions Négrières Francaises au XVIIIe Siècle*, ed. Serge Daget, 2 vols. (Paris, 1978–84); Hall, *Africans in Colonial Louisiana*, chs. 2–3, esp. figure 2 on 35 and table 2 on 60. Daniel Usner estimates the number of Africans imported between 1718 and 1731 to be about 7,000 (*Indians, Settlers, & Slaves*, 33–34), while Thomas N. Ingersoll counts them as 5,544 ("The Slave Trade and the Ethnic Diversity of Louisiana's Slave Community," *LH*, 28 [1996], 134).

9. Hall, *Africans in Colonial Louisiana*, 41–95; Usner, *Indians, Settlers, & Slaves*, 33; Peter Caron, "'Of a nation which others do not understand': Bambara Slaves and African Ethnicity in Colonial Louisiana, 1718–60," *S&A*, 18 (1997), 98–121. For the French slave trade, see Robert Louis Stein, *The French Slave Trade in the Eighteenth Century: An Old Regime Business* (Madison, Wisc., 1979).

10. Hall, *Africans in Colonial Louisiana*, 41–55, 128–29; Usner, "From African Captivity," 36–37, quotation on 36. For a different understanding of the nationality of the Africans who arrived in Louisiana during the 1720s and a well-placed caution "that the national or ethnic labels of slaves in Louisiana [like Bambara] were flexible and subject to different meanings and interpretations depending on the speaker, the language and the context of usage," see Caron, "Bambara Slaves and African Ethnicity in Colonial Louisiana," 98–121, quotation on 115.

11. McGowan, "Creation of a Slave Society," 45–47; Usner, *Indians, Settlers, & Slaves*, 28–29; Thomas N. Ingersoll, "Old New Orleans: Race, Class, Sex, and Order in the Early Deep South, 1718–1819," unpublished doctoral diss., University of California, Los Angeles, 1991, 31, table 2.

12. Maduell, comp. and trans., *Census Tables*, 25–76; Usner, *Indians, Settlers, & Slaves*, 34–36, 41–50, 59–63, 82, and esp. table 2; Hall, *Africans in Colonial Louisiana*, 6–8, 10, 73–74, 99–100, 160; McGowan, "Creation of a Slave Society," ch. 2.

13. Hall, *Africans in Colonial Louisiana*, ch. 3; Usner, *Indians, Settlers, & Slaves*, 37–41; Usner, "From African Captivity," 28, 33. Many of the first arrivals chanced ashore in the midst of the French campaign against the Spanish at Pensacola. They were immediately put to work supporting this doomed military exercise, and, in return for their services, most were left without food and clothing by the hapless French soldiery. For a first-hand account, see Charles Le Gac, *Immigration and War: Louisiana, 1718–1721*, ed. and trans., Glenn R. Conrad (Lafayette, La., 1970). Hall documents mortality rates of less than 4 percent for slaves in Louisiana arriving before 1724. Hall, *Africans in Colonial Louisiana*, 72–73, 382–85.

14. Mettas, *Repértoiré des expéditions négrières francaises*, number 2895. *Miss. Arch*, 2: 659–60, 668–69; Usner, *Indians, Settlers, & Slaves*, 37–40, quotation on 40; Hall, *Africans in Colonial Louisiana*, 88–89; for an earlier voyage of the *Venus*, ibid., 84–85; Ingersoll, "Old New Orleans," 202.

15. Mettas, *Repértoiré des expéditions négrières francaises;* Ingersoll, "Old New Orleans," 48; *Miss. Arch*, 2: 620, 638, 668–69; Hall, *Africans in Colonial Louisiana*, 171–72, esp. table 7; Usner, *Indians, Settlers, & Slaves*, 47–50.

16. Hall, *Africans in Colonial Louisiana*, ch. 3; Usner, *Indians, Settlers, & Slaves*, 37–40; McGowan, "Creation of a Slave Society," 54–57.

17. Maduell, comp. and trans, *Census Tables*, 113, 123; *Miss. Arch*, 3: 179–81; Usner, *Indians, Settlers, & Slaves*, 46–49; Hall, *Africans in Colonial Louisiana*, 9, 73–74; Ingersoll, "Old New Orleans," 31–33, table 2.

18. Usner, *Indians, Settlers, & Slaves*, 55–56; Usner, "From African Captivity," 32–36, quotations on 32, 34. In 1732 thirty-seven of the more than 250 black slaves residing in the city belonged to white craftsmen. Also Hall, *Africans in Colonial Louisiana*, 126–27, 132–39; Henry P. Dart, "The Slave Depot of the Company of the Indies at New Orleans," *LHQ*, 9 (1927), 286–87; Samuel Wilson, Jr., "The Plantation of the Company of the Indies," *LH*, 31 (1990), 161–75; *Miss. Arch*, 2: 230, 494, 553–54, 599, 602, 626–27, 639; 3: 779, quotation on 2: 592.

19. *Miss. Arch*, 2: 230, 599, quotation on 3: 779; Usner, *Indians, Settlers, & Slaves*,

55–56; Usner, "From African Captivity," 34–35; Hall, *Africans in Colonial Louisiana,* 132–39.

20. The evidence of Samba's participation in the Fort d'Arguin insurrection, as Gwendolyn Mildo Hall observes, is frail and contradictory, but Samba convinced the French he was dangerous enough to be enslaved and deported. *Africans in Colonial Louisiana,* 109–10; Usner, "From African Captivity," 37; Du Pratz, *History of Louisiana,* 77–79. On the Afro-French community in St. Louis and other enclaves on the Senegal, see Philip D. Curtin, *Economic Change in Precolonial Africa: Senegambia in the Era of the Slave Trade* (Madison, Wisc., 1975), 113–21.

21. Hall, *Africans in Colonial Louisiana,* 100, 122–26; Usner, "From African Captivity," 29; McGowan, "Creation of a Slave Society," ch. 2; Jacob M. Price, *France and the Chesapeake: A History of the French Tobacco Monopoly, 1674–1791,* 2 vols. (Ann Arbor, Mich., 1973), 1: 247–67, 302–28, esp. 323–24; Jack D. L. Holmes, "Indigo in Colonial Louisiana and the Floridas," *LH,* 8 (1967), 329; *Miss. Arch,* 2: 534–35; Heloise H. Cruzat, ed., "The Jonchere Concession, October 26, 1719," *LHQ,* 11 (1928), 553–56; Jay Higginbotham, "The Chaumont Concession: A French Plantation on the Pasagoula," *JMH,* 36 (1974), 353–62.

22. *Miss. Arch,* 2: 625; 3: 523–26; Donnan, *Slave Trade,* 4: 638–42.

23. But even in the areas of the heaviest concentration of slaves, the slave population was spread thin. Only one-quarter of the free population of the colony owned slaves, and no more than fifteen individuals owned more than twenty. Maduell, comp. and trans., *Census Tables,* 121–22; Usner, "From African Captivity," 30–31; John Clarke, *New Orleans, 1718–1812, An Economic History* (Baton Rouge, La., 1970), 24–25 n27.

24. For early attempts to keep Africans and Indians apart, see Hall, *Africans in Colonial Louisiana,* 97–104, 117–18; Usner, *Indians, Settlers, & Slaves,* 56–59, quotation on 59.

25. Usner, *Indians, Settlers, & Slaves,* 158–59; Price, *France and the Chesapeake,* 1: 247–67, 302–28; Du Pratz, *History of Louisiana,* 192–222. For parallel developments in West Florida, see Robin F. A. Fabel, *The Economy of British West Florida, 1763–1783* (Tuscaloosa, Ala., 1988), 117–19.

26. Du Pratz, *History of Louisiana,* 189–216; Fabel, *Economy of British West Florida,* 113; Usner, *Indians, Settlers, & Slaves,* 159–61; Holmes, "Indigo in Colonial Louisiana and Florida," 329–49; Clark, *New Orleans,* 56, 61–87; Hall, *Africans in Colonial Louisiana,* 124–26.

27. Brasseaux, "Slave Regulations," 141–42; McGowan, "Creation of a Slave Society," 126–27; Hall, *Africans in Colonial Louisiana,* 127–28.

28. Ingersoll, "Slave Codes and Judicial Practice in New Orleans," 30–33; McGowan, "Creation of a Slave Society," 48–57, 118–26; quotation in Mary Veronica Micele, "The Influence of the Roman Catholic Church on Slavery in Colonial Louisiana under French Domination, 1718–1763," Unpublished doctoral diss., Tulane University, 1979, 140; Gayarré, *History of Slavery in Louisiana,* 3: 75–76.

29. *Miss. Arch,* 2: 573–74; 4: 317–21; Heloise H. Cruzat, trans., "Records of the

Superior Council of Louisiana," *LHQ*, quotation on 3: 414, also 443–44; *ibid.*, 19: 768–72; Hall, *Africans in Colonial Louisiana*, 97–98; Usner, "From African Captivity," 40–44, and Usner, *Indians, Settlers, & Slaves*, 58–59, 93. See "Trial and Sentence of Biron, Runaway Negro Slave, Before the Superior Council of Louisiana, 1728," *LHQ*, 8 (1925), 23–27; Ingersoll, "Old New Orleans," 214–16.

30. Brasseaux, "Slave Regulations," 144–45; McGowan, "Creation of a Slave Society," 53–57; Hall, *Africans in Colonial Louisiana*, 142–59. Also see Henry P. Dart, ed., "Cabildo Archives French Period, No. IX," *LHQ*, 4 (1921), 224. For a different view, see Ingersoll, "Slave Codes and Judicial Practice in New Orleans," 35.

31. Hall, *Africans in Colonial Louisiana*, ch. 4; Woods, *French-Indian Relations on the Southern Frontier*, 95–109, and "The French and Natchez Indians in Louisiana, 1700–1731," *LH*, 19 (1978), 413–35; Usner, *Indians, Settlers, & Slaves*, 65–75; McGowan, "Creation of a Slave Society," ch. 3; John Delanglez, "The Natchez Massacre and Governor Perier," *LHQ*, 17 (1934), 631–33; *Miss. Arch.*, 1: 54–56; 61–70, 71–76, 77–81.

32. Woods, *French-Indian Relations the Southern Frontier*, 95–109, and "French and Natchez Indians in Louisiana," 413–35; Hall, *Africans in Colonial Louisiana*, ch. 4, quotation on 104; Usner, *Indians, Settlers, & Slaves*, 65–75; John A. Green, "Governor Perier's Expedition against the Natchez Indians," *LHQ*, 19 (1936), 547–77; McGowan, "Creation of a Plantation Society," ch. 3, quotation on 104.

33. Du Pratz, *History of Louisiana*, 77–79, 92; Hall, *Africans in Colonial Louisiana*, ch. 4; Usner, *Indians, Settlers, & Slaves*, 74–75; McGowan, "Creation of a Slave Society," 102–3; *Miss. Arch.*, 4: 81–82; also see another apparently unrelated conspiracy, *ibid.*, 4: 115–16.

34. Hall, *Africans in Colonial Louisiana*, 103; McGowan, "Creation of a Slave Society," ch. 3; Rowland C. McConnell, *Negro Troops of Antebellum Louisiana: A History of the Battalion of Free Men of Color* (Baton Rouge, La., 1968), 3–14; quotation in Gayarré, *History of Louisiana*, 1: 435.

35. For the initial development of the free black population in Louisiana, see Ingersoll, "Old New Orleans," 216.

36. The accepted anthropological designation for these communities is "triracial isolates." Scholars have traced their origins to Virginia and North Carolina in the seventeenth century and then their expansion into South Carolina, Kentucky, and Tennessee with various branches moving north and south. A recent survey by Virginia Easley DeMarce provides an excellent overview; "'Verry Slitly Mixt': Tri-Racial Isolate Families of the Upper South—A Genealogical Study," *NGSQ*, 80 (1992), 5–35.

37. Rachel N. Klein, *Unification of a Slave State: The Rise of the Planter Class in the South Carolina Backcountry, 1760–1808* (Chapel Hill, N.C., 1990), 18–21, 62–72.

38. For Johnson's whitening see J. Douglas Deal, *Race and Class in Colonial Virginia: Indians, Englishmen, and Africans on the Eastern Shore of Virginia during the Seventeenth Century* (New York, 1993), 258–69, esp. 277. See, for example, the case of Gideon Gibson, a mulatto slaveholder who during the mid-eighteenth century was in the process of transforming himself from "black" to "white." Winthrop D. Jordan, *White over Black: American Attitudes toward the Negro, 1550–1812* (Chapel

Hill, N.C., 1968), 171–74; Klein, *Unification of a Slave State,* 69–71; Robert L. Meriwether, *The Expansion of South Carolina, 1729–1765* (Kingsport, Tenn., 1940), 90, 96. As a group, free people of color were getting lighter in the Chesapeake during the late seventeenth century and into the eighteenth, perhaps as part of a conscious strategy of successful free men who married white women. See, for example, Deal, *Race and Class,* 187, 276 n. 20.

39. Warren M. Billings, "The Cases of Fernando and Elizabeth Key: A Note on the Status of Blacks in Seventeenth-Century Virginia," *WMQ,* 30 (1973), 467–74. The case of Don Francisco Condelarium was brought to my attention by Richard Haynie of the Northumberland County, Virginia, Historical Society. The case can be found in Northumberland County Order Book, 1678–98, part 2, 550, in the Society's collections.

Part II. Slave Societies: The Plantation Generations

1. Lorena S. Walsh, "A 'Place in Time' Regained: A Fuller History of Colonial Chesapeake Slavery through Group Biography," in Larry E. Hudson, Jr., ed., *Working toward Freedom: Slave Society and the Domestic Economy in the American South* (Rochester, N.Y., 1994), 14, 26–27 n18; Philip Morgan, "Three Planters and Their Slaves: Perspectives on Slavery in Virginia, South Carolina, and Jamaica, 1750–1790," in Winthrop D. Jordan and Sheila L. Skemp, eds., *Race and Family in the Colonial South* (Jackson, Miss., 1987), 65. Abolitionists made much of the animalistic names applied to slaves. See, for example, John Hepburn, "The American Defense of the Christian Golden Rule," in Roger Bruns, ed., *Am I Not a Man and a Brother: The Antislavery Crusade of Revolutionary America, 1688–1788* (New York, 1977), 19.

2. Edgar T. Thompson, *Race Relations and the Race Problem: A Definition and an Analysis* (Chapel Hill, N.C., 1939), and *Plantation Societies, Race Relations, and the South* (Durham, N.C., 1975); also, Lloyd Best, "The Mechanism of Plantation Type Economies: Outline of a Model of Pure Plantation Economy," *SES,* 17 (1968), 283–326.

3. Philip D. Curtin, *The Rise and Fall of the Plantation Complex: Essays in Atlantic History* (Cambridge, UK, 1990), chs. 1–8; Sidney W. Mintz, *Sweetness and Power: The Place of Sugar in Modern History* (New York, 1985), ch. 3; Charles Verlinden, *The Beginnings of Modern Colonization: Eleven Essays with an Introduction* (Ithaca, N.Y., 1970); J. H. Galloway, *The Sugar Cane Industry: An Historical Geography from Its Origins to 1914* (Cambridge, UK, 1989), ch. 7, and Galloway, "The Mediterranean Sugar Industry," *GR,* 67 (1977), 177–94; William D. Phillips, Jr., "Sugar Production and Trade in the Mediterranean at the Time of the Crusades," in Vladimir P. Goss and Christine Verzár Bornstein, eds., *The Meeting of Two Worlds: Cultural Exchange during the Period of the Crusades* (Kalamazoo, Mich., 1986), 393–406; Michael M. Craton, "The Historical Roots of the Plantation Model," *S&A,* 5 (1984), 189–221.

4. Curtin, *The Rise and Fall of the Plantation Complex,* ch. 2; T. Bentley Duncan, *Atlantic Islands: Madeira, the Azores, and the Cape Verdes in the Seventeenth-Cen-*

tury Commerce and Navigation, 1470–1655 (Chicago, 1972); Robert Garfield, *A History of São Tomé* (San Francisco, 1992).

5. Quotation in Morgan Godwyn, *The Negro's and Indians Advocate* (London, 1680), 36.

6. Dell Upton, "White and Black Landscapes in Eighteenth-Century Virginia," in Robert Blair St. George, ed., *Material Life in America, 1600–1860* (Boston, 1988), 357–69; Terrence W. Epperson, "Race and the Disciplines of the Plantation," *HArch,* 24 (1990), 29–36; Rhys Isaac, *The Transformation of Virginia, 1740–1790* (Chapel Hill, N.C., 1982), 34–42; John Michael Vlach, *Back of the Big House: The Architecture of Plantation Slavery* (Chapel Hill, N.C., 1993); B. W. Higman, *Jamaica Surveyed: Plantation Maps and Plans of the Eighteenth and Nineteenth Centuries* (Kingston, 1988).

7. Gilberto Freyre, *The Masters and the Slaves,* 2nd ed. (Berkeley, Cal., 1986); Eugene D. Genovese, *The Political Economy of Slavery: Studies in the Economy and Society of the Slave South* (New York, 1966), and *Roll, Jordan, Roll: The World the Slaves Made* (New York, 1974).

8. No one more fully captures the violence of plantation slavery than Kenneth M. Stampp, *The Peculiar Institution: Slavery in the Ante-Bellum South* (New York, 1963), ch. 4, entitled "To Make Them Stand in Fear." Robin Blackburn counterpoints the difference between the seemingly endless atrocities committed in the religious war of the early modern era and the commonplace violence meted out to the poor and criminal in workhouses and jails, on one hand, and the violence that underpinned slave society, on the other. *The Making of New World Slavery: From the Baroque to the Modern, 1492–1800* (London, 1997), 314, 344–47.

9. Elsa V. Goveia, "The West Indian Slave Laws of the Eighteenth Century," *Revista de ciencias sociales,* 4 (1960), 75–106; Genovese, *Roll, Jordan, Roll,* 25–48; Alan Watson, *Slave Law in the Americas* (Athens, Ga., 1989); Mark V. Tushnet, *The American Law of Slavery, 1810–1860: Considerations of Humanity and Interest* (Princeton, N.J., 1981); Thomas D. Morris, *Southern Slavery and the Law, 1619–1860* (Chapel Hill, N.C., 1996).

10. Freyre, *The Masters and the Slaves;* Genovese, *Roll, Jordan, Roll;* Willie Lee Rose, "The Domestication of Domestic Slavery," in Rose, *Slavery and Freedom,* ed. William W. Freehling (New York, 1982), 18–36.

11. Winthrop D. Jordan, *White over Black: American Attitudes toward the Negro, 1550–1812* (Chapel Hill, N.C., 1968), esp. pts. 1–2.

12. Quotation in *Laurens Papers,* 10: 2–3. Philip Morgan analyzes the incident from another perspective in "Three Planters and Their Slaves," 56–58.

13. Robin C. C. Law, *The Oyo Empire, c.1600-c.1836: A West African Imperialism in the Era of the Atlantic Slave Trade* (Oxford, UK, 1977); Law, *The Slave Coast of West Africa, 1550–1750: The Impact of the Atlantic Slave Trade on an African Society* (Oxford, UK, 1991), and Law, "Trade and Politics behind the Slave Coast: The Lagoon Traffic and the Rise of Lagos, 1500–1800," *JAH,* 24 (1983), 321–48; David Northrup, *Trade without Rulers: Pre-Colonial Economic Development in South-Eastern Nigeria* (Oxford, UK, 1978); Walter Rodney, *A History of the Upper*

Guinea Coast, 1545–1800 (Oxford, UK, 1970); Joseph C. Miller, *Way of Death: Merchant Capitalism and the Angolan Slave Trade, 1730–1830* (Madison, Wisc., 1988), esp. chs. 8–9, and Miller, "A Marginal Institution on the Margin of the Atlantic System: The Portuguese Southern Atlantic Slave Trade in the Eighteenth Century," in Barbara L. Solow, ed., *Slavery and the Rise of the Atlantic System* (Cambridge, Mass., 1991), 120–50.

14. Historians of the slave trade—following a tradition blazed by scholars of European migration that emphasized fine differences between English and French, Czechs and Poles, Scotch-Irish and Irish Catholics, or Ashkenazie and Sephardic Jews—have recently turned their attention to ethnic or national differences among Africans, distinguishing between Bambara and Igbo peoples. However, distinctions among Africans between agriculturalists and pastoralists, peasants and merchants, slaves and slaveholders still remain unstudied. Little has been written about the social standing—free and slave, peasant and paramount—of those swept up in the slave trade in the plantation period.

15. Miller, *Way of Death,* 162–64; Herbert S. Klein, "African Women in the Atlantic Slave Trade," in Claire C. Robertson and Martin A. Klein, eds., *Women and Slavery in Africa* (Madison, Wisc., 1983), 29–38; David Geggus, "Sex Ratio, Age and Ethnicity in the Atlantic Slave Trade: Data from French Shipping and Plantation Records," *JAH,* 30 (1989), 23–44. David Eltis and Stanley L. Engerman, "Was the Slave Trade Dominated by Men?" *JIH,* 23 (1992), 237–57, and Eltis and Engerman, "Fluctuations in Sex and Age Ratios in the Transatlantic Slave Trade, 1663–1864," *EHR,* 46 (1993), 308–23, find a smaller imbalance between men and women than previous studies, but still affirm that males constituted the largest category. Quotation in Donnan, *Slave Trade,* 2: 327.

16. Addressing the movement of Africans to the Americas prior to 1680, John Thornton argues that the transfer of Africans was remarkably direct and created homogenous populations. In the Americas, Thornton maintains, slaves on any given plantation "would have no shortage of people from their own nation with whom to communicate and perhaps to share elements of common culture." (John Thornton, *Africa and Africans in the Making of the Atlantic World, 1400–1680* [Cambridge, UK, 1992], 192–205, quotation on 197.) Thornton's case for homogeneity has recently received powerful support from two quarters. First, David Eltis and David Richardson, analyzing a new, more inclusive slave-trade data base, have discovered that large channels of trade connected African and the Americas along very specific lines, and subsidiary channels created even more specific connections. In short, the "pattern of West African arrivals in the Americas was far from random" (David Eltis and David Richardson, "The 'Numbers Game' and Routes to Slavery," and "West Africa and the Transatlantic Slave Trade: New Evidence of Long-Run Trends," in *S&A,* 18 [1997], 5–8, 16–35, quotation on 20.) Second, a series of regional studies of slavery in the Americas have uncovered patterns which indicate the numerical dominance of particular African nations or ethnicities (Gwendolyn Midlo Hall, *Africans in Colonial Louisiana: The Development of Afro-Creole Culture in the Eighteenth Century* [Baton Rouge, La., 1992]; David P. Geggus, "Sugar and Coffee Cultivation in Saint

Domingue and the Shaping of the Slave Labor Force," in Ira Berlin and Philip D. Morgan, eds., *Cultivation and Culture: Labor and the Shaping of Slave Life in the Americas* [Charlottesville, Va., 1993], 79–86; and, perhaps most fully, Douglas B. Chambers, "'He Is an African but Speaks Plain': Historical Creolization in Eighteenth-Century Virginia," in Alusine Jalloh and Stephen E. Maizlish, eds., *Africa and the African Diaspora* [College Station, Tex., 1996], 100–33, esp. n34; "'My Own Nation': Igbo Exiles in the Diaspora," *S&A,* 18 [1997], 72–97). But doubts about how these macro-patterns effected the construction of the slave populations of the New World in particular areas or on particular plantations have been raised by Philip D. Morgan and Peter Caron, who see the movement of Africans to the New World into various regions, in Morgan's words, as a much more "fluid, evanescent" process. I have drawn heavily on Morgan's analysis. Philip D. Morgan, "The Cultural Implications of the Atlantic Slave Trade: African Regional Origins, American Destinations and New World Developments," and Peter Caron, "'Of a Nation Which Others Do Not Understand': Bambara Slaves and African Ethnicity in Colonial Louisiana, 1718–60," *S&A,* 18 (1997), 122–45, 98–121. A close analysis of the holding of a single planter family over more than a century reveals how, even when slaves derived from a single catchment area, changes in the slave trade over time, the entry of small groups from other parts of Africa, and the internal sale and movement of slaves prevented the direct transfer of any single African nation or culture to the Americas. Lorena S. Walsh, *From Calabar to Carter's Grove: A History of a Virginia Slave Community* (Charlottesville, Va., 1997).

17. Philip D. Curtin, *Economic Change in Precolonial Africa: Senegambia in the Era of the Slave Trade* (Madison, Wisc., 1975), ch. 1; George E. Brooks, *Landlords and Strangers: Ecology, Society, and Trade in West Africa, 1000–1630* (Boulder, Col., 1993), chs. 1, 4; James F. Searing, *West African Slavery and Atlantic Commerce: The Senegal River Valley, 1700–1860* (Cambridge, UK, 1993); Northrup, *Trade without Rulers,* ch. 1, 7, 14–16; Law, *Slave Coast,* ch. 2; Elizabeth Isichei, *A History of the Igbo People* (New York, 1976).

18. John S. Mbiti, *African Religions and Philosophy* (1969); E. Geoffrey Parinder, *Religion in Africa,* 3rd ed. (Baltimore, 1974); Newell S. Booth, Jr., ed., *African Religions: A Symposium* (New York, 1977); and Robin Horton, *Patterns of Thought in Africa and the West: Essay on Magic, Religion, and Science* (Cambridge, 1993); Mechal Sobel, *The World They Made Together: Black and White Values in Eighteenth-Century Virginia* (Princeton, N.J., 1987).

19. While historians have become comfortable with the notion that "creole" identities are constructed, they frequently contrast the hybrid nature of the creole identity to that of the African, imputing a purity to the point of origins. The formulation of "African to Creole," which has guided so much of the study of the beginnings of African-American life, suggests a process of making from a product that had been made. The premise here is that Igbo nationality, to cite one case, is as much a construction as Afro-Virginian, and the process of nation formation in Africa should not be obscured by the process of creolization in the Americas. The point is made for a

later period in Leroy Vail, ed., *The Creation of Tribalism in Southern Africa* (London, 1989).

20. Philip D. Curtin, *The Atlantic Slave Trade: A Census* (Madison, Wisc., 1969), 275–82; James A. Rawley, *The Transatlantic Slave Trade: A History* (New York, 1981), ch. 12; Joseph C. Miller, "Overcrowded and Undernourished: The Techniques and Consequences of Tight-Packing in the Portuguese Southern Atlantic Slave Trade," in Serge Daget, ed., *La derniere traite à l'esclavage,* 2 vols. (Paris/Nantes, 1988), 395–425. Herbert S. Klein and Stanley L. Engerman summarize and interpret the most recent data respecting slave mortality in the Middle Passage, noting extreme variability through the trade but a general decline in mortality rates over time. "Long Term Trends in African Mortality in the Transatlantic Slave Trade," *S&A,* 18 (1997), 36–48.

21. For the large question of the "creation" and "recreation" of nationality and ethnicity, see Kathleen Neils Conzen et al., "The Invention of Ethnicity: A Perspective from the USA," *Journal of American Ethnic History,* 12 (1992), 3–41; Werner Sollors, *Beyond Ethnicity: Consent and Descent in American Culture* (New York, 1986), and Sollors, ed., *The Invention of Ethnicity* (New York, 1989).

22. The literature on slave rebellion is vast. Any understanding must start with Herbert Aptheker, *American Negro Slave Revolts,* 5th ed. (New York, 1983); Eugene D. Genovese, *From Rebellion to Revolution: Afro-American Slave Revolts in the Making of the Modern World* (Baton Rouge, La., 1979); Michael Craton, *Testing the Chains: Resistance to Slavery in the British West Indies* (Ithaca, N.Y., 1982).

23. Eltis and Richardson, "West Africa and the Transatlantic Slave Trade," 16–35.

24. Morgan, "The Cultural Implications of the Atlantic Slave Trade," 122–45.

25. C. Vann Woodward, *American Counterpoint: Slavery and Racism in the North–South Dialogue* (Boston, 1971), ch. 3; Russell R. Menard, "The Maryland Slave Population, 1658 to 1730: A Demographic Profile of Blacks in Four Counties," *WMQ,* 32 (1975), 29–54.

26. Quoted in Frank J. Klingberg, *An Appraisal of the Negro in Colonial South Carolina: A Study of Americanization* (Washington, D.C., 1941), 106.

5. The Tobacco Revolution in the Chesapeake

1. On the rise of the planter class in the Chesapeake, see Edmund S. Morgan, *American Slavery, American Freedom: The Ordeal of Colonial Virginia* (New York, 1975), ch. 15; Bernard Bailyn, "Politics and Social Structure in Virginia," in James Morton Smith, ed., *Seventeenth-Century America: Essays in Colonial History* (Chapel Hill, N.C., 1959), 90–115; Allan Kulikoff, *Tobacco and Slaves: The Development of Southern Cultures in the Chesapeake, 1680–1800* (Chapel Hill, N.C., 1986), pt. II, esp. ch. 7. John J. McCusker and Russell R. Menard, *The Economy of British America, 1607–1789* (Chapel Hill, N.C., 1985), ch. 6, provides an informed overview of the Chesapeake economy.

2. William Waller Hening, comp., *The Statutes at Large: Being a Collection of All the Laws of Virginia,* 13 vols. (Richmond, 1819–1823), 2: 283, 404, 440, quotation on 346; Morgan, *American Slavery, American Freedom,* 330.

3. Kulikoff, *Tobacco and Slaves,* 37–42, 65, 319–20; Kulikoff, "A 'Prolifick' People: Black Population Growth in the Chesapeake Colonies, 1700–1790," *SS,* 16 (1977), 391–96, 403–5; and Kulikoff, "The Origins of Afro-American Society in Tidewater Maryland and Virginia, 1700 to 1790," *WMQ,* 35 (1978), 229–31; Russell R. Menard, "The Maryland Slave Population, 1658 to 1730: A Demographic Profile of Blacks in Four Counties," *WMQ,* 32 (1975), 30–32; Menard, "From Servants to Slaves: The Transformation of the Chesapeake Labor System," *SS,* 16 (1977), 359–71, 381–82; Darrett B. Rutman and Anita H. Rutman, *A Place in Time: Middlesex County, Virginia, 1650–1750* (New York, 1984), 72; Wesley Frank Craven, *White, Red, and Black: The Seventeenth-Century Virginian* (Charlottesville, Va., 1971), 86–103; quotation in Marion Tinling, ed., *The Correspondence of the Three William Byrds of Westover, Virginia, 1684–1776,* 3 vols. (Charlottesville, Va., 1977), 2: 487.

4. Kulikoff, *Tobacco and Slaves,* 319–24; Menard, "From Servant to Slaves," 366–69; Walter Minchinton, Celia King, and Peter Waite, *Virginia Slave Trade Statistics, 1698–1775* (Richmond, 1984); Craven, *White, Red, and Black,* 86–7; Susan Westbury, "Analyzing a Regional Slave Trade: The West Indies and Virginia, 1668–1775," *S&A,* 7 (1986), 241–56. Herbert S. Klein maintains that West Indian re-exports remained the majority into the first two decades of the eighteenth century, see "Slaves and Shipping in Eighteenth-Century Virginia," *JIH,* 3 (1975), 384–85.

5. Menard, "Maryland Slave Population," 49–53; Kulikoff, "A 'Prolifick' People," 393–96; Darold D. Wax, "Black Immigrants: The Slave Trade in Colonial Maryland," *MHM,* 73 (1978), 30–5; Klein, "Slaves and Shipping in Eighteenth-Century Virginia," 383–412; Donald M. Sweig, "The Importation of African Slaves to the Potomac River, 1732–1772," *WMQ,* 42 (1985), 507–24.

6. John Thornton, *Africa and Africans in the Making of the Atlantic World, 1440–1680,* 2nd ed. (Cambridge, UK, forthcoming), ch. 11; Kulikoff, *Tobacco and Slaves,* ch. 8; Sylvia R. Frey, *Water from the Rock: Black Resistance in the Revolutionary Age* (Princeton, N.J., 1991), ch. 1, esp., 28–44; Eric Klingelhofer, "Aspects of Early Afro-American Material Culture: Artifacts from the Slave Quarters at Garrison Plantation," *HArch,* 21 (1987), 112–19; quotation in John C. Van Horne, ed., *Religious Philanthropy and Colonial Slavery: The American Correspondence of the Associates of Dr. Bray, 1717–1777* (Urbana, Ill., 1985), 99–101; Allan D. Austin, ed., *African Muslims in Antebellum America: A Source Book* (New York, 1984).

7. Kulikoff, *Tobacco and Slaves,* 320–21, 325–27; Kulikoff, "A 'Prolifick' People," 392–406; Menard, "The Maryland Slave Population," 30–35, 38–49; and Craven, *White, Red, and Black,* 98–101; Darrett B. Rutman and Anita H. Rutman, "'More True and Perfect Lists': The Reconstruction of Censuses for Middlesex County, Virginia, 1668–1704," *VMHB,* 88 (1980), 55, and Darrett B. Rutman, Charles Wetherman, and Anita H. Rutman, "Rhythms of Life: Black and White Seasonality in the Early Chesapeake," *JIH,* 11 (1980), 36–38.

8. Quoted in Lorena Walsh, "A 'Place in Time' Regained: A Fuller History of

Colonial Chesapeake Slavery through Group Biography," in Larry E. Hudson, Jr., ed., *Working toward Freedom: Slave Society and Domestic Economy in the American South* (Rochester, N.Y., 1994), 14; Lorena S. Walsh, *From Calabar to Carter's Grove: A History of a Virginia Slave Community* (Charlottesville, Va., 1997), 34; A "new Negro," declared a visitor to Maryland in 1747 with the finality gained by long experience, "must be broke." Kulikoff, *Tobacco and Slaves*, 325.

9. For the names of Carter's slaves, see Inventory, Estate of Robert Carter, Esq., Carter papers in the Alderman Library, University of Virginia, Charlottesville. The naming of Chesapeake slaves is discussed in Kulikoff, *Tobacco and Slaves*, 325–26; Mechal Sobel, *The World They Made Together: Black and White Values in Eighteenth-Century Virginia* (Princeton, N.J., 1987), ch. 11.

10. Gerald W. Mullin, *Flight and Rebellion: Slave Resistance in Eighteenth-Century Virginia* (New York, 1972), chs. 1–3; Kulikoff, *Tobacco and Slaves*, esp. 319–34; Menard, "The Maryland Slave Population," 29–54; Lois Green Carr and Lorena S. Walsh, "Economic Diversification and Labor Organization in the Chesapeake, 1650–1820," in Stephen Innes, ed., *Work and Labor in Early America* (Chapel Hill, N.C., 1988), 144–88. Quotations in Hugh Jones, *The Present State of Virginia, from Whence Is Inferred a Short View of Maryland and North Carolina*, ed. Richard L. Morton (Chapel Hill, N.C., 1956), 75–76, and Philip Alexander Bruce, *Institutional History of Virginia in the Seventeenth Century*, 2 vols. (New York, 1910), 1: 9. Before 1740 most Chesapeake slaves lived in units of less than ten slaves, and the quarters to which the newly arrived Africans were assigned were generally smaller than the average. Kulikoff, *Tobacco and Slaves*, 320, 331.

11. Hening, comp., *Statutes at Large*, 3: 447–62; 4: 126–34; "Management of Slaves, 1672," *VMHB*, 7 (1900), 314.

12. Quotation in J. Douglas Deal, *Race and Class in Colonial Virginia: Indians, Englishmen, and Africans on the Eastern Shore during the Seventeenth Century* (New York, 1993), 331–32. See above chapter 1, p. 44. New laws also prevented slaves from gathering together outside of their owner's estate for more than four hours. Hening, comp., *Statutes at Large*, 2: 492–93. For the powerful force of social and verbal isolation, see Paul Edwards, ed., *The Life of Olaudah Equiano or Gustavus Vassa: The African* (New York, 1969), 54.

13. Mullin, *Flight and Rebellion*, 14–16: Kulikoff, *Tobacco and Slaves*, 319–22; Kulikoff, "Origins of Afro-American Society," 230–35; Wax, "Black Immigrants," 30–45; Walsh, *From Calabar to Carter's Grove*, ch. 2; David Hackett Fischer and James C. Kelly, *Away, I'm Bound Away: Virginia and the Westward Movement* (Richmond, 1993), 30–33, quotation on 31. For the collapse of African nationality into the term "new Negro," see Michael Mullin, *Africa in America: Slave Acculturation and Resistance in the American South and the British Caribbean, 1736–1831* (Urbana, Ill., 1992), 3, quotation on 24. For another perspective which sees the cultural preeminence of Igbo peoples in the Chesapeake, particularly in the second quarter of the eighteenth century, see Douglas B. Chambers, "'He Is an African but Speaks Plain': Historical Creolization in Eighteenth-Century Virginia," in Alusine Jalloh and Stephen Maizlish, eds., *Africa and the African Diaspora* (College Station,

Tex., 1996), 100–33, and "'My Own Nation': Igbo Exiles in the Diaspora," *S&A,* 18 (1997), 73–97.

14. Mullin, *Flight and Rebellion,* 9–10; Philip D. Morgan and Michael L. Nicholls, "Slaves in Piedmont Virginia, 1720–1790," *WMQ,* 46 (1989), 211–12; Winthrop D. Jordan, "Planter and Slave Identity Formation: Some Problems in the Comparative Approach," in Vera Rubin and Arthur Tuden, eds., *Comparative Perspectives on Slavery in New World Plantation Societies, Annals of New York Academy of Sciences,* 292 (1977), 38–39.

15. A. Leon Higginbotham, Jr., *In the Matter of Color: Race and the American Legal Process, The Colonial Period* (New York, 1978), 22–30; Marvin L. Michael Kay and Lorin Lee Cary, *Slavery in North Carolina: 1748–1775* (Chapel Hill, N.C. 1995), chs. 2–3; Philip J. Schwarz, *Twice Condemned: Slaves and the Criminal Laws of Virginia, 1705–1865* (Baton Rouge, La., 1988), 13–26, 72–82, see p. 82 for increasingly severe penalties for slave criminals. Donna J. Spindel, *Crime and Society in North Carolina, 1663–1776* (Baton Rouge, La., 1989), 13–26, 54–55, 60–62, 65–66, 72–82, 133–37; Morgan, *American Slavery, American Freedom,* 311–15; Kathleen M. Brown, *Good Wives, Nasty Wenches, and Anxious Patriarchs: Gender, Race, and Power in Colonial Virginia* (Chapel Hill, N.C., 1996), 350–55; Rutman and Rutman, *A Place in Time,* 170–177, esp. 173. For Byrd (who also used the "bit"), see Louis B. Wright and Marion Tinling, eds., *The Secret Diary of William Byrd of Westover, 1709–1712* (Richmond, Va., 1941), 112, 117; and for Carter, see Lancaster County, Virginia, Order Book #5, 1702–13, p. 185; Robert Carter to Robert Jones, 10 Oct. 1727, Carter Papers, University of Virginia Library, Charlottesville (both citations courtesy of Emory Evans); Schwarz, *Twice Condemned,* 80–1.

16. Hening, comp., *Statutes at Large,* 2: 270, 299–300, 481–82; 3: 86–87, 447–62; 4: 132. See the difference between an early nonracial law respecting the punishment of servants. *Ibid.,* 1: 538. Thomas D. Morris, *Southern Slavery and the Law, 1619–1860* (Chapel Hill, N.C., 1996), 163–69. As slaves became subject to more violent punishment, they lost much of the traditional protections afforded the accused under English law. Hening, comp., *Statutes at Large,* 3: 102–3, 269–70; 4: 127.

17. Carr and Walsh, "Economic Diversification and Labor Organization in the Chesapeake, 1650–1820," 157–61; Walsh, *From Calabar to Carter's Grove,* 85–86, 93–94.

18. Quotations in Philip V. Fithian, *Journal and Letters of Philip Vickers Fithian, 1773–1774: A Plantation Tutor of the Old Dominion,* ed. Hunter D. Farish (Williamsburg, Va., 1943), 73, 98, and Edmund S. Morgan, *Virginians at Home: Family Life in the Eighteenth Century* (Charlottesville, Va., 1963), 53–54; Dell Upton, "White and Black Landscapes in Eighteenth-Century Virginia," in Robert Blair St. George, ed., *Material Life in America* (Boston, 1988), 362–68; Terrence W. Epperson, "Race and the Disciplines of the Plantation," *HArch,* 24 (1990), 29–36. Also see the occupational structure of George Washington's Mount Vernon estate, Donald Jackson and Dorothy Twohig, eds., *The Diaries of George Washington,* 4 vols. (Charlottesville, Va., 1978), 4: 277–83. The fullest view of the operation of an eighteenth-century Chesapeake plantation town can be gained in Jack P. Greene, ed., *The Diary of*

Colonel Landon Carter of Sabine Hall, 1752–1778, 2 vols. (Charlottesville, Va., 1965), and its architecture can be glimmered in Thomas T. Waterman, *The Mansions of Virginia, 1706–1776* (Chapel Hill, N.C., 1946), also Brown, *Good Wives,* ch. 8; Rhys Isaac, *The Transformation of Virginia, 1740–1790* (Chapel Hill, N.C., 1982), chs. 1–2.

19. Although formulated with reference to the years prior to the Civil War, insights into the planters' ideology can be gleaned from Eugene D. Genovese, *Roll, Jordan, Roll: The World the Slaves Made* (New York, 1974). Quotation in Mullin, *Flight and Rebellion,* vii.

20. The close supervision of slaves by resident planters can be viewed in the operation of Landon Carter's vast estate. See, for example, Greene, ed., *Diary of Colonel Landon Carter,* 1: 422, 497, 502; Kulikoff, *Tobacco and Slaves,* 337–39, 382–86; Walsh, "Slaves and Tobacco in the Chesapeake," 172, 176–80; Lorena S. Walsh, "Plantation Management in the Chesapeake, 1620–1820," *JEH,* 49 (1989), 393–96, esp. 394 n2. "Black slaves, not white servants, made most of the largest individual crops recorded, and most of these efficient workers were Africans, not creoles." Lorena S. Walsh, "Slave Life, Slave Society, and Tobacco Production in the Tidewater Chesapeake, 1620–1820," in Ira Berlin and Philip D. Morgan, eds., *Cultivation and Culture: Labor and the Shaping of Slave Life in the Americas* (Charlottesville, Va., 1993), 176; Philip D. Morgan, "Task and Gang Systems: The Organization of Labor on New World Plantations," in Innes, ed., *Work and Labor in Early America,* 198–201, 203–4.

21. Quotation in Hening, comp., *Statutes at Large,* 3: 102–3. Also see Mullin, *Flight and Rebellion,* 118–19, and Mullin, *Africa in America,* 138–39, 149–50; Greene, ed., *Diary of Colonel Landon Carter,* 1: 390, 396. Thomas Jefferson's slaves worked their own gardens and provision grounds, but when they planted tobacco, Jefferson was quick to object. Edwin M. Betts, ed., *Thomas Jefferson's Farm Book* (New York, 1953), 268–69; Mary Beth Norton, *Liberty's Daughters: The Revolutionary Experience of American Women, 1750–1800* (New York, 1980), 32. For the implication of the restrictions on slave property-holding on slave family life and particularly on the role of slave men as "providers," see Brown, *Good Wives,* 183–84.

22. Quotation in Philip D. Morgan "Slave Life in Piedmont Virginia," in Lois Green Carr, Philip D. Morgan, and Jean B. Russo, eds., *Colonial Chesapeake Society* (Chapel Hill, N.C., 1988), 468–69; Walsh, "Slaves and Tobacco in the Chesapeake," 176–77, 180; Mullin, *Africa in America,* 149–54, and Mullin, *Flight and Rebellion.* For legislation against slave property-holding, see Hening, comp., *Statutes at Large,* 3: 103, 459–60; Walter Clark, ed., *The State Records of North Carolina,* 16 vols. (Winston, N.C., 1895–1906), 23: 194–95.

23. W. N. Sainsbury et al., eds., *Calendar of State Papers, Colonial Series, America and West Indies,* 40 vols. (London, 1860–1969), 25: 83; 33: 192, 297–98; 36: 333–36, 414–15; 37: 277; 38: 41; H. R. McIlwaine et al., eds., *Executive Journals of the Council of Colonial Virginia,* 6 vols. (Richmond, 1925–54), 3: 234–36, 242–43, 574–75; quotation on 3: 574; 4: 20, 29, 31, 228 (courtesy of Emory Evans).

24. See, for example, Olaudah Equiano's resistance to having his name changed. Edwards, ed., *The Life of Olaudah Equiano,* 56–57. Quotation in "Eighteenth-Cen-

tury Maryland as Portrayed in the 'Itinerant Observations' of Edward Kimber,"
MHM, 51 (1956), 327–28.

25. Mullin, *Flight and Rebellion,* 39–45; Sobel, *The World They Made Together,*
95; Kulikoff, *Tobacco and Slaves,* 328–29, 352; Mullin, *Africa in America,* 39, 44–45.
Quotations in Michael Mullin, ed., *American Negro Slavery: A Documentary History* (New York, 1976), 83, and in William K. Boyd, ed., *William Byrd's Histories of
the Dividing Line betwixt Virginia and North Carolina* (Raleigh, N.C., 1929), 56.
Mullin enlarges the connection between violent resistance to slavery—flight, maroonage, and insurrection—and the arrival of Africans in the Americas in *Africa in
America,* ch. 2.

26. Kulikoff, *Tobacco and Slaves,* 328–29; Mullin, *Flight and Rebellion,* 42–44;
Mullin, *Africa in America,* 44–45. Once winter set in, planters found runaway slaves
returning of their own accord. See Robert Carter to Robert Jones, 10 Oct. 1729,
Carter Letterbooks, University of Virginia; Walsh, "Slaves and Tobacco," 176–79;
Kay and Cary, *Slavery in North Carolina,* 122.

27. The story of runaways is best told by the slaveholders who chased them. A
systematic, but still incomplete, collection of advertisements for fugitive slaves is
Lathan A. Windley, comp., *Runaway Slave Advertisements: A Documentary History
from the 1730s to 1790,* 4 vols. (Westport, Conn., 1983).

28. Philip D. Morgan, "Slave Life in Piedmont, Virginia, 1720–1800," 433–84, and
Morgan and Michael L. Nicholls, "Slaves in Piedmont Virginia, 1720–1790," *WMQ,*
46 (1989), 211–51; Walsh, *From Calabar to Carter's Grove,* 204–15. The expansion of
Chesapeake slavery also pushed into North Carolina: Kay and Cary, *Slavery in North
Carolina,* 19–22.

29. Morgan, "Slave Life in Piedmont Virginia," 444–47; Kay and Cary, *Slavery in
North Carolina,* 25–26; Morgan and Nicholls, "Slaves in Piedmont Virginia," 215,
217–33, esp. 229–30, quotation on 221; quotation in Van Horne, ed., *Religious Philanthropy,* 219.

30. Walsh, *From Calabar to Carter's Grove,* 204–11; Morgan, "Slave Life in
Piedmont Virginia," 438–54.

31. Emory G. Evans, ed., "A Question of Complexion: Documents Concerning
the Negro and the Franchise in Eighteenth-Century Virginia," *VMHB,* 71 (1963), 414.

32. Winthrop D. Jordan, *White over Black: American Attitudes toward the Negro, 1550–1812* (Chapel Hill, N.C., 1968), 122–26; Ira Berlin, *Slaves without Masters:
The Free Negro in the Antebellum South* (New York, 1974), 6–9; Douglas Deal, "A
Constricted World: Free Blacks on Virginia's Eastern Shore, 1680–1750," in Carr,
Morgan, and Russo, eds., *Colonial Chesapeake Society,* 276–79; Michael L. Nicholls,
"Passing Through This Troublesome World: Free Blacks in the Early Southside,"
VMHB, 92 (1984), 51–53; Brown, *Good Wives,* chs. 4, 7; Kay and Cary, *Slavery in
North Carolina,* 66–68.

33. Hening, comp., *Statutes at Large,* 2: 481, 490, 492–93, 3: 86–88, 102, 172, 238,
250, 269, 298, 453–54. In 1723 manumission became the prerogative of the governor
and the Council in Virginia. *Ibid.,* 4: 132. In 1752 Maryland banned testamentary
manumission. William Hand Browne et al., eds., *Archives of Maryland* (Baltimore,
1884–1972), 50: 76.

34. See above, pp. 90–91.

35. A 1755 Maryland census, the only known prerevolutionary enumeration of free black people in the region, counted slightly more than 1,800 free persons of African descent, about 4 percent of Maryland's black population and less than 2 percent of its free population. *Gentlemen's Magazine and Historical Chronicle,* 34 (1764), 261. Although no other Chesapeake colony took a similar census, there is no evidence that any contained a larger proportion of black free people than Maryland. Petition from Petersburg, 11 Dec. 1805, Legislative Petitions, Virginia State Library, Richmond; *Proceedings and Debates of the Convention of North-Carolina Called to Amend the Constitution of the State* (Raleigh, 1835), 351.

36. *Gentlemen's Magazine,* 34 (1764), 261. In Virginia, slaves petitioning for manumission—the only avenue left open to them—emphasized their descent from a European or Native-American ancestor. Brown, *Good Wives,* 223–24.

37. Deal, "A Constricted World," 292–93, 302; Brown, *Good Wives,* 227–36. One-sixth of the adult free black population of Maryland in 1755 were crippled or elderly. *Gentlemen's Magazine,* 34 (1764), 261.

38. Breen and Innes, *"Myne Owne Ground";* Deal, "A Constricted World," 275–305; Philip J. Schwarz, "Emancipators, Protectors, and Anomalies: Free Black Slaveowners in Virginia," *VMHB,* 95 (1987), 317–38; Brown, *Good Wives,* 225–27, 238–41.

39. Morgan, "Slave Life in Piedmont Virginia," 461–64, quotation on 462; Nicholls, "Passing Through This Troublesome World," 55–58. Brown, *Good Wives,* 411–16.

40. Mullin, *Flight and Rebellion,* ch. 3; Kulikoff, *Tobacco and Slaves,* 345–80; quotation in *Runaway Advertisements,* 1: 175–76 (Williamsburg *Virginia Gazette* [Dixon & Hunter], 30 Mar. 1776).

41. Kulikoff, *Tobacco and Slaves,* 336–39; Kulikoff, "A 'Prolifick' People," 393–96, 405; Menard, "Maryland Slave Population," 42–54; Menard, "From Servants to Slave," 387–88.

42. Kulikoff, *Tobacco and Slaves,* ch. 9, esp. 359–80; Kulikoff, "The Beginnings of the Afro-American Family in Maryland," in Aubrey C. Land et al., eds., *Law, Society, and Politics in Early Maryland* (Baltimore, 1977), 177–96; Kulikoff, "A 'Prolifick' People," 401–3, 405–14, and "Origins of Afro-American Society," 246–53; and quotations in Betts, ed., *Thomas Jefferson's Farm Book,* pt. 2: 46 and also 12–13, 21, 24–26, 42–46; and Morgan and Nicholls, "Slaves in Piedmont Virginia," 235, 230–38.

43. Morgan, "Slave Life in Piedmont Virginia," 434–64; Morgan and Nicholls, "Slaves in Piedmont Virginia," 221–47.

44. Van Horne, ed., *Religious Philanthropy,* 100.

45. Quotation in Charles Ball, *Slavery in the United States: A Narrative of the Life and Adventures of Charles Ball* (Lewistown, Pa., 1837), 23; Kulikoff, *Tobacco and Slaves,* 333–34; quotation in Jones, *The Present State of Virginia,* 75–77.

46. Quotations in Mullin, *Africa in America,* 269, and Greene, ed., *Diary of Colonel Landon Carter,* 2: 919; Herbert G. Gutman, *The Black Family in Slavery and Freedom, 1750–1925* (New York, 1976), 75–78.

47. Robert Carter to Samuel Carter, 10 Mar. 1781, Robert Carter Letterbooks, 4:

48; Robert Carter to John Pound, 16 March 1779, to Fleet Cox, 2 Jan. 1788, and to George Newman, 29 Dec. 1789, typescript, Robert Carter Papers, Duke University, Durham, N.C.; Greene, ed., *Diary of Colonel Landon Carter,* 1: 329–30, 348; 2: 648, 845, 1109; Daniel Dulany to Robert Carter, 18 Dec. 1768, Colonial Papers, Maryland Historical Society, Baltimore; Herbert G. Gutman, *The Black Family in Slavery and Freedom, 1750–1825* (New York, 1976), 347; Kulikoff, *Tobacco and Slaves,* 339–41, 346, 353–80; Mullin, *Flight and Rebellion,* 129; Morgan, "Slave Life in Piedmont Virginia," 469; Brown, *Good Wives,* 357–61; Norton, *Liberty's Daughters,* 68–70; quotation in *Runaway Advertisements,* 2: 22 (Annapolis *Maryland Gazette,* 6 Feb. 1755); 2: 67 (Annapolis *Maryland Gazette,* 2 Oct. 1766).

48. Sobel, *The World They Made Together,* ch. 9; Walsh, *From Calabar to Carter's Grove,* 115–16, 159–68; William M. Kelso, *Kingsmill Plantations, 1619–1800: Archaeology of Country Life in Colonial Virginia* (Orlando, Fla., 1984); Steven L. Jones, "The African-American Tradition in Vernacular Architecture," in Theresa A. Singleton, *The Archeology of Slavery and Plantation Life* (San Diego, Cal., 1985), 195–214.

49. Carville V. Earle, *The Evolution of a Tidewater Settlement System: All Hallow's Parish, Maryland, 1650–1783* (Chicago, 1975), 18; quotation in Browne et al., eds. *Archives of Maryland,* 38: 48.

50. Kulikoff, *Tobacco and Slaves,* ch. 9, esp. 358–80, and Kulikoff, "Afro-American Family," 186–87; Isaac, *Transformation of Virginia,* 328–41; Mary Beth Norton, Herbert G. Gutman, and Ira Berlin, "The Afro-American Family in the Age of Revolution," in Ira Berlin and Ronald Hoffman, eds., *Slavery and Freedom in the Age of the American Revolution* (Charlottesville, Va., 1983), 175–91.

51. Sobel, *The World They Made Together,* ch. 9; Upton, "White and Black Landscapes in Eighteenth-Century Virginia," 357–69; Isaac, *Transformation of Virginia,* 357–68; Walsh, *From Calabar to Carter's Grove,* 7–10, 75, 181–82.

52. Walsh, *Calabar to Carter's Grove,* 85–86.

53. Quotation in Lorena S. Walsh, "Work and Resistance in the New Republic: The Case of the Chesapeake, 1770–1820," in Mary Turner, ed., *From Chattel Slaves to Wage Slaves: The Dynamics of Labour Bargaining in the Americas* (Kingston, 1995), 110.

54. Walsh, "Slaves and Tobacco in the Chesapeake," 177.

55. *Ibid.,* 177–84.

56. McCusker and Menard, *The Economy of British America,* 128–33; Paul G. E. Clemens, *The Atlantic Economy and Colonial Maryland's Eastern Shore: From Tobacco to Grain* (Ithaca, N.Y., 1980), 168–223; David Klingaman, "The Significance of Grain in the Development of the Tobacco Colonies," *JEH,* 29 (1969), 268–78; Carville Earle and Ronald Hoffman, "Staple Crops and Urban Development in the Eighteenth-Century South," *PAH,* 10 (1976), 7–78; Walsh, "Plantation Management in the Chesapeake, 1620–1820," 393–400; Carr and Walsh, "Economic Diversification and Labor Organization," 147–48; Walsh, "Slaves and Tobacco in the Chesapeake," 179–86.

57. Earle and Hoffman, "Staple Crops and Urban Development"; Menard and

McCusker, *The Economy of British America,* 129–133. For iron works, see Ronald Lewis, *Coal, Iron, and Slaves: Industrial Slavery in Maryland and Virginia, 1715–1865* (Westport, Conn., 1979).

58. Walsh, "Slaves and Tobacco in the Chesapeake," 186–87; quotation in Billy G. Smith and Richard Wojtowicz, eds., *Blacks Who Stole Themselves: Advertisements for Runaways in the Pennsylvania Gazette, 1728–1790* (Philadelphia, 1989), 108 (5 Aug. 1772), 118 (27 Apr. 1774); Carr and Walsh, "Economic Diversification and Labor Organization," 163, 166–75; David W. Galenson, *White Servitude in Colonial America: An Economic Analysis* (New York, 1981), 51–64. Allan Kulikoff has estimated that the proportion of blacks working as agricultural laborers dropped from 90 to 82 percent between 1733 and 1776. "Tobacco and Slaves: Population, Economy, and Society in Eighteenth-Century Prince George's County, Maryland," unpub. doctoral diss., Brandeis University, 1976, 235–39. For women's work, see Carole Shammas, "Black Women's Work and the Evolution of Plantation Society in Virginia," *LHist,* 26 (1985), 5–28.

59. Carville Earle and Ronald Hoffman, "The Urban South: The First Two Centuries," in Blair A. Brownell and David R. Goldfield, eds., *The City in Southern History: The Growth of Urban Civilization in the South* (Port Washington, N.Y., 1977), 23–51; Edward C. Papenfuse, *In Pursuit of Profit: The Annapolis Merchants in the Era of the American Revolution, 1763–1805* (Baltimore, 1975), ch. 1; Thomas M. Preisser, "Alexandria and the Evolution of the Northern Virginia Economy, 1749–1776," *VMHB,* 89 (1981), 282–93; Kay and Cary, *Slavery in North Carolina,* 27–28.

60. Earle and Hoffman, "The Urban South"; Mullin, *Flight and Rebellion,* 87–88, 124–27; and Gray, *So. Ag.,* 2: 602–17. Although the best study of slave hiring in the Chesapeake region focuses on the post-Revolution years, the forces promoting slave hire after the war suggest that the practice predated the Revolution. See Sarah S. Hughes, "Slaves for Hire: The Allocation of Black Labor in Elizabeth City County, Virginia, 1782 to 1810," *WMQ,* 35 (1978), 260–86.

61. Greene, ed., *Diary of Colonel Landon Carter,* 1: 390, 2: 871; John C. Fitzpatrick, ed., *The Writings of George Washington,* 39 vols. (Washington, D.C., 1931–44), 31: 186–89, 32: 437–38, 474–75, 33: 201–2, 336–7); Morgan, "Slave Life in Piedmont Virginia," 465–67.

62. Betts, ed., *Jefferson's Farm Book,* 268–69; Morgan, "Slave Life in Piedmont Virginia," 466–68; Gregory A. Stiverson and Patrick H. Butler, eds., "Virginia in 1732: The Travel Journal of William Hugh Grove," *VMHB,* 85 (1977), 32, 40; Ronald L. Lewis, "Slave Families at Early Chesapeake Iron Works," *VMHB,* 86 (1978), 172–73, 176–79; Walsh, *From Calabar to Carter's Grove,* 182–203; quotation in Kulikoff, "Afro-American Family," 247, 250.

63. Quotation in Greene, ed., *Diary of Colonel Landon Carter,* 1: 484; quotation in *Runaway Advertisements,* 2: 45–46 (Annapolis *Maryland Gazette,* 2 July 1762); Kulikoff, "Afro-American Family," 185–86; Jordan, *White over Black,* 405 n7; Mullin, *Flight and Rebellion,* 83–139; Walsh, *From Calabar to Carter's Grove,* ch. 6; "Description of Servants, 1772," Northampton Furnace, Ridgely Account Books, Maryland Historical Society, Baltimore; and Lewis, *Coal, Iron and Slaves,* 82–84,

162–63; quotation in John Brickell, *The Natural History of North Carolina* (Dublin, 1737), 275.

64. Farish, ed., *Journal of Philip Fithian,* 184–85, 199–200.

65. Michael Anesko, "So Discreet a Zeal: Slavery and the Anglican Church in Virginia, 1680–1730," *VMHB,* 93 (1985), 247–78; Jerome W. Jones, "The Established Virginia Church and the Conversion of Negroes and Indians, 1620–1760," *JNH,* 46 (1961), 12–23. For the Williamsburg school, see Thad W. Tate, *The Negro in Eighteenth-Century Williamsburg* (Williamsburg, Va., 1965), 73–85.

66. Isaac, *The Transformation of Virginia, 1740–1790,* 151–54; George William Pilcher, "Samuel Davies and the Instruction of Negroes in Virginia," *VMHB,* 74 (1966), 293–300; John B. Boles, "Introduction," in Boles, ed., *Master & Slave in the House of the Lord: Race and Religion in the American South, 1740–1870* (Lexington, Ky., 1988), 5–6; Sobel, *The World They Made Together,* 180–91; Christine Leigh Heyrman, *Southern Cross: The Beginnings of the Bible Belt* (New York, 1997), 46–52; Robert M. Calhoon, *Evangelicals and Conservatives in the Early South, 1740–1861* (Columbia, S.C., 1988), 14–20; quotation in Samuel Davies, *Letters from the Reverend Samuel Davies, Showing the State of Religion in Virginia, Particularly among the Negroes* (London, 1757), 10.

67. Luther P. Jackson, "Religious Development of the Negro in Virginia from 1760 to 1860," *JNH,* 16 (1931), 168–239; Mechal Sobel, *Trabelin' On: The Slave Journey into an Afro-Baptist Faith* (Westport, Conn., 1979), and Sobel, *The World They Made Together,* 199–203, 207–12. Quotation in *Runaway Advertisements,* 1: 56 (Williamsburg *Virginia Gazette* [Purdie and Dixon], 1 Oct. 1767), and 1:109 (Williamsburg *Virginia Gazette* [Purdie and Dixon] 27 Feb., 1772). Also see *ibid.,* 1: 98 (Williamsburg *Virginia Gazette* [Purdie and Dixon], 11 July 1771). Slaveholders also recognized the connection between conversion and resistance, telling one Anglican missionary in 1770 that "since we got to baptizing them they are become insolent and Idle, Runaways, etc.," Van Horne, ed., *Religious Philanthropy,* 289; Sylvia R. Frey, "'The Year of Jubilee Is Come': Black Christianity in the Plantation South in Post-Revolution America," in Ronald Hoffman and Peter J. Albert, eds., *Religion in a Revolutionary Age* (Charlottesville, Va., 1994), 90–91.

68. *Runaway Advertisements,* 1: 149–50 (Williamsburg *Virginia Gazette* [Purdue & Dixon]), 30 June 1774).

6. The Rice Revolution in the Lowcountry

1. *Historical Statistics,* 2: 1192–93; John J. McCusker and Russell R. Menard, *The Economy of British America, 1607–1789* (Chapel Hill, N.C., 1985), 175–79; Peter A. Coclanis, *The Shadow of a Dream: Economic Life and Death in the South Carolina Low Country: 1670–1920* (New York, 1988), ch. 3; R. C. Nash, "South Carolina and the Atlantic Economy in the Late Seventeenth and Eighteenth Centuries," *EHR,* 45 (1992), 680; Peter H. Wood, *Black Majority: Negroes in Colonial South Carolina from 1670 through the Stono Rebellion* (New York, 1974), 55–62; Gray, *So. Ag.,* 1: 277–90; Converse D. Clowse, *Economic Beginnings in Colonial South Carolina,*

1670–1730, 122–32; Julia Floyd Smith, *Slavery and Rice Culture in Low Country Georgia, 1750–1860* (Knoxville, Tenn., 1985), 15–29; Russell R. Menard argues that the lowcountry was transformed from a society with slaves to a slave society prior to the rice revolution. "The Africanization of the Lowcountry Labor Force, 1670–1730," in Winthrop D. Jordan and Sheila L. Skemp, eds., *Race and Family in the Colonial South* (Jackson, Miss., 1987), 92.

2. Coclanis, *Shadow of a Dream*, 80–81; Clowse, *Economic Beginnings of Colonial South Carolina*, 122–32, 167–71, 220–21, 231–35, 256–58; Wood, *Black Majority*, 35–62; Gray, *So. Ag.*, 1: 277–79, 289–90; James M. Clifton, "Golden Grains of White: Rice Planting on the Lower Cape Fear," *NCHR*, 50 (1973), 368–78, and Clifton, "The Rice Industry in Colonial America," *AH*, 55 (1981), 266–83; Sam B. Hilliard, "Antebellum Tidewater Rice Culture in South Carolina and Georgia," in James R. Gibson, ed., *European Settlement and Development in North America: Essays on Geographical Change in Honour and Memory of Andrew Hill Clark* (Toronto, 1978), 94–110; Douglas C. Wilms, "The Development of Rice Culture in 18th Century Georgia," *Southeastern Geographer*, 12 (1972), 45–57; Joyce E. Chaplin, "Tidal Rice Cultivation and the Problem of Slavery in South Carolina and Georgia, 1760–1815," *WMQ*, 49 (1992), 29–61.

3. Peter H. Wood, "'More Like a Negro Country': Demographic Patterns in Colonial South Carolina, 1700–1740," in Stanley L. Engerman and Eugene D. Genovese, eds., *Race and Slavery in the Western Hemisphere: Quantitative Studies* (Princeton, N.J., 1975), 131–45, quotation on 132, and Wood, *Black Majority*, 13–91; Coclanis, *Shadow of a Dream*, 64–65; Daniel C. Littlefield, *Rice and Slaves: Ethnicity and the Slave Trade in Colonial South Carolina* (Baton Rouge, La., 1981); Russell R. Menard, "Slave Demography in the Lowcountry, 1670–1740: From Frontier Society to Plantation," *SCHM*, 96 (1995), 291–302; David Richardson, "The British Slave Trade to Colonial South Carolina," *S&A*, 12 (1991), 125–72; Philip D. Morgan, ed., "Profile of a Mid-Eighteenth Century South Carolina Parish: The Tax Return of Saint James' Goose Creek," *SCHM*, 81 (1980), 51–65; *Historical Statistics*, 2: 1168. For the development of slavery and a plantation order in colonial Georgia, see Darold D. Wax, "'New Negroes Are Always in Demand': The Slave Trade in Eighteenth-Century Georgia," *GHQ*, 68 (1984), 193–200; Betty Wood, *Slavery in Colonial Georgia, 1730–1775* (Athens, Ga., 1984), 91–98, and Wood, "Some Aspects of Female Resistance to Chattel Slavery in Low Country Georgia, 1763–1815," *HJ*, 30 (1987), quotation on 604. For the growth of rice culture in East Florida and the growth of the black population in Florida under British rule between 1763 and 1784, see J. Leitch Wright, Jr., "Blacks in British East Florida," *FHQ*, 54 (1976), 426–42, and Daniel F. Schafer, "'Yellow Silk Ferret Tied Round Their Wrists': African Americans in British East Florida, 1763–1784," in David R. Colburn and Jane L. Landers, eds., *The African American Heritage of Florida* (Gainesville, Fla., 1995), 71–99, quotation on 76; also Donnan, *Slave Trade*, 4: 382.

4. William R. Snell, "Indian Slavery in Colonial South Carolina, 1671–1795," unpub. doctoral diss., University of Alabama, 1972; Wood, "The Changing Population of the Colonial South," in Peter H. Wood, Gregory A. Waselkov, and

M. Thomas Hatley, eds., *Powhatan's Mantle: Indians in the Colonial Southeast* (Lincoln, Neb., 1989), 47.

5. Littlefield, *Rice and Slaves,* ch. 2; W. Robert Higgins, "Charleston: Terminus and Entrepôt of the Colonial Slave Trade," in Martin L. Kilson and Robert I. Rotberg, eds., *The African Diaspora* (Cambridge, Mass., 1976), 115; Wood, "'More Like a Negro Country,'" 144; Menard, "Africanization of the Lowcountry," 93–94. With the beginning of slavery in Georgia in the 1750s, many of the slaves entering that colony came from South Carolina. By the 1760s, however, Georgia planters also imported their slaves directly from Africa, and most slaves were "African born." Harold E. Davis, *The Fledgling Province: Social and Cultural Life in Colonial Georgia, 1733–1776* (Chapel Hill, N.C., 1976), 131.

6. Littlefield, *Rice and Slaves,* 8–11; "'More Like a Negro Country,'" 149–54; Coclanis, *Shadow of a Dream,* 60, 243–44 n44; Higgins, "Charleston: Terminus and Entrepôt," 118–27; Darold D. Wax, "Preferences for Slaves in Colonial America," *JNH,* 58 (1973), 388–99; Wood, *Slavery in Colonial Georgia,* 103. Philip D. Curtin, *The Atlantic Slave Trade: A Census* (Madison, Wisc., 1969), 143, 156–57; *Laurens Papers,* 1: 275, 294–95, 331; 2: 179–82, 186, 230, 357, 400–2, 423, 437; 4: 192–93. On the age and sex preferences of South Carolina planters, see Donnan, *Slave Trade,* 4: 329; *Laurens Papers,* 1: 295 (quotation), 2: 186, 204, 230, 278, 315, 348, 357, 400–2. By the 1720s the sex ratio of South Carolina slaves was normally 120 or more, and it continued to increase during the next decade. Wood, *Black Majority,* 153, 160, 164–65; Littlefield, *Race and Slaves,* 58–59. Developments in Georgia followed the pattern established in South Carolina, Wood, *Slavery in Colonial Georgia,* 108.

7. Coclanis, *Shadow of a Dream,* 98; Morgan, "A Mid-Eighteenth Century South Carolina Parish," 51–65; Russell R. Menard, "Slavery, Economic Growth, and Revolutionary Ideology in the South Carolina Lowcountry," in Ronald Hoffman et al., eds., *The Economy of Early America: The Revolutionary Period, 1763–1790* (Charlottesville, Va., 1988), 262–65. The units in which Georgia slaves resided were considerably smaller than those in South Carolina, but growing rapidly. Wood, *Slavery in Colonial Georgia,* 104–8. For the Cape Fear area, see Marvin L. Michael Kay and Lorin Lee Cary, *Slavery in North Carolina, 1748–1775* (Chapel Hill, N.C., 1995), 23–24.

8. For an excellent contemporary description of the process of rice cultivation and its changing technology, see William Butler, "Observations on the Culture of Rice, 1786," South Carolina Historical Society, Charleston; Joseph W. Barnwell, ed., "Diary of Timothy Ford, 1785–1786," *SCHM,* 13 (1912), 182–84; Gray, *So. Ag,* 1: 281–97; Hilliard, "Antebellum Tidewater Rice Culture," 109–10. Quotation in Evangeline Walker Andrews and Charles M. Andrews, eds., *Journal of a Lady of Quality* (New Haven, Conn., 1934), 194.

9. Coclanis, *Shadow of a Dream,* 78–83, 94–110; Menard, "South Carolina Lowcountry," 250–54, quotation on 252; Richardson, "British Slave Trade to Carolina," 132–34; Joyce E. Chaplin, *An Anxious Pursuit: Agricultural Innovation and Modernity in the Lower South, 1730–1815* (Chapel Hill, N.C., 1993), 187–92; Alan Gallay, *The Formation of a Planter Elite: Jonathan Bryan and the Southern Colonial Frontier* (Athens, Ga., 1989), 61.

10. Gray, *So. Ag.*, 1: 290–93; McCusker and Menard, *Economy of British America*, 185–87; Chaplin, *Anxious Pursuit*, 190–208; Nash, "Atlantic Economy," 679–80; Menard, "South Carolina Lowcountry," 254–55, 257 (table 1).

11. Gray, *So. Ag.*, 1: 293–97; David L. Coon, "Eliza Lucas Pinckney and the Reintroduction of Indigo Culture in South Carolina," *JSoH*, 42 (1976), 61–76; Chaplin, *Anxious Pursuit*, 193–202; G. Terry Sharrer, "The Indigo Bonanza in South Carolina, 1740–90," *T&C*, 12 (1971), 449–52, and Sharrer, "Indigo in Carolina, 1671–1796," *SCHM*, 72 (1971), 94–103; David H. Rembert, Jr., "The Indigo of Commerce in Colonial North America," *Economic Botany*, 33 (1979), 128–34.

12. Johann David Schoepf, *Travels in the Confederation 1783–1784*, trans. and ed. Alfred J. Morrison, 2 vols. (Philadelphia, 1911), 2: 157–59; Chaplin, *Anxious Pursuit*, 198–99; Schafer, "'Yellow Silk Ferret Tied Round Their Wrists,'" 79–81.

13. Wood, "'More Like a Negro Country,'" 153–64; Coclanis, *Shadow of a Dream*, 39–47; Menard, "Slave Demography in the Lowcountry," 294–301; Philip D. Morgan, "Afro-American Cultural Change: The Case of Colonial South Carolina Slaves," paper presented at the annual meeting of the Organization of American Historians, held in New Orleans, April 1979, 3–6, esp. tables 1, 4, 7 (courtesy of the author). But by the 1750s there were large number of native-born slaves in South Carolina, see Governor James Glen writing in 1751: Many slaves "are natives of Carolina, who have no notion of liberty, nor no longing after any other country." H. Roy Merrens, ed., *The Colonial South Carolina Scene: Contemporary Views, 1697–1774* (Columbia, S.C., 1977), 183. As the black population began to increase naturally, slaveholders demonstrated concern for their slaves' family life. *Laurens Papers*, 4: 595–96, 625; 5: 370; Coclanis, *Shadow of a Dream*, 43–45; McCusker and Menard, *Economy of British America*, 181; quotations in Littlefield, *Rice and Slaves*, 67–68, and Menard, "South Carolina Lowcountry," 261.

14. Philip Morgan, "Three Planters and Their Slaves: Perspectives on Slavery in Virginia, South Carolina, and Jamaica, 1750–1790," in Jordan and Skemp, eds. *Race and Family in the Colonial South*, 65.

15. Frank J. Klingberg, ed., *The Carolina Chronicle of Dr. Francis Le Jau, 1706–1717* (Berkeley, Cal., 1956), 54–55, 121–22, 129–30, quotations on 55, 108; quotation in George F. Jones, ed., "John Martin Boltzius's Trip to Charleston, October 1742," *SCHM*, 82 (1981), 93; Morgan, "Three Planters and Their Slaves," 63–65.

16. Thomas J. Cooper and David J. McCord, comps., *The Statutes at Large of South Carolina*, 10 vols. (Columbia, S.C., 1837–41), 7: 346–47, 410–11; Thomas D. Morris, *Southern Slavery and the Law, 1619–1860* (Chapel Hill, N.C., 1996), 164–65, 169–70.

17. Wood, *Black Majority*, ch. 12; Edward A. Pearson, "'A Countryside Full of Flames': A Reconsideration of the Stono Rebellion and Slave Rebelliousness in the Early Eighteenth-Century South Carolina Lowcountry," *S&A*, 17 (1996), 22–50.

18. John C. Van Horne, *Religious Philanthropy and Colonial Slavery: The American Correspondence of the Associates of Dr. Bray, 1717–1777* (Urbana, Ill., 1985), 112, 116; Klingberg, ed., *Carolina Chronicle of Dr. Francis Le Jau*, 69–70, 74.

19. George C. Rogers, Jr., *Charleston in the Age of the Pinckneys* (Norman, Okla., 1969); Coclanis, *Shadow of a Dream*, 5–11; Carl Bridenbaugh, *Myths and*

Realities: Societies of the Colonial South (Baton Rouge, La., 1952), 59–60, 76–94; Frederick P. Bowes, *The Culture of Early Charleston* (Chapel Hill, N.C., 1942). For Charles Town's population, see Coclanis, *Shadow of a Dream*, 114, 18 n14; R. C. Nash, "Urbanization in the Colonial South, Charleston, South Carolina as a Case Study," *JUH* 19 (1992), 3–29. South Carolina's wealth is variously calculated by Alice Hanson Jones, *Wealth of a Nation To Be: The American Colonies on the Eve of the American Revolution* (New York, 1980); Peter A. Coclanis, "The Wealth of British America on the Eve of the Revolution," *JIH*, 21 (1990), 245–60; Menard, "South Carolina Lowcountry," 265–67.

20. Clues for the origins of lowcountry paternalism can be found in McCusker and Menard, *Economy of British America*, 183–84; Morgan, "Three Planters and Their Slaves," 37–42, 54–68. For the interplay of quasi-absenteeism and planter ideology in the nineteenth century, see William W. Freehling, *Prelude to Civil War: The Nullification Controversy in South Carolina, 1813–1836* (New York, 1966), 65–70; Michael P. Johnson, "Planters and Patriarchy: Charleston, 1800–1860," *JSoH*, 46 (1980), 45–72. The development of a unique style of plantation architecture provides a measure of the growing confidence of the planter class, see Samuel Gaillard Stoney, *Plantations of the Carolina Low Country* (Charleston, S.C., 1938), and Mills Lane, *Architecture of the Old South: South Carolina* (Savannah, Ga., 1984).

21. William L. Van Deburg, *The Slave Drivers: Black Agricultural Labor* (Westport, Conn., 1979), provides basic information on this understudied figure.

22. Philip D. Morgan, "Task and Gang Systems: The Organization of Labor on New World Plantations," in Stephen Innes ed., *Work and Labor in Early America* (Chapel Hill, N.C., 1988), 191–92; Morgan, "Work and Culture: The Task System and the World of Lowcountry Blacks 1700–1880," *WMQ*, 39 (1982), 563–99.

23. See above note 20, also Joyce E. Chaplin, "Slavery and the Principle of Humanity: A Modern Idea in the Early Lower South," *JSH*, 24 (1990), 299–315. Henry Laurens considered his slaves "poor Creatures who look up to their Master as their Father, their Guardian, & Protector." *Laurens Papers*, 8: 618. For a close inspection of the operation of the patriarchal ideal on the plantations of Henry Laurens, see Robert Olwell, "'A Reckoning of Accounts': Patriarchy, Market Relations, and Control on Henry Laurens's Lowcountry Plantations, 1762–1785," in Larry Hudson, Jr., *Working toward Freedom: Slave Society and Domestic Economy in the American South* (Rochester, N.Y., 1994), 38–40; Maurice Crouse, ed., "The Letterbook of Peter Manigault, 1763–1773," *SCHM*, 70 (1969), 181–84; Josiah Smith to George Austin, 25 Feb. 1772, quotation in 22 July 1774, Josiah Smith Letterbook, Southern Historical Collection, University of North Carolina.

24. Jane G. Landers, "Acquisition and Loss on a Spanish Frontier: The Free Black Homesteaders of Florida, 1784–1821," *S&A*, 17 (1996), 88–89; Wilbur H. Siebert, "The Departure of the Spaniards and Other Groups from East Florida, 1763–1764," *Florida Historical Society*, 19 (1940), 146; Robert L. Gold, "The Settlement of the East Florida Spaniards in Cuba, 1763–1766," *FHQ*, 42 (1964), 216–17. Also see chapter 3, note 35 above.

25. Alexander Hewatt, *An Historical Account of the Rise and Progress of the Colonies of South Carolina and Georgia*, 2 vols. (London, 1779), 1: 120. Hewatt's

judgment was shared by many: "The rice can only be cultivated by negroes," declared La Rochefauld-Liancourt in 1799. *Travels through the United States of North America,* 2 vols. (London, 1799), 1: 622; John Drayton, *A View of South-Carolina, as Respects Her Natural and Civil Concerns* (Charleston, 1802), 147.

26. Coclanis, *Shadow of a Dream,* 114–16; also Nash, "Urbanization in the Colonial South," 3–29; Betty Wood, *Women's Work, Men's Work: The Informal Slave Economies of Lowcountry Georgia* (Athens, Ga., 1995), 7, 192 n19–20.

27. Philip D. Morgan, "Black Life in Eighteenth-Century Charleston," *PAH,* new ser., 1 (1984), 188–90; Coclanis, *Shadow of a Dream,* 6.

28. Wood, *Women's Work, Men's Work,* 105–7; Morgan, "Charleston," 190; Charles Town *South-Carolina Gazette,* 29 Apr. 1732.

29. Carl Bridenbaugh, *Colonial Craftsmen* (New York, 1950), 139–41, and Bridenbaugh, *Cities in Revolt: Urban Life in America, 1743–1776* (New York, 1964), 88–89, 244, 274, 285–86; Richard B. Morris, *Government and Labor in Early America* (New York, 1946), 183–85; Leila Sellers, *Charleston Business on the Eve of the American Revolution* (Chapel Hill, N.C., 1934), 99–108; John Donald Duncan, "Servitude and Slavery in Colonial South Carolina, 1670–1776," unpub. doctoral diss., Emory University, 1971, 439–46; Kenneth Coleman, *Colonial Georgia, A History* (New York, 1976), 229–30; Morgan, "Charleston," 200–5; Wood, *Women's Work, Men's Work,* ch. 5; Wood, *Slavery in Georgia,* 131–32, 143–45; Peter H. Wood, "'Taking Care of Business' in Revolutionary South Carolina: Republicanism and The Slave Society," in Jeffrey J. Crow and Larry E. Tise, eds., *The Southern Experience in the American Revolution* (Chapel Hill, N.C., 1978), 273; Hewatt, *Account of South Carolina and Georgia,* 2: 97; Allen D. Candler et al., eds., *The Colonial Records of the State of Georgia,* 32 vols. (Atlanta, Ga., 1912), 18: 277–82; Charles S. Henry, comp., *A Digest of All the Ordinances of Savannah* (Savannah, Ga., 1854), 94–97; Cooper and McCord, comps., *Statutes at Large of South Carolina,* 2: 22–23; 7: 385–87, 9: 692–97; Donald R. Lennon and Ida Brooks Kellam, eds., *The Wilmington Town Book, 1743–1778* (Raleigh, N.C., 1973), 165–66; quotation in Barnwell, ed., "Diary of Timothy Ford," 142.

30. Philip D. Morgan has made the best estimates of slave skill in colonial Charles Town. One calculation, based on a listing of inventoried slaves, places the proportion of slaves engaged in skilled labor at 63 percent in 1770 (down from 73 percent) a decade earlier. Another calculation based on the information in advertisements for runaway slaves places the proportion engaged in skilled labor at 43 percent (down from 50 percent in 1760). The proportion of slaves skilled increased from 9 to 10 percent in 1730 to 13 to 16 percent in the 1770s. Philip D. Morgan, "Colonial South Carolina Runaways: Their Significance for Slave Culture," *S&A,* 6 (1985), 63. The rise of the slave artisanry can be traced in the struggle between white tradesmen and slaveholders over the employment of skilled slaves, a struggle complicated by the fact that many white tradesmen *were* slaveholders. Wood, *Women's Work, Men's Work,* chs. 5 and 7. Quotation in Morris, *Government and Labor in Early America,* 184, generally 182–88. Quotation in *Runaway Advertisements,* 4: 59 (Savannah *Georgia Gazette,* 16 Nov. 1774).

31. See note 30 above and sale of estate of gunsmith Joseph Massey, which

included "A Negro Man and Boy Which Can Work at the Gunsmith's Trade."
Charles Town *South-Carolina Gazette,* 25 June 1737, cited in Duncan, "Servitude
and Slavery," 192–93, and also 437–39. E. Milby Burton, *Charleston Furniture, 1700–
1825* (Charleston, 1955), 10, and Burton, *South Carolina Silversmiths, 1690–1860*
(Rutland, Vt., 1968), 207–8. The regulations governing slave artisans and porters in
the Charles Town *South-Carolina Gazette,* 25 Dec. 1740, 9 July 1750, 3 June 1751, and
14 Nov. 1761, provides telling evidence, as do the complaints on failure to enforce the
regulations, see *ibid.,* 14 Nov 1763, all cited in Duncan, "Servitude and Slavery,"
440–41.

 32. "Presentments of the Charles Town Grand Jury, 1733–1734," *SCHM,* 25
(1924), 193; Wood, *Black Majority,* 209 n48; Wood, *Women's Work, Men's Work,*
82–83, 101–21; Morgan, "Charleston," 191–94; Wood, *Slavery in Colonial Georgia,*
chs. 8–9; quotation in Peter H. Wood, "'Taking Care of Business,'" 273; Morris,
Government and Labor in Early America, quotation on 185. Cooper and McCord,
comps., *South Carolina Statutes at Large,* 2: 22–23; 3: 395–99, 456–61; 7: 343, 345–47,
356–68, 385–97, 412–13; Lennon and Kellam, eds., *Wilmington Town Book,* 165–69,
204–5, 210–11, 219–21, 225–29, 234, 238, for the various regulations governing the
slaves' living out and hiring out. For slaves pocketing their earnings, see *Laurens
Papers,* 10: 201.

 33. Savannah *Georgia Gazette,* 6 July 1768; Wood, *Women's Work, Men's Work,*
128–31; Morgan, "Charleston," 192–93.

 34. Wood, *Women's Work, Men's Work,* ch. 4; Robert Olwell, "'Loose, Idle, and
Disorderly': Slave Women in the Eighteenth-Century Charleston Marketplace," in
David Barry Gaspar and Darlene Clark Hine, eds., *More than Chattel: Black Women
and Slavery in the Americas* (Bloomington, Ind., 1996), 97–110; Morgan, "Charles-
ton," 191–97; "Presentments of the Charles Town Grand Jury, 1733–1734," 194–95;
Charles Town *South-Carolina Gazette,* 14 Nov. 1761, 10 Oct. 1763, 25 Jan. 1770
(quotation); 24 Sept. 1772; Charles Town *City Gazette,* 23 Mar. 1734, 19 Mar. 37, 24
Sept. 1772 (quotation); Charles Town *South Carolina Gazette and Country Journal,* 3
Mar. 1773, 1 June 1773.

 35. Jones, ed., "John Martin Boltzius's Trip to Charleston," 104, 106–7, quotation on 101; "Letter from Mr. John Martin Bolzius to Revd. Mr. Whitefield," 24 Dec.
1745, in Candler, ed., *Colonial Records of Georgia,* 24: 434–44; Charles Town *South
Carolina Gazette,* 17 Sept. 1772.

 36. Quotes in Charles Town *South Carolina Gazette,* 17 Sept. 1772, and Jones,
ed., "John Martin Boltzius's Trip to Charleston," 101; Mark Anthony De Wolfe
Howe, ed., "Journal of Josiah Quincy, Junior," *Massachusetts Historical Society
Proceedings,* 49 (1915–1916), 424–81, 463; Winthrop D. Jordan, "American Chiaroscuro: The Status and Definition of Mulattoes in the British Colonies," *WMQ,* 19
(1962), 193–200.

 37. Quotations in Charles Town *South-Carolina Gazette* in Robert M. Weir,
Colonial South Carolina: A History (Millwood, N.Y., 1983), 190, and Charles Town
South-Carolina and American General Gazette, 6 Jan. 1775; Howe, ed., "Journal of
Josiah Quincy, Junior," 424–81; Henry, comp., A *Digest of All the Ordinances of*

Savannah, 95–97; Alexander Edwards, comp., *Ordinances of the City Council of Charleston* (Charleston, S.C., 1802), 65–68; Cooper and McCord, comps., *Statutes at Large of South Carolina,* 7: 363, 380–81, 393; Lennon and Kellam, eds., *Wilmington Town Book,* xxx–xxxi, 165–68, 204–5; Duncan, "Servitude and Slavery," 467–69, 481–84; and Sellers, *Charleston Business,* 99–102, 106–8.

38. Wood, *Women's Work, Men's Work,* 70–79, 135–37, and Wood, *Slavery in Colonial Georgia,* 85, 114–15, 159–62; Morgan, "Charleston," 206–8, 222–29; Lennon and Kellam, eds., *Wilmington Town Book,* 168–69, 187, 205–14, 234, 238; Alan D. Watson, "Impulse toward Independence: Resistance and Rebellion among North Carolina Slaves, 1750–1775," *JNH,* 63 (1978), 319. When Flora ran off to Savannah in 1774, her owner "supposed" her "to be haboured under the Bluff by sailors." *Runaway Advertisements,* 4: 53 (Savannah *Georgia Gazette,* 13 July 1774). For laws against trading with slaves, see Cooper and McCord, comps., *South Carolina Statutes at Large,* 3: 163, 7: 353, 367.

39. Harvey H. Jackson, "Hugh Bryan and the Evangelical Movement in Colonial South Carolina," *WMQ,* 43 (1986), 594–614; Allan Gallay, "The Origins of the Slaveholders' Paternalism: George Whitefield, the Bryan Family, and the Great Awakening in the South," *JSoH,* 53 (1987), 369–94; Charles S. Bolton, *Southern Anglicanism: The Church of England in Colonial South Carolina* (Westport, Conn., 1982), 118; John C. Van Horne, "Impediments to the Christianization and Education of Blacks in Colonial America: The Case of the Associates of Dr. Bray," *HMPEC,* 50 (1981), 243–69. James B. Lawrence, "Religious Education of the Negro in the Colony of Georgia," *GHQ,* 14 (1930), 41, 47–51.

40. The handful of black men and women who gained legal freedom were closely allied with the planter class, often as the product of a sexual liaison. Robert Olwell, "Becoming Free: Manumission and the Genesis of a Free Black Community in South Carolina, 1740–90," *S&A,* 17 (1996), 1–19; Wood, *Black Majority,* 100–3; Weir, *Colonial South Carolina,* 199–200; Coclanis, *Shadow of a Dream,* 256 n123, 115; Morgan, "Charleston," 188, 193–94; Marina Wikramanayake, *A World in Shadow: The Free Black in Antebellum South Carolina* (Columbia, S.C., 1973), ch. 1. A sample of manumissions taken from South Carolina records between 1729 and 1776 indicates that two-thirds of the slaves freed were female and one-third of the slaves freed were of mixed racial origins at a time when the slave population of South Carolina was disproportionately male and black. Duncan, "Servitude and Slavery," 395–98. For the free black population of East Florida, see John J. TePaske, "The Fugitive Slave: Intercolonial Rivalry and Spanish Slave Policy, 1687–1764," in *Eighteenth-Century Florida and Its Borderlands,* ed. Samuel Proctor (Gainesville, Fla., 1975), 11.

41. Charles Town *South-Carolina Gazette,* 24 May 1773; Duncan, "Servitude and Slavery," quotation on 234, also see 233–37; Klaus G. Loewald et al., eds., "Johann Martin Bolzius Answers a Questionnaire on Carolina and Georgia," WMQ, 14 (1957), quotation on 236; Cooper and McCord, comps., *Statutes at Large of South Carolina,* 7: 396–412; Wood, *Women's Work, Men's Work,* ch. 6.

42. *Laurens Papers,* quotation on 5: 53; Wood, "'Taking Care of Business,'" 277–78.

43. Winthrop D. Jordan, *White over Black: American Attitudes toward the Negro, 1550–1812* (Chapel Hill, N.C., 1968), 144–50, 167–78, and Jordan, "American Chiaroscuro," 186–200, quotation on 187; Wood, *Black Majority*, 100–3; Coclanis, *Shadow of a Dream*, 256 n123. A sample of manumissions taken from the South Carolina records between 1729 and 1776 indicates that two-thirds of the slaves freed were female and one-third of the slaves freed were of mixed racial origins at a time when the slave population of South Carolina was disproportionately male and black. Duncan, "Servitude and Slavery," 395–98; Olwell, "Becoming Free." 5–7.

44. *Runaway Advertisements,* 3: 650–1 (Charles Town *South Carolina Gazette and Country Journal,* 21 Nov. 1769).

45. Theresa A. Singleton, "The Archeology of Afro-American Slavery in Coastal Georgia: A Regional Perception of Slave Household and Community Patterns," unpub. doctoral diss., University of Florida, 1980; Thomas R. Wheaton and Patrick H. Garrow, "Acculturation and the Archeological Record in the Carolina Lowcountry"; Lynne G. Lewis, "The Planter Class: The Archeological Record at Drayton Hall"; Kenneth E. Lewis, "Plantation Layout and Function in the South Carolina Lowcountry"; and Steven L. Jones, "The African-American Tradition in Vernacular Architecture," all in Theresa A. Singleton, ed., *The Archeology of Slavery and Plantation Life* (San Diego, 1985), 35–65, 121–40, 199–200, 239–59; quotations in Philip D. Morgan and George D. Terry, "Slavery in Microcosm: A Conspiracy Scare in Colonial South Carolina," *SS,* 21 (1982), 128; Daniel L. Schafer, "Plantation Development in British East Florida: A Case Study of the Earl of Egmont," *FHQ,* 63 (1984), 176–77; Margaret Washington Creel, *"A Peculiar People": Slave Religion and Community-Culture among the Gullahs* (New York, 1988). "In all Country Settlements," observed Alexander Garden in 1740, "they live in contiguous Houses and often 2, 3 or 4 Famillys of them in One House . . . They labour together and converse almost wholly among themselves." Frank J. Klingberg, *An Appraisal of the Negro in Colonial South Carolina* (Washington, D.C., 1941), 106.

46. *Laurens Papers,* 3: 203, 5: 370. Laurens was only one of many planters who recognized that "a breeding Woman" might "in ten Years time . . . double her worth in her own Children." *Ibid.,* 5: 370. Quotation in Klingberg, *An Appraisal of the Negro in Colonial South Carolina,* 106.

47. Loewald et al., eds., "Bolzius Questionnaire," quotation on 236. Cheryll Ann Cody, "A Note on Changing Patterns of Slave Fertility in the South Carolina Rice District, 1735–1865,'" *SS* 16 (1977), 457–63, and Cody, "Slave Demography and Family Formation: A Community Study of the Ball Family Plantations, 1720–1896," unpub. doctoral diss., University of Minnesota, 1982; Schafer, "'Yellow Silk Ferret Tied Round Their Wrists,'" 88–90; Littlefield, *Rice and Slaves,* 64–65.

48. Cooper and McCord, comps., *Statutes at Large of South Carolina,* 7: 397. The 1755 Georgia slave code, which was modeled on the 1740 South Carolina law, also allowed slaves to have Sunday to themselves. Wood, *Women's Work, Men's Work,* 15, 49–50. "Letters of the Honorable James Habersham," *GHC,* 6 (1904), 190–91.

49. *Laurens Papers,* 12: 368; Mark Catesby, *The Natural History of Carolina,*

Florida and the Bahama Islands, 2 vols. (London, 1731–43), xviii; quotation in Andrews, ed., *Journal of a Lady of Quality,* 176–77.

50. Quotation in *Laurens Papers,* 5: 99–100; Creel, *"A Peculiar People,"* 68; Loewald et al., eds., "Bolzius Questionnaire," 256–60; Charles Town Grand Jury Presentment, January 1772, SCDA&H.

51. Grand Jury Presentment, Beaufort, 1775, SCDA&H. The easy fraternization of plantation slaves and white nonslaveholders, often disreputable in the eyes of the planter class, became evident in the South Carolina General Assembly's investigation of a slave conspiracy in 1749. Morgan and Terry, "Slavery in Microcosm," 121–45. On trading, see Wood, *Women's Work, Men's Work,* ch. 3. For the repeated passage of laws prohibiting slaves from independently planting certain crops or from keeping stock, see Cooper and McCord, eds., *South Carolina Statutes at Large,* 3: 163, 7: 353, 367–68, 382, 409.

52. *Laurens Papers,* 4: 41, 616; 5: 19–20, 41, 57; C. C. Lucas to Charles Pinckney, 30 Jan. 1745/46, Pinckney Papers, Manuscript Division, Library of Congress, Washington, D.C.; Wood, *Women's Work, Men's Work,* 61–70; Morgan, "Work and Culture," 572–73; Morgan, "Task and Gang Systems," 208–12; Morgan, "Task and Gang Systems: The Organization of Labor on Plantations," in Elise Marienstras and Barbara Karsky, eds., *Autre temps, autre espace: Etudes sur l'Amerique pre-industrelle* (Nancy, 1986), 147–64; Olwell, "'A Reckoning of Accounts,'" 33–52; Chaplin, "Tidal Rice Cultivation and the Problem of Slavery in South Carolina and Georgia, 1760–1815," 33; Schafer, "'Yellow Silk Ferret Tied Round Their Wrists,'" 90.

53. Morgan, "Work and Culture," 563–99; Morgan, "Task and Gang Systems," 191–92.

54. See, for example, Chaplin, *Anxious Pursuit,* 230–31.

55. Schafer, "'Yellow Silk Ferret Tied Round Their Wrists,'" 81–2, 87; *Laurens Papers,* 5:227; Richard Hutson to Mr. Croll, 22 Aug. 1767, Richard Hutson Letters, Southern History Collection, University of North Carolina Library, Chapel Hill.

56. James M. Clifton, "The Rice Driver: His Role in Slave Management," *SCHM,* 82 (1981), 331–53; Duncan, "Servitude and Slavery," 427–28. As Philip Morgan notes in his analysis of South Carolina runaways, "Drivers were conspicuously absent from the ranks of the skilled runaways." "Colonial South Carolina Runaways," 63.

57. Schoepf, *Travels through the Confederation,* 2: 157–52, 221; Chaplin, *Anxious Pursuits,* 198–99.

58. See, for example, advertisement in Charles Town *South-Carolina Gazette,* 3 Apr. 1762; Donnan, *Slave Trade,* 4: 288. Also Wood, *Black Majority,* 103–24, 196–211, 229–33; Schafer, "British East Florida," 175–77; Menard, "Africanization," 98–99; Hewatt, *Account of South Carolina and Georgia,* 2: 97; Morgan and Terry, "Slavery in Microcosm," 131–36. For the introduction of machines to increase production, improve efficiency, and ease the burden on slaves, see Chaplin, *Anxious Pursuit,* ch. 5, esp. 137–38.

59. Quoted in Schafer, "'Yellow Silk Ferret Tied Round Their Wrists,'" 77–78, 83; *Laurens Papers,* 5: 370.

60. Morgan and Terry, "Slavery in Microcosm," 121–45, quotation on 135; Schafer, "'Yellow Silk Ferret Tied Round Their Wrists,'" 78.

61. *Laurens Papers,* 5: 567–68.

62. Herbert Aptheker, "Maroons within the Present Limits of the United States," *JNH,* 24 (1939), 167–84; Duncan, "Servitude and Slavery," ch. 15; Morgan, "Colonial South Carolina Runaways," 58. Also Candler et al., eds., *Colonial Records of Georgia,* 12: 325–32; 19, pt. 1: 185.

63. Rachel N. Klein, *Unification of a Slave State: The Rise of the Planter Class in the South Carolina Backcountry, 1760–1808* (Chapel Hill, N.C., 1990), 18–21, 62–72. Robert L. Meriwether, *The Expansion of South Carolina, 1729–1765* (Kingsport, Tenn., 1940), 90, 96.

64. For planter preferences, see above note 5. The continual arrival of Africans into the lowcountry and the purchase of slaves in large groups enabled slaves not only to maintain a generalized knowledge of Africa but specific nationalities and ethnicities. In 1737 a South Carolina planter attempting to find a fugitive reminded his fellows that "as there is abundance of Negroes in this Province of that Nation, he may chance to be habour'd among some of them." *Runaway Advertisements,* 3: 29 (Charles Town *South Carolina Gazette* [Timothy], 6–13 July 1737). If slaveholders sensed the significance of national or ethnic solidarities, slaves valued them even more. Africans ran away in national groups often enough in the lowcountry to make masters wary of national or ethnic solidarities. *Runaway Advertisements,* 3: 23 (Charles Town *South Carolina Gazette* [Timothy], 3: 23 [out of the same cargo, 11 Sept. 1736]; 3: 341–42 (31 Oct. 1774). Runaways found a safe harbor with slaves of their own nation. (Littlefield, *Rice and Slaves,* 126.) The steady stream of Africans entering the lowcountry renewed the slaves' knowledge of West African life. Solidarities derived from Africa also appear to have influenced marriage patterns and other forms of social action. *Runaway Advertisements,* 3: 7 (Charles Town *South-Carolina Gazette,* 9–16 June 1733); quotation on 3: 467–68 (Charles Town *South-Carolina and American General Gazette,* 17–24 Feb. 1775). For Oswald, see Alexander Peter Kup, *A History of Sierra Leone 1400–1787* (Cambridge, UK, 1961), 190–91; *Laurens Papers,* 4: 585; 5: 370; Schafer, "'Yellow Silk Ferret Tied Round Their Wrists,'" 79–85.

65. Van Horne, ed., *Religious Philanthropy,* 138, 115–16. Beginning in 1727 and continuing into the nineteenth century, the South Carolina legislature attempted to force planters to maintain the presence of a white man on the plantations. Cooper and McCord, comps., *South Carolina Statutes at Large,* 2: 272–74; Loewald et al., eds., "Bolzius Questionnaire," 234; Charles Town *South-Carolina Gazette,* 2 June 1766, 31 Jan. 1771. "All my expense was upon Negroes who are walking about, no white face belonging to the plantation but an overseer." Daniel F. Schafer, "'Yellow Silk Ferret Tied Round Their Wrists,'" 76.

66. Quotation in Hewatt, *Account of South Carolina and Georgia,* 2: 100.

67. Allan Gallay, "The Origins of the Slaveholders' Paternalism: George White-field, the Bryan Family, and the Great Awakening in the South," *JSoH,* 53 (1987), 369–94; Gallay, "Planters and Slaves in the Great Awakening," in John Boles, ed., *Masters and Slaves in the House of the Lord: Race and Religion in the American South, 1740–1870* (Lexington, Ky., 1988), 19–36; Gallay, *The Formation of a Planter*

Elite, 30–54; Sylvia R. Frey, "Shaking the Dry Bones: The Dialectic of Conversion," in Ted Ownby, ed., *Black and White Cultural Interaction in the Antebellum South* (Jackson, Miss., 1993), 26–28; Daniel T. Morgan, "The Great Awakening in South Carolina, 1740–1775," *South Atlantic Quarterly,* 70 (1971), 595; Harvey H. Jackson, "Hugh Bryan and the Evangelical Movement in Colonial South Carolina," *WMQ,* 43 (1986), 594–614.

68. *Runaway Advertisements,* 3: 82 (Charles Town *South Carolina Gazette* [Timothy], 11–18 April 1748), 4: 22 (Savannah *Georgia Gazette,* 3 June 1767), 62 (Savannah *Georgia Gazette,* 19 Apr. 1775).

69. Wood, *Black Majority,* 181–85; Cheryll Ann Cody, "There Was No 'Absolom' on the Ball Plantations: Slave-Naming Practices in the South Carolina Low Country, 1720–1865," *AHR,* 92 (1987), 563–96, and Cody, "Naming, Kinship, and Estate Dispersal: Notes on Slave Family Life on a South Carolina Plantation, 1786–1833," *WMQ,* 39 (1982), 192–211; Mary Beth Norton, Herbert G. Gutman, and Ira Berlin, "The Afro-American Family in the Age of Revolution," in Ira Berlin and Ronald Hoffman, eds., *Slavery and Freedom in the Age of the American Revolution* (Charlottesville, Va., 1983), 180–83.

70. Wood, *Black Majority,* esp. ch. 6; Lorenzo Dow Turner, *Africanisms in the Gullah Dialect* (Chicago, 1949); William R. Bascom, "Acculturation among the Gullah Negroes," *AA,* 43 (1941), 43–50; Klingberg, *An Appraisal of the Negro in South Carolina,* 20n, 138n; Hennig Cohen, "Slave Names in Colonial South Carolina," *American Speech,* 28 (1952): 102–7; Cody, "There Was No 'Absolom' on the Ball Plantation," 575.

71. John Michael Vlach, *The Afro-American Tradition in Decorative Arts* (Cleveland, 1978); Vlach, *Charleston Blacksmith: The Work of Philip Simmons* (Athens, Ga., 1981); Dale Rosengarten, *Row upon Row: Sea Grass Baskets of the South Carolina Lowcountry* (Columbia, S.C., 1986).

72. Creel, *"A Peculiar People,"* 101, 373 n43 and 44; also James Barclay, *The Voyages of and Travels of James Barclay* (London, 1777), 27.

73. Johann Ewald, *Diary of the American War,* ed. and trans. Joseph P. Justin (New Haven, Conn., 1979), 199, 203. On Gullah, see Turner, *Africanisms in the Gullah Dialect;* Frederic G. Cassidy, "The Place of Gullah," *American Speech,* 55 (1980), 3–16, and Cassidy, "Some Similarities between Gullah and Caribbean Creoles," in Michael B. Montgomery and Guy Bailey, eds., *Language Variety in the South: Perspectives in Black and White* (University, Ala., 1986), 30–37.

74. Klingberg, *An Appraisal of the Negro in Colonial South Carolina,* 116–17; Van Horne, ed., *Religious Philanthropy,* 104, 228–29; and Petition of John and William Morriss, 1791, and Petition from Camden Negroes, 1793, South Carolina Legislative Papers, SCDA&H. Lawrence, "Religious Education of the Negroes in the Colony of Georgia," 43–57.

75. The transcendent role of market women is glimpsed in the remarks of a "Stranger." Charles Town *South Carolina Gazette,* 24 Sept. 1772. For one planter's attempt to keep boatmen from mixing with his plantation hands, see *Laurens Papers,* 3: 509; 4: 298–99, 319, 616, 633, 661; 5: 2–3; and Sellers, *Charleston Business,* 106–8.

76. David, quoted in Morgan, "Charleston," 208–9.

77. Laurens Papers, 10: 206–8, 231–32; Frey, *Water from the Rock,* 54–56, and Frey, "Shaking the Dry Bones: The Dialectic of Conversion," 30; Robert A. Olwell, "'Domestick Enemies': Slavery and Political Independence in South Carolina, May 1775–March 1776," *JSoH, 55* (1989), 29–34.

7. Growth and the Transformation of Black Life in the North

1. Quotation in Gary B. Nash, *Forging Freedom: The Formation of Philadelphia's Black Community, 1720–1840* (Cambridge, Mass., 1988), 10.

2. Ernst Van Den Boogaart, "The Servant Migration to New Netherland, 1624–1664," in P. C. Emmer, ed., *Colonialism and Migration; Indentured Labour before and after Slavery* (Dordrecht, 1986), 58; Graham Russell Hodges, *Slavery and Freedom in the Rural North: African Americans in Monmouth County, New Jersey, 1665–1865* (Madison, Wisc., 1996), 11–14; Robert V. Wells, *The Population of the British Colonies in America before 1776* (Princeton, N.J., 1975), 112.

3. Richard S. Dunn, "Servants and Slaves: The Recruitment and Employment of Labor," in Jack P. Greene and J. R. Pole, eds., *Colonial British North America: Essays in the New History of the Early Modern Era* (Baltimore, 1984), 157–94; Bernard Bailyn, "The Idea of Atlantic History," *Itinerario, 20* (1996), 19–44.

4. Nash, *Forging Freedom,* 9; Gary B. Nash and Jean R. Soderlund, *Freedom by Degrees: Emancipation in Pennsylvania and Its Aftermath* (New York, 1991), 14–16; Jean R. Soderlund, *Quakers & Slavery: A Divided Spirit* (Princeton, N.J., 1985), 64; and Soderlund, "Black Importation and Migration into Southeastern Pennsylvania, 1682–1810," *PAPS, 133* (1989), 144–47; Elaine F. Crane, *A Dependent People: Newport, Rhode Island, in the Revolutionary Era* (New York, 1985), 76; Shane White, *Somewhat More Independent: The End of Slavery in New York City, 1770–1810* (Athens, Ga., 1991), 3–4, 25–27; Edgar J. McManus, *A History of Negro Slavery in New York* (Syracuse, N.Y., 1966), 25; Wells, *Population of the British Colonies,* 112–15, 135–36.

5. Boogaart, "Servant Migration," 65–71; U.S. Bureau of the Census, *A Century of Population Growth* (Washington, D.C., 1909), 150–51, 156–57; Gary B. Nash, *The Urban Crucible: Social Change, Political Consciousness, and the Origins of the American Revolution* (Cambridge, Mass., 1979), 13–15, 106–111, 320–21; Nash, "Slaves and Slaveowners in Colonial Philadelphia," *WMQ, 30* (1973), 223–56; Nash and Soderlund, *Freedom by Degrees,* 14–16; Soderlund, *Quakers & Slavery,* 58, 64; Thomas J. Archdeacon, *New York City, 1664–1710: Conquest and Change* (Ithaca, N.Y., 1976), 46–47; Lorenzo Johnston Greene, *The Negro in Colonial New England* (New York, 1971), 78, 81–82, 84–88, 92–93; David E. Van Deventer, *The Emergence of Provincial New Hampshire, 1623–1741* (Baltimore, 1976), 113–14; Lynne Withey, *Urban Growth in Colonial Rhode Island: Newport and Providence in the Eighteenth Century* (Albany, N.Y., 1984), 71; Crane, *A Dependent People,* 49–52; Bruce C. Daniels, *Dissent and Conformity on Narragansett Bay: The Colonial Rhode Island Town* (Middletown, Conn., 1983), 57–59; Jackson Turner Main, *Society and Economy in Colonial Connecticut* (Princeton, N.J., 1985), 82, 181, 269, 283–84, 294–95, 305, esp. 366.

6. Nash and Soderlund, *Freedom by Degrees,* 16–20; Soderlund, *Quakers & Slavery,* 58–59, 64.

7. Richard B. Morris, *Government and Labor in Early America* (New York, 1946), 182–84; Nash, *Forging Freedom,* 11; Nash, *The Urban Crucible,* 107–9, 320–21; Nash, "Slaves and Slaveowners in Colonial Philadelphia," 248–52 and table 8; Nash and Soderlund, *Freedom by Degrees,* 21–22; Jean R. Soderlund, "Black Women in Colonial Pennsylvania," *PMHB,* 107 (1983), 51–54; Arthur Zilversmit, *The First Emancipation: The Abolition of Slavery in the North* (Chicago, 1967), 36–40; Archdeacon, *New York City,* 89–90, esp. 89 n16; Michael Kammen, *Colonial New York: A History* (New York, 1975), 182; Greene, *Negro in New England,* 111–19; Carl Bridenbaugh, *Cities in Revolt: Urban Life in America, 1743–1776* (New York, 1955), 88, 285–86; White, *Somewhat More Independent,* 12. For the success of white cartmen in excluding black competitors, see Graham Russell Hodges, *New York City Cartmen, 1667–1850* (New York, 1986), 25–26, 152–59. Quotation in Patrick M'Robert, "Tour through Part of the North Provinces of America," ed. Carl Bridenbaugh, *PMHB,* 59 (1935), 142.

8. Quotation in Morris, *Government and Labor in Early America,* 183. Also John F. Watson, *Annals of Philadelphia,* 2 vols. (Philadelphia, 1830), 1: 98; Herbert L. Osgood, ed., *Minutes of the Common Council of the City of New York, 1675–1776,* 8 vols. (New York, 1905), 1: 136–37; Leonard P. Stavisky, "Negro Craftsmen in Early America," *AHR,* 54 (1949), 315–25; Nash, *Urban Crucible,* 107–9, 320–21; Kammen, *Colonial New York,* 182; Hodges, *New York City Cartmen,* 25–26; Greene, *Negro in New England,* 111–19.

9. John E. Pomfret, *Colonial New Jersey: A History* (New York, 1973), 210; McManus, *New York Slavery,* 42–44; Nash and Soderlund, *Freedom by Degrees,* 33–36; Greene, *Negro in New England,* 321; Christian McBurney, "The South Kingston Planters: Country Gentry in Colonial Rhode Island," *RIH,* 45 (1987), 86–90.

10. Peter O. Wacker and Paul G. E. Clemens, *Land Use in Early New Jersey: A Historical Geography* (Newark, N.J., 1995), 100–1; Hodges, *Rural North,* ch. 2, esp. 45–46.

11. Wacker and Clemens, *Land Use in Early New Jersey,* ch. 7, esp. 244; Hodges, *Rural North,* ch. 2.

12. Hodges, *Rural North,* 47–48. For Truth's experience as a slave in New York's Ulster County, see Nell Irvin Painter, *Sojourner Truth: A Life, A Symbol* (New York, 1996), chs. 2, 18, esp. 171–72.

13. Quotation in Nash, *Forging Freedom,* 9–11; Soderlund, "Black Importations," 146; Sharon V. Salinger, *"To Serve Well and Faithfully": Labor and Indentured Servants in Pennsylvania, 1682–1800* (Cambridge, UK, 1987), 140; James B. Lydon, "New York and the Slave Trade, 1700–1774," *WMQ,* 35 (1978), 387–88; Hodges, *Rural North,* 8.

14. Nash, "Slaves and Slaveowners in Colonial Philadelphia," 226–32; Nash, *Forging Freedom,* 10–11; Soderlund, "Black Importation," 145–46; Hodges, *Rural North,* 8; Lydon, "New York and the Slave Trade," 387–88; Darold D. Wax, "Quaker Merchants and the Slave Trade in Colonial Pennsylvania," *PMHB,* 86 (1962), 145; Wax, "Africans on the Delaware: The Pennsylvania Slave Trade, 1759–1765," *PH,* 50

(1983), 38–49; Wax, "Negro Imports into Pennsylvania, 1720–1766," 256–57, 280–87; Wax, "The Negro Slave Trade in Colonial Philadelphia," unpub. doctoral diss., University of Washington, 1962, 32.

15. Quotation in Nash, *Forging Freedom*, 11.

16. William D. Piersen, *Black Yankees: The Development of an Afro-American Subculture in Eighteenth-Century New England* (Amherst, Mass., 1988), 7.

17. See, for example, Philadelphia *Pennsylvania Gazette*, 17 June 1734 and 21 Feb. 1776, in Billy G. Smith and Richard Wojtowicz, eds., *Blacks Who Stole Themselves: Advertisements for Runaways in the Pennsylvania Gazette, 1728–1790* (Philadelphia, 1989), 18, 128; *Philadelphia Journal*, 27 May 1762, quoted in Vivienne L. Kruger, "Born to Run: The Slave Family in Early New York, 1626–1827," unpub. doctoral diss., Columbia University, 1985, 68.

18. Piersen, *Black Yankees*, 6–8, 179 n19.

19. Quotation in Watts, *Letterbook of John Watts*, 31; Edgar J. McManus, *Black Bondage in the North* (Syracuse, N.Y., 1973), 38–39; Wells, *Population of the British Colonies*, 74–75, 85–86, 93–94, 102–4, 138–40, 274; White, *Somewhat More Independent*, 12–13 n24; Evarts B. Greene and Virginia D. Harrington, *American Population before the Federal Census of 1790* (New York, 1932), 95–104; Wax, "Preference for Slaves in Colonial America," 400–1; U.S. Bureau of the Census, *A Century of Population Growth*, 149–84; Greene, *Negro in New England*, 93–96; Main, *Society and Economy in Colonial Connecticut*, 178–79, 197, Appendix 5A; Kruger, "Born to Run," 43, also 305; Hodges, *Rural North*, 16–17. The sex ratio in Philadelphia, however, tended to be balanced. See Nash and Soderlund, *Freedom by Degrees*, 23–24.

20. Susan E. Klepp, *Philadelphia in Transition: A Demographic History of the City and Its Occupational Groups, 1720–1830* (New York, 1989), 233, and Klepp, "Seasoning and Society: Racial Differences in Mortality in Eighteenth-Century Philadelphia," *WMQ*, 51 (1994), 474, 477–506; Nash and Soderlund, *Freedom by Degrees*, 15, 24–25; Nash, *Forging Freedom*, 33–34; White, *Somewhat More Independent*, 88–92; Kruger, "Born to Run," 424–31; John B. Blake, *Public Health in the Town of Boston, 1630–1822* (Cambridge, Mass., 1959), chs. 5–6; Piersen, *Black Yankee*, 19–21; Crane, *A Dependent People*, 80. The majority of slaveholders in Boston, Philadelphia, and New York owned only one or two slaves, and a tiny fraction of a percent owned more than nine, Gary Nash, "Forging Freedom: The Emancipation Experience in the Northern Seaport Cities, 1775–1820," in Ira Berlin and Ronald Hoffman, eds., *Slavery and Freedom in the Age of the American Revolution* (Charlottesville, Va., 1983), 27–30, esp. tables 6–7; White, *Somewhat More Independent*, 88–92; Hodges, *Rural North*, 15–18.

21. Although focused on colonial New York, the fullest discussion of the slave family in the North is Kruger, "Born to Run," esp. ch. 4. Also McManus, *Slavery in the North*; Nash, *Forging Freedom*, 11–16; Nash and Soderlund, *Freedom by Degrees*, 25; Nash, *Forging Freedom*, 33; Klepp, "Seasoning and Society," 475–77; Main, *Colonial Connecticut*, 178–79; Joyce D. Goodfriend, *Before the Melting Pot: Society and Culture in Colonial New York City, 1664–1730* (Princeton, N.J., 1992), 118.

Quotation in Kruger, "Born to Run," 329. Between 1767 and 1775 fewer than 100 black children were born and survived in Philadelphia, while at the same time some 679 slaves and free blacks died in the city.

22. Quotation in McManus, *Black Bondage in the North,* 38; Bridenbaugh, *Cities in Revolt,* 88, 285–86, and *Cities in the Wilderness,* 163, 200–01; Nash, "Slaves and Slaveowners in Colonial Pennsylvania," 243–44; Archdeacon, *New York City,* 89–90; Nash and Soderlund, *Freedom by Degrees,* 27–29; Rossiter, *A Century of Population Growth,* 170–80; McManus, *New York Slavery,* 44–45, and *Black Bondage in the North,* 37–39; Crane, *A Dependent People,* 77; Main, *Colonial Connecticut,* 177–79; and Wells, *Population in the British Colonies,* 116–23; Nash and Soderlund, *Freedom by Degrees,* 32. The low ratio of women to children may have been the result of high child mortality as well as low fertility. In 1788 J. B. Brissot de Warville observed, "Married Negroes certainly have as many children as whites, but it has been observed that in the cities the death rate of Negro children is higher." Briscot de Warville, *New Travels in the United States of America, 1788,* ed. Durand Echeverria (Cambridge, Mass., 1964), 232n. The shortage of African women and a sexual balance among Indians and, to a lesser extent, whites that favored women encouraged black men to marry Indian and, occasionally, white women, especially in New England; Winthrop D. Jordan, "American Chiaroscuro: The Status and Definition of Mulattoes in the British Colonies," *WMQ,* 19 (1962), 197–98, esp. n28.

23. Kruger, "Born to Run," 169–76, ch. 7, esp. 321–38; Klepp, *Philadelphia in Transition,* 475–76; Nash and Soderlund, *Freedom by Degrees,* 23–26; Soderlund, "Black Importation," 147–48. Franklin quoted in Nash and Soderlund, *Freedom by Degrees,* xii.

24. Charles Z. Lincoln, William H. Johnson, and A. Judd Northrop, comps., *The Colonial Laws of New York from the Year 1664 to the Revolution,* 5 vols. (Albany, N.Y., 1894–96), 1: 764–65; Bernard Bush, comp., *Laws of the Royal Colony of New Jersey, 1703–1756, New Jersey Archives,* 3rd ser., 5 vols. (Trenton, N.J., 1977–86), 2: 130–37; James T. Mitchell and Henry Flanders, comps., *The Statutes at Large of Pennsylvania from 1682 to 1801,* 17 vols. (Harrisburg, 1896–1915), 4, 59–64; J. H. Trumball and C. J. Hoadly, eds., *The Public Records of Connecticut,* 15 vols (Hartford, 1850–90), 4: 375–76, 408; 5: 233; John R. Bartlett, ed., *Records of the Colony of Rhode Island and Providence Plantations,* 10 vols. (Providence, 1857), 2: 251–53; Zilversmit, *The First Emancipation,* 16–19; Goodfriend, *Before the Melting Pot,* 116–17; Nash and Soderlund, *Freedom by Degrees,* 61–62.

25. "Throughout the pre-Revolutionary period," write Gary B. Nash and Jean R. Soderlund in their study of Pennsylvania, "manumissions were rare." Nash and Soderlund tell of the excruciatingly slow exodus of black people from bondage in one of the few places where the issue of slavery's legitimacy had been raised. Nash and Soderlund, *Freedom by Degrees,* ch. 2, quotation on 57. Nash, *Forging Freedom,* 32–37. Of the 437 slaves freed by their masters in a sample of testamentary declarations from 1669 to 1829, only nineteen were freed between 1669 and 1717 and only 103 were freed between 1717 and 1771, Kruger, "Born to Run," ch. 10, esp. 593–97. Also see White, *Somewhat More Independent,* 153; Hodges, *Rural North,* 61–62.

26. Census takers failed to differentiate between free and slave blacks in the northern colonies. The statement by one historian of New York slavery that "free blacks before the first federal census in 1790 were generally either not enumerated by census takers or were mistakenly counted as slaves" appears to be true for other northern colonies. Kruger, "Born to Run," 601. See also Greene, *Negro in New England,* 97; Goodfriend, *Before the Melting Pot,* 13, 115–117; Shane White, "'We Dwell in Safety and Pursue Our Honest Callings': Free Blacks in New York City, 1783–1810," *JAmH,* 75 (1988), 448. The best assessment of the size of the North's free black population prior to the Revolution has been made by Jean Soderlund from the manumission records in Philadelphia. Soderlund estimates that in 1767 there were fifty-seven free blacks in Philadelphia, who made up about 4 percent of the city's black population. The free black population increased rapidly in the years that followed, with the beginning of Quaker manumissions, but still in 1775 Soderlund calculates there were 114 free blacks in Philadelphia, who composed 14 percent of a greatly reduced black population. Free blacks made up an even smaller percentage of the black population in the countryside. Soderlund, "Black Importation," 148, 151. The Quakers' decision to rid themselves of slavery created a small spurt of manumissions in the years prior to the Revolution. See Nash and Soderlund, *Freedom by Degrees,* ch. 2 and 74–88; Nash, *Forging Freedom,* 32–36; Kruger, "Born to Run," 52–56, 608–14; John Cox, Jr., *Quakerism in the City of New York* (New York, 1930), 59–60; Hodges, *Rural North,* 62–63.

27. Greene, *Negro in New England,* ch. 11; Piersen, *Black Yankees,* 46–48; Mitchell and Flanders, comps., *Statutes at Large of Pennsylvania,* 4: 49–64; Lincoln, Johnson, and Northrup, eds., *Colonial Laws of New York,* 1: 761–67; Hodges, *Rural North,* 23; Kruger, "Born to Run," ch. 10; Zilversmit, *The First Emancipation,* 16–19.

28. See, for example, Lincoln, Johnson, and Northrup, eds., *Colonial Laws of New York,* 2: 679–81; Bush, comp., *Laws of New Jersey,* 2: 28–29.

29. John Hepburn, "The American Defense of the Christian Golden Rule," in Roger Bruns, ed., *Am I Not a Man and a Brother: The Antislavery Crusade of Revolution America, 1688–1788* (New York, 1977), 19. The point is made more fully in Klepp, "Seasoning and Society," 487. The number of free people of African descent with surnames declined after the Dutch were ousted from New Netherland. See Kruger, "Born to Run," 61 n22.

30. "'The Outcasts of the Nations of the Earth': The New York Conspiracy of 1741 in Atlantic Perspective," in Peter Linebaugh and Marcus Rediker, *The Many-Headed Hydra: The Adventures of the Atlantic Proletariat* (Boston: Beacon Press, forthcoming); Thomas J. Davis, *A Rumor of Revolt: The "Great Negro Plot" in Colonial New York* (New York, 1985); Daniel Horsmanden, *The New York Conspiracy,* ed. Thomas J. Davis (Boston, 1971).

31. James Oliver Horton and Lois E. Horton, *In Hope of Liberty: Culture, Community and Protest among Northern Free Blacks, 1700–1860* (New York, 1997), 16–17, 78–79.

32. Hodges, *Rural North,* 66–69; Pierson, *Black Yankees,* 49–61; John Van Horne, "Impediments to the Christianization and Education of Blacks in Colonial

America," *HMPEC,* 50 (1981), 260; Lawrence W. Towner, "'A Fondness for Freedom': Servant Protest in Puritan Society," *WMQ,* 19 (1962), 201–19; Franklin B. Dexter, ed., *The Literary Diary of Ezra Stiles,* 3 vols. (New York, 1901), 1: 247–48, 294, 355, 415, quotation on 213–14; John C. Van Horne, ed., *Religious Philanthropy and Colonial Slavery: The American Correspondence of the Associates of Dr. Bray, 1717–1777* (Urbana, Ill., 1985), 193–94, 220–21, 239–40, 247–48, 271–72, 315, 326. From among the slaves who attended SPG schools and registered their marriages at the Anglican churches, a small cadre of leaders began to emerge. In Newport, John Quamino, who had "tasted the Grace of the Lord Jesus" and wished "that his Relations and Countrymen in Africa might come to the knowledge of and taste the same blessed thing," led his fellow slaves in prayer in the home of a pious Newport Congregationist. Quamino and another African-born slave, Bristol Yamma, were later sent to Princeton to study.

33. Goodfriend, *Before the Melting Pot,* 122–27, quotation on 122; Kenneth Scott, "The Slave Insurrection in New York in 1712," *NYHQ,* 45 (1961): 43–74, quotation on 47.

34. Quoted in the Philadelphia *Pennsylvania Gazette,* 22 June 1769, in Smith and Wojtowicz, eds., *Blacks Who Stole Themselves,* 92.

35. Piersen, *Black Yankees,* ch. 9. For resistance tied to African ways, see Robert C. Twombly, "Black Resistance to Slavery in Massachusetts," in William L. O'Neill, ed., *Insights and Parallels: Problems and Issues of American Social History* (Minneapolis, 1973), 26–32, and, for various association names, see Dorothy Porter, ed., *Early Negro Writing, 1760–1837* (Boston, 1971). Also James Deetz, *In Small Things Forgotten: The Archaeology of Early American Life* (Garden City, N.Y., 1977), 140–42; Vernon G. Baker, "Archeological Visibility of Afro-American Culture: An Example from Black Lucy's Garden, Andover, Massachusetts," in Robert Schuyler, ed., *Archaeological Perspectives on Ethnicity in America* (Farmingdale, N.Y., 1980), 34–35.

36. African slaves—many of whom did not yet speak English and still carried tribal names and markings—composed the majority of the participants in the New York slave insurrection of 1712, although most of the city's slaves were creoles. Scott, "Slave Insurrection in New York in 1712," 43–74, esp. 62–67.

37. Although they shared elements with other ceremonies of role reversal, Election Day and Pinkster Day were celebrated at different times of the year. My discussion is drawn from Joseph P. Reidy, "'Negro Election Day,' and Black Community Life in New England, 1750–1860," *MP,* 1 (1978): 102–17; Piersen, *Black Yankees,* ch. 10, 136; Shane White, "Pinkster: Afro-Dutch Syncretization in New York City and the Hudson Valley," *JAF,* 102 (1989), 68–75; White, *Somewhat More Independent,* 95–106; White, "Pinkster in Albany, 1803: A Contemporary Description," *NYH,* 70 (1989), 191–99; White, "'It Was a Proud Day': African Americans, Festivals, and Parades in the North, 1741–1834," *JAmH,* 81 (1994), 13–50; A. J. Williams-Myers, "Pinkster Carnival: Africanisms in the Hudson River Valley," *Afro-Americans in New York Life and History,* 9 (1985), 7–17; Woods, "The Negro in Early Pennsylvania," 451; and Alice Morse Earle, *Colonial Days in Old New York* (New York, 1896), 195–201; David Steven Cohen, "In Search of Carolus Africanus Rex: Afro-Dutch

Folklore in New York and New Jersey," *JAAHGS,* 5 (1984), 149–63. The name "Pink-ster" was originally related to the Dutch word for Whitsuntide or Pentecost—*Pfingsten* in German, according to White, *Somewhat More Independent,* 95. For comparative perspective see John Thornton, *Africa and Africans in the Making of the Atlantic World, 1400–1680* (Cambridge, UK, 1992), 202–5.

38. Quotations in Piersen, *Black Yankees,* 121; White, *Somewhat More Independent,* 97.

39. Quotations in Piersen, *Black Yankees,* 122–24.

40. Robert Dirks, *The Black Saturnalia: Conflict and Its Ritual Expression on British West Indian Slave Plantations* (Gainesville, Fla., 1987). Also Wayne K. Durrell, "Routine of Seasons: Labour Regimes and Social Ritual in an Antebellum Plantation Community," *S&A* 16 (1995), 161–87.

41. Piersen, *Black Yankees,* 129

42. Zilversmit, *First Emancipation,* 100–2, quotation on 101; Herbert Aptheker, ed., *A Documentary History of the Negro People in the United States,* 2 vols. (New York, 1951), 1: 6–9, quotation on 8; quotation in Benjamin Quarles, *The Negro in the American Revolution* (Chapel Hill, 1961), 39–40. Also see Bruns, ed., *Am I Not a Man and a Brother,* 337–40.

43. Hodges, *Rural North,* 90–92, quotation on 90.

44. Aptheker, ed., *Documentary History of the Negro People,* 1: 8–9, quotation on 8; Sidney Kaplan, "The 'Domestic Insurrections' of the Declaration of Independence," *JNH,* 61 (1976), 249–50; Zilversmit, *The First Emancipation,* 101, 112.

8. Stagnation and Transformation in the Lower Mississippi Valley

1. Thomas N. Ingersoll, "The Slave Trade and the Ethnic Diversity of Louisiana's Slave Community," *LH,* 37 (1996), 135–42; Gwendolyn Midlo Hall, *Africans in Colonial Louisiana: The Development of Afro-Creole Culture in the Eighteenth Century* (Baton Rouge, La., 1992), 160, 180–83; Daniel H. Usner, Jr., *Indians, Settlers, & Slaves in a Frontier Exchange Economy: The Lower Mississippi Valley before 1783* (Chapel Hill, N.C., 1992), 109. Only one shipment of African slaves is listed in Jean Mettas, *Repértoire des Expéditions Négrières Francaises au XVIIIe Siècle,* 2 vols.

2. Ingersoll, "Slave Trade and Ethnic Diversity," 140–45; Paul F. Lachance, "The Politics of Fear: French Louisiana and the Slave Trade, 1786–1809," *PS,* 1 (1979), 166–67, 196; Robin F. A. Fabel, "Anglo-Spanish Commerce in New Orleans during the American Revolutionary Era," in William S. Coker and Robert R. Rea, eds., *Anglo-Spanish Confrontation on the Gulf Coast during the American Revolution* (Pensacola, Fla., 1982), 25–53.

3. Antoine-Simon Le Page Du Pratz, *The History of Louisiana,* ed. Joseph G. Tregle, Jr. (Baton Rouge, La., 1975), 376–87, quotation on 380–81; James Thomas McGowan, "Creation of a Slave Society: Louisiana Plantations in the Eighteenth Century," unpub. doctoral diss., University of Rochester, 1976, 111–15.

4. McGowan, "Creation of a Slave Society," 126–28.

5. Du Pratz, *History of Louisiana,* 381, 386; Hall, *Africans in Colonial Louisiana,*

168–71, 304–5; McGowan, "Creation of a Slave Society," 119–21; Thomas N. Ingersoll, "Old New Orleans: Race, Class, Sex, and Order in the Early Deep South, 1718–1819," unpub. doctoral diss., University of California, Los Angeles, 1991, 208–9; Mary Veronica Micele, "The Influence of the Roman Catholic Church on Slavery in Colonial Louisiana under French Domination, 1718–1763," unpub. doctoral diss., Tulane University, 1979, 65–94; Jean Delanglez, *The French Jesuits in Lower Louisiana, 1700–1763* (Washington, D.C., 1935), 136; Emily Clark, "'By All the Conduct of Their Lives': A Laywomen's Confraternity in New Orleans, 1730–1744," *WMQ,* 54 (1997), 779–92; Gary B. Mills, *The Forgotten People: Cane River's Creoles of Color* (Baton Rouge, La., 1977), 2–3, 7.

6. McGowan, "Creation of a Slave Society," 116–32, quotation on 127; Hall, *Africans in Colonial Louisiana,* 183–86, quotation on 175; Ingersoll, "The Slave Trade and Ethnic Diversity," 138. On enforcement of the *Code Noir*'s provisions respecting the sanctity of the family, see Carl A. Brasseaux, "The Administration of the Slave Regulations in French Louisiana, 1724–1766," *LH,* 21 (1980), 141–42, 147–48.

7. Hall, *Africans in Colonial Louisiana,* 9–10, 175–77, 182–83, table 8; Usner, *Indians, Settlers, & Slaves,* 108; Acosta Rodriguez, *La problacion de la Luisiana espanola (1763–1803)* (Madrid, 1979), 110.

8. Hall, *Africans in Colonial Louisiana,* 250–51; Jacob M. Price, *France and the Chesapeake: A History of the French Tobacco Monopoly, 1674–1791,* 2 vols. (Ann Arbor, Mich., 1973), 1: ch. 13, esp. 357; John G. Clark, *New Orleans, 1718–1812: An Economic History* (Baton Rouge, La., 1970), 56; Brian E. Coutts, "Boom and Bust: The Rise and Fall of the Tobacco Industry in Spanish Louisiana, 1770–1790," *Americas,* 42 (1986), 289–309.

9. Usner, *Indians, Settlers, & Slaves,* ch. 4, esp. 106, 159; Clark, *New Orleans,* chs. 9–10, esp. 181–82; Hall, *Africans in Colonial Louisiana,* 252–53, 276–77; Jack D. L. Holmes, "Indigo in Colonial Louisiana and Florida," *LH,* 8 (1967), 333; Henry P. Dart and Laura L. Porteous, ed. and trans., "A Louisiana Indigo Plantation on Bayou Teche, 1773," *LHQ,* 9 (1926), 565–89. On the comparative success of indigo production in West Florida, see Robin F. A. Fabel, *The Economy of British West Florida, 1763–1783* (Tuscaloosa, Ala., 1988), 112–14.

10. J. Zitomersky, "Urbanization in French Colonial Louisiana (1706–1766)," *Annales, de demographie historique* (1974), 263–278; Usner, *Indians, Settlers, & Slaves,* 48–54.

11. Ingersoll, "Old New Orleans," 341; Kimberly S. Hanger, "Household and Community Structure among the Free Population of Spanish New Orleans, 1778," *LH,* 30 (1989), 63–79.

12. Clark, *New Orleans,* 47–53; Hall, *Africans in Colonial Louisiana,* 175–76; Usner, "From African Captivity to American Slavery," 39n.

13. Hall, *Africans in Colonial Louisiana,* 250; Usner, *Indians, Settlers, & Slaves,* ch. 5; Clark, *New Orleans,* 57–59; John Hebron Moore, "The Cyprus Lumber Industry in the Lower Mississippi Valley during the Colonial Period," *LH,* 24 (1983), 25–47; Jack D. L. Holmes, "Livestock in Spanish Natchez," *JMH,* 23 (1961), 15–37; McGowan, "Creation of a Slave Society," 135–45; Robert R. Rea, "Planters and

Plantation in British West Florida," *AR*, 29 (1976), 220–35, esp. 231–34; Fabel, *Economy of West Florida*, ch. 5. For the 1763 census, see Jacqueline Voorhies, comp., *Some Late Eighteenth-Century Louisianans: Census Records, 1758–1796* (Lafayette, La., 1973), 1–107. On the use of black overseers, see McGowan, "Creation of a Slave Society," 137, 181.

14. Laura L. Porteus, trans., "The Documents in Loppinot's Case, 1774," *LHQ*, 12 (1929), 82.

15. Henry P. Dart, ed., "Cabildo Archives," *LHQ*, 3 (1920), 89–91; Hall, *Africans in Colonial Louisiana*, ch. 7, esp. 160–63, 181–90; 202–3; Gerard L. St. Martin, ed. and trans., "A Slave Trial in Colonial Natchitoches," *LH*, 28 (1987), 63–89, esp. 66–68, 71–74.

16. Usner, *Indians, Settler, & Slaves*, 227–34.

17. Quotation in Porteus, trans., "Loppinot's Case, 1774," 106. Opponents of the slaves' free Sunday admitted this "abuse is tolerated because from time immemorial, with the general consent of the masters and connivance of the Superiors, slaves have labored without interruption in the presence of, and with the knowledge and consent of Magistrates." *Ibid.*, 106–7; Francisco Bouligny quoted in Alcée Fortier, *A History of Louisiana*, 3 vols. (New York, 1904), 2: 35–36; Hall, *Africans in Colonial Louisiana*, 176–77.

18. McGowan, "Creation of a Slave Society," 136–45, 152–55, 181–193; Jean-François-Benjamin de Montigny, "History of Louisiana," in Benjamin F. French, ed., *Historical Collections of Louisiana*, 5 vols. (New York, 1846–53), 5: 119–22, quotation on 120–21; Porteus, trans., "Loppinot's Case, 1774," 109; Francisco Bouligny quoted in Fortier, *A History of Louisiana*, 2: 36.

19. Micele, "Catholic Church," 96, 139–40.

20. Thomas N. Ingersoll, "Slave Codes and Judicial Practice in New Orleans, 1718–1807," *LHR*, 13 (1995), 29.

21. Ingersoll, "Slave Codes and Judicial Practice," 40–41, 47–51. The 1751 code is abstracted in Charles Gayarré, *History of Louisiana*, 4 vols. (New York, 1854), 2: 360–65.

22. Ingersoll, "Slave Codes and Judicial Practice," 29–31, 36–38; Gayarré, *History of Louisiana*, 2: 360–65; McGowan, "Creation of a Slave Society," 140.

23. Francisco Bouligny quoted in Fortier, *A History of Louisiana*, 2: 36; St. Martin, trans., "Slave Trial," 71–72.

24. Montigny, "Historical Memoirs of M. Dumont," in French, ed., *Historical Collections of Louisiana*, 5: 119–22; McGowan, "Creation of a Slave Society," 141.

25. Montigny, "Historical Memoirs of M. Dumont," in French, ed., *Historical Collections of Louisiana*, 5: 119–22, quotation on 120.

26. The most complete discussion of the Indian trade can be found in Usner, *Indians, Settlers, & Slaves*, and Usner, "Indian-Black Relations in Colonial and Antebellum Louisiana," in Stephan Palmié, ed., *Slave Culture and Cultures of Slavery* (Knoxville, Tenn., 1995), 145–61.

27. Quotations in Porteus, trans., "Loppinot's Case, 1774," 56, 71, also see 109; McGowan, "Creation of a Slave Society," 186–87, 206. On the laws enjoining slaves

trading independently, Brasseaux, "Administration of Slave Regulations," 145–46, 156.

28. Hall, *Africans in Colonial Louisiana,* 305–6.

29. Usner, *Indians, Settlers, & Slaves,* ch. 5, esp. 165–68; St. Martin, ed., "Slave Trial," 65–67.

30. St. Martin, ed., "Slave Trial," 79; Din and Harkins, *New Orleans Cabildo,* 156–57. The court affirmed that "on legal holidays the Negroes do not need permits from their masters to communicate with each other nor for any private work they do." Thomas N. Ingersoll, "Free Blacks in a Slave Society: New Orleans, 1718–1812," *WMQ,* 48 (1991), 181–82, esp. n34; Kimberly S. Hanger, "Avenues to Freedom to New Orleans' Black Population, 1769–1779," *LII,* 31 (1990), 241 n10; Burson, *Stewardship of Don Estaban Miró,* 112.

31. Din and Harkins, *New Orleans Cabildo,* 5–6; Lawrence Kinnaird, *Spain in the Mississippi Valley, 1765–1794,* 4 vols. (Washington, D.C., 1946–49), 1: 196. Also Hanger, "Avenues to Freedom," 239.

32. Quotation in French, ed., *Historical Collections of Louisiana,* 5: 120–21; Porteus, ed. and trans., "Loppinot's Case, 1774," 79, 106; Usner, *Indians, Settlers, & Slaves,* 40, 201, 215.

33. Jerah Johnson, "New Orleans's Congo Square: Urban Setting for Early Afro-American Culture Formation," *LH,* 32 (1991), 117–33; Henry P. Dart, "Cabarets of New Orleans in the French Colonial Period," *LHQ,* 19 (1936), 578–83. The best description of Congo Square is one drawn by Benjamin Latrobe in the early nineteenth century. See Edward C. Carter II, John C. Van Horne, and Lee W. Formwalt, eds., *The Journals of Benjamin Henry Latrobe, 1799–1820,* 3 vols. (New Haven, Conn., 1980), 3: 185, 203–4. A summary view drawn from the accounts of nineteenth-century travelers, David C. Estes, "Traditional Dances and Processions of Blacks as Witnessed by Antebellum Travelers," *Louisiana Folklore Miscellany,* 6 (1990), 1–14.

34. A visitor to New Orleans at the turn of the century declared disgustedly that the "canaille, white and black, free and slave, mingled indiscriminately." Berquin Duvallon, *Vue de la colonie du Mississippi, ou des provinces de Louisiana et Floride* (Paris, 1803), in James A. Robertson, ed., *Louisiana under Spain, France, and the United States, 1785–1807,* 2 vols. (Cleveland, 1911), 1: 216. "There is almost no street, inside or outside the portals of the City, that does not have a cabaret," declared petitioners to the Calbildo in 1800. "These public houses are always filled with soldiers, seamen, workers and slaves," Ronald R. Morazan, "Letters, Petitions, and Decrees of the Cabildo of New Orleans, 1800–1803: Edited and Translated," 2 vols., unpub. doctoral diss., Louisiana State University, 1972, 49–50.

35. Pintard, "New Orleans in 1801," 232; Usner, *Indians, Settlers, & Slaves,* 202.

36. The twentieth-century romanaticization of New Orleans's history has confounded the subject of sex and sexuality in the lower Mississippi Valley. Henry Asbury, *The French Quarter: An Informal History of the New Orleans Underworld* (New York, 1936). It is further complicated by the unreliability of censuses which presume to enumerate "mulattoes." Any discussion, however, must begin with the historically imbalanced sex ratios of Europeans and European-Americans (among

whom men were in the majority), and Africans and African Americans (among whom women were in the majority). The relationships which grew from that demographic imbalance took a variety of forms over the first century and a half of settlement, and are reviewed in Donald E. Everett, "Free Persons of Color in Colonial Louisiana," *LH,* 7 (1966), 33–36; Jack D. L. Holmes, "Do It! Don't Do It!: Spanish Laws on Sex and Marriage," in Edward F. Haas, ed., *Louisiana's Legal Heritage* (New Orleans, 1983), 20–25, and Holmes, "The Role of Blacks in Spanish Alabama: The Mobile District, 1780–1813," *AHQ,* 37 (1975), 10–12; Carl A. Brasseaux, "The Moral Climate of French Colonial Louisiana, 1699–1763," *LH,* 27 (1986), 27–41; Kimberly S. Hanger, *Bounded Lives, Bounded Places: Free Black Society in Colonial New Orleans, 1769–1803* (Durham, N.C., 1997), 34–38; Paul F. Lachance, "The Formation of a Three-Caste Society: Evidence from Wills in Antebellum New Orleans," *SSH,* 18 (1994), 212–13, esp. 222; Gayarré, *History of Louisiana,* 3: 57–71. Each in its own way makes the case for the tradition of open and unapologetic acceptance of interracial sex between black and white in New Orleans. Daniel Usner adds Native Americans to the mixture. Differences arose in the way French, Spanish, and Americans dealt with interracial sex and its product, people of color. For a useful comparison with developments in French Saint Domingue, see John D. Garrigus, "'Sons of the Same Father': Gender, Race, and Citizenship in French Saint-Domingue," in Christine Adams, Jack R. Censer, and Lisa Jane Graham, eds., *Visions and Revisions of Eighteenth Century France* (University Park, Penn., 1997), 145–49. Assessing the actuality of racial mixing is an all but impossible task, but see Voorhies, *Some Late Eighteenth Century Louisianans,* 1–107, and the general undercount of Louisiana censuses. Hanger, "Avenues to Freedom," 238–39, and *Bounded Lives, Bounded Places,* 113–14; Ingersoll, "Free Blacks in a Slave Society," 187 n52. But Hall notes that concubines of white men were promoted from "black" to "mulatto." *Africans in Colonial Louisiana,* 239–40, 264–65.

37. Ronald R. Morazan, ed., "'Quadroon' Balls in the Spanish Period," *LH,* 14 (1973), 310–15; Henry A. Kmen, *Music in New Orleans: The Formative Years, 1791–1841* (Baton Rouge, La., 1966), ch. 2, esp. 42–46; Din and Harkins, *New Orleans Cabildo,* 173–75. Also see Samuel Kinser, *Carnival, American Style: Mardi Gras at New Orleans and Mobile* (Chicago, 1990).

38. See above note 36. Quotations in Hall, *Africans in Colonial Louisiana,* 379–80; Holmes, "Do It! Don't Do It," 44; Micele, "Catholic Church," 154.

39. Everett, "Free Persons of Color in Colonial Louisiana," 36–39; Holmes, "Do It! Don't Do It!" 22–24; Ronald R. Morazan, ed., "'Quadroon' Balls in the Spanish Period," *LH,* 14 (1973), 310–15; Henry A. Kmen, *Music in New Orleans: The Formative Years, 1791–1841* (Baton Rouge, La., 1966), 42–48; Paul Lachance, "Intermarriage and French Cultural Persistence in Late Spanish and Early American New Orleans," *HSSH,* 15 (1982), 76–77; and Harkins, *New Orleans Cabildo,* 173–76; Roulhac Toledano and Mary Louise Christovich, eds., *New Orleans Architecture,* 8 vols. (Gretna, La., 1971–), 6: 90–94; Joseph G. Tregle, Jr., "Creoles and Americans," in Hirsh and Logsdon, eds., *Creole New Orleans,* 149–50; Lois V. M. Gould, "In Full Enjoyment of their Liberty: The Free Women of Color of the Gulf Ports of New

Orleans, Mobile, and Pensacola, 1769–1860," unpub. doctoral diss., Emory University, 1991, 215–33.

40. In 1788 fire destroyed a large portion of New Orleans. Of the 496 claims submitted to the Spanish government, 51 were from free women of color, and they averaged 1,770 pesos; 21 were from free men of color, and they averaged 1,723 pesos. Kimberly S. Hanger, "'The Fortunes of Women in America': Spanish New Orleans's Free Women of African Descent and Their Relations with Slave Women," in Patrica Morton, ed., *Discovering the Women in Slavery: Emancipating Perspectives on the American Past* (Athens, Ga., 1996), 169.

41. Hall, *Africans in Colonial Louisiana,* ch. 6, esp. the discussion of creole language, pp. 161–69, 187–200, quotation on 324–25; quotation in Ingersoll, "Slave Codes and Judicial Practice," 48; Berquin-Duvallon, *Vue de la colonie du Mississippi,* in Robertson, ed., *Louisiana under the Rule of Spain, France, and the United States,* 1: 184.

42. Gayarré, *History of New Orleans,* 2: 359–65, quotation on 364.

43. On the shortage of foodstuffs in New Orleans, see Clark, *New Orleans,* 160, and again 257–58.

44. Usner summarizes Spanish and British policies in *Indians, Settlers, & Slaves,* ch. 4. But also see Gilbert C. Din, *The Canary Islanders of Louisiana* (Baton Rouge, La., 1988), 15–83, and "Spanish Immigration to a French Land," *RL,* 5 (1976), 63–80; Carl A. Brasseaux, *The Founding of New Acadia: The Beginnings of Arcadian Life in Louisiana, 1775–1803* (Baton Rouge, La., 1987); Fabel, *Economy of British West Florida,* 6–21; Clark, *New Orleans,* 181–201, 222–25; Coutts, "Boom and Bust," 289–309; Lachance, "The Politics of Fear: French Louisiana and the Slave Trade," 164; Ingersoll, "Slave Trade and Ethnic Diversity," 133–51. Quotation in Mark Van Doren, ed., *The Travels of William Bartram* (New York, 1928), 339.

45. Roland C. McConnell, *Negro Troops of Antebellum Louisiana: A History of the Battalion of Free Men of Color* (Baton Rouge, La., 1968), 5–12, and McConnell, "Louisiana's Black Military History, 1729–1865," in Robert R. McDonald, John R. Kemp, and Edward F. Haas, eds., *Louisiana's Black Heritage* (New Orleans, 1979), 32–35; Kimberly S. Hanger, "A Privilege and Honor to Serve: The Free Black Militia of Spanish New Orleans," *Military History of the Southwest,* 21 (1991), 67–68; Usner, *Indians, Settlers, & Slaves,* 82–87.

46. John Preston Moore, *Revolt in Louisiana: The Spanish Occupation, 1766–1770* (Baton Rouge, La., 1976); David K. Texada, *Alejandro O'Reilly and the New Orleans Rebels* (LaFayette, La., 1970).

47. Jack D. L. Holmes, *Honor and Fidelity: The Louisiana Infantry Regiment and the Louisiana Militia Companies, 1766–1821* (Birmingham, Ala., 1965), 17; Hanger, "A Privilege and Honor," 74.

48. In Cuba, O'Reilly had reorganized the colored militia after the disastrous loss of Havana to the British in 1762, creating three full battalions of 800 men in the capital and other units in the provinces. Herbert S. Klein estimates that one of every five free men of color in Cuba served in the militia. Some 160 of these accompanied O'Reilly's expedition to Louisiana in 1769. Klein, "The Colored Militia of Cuba,

1568–1868," *CS,* 6 (July 1966), 17–27, esp. 19–20; Leon Campbell, "The Changing Racial and Administrative Structure of the Peruvian Military under the Late Bourbons," *Americas,* 32 (1975), 117–33; Allen J. Keuthe, *Military Reform and Society in New Granada, 1773–1808* (Gainesville, Fla., 1978); Lyle N. McAlister, *The "Fuero Militar" in New Spain, 1764–1800* (Gainesville, Fla., 1957). One militia captain distinguished his unit, the "Battalion of Octoroons" from the "Battalion of Quadroons." Morazan, ed., "Quadroon Balls," 312.

49. McConnell, *Negro Troops,* 17–22, quotation on 42; Hanger, "A Privilege and Honor," 59–86; Hanger, *Bounded Lives, Bounded Places,* ch. 4, esp. 117–19; Everett, "Free Persons of Color in Colonial Louisiana," 41–43; Harold E. Sterkx, *Free Negro in Ante-Bellum Louisiana* (Rutherford, N.J., 1972), 73–79; Gilbert C. Din, "Cimarrones and the San Malo Band in Spanish Louisiana," *LH,* 21 (1980), 240–43. The militia's roster for 1770 counted 61 free pardos and 238 free morenos within twelve miles of New Orleans. Hanger, *Bounded Lives, Bounded Places,* 23, 114, 184 n11. By 1781, 271 went into battle at Pensacola, organized in the traditional Spanish manner by color—moreno and pardo. Under Spanish control the militia grew rapidly. The force in New Orleans increased from 89 men in 1779 to 469 in 1801. *Ibid.,* 120, 159–60. By 1790 a second company of pardo militia had been established, also with its own officers. Holmes, *Honor and Fidelity,* 20.

50. For the restrictive nature of French regulation of manumission, see Hans W. Baade, "The Law of Slavery in Spanish Luisiana, 1769–1803," in Edward F. Haas, ed., *Louisiana's Legal Heritage* (New Orleans, 1983), 49–50, 60; Everett, "Free Persons of Color in Colonial Louisiana," 22–23; Ingersoll, "Slave Codes and Judicial Practice," 34–35, 38–39, and Ingersoll, "Free Blacks in a Slave Society," 177. The relevant sections of the *Code Noir* can be found in Gayarré, *History of Louisiana,* 1: 539.

51. Baade, "The Law of Slavery in Spanish Luisiana," 46–60; Everett, "Free People of Color in Colonial Louisiana," 29–33; Hanger, "Avenues to Freedom," 244–45. Prior to 1769 fewer than 60—about one a year—gratuitous slaveholder-sponsored manumissions were registered in French Louisiana. Ingersoll, "Slave Codes and Judicial Practice," 39. In the absence of a similar growth in the free colored population in West Florida—where, in 1767, the British enacted a slave code that severely limited manumission—testifies to the importance of Spanish governance and the laws and customs regulating manumission. Fabel, *Economy of British West Florida,* 23–25.

52. Hanger, "Avenues to Freedom," 243–45, 249–52; Everett, "Free Persons of Color in Colonial Louisiana," 45–47; Ingersoll, "Free Blacks in a Slave Society," 186–88. McGowan, "Creation of a Slave Society," 201–5; Hanger, *Bounded Lives, Bounded Places,* 26–33; Hall, *Africans in Colonial Louisiana,* 258–60, 266–74.

53. Hanger, "Avenues to Freedom," 246–54, and Hanger, "'The Fortunes of Women in America,'" 156–59; Ingersoll, "Free Blacks in a Slave Society," 186.

54. Baade, "Law of Slavery in Spanish Luisiana," 48–63, 67–70; Herbert S. Klein, *Slavery in the Americas: A Comparative Study of Virginia and Cuba* (Chicago, 1967), 57–65, 196–200; Leslie B. Rout, Jr., *The African Experience in Spanish America, 1502 to the Present Day* (Cambridge, UK, 1976), 87–93; Everett, "Free Persons of Color in Colonial Louisiana," 43–45; Ingersoll, "Free Blacks in a Slave Society," 180–80, 183–

84; Hanger, "Avenues of Freedom," 240–45; 262–63; Hanger, "Origins of New Or-leans's Free Creoles of Color," in James H. Dormon, ed., *Creoles of Color of the Gulf South* (Knoxville, Tenn., 1996), 6–7, 17–23; Hanger, *Bounded Lives, Bounded Places,* 42–51.

55. Baade, "Law of Slavery in Spanish Luisiana," 67–70; Ingersoll, "Free Blacks in a Slave Society," 183–86; Everett, "Free Persons of Color in Colonial Louisiana," 45–46. Slaveowners contested one-fifth of all purchases of freedom. Hanger, *Bounded Lives, Bounded Places,* 25–26.

56. Hanger, "Avenues to Freedom," 244–47.

57. *Ibid.,* 243–45, 248, 252, 258–63.

58. *Ibid.,* 239; McGowan, "Creation of a Slave Society," 196. Hall, *Africans in Colonial Louisiana,* 239–40, 258–59. Hanger, "Avenues to Freedom," 239.

Part III. Slave and Free: The Revolutionary Generations

1. R. R. Palmer, *The Age of the Democratic Revolution: A Political History of Europe and America, 1760–1800,* 2 vols. (Princeton, N.J., 1959–1964); E. J. Hobsbawm, *The Age of Revolution: Europe, 1789–1848* (New York, 1962); Robin Blackburn, *The Overthrow of Colonial Slavery, 1776–1848* (London, 1988); C. L. R. James, *The Black Jacobins: Toussaint L'Overture and the San Domingo Revolution,* 2nd ed. (New York 1963); David Brion Davis, *The Problem of Slavery in the Age of Revolution, 1770–1823* (Ithaca, N.Y., 1975); Michael Mullin, "British Caribbean and North American Slaves in an Era of War and Revolution, 1775–1807," in Jeffrey J. Crow and Larry E. Tise, ed., *The Southern Experience in the American Revolution* (Chapel Hill, N.C., 1978); David Barry Gaspar and David Patrick Geggus, eds., *A Turbulent Time: The French Revolution and the Greater Caribbean* (Bloomington, Ind., 1997). The pioneering work that demonstrated rapid movement of revolution-ary ideas through the Atlantic is Julius Sherrard Scott III, "The Common Wind: Currents of Afro-American Communication in the Era of the Haitian Revolution," unpub. doctoral diss., Duke University, 1986.

2. Benjamin Quarles, *The Negro in the American Revolution* (Chapel Hill, N.C., 1961); Sylvia R. Frey, *Water from the Rock: Black Resistance in a Revolutionary Age* (Princeton, N.J., 1991); Winthrop D. Jordan, *White over Black: American Atti-tudes toward the Negro 1550–1812* (Chapel Hill, N.C., 1968), 269–314; Ira Berlin and Ronald Hoffman, eds., *Slavery and Freedom in the Age of the American Revolution* (Charlottesville, Va., 1983).

3. Quotation in Philip Foner, ed., *The Complete Writings of Thomas Paine,* 2 vols. (New York, 1945), 2: 15–19; Jordan, *White over Black,* 291–94.

4. Rhys Isaac, *The Transformation of Virginia, 1740–1790* (Chapel Hill, N.C., 1982); James D. Essig, *The Bonds of Wickedness: American Evangelicals against Slavery, 1770–1808* (Philadelphia, 1982); Christine Leigh Heyrman, *Southern Cross: The Beginnings of the Bible Belt* (New York, 1997); Donald G. Mathews, *Slavery and Methodism: A Chapter in American Morality, 1780-1845* (Princeton, N.J., 1965), chs. 1–3.

5. Rolando Mellafe, *Negro Slavery in Latin America,* trans. J. W. S. Judge

(Berkeley, Cal., 1975), 105–11; Scott, "The Common Wind," 146–58; David Patrick Geggus, "Slave Resistance in the Spanish Caribbean in the Mid-1790s," in Gaspar and Geggus, eds., *A Turbulent Time,* 136–37, and Geggus, "The French and Haitian Revolutions, and Resistance to Slavery in the Americas: An Overview," *RFHOM,* 76 (1989), 119–20; James Thomas McGowan, "Creation of a Slave Society: Louisiana Plantations in the Eighteenth Century," unpub. doctoral diss., University of Rochester, 1976, 296–318; Thomas N. Ingersoll, "Slave Codes and Judicial Practice in New Orleans, 1718–1807," *LHR,* 13 (1995), 55–56.

6. Blackburn, *The Overthrow of Colonial Slavery,* 163–264; James, *Black Jacobins;* David Patrick Geggus, "Slavery, War, and Revolution in the Greater Caribbean, 1789–1815," in Gaspar and Geggus, eds., *A Turbulent Time,* 1–50. For a deft summary of how events in France shaped the demise of slavery in Saint Domingue, see Carolyn E. Fick, "The French Revolution in Saint Domingue: A Triumph or a Failure?," in *ibid.,* 51–75.

7. James, *Black Jacobins;* Carolyn E. Fick, *The Making of Haiti: The Saint Domingue Revolution from Below* (Knoxville, Tenn., 1990); Gaspar and Geggus, eds., *A Turbulent Time;* Scott, "Common Wind," ch. 5.

8. Duncan J. MacLeod, *Slavery, Race, and the American Revolution* (London, 1974); Barbara Jeanne Fields, "Slavery, Race and Ideology in the United States of America," *NLR,* 181 (1990), 95–118.

9. Three recent studies of manumission reveal the complexity of the process and the ability of slaves and slaveowners to employ manumission to their own advantage. Kimberly S. Hanger, *Bounded Lives, Bounded Places: Free Black Society in Colonial New Orleans, 1769–1803* (Durham, N.C., 1997); Gary B. Nash and Jean R. Soderlund, *Freedom by Degrees: Emancipation in Pennsylvania and Its Aftermath* (New York, 1991); T. Stephen Whitman, *The Price of Freedom: Slavery and Manumission in Baltimore and Early National Maryland* (Lexington, Ky., 1997).

10. Shane White, "'It was a Proud Day': African Americans, Festivals, and Parades in the North, 1741–1834," *JAmH,* 81 (1994), 13–50.

11. Frey, *Water from the Rock,* ch. 6, provides an overview of the African-American diaspora in the Age of Revolution.

9. The Slow Death of Slavery in the North

1. Arthur Zilversmit, *The First Emancipation: The Abolition of Slavery in the North* (Chicago, 1967), chs. 5–8; William O'Brien, "Did the Jennison Case Outlaw Slavery in Massachusetts?" *WMQ,* 17 (1960), 219–41; John D. Cushing, "The Cushing Court and the Abolition of Slavery in Massachusetts: More Notes on the 'Quock Walker Case,'" *AJLH,* 5 (1961), 118–44; Arthur Zilversmit, "Quok Walker, Mumbet, and the Abolition of Slavery in Massachusetts," *WMQ,* 25 (1968), 614–24; Elaine MacEacheren, "Emancipation of Slavery in Massachusetts: A Reexamination, 1770–1790," *JNH,* 55 (1970), 289–306.

2. Zilversmit, *The First Emancipation,* chs. 5–6; Larry R. Gerlach, ed., *New Jersey in the American Revolution, 1763–1783: A Documentary History* (Trenton, N.J., 1975), 147–50.

3. Benjamin Quarles, *The Negro in the American Revolution* (Chapel Hill, N.C., 1961), ch. 10; Graham Russell Hodges, *Slavery and Freedom in the Rural North: African Americans in Monmouth County, New Jersey, 1665–1865* (Madison, Wisc., 1996), 109 n27. For refugeeing, see Trenton *New Jersey Gazette,* 5 June 1780; Chatham *New Jersey Journal,* 13 June 1780; Philadelphia *Pennsylvania Post,* 23 June 1780.

4. Vivienne L. Kruger, "Born to Run: The Slave Family in Early New York, 1626–1827," unpub. doctoral diss., Columbia University, 1985, 648–49, quotation on 660.

5. Quarles, *Negro in the American Revolution,* vii–ix, 9–12, 16–18, 51–56, 68–74; Leonard Lundlin, *Cockpit of the Revolution: The War for Independence in New Jersey* (Princeton, N.J., 1940), 153–65; Hodges, *Rural North,* 92–95, quotation in Philadelphia *Pennsylvania Gazette,* 17 July 1776, in Billy G. Smith and Richard Wojtowicz, comps., *Blacks Who Stole Themselves: Advertisements for Runaways in the Pennsylvania Gazette, 1728–1790* (Philadelphia, 1989), 129–30, 132–33, 144.

6. Quarles, *American Revolution,* vii–ix, 9–12, 16–18, 51–56, 68–74; Gary B. Nash, *Forging Freedom: The Formation of Philadelphia's Black Community, 1720–1840* (Cambridge, Mass., 1988), 49; Hodges, *Rural North,* 94–103, and Hodges, "Black Revolt in New York and the Neutral Zone," in William Pencak and Paul Gilje, eds., *New York in the Age of the Constitution* (Cranberry, N.J., 1993), 20–47.

7. Kruger, "Born to Run," ch. 11; Shane White, *Somewhat More Independent: The End of Slavery in New York City, 1770–1810* (Athens, Ga., 1991), 131, 141–43; quotation in New *Jersey Gazette,* 28 October 1778, in *ibid,* 131; Nash, *Forging Freedom,* 46–57; Gary B. Nash and Jean R. Soderlund, *Freedom by Degrees: Emancipation in Pennsylvania and Its Aftermath* (New York, 1991), 76–77, 88–89, 95, 138–39; quotations in Smith and Wojtowicz, comp., *Blacks Who Stole Themselves,* 129–30, also see 132–33, 144; "Official Letters of Major General James Pattison," *Collections of the New-York Historical Society for the Year 1875* (New York, 1876), 397; Trenton *New Jersey Gazette,* 5 June 1780.

8. White, *Somewhat More Independent* (Athens, Ga., 1991), 131, 141–43; Quarles, *The American Revolution,* esp. chs. 5–6; Kruger, "Born to Run," ch. 11; Hodges, "Black Revolt in New York and the Neutral Zone," 28; Nash, *Forging Freedom,* 46–57; Nash and Soderlund, *Freedom by Degrees,* 76–77, 88–89, 95, 138–39; quotations in Smith and Wojtowicz, comps., *Blacks Who Stole Themselves,* 129–30, 132–33, 144.

9. Nash, *Forging Freedom,* 57–60; Nash and Soderlund, *Freedom by Degrees,* 95–96; White, *Somewhat More Independent,* ch. 5, esp. 134–38.

10. Quotation in Nash, *Forging Freedom,* 64–65.

11. Roger Bruns, ed., *Am I Not a Man and a Brother: The Antislavery Crusade of Revolutionary America, 1688–1788* (New York, 1977), quotation on 428–29; Herbert Aptheker, ed., *A Documentary History of the Negro People in the United States,* 2 vols. (New York, 1951), 1: 9–12; Nash, *Forging Freedom,* 62–65; Nash and Soderlund, *Freedom by Degrees,* 112–13, 133.

12. Nash, *Forging Freedom,* 44, 50, 67–70. Zilversmit, *First Emancipation,* ch. 5, esp. 124–37; Nash and Soderlund, *Freedom by Degrees,* esp. ch. 4, quotation on 101.

13. Slaveholders developed a variety of stratagems to delay and defeat the purpose of abolition. They sold slaves out of the state and shipped pregnant women to slave states, so children would be born in slavery. Nash and Soderlund, *Freedom by Degrees*, 111–15.

14. White, *Somewhat More Independent*, 141–47. Escapes and manumission reduced the slave population of Philadelphia by two-thirds between 1767 and 1788. Nash and Soderlund, *Freedom by Degrees*, 139. "Abolition societies"—formed in Pennsylvania in 1784, and later in New York—became springboards for freedom suits. Judicial action was generally initiated by free and slave blacks and implemented by a society's white membership. Nash and Soderlund, *Freedom by Degrees*, 119–23. On arson, see Nash, *Forging Freedom*, 174–75; White, *Somewhat More Independent*, 65.

15. Zilversmit, *First Emancipation*, chs. 3–5, esp. 134–35.

16. *Ibid.*, 128–29, 133–35; Nash and Soderlund, *Freedom by Degrees*, 102; Philadelphia *Pennsylvania Packet*, 31 Jan. 1781, 5, 21 Feb. 1781.

17. Zilversmit, *First Emancipation*, 16–17, 121–24, 150, 180–82, 193–94; Hodges, *Rural North*, ch. 4; Kruger, "Born to Run," 724–27. In New York, a special legislative enactment allowed slaveholders to divest themselves of slave children between 1799 and 1804 with the expectation that they would be indentured to them by the overseers of the poor, who would pay the cost of each child's support at the rate of $3.50 a month. The abandonment program was itself abandoned in 1804 as too expensive. In 1817 lawmakers abolished slavery in New York as of July 4, 1827, but the law did not apply to children born into slavery between 1799 and 1827, and they would have to serve out their indentures. *Ibid.*, ch. 13; McManus, *Slavery in New York*, 161–88.

18. Nash, *Forging Freedom*, 71–72; Hodges, *Rural North*, 123–26. Historians of slavery in New York dispute the impact of manumission. See White, *Somewhat More Independent*, 27–30 and 46–50, and Kruger, "Born to Run," 724–84; also Harry B. Yoshpe, "Record of Slave Manumissions in New York during the Colonial and Early National Periods," *JNH*, 26 (1941), 78–101. For the bargaining between slave and slaveholder, see White, *Somewhat More Independent*, 49–50, 106–11, 144; Kruger, "Born to Run," ch. 12, esp. 756–67. The traditional right of slaves in New York to choose their own masters greatly strengthened the slaves' hand in this negotiation, see White, *Somewhat More Independent*, 106–11; Zilversmit, *First Emancipation*, 190–92; C. W. Larison, *Silvia DuBois, A Biografy of the Slave Who Whipt Her Mistres and Gand Her Fredom*, ed. and trans., Jared C. Lobdell (New York, 1988), 54; Philadelphia *Pennsylvania Gazette*, 3 Dec. 1794.

19. White, *Somewhat More Independent*, 28–29; Nash and Soderlund, *Freedom by Degrees*, ch. 5, and 26, 156–57; Hodges, *Rural North*, ch. 4, esp. 125–26; Kruger, "Born to Run," ch. 12, quotations on 757 and 212; quotations in Yoshpe, "Record of Slave Manumissions," 85; in Philip Morgan, "Black Society in the Lowcountry, 1760–1810," in Ira Berlin and Ronald Hoffman, eds., *Slavery and Freedom in the Age of the American Revolution* (Charlottesville, Va., 1983), 84–85 n3.

20. Smith and Wojtowicz, comps., *Blacks Who Stole Themselves*, 135, 141, 151; Nash and Soderlund, *Freedom by Degrees*, 139–41.

21. White, *Somewhat More Independent,* 117–118, quotation on 117; Nash and Soderlund, *Freedom by Degrees,* 115–36.

22. In New York, almost three-quarters of the owners of fugitives who presumed to know their slaves' destinations or motives presumed their slaves to be passing as free, rather than visiting or simply avoiding punishment. White, *Somewhat More Independent,* 132–34, quotations on 125–26. Compare this to South Carolina runaways whom masters estimated were four times more likely to be visiting than to make a permanent escape. Philip D. Morgan, "Colonial South Carolina Runaways: Their Significance for Slave Culture," *S&A,* 6 (1985), 68.

23. White, *Somewhat More Independent,* ch. 5, esp., 146–48; quotation in Smith and Wojtowicz, comps., *Blacks Who Stole Themselves,* 142.

24. White, *Somewhat More Independent,* 3–15, 153, quotation on 14; Shane White, "'We Dwell in Safety and Pursue Our Honest Callings': Free Blacks in New York City, 1783–1860," *JAmH,* 75 (1988), 448; Hodges, *Rural North,* 117–19.

25. Nash and Soderlund, *Freedom by Degrees,* 32–36, 143–154, 160–63, also ch. 1, esp. 5, 43–49; Kruger, "Born to Run," 92, 747; White, *Somewhat More Independent,* chs. 1–3; Peter O. Wacker, *Land and People: A Cultural Geography of Preindustrial New Jersey: Origins and Settlement Patterns* (New Brunswick, N.J., 1975), 190.

26. Nash and Soderlund, *Freedom by Degrees,* chs. 6–7, esp. 194–95.

27. Kruger, "Born to Run," 158, table 8; White, *Somewhat More Independent,* 46; White, "'We Dwell in Safety," 451–52; Nash and Soderlund, *Freedom by Degrees,* 173–83; Nash, *Forging Freedom,* 76–78.

28. Gary B. Nash, "Forging Freedom: Emancipation Experience in the Northern Seaport Cities, 1775–1820," in Berlin and Hoffman, eds., *Slavery and Freedom,* 20–27, and Nash, *Forging Freedom,* 79–88; White, *Somewhat More Independent,* 192–94; Kruger, "Born to Run," 437–47. Also Quarles, *American Revolution,* 51–52; Nash and Soderland, *Freedom by Degrees,* 90; William D. Pierson, *Black Yankees: The Development of an Afro-American Subculture in Eighteenth-Century New England* (Amherst, Mass., 1988), 34–35. Some 90 percent of 580 manumitted slaves drawn from a sample of 2,000 whose names were listed in New York's manumission records between 1701 and 1831 had names different from their manumitters. Kruger, "Born to Run," 444–45.

29. White, *Somewhat More Independent,* 192–94; Kruger, "Born to Run," 911–13.

30. Paul G. E. Clemens and Lucy Simler, "Rural Labor and Farm Household in Chester County, Pennsylvania, 1750–1820," in Stephen Innes, ed., *Work and Labor in Early America* (Chapel Hill, N.C., 1988), 106–43; Nash and Soderlund, *Freedom by Degrees,* 187–91; Hodges, *Rural North,* 120–21, 126–29; quotation in Peter O. Wacker and Paul G. E. Clemens, *Land Use in Early New Jersey: A Historical Geography* (Newark, N.J., 1995), 103, also 258.

31. Nash and Soderlund, *Freedom by Degrees,* 182–93, quotation on 189; Clemens and Simler, "Rural Labor and Farm Household in Chester County, Pennsylvania, 1750–1820," 106–23.

32. Ira Berlin, "The Structure of the Free Negro Caste in the Antebellum United

States," *JSH,* 9 (1975), 300; Nash, "Forging Freedom," 4–15; Nash, *Forging Freedom,* 72; White, *Somewhat More Independent,* 153–56, quotation on 154.

33. "Book of Negroes," National Archives, RG 360; Graham R. Hodges, *The Black Loyalist Directory: African Americans in Exile in the Age of Revolution* (New York, 1996); Ellen G. Wilson, *The Loyal Blacks* (New York, 1976), ch. 3; Hodges, *Rural North,* 101–3; Eldon Jones, "The British Withdrawal from the South," 1781–1785, in W. Robert Higgins, ed., *The Revolutionary War in the South: Power, Conflict, and Leadership* (Durham, N.C., 1979), 268–85.

34. Berlin, "Structure of the Free Negro Caste," 300; Nash, *Forging Freedom,* 136–40, 142–44; Nash, "Forging Freedom," 8–11. Prior to the American Revolution, there was little identification between the North and freedom among fugitive slaves. In 1767 a fugitive from Savannah was noted to be headed to some Caribbean island as he "has formerly attempted to get off for the West Indies." *Runaway Advertisements,* 4: 24 (Savannah *Georgia Gazette,* 16 Sept. 1767). A year later, Billie, who escaped from the Neabsco Iron-Works in northern Virginia, was thought to be "bound for Charles-Town, or to some place in Carolina, where he expects to be free." Smith and Wojtowicz, comps., *Blacks Who Stole Themselves,* 89. Even during the Revolution, numerous slaves ran southward; see, for example, the case of Nat who fled from southern Maryland to South Carolina. Lorena S. Walsh, "Rural African Americans in the Constitutional Era in Maryland," *MHM,* 84 (1989), 334, 336.

35. John Baur, "International Repercussions of the Haitian Revolution," *Americas,* 26 (1970), 394–418; Alfred N. Hunt, *Haiti's Influence on Antebellum America: Slumbering Volcano in the Caribbean* (Baton Rouge, La., 1988), ch. 3; Gabriel Débien and René Le Gardeur, "The Saint-Domingue Refugees in Louisiana, 1792–1804," in Carl A. Brasseaux and Glenn R. Conrad, eds., *The Road to Louisiana: The Saint-Domingue Refugees, 1792–1809,* trans. David Cheramie (Lafayette, La., 1992), 113–17; James Oliver Horton and Lois E. Horton, *In Hope of Liberty: Culture, Community and Protest among Northern Free Blacks, 1700–1860* (New York, 1997), 109–10; White, *Somewhat More Independent,* 31–32, 155–56; White, "'We Dwell in Safety,'" 450; Nash, *Forging Freedom,* 140–44, 174–76. In Philadelphia, slaveholders freed their slaves under Pennsylvania law but quickly turned around and bound them into long-term indentures. During the 1790s French immigrant slaveholders indentured nearly 500 slaves in Philadelphia. Nash and Soderlund, *Freedom by Degrees,* 180–81.

36. Arthur O. White, "The Black Leadership Class and Education in Antebellum Boston," *JNE,* 42 (1973), 507; Nash, *Forging Freedom,* 174–76, 180–83.

37. Nash, "Forging Freedom," 5–7, esp. table 2; Nash, *Forging Freedom,* 143; [Jeremy Belknap], "Queries Respecting the Slavery and Emancipation of Negroes in Massachusetts," *Collections of the Massachusetts Historical Society,* ser. 1, 4 (1795), 206; quotation in Stuart M. Blumin, *The Urban Threshold: Growth and Change in a Nineteenth-Century Urban Community* (Chicago, 1976), 24. For a slightly different pattern in Pennsylvania, where most of the migrants derived from the states to the south, see Jean R. Soderlund, "Black Importation and Migration into Southeastern Pennsylvania," *PAPS,* 133 (1989), 150–52.

38. Nash, *Forging Freedom,* 138, 142–43; Kruger, "Born to Run," 131.

39. During the colonial period, the balance in favor of men was always greater in the countryside than in the city, but even cities had sex ratio's favoring men in the eighteenth century. In 1746 in New York City, for example, the sex ratio of black men to women was 127 to 100. Kruger, "Born to Run," 305, 370–71 n11; Nash, "Forging Freedom," 11–12. That changed dramatically by the time of the Revolution and even more dramatically following the Revolution. *Ibid.*, 11–15, esp. table 3; also *Returns of the Whole Number of Persons within the Several Districts of the United States* (Washington, D.C., 1801); *Census for 1820* (Washington, D.C., 1821). The meaning of the census enumerations, however, has been contested. Gary Nash argues that official records exaggerated the female majority. Many men were away at sea when census takers called. Men, more often than women, avoided being counted. Nash, *Forging Freedom*, 135–36. Also see W. Jeffrey Bolster, *Black Jacks: African American Seamen in the Age of the Sail* (Cambridge, Mass., 1997), 2–6, 159–65, Kruger, "Born to Run," 312, table 3, 908.

40. Salinger, "Artisans, Journeymen, and the Transformation of Labor," 66–68; Nash and Soderlund, *Freedom by Degrees*, 118–20, 138–40; White, *Somewhat More Independent*, 33–36.

41. Nash, *Forging Freedom*, 74–75, 152–53, quotation on 146; White, *Somewhat More Independent*, 156–58, 163–64; White, "'Dwell in Safety,'" 457–59; Leon F. Litwack, *North of Slavery: The Negro in the Free States* (Chicago, 1961), 154.

42. Nash, *Forging Freedom*, 146, 149; White, *Somewhat More Independent*, 157–58; White, "'Dwell in Safety,'" 453–54.

43. Nash, *Forging Freedom*, 144–46; Howard B. Rock, ed., *The New York City Artisan, 1789–1825* (Albany, N.Y., 1989), 39–40; Paul A. Gilje and Howard B. Rock, "'Sweep O! Sweep O!': African-American Chimney Sweeps and Citizenship in the New Nation," *WMQ*, 51 (1994), 507–32.

44. Bolster, *Black Jacks*, 3–38, 113–16; Nash, *Forging Freedom*, 146; Nash, "Forging Freedom," 8–10; White, *Somewhat More Independent,*, 159–60; White, "'Dwell in Safety,'" 453–54; Ira Dye, "Early American Merchant Seafarers," *PAPS*, 120 (1976), 331–36.

45. Julie Winch, *Philadelphia's Black Elite: Activism, Accommodation, and the Struggle for Autonomy, 1787–1848* (Philadelphia, 1988), ch. 1; Nash, *Forging Freedom*, 74, 148–50, 153–54; White, *Somewhat More Independent*, 160–61; White, "'Dwell in Safety,'" 453–55. On Forten, see Robert Purvis, *Remarks on the Life and Character of James Forten Delivered at Bethel Church, March 30, 1842* (Philadelphia, 1842).

46. Nash, *Forging Freedom*, 149–52; White, *Somewhat More Independent*, 158–66; Winch, *Philadelphia's Black Elite*, 17–147.

47. William H. Robinson, ed., *The Proceedings of the Free, African Union Society and the African Benevolent Newport, Rhode Island, 1780–1824* (Providence, 1976), x–xi, and also list of births and deaths of free blacks; White, *Somewhat More Independent*, 166–71; Nash, *Forging Freedom*, 75–76. One of the first matters of business of Philadelphia's Free African Society, founded in 1787, was to establish "a regular mode of procedure with respect to . . . marriages." William Douglass, *Annals*

of the First African Church in the United States of America (Philadelphia, 1862), 34–42.

48. Quotation in Nash, *Forging Freedom*, 74–75, 158–60.

49. Nash, *Forging Freedom*, 298–99 n1. For the small size of black households in Newport, see Elaine F. Crane, *A Dependent People: Newport, Rhode Island, in the Revolutionary Era* (New York, 1985), 82.

50. Nash, "Forging Freedom," 31–33; Nash, *Forging Freedom,* 158–60; White, *Somewhat More Independent,* 166–71.

51. Nash, "Forging Freedom," 33–40; Nash, *Forging Freedom,* 162–63; Kruger, "Born to Run," 918–20.

52. Susan E. Klepp, "Seasoning and Society: Racial Differences in Mortality in Eighteenth-Century Philadelphia," *WMQ*, 51 (1994), 496–502.

53. Nash, "Forging Freedom," 31–33, 39–40; White, *Somewhat More Independent,* 34–39, 47–53; Nash, "Forging Freedom," 33–40; Nash, *Forging Freedom,* 163. For the lag in the formation of independent black households in the countryside, see Kruger, "Born to Run," 897.

54. Horton and Horton, *In Hopes of Liberty,* 107–8; G. S. Rowe, "Black Offenders, Criminal Courts, and Philadelphia Society in the Late Eighteenth Century," *JSH,* 22 (1989), 685–712; Nash, *Forging Freedom,* 214. Household independence for black people also occurred simultaneously with the opening of the first soup kitchens by the newly formed Society for Supplying the Poor with Soup in Philadelphia. *Ibid.,* 216; Carl D. Oblinger, "Alms for Oblivion: The Making of a Black Underclass in Southeastern Pennsylvania, 1780–1860," in John E. Bodnar, ed., *The Ethnic Experience in Pennsylvania* (Lewisburg, Pa, 1973), 94–120.

55. Within these neighborhoods, black people occupied the meanest quarters. Although they shared the same streets and courtyards with workingclass white families, black people lived disproportionately in cellar rooms and attic apartments. Overcrowding—along with the absence of sanitation and potable water—bred disease, assuring that the high rates of morbidity and mortality that dogged black people in slavery would remain a part of black life in freedom. Unable to bear enough children who survived infancy to reproduce itself, the urban black population depended on new arrivals from the countryside to sustain its numbers. Nash, *Forging Freedom,* 163–71; Nash, "Forging Freedom," 40–43; Emma J. Lapansky, "South Street Philadelphia, 1762–1854: A Haven for Those Low in the World," unpub. doctoral diss., University of Pennsylvania, 1975; Norman J. Johnson, "The Caste and Class of the Urban Form of Historic Philadelphia," *Journal of the American Institute of Planners,* 32 (1966), 334–49.

56. Nash, *Forging Freedom,* 94, 109; Carol V. R. George, *Segregated Sabbaths: Richard Allen and the Emergence of Independent Black Churches, 1760–1840* (New York, 1973), 49; Daniel Perlman, "Organizations of the Free Negro in New York City, 1800–1860," *JNH* 56 (1971), 182–83; Robinson, ed., *Free African Union Society;* Douglass, *Annals of the First African Church,* 33–42. For an earlier attempt to establish "The Negro Burying Ground in the Potters Field" in New York, see Osgood,

comp., *Minutes of the Common Council*, 1: 554, 598, 610, 663, 710, 739, 769; 2: 22, 112, 134, 151, 158, 218, 221, 264.

57. Nash, *Forging Freedom*, 109–33; Will B. Gravely, "The Rise of African Churches in America (1786–1822): Re-examining the Contexts," *JRT*, 14 (1984), 58–73, and "African Methodism and the Rise of Black Denominationalism," in Russell E. Richey and Kenneth E. Rowe, eds., *Rethinking Methodist History: A Bicentennial Consultation* (Nashville, 1985), 111–24; also George, *Segregated Sabbaths*, chs. 2–3; Milton C. Sernett, *Black Religion and American Evangelicalism: White Protestants, Plantation Missions, and the Flowering of Negro Christianity, 1787–1865* (Metuchen, N.J., 1975), chs. 4–5.

58. Quotation in "The Causes and Motives for Establishing St. Thomas's African Church of Philadelphia," in Douglas, *Annals of the First African Church*, 93–95, Nash, *Forging Freedom*, ch. 4.

59. Nash, *Forging Freedom*, 191–93.

60. Quotation in Robinson, ed., *Free African Union Society*, xi–xii. Also see Horton and Horton, *In Hopes of Freedom*, 70–71; Nash, *Forging Freedom*, 202–10; Harry L. Silcox, "Delay and Neglect: Negro Public Education in Antebellum Philadelphia, 1800–1860," *PMHB*, 97 (1973), 44–45; Melvin H. Buxbaum, "Cyrus Bustill Addresses the Blacks of Philadelphia," *WMQ*, 29 (1972), 102–8; Charles C. Andrews, *History of the New-York African Free-Schools* (New York, 1830).

61. Quotation in Nash, *Forging Freedom*, 64–65, also see 180–83. Also see James Forten, *A Series of Letters by a Man of Color* (Philadelphia, 1913), rpt. in Herbert Aptheker, ed., *A Documentary History of the Negro People in the United States* (New York, 1951). Some black men continued to vote, usually supporting the Federalist Party, whose members were prominent in the manumission societies. Ottley and Weatherby, eds., *Negro in New York*, 53–56; Daniel Perlman, "Organizations of the Free Negro in New York City, 1800–1860," *JNH*, 56 (1971), 181–97; Herman Bloch, "The New York Negro's Battle for Political Rights, 1777–1865," *IRSH*, 11 (1964), 65–80; Robert J. Cottrol, *The Afro-Yankees: Providence's Black Community in the Antebellum Era* (Westport, Conn., 1982).

62. Winch, *Philadelphia's Black Elite*, 6–7, 19, 22–24; Litwack, *North of Slavery*, 18–19, 25; Shane White, "'It was a Proud Day': African Americans, Festivals, and Parades in the North, 1741–1834," *JAmH*, 81 (1994), 13–50.

63. White, *Somewhat More Independent*, ch. 7, esp. 194–206; Nash, *Forging Freedom*, 217–33.

64. White, *Somewhat More Independent*, 144–45; Paul A. Gilje, *The Road to Mobocracy: Popular Disorder in New York City, 1763–1834* (Chapel Hill, N.C., 1987), 147–50. Another measure of difference between the respectables and the lower orders within black society can be seen in the reaction to the execution of two black criminals, John Joyce and Peter Mathias, in Philadelphia in 1808. When the angry crowd of black men and women stormed the gallows and assaulted the hangman, Richard Allen defended the justice of the proceedings. *Confessions of John Joyce, alias Davis, Who Was Executed on May, the 14th of March 1808* (Philadelphia, 1808),

and Michael Meranze, *Laboratories of Virtue: Punishment, Revolution, and Authority in Philadelphia, 1760–1835* (Chapel Hill, N.C., 1996), 33–34.

65. The Newport Free African Society in 1787 corresponded with the white colonizationist William Thornton respecting its "earnest desire of returning to Affrica and settling there" and proposed sending a delegation to see if land could be purchased with an eye toward settlement. But see the correspondence from black Bostonians and Philadelphians indicating their opposition even to these initial explorations. Robinson, ed., *Free African Union Society,* 16–18, 29.

66. Nash, *Forging Freedom,* 97–98, 103, 115–16, quotation on 98; Minutes of the Free African Society in Douglass, *Annals of the First African Church,* 17–19; Robinson, ed., *Free African Union Society.*

10. The Union of African-American Society in the Upper South

1. For the politicization of slave society in the Chesapeake during the years immediately before the Revolution, see Sylvia R. Frey, *Water from the Rock: Black Resistance in a Revolutionary Age* (Princeton, N.J., 1991), ch. 2.

2. Benjamin Quarles, *The Negro in the American Revolution* (Chapel Hill, N.C., 1961), ch. 2; Sylvia R. Frey, "Between Slavery and Freedom: Virginia Blacks in the American Revolution," *JSoH,* 49 (1983), 376–78, 387–88.

3. Frey, *Water from the Rock,* 161–62; Quarles, *Negro in the American Revolution,* 24–26; Ronald Hoffman, *A Spirit of Dissension: Economics, Politics, and the Revolution in Maryland* (Baltimore, 1973), 148, 152–57, 188; Louis Morton, *Robert Carter of Nomini Hall: A Virginia Tobacco Planter of the Eighteenth Century* (Charlottesville, Va., 1941), 55–56; quotation in W. W. Abbot, ed., *The Papers of George Washington: Revolutionary War Series,* 4 vols. (Charlottesville, Va., 1985–91), 2: 479–80.

4. Quarles, *Negro in the American Revolution,* 26–32. Sylvia Frey considers the estimate of 800 fugitives to Dunmore to be a serious undercount. Frey, "Between Slavery and Freedom," 378–79. Also Williamsburg *Virginia Gazette,* 17 Nov. 1775 (Purdie); and 2 Dec. 1775 (Purdie & Nicholson); Robert Carter Daybook, 12 July 1776, vol. 13: 175–80, Duke University Library.

5. J. A. Robinson, "British Invade the Chesapeake, 1777," in Ernest McNeill Ellen, ed., *Chesapeake Bay in the American Revolution* (Centerville, Md., 1981), 341–77.

6. Frey, *Water from the Rock,* 145–48, 158–60, quotation on 148. Despite numerous precautions taken by slaveowners—including direct, personal pleas for slave loyalty—the number of runaways increased steadily. When British officers came ashore, it shot up sharply, as with a May 1779 expedition in which the British carried off upward of a thousand slaves. Quotation in William T. Hutchinson and William M. E. Rachal, eds., *The Papers of James Madison,* 17 vols. (Chicago, 1962–), 2: 293; 3: 111.

7. Frey, "Between Slavery and Freedom," 376, 381–83; Quarles, *Negro in the American Revolution,* ch. 7, esp. 118–19; Walter Clark, ed., *The State Records of*

North Carolina, 26 vols. (Raleigh, N.C., 1886–1907), 25: 138; Thad W. Tate, *The Negro in Eighteenth-Century Williamsburg* (Williamsburg, Va., 1965), 219. Quotations in Williamsburg *Virginia Gazette*, 3 Oct. 1777 (Purdie), and Hutchinson and Rachal, eds., *Madison Papers*, 2: 293. John C. Fitzpatrick, ed., *The Writings of George Washington, 1745–1799*, 39 vols. (Washington, D.C., 1931–44), 22: 14.

8. Hutchinson and Rachal, eds., *Madison Papers*, 7: 304; Williamsburg *Virginia Gazette*, 26 Sept. 1777; Frey, *Water from the Rock*, 148, 151, 159–60.

9. Quarles, *Negro in the American Revolution*, 116–118, 122–130; Frey, "Between Slavery and Freedom," 379–84, 88–90, and Frey, *Water from the Rock*, quotations on 149–58, 165.

10. Frey, *Water from the Rock*, 153–54, 163–69, quotations on 167. Frey "Between Slavery and Freedom," 377–82, quotation in James Ballagh, ed., *The Letters of Richard Henry Lee*, 2 vols. (New York, 1911–14), 2: 256.

11. Frey, "Between Slavery and Freedom," 388–90; Frey, *Water from the Rock*, 153–55, 157–59, quotation on 163.

12. Quarles, *Negro in the American Revolution*, 13–14, 55–60, and chs. 5–6; Frey, "Between Slavery and Freedom," 383–85.

13. Frey, "Between Slavery and Freedom," 389–94, quotation on 389; Lorena S. Walsh, "Rural African Americans in the Constitutional Era in Maryland, 1776–1810," *MHM*, 84 (1989), 329.

14. Correspondence file, 1781–84, Great Dismal Swamp Land Company, Duke University; Frey, *Water from the Rock*, 160–61; Hoffman, *A Spirit of Dissension*, quotation on 147–48, also 185, 188–89.

15. Frey, *Water from the Rock*, 148, 159–60; 166–7; Richard Dunn, "Black Society in the Chesapeake," in Ira Berlin and Ronald Hoffman, eds., *Slavery and Freedom in the Age of the American Revolution* (Charlottesville, Va., 1983), 56–59; Lorena S. Walsh, "Plantation Management in the Chesapeake, 1620–1820," *JEH*, 49 (1989), 400–1; also David John Mays, ed., *The Letters and Papers of Edmund Pendleton*, 2 vols. (Charlottesville, Va., 1967), 1: 366.

16. Walsh, "Rural African Americans," 327–36; Lorena Walsh, "Slave Life, Slave Society, and Tobacco Production in the Chesapeake, 1620–1820," in Ira Berlin and Philip D. Morgan, eds., *Cultivation and Culture: Labor and the Shaping of Slave Life in the Americas* (Charlottesville, Va., 1993), 188–91.

17. Walsh, "Plantation Management," 401; Walsh, "Slave Life, Slave Society, and Tobacco Production," 188–89; Lois Green Carr and Lorena S. Walsh, "Economic Diversification and Labor Organization in the Chesapeake, 1650–1820," in Stephen Innes, ed., *Work and Labor in Early America* (Chapel Hill, N.C., 1988), 175–78; Lois Green Carr, "Diversification in the Colonial Chesapeake: Somerset County, Maryland, in Comparative Perspective," in Lois Green Carr, Philip D. Morgan, and Jean B. Russo, eds., *Colonial Chesapeake Society* (Chapel Hill, N.C., 1988), 342–82; Walsh, "Rural African Americans," 327–41; Mary Beth Norton, *Liberty's Daughters: The Revolutionary Experience of American Women, 1750–1800* (Boston, 1980), 164–65; Paul G. E. Clemens, *The Atlantic Economy and Colonial Maryland's Eastern Shore: From Tobacco to Grain* (Ithaca, N.Y., 1980), 168–206.

18. Walsh, "Rural African Americans," 327–36; Walsh, "Slave Life, Slave Society, and Tobacco Production," 187–89; quotation in Norton, *Liberty's Daughters,* 165. For night work, see Carr and Walsh, "Economic Diversification and Labor Organization," 159–60 esp. n31.

19. Walsh, "Rural Africa Americans," 328–37. William Elson's fate is described in Allan Kulikoff, *Tobacco and Slaves: The Development of Southern Cultures in the Chesapeake, 1680–1800* (Chapel Hill, N.C., 1986), 390–91.

20. Frey, "Between Slavery and Freedom," 394–97.

21. Philip D. Morgan and Michael Nicholls, "Runaway Slaves in Eighteenth-Century Virginia," paper delivered at the Organization of American Historians meeting, 1990, 4 n4 esp. table 1 (courtesy of the authors); Allan Kulikoff, "Uprooted Peoples: Black Migrants in the Age of the American Revolution, 1790–1820," in Berlin and Hoffman, eds., *Slavery and Freedom in the Age of the American Revolution,* 144.

22. *Historical Statistics,* 2: 756.

23. Jean B. Lee, *The Price of Nationhood: The American Revolution in Charles County* (New York, 1994), 253; Lorena S. Walsh, "Work and Resistance in the New Republic: The Case of the Chesapeake, 1770–1820," in Mary Turner, ed., *From Chattel Slaves to Wage Slaves: The Dynamics of Labour Bargaining in the Americas* (Kingston, 1995), 97; Fitzpatrick, ed., *Writings of Washington,* 37: 256–68, quotation on 338; Donald Jackson and Dorothy Twohig, eds., *The Diaries of George Washington,* 4 vols. (Charlottesville, Va., 1978), 4: 227–83.

24. Donald L. Robinson, *Slavery in the Structure of American Politics, 1765–1820* (New York, 1971), 82–83; *Md. Law,* 1783, c. 23; William Waller Hening, comp., *Statutes at Large, Being a Collection of All the Laws of Virginia,* 13 vols. (Richmond, Va., 1800–23), 11: 24–25; Dunn, "Black Society in the Chesapeake," 52.

25. Christopher Phillips, *Freedom's Port: The African American Community in Baltimore, 1790–1860* (Urbana, Ill., 1997), 46; Dunn, "Black Society in the Chesapeake," 62–66; Kulikoff, "Uprooted Peoples," 148–51; Lee, *The Price of Nationhood,* 252–53; Michael Tadman, *Speculators and Slaves: Masters, Traders, Slaves in the Old South* (Madison, Wisc., 1989), 12; Lorena S. Walsh, *From Calabar to Carter's Grove: A History of a Virginia Slave Community* (Charlottesville, Va., 1997), ch. 6; Ellen Eslinger, "The Shape of Slavery on the Kentucky Frontier, 1775–1800," *RKHS,* 92 (1994), 1–23; Anita S. Goodstein, "Black History on the Nashville Frontier, 1780–1810," *THQ,* 38 (1979), 401–20; quotation in Merton L. Dillon, *Benjamin Lundy and the Struggle for Negro Freedom* (Urbana, Ill., 1966), 6. Most Chesapeake slaves were taken to Kentucky and Tennessee but also to the lowcountry of South Carolina and Georgia. In the period from 1780 to 1810, between 75,000 (Kulikoff) and 115,000 (Tadman) exited the region. Kulikoff, "Uprooted Peoples," 148; Tadman, *Speculators and Slaves,* 12; David Hackett Fischer and James C. Kelly, *Away, I'm Bound Away: Virginia and the Westward Movement* (Richmond, Va., 1993), 97–98.

26. For the westward movement of the slave population see Dunn, "Black Society in the Chesapeake," 54–67; Allan Kulikoff, "The Colonial Chesapeake: Seedbed of

Antebellum Southern Culture," *JSoH,* 45 (1979), 513–23; Gail S. Terry, "Sustaining the Bonds of Kinship in a Trans-Appalachian Migration, 1790–1811: The Cabell-Beckinridge Slaves Move West," *VMHB,* 102 (1994), 455–80; Eslinger, "Shape of Slavery on the Kentucky Frontier," 1–23. For apprenticing slaves, see Edwin M. Betts, ed., *Thomas Jefferson's Farm Book* (New York, 1953), 466, and Kulikoff, *Tobacco and Slaves,* 373. The slaves' willingness to flee at the first sign that they would be sold—and the slaveowners' appreciation of that threat—is discussed in T. Stephen Whitman, *The Price of Freedom: Slavery and Manumission in Baltimore and Early National Maryland* (Lexington, Ky., 1997), 25.

27. Carr and Walsh, "Economic Diversification and Labor Organization in the Chesapeake," 182; Walsh, "Rural African Americans," 337; Walsh, "Slave Life, Slave Society, and Tobacco Production," 170–3, 190.

28. Walsh, "Rural African Americans," 337–38.

29. Clemens, *The Atlantic Economy and Colonial Maryland's Eastern Shore;* David Klingaman, "The Significance of Grain in the Development of the Tobacco Colonies," *JEH,* 29 (1969), 268–78; Carville Earle and Ronald Hoffman, "Staple Crops and Urban Development in the Eighteenth-Century South," *PAH,* 10 (1976), 7–78; Harold B. Gill, Jr., "Wheat Culture in Colonial Virginia," *AH,* 52 (1978), 380–93; Walsh, "Plantation Management," 393–400; Carr and Walsh, "Economic Diversification and Labor Organization," 147–48; Walsh, "Slaves and Tobacco in the Chesapeake," 179–186.

30. The linkages are elaborated fully in Earle and Hoffman, "Staple Crops and Economic Development," 26–51. Also see Walsh, "Slaves and Tobacco in the Chesapeake," 184–85.

31. Kulikoff, *Tobacco and Slaves,* 342–44, 404–6; Walsh, "Rural African Americans," 330–32; Walsh, "Slave Life, Slave Society, and Tobacco Production," 193–94, 197–99; Dunn, "Black Society in the Chesapeake," 77–78; Kulikoff, "Uprooted Peoples," 153–66; Lee, *Price of Nationhood,* 252–53. For the near ubiquity of slave hire, see Sarah S. Hughes, "Slaves for Hire: The Allocation of Black Labor in Elizabeth City County, Virginia, 1782 to 1810," *WMQ,* 35 (1978), 260–86.

32. See Fitzpatrick, ed., *Writings of Washington,* 5: 3, 355–56, for the use of a mixed labor force of free and slave.

33. Walsh, "Plantation Management," 404–6; Walsh, "Slaves and Tobacco in the Chesapeake," 185–99, for what Walsh calls the Chesapeake's "second system of agriculture," 185; Philip D. Morgan, "Task and Gang Systems: The Organization of Labor on New World Plantations," in Innes, ed., *Work and Labor in Early America,* 200.

34. Quotation in W. W. Abbot, ed., *The Papers of George Washington: Presidential Series,* 6 vols. (Charlottesville, Va., 1987—), 1: 223; Jackson and Twohig, eds., *Diaries of Washington,* 5: 9–10.

35. Quotations in Walsh, "Slave Life, Slave Society, and Tobacco Production," 188–89, 196–97; William Strickland, *Journal of a Tour in the United States of America, 1794–1795,* ed. by J. E. Strickland (New York 1971), 33–34.

36. Kulikoff, *Tobacco and Slaves,* 337–43, 394, 397–401; Dunn, "Black Society in the Chesapeake," 67–82. Quotation in *Runaway Advertisements,* 2: 26 (Annapolis *Maryland Gazette,* 11 Nov. 1756).

37. Kulikoff, *Tobacco and Slaves,* 397–406; Carr and Walsh, "Economic Diversification and Labor Organization in the Chesapeake," 176–8; Bayly E. Marks, "Skilled Blacks in Antebellum St. Mary's County, Maryland," *JSoH,* 53 (1987), 545–52; Fitzpatrick, ed., *Writings of Washington,* 31: 465.

38. Ronald L. Lewis, *Coal, Iron, and Slaves: Industrial Slavery in Maryland and Virginia, 1715–1865* (Westport, Conn., 1979), and Lewis, "The Use and Extent of Slave Labor in the Chesapeake Iron Industry: The Colonial Era," *LHist,* 17 (1977), 388–405; Charles B. Dew, "David Ross and the Oxford Iron Works: A Study of Industrial Slavery in the Early Nineteenth-Century South," *WMQ,* 31 (1974), 189–224.

39. Quotations in Walsh, "Work and Resistance in the New Republic," 113, and in Fitzpatrick, ed., *The Writings of Washington,* 32: 65–66; Petition from Charlotte County, 20 Dec. 1810, Legislative Petitions, Virginia State Library; William Tatham, *An Historical and Practical Essay on the Culture and Commerce of Tobacco* (London, 1800), rpt. in G. Melvin Herdon, *William Tatham and the Cultivation of Tobacco* (Coral Gables, Fla., 1969), 102–5. The continued importance of the slaves' economy as well as its limitations is revealed by the dispute at Mount Vernon when Washington changed the slaves' allowance from unsifted to sifted meal. Slaves, who used the hulls of the unsifted meal to feed their fowl, objected strenuously and forced Washington to reconsider. Fitzpatrick, ed., *The Writings of Washington,* 32: 437–38, 474–75.

40. Quotation in Morgan, "Task and Gang," 213; Walsh, "Work and Resistance in the New Republic," 102–3; Jackson and Twohig, eds., *Diaries of George Washington,* 5: 145.

41. Kulikoff, *Tobacco and Slaves,* 399–401; Carr and Walsh, "Economic Diversification and Labor Organization," 161, 176–83; Walsh, "Slave Life, Slave Society, and Tobacco Production," 186; Carole Shammas, "Black Women's Work and the Evolution of Plantation Society in Virginia," *LHist,* 26 (1985), 5–28; Mary Beth Norton, "'What an Alarming Crisis Is This': Southern Women in the American Revolution," in Jeffrey J. Crow and Larry E. Tise, eds., *The Southern Experience in the American Revolution* (Chapel Hill, N.C., 1978), 203–34.

42. Mary Beth Norton, Herbert Gutman, and Ira Berlin, "Afro-American Family in the Age of Revolution," in Berlin and Hoffman, eds., *Slavery and Freedom in the Age of the Revolution,* 181–82; Dew, "David Ross and the Oxford Iron Works," 212–13; Kulikoff, *Tobacco and Slaves,* 373; Robert Carter to Newyear Branson, 22 Aug. 1788, Carter Letterbooks, Duke University Library.

43. Quotation in Richard Parkinson, *A Tour in America in 1798, 1799, and 1800,* 2 vols. (London, 1805), 2: 448; Jack P. Greene, ed. *The Diary of Colonel Landon Carter of Sabine Hall, 1752–1778,* 2 vols. (Charlottesville, Va., 1965), 2: 648. For Jefferson's opposition to "broad" wives, see Betts, ed., *Thomas Jefferson's Garden*

Book, 450; also Brenda E. Stevenson, *Life in Black and White: Family and Community in the Slave South* (New York, 1996).

44. Quotation in Herbert G. Gutman, *The Black Family in Slavery and Freedom, 1750–1825* (New York, 1976), 158–59.

45. Walsh, "Rural African Americans," 335; Norton, *Liberty's Daughters,* 29–33. See also Robert Carter to Samuel Carter, 10 Mar. 1781, Carter Letterbook, 4: 48, Duke University Library, Durham, N.C.

46. Sylvia R. Frey, "'Shaking the Dry Bones': The Dialectic of Conversion," in Ted Ownby, ed., *Black and White: Cultural Interaction in the Antebellum South* (Jackson, Miss., 1993), 23–44, and Frey, "'The Year of Jubilee Is Come': Black Christianity in the Plantation South in Post-Revolution America," in Ronald Hoffman and Peter J. Albert, eds., *Religion in a Revolutionary Age* (Charlottesville, Va., 1994), 94–124; Russell E. Rickey, "From Quarterly to Camp Meeting: A Reconsideration of Early American Methodism," *Methodist History,* 23 (1985), 199–213, esp. 205–6; Frey, *Water from the Rock,* ch. 8. Christine Leigh Heyrman observes that black women outnumbered black men in the early Baptist and Methodist churches three to two. *Southern Cross: The Beginnings of the Bible Belt* (New York, 1997), 217–18.

47. Elmer T. Clark et al., eds., *The Journal and Letters of Francis Asbury,* 3 vols. (Nashville, Tenn., 1958), 1: 403, 593; 3: 15. Quotations in *Runaway Advertisements,* 1: 269–70 (Williamsburg *Virginia Gazette* [Purdie], 1 May 1778), 421 (Richmond *Virginia Gazette and General Advertizer* [Davis], 27 Oct. 1790]; 2: 401 (*Maryland Journal and Baltimore Advertiser,* 8 Jan. 1790). For an estimate of African-American membership in the Baptist, Methodist, and Presbyterian Church in 1810, see Heyrman, *Southern Cross,* 5, 23, 46, 218–20, 262–63.

48. Quotation in Heyrman, *Southern Cross,* 47.

49. Carville Earle and Ronald Hoffman, "The Urban South: The First Two Centuries," in Blaine A. Brownell and David R. Goldfield, eds., *The City in Southern History: The Growth of Urban Civilization in the South* (Port Washington, N.Y., 1977), 23–51; Marianne B. Sheldon, "Black-White Relations in Richmond, Virginia, 1782–1820," *JSoH,* 45 (1979), 26–44; Phillips, *Freedom's Port,* 10–16, 57–59; G. Terry Sharrer, "Flour Milling in the Growth of Baltimore, 1750–1830," *MHM,* 71 (1976), 322–33; Earle and Hoffman, "Staple Crops and Urban Development," 7–78; Walsh, "Slave Life, Slave Society, and Tobacco Production," 191.

50. Earle and Hoffman, "Staple Crops and Urban Development," 51–57; Joseph A. Goldenberg, *Shipbuilding in Colonial America* (Charlottesville, Va., 1976), 118–20; Walsh, "Slave Life, Slave Society, and Tobacco Production," 191–92; Lewis, *Coal, Iron, and Slaves,* 21–26, 199–227; Kulikoff, *Tobacco and Slaves,* 414–16; Charles G. Steffen, "The Pre-Industrial Iron Worker: Northampton Iron Works, 1780–1820," *LHist,* 20 (1979), 93–95; Dew, "David Ross and the Oxford Iron Works," 195, 198–99, 206–214.

51. Frey, *Water from the Rock,* 216–18; Jacob Price, "Economic Function and the Growth of American Port Towns in the Eighteenth Century," *PAH,* 8 (1974), 176; Whitman, *The Price of Freedom,* 10; Phillips, *Freedom's Port,* 14–15; James Sidbury,

"Slave Artisans in Richmond, Virginia, 1780–1810," in Howard B. Rock, Paul A. Gilje, and Robert Asher, eds., *American Artisans: Crafting Social Identity, 1750–1850* (Baltimore, 1995), 48–62; Michael L. Nicholls, "Recreating White Virginia," in Lois Green Carr, ed., *The Chesapeake and Beyond* (Crownsville, Md., 1992), 27–28; also Frey, *Water from the Rock,* 216–18; Dunn, "Black Society in the Chesapeake," 62.

52. Sheldon, "Richmond Black-White Relations," 29; Whitman, *The Price of Freedom,* 11–12, 18–19; Phillips, *Freedom's Port,* 19–20.

53. Walsh, "Slave Life, Slave Society, and Tobacco Production," 191–92, 354 n43; Sidbury, "Slave Artisans in Richmond," 56–60; Tommy L. Bogger, *Free Blacks in Norfolk, 1790–1860: The Darker Side of Freedom* (Charlottesville, Va., 1997), 20–21; Whitman, *Price of Freedom,* 14–16; Phillips, *Freedom's Port,* 16, 18–19, 22–24, 32; quotation in Petition from Henrico Country, 8 June 1782, Legislative Papers, Virginia State Library, Richmond; Hening, comp., *Statutes at Large,* 11: 57–59; Loren Schweninger, "The Underside of Slavery: The Internal Economy, Self-Hire, and Quasi-Freedom in Virginia 1780–1865," *S&A,* 12 (1991), 2–3; Nicholls, "Recreating White Virginia," 28–29.

54. Whitman, *The Price of Freedom,* 24, 62, 90–91, and Whitman, "Diverse Good Causes: Manumission and the Transformation of Urban Slavery," *SSH,* 19 (1995), 352–53; Phillips, *Freedom's Port,* 19, 24; quotation in Richmond *Virginia Gazette and General Advertiser* (Augustine Davis), 5 Nov. 94, courtesy of Michael Nicholls.

55. Sidbury, "Slave Artisans in Richmond," 50, and Tina H. Sheller, "Freemen, Servants, and Slaves: Artisans and Craft Structure of Revolutionary Baltimore Town," 24–32, both in Rock, Gilje, and Asher, eds., *American Artisans;* Whitman, *The Price of Freedom,* 11–13, and Whitman, "Diverse Good Causes," 336–37; Phillips, *Freedom's Port,* 16–19.

56. Whitman, *The Price of Freedom,* ch. 1, and Whitman "Diverse Good Causes," 336–37; Sidbury, "Slave Artisans in Richmond," 50, and Sheller, "Freemen, Servants, and Slaves," 24–32; Gary L.Browne, *Baltimore in the Nation, 1789–1861* (Chapel Hill, N.C., 1939), 58–59.

57. Suzanne Lebsock, *Free Women of Petersburg: Status and Culture in a Southern Town, 1784–1860* (New York, 1984), 139, 182, quotation on 99; Parkinson, *A Tour in America in 1798, 1799, and 1800,* 2: 433; *Runaway Advertisements,* 1: 211–12 (Richmond *Virginia Gazette* or *Weekly Advertiser* [Nicholson and Prentice], 19 Jan. 1782). Nicholls, "Recreating White Virginia," 27–28, see 30 for market regulations.

58. Lebsock, *Free Women of Petersburg,* 182; Whitman, *The Price of Freedom,* 19.

59. Fitzpatrick, ed., *The Writings of Washington,* 33: 394–95.

60. *Gentlemen's Magazine and Historical Chronicle,* 34 (1764), 261; Petition from Petersburg, 11 Dec. 1805, Legislative Petitions, Virginia State Library; *Proceedings and Debates of the Convention of North-Carolina Called to Amend the Constitution of the State* (Raleigh, 1835), 351.

61. Quarles, *Negro in the American Revolution,* 111–57; quotation in Petition from Henrico County, 1781, Legislative Petitions, Virginia State Library.

62. Quarles, *Negro in the American Revolution,* 115–19, and ch. 6; Luther P.

Jackson, "Virginia Negro Soldiers and Seamen in the American Revolution," *JNH*, 27 (1942), 274–5; Frey, "Between Slavery and Freedom," 375–98, and Frey, *Water from the Rock,* ch. 6; Hening, comp., *Statutes at Large,* 8: 103; 9: 308–9; Morgan and Nicholls, "Runaway Slaves in Eighteenth-Century Virginia," 10–12.

63. Changes in the manumission laws are summarized in Ira Berlin, *Slaves without Masters: The Free Negro in the Antebellum South* (New York, 1974), 29–30.

64. Daniel Coker, *Dialogue between a Virginian and an African Minister* (Baltimore, 1810).

65. Whitman, *The Price of Freedom,* ch. 6; Phillips, *Freedom's Port,* 37–42; Christopher Phillips, "The Roots of Quasi-Freedom: Manumission and Term Slavery in Early National Baltimore," *SS,* new ser., 4 (1993), 39–66; Lebsock, *Free Women of Petersburg,* 91, 94–95.

66. Catterall, *Judicial Cases,* 1: 183–5; 317; 4, 114; Anne Arundel Misc. Manumission, 4 Jan. 1802, Maryland State Archives, Annapolis; quotation in [John S. Tyson], *Life of Elisha Tyson, Philanthropist* (Baltimore, 1825), 25.

67. Whitman, *The Price of Freedom,* 99–110; Phillips, "Roots of Quasi-Freedom," 53–58; Lee, *Price of Nationhood,* 209–10; Bogger, *Free Blacks in Norfolk,* 11–19.

68. Phillips, *Freedom's Port,* 24–25, 46–53; Whitman, *The Price of Freedom,* ch. 5; Bogger, *Free Blacks in Norfolk,* 12–20; Lebsock, *Free Women of Petersburg,* 95–96.

69. [Tyson], *Life of Elisha Tyson,* 15; S. Greaves (?) to Meirs Fisher, 27 May 1790, Robert Pleasants to James Pemberton, letterbook copy, 22 Apr. 1795, PAS ; Catterall, ed., *Judicial Cases Concerning Slavery,* 1: 109–10; 2: 18–19, 54; 4: 2–5, 49–52, 54; Phillips, *Freedom's Port,* 35–36; Bogger, *Free Blacks in Norfolk,*94–97; Peter Wallenstein, "Indian Foremothers: Race, Sex, Slavery, and Freedom in Early Virginia," in Catherine Clinton and Michele Gillespie, eds., *The Devil's Lane: Sex and Race in the Early South* (New York, 1997), 61–73. Also see Michael L. Nicholls, "Passing through This Troublesome World: Free Blacks in the Early Southside," *VMHB,* 92 (1984), 59–60.

70. Whitman, *The Price of Freedom,* 63–68; Phillips, *Freedom's Port,* 35–36; Lee, *Price of Nationhood,* 210–16. Still, freedom was not easily secured, as William and Mary Butler's owners dug deep into their pockets to fight the suit. When they failed, their lawyers declined to act on the court's decision and delayed long enough to sell some of the Butlers into permanent slavery. Walsh, "Rural African Americans," 335.

71. Both Whitman and Phillips emphasized this point, see for example, Whitman, *The Price of Freedom,* ch. 2, esp. 72, and Phillips, *Freedom's Port,* 46.

72. Annapolis *Maryland Gazette,* 9 Aug. 1792.

73. Greene, ed., *Diary of Landon Carter,* 2: 777, 1012, 1051–52; Baltimore *Maryland Journal,* 25 June 1793; Annapolis *Maryland Gazette,* 6 May 1790; Richmond *Virginia Gazette,* 2 May 1792; Richmond *Virginia Gazette,* 26 Dec. 1777; Annapolis *Maryland Gazette,* 6 July 1797.

74. [The Reverend] Thurston to Robert Carter, 5 Aug. 1796, Robert Carter Papers, Library of Congress.

75. Frances S. Childs, *French Refugee Life in the United States, 1790–1800* (Balti-

more, 1940), 15, 89–90; Bogger, *Free Blacks in Norfolk,* 25–27; James Sidbury, "Saint Domingue in Virginia: Ideology, Local Meanings, and Resistance to Slavery, 1790–1800," *JSoH,* 53 (1997), 534–35, 538; Walter C. Hartridge, "The Refugees from the Island of St. Domingo in Maryland," *MHM,* 38 (1943), 103–8; Phillips, *Freedom's Port,* 70–72, 87–88.

76. Berlin, *Slaves without Masters,* 45–49, and 48 n47.

77. Whitman, *The Price of Freedom,* 93; Phillips, *Freedom's Port,* 54–55, 91–92. The manumission of men and women in roughly equal numbers and the movement toward numerical sexual equality was counter to patterns of manumission throughout the hemisphere. Herbert S. Klein, *African Slavery in Latin America and the Caribbean* (New York, 1986), 156–57. The phenomena may have been confined to Maryland. See Lebsock, *Free Women of Petersburg,* 95–96, 281–83 n18–25; Bogger, *Free Blacks in Norfolk,* 21, for the traditional numerical dominance of manumitted women in at least one Virginia city.

78. Whitman, *The Price of Freedom,* 95; Phillips, *Freedom's Port,* 62–63.

79. Whitman, *The Price of Freedom,* 11–12, 24, 24–27; Phillips, *Freedom's Port,* ch. 2.

80. Berlin, *Slaves without Masters,* ch. 4.

81. *Ibid.,* 51–52; Phillips, *Freedom's Port,* 88–92.

82. Quotation in Petition from Petersburg, 11 Dec. 1805, Legislative Petitions, Virginia State Library; Berlin, *Slaves without Masters,* 54–55; Dunn, "Black Society in the Chesapeake," 75–77; Lebsock, *Free Women of Petersburg,* 7; Michael L. Nicholls, "Recreating White Virginia," 27–28; Harry M. Ward and Harold E. Greer, Jr., *Richmond during the Revolution, 1775–1783* (Charlottesville, Va., 1977), 8.

83. Phillips, *Freedom's Port,* 60, 91–101.

84. *Ibid.,* 60; Walsh, *From Calabar to Carter's Grove,* 217–18.

85. Phillips, *Freedom's Port,* 73–81, 108–9, 121; Bogger, *Free Blacks in Norfolk,* ch. 3.

86. Phillips, *Freedom's Port,* 32, 83–84, quotation on 83.

87. Tate, *The Negro in Eighteenth-Century Williamsburg;* ch. 4; Bogger, *Free Blacks in Norfolk,* 145–48; Lebsock, *Free Women of Petersburg,* 9; Sidbury, "Slave Artisans in Richmond," 57; Phillips, *Freedom's Port,* ch. 5.

11. Fragmentation in the Lower South

1. Ronald Hoffman, "The 'Disaffected' in the Revolutionary South," in Alfred F. Young, ed., *The American Revolution: Explorations in the History of American Radicalism* (De Kalb, Ill., 1976), 273–316; John Shy, "The American Revolution: The Military Conflict Considered as a Revolutionary War," in Stephen G. Kurtz and James H. Hutson, eds., *Essays on the American Revolution* (Chapel Hill, N.C., 1973), 121–56, and Shy, "British Strategy for Pacifying the Southern Colonies, 1778–1781," in Jeffrey J. Crow and Larry E. Tise, eds., *The Southern Experience in the American Revolution* (Chapel Hill, N.C., 1978), 155–73; John S. Pancake, *This Destructive War: The British Campaign in the Carolinas, 1780–1782* (University, Ala.,

1985). For the backcountry, see Rachel N. Klein, *Unification of a Slave State: The Rise of the Planter Class in the South Carolina Backcountry, 1760–1808* (Chapel Hill, N.C., 1990), ch. 3. In addition, pirates and privateers raided the coast, carrying off numerous slaves. Daniel F. Schafer, "'Yellow Silk Ferret Tied Round Their Wrists': African Americans in British East Florida, 1763–1784," in David R. Colburn and Jane L. Landers, eds., *The African American Heritage of Florida* (Gainesville, Fla, 1995), 94.

2. Josiah Smith to James Poyas, quotation in 18 May 1775, also 16 June 1775, Josiah Smith Letterbooks, Southern Historical Collection, University of North Carolina; quotation in *Runaway Advertisements,* 3: 345 (Charlestown *South-Carolina Gazette* [Timothy], 7 Nov. 1775).

3. Sylvia R. Frey, *Water from the Rock: Black Resistance in a Revolutionary Age* (Princeton, N.J., 1991), 54–59, quotation on 57; Robert A. Olwell, "'Domestick Enemies': Slavery and Political Independence in South Carolina, May 1775–March 1776," *JSoH,* 55 (1989), 32–33; M. Foster Farley, "The South Carolina Negro in the American Revolution, 1775–1783," *SCHM,* 79 (1978), 76–77; Benjamin Quarles, *The Negro in the American Revolution* (Chapel Hill, N.C., 1961), 14, 124–27; Philip D. Morgan, "Black Life in Eighteenth-Century Charleston," *PAH,* new ser., 1 (1984), 218 n95, and Morgan, "Black Society in the Lowcountry, 1760–1810," in Ira Berlin and Ronald Hoffman, eds., *Slavery and Freedom in the Age of the American Revolution* (Charlottesville, Va., 1983), 108–9; Peter H. Wood, "'Taking Care of Business' in Revolutionary South Carolina: Republicanism and the Slave Society," in Crow and Tise, eds., *Southern Experience,* 278; Jeffrey J. Crow, *The Black Experience in Revolutionary North Carolina* (Raleigh, N.C., 1977), 56–58. Vigilance paid off, as planters unearthed numerous plots "to take the Country by killing whites." *Laurens Papers,* 10: 162–63.

4. Frey, *Water from the Rock,* 57–60; *Laurens Papers,* 10: 320–22, and quotation on 10: 162–63; Robert M. Weir, *Colonial South Carolina: A History* (Millwood, N.Y., 1983), 200–3; Morgan, "Charleston," 213–14; Wood, "Taking Care of Business," 284–87, quotation on 292 n49; Olwell, "'Domestick Enemies,'" 33–35, 38–39n.

5. Frey, *Water from the Rock,* 61; Lilla M. Hawes, ed., "The Papers of Lachan McIntosh, 1774–1799," *GHQ,* 39 (1955), 54. For the flight of a family group see, *Runaway Advertisements,* 3: 343 (*Charles Town South-Carolina Gazette* [Timothy], 13 March 1775).

6. Olwell, "'Domestick Enemies,'" 21–48, for a full explication of the slaveholders' fear of a British–slave alliance. Also see Frey, *Water from the Rock,* quotation on 59, 64–65; Crow, *Black Experience in N.C.,* quotation on 58–59; Jeffrey J. Crow, "Slave Rebelliousness and Social Conflict in North Carolina, 1775 to 1802," *WMQ,* 37 (1980), 83–85; Peter H. Wood, "'The Dream Deferred': Black Freedom Struggles on the Eve of White Independence," in Gary Y. Okihiro, ed., *In Resistance: Studies in African, Caribbean, and Afro-American History* (Amherst, Mass., 1986), 178–79; Alan D. Watson, "Impulse toward Independence: Resistance and Rebellion among North Carolina Slaves, 1750–1775," *JNH,* 63 (1978), quotation on 324–25. Also *Laurens Papers,* 10: 546–49, 576–77. When Patriot militiamen raided Sullivan's Island

in December 1775, they also arrested several white people. "Journal of the Council of Safety," *Collections of the South Carolina Historical Society,* 3: 62–3, 75, 84, 89, 103–105, 145.

7. David George, "An Account of the Life of Mr. David George," in John Rippon, ed., *The Annual Baptist Register* (London, 1794), 473–80; Mary Beth Norton, *Liberty's Daughters: The Revolutionary Experience of American Women, 1750–1800* (Boston, 1980), 209–12; Josiah Smith to George Applely, 2 Dec. 1780, Josiah Smith Letterbooks; *Runaway Advertisements,* 3: 375 (Charleston *Gazette of the State of South-Carolina* [Timothy and Boden], 13 Oct. 1779).

8. Thomas Pinckney to Eliza Pinckney, 17 May 1779, Pinckney Family Papers, South Carolina Historical Society; *Runaway Advertisements,* 3: 569 (Charleston *South-Carolina and American General Gazette,* 6 Sept. 1780, 21 Oct. 1780); 3: 580 (Charleston *Royal Gazette,* 16–19 May 1781); 3: 584 (Charleston *Royal Gazette,* 11–14 July 1781); 4: 79 (Savannah *Royal Georgia Gazette,* 7 Sept. 1780); Frey, *Water from the Rock,* 92–95; Josiah Smith to George Applely, 2 Dec. 1780, Josiah Smith Letterbooks. For the Indian connection, see Michael Mullin, "British Caribbean and North American Slaves in an Era of War and Revolution, 1775–1807," in Crow and Tise, *Southern Experience,* 261.

9. Quotation in Frey, *Water from the Rock,* 65–66; Crow, "Slave Rebelliousness," 86–88; Betty Wood, "Some Aspects of Female Resistance to Chattel Slavery in Low Country Georgia, 1763–1815," *HJ,* 30 (1987), 612; quotation on George Smith McCowen, Jr., *The British Occupation of Charleston, 1780–82* (Columbia, S.C., 1972), 44. For the new tone of runaway advertisements see, for example, *Runaway Advertisements,* 3: 529, 571 (Charleston *South-Carolina and American General Gazette,* 16 Apr. 1778, 4 Nov. 1780); 4: 83–84 (Savannah *Royal Georgia Gazette,* 18 Jan. 1781).

10. *Slave Advertisements,* 3: 579 (Charleston *Royal Gazette,* 21–24 Mar. 1781).

11. Quotations in Daniel E. Meaders, "South Carolina Fugitives as Viewed through Local Colonial Newspapers with Emphasis on Runaway Notices, 1732–1801," *JNH,* 60 (1975), 309; *Runaway Advertisements,* 3: 487 (Charleston *South-Carolina and American General Gazette,* 25 Sept.–2 Oct. 1776); 3: 584 (Charleston *Royal Gazette,* 11–14 July 1781).

12. Frey, *Water from the Rock,* quotation on 101–102; *Runaway Advertisements,* 3: 566 (Charleston *South-Carolina and American General Gazette,* 19 Jan. 1780).

13. Frey, *Water from the Rock,* quotation on 113–14.

14. McCowen, *British Occupation of Charleston,* 2, 33–34, 98, and esp. ch. 5; Sylvia R. Frey, "The British and the Black: A New Perspective," *The Historian,* 38 (1976), 230–32; Frey, *Water from the Rock,* 96–98, 100.

15. Schafer, "'Yellow Silk Ferret Tied Round Their Wrists,'" 94–95; McCowen, *British Occupation of Charleston,* 2, 33–34, 98, and esp. ch. 5; Frey, *Water from the Rock,* 96–98, 100, and Frey, "British and the Black," 230–23; Crow, *Black Experience in N.C.,* 72–75. On March 14, 1781, the Charleston *Royal Gazette* listed some 600 blacks employed by the army as everything from patrons to carpenters and blacksmiths.

16. Frey, *Water from the Rock,* 136–40, and "The British and the Black," 229–32; Crow, *Black Experience in N.C.,* 75–79, and Crow, "Slave Rebelliousness," 87–88. See the last on the use of foragers by the British army in North Carolina and Cornwallis's efforts to disarm blacks. Franklin and Mary Wickwire, *Cornwallis: The American Adventure* (Boston, 1970), 142–43. For Dunmore's next adventure, see Wright, *Florida in the American Revolution,* 118–20; J. Barton Starr, *Tories, Dons, and Rebels: The American Revolution in British West Florida* (Gainesville, Fla, 1976), 220–21.

17. Roger Norman Buckley, *Slaves in Red Coats: The British West India Regiments, 1795–1815* (New Haven, Conn., 1979).

18. Frey, *Water from the Rock,* 88. More than any other British field commander, General Charles Cornwallis considered the possibility of creating an army of former slaves. Although he ultimately rejected that course, during his drive through North Carolina Cornwallis transformed the black people who trailed his army into foraging units. They did their job too well, and he ordered that "no Negroe shall be Suffred to Carry Arms on any pretence." Even that failed to stop the former slaves, and at last Cornwallis called a halt to the "Shameful Maurauding" and "Scandalous Crimes." His reversal came too late. The mobilization of black stragglers had already had a powerful affect, and one North Carolina slaveholder was certain that Cornwallis could have raised an army of "500 Negroes" in Wilmington alone. Crow, "Slave Rebelliousness," 88–89.

19. Frey, *Water from the Rock,* 94–95.

20. McCowen, *British Occupation of Charleston,* 33–34; Frey, *Water from the Rock,* 82. Quarles, *Negro in the American Revolution,* 107–110 also n29 (slaves as bounties). For refugeeing to West Florida, see Wright, *Florida in the American Revolution,* 10–12, 14, 37–39, 43–44, 46. Jane Landers, "Spanish Sanctuary: Fugitive Slaves in Florida, 1687–1790," *FHQ,* 62 (1984), 303, notes that some 8,000 slaves were taken to East Florida. Wright, "Blacks in British East Florida," *FHQ,* 54 (1976), 427; Schafer, "'Yellow Silk Ferret Tied Round Their Wrists,'" 94; Gwendolyn Midlo Hall, *Africans in Colonial Louisiana: The Development of Afro-Creole Culture in the Eighteenth Century* (Baton Rouge, La., 1992), 283–84; Caroline M. Burson, *The Stewardship of Don Estaban Miró, 1782–1792* (New Orleans, 1942), 106; Starr, *Tories, Dons, and Rebels,* 49. See above, pp. 326–27.

21. Frey, *Water from the Rock,* 89–91, 111–127; Hawes, ed., "Minute Book, Savannah Board of Police, 1779," *GHQ,* 45 (1961), 245–57; McCowen, *British Occupation of Charleston,* 93–94.

22. Frey, *Water from the Rock,* 120–21; Morgan, "Lowcountry," 109.

23. Frey, *Water from the Rock,* 93–95, 120–128.

24. David Ramsey, *History of South Carolina,* 2 vols. (Charleston, 1808), 1: 334.

25. Quarles, *Negro in the American Revolution,* 60–67; Farley, "South Carolina Negro," 80–82; Klein, *Unification of a Slave State,* 106–7.

26. Frey, *Water from the Rock,* 85–86, 94, 112–13, 193; Quarles, *Negro in the American Revolution,* 126–28; Schafer, "'Yellow Silk Ferret Tied Round Their Wrists,'" 95–97; William T. Hutchinson and William M. E. Rachal, eds., *The Papers*

of James Madison, 17 vols. (Chicago, 1962), 2: 55–57. In 1780 Virginia exempted Georgia and South Carolina slaveholders from the state's prohibition on the importation of slaves. William W. Hening, eds., *The Statutes at Large: Being a Collection of All the Laws of Virginia,* 18 vols. (Richmond, 1809–23), 10: 307–8; William L. Saunders, ed., *Colonial Records of North Carolina,* 10 vols. (Raleigh, 1886–90), 10: 567, 569.

27. Wilbur Henry Siebert, ed., *Loyalists in East Florida, 1774 to 1785,* 2 vols. (Deland, Fla., 1929), 2: 134.

28. Quarles, *Negro in the American Revolution,* 102–108; Frey, *Water from the Rock,* 68; Joyce E. Chaplin, *An Anxious Pursuit: Agricultural Innovation and Modernity in the Lower South, 1730–1815* (Chapel Hill, N.C., 1993), 235.

29. Quarles, *Negro in the American Revolution,* 107–10; Farley, "South Carolina Negro," 78; Frey, *Water from the Rock,* 104–5. For impressment of slaves in South Carolina, see William Edwin Hemphill et al., eds., *Journals of the General Assembly and House of Representatives, 1776–1780* (Columbia., S.C., 1970), 114, 197–98, 254. Thomas J. Cooper and David J. McCord, comps., *The Statutes at Large of South Carolina,* 10 vols. (Columbia, S.C., 1837–41), 4: 428–29.

30. McCowen, *British Occupation of Charleston,* 108; Quarles, *Negro in the American Revolution,* ch. 6; Klein, *Unification of a Slave State,* 106–7.

31. See, for example, *Runaway Advertisements,* 4: 81 (Savannah *Royal Georgia Gazette,* 12 Oct. 1780).

32. Frey, *Water from the Rock,* 168; Jerome J. Nadelhaft, *The Disorders of War: The Revolution in South Carolina* (Orono, Maine, 1981), 63, 72; Klein, *Unification of a Slave State,* 95–104; Chaplin, *Anxious Pursuit,* 322–23. Quotations in Morgan, "Lowcountry," 109, 136–39 esp. n99; in Norton, *Liberty's Daughter's,* 208–9, and in Michael Mullin, "British Caribbean and North American Slaves in an Era of War and Revolution, 1775–1807," in Crow and Tise, eds., *Southern Experience,* 239–41.

33. Quotation in Frey, *Water from the Rock,* 114–15. Also Quarles, *Negro in the American Revolution,* 121.

34. Charles Town *South-Carolina and American General Gazette,* 20 Jan. 1781; Chaplin, *Anxious Pursuit,* 324–25.

35. Eliza Pinckney to Thomas Pinckney, 17 May 1779, Pinckney Family papers, South Carolina Historical Society, Charleston; Eliza Pinckney to ?, 25 Sept. 1780, Pinckney Family Papers, Library of Congress; Josiah Smith to ?, 2 Dec. 1780, 15 Mar. 1781, Josiah Smith Letterbooks; Norton, *Liberty's Daughters,* 211–12; quotation in Morgan, "Lowcountry," 109–110; Nadelhaft, *Disorders of War,* 64; McCowen, *British Occupation of Charleston,* 104; quotation in Joyce E. Chaplin, "Creating a Cotton South in Georgia and South Carolina, 1760–1815," *JSoH,* 57 (1991), 181–82.

36. James Harold Easterbye, *Wadoo Barony: Its Fate as Told in the Colleton Papers, 1773–1793* (Columbia, S.C., 1952), 4; Frey, *Water from the Rock,* 114–16; Norton, *Liberty's Daughters,* 212. For the general problem of disorder on the plantation, see Joyce E. Chaplin, "Tidal Rice Cultivation and the Problem of Slavery in South Carolina and Georgia, 1760–1815," *WMQ,* 49 (1992), 38–39.

37. Josiah Smith to ?, 15 Mar. 1781, Josiah Smith Letterbooks; Norton, *Liberty's Daughter's,* 207–12, quotations on 208 and 212; Chaplin, *Anxious Pursuit,* 234–35; Chaplin, "Creating a Cotton South," 181–82.

38. Gray, *So. Ag.,* 1: 593–94; Frey, *Water from the Rock,* 208–09; G. Terry Sharrer, "The Indigo Bonanza in South Carolina, 1740–90," *T&C,* 12 (1971), 455.

39. Chaplin, "Creating a Cotton South," 178–79, 181–83, and Chaplin, *Anxious Pursuit,* 157–58. On gardens, see Rouchefoucault Liancourt, *Travels through the United States of North America . . . in the Years 1795, 1796, and 1797,* 2 vols. (London, 1799), 1: 599.

40. Chaplin, *Anxious Pursuit,* 208–20; Chaplin, "Creating a Cotton South," 182–86.

41. Josiah Smith to ?, 15 Mar. 1781, Josiah Smith Letterbooks; Frey, *Water from the Rock,* 117–18; Morgan, "Lowcountry," 111–13. Still, slaves were able to supply the market in Charleston and other rice ports through their gardening and marketing.

42. McCowen, *British Occupation of Charleston,* 33–34; Frey, *Water from the Rock,* 82–86; Morgan, "Lowcountry," 111–13.

43. Quarles, *Negro in the American Revolution,* 163–66; Frey, *Water from the Rock,* 105–6, 119, 172–82; Ellen G. Wilson, *The Loyal Blacks* (New York, 1976), 31, ch. 3; Kenneth Coleman, *The American Revolution in Georgia, 1763–1789* (Athens, Ga., 1958), 145–46; Eldon Jones, "The British Withdrawal from the South, 1781–1785," in W. Robert Higgins, ed., *The Revolutionary War in the South: Power, Conflict, and Leadership* (Durham, N.C., 1979), 268, 284; Phyllis R. Blakeley, "Boston King: A Negro Loyalist Who Sought Refuge in Nova Scotia," *Dalhousie Review,"* 48 (1968), 347–56; Julius Sherrard Scott III, "The Common Wind: Currents of Afro-American Communication in the Era of the Haitian Revolution," unpub. doctoral diss., Duke University, 1986, 86–90.

44. Morgan, "Lowcountry," 110–11. For contemporary estimates, see Charleston *South-Carolina Gazette and General Advertizer,* 29 Nov.–2 Dec. 1783; Moultrie, *Memoirs,* 2: 356; Julian P. Boyd et al., eds., *The Papers of Thomas Jefferson,* 21 vols. (Princeton, N.J., 1953—), 8: 199. For Florida slaves, see Landers, "Spanish Sanctuary: Fugitives in Florida," 304–13; Starr, *Tories, Dons, and Rebels,* 48–50, 229–32.

45. "Miscellaneous Papers of James Jackson," *GHQ,* 37 (1953), 78; Coleman, *American Revolution in Georgia,* 145–46; Frey, *Water from the Rock,* 106, 174–79.

46. Morgan, "Lowcountry," 111; Wright, *Florida in the American Revolution,* ch. 10; Jane L. Landers, "Traditions of African American Freedom and Community in Colonial Florida," in Colburn and Landers, eds., *African American Heritage of Florida,* 25–26; Frey, *Water from the Rock,* 179–80; Nadelhaft, *Disorders of War,* 156.

47. Max Farrand, ed., *The Records of the Federal Convention of 1787,* 5 vols. (New Haven, Conn., 1911), 2: 371. Also Chaplin, *Anxious Pursuit,* 119.

48. "Letters of Joseph Clay Merchant of Savannah, 1776–1793," *GHSC,* 8 (1913), 167–75; quotation on 211; Klein, *Unification of a Slave State,* 114–115; Nadelhaft, *Disorders of War,* 145–57; Frey, *Water from the Rock,* 206–10, quotation on 208;

Chaplin, "Tidal Rice Cultivation and the Problem of Slavery," 38–39; Chaplin, *Anxious Pursuit,* 236–38, also Gray, *So. Ag.,* 1: 277–90, 2: 595–96; Coclanis, *Shadow of a Dream,* 133–34.

49. Quotation in Morgan, "Lowcountry," 109, 120. The ability to secede en masse continued to be a major weapon in the slaves' hands. In 1786 a Georgia planter reported that "all my working Negroes left me last night," he supposed because of "the short prospect of provision." Chaplin, *Anxious Pursuit,* 268–70, and Chaplin, "Tidal Rice Cultivation and the Problem of Slavery in South Carolina and Georgia," 54.

50. Morgan, "Lowcountry," 138–40, esp. 139n; Nadelhaft, *Disorders of War,* 132; Quarles, *Negro in the American Revolution,* 174–75; Frey, *Water from the Rock,* 226–228, quotation on 227; Mullin, "British Caribbean and North American Slaves," 240–41. As measured by the number of advertisements placed in the Savannah *Georgia Gazette,* the number of runaways increased substantially after the war. Wood, "Female Resistance," 613–15. Wartime banditry also continued, see Robert M. Weir, "'The Violent Spirit': The Reestablishment of Order, and the Continuity of Leadership in Post-Revolutionary South Carolina," in Ronald Hoffman et al., eds., *An Uncivil War: The Southern Backcountry during the American Revolution* (Charlottesville, Va., 1985), 70–98; Klein, *Unification of a Slave State,* 116–18.

51. Klein, *Unification of a Slave State,* ch. 7; Alfred N. Hunt, *Haiti's Influence on Antebellum America: Slumbering Volcano in the Caribbean* (Baton Rouge, La., 1988), ch. 3; Frances S. Childs, *French Refugee Life in the United States, 1790–1800* (Baltimore, 1940); David Brion Davis, *The Problem of Slavery in the Age of Revolution, 1770–1823* (Ithaca, N.Y., 1975), 113–63.

52. Morgan, "Lowcountry," 138–39. For the post-war consolidation of planter authority, see Klein, *Unification of a Slave State,* chs. 4–5, and for suppression of bandits, 114–18; Nadelhaft, *Disorders of War,* 132; Loren Schweninger, "Slave Independence and Enterprise in South Carolina, 1780–1865," *SCHM,* 93 (1992), 116–17.

53. Frey, *Water from the Rock,* 211, 227–28; William Dusinberre, *Them Dark Days: Slavery in the American Rice Swamps* (New York, 1996), 255. Planters also used other, more subtle incentives to create a new social order, see Joyce E. Chaplin, "Slavery and the Principle of Humanity: A Modern Idea in the Early Lower South," *JSH,* 24 (1990), 309–10.

54. Coclanis, *The Shadow of a Dream,* ch. 4; Chaplin, *Anxious Pursuit,* ch. 7. On the switch from inland to tidal rice production, see Gray, *So. Ag.,* 1: 279–28, 2: 721; Chaplin, "Tidal Rice Cultivation and the Problem of Slavery," 29–61; Morgan, "Lowcountry," 98–107; Johann David Schopf, *Travels in the Confederation, 1783–1784,* ed. and trans. Alfred J. Morrison, 2 vols. (Philadelphia, 1911), 2: 181–82, quotation on 221.

55. Jane G. Landers, "Rebellion and Royalism in Spanish Florida: The French Revolution on Spain's Northern Frontier," in David Barry Gaspar and David Patrick Geggus, eds., *A Turbulent Time: The French Revolution and the Greater Caribbean* (Bloomington, 1997), 156–77; Landers, "Acquisition and Loss on a Spanish Frontier: The Free Black Homesteaders of Florida, 1784–1821," *S&A,* 17 (1996), 85–101; Lan-

ders, "Black Society in Spanish St. Augustine, 1784–1821," unpub. doctoral diss., University of Florida, 1988; Susan R. Parker, "'Men without God or King': Rural Planters of East Florida, 1784–1790," *FHQ,* 69 (1990), 135–55.

56. G. Terry Sharrer, "Indigo in Carolina, 1671–1796," *SCHM,* 72 (1971), 94–103; John J. Winberry, "Repudiation of Carolina Indigo," *SCHM,* 80 (1979), 242–50; Chaplin, *Anxious Pursuit,* 205–6; Morgan, "Lowcountry," 106.

57. Gray, *So. Ag.,* 2: 609; Chaplin, *Anxious Pursuit,* 208–226, 291–319; also John Hebron Moore, "Cotton Breeding in the Old South," *AH,* 30 (1956), 96–97. For sea island cotton see Charles F. Kovacik and Robert E. Mason, "Changes in the South Carolina Sea Island Cotton Industry," *Southeastern Geographer,* 25 (1985), 77–104; Frey, *Water from the Rock,* 212–13, 220–22.

58. "Letters of Joseph Clay," 194–95, quotation on 187; Morgan, "Lowcountry," 84–89, 132; Frey, *Water from the Rock,* 211–13.

59. Patrick S. Brady, "The Slave Trade and Sectionalism in South Carolina, 1787–1808," *JSoH,* 38 (1972), 612–14.

60. Frey, *Water from The Rock,* 180–85, 213; Schafer, "'Yellow Silk Ferret Tied Round Their Wrists,'" 97; *Runaway Advertisements,* 4: 104–5, 111 (Savannah *Gazette of the State of Georgia,* 7 May 1783, 22 Jan. 1784); 3: 403 (Charleston *State Gazette of South-Carolina* [Timothy], 22 Jan. 1787). Similarly, in 1787 a North Carolina slaveholder tried to recover a fugitive proportedly at large since February 1781, who was reported to have been sent from Wilmington to Charleston by the British, "where he sometimes passed for a freeman, and hired himself as such." Some slaveholders attempted to recover slaves who had taken refuge with the Indians; see Theodora J. Thompson and Rosa S. Lumpkin, eds., *Journal of the House of Representatives, 1783–1784* (Columbia., S.C., 1977), 530. Finally, slaveholders opened negotiations with slaves who had taken refuge in Florida; one slave told his master's envoy that he might return "willingly . . . but not at present." Morgan, "Lowcountry," 110.

61. Morgan, "Lowcountry," 84–86 quotation in n3; Robert William Fogel and Stanley L. Engerman, "Philanthropy at Bargain Prices: Notes on the Economics of Gradual Emancipation," *JLS,* 3 (1974), 381–83; Chaplin, "Creating a Cotton South," 186–87, and Chaplin, *Anxious Pursuit,* 290–91; G. Melvin Herndon, "Samuel Edward Butler of Virginia Goes to Georgia, 1784," *GHQ,* 52 (1968), 115–31; Allan Kulikoff, "Uprooted Peoples: Black Migrants in the Age of the American Revolution, 1790–1820," in Berlin and Hoffman, eds., *Slavery and Freedom in the Age of the American Revolution,* 149.

62. Morgan, "Lowcountry," 84–92, 132; Brady, "Slave Trade and Sectionalism in South Carolina," 612–14; Kulikoff, "Uprooted Peoples," 149–51; Chaplin, *Anxious Pursuit,* 320–22.

63. Winthrop D. Jordan, *White over Black: American Attitudes toward The Negro, 1550–1812* (Chapel Hill, N.C., 1968), 325–31.

64. Morgan, "Lowcountry," 93–96. "The best tidal swamp was worth at least twice as much as inland swamp—up to four times as much if improved." Chaplin, "Tidal Rice Cultivation and the Problem of Slavery," 36–46 quotation on 43, and

Chaplin, *Anxious Pursuit,* 237–76, indicates that the enormous capital investment in tidal rice production squeezed out smaller planters and barred the entry of newcomers.

65. Klein, *Unification of a Slave State,* 21–26, 151–53, 247–68; Chaplin, *Anxious Pursuit,* 277–80, 285–88, 321–22; Morgan, "Lowcountry," 83–85; Frey, *Water from the Rock,* 213–15, also Gray, *So. Ag.,* 1: 438, 444–46.

66. Morgan, "Lowcountry," 118–20; Chaplin, "Tidal Rice Cultivation and the Problem of Slavery," 55–56, and Chaplin, *Anxious Pursuits,* ch. 7, esp. 266–70; quotation in Dusinberre, *Them Dark Days,* 274–75. The drivers' authority also grew because of an increase in absenteeism among owners, who increasingly withdrew to Charleston and also spent more time living abroad. Luigi Castiglioni, an Italian nobleman who visited the lowcountry after the war, believed most planters were "raised in England" and lived "for the most part in Charleston, visiting their lands two or three times a year." Luigi Castiglioni, *Viaggio: Travels in the United States of North America, 1785–1787,* ed. and trans. Antonio Pace (Syracuse, N.Y., 1983), 164.

67. Morgan, "Work and Culture," 575; Wood, *Women's Work, Men's Work,* 16–17; Chaplin, *Anxious Pursuits,* 231, 269, 326–67.

68. Mullin, "British Caribbean and North American Slaves in an Era of War and Revolution," 249; Morgan, "Lowcountry," 105–8; Chaplin, "Tidal Rice Cultivation and the Problem of Slavery," 56–57; quotation in Richard K. Murdock, ed., "Letters and Papers of Dr. Daniel Turner: A Rhode Islander in South Georgia," *GHQ,* 54 (1970), 102.

69. Morgan, "Lowcountry," 105–6. For the resistance of former lowcountry slaves to the gang labor system preferred by upcountry planters, see Chaplin, *Anxious Pursuit,* 122–23, 324–25, 327; Drew Gilpin Faust, *James Henry Hammond and the Old South: A Design for Mastery* (Baton Rouge, La., 1982), ch. 5.

70. Morgan, "Lowcountry," 97, 99–105; Chaplin, *Anxious Pursuit,* 236–73, 353–55. For sexual division of labor, see Chaplin, "Tidal Rice Cultivation and the Problem of Slavery," 33, 47–48, 49, 55, and for women's occupations, Norton, *Liberty's Daughters,* 29–33.

71. Morgan, "Lowcountry," 97–108; Ira Berlin, "The Slaves' Changing World," in James O. Horton and Lois E. Horton, eds., *A History of the African American People* (New York, 1995), 42–59.

72. Chaplin, *Anxious Pursuit,* 126–27, 270–71.

73. Petition of James Brock(?) et al., nd, Petition Collection, South Carolina General Assembly Papers, South Carolina Department of Archives and History, Columbia; Morgan, "Lowcountry," 122–24; Morgan, "Charleston," 194–95; Schweninger, "Slave Independence and Enterprise in South Carolina," 105–7, quotation on 105.

74. Robert Olwell, "'A Reckoning of Accounts': Patriarchy, Market Relations, and Control on Henry Lauren's Lowcountry Plantations, 1762–1785," in Larry E. Hudson, Jr., *Working toward Freedom: Slave Society and Domestic Economy in the American South* (Rochester, N.Y., 1994), 38–40; quotation in Schweninger, "Slave Independence and Enterprise," 105. Wood, *Women's Work, Men's Work,* 77, for nearly the same complaint. Also Cooper and McCord, comps., *The Statutes at Large*

of South Carolina, 7: 434–35; Austin S. Clayton, comp., *A Compilation of Laws of Georgia* (Augusta, 1812), 133, 332–33; Morgan, "Lowcountry," 122–24; Chaplin, *Anxious Pursuit,* 325–26, 336; John Campbell, "As 'a Kind of Freeman': Slaves Market-Related Activities in the South Carolina Upcountry, 1800–1860," in Ira Berlin and Philip D. Morgan, eds., *The Slaves' Economy: Independent Production by Slaves in the Americas* (London, 1991), 131–69.

75. Chaplin, *Anxious Pursuit,* 218–19, 325–26, 333, 336–37.

76. Morgan, "Lowcountry," 92, 129–31; Chaplin, *Anxious Pursuit,* 321.

77. Morgan, "Lowcountry," 132.

78. *Ibid.,* 84–89; Wood, "Female Resistance," 606–7; Kulikoff, "Uprooted Peoples," 154; Chaplin, *Anxious Pursuit,* 321–22.

79. Chaplin, "Tidal Rice Cultivation and the Problem of Slavery," 57–59, and Chaplin, *Anxious Pursuit,* 270–73. On the slaves' sacred space, see, Margaret Washington Creel, "Gullah Attitudes toward Life and Death," in Joseph E. Holloway, ed., *Africanisms in American Culture* (Bloomington, Ind., 1990), 69–97, and Creel, *"A Peculiar People,"* 179.

80. Morgan, "Lowcountry," 124–29.

81. John Lambert, *Travels through Lower Canada and the United States of North America* (London, 1810), 2: 403; Schopf, *Travels in the Confederation,* 2: 201–2; *Laurens Papers,* 10: 201.

82. Quotation in Schweninger, "Slave Independence and Enterprise," 114; Morgan, "Lowcountry," 123–24; Wood, *Women's Work, Men's Work,* chs. 4–5 (for population of Savannah, see 211–12 n6). See especially the struggle to regulate the sale of badges for slaves. *Ibid.,* 94–96.

83. Wood, *Women's Work, Men's Work,* ch. 7; Whittington B. Johnson, *Black Savannah, 1788–1864* (Fayetteville, Ark., 1996), 91, 93–94, 96.

84. Morgan, "Charleston," 191–93, esp. 192 n10. Quotation in Schweninger, "Slave Independence and Enterprise," 108; Lilla M. Hawes, ed., *Papers of Lachlan McKintoch, 1774–1779,* GHSC (Savannah, 1957), 12: 88; Thompson and Lumpkin, eds., *Journals of the House of Representatives of South Carolina, 1783–1784,* 237; James Howard Brewer, "Legislation Designed to Control Slavery in Wilmington and Fayetteville," *NCHR,* 30 (1953), 163–64; Michele K. Gillespie, "Planters in the Making: Artisanal Opportunity in Georgia, 1790–1830," in Howard B. Rock, Paul A. Gilje, and Robert Asher, eds., *American Artisans: Crafting Social Identity, 1750–1850* (Baltimore, 1995), 40–47.

85. Wood, *Women's Work, Men's Work,* 129–132, quotation on 129. The town in question was Savannah.

86. "Letters Showing the Rise and Progress of the Early Negro Churches in Georgia and the West Indies," *JNH,* 1 (1916), 65–72; Walter H. Brooks, "Priority of the Silver Bluff Church and Its Promoters," *JNH,* 7 (1922), 172–96; Allan Gallay, "Planters and Slaves in the Great Awakening," in John B. Boles, ed., *Masters and Slaves in the House of the Lord: Race and Religion in the American South, 1740–1870* (Lexington, Ky., 1988), 33–34; Johnson, *Black Savannah,* 8–11.

87. Morgan, "Lowcountry," 115–17, 122; Marina Wikramanayake, *A World in*

Shadow: The Free Black in Antebellum South Carolina (Columbia, S.C., 1973), ch. 2; Robert Olwell, "Becoming Free: Manumission and the Genesis of a Free Black Community in South Carolina," *S&A,* 17 (1996); Wood, *Women's Work, Men's Work,* 122–25.

88. Papers Relating to Santo Domingo, 1791–1793; Petition from Charleston 11 Dec. 1797, ? Sept. 1798, South Carolina Archives; Rusticus Letters, 1794, South Carolina Historical Society; Charleston *City Gazette,* Aug–Dec. 1793; Proceeding of the Savannah City Council, 5 July 1795, Savannah City Hall; Hunt, *Haiti's Influence on Antebellum America,* ch. 3; Wood, *Women's Work, Men's Work,* 223 n. 13; Charles Fraser, *Reminiscences of Charleston* (Charleston, 1854), 43–44; Johnson, *Black Savannah,* 109–110; Ira Berlin, *Slaves without Masters: The Free Negro in the Antebellum South* (New York, 1974), 35–36; George D. Terry, "South Carolina's First Negro Seamen Acts, 1793–1803," *Proceedings of the South Carolina Historical Association,* (1980), 78–93.

89. *Runaway Advertisements,* 3: 410–411 (Charleston *State Gazette of South-Carolina* [Timothy], 5 Apr. 1790).

90. The imperfect record of South Carolina manumission during the eighteenth century yields some 379 examples of slaves gaining their freedom. Of those, some 199, or 53 percent, were recorded after 1775. Olwell, "Becoming Free," 5; Wikramanayake, *A World in Shadow,* ch. 1; Coclanis, *Shadow of a Dream,* 115.

91. Olwell, "Becoming Free," 5–7; Morgan, "Lowcountry," 116, 122.

92. John Donald Duncan, "Servitude and Slavery in Colonial South Carolina, 1670–1776," unpub. doctoral diss., Emory University, 1971, 398; Olwell, "Becoming Free," 5–7.

93. The number of slaves purchasing their freedom also increased sharply following the Revolution. Olwell, "Becoming Free," 10–11.

94. Successful fugitives seemed to share many of the characteristics of manumittees. In the words of one slaveholder, they were creoles who were "tolerably free from the common Negro dialect." *Runaway Advertisements,* 3: 410 (Charleston *State Gazette of South Carolina* [Timothy], 18 Feb. 1790), 3: 410.

95. Michael P. Johnson and James L. Roark, *Black Masters: A Free Family of Color in the Old South* (New York, 1984), 3–4; Wikramanayake, *World in Shadow.*

96. Morgan, "Charleston," 205–6; Loren Schweninger, *Black Property Owners in the South, 1790–1915* (Urbana, Ill., 1990), 20–21.

97. E. Horace Fitchett, "The Origin and Growth of the Free Negro Population of Charleston, South Carolina," *JNH,* 26 (1941), 421–437, and Fitchett, "The Traditions of the Free Negro in Charleston, South Carolina," *ibid.,* 25 (1940), 148.

98. See, for example, "Eighteenth Century Petition of South Carolina Negroes," *JNH,* 31 (1946), 98–99.

99. Rouchefoucault Liancourt, *Travels through the United States,* 602; Larry Koger, *Black Slaveowners: Free Black Slave Masters in South Carolina, 1790–1860* (Jefferson, N.C., 1985), 13–14; Schweninger, *Black Property Owners in the South,* 23; Johnson, *Black Savannah,* 79–81.

100. On passing, see Koger, *Black Slaveowners,* 14–16.

101. *Rules and Regulations of the Brown Fellowship Society, Established at Charleston, South Carolina, November 1, 1790* (Charleston, 1844); Fitchett, "The Traditions of the Free Negro," 139–52, quotation on 144; Robert L. Harris, Jr., "Charleston's Free Afro-American Elite: The Brown Fellowship Society and the Humane Brotherhood," *SCHM,* 82 (1981), 289–310.

12. Slavery and Freedom in the Lower Mississippi Valley

1. D. Clayton James, *Antebellum Natchez* (Baton Rouge, La., 1968), 17–18; J. Leitch Wright, Jr., *Florida in the American Revolution* (Gainesville, Fla., 1975), 10–12, 14, 22–23, 46. As a result of refugeeing, the wartime population of West Florida doubled and that of East Florida quintupled. *Ibid.,* 21.

2. Wright, *Florida in the American Revolution,* 46–52, 76–77, 131; John W. Caughey, "Willing's Expedition Down the Mississippi, 1778," *LHQ,* 15 (1932), 5–36; J. Barton Starr, *Tories, Dons, and Rebels: The American Revolution in British West Florida* (Gainesville, Fla., 1976), ch. 3; Gwendolyn Midlo Hall, *Africans in Colonial Louisiana: The Development of Afro-Creole Culture in the Eighteenth Century* (Baton Rouge, La., 1992), 301–3; Robin F. A. Fabel, *The Economy of British West Florida, 1763–1783* (Tuscaloosa, Ala., 1988), 31. The British also armed slaves to defend West Florida against a Spanish invasion. Robert R. Rea, "Planters and Plantations in British West Florida," *AR,* 29 (1976), 226. On the aborted slave rebellion in Baton Rouge in the summer of 1776, see Mrs. Rowland Dunbar, ed., *Life and Letters and Papers of William Dunbar, 1749–1810* (Jackson, Miss., 1930), 26–28; Margaret Fisher Dalrymple, ed., *The Merchant of Manchac: The Letterbooks of John Fitzpatrick, 1768–1790* (Baton Rouge, La., 1978), 204.

3. Wright, *Florida in the American Revolution,* chs. 5–7, and 108–9; Fabel, *Economy of British West Florida,* 38–39. On the role of the free black militiamen, see Jack D. L. Holmes, *Honor and Fidelity: The Louisiana Infantry Regiment and the Louisiana Militia Companies, 1766–1821* (Birmingham, Ala., 1965), 29–36, 54–59; Kimberly S. Hanger, "A Privilege and Honor to Serve: The Free Black Militia of Spanish New Orleans," *Military History of the Southwest,* 21 (1991), 59–65. The British also armed black men, many of them slaves, in defense of Mobile and Pensacola, see Rea, "Planters and Plantations in British West Florida," 226.

4. Hall, *Africans in Colonial Louisiana,* 305–6; Gilbert C. Din, "Cimarrones and the San Malo Band in Spanish Louisiana," *LH,* 21 (1980), 237–62. For an attempt by British and French planters to establish a mutually beneficial exchange of runaway slaves, see Fabel, *Economy of British West Florida,* 28–29; Dalrymple, ed., *Merchant of Manchac,* 110–11, 130–31, 235, 245, 291–92.

5. Hall, *Africans in Colonial Louisiana,* ch. 7; Daniel H. Usner, Jr., *Indians, Settlers, & Slaves in a Frontier Exchange Economy: The Lower Mississippi Valley before 1783* (Chapel Hill, N.C., 1992), 136–38; Din, "Cimarrones," 240–45; Thomas N. Ingersoll, "Old New Orleans: Race, Class, Sex, and Order in the Early Deep South, 1718–1819," unpub. doctoral diss., University of California, Los Angeles, 1991, 484–92.

6. Hall, *Africans in Colonial Louisiana,* 202–12, 218–20, 222; Din, "Cimarrones," 247–48. In addition to cooperating with plantation slaves, maroons also dealt with white planters and merchants. See, for example, the mill operator who hired maroons, in Laura L. Porteous, ed., "Index to the Spanish Judicial Records," *LHQ,* 16 (1933), 516–20, and *ibid.,* 20 (1937), 841–65; Caroline M. Burson, *The Stewardship of Don Estaban Miró, 1782–1792* (New Orleans, 1942), 110–19.

7. Hall, *Africans in Colonial Louisiana,* 205–15; Din, "Cimarrones," 247–50; Usner, *Indians, Settlers, & Slaves,* 140–41; James Thomas McGowan, "Creation of a Slave Society: Louisiana Plantations in the Eighteenth Century," unpub. doctoral diss., University of Rochester, 1976, 228–41.

8. Hall, *Africans in Colonial Louisiana,* 226–35.

9. *Ibid.,* ch. 7, esp. 266; Din, "Cimarrones," 248. For the effects of San Maló on plantation discipline in West Florida, see Fabel, *Economy of British West Florida,* 130.

10. Roland C. McConnell, *Negro Troops of Antebellum Louisiana: A History of the Battalion of Free Men of Color* (Baton Rouge, La., 1968), 17–22, 41–43; Holmes, *Honor and Fidelity,* 17, 32–33, 48, 54–57, quotation on 54; Hanger, "A Privilege and Honor," 66–78; Hanger, *Bounded Lives, Bounded Places: Free Black Society in Colonial New Orleans, 1769–1803* (Durham, N.C., 1997), ch. 4, esp. 119–22; Harold E. Sterkx, *Free Negro in Ante-Bellum Louisiana* (Rutherford, N.J., 1972), 73–79. When the English captured several black militiamen at the battle of Mobile and sold them to the Indians, Spanish authorities were quick to ransom them. Burson, *Stewardship of Don Estaban Miró,* 42.

11. Hanger, "A Privilege and Honor," 59–79, and Hanger, *Bounded Lives, Bounded Places,* ch. 4; McConnell, *Negro Troops of Antebellum Louisiana,* ch. 2; Holmes, *Honor and Fidelity;* Sterkx, *Free Negro in Ante-Bellum Louisiana,* 73–79. Although free colored militiamen served under officers of their own color, black and brown, both pardo and moreno units had white "advisors."

12. Kimberly S. Hanger, "Origins of New Orleans's Free Creoles of Color," in James H. Dormon, ed., *Creoles of Color in the Gulf South* (Knoxville, Tenn., 1996), 7–9, esp. table 1; Ingersoll, "Old New Orleans," 592–93.

13. Hanger, "Avenues to Freedom," 247, 257; Hanger, "Origins," 8–9; Hanger, *Bounded Lives, Bounded Places,* 12, 26–33; Thomas N. Ingersoll, "Free Blacks in a Slave Society: New Orleans, 1718–1812," *WMQ,* 48 (1991), 186–87; McGowan, "Creation of a Slave Society," ch. 4.

14. Hanger, "Avenues to Freedom," 261–63, and Hanger, "Origins," 8–27; Ingersoll, "Free Blacks in a Slave Society," 180–89.

15. The point is made sharply in Thomas N. Ingersoll, "Slave Codes and Judicial Practice in New Orleans, 1718–1807," *LHR,* 13 (1995), 42, 45.

16. McGowan, "Creation of a Slave Society," 201; Ingersoll, "Free Blacks in a Slave Society," 183; Hanger, "Origins," 8–9; Sterkx, *Free Negro in Ante-Bellum Louisiana,* 36–51; Paul F. Lachance, "The Formation of a Three-Caste Society: Evidence from Wills in Antebellum New Orleans," *SSH,* 18 (1994), 234; Thomas M. Fiehrer, "The African Presence in Colonial Louisiana: An Essay on the Continuity of Carib-

bean Culture," in Robert R. McDonald, John R. Kemp, and Edward F. Haas, eds., *Louisiana's Black Heritage* (New Orleans, 1979), 23–24.

17. For New Orleans: McGowan, "Creation of a Slave Society," 196–203; Lawrence Kinnaird, *Spain in the Mississippi Valley, 1765–1794,* 3 vols. (Washington, D.C., 1946–49), 2: 196; *New Orleans in 1805, A Directory and Census* (New Orleans, 1936); and a summary table in Hanger, "Avenues to Freedom," 239; for Mobile: Kinnaird, *Spain in the Mississippi Valley,* 2: 196; Virginia Meacham Gould, "The Free Creoles of Color of the Antebellum Gulf Ports of Mobile and Pensacola: A Struggle for the Middle Ground," in Dormon, ed., *Creoles of Color,* 33–35; for Pensacola: *ibid.;* Jack D. L. Holmes, "The Role of Blacks in Spanish Alabama: The Mobile District, 1780–1813," *AHQ,* 37 (1975), 8; William Coker and Douglas Inglis, *The Spanish Census of Pensacola, 1784–1820: A Genealogical Guide to Spanish Pensacola* (Pensacola, Fla., 1980); Duvon C. Corbitt, "The Last Spanish Census of Pensacola, 1820," *FHQ,* 24 (1945), 30–32; Pablo Tornero Tinajero, "Estudio de la poblacion de Pensacola, (1784–1820)," *Annurio de Estudios Americans,* 34 (1977), 537–61.

18. Français-Xavier Martin, comp., *A General Digest of the Acts of the Legislature of the Late Territory of Orleans and the State of Louisiana,* 3 vols. (New Orleans, 1816), 1: 608; Ira Berlin, *Slaves without Masters: The Free Negro in the Antebellum South* (New York, 1974), 123; Ingersoll, "Free Blacks in a Slave Society," 196–98, and Ingersoll, "Slave Codes and Judicial Practice," 60–61; Hans W. Baade, "The Law of Slavery in Spanish Luisiana, 1769–1803," in Edward F. Haas, ed., *Louisiana's Legal Heritage* (New Orleans, 1983), 71–74.

19. Carl A. Brasseaux and Glenn R. Conrad, eds., *The Road to Louisiana: The Saint-Domingue Refugees, 1792–1809,* trans. David Cheramie (Lafayette, La., 1992); Alfred N. Hunt, *Haiti's Influence on Antebellum America: Slumbering Volcano in the Caribbean* (Baton Rouge, La., 1988), ch. 3; Dunbar Rowland, ed., *Official Letter Books of W. C. C. Claiborne, 1801–1816,* 6 vols. (Jackson, Miss., 1917), 4: 381–82, 391–93, 409; 5: 1–3, 30–31.

20. For New Orleans: Hanger, "Avenues to Freedom," 239, and Hanger, "Origins," 2; Lachance, "The Formation of a Three-Caste Society," 234; McGowan, "Creation of a Slave Society," 196–97. For Mobile: Kinnaird, *Spain in the Mississippi Valley,* 2: 196. For Pensacola: Coker and Inglis, *The Spanish Census of Pensacola;* Corbitt, "The Last Spanish Census of Pensacola, 30–32; Tinajero, "Estudio de la poblacion de Pensacola," 537–61.

21. Hanger, "Avenues to Freedom," 245–47; Hanger, "Origins," 8–10; and Hanger, "'The Fortunes of Women in America': Spanish New Orleans's Free Women of African Descent and Their Relations with Slave Women," in Patricia Morton, ed., *Discovering the Women in Slavery: Emancipating Perspectives on the American Past* (Athens, Ga., 1996), 156–59; Ingersoll, "Free Blacks in a Slave Society," 186–87; McGowan, "Creation of a Slave Society," 201–2; Hanger, *Bounded Lives, Bounded Places,* 41–53.

22. Carl A. Brasseaux and Glenn R. Conrad, "Introduction," in Brasseaux and Conrad, eds., *Road to Louisiana,* xiii; Paul Lachance, "The 1809 Immigration of Saint-Domingue Refugees to New Orleans: Reception, Integration, and Impact," in

ibid., 247–48, and Lachance, "The Formation of a Three-Caste Society," 226, 234. In 1820 the sex ratio for white people in New Orleans was 246, and 44 for free colored people. See *ibid.,* 224.

23. Carl A. Brasseaux, "Creoles of Color in Louisiana's Bayou Country, 1766–1877," in Dormon, ed., *Creoles of Color,* 67–75; Gary B. Mills, *The Forgotten People: Cane River's Creoles of Color* (Baton Rouge, La., 1977), prologue and ch. 1.

24. Paul F. Lachance, "The Foreign French," in Arnold R. Hirsch and Joseph Logsdon, eds., *Creole New Orleans: Race and Americanization* (Baton Rouge, La., 1992), 116.

25. Quotation in C. C. Robin, *Voyage to Louisiana, 1803–1805,* trans. Stuart O. Landry (New Orleans, 1966), 248.

26. Jerah Johnson, "Colonial New Orleans: A Fragment of the Eighteenth-Century French Ethos," in Hirsch and Logsdon, eds., *Creole New Orleans,* 52–53.

27. Ingersoll, "Free Blacks in a Slave Society," 189, 198–99; Brasseaux, "Creoles of Color in Louisiana's Bayou Country," 69–71; Roulhac Toledano and Mary Louise Christovich, eds., *New Orleans Architecture,* 8 vols. (Gretna, La., 1971–80), 6: ch. 16.

28. Hanger, *Bounded Lives, Bounded Places,* ch. 2, esp. 58–59; Berquin-Duvallon, *Vue de la colonie espagnole du Mississippi,* as quoted in Paul Alliot, "Historical and Political Reflections on Louisiana," in James A. Robertson, ed., *Louisiana Under the Rule of Spain, France, and the United States, 1785–1807,* 2 vols. (Cleveland, Ohio, 1911), 1: 219; Lachance, "The Foreign French," 124.

29. Kimberly S. Hanger, "Household and Community Structure among the Free Population of Spanish New Orleans, 1778," *LH,* 30, (1989),72–74; Hanger, "'The Fortunes of Women in America,'" 159–65; and Hanger, *Bounded Lives, Bounded Places,* 69–87.

30. Caryn Cossé Bell expands on the egalitarian tradition within the free black community in *Revolution, Romanticism, and the Afro Creole Protest Tradition in Louisiana, 1718-1868* (Baton Rouge, La., 1997), and Arnold R. Hirsch and Joseph Logsdon, "Franco Africans and African Americans: Introduction," in Hirsch and Logsdon, eds., *Creole New Orleans.* Hirsch and Logsdon emphasize the difference between the exclusivity of free people of color in Charleston and their more expansive counterparts in New Orleans, 191–97.

31. Burson, *Stewardship of Don Estaban Miró,* 124–43; John G. Clark, *New Orleans, 1718–1812: An Economic History* (Baton Rouge, La., 1970), 183–86; Usner, *Indians, Settlers, & Slaves,* 108–11; Carl A. Brasseaux, *The Founding of New Acadia: The Beginnings of Acadian Life in Louisiana, 1765–1803* (Baton Rouge, La., 1987); Andrew S. Walsh and Robert V. Wells, "Population Dynamics in the Eighteenth-Century Mississippi River Valley: Acadians in Louisiana," *JSH,* 11 (1978), 521–45; Gilbert C. Din, "Early Spanish Colonization Efforts in Louisiana," *LS,* 11 (1972), 31–49, and "Spain's Immigration Policy and Efforts in Louisiana during the American Revolution," *ibid.,* 14 (1975), 241–75; Fabel, *Economy of British West Florida,* 6–21; Starr, *Tories, Dons, and Rebels,* 33–34; Clinton N. Howard, *British Development of West Florida, 1763–1769* (Berkeley, Ca., 1947), 50–101.

32. Hall, *Africans in Colonial Louisiana,* 277–78; Lachance, "Politics of Fear," 196; Fiehrer, "The African Presence in Colonial Louisiana," 11; Robert L. Paquette, "Revolutionary Saint Domingue in the Making of Territorial Louisiana," in David Barry Gaspar and David Patrick Geggus, eds., *A Turbulent Time: The French Revolution and the Greater Caribbean* (Bloomington, Ind., 1997), 222 n25.

33. Usner, *Indians, Settlers, & Slaves,* ch. 4; Hall, *Africans in Colonial Louisiana,* 276–77; Clark, *New Orleans,* 189–92; Arthur P. Whitaker, "The Commerce of Louisiana and the Floridas at the End of the Eighteenth Century," *HAHR,* 8 (1928), 190–203; Jack D. L. Holmes, "Some Economic Problems of Spanish Governors of Louisiana," *HAHR,* 42 (1962), 524–27, 529–31, 536; Brian E. Coutts, "Boom and Busts: The Rise and Fall of the Tobacco Industry in Spanish Louisiana, 1770–1790," *Americas,* 42 (1986), 289–309; Robin F. A. Fabel, "Anglo-Spanish Commerce in New Orleans during the American Revolutionary Era," in William S. Coker and Robert R. Rea, eds., *Anglo-Spanish Confrontation on the Gulf Coast during the American Revolution* (Pensacola, Fla., 1982), 32–35; Brian Coutts, "Flax and Hemp in Spanish Louisiana, 1777–1783," *LH,* 26 (1985), 129–39; John Hebron Moore, "The Cyprus Lumber Industry in the Lower Mississippi Valley during the Colonial Period," *LH,* 24 (1983), 42.

34. Ingersoll, "Slave Codes and Judicial Practice," 47–53; Baade, "Law of Slavery in Spanish Luisiana," 63–66; Gilbert C. Din and John E. Harkins, *The New Orleans Cabildo: Colonial Louisiana's First City Government, 1769–1803* (Baton Rouge, La., 1996), 160–62; McGowan, "Creation of a Slave Society," 242–43. The 1777 code never received royal approval, rendering it moot.

35. Hall, *Africans in Colonial Louisiana,* 213–36; Din, "Cimarrones," 244–62, and Din and Harkins, *New Orleans Cabildo,* 156–59, 162–63, 166–69; McConnell, *Negro Troops,* 22–23; Burson, *Stewardship of Don Estaban Miró,* 214–20; Charles Gayarré, *History of Louisiana,* 4 vols. (New York, 1854–66), 3: 57–66; Usner, *Indians, Settlers, & Slaves,* 140–41; McGowan, "Creation of a Slave Society," 233–42.

36. Paul Lachance, "The Politics of Fear: French Louisiana and the Slave Trade, 1789–1809," *PS,* 1 (1979), 162–97; Thomas N. Ingersoll, "The Slave Trade and the Ethnic Diversity of Louisiana's Slave Community," *LH,* 37 (1996), 143–61; Din and Harkins, *New Orleans Cabildo,* 175–80.

37. Ingersoll, "The Slave Trade and the Ethnic Diversity," 143–61, and Ingersoll, "Old New Orleans," 685–97; Lachance, "The Politics of Fear," 166–97; Clark, *New Orleans,* 165, 176–77, 317–18; Hall, *Africans in Louisiana,* 278–80; Jack D. L. Holmes, *Gayoso: The Life of a Spanish Governor in the Mississippi Valley, 1789–1799* (Baton Rouge, La., 1965), 219; Alcée Fortier, *A History of Louisiana,* 3 vols. (New York, 1904), 2: 39; Clarence E. Carter, ed., *The Territorial Papers of the United States,* 26 vols. (Washington, D.C., 1934–), 9: 209–14, 405–7.

38. Hall, *Africans in Colonial Louisiana,* 283–84; Burson, *Stewardship of Don Estaban Miró,* 106; Starr, *Tories, Dons, and Rebels,* 49; Ingersoll, "Old New Orleans," 652, and Ingersoll, "The Slave Trade and the Ethnic Diversity," 147–61; Lachance, "The Politics of Fear," 166–67, 180–81, 183–86, 196; Patrick S. Brady, "The

Slave Trade and Sectionalism in South Carolina, 1787–1808," *JSoH,* 38 (1972), 616 n37; Fabel, *Economy of British West Florida,* 29–38, 44–46, 66–69, 105–6, 108, 214–36, quotation on 37; Dalrymple, ed., *Merchant of Manchac,* 20, 213, 244, 295.

39. Hall, *Africans in Colonial Louisiana,* chs. 8–9, esp. 285–86; Ingersoll, "The Slave Trade and Ethnic Diversity," 151; Lachance, "The Politics of Fear," 167, 180, 182, 196–97; James, *Antebellum Natchez,* 45; Fabel, *Economy of British West Florida,* ch. 2; Catterall, *Judicial Cases,* 4: 524–25.

40. Clark, *New Orleans,* chs. 10–11, esp. 183–92; Burson, *Stewardship of Don Estaban Miró,* 74; Jack D. L. Holmes, "Indigo in Colonial Louisiana and the Floridas," *LH,* 8 (1967), 335–40, and Holmes, *Gayoso,* 91–98; James, *Antebellum Natchez,* 48–51; Coutts, "Boom and Bust," 305–9.

41. The redistribution of sugar production in the Americas in the wake of Saint Domingue can be captured in Stuart B. Schwartz, *Sugar Plantations in the Forming of Brazilian Society, Bahia, 1550–1835* (Cambridge, UK, 1985), 164; Patrick J. Carroll, *Blacks in Colonial Veracruz: Race, Ethnicity, and Regional Development* (Austin, Tex., 1992), 54–55; Franklin Knight, *Slave Society in Cuba during the Nineteenth Century* (Madison, Wisc., 1970), 12.

42. René J. Gardeur, Jr., "The Origins of the Sugar Industry in Louisiana," in *Green Fields: Two Hundred Years of Louisiana Sugar* (Lafayette, La., 1980), 1–28; Clark, *New Orleans,* 202–3, 217–20; J. Carlyle Sitterson, *Sugar Country: The Cane Sugar Industry in the South, 1753–1950* (Lexington, Ky., 1953), 11–12; Arthur P. Whitaker, *The Mississippi Question, 1795–1803* (New York, 1934), 131–32; Lachance, "Politics of Fear," 170 n26, 192, and Lachance, "The 1809 Immigration of Saint-Domingue Refugees," 271. For the problems of growing sugar with a six-month growing cycle, see Alliot, "Historical and Political Reflections on Louisiana," in Robertson, ed., *Louisiana,* 1: 61–63; James Pitot, *Observations on the Colony of Louisiana from 1796 to 1802,* trans. Henry C. Pitot (Baton Rouge, La., 1979), 73–76, 115–16.

43. Clark, *New Orleans,* 202–3, 217–20; James, *Antebellum Natchez,* 48–52; John Hebron Moore, *The Emergence of the Cotton Kingdom of the Old Southwest* (Baton Rouge, La., 1988), 1–17; Holmes, *Gayoso,* 96–101; Fortier, *A History of Louisiana,* 2: 29–30; Jack D. L. Holmes, "Cotton Gins in the Spanish Natchez District 1795–1800," *JMH,* 31 (1969), 159–171; quotation in Andrew Ellicott, *The Journal of Andrew Ellicott* (Chicago, 1962 [1803]), 133.

44. Ronald L. F. Davis, *The Black Experience in Natchez, 1720–1880* (Natchez, Miss., 1993), 44–50; Samuel Wilson, Jr., "Architecture of Early Sugar Plantations," in *Green Fields,* 51–82; Morton Rothstein, "The Natchez Nabobs: Kinship and Friendship in an Economic Elite," in Hans Trefousse, ed., *Essays in Honor of Arthur C. Cole* (New York, 1977), 97–112; quotation in Lachance, "Politics of Fear," 162. When the new American governor arrived in Louisiana in 1804, he found "but one sentiment throughout the Province—*they must import more Slaves, or the Country was ruin'd forever.*" Carter, ed., *Territorial Papers,* 9: 340.

45. Lachance, "The Politics of Fear," 186–97; Clark, *New Orleans,* 222–25; Ingersoll, "The Slave Trade and Ethnic Diversity," 133, and Ingersoll, "Old New Orleans," 578; Brady, "The Slave Trade and Sectionalism in South Carolina," 616.

46. Hall, *Africans in Colonial Louisiana,* ch. 9, and 252 (Hall maintains most of the new arrivals were, like the previous influx, from Senegambia), 288; Allan Kulikoff, "Uprooted Peoples: Black Migrants in the Age of the American Revolution, 1790–1820," in Ira Berlin and Ronald Hoffman, eds., *Slavery and Freedom in the Age of the American Revolution* (Charlottesville, Va., 1983), 149, 162–63; Davis, *The Black Experience in Natchez,* 10–13, 16, esp. table 1; Ingersoll, "Old New Orleans," 545–46, and Ingersoll, "The Slave Trade and Ethnic Diversity," 154–55; James, *Antebellum Natchez,* 41–43, 45–46, esp. 46; Fabel, *Economy of British West Florida,* 37–38; Dalrymple, ed., *Merchant of Manchac,* 425–31.

47. Hall, *Africans in Colonial Louisiana,* ch. 9, and 252; Davis, *The Black Experience in Natchez,* 10–13; Jack D. L. Holmes, "The Abortive Slave Revolt at Pointe Coupée, Louisiana, 1795," *LH,* 11 (1970), 342–43. In 1784 Farrar pressed the Spanish Crown for permission to import slaves directly from Africa. Hall, *Africans in Colonial Louisiana,* 280–81.

48. Davis, *The Black Experience in Natchez,* 10–12, 15; Kulikoff, "Uprooted Peoples," 154, 162–63, esp. n35; Hall, *Africans in Colonial Louisiana,* 295–301; 363–64; Ingersoll, "Old New Orleans," 539–43; McGowan, "Creation of a Slave Society," 271 n24.

49. LaChance, "Politics of Fear," 173; McGowan, "Creation of a Slave Society," 245–52; Robin, *Voyage to Louisiana,* 238. For the trials of one newly imported African, see Terry Alford, *Prince among Slaves* (New York, 1977), ch. 3.

50. Ingersoll, "Slave Codes and Judicial Practice," 54–60; Baade, "Law of Slavery in Spanish Louisiana," 70–74; Lachance, "Politics of Fear," 178–79; James D. Padgett, ed., "A Decree for Louisiana, Issued by the Baron de Carondelet, June 1, 1795," *LHQ,* 20 (1937), 590–605; quotation in Ronald R. Morazan, "Letters, Petitions, and Decrees of the Cabildo of New Orleans, 1800–1803: Edited and Translated," 2 vols., unpub. doctoral diss., Louisiana State University, 1972, 1: 179–80, 185.

51. Berquin-Duvallon, *Vue de la colonie espagnole du Mississippi,* as quoted in Alliot, "Historical and Political Reflections on Louisiana," 1: 118–22; Edward C. Carter II, John C. Van Horne, and Lee W. Formwalt, eds., *The Journals of Benjamin Henry Latrobe, 1799–1820,* 3 vols. (New Haven, Conn., 1980), 3: 171–72, 291, quotation on 201. Viewed from the perspective of the nineteenth century, slaves in the lower Mississippi Valley maintained an active internal economy. Roderick A. McDonald, "Independent Economic Production by Slaves on Antebellum Louisiana Sugar Plantations," in Ira Berlin and Philip D. Morgan, eds., *Cultivation and Culture: Labor and the Shaping of Slave Life in the Americas* (Charlottesville, Va., 1993), 273–302, and McDonald, *The Economy and Material Culture of Slaves: Goods and Chattels on the Sugar Plantation of Jamaica and Louisiana* (Baton Rouge, La., 1993), chs. 2, 4; Virginia Meachum Gould, "'If I Can't Have My Rights, I Can Have My Pleasures, and If They Won't Give Me Wages, I Can Take them': Gender and Slave Labor in Antebellum New Orleans," in Morton, ed., *Discovering the Women in Slavery,* 188–90.

52. Carter et al., eds., *Journals of Latrobe,* 3: 201.

53. McDonald, *The Economy and Material Culture of Slaves,* 12–14, 60–61;

McDonald, "Independent Economic Production by Slaves," 277–78, 284–85; Berquin-Duvallon, *Vue de la colonie espagnole du Mississippi,* and Perrin du Lac, *Voyage,* as quoted in Robertson, ed., *Louisiana,* 1: 181–84.

54. Berquin-Duvallon, *Vue de la colonie espagnole du Mississippi,* as quotation in Alliot, "Historical and Political Reflections on Louisiana," 1: 121; Daniel H. Usner, Jr., "Indian-Black Relations in Colonial and Antebellum Louisiana," in Stephan Palmié, *Slave Cultures and the Cultures of Slavery* (Knoxville, Tenn., 1995), 155–56; and Usner, "American Indians on the Cotton Frontier: Changing Economic Relations With Citizens and Slaves in the Mississippi Territory," *JAmH,* 72 (1985), 306–12, quotations on 311.

55. Randy J. Sparks, "Religion in Amite County, Mississippi," in John B. Boles, ed., *Masters & Slaves in the House of the Lord: Race and Religion in the American South, 1740–1870* (Lexington, Ky., 1988), 59–60.

56. Ernest R. Liljegren, "Jacobinism in Spanish Louisiana, 1792–1797," *LHQ,* 22 (1939), 47–97; Kimberly Hanger, "Conflicting Loyalties: The French Revolution and People of Color in Spanish New Orleans," *LH,* 34 (1993), 5–33.

57. Liljegren, "Jacobinism in Spanish Louisiana," 47–97; quotation in Everett, "Free Persons of Color in Colonial New Orleans," 41.

58. Hall, *Africans in Colonial Louisiana,* 347–48; McGowan, "Creation of a Plantation Society," ch. 7; Lachance, "Politics of Fear," 165–66; Hunt, *Haiti's Influence on Antebellum America,* 25–27; Gabriel Debien and René Le Gardeur, "The Saint-Domingue Refugees in Louisiana, 1792–1804," in Brasseaux and Conrad, eds., *The Road to Louisiana,* 113–243.

59. McGowan, "Creation of a Slave Society," 297–99; Holmes, *Honor and Fidelity,* 54–59; Hanger, "A Privilege and Honor," 68–69, 80–82, and Hanger, *Bounded Lives, Bounded Places,* 114, 117–25; Hall, *Africans in Colonial Louisiana,* 324. Whatever Carondolet expected of the colored militiamen, he had no trust in the French planters, from whom he declared that "little or nothing could be counted on." Baron de Carondelet, "Military Report on Louisiana and West Florida," in Robertson, ed., *Louisiana,* 1: 328; Thomas M. Fiehrer, "The Baron de Carondelet as an Agent of Bourbon Reform: A Study of Spanish Colonial Administration in the Years of the French Revolution," unpub. doctoral diss., Tulane University, 1977, 466–96.

60. McGowan, "Creation of a Slave Society," 297–318; Ingersoll, "Old New Orleans," 645–50, and Ingersoll, "Slave Codes and Judicial Practice," 55–56; Liljegen, "Jacobinism in Spanish Louisiana," 51 n15, 79–83; Lachance, "Politics of Fear," 174. Carondelet's actions were part of a larger attempt to reform slavery within the Spanish empire. In 1789 Charles III issued a new slave code, *Código Negro,* which reflected both the humanitarian impulse and the fear of revolution from below by providing slaves with extraordinary protection from their owners. Slaveholders throughout the empire—including Louisiana—objected immediately. The code never went into effect, and it was withdrawn in 1794, but slaves learned of its provisions or at least its general purposes. Some took it as the beginnings of a general emancipation, and it was a source of considerable unrest and insurrectionary activity throughout the Spanish Caribbean. In 1792 Carondelet issued his own edict on the treatment

of slaves. It was very much in the spirit of the *Código*, and it faced the same opposition from planters. Historians have disagreed about the role of the *Código* and Carondelet's code. The preponderance of evidence suggests that neither provided slaves with much practical protection. But their existence added to the slaves' belief that their status would soon change. Rolando Mellafe, *Negro Slavery in Latin America*, trans. J. W. S. Judge (Berkeley, Cal., 1975), 105–11; Julius Sherrard Scott III, "The Common Wind: Currents of Afro-American Communication in the Era of the Haitian Revolution," unpub. doctoral diss., Duke University, 1986, 146–58; David Patrick Geggus, "Slave Resistance in the Spanish Caribbean in the mid-1790s," in Gaspar and Geggus, eds., *A Turbulent Time*, 136–37; McGowan, "Creation of a Slave Society," 296–311; Ingersoll, "Slaves Codes and Judicial Practice," 55–56.

61. Gayarré, *History of Louisiana,* 3: 301–5. In 1792 the French National Assembly extended full civil rights to free people of color, and in 1794 it abolished slavery. In May 1802 France abrogated the earlier emancipation, reestablishing slavery in the French colonies. Georges Lefebvre, *The French Revolution,* 2 vols. (New York, 1969), 2: 130; C. L. R. James, *Black Jacobins: Toussaint L'Ouverture and the San Domingo Revolution,* rev. ed. (New York, 1963), 139–40, and Carolyn E. Fick, *The Making of Haiti: The Saint Domingue Revolution from Below* (Knoxville, Tenn., 1990). The effect of rumors of emancipation are discussed in Michael Craton, "Slave Culture, Resistance and the Achievement of Emancipation in the British West Indies," in James Walvin, *Slavery and British Society, 1776–1838* (London, 1982), 105–6; David Patrick Geggus, "Slavery, War, and Revolution in the Greater Caribbean, 1789–1815," in Gaspar and Geggus, eds., *A Turbulent Time,* 8–18.

62. Stephen Webre, "The Problem of Indian Slavery in Spanish Louisiana, 1769–1803," *LH,* 25 (1984), 117–35, reviews the entire controversy over "Indian" slavery, but see esp. 124–32. In 1769, as one of his first acts upon restoring Spanish control over Louisiana, Alexjandro O'Reilly ordered Indian slavery—officially abolished under French rule—to be terminated without condition. Kinnaird, *Spain in the Mississippi Valley,* 1: 89–90, 125–26; Usner, *Indians, Settlers, & Slaves,* 99–33. The question of racial identity—what was a "mulatto"—appeared in a variety of guises as the crisis of the 1790s deepened. In the Pointe Coupée district, an attempt was made to redefine "grif" (a mixture of Indian and African). Hall, *Africans in Colonial Louisiana,* 262–66. The matter was resolved, at least formally, in 1810 when the court ruled "a negro of unmixed blood raises a presumption of slavery" but "persons of color are presumed to be free." Catterall, *Judicial Case,* 3: 392.

63. Webre, "The Problem of Indian Slavery," 127–31, quotation on 130.

64. *Ibid.,* 130–35; Gayarré, *History of Louisiana,* 3: 335; McGowan, "Creation of a Slave Society," 311–19. Indian slaves still petitioned for freedom following Louisiana's accession to the United States. Thomas D. Morris, *Southern Slavery and the Law, 1619–1860* (Chapel Hill, N.C., 1996), 20–21; Usner, *Indians, Settlers, & Slaves,* 133 n47.

65. Hall, *Africans in Louisiana,* 253–56, ch. 10; Burson, *Stewardship of Don Estaban Miró,* 121–22; LaChance, "Politics of Fear," 170–71; Din and Harkins, *New Orleans Cabildo,* 169; Holmes, "Slave Revolt at Pointe Coupée," 341–62; Ulysses S.

Ricard, Jr., "The Pointe Coupée Slave Conspiracy of 1791," in Patricia Galloway and Philip Boucher, eds., *Proceedings of the Fifteenth Meeting of the French Colonial Historical Society* (1992); McGowan, "Creation of a Slave Society," ch. 8; Sterkx, *Free Negro in Ante-Bellum Louisiana,* 91–93; McConnell, *Negro Troops,* 27–28; Carter, ed., *Territorial Papers,* 9: 575–76; James H. Dormon, "The Persistent Specter: Slave Rebellion in Territorial Louisiana," *LH,* 28 (1977), 389–93; Juan Jose Andreu Ocariz, *Movimientos Rebeldes de los Esclavaos Negros el Dominino Español en Luisiana* (Zaragoza, 1977), 75–86, 97–106, 117–77; Hanger, "Conflicting Loyalties," esp. 12–13 n21; Debien and Le Gardeur, "Saint-Domingue Refugees in Louisiana," 175–83; Scott, "The Common Wind," 234–35, 265–74.

66. No one has sorted through all of the various conspiracies, rumors of conspiracies, and the actual acts of rebellion during the 1790s. Until that is done, the nature of the threat to Spanish rule or the slave society cannot be gauged with any accuracy. However, these threats were taken with the utmost seriousness by Spanish authorities and the largely French planter class, and on the basis of official adjudication, hundreds of men and women were jailed, imprisoned, deported, lashed, and hung. See above, note 68.

67. Hall, *Africans in Colonial Louisiana,* 317–19, ch. 11; Holmes, "Slave Revolt at Pointe Coupée," 341–62; McGowan, "Creation of a Slave Society," ch. 8; Ocariz, *Movimientos Rebeldes de los Esclavaos Negros,* 117–77.

68. Hanger, "Conflicting Loyalties," 12–33, quotation on 25; Hanger, "Fortunes of Women in America," 158–59. Also see the case of Charles L'Ange, McGowan, "Creation of a Slave Society," 320–27. Free colored militiamen continued their historic role as supports of the slaveholding status quo elsewhere in the greater Caribbean. David Geggus, "The French and Haitian Revolutions, and Resistance to Slavery in the Americas: An Overview," *RFHOM,* 76 (1989), 111 n17.

69. Berlin, *Slaves without Masters,* 117–20; Carter, ed., *Territorial Papers,* 9: 174–75; Rowland, ed., *Claiborne Letter Books,* 2: 217–19.

70. Berlin, *Slaves without Masters,* 120–21; Bell, *Revolution, Romanticism, and the Afro-Creole Protest Tradition in Louisiana,* 33–36; quotation in Lachance, "1809 Immigration of Saint-Domingue Refugees," 121; Jane Lucas de Grummond, *Renato Beluche: Smuggler, Privateer, and Patriot, 1780–1860* (Baton Rouge, La., 1983), ch. 5; Stanley Faye, "Privateers of Guadeloupe and Their Establishment in Barataria," *LHQ,* 23 (1940), 431–34.

71. Martin, comp., *Orleans Law,* 1: 620, 640–42, 648, 656, 660; 2: 104, 326–32; Berlin, *Slaves without Masters,* 122–23; Ingersoll, "Free Blacks in New Orleans," 196–98; Ingersoll, "Slave Codes and Judicial Practice," 60–61; Baade, "Law of Slavery in Spanish Luisiana," 71–74.

72. Dormon, "The Persistent Specter," 393–404.

Epilogue: Making Race, Making Slavery

1. Robert J. Steinfeld, *The Invention of Free Labor: The Employment Relation in English and American Law and Culture, 1350–1870* (Chapel Hill, N.C., 1991); Eric

Foner, *Free Soil, Free Labor, Free Men: The Ideology of the Republican Party before the Civil War* (New York, 1970); Richard H. Sewell, *Ballots for Freedom: Antislavery Politics in the United States, 1837–1860* (New York, 1976).

2. Larry E. Tise, *Proslavery: A History of the Defense of Slavery in America, 1701–1840* (Athens, Ga., 1987); Eugene D. Genovese, *The World the Slaveholders Made: Two Essays in Interpretation* (New York, 1969); Drew Faust, *A Sacred Circle: The Dilemma of the Intellectual in the Old South, 1840–1860* (Baltimore, 1977), and Faust, ed., *The Ideology of Slavery: Proslavery Thought in the Antebellum South* (Baton Rouge, La., 1981).

3. Leon F. Litwack, *North of Slavery: The Negro in the Free States* (Chicago, 1961); James Oliver Horton and Lois E. Horton, *In Hope of Liberty: Culture, Community, and Protest among Northern Free Blacks, 1700–1860* (New York, 1997); Leonard P. Curry, *The Free Black in Urban America, 1800–1850: The Shadow of the Dream* (Chicago, 1981).

4. Michael Tadman, *Speculators and Slaves: Masters, Traders, and Slaves in the Old South* (Madison, Wisc., 1989), 5–7, 12, 19–46, 225–27, 237–47.

5. Joseph P. Reidy, "Obligation and Right: Patterns of Labor, Subsistence, and Exchange in the Cotton Belt of Georgia, 1790–1860," and Steven F. Miller, "Plantation Labor Organization and Slave Life on the Cotton Frontier: The Alabama-Mississippi Black Belt, 1815–1840," in Ira Berlin and Philip D. Morgan, eds., *Cultivation and Culture: Labor and the Shaping of Slave Life in the Americas* (Charlottesville, Va., 1993), 138–69.

6. Litwack, *North of Slavery*, ch. 1; Ira Berlin, *Slaves without Masters: The Free Negro in the Antebellum South* (New York, 1974), ch. 3. The slaveholders' counterattack is put in the context of the reaction to the French Revolution by Larry Tise, *Proslavery*, chs. 7–8.

7. Litwack, *North of Slavery*, ch. 2; Berlin, *Slaves without Masters*, ch. 10.

8. James D. Essig, *The Bonds of Wickedness: American Evangelicals against Slavery, 1770–1808* (Philadelphia, 1982); Christine Leigh Heyrman, *Southern Cross: The Beginnings of the Bible Belt* (New York: 1997), 46–49, 92–94, 138; Mathews, *Slavery and Methodism*, chs. 1–3; Forest F. Wood, *The Arrogance of Faith: Christianity and Race in America from the Colonial Era to the Twentieth Century* (New York, 1990); quotation in Betty Wood, "'For Their Satisfaction or Redress': African Americans and Church Discipline in the Early South," in Catherine Clinton and Michele Gillespie, eds., *The Devil's Lane: Sex and Race in the Early South* (New York, 1997), 112.

9. Benjamin Quarles, "The Revolutionary War as a Black Declaration of Independence," in Berlin and Hoffman, eds., *Slavery and Freedom in the Age of the American Revolution*, 283–305.

10. Herbert Aptheker, *American Negro Slave Revolts*, 5th ed. (New York, 1983), chs. 4–5, 9; Douglas R. Egerton, *Gabriel's Rebellion: The Virginia Slave Conspiracies of 1800 and 1802* (Chapel Hill, N.C., 1993), and Egerton, "'Fly across the River': The Easter Slave Conspiracy of 1802," *NCHR*, 68 (1991), 87–110; Thomas C. Parramore, "Aborted Takeoff: A Critique of 'Fly across the River,'" *NCHR*, 68 (1991), 111–21;

Jeffrey J. Crow, "Slave Rebelliousness and Social Conflict in North Carolina, 1775 to 1802," *WMQ*, 37 (1980), 79–102; John Scott Strickland, "The Great Revival and Insurrectionary Fears in North Carolina: An Examination of Antebellum Southern Society and Slave Revolt Panics," in Orville Burton and Robert C. McMath, eds., *Class, Conflict, and Consensus: Antebellum Southern Community Studies* (Westport, Conn., 1982), 57–95; Juan Jose Andreu Ocariz, *Movimientos Rebeldes de los Esclavaos Negros el Dominino Espanol en Luisiana* (Zaragoza, 1977), 117–77; Robert L. Paquette, "Revolutionary Saint Domingue in the Making of Territorial Louisiana," in Gaspar and Geggus, eds., *A Turbulent Time*, 216–20, quotation on 220; James H. Dormon, "The Persistent Specter: Slave Rebellion in Territorial Louisiana," *LH*, 28 (1977), 389–404.

11. Paul A. Gilje, *The Road to Mobocracy: Popular Disorder in New York City, 1763–1834* (Chapel Hill, N.C., 1987), 147–49; Shane White, *Somewhat More Independent: The End of Slavery in New York City, 1770–1810* (Athens, Ga., 1991), 144–45. Despite the rioter's efforts and those of the New York Manumission Society, the slaves were removed to Baltimore, where their owner employed them in her cigar factory. T. Stephen Whitman, *The Price of Freedom: Slavery and Manumission in Baltimore and Early National Maryland* (Lexington, Ky., 1997), 23.

12. Frank A. Cassell, "Slaves of the Chesapeake Bay Area and the War of 1812," *JNH*, 57 (1972), 144–55; Christopher T. George, "Mirage of Freedom: African Americans in the War of 1812," *MHM*, 91 (1996), 428–50; John N. Grant, "Black Immigrants into Nova Scotia, 1776–1815, *JNH*, 58 (1973), 253–70; Robin Winks, *The Blacks in Canada: A History* (New Haven, Conn., 1971), 114–24; John McNish Weiss, *Free Black American Settlers in Trinidad, 1815–1816* (London, 1995).

13. James O. Killen, ed., *The Trial Record of Denmark Vesey* (Boston, 1970); John Lofton, *Insurrection in South Carolina: The Turbulent World of Denmark Vesey* (Yellow Springs, Ohio, 1964); Robert S. Starobin, ed., *Denmark Vesey: The Slave Conspiracy of 1822* (Englewood Cliffs, N.J., 1970).

14. The most important post-Vesey rebellion, Nat Turner's insurrection in 1831, did not draw upon the ideology of the Age of Revolution but instead had its roots in a mixture of African and Christian millennialism.

15. George M. Fredrickson, *The Black Image in the White Mind: The Debate on Afro-American Character and Destiny, 1817–1914* (New York, 1971), esp. ch. 3; William R. Stanton, *The Leopard's Spots: Scientific Attitudes toward Race in America, 1815–59* (Chicago 1960).

16. Fredrickson, *The Black Image*, 2–3; Tise, *Proslavery*, 3, 5–6, 11–14; Faust, *A Sacred Circle*.

17. David R. Roediger, *The Wages of Whiteness: Race and the Making of the American Working Class* (London, 1991); and Alexander Saxton, *The Rise and Fall of the White Republic: Class-politics and Mass Culture in Nineteenth-Century America* (New York, 1990). For the change in the suffrage see, Litwack, *North of Slavery*, 74–86.

18. Fredrickson, *The Black Image*, chs. 3–5; Eugene H. Bertwanger, *The Frontier*

against Slavery: Western Anti-Negro Prejudice and the Slavery Extension Controversey (Urbana, Ill., 1967); Eric Foner, *Politics and Ideology in the Age of the Civil War* (New York, 1980), ch. 5.

19. Winthrop D. Jordan, *White over Black: American Attitudes toward the Negro, 1550–1812* (Chapel Hill, N.C., 1968), chs. 11–14; Faust, *A Sacred Circle.*

Acknowledgments

In a financial system predicated on debt, it has become the custom to extend credit to the most profligate. Rather than face a term in debtor's prison, the fiscally irresponsible are encouraged to continue in their dissolute ways. Fortunately, this strange fiduciary principle has been extended to the life of the mind, for it is understood that acknowledging intellectual debts, rather than halting the massing of obligations, invites their accumulation. In hopes of encouraging still further this strange—but most wonderful—system of intellectual bookkeeping, I herein confess that my accounts are badly overdrawn and admit they will never be paid in full. I cheerfully await sentencing.

My first debt is to my colleagues on the Freedmen and Southern Society Project. For more than twenty years I have been privileged to be part of that remarkable cadre of scholars at the University of Maryland whose close investigations of slavery's last minutes raised questions about slavery's first hours. Leslie S. Rowland, Joseph P. Reidy, Barbara Jeanne Fields, Steven Hahn, Steven F. Miller, Julie Saville, Thavolia Glymph, John C. Rodrigue, Michael Honey, Leslie A. Schwalm, Susan O'Donovan, and Wayne K. Durrill—in dozens of lunchtime conversations—pressed the case for a new history of slavery with probing queries about the nature of the society that emancipation demolished. If nothing else, this book is an attempt to put some of those questions to rest.

Trailing the history of slavery in the United States from its nineteenth-century conclusion to its seventeenth-century beginnings, I have been guided by the extraordinarily rich studies of slavery in colonial America. In rejecting static models of social relations and focusing on dynamic institutions and social structures, students of the colonial and revolutionary periods have written some of the best histories of American slavery. What emerges from their work is conclusive evidence that black life in mainland North America changed rapidly, for the status and culture of peoples of African descent varied remarkably over time and differed

486

from place to place, as did the meaning imputed to blackness and white-ness. These scholars, with their careful attention to changing circum-stances, offered clues as to how a historicized study of African-American life in the United States might be written and profoundly shaped my own thinking on the subject.

While I have learned from the new history of slavery, I have also drawn upon the lessons of the old. Five works have been especially im-portant. John Hope Franklin's monumental *From Slavery to Freedom* defined the study of African-American life for my generation; Kenneth M. Stampp's *The Peculiar Institution,* more than any other study of slavery, broke the back of the racist scholarship in which the history of slavery was entrapped; Eugene D. Genovese's *Roll, Jordan, Roll* elevated the history of slavery—and all of American history—by his seeing the slaves as a class in, and occasionally for, themselves; Herbert G. Gut-man's *The Black Family in Slavery and Freedom* connected the history of enslaved workers to the making of the American working class; Nathan I. Huggins's *Black Odyssey* demonstrated that the slave experience must be understood from the inside out as well as the outside in.

In 1989 the University of Maryland hosted a conference to study how work—particularly the slaves' independent economies—shaped slave culture in the Americas. The papers presented over that long weekend were published in two volumes, which I edited with Philip D. Morgan. Those volumes, and subsequent correspondence with the participants and my fellow editor, forced me to rethink my understanding of slavery, especially the economic basis of the slaves' culture. It also eventuated in a series of papers on various aspects of slavery and slave historiography delivered at the Southern Historical Association Meeting in Atlanta, the Center for the Study of Southern Culture at the University of Mississippi, the Atlantic Seminar at The Johns Hopkins University, the Ecole des Hautes Etudes, the College of William and Mary, and the seminar on Af-rica in the Americas at my own university. Critics of those essays helped me clarify my thoughts in a variety of ways. I am deeply appreciative of their numerous thoughtful interventions.

In 1995 an invitation from Marcus B. Rediker and Joe William Trot-ter allowed me to draw these miscellaneous essays together as the E. P. Thompson lectures at the University of Pittsburgh and Carnegie-Mellon University. For that opportunity, as well as their warm hospitality and even warmer criticism, I owe a hearty thanks to Professors Rediker and

Trotter and their colleagues and students. I later published one of my lectures in the Institute of Early American History and Culture's *William and Mary Quarterly*. I am particularly grateful to the Institute's director, Ronald Hoffman, and the *Quarterly's* editor, Michael McGiffert. Their dedication to the highest scholarly standards have made the *William and Mary Quarterly* the benchmark for the best of American historical scholarship.

An extraordinary year at the Center for Advanced Studies in the Behavioral Sciences at Palo Alto provided the time for searching reflection in an environment which, despite the occasional shaking of the earth, encouraged an open rethinking of established truths. Like a generation of fellows, I owe a special debt of gratitude to the staff of the Center and most especially to its associate director, Robert Scott, whose years at the Center have not only provided deep insight into the quixotic manner in which knowledge is produced but also allowed him to perfect a wicked—if not quite legal—volleyball serve. Two brief stints as dean at the University of Maryland did nothing to speed the completion of this volume. But in ever so many ways, the questions and prodding of colleagues and coworkers—most of whom viewed slavery from very different disciplinary perspectives—improved this volume.

When this manuscript neared a publishable form, it was read in its entirety by Eric Foner, Steven Hahn, Ronald Hoffman, Susan O'Donovan, and Marie Schwartz, whose numerous queries necessitated reformulations, always for the better. In addition, Lois E. Horton, James O. Horton, and Shane White read the chapters on the North and offered suggestions based upon their own studies of eighteenth- and nineteenth-century black life. Emory Evans, Michael Nicholls, and Lorena Walsh have done the same for the chapters on the Chesapeake and Upper South, as did Edward Pearson for lowcountry South Carolina and the Lower South and Daniel H. Usner, Jr., for the lower Mississippi Valley. Michael Nicholls was especially generous in sharing his deep knowledge of the growth of eighteenth-century Chesapeake cities. Alfred F. Young reviewed the section on the Age of Revolution and gave me the benefit of his extraordinary understanding of that period. Joseph C. Miller elevated my textbook knowledge of African history, and, at the last, Stanley Engerman read the entire manuscript and saved me from numerous howlers. Sad to say much of this good advice was ignored or rejected, and—although doubtless guilty by association—these generous friends and colleagues bear no responsibility for errors of commission and omission that remain.

No one need tell this author the difficulties of the endgame. David Hostetter, Terrie Hruzd, Cynthia Kennedy, Shelley Sperry, and Linda Sargent took time from their own studies to assist in the final preparation of the volume, checking footnotes, compiling statistics, and formatting word processing disks. Diane West's steady typing and cheerful demeanor helped with the final preparation of the manuscript, while I was otherwise occupied with the affairs of the College of Arts and Humanities. Megan Gelstein of WGBH in Boston allowed me to review the extraordinary collection of images the Africa in America project has amassed in preparation for its monumental documentary history of slavery. Joyce Seltzer and Susan Wallace Boehmer, my editors at Harvard University Press, "made book" and made this book better by their enthusiasm, encouragement, and sharp editorial pencils. A short term at the Research School of Social Sciences at the Australian National University provided the solitude for reading the final proofs and the unsettling experience of finding, at the last, many questions unanswered. For both, I thank Paul Bourke, the director of the history section of the Institute for Advanced Studies, and Douglas Craig of the history department of Australian National University.

Lisa, Richard, and Jill kept me alert to the long shadow slavery cast in the twentieth century, and Martha, who lived with this book longer than anyone should reasonably be required to, sustained the entire enterprise and made it all worthwhile. This book is hers, with love.

Index

DATE DUE

SEP 2 1 2022	

BRODART, CO.   Cat. No. 23-221